International Business Ethics

Stephan Rothlin • Dennis McCann

International Business Ethics

Focus on China

Springer

Stephan Rothlin
School of Distance Education
University of International Business
and Economics
Beijing, China

Dennis McCann
College of Liberal Arts and Sciences
Silliman University
Dumaguete, Philippines

ISBN 978-3-662-47433-4 ISBN 978-3-662-47434-1 (eBook)
DOI 10.1007/978-3-662-47434-1

Library of Congress Control Number: 2015943400

Springer Heidelberg New York Dordrecht London

Cover illustration: Ancient Observatory, Beijing; picture: Klaus Pichler. www.pichlerphoto.ch.

Printed on acid-free paper

Springer-Verlag GmbH Berlin Heidelberg is part of Springer Science+Business Media (www.springer.com)

Foreword, Acknowledgments, and Dedication

With the emergence of an increasingly interconnected and globalized business world, business leaders, the companies they manage, and the government bodies that regulate them must face a host of ethical questions. The individuals exercising responsibility are challenged to make the right decisions often under considerable pressure and constraints of time and money. While the academic field of business ethics has developed within American and European contexts at the intersection of liberal arts and business education, the rapidly growing economies of Asia have had a decisive impact in broadening its scope. In fact, the growing importance of economic developments in India and in China suggests the likelihood that a paradigm shift is under way in international business ethics. If the immediate past was dominated by approaches modeled primarily along Western lines, the future will surely challenge us to develop truly international perspectives on the conduct of business, based on a growing appreciation of Asian cultures and moral philosophies. Since Asian businesses will continue to play a dynamic and sometimes unsettling role in evermore interlinked markets, it becomes important for everyone involved to understand Asian assumptions about doing business ethically and responsibly.

International Business Ethics: Focus on Asia *is meant to address this need, by building on the momentum of the last 50 years in the field of applied ethics, relating ethical theories to various problems of morality and law that arise in business, but now shifting the focus to the discussion of Asian problems and solutions. While the case study approach was certainly prominent in the development of theories and analyses in the academic field of business ethics, business education as a whole tended to interpret its guidelines primarily in tune with conventional theories of business economics. We hope the 20 case studies that we have developed for this book will show the limits of relying on models derived exclusively from Western assumptions about ethics and economics. With the emerging countries of Asia playing a more decisive role on the world stage, it becomes necessary not only to make business ethics more* international *but also to explore systematically the extremely rich but still largely ignored treasures of Asian moral and practical wisdom. In selecting our case studies, and developing the resources implicit in them, we have, of course, given great prominence to China while also trying to honor the variety of cultural perspectives evident in other areas of east Asia.*

International Business Ethics *provides opportunities to explore the ethical issues that entrepreneurs, corporate decision-makers, and government officials in Asia have had to face over the past decade. In addition to the uneven patterns of economic and social development, our case studies show them struggling with environmental disasters, some manmade, others not; various forms of corruption, rampant in some areas, still lingering in others; unfair competition; product safety failures; as well as a host of abuses in the area of working conditions, labor rights, and deceptive practices. The global financial crisis that hit like a tsunami in 2008 serves as a reminder of how devastating the consequences can be when markets are set adrift without any ethical compass. While it is of course impossible to overhaul a financial system overnight, the approaches to business management, ethics, and economics featured in this book demonstrate that it is possible to conceive the conduct of business and the administration of government institutions within a system that actually assists the development of the "real economy." International finance, and the full range of institutions that depend upon its services, should not be rigged to benefit only a small number of privileged people but rather the greater society. Like all business enterprises, international finance should make a contribution to the "common good."*

Our hope is that by creating case studies reflecting Asian business concerns, and by offering an approach to business ethics that we believe synthesizes the best of Western and Chinese moral philosophy, we will meet the needs of our students at least half way, as they seek to prepare themselves for careers in international business and other institutions. We also hope that our efforts will be useful to readers and business practitioners in Europe and North America who are trying to do business in Asia and who are seeking a way through all the advice they've been getting—some bad and some good—about doing business here. We reject the notion that in order to succeed in business in Asia, you must leave your moral principles behind and prepare to operate in an environment where anything goes. One lesson to be drawn from our case studies is that alongside the dramatic economic progress being made in Asia, there is also a dramatic increase in concern for doing business with integrity, adhering to the rule of law, and cooperating with various government agencies in the struggle against corruption. Those who ignore the changes under way in Asia do so at their own peril.

This book began as an attempt to revise the first edition of International Business Ethics: Becoming a Top-Notch Player *(2004) that Stephan Rothlin had published with Renmin University Press in Beijing. Dennis McCann adopted the book for his courses in business ethics in Hong Kong, and after being introduced to its author, they began their long journey together in Asia focused on the development of ethical approaches geared to Asian contexts. We are grateful for the support from the research team at the CIBE, the Center for International Business Ethics, Beijing, in assisting us with case studies, namely, Yang Hengda, Marta Caccamo, Catherine Malone, Li Xiaosong, Yang Fang, and Gao Huan. We have also benefited from the resources of Rothlin*

International Management Consulting Company, Ltd., Hong Kong and Beijing, with the support of Alice Wurmboeck, Lana Ho, Constantin Landers, Marcela Mimica, Anna Moeller, Zhou Shoujin, Ignatius Wang, and Lorenz Long.

Finally, we dedicate this book to Mr. Zhu Rongji the former Prime Minister of the People's Republic of China who convincingly argued for the kind of honesty and integrity within business and government that we attempt to promote here. We have been inspired by his struggle against the widespread cultures of nepotism, lack of transparency and corruption, and by his insistence that these are not the last word in the history of Asian development.

April 16, 2015 Stephan Rothlin
Dennis McCann

Contents

About the Authors

Stephan Rothlin is the founder and chief executive officer of Rothlin International Management Consulting, Ltd. (RIMAC), and formerly general secretary and vice director of the Center for International Business Ethics (CIBE) at the University of International Business and Economics in Beijing. He also serves as chairman of the Association of International Business Ethics of Hong Kong (AIBE). Born in Zurich, Switzerland, and educated in various universities throughout Europe in the disciplines of philosophy, economics, sociology, and ethics, Dr. Rothlin ultimately obtained his PhD at the State University of Innsbruck, Austria, in business ethics in 1991.

Between 1992 and 1998 he taught business ethics in the Institute of Management and Economics at the University of Zurich. In 1998 he moved to Beijing, where he taught international business ethics at several universities, including Renmin University (Finance and Business School), Peking University (BiMBA-program), Beijing Institute of Technology, the University of International Business and Economics, and the Central Party School in Beijing. He is a permanent visiting fellow at the Institute for Empirical Research in Economics at the University of Zurich and is welcomed as a regular visiting professor at a number of business schools in Asia, Europe, and the USA.

Dr. Rothlin's main research focus is the development of international business ethics in Asia, with a special focus on China. In cooperation with Peking University Press, he directs a series of translations of major business ethics textbooks into Chinese. In 2004, Renmin University Press published his book *Becoming A Top-Notch Player*. He has considerable experience in cross-cultural projects and is fluent in six languages: German, French, Italian, Spanish, English, and Mandarin Chinese.

Dennis McCann is director of research at Rothlin International Management Consulting, Ltd. (RIMAC), and formerly director of the Case Study Institute at the Center for International Business Ethics at the University of International Business and Economics in Beijing. Professor emeritus of Agnes Scott College, Atlanta/Decatur, Georgia, USA, Dr. McCann obtained a PhD from the University of Chicago Divinity School in 1976 and an STL from the Gregorian University, Rome, Italy, in

1971. He taught business ethics in the USA for over 30 years and has been involved in research, lecturing, and teaching business ethics in China and Southeast Asia for the past 15 years. Dr. McCann is particularly concerned with identifying culturally appropriate teaching materials for Asia, based on his ongoing research in the fields of philosophy and religious studies. Dr. McCann was formerly the director of research and development at the Hong Kong America Centre (HKAC) during his Fulbright year (2005–2006) and served as visiting professor in the Department of Philosophy and Religion, Hong Kong Baptist University (2006–2008). Dr. McCann served as executive director of the Society of Christian Ethics, the premier academic association for professors of religious ethics in the USA (1996–2001). He is the author of several books and dozens of scholarly articles, most recently the coauthor, with Prof. Lee Kam-hon and Ms. Mary Ann Ching Yuen, of *Christ and the Business Culture*, published in 2012 by the Center for the Study of Religion and Chinese Society (CSRCS), Chinese University Press in Hong Kong. Over the past 15 years Dr. McCann has taught, given workshops, and lectured in universities in Hong Kong, China, the Philippines, Malaysia, Japan, Thailand, Indonesia, and India.

Chapter 1
Becoming a Top-Notch Player

1.1 Prelude

International Business Ethics: Focus on China begins with an attempt to shift the rhetorical context in which we—students, teachers, and other readers—think about business. We believe that too many of us regard business as war by other means. Lacking a realistic experience of the devastation caused by wars, we make a fundamental "category mistake" by using this metaphor to justify or ignore most of the morally questionable activities that go on in business. The basic argument of the book means to shift from warlike attitudes that make predatory behavior seems normal and legitimate to a recognition that business competition is more like what we experience in sports, where players know the rules and normally are committed to abide by them. Our first chapter attempts to establish the ethical significance of becoming a "top-notch player" in business, by taking a closer look at the kind of game that business is. The field of business ethics turns out to be more like a football pitch than a battlefield. While it is debatable whether "all's fair in love and war," certainly nowhere is it true that all's fair in business.

The bribery and other forms of corruption in professional sports such as football are an important challenge to international business ethics. Why is match-fixing universally condemned, though occasionally practiced? Is there more to sports than winning in order to cash in on it? What is sportsmanship? Could it be that international business ethics is analogous to the sportsmanship ethic that is promoted in football and other professional sports? In this chapter, we will examine the recent wave of scandals in FIFA football. What may these scandals tell us about the challenges faced by anyone hoping to improve international business ethics in China and East Asia?

S. Rothlin, D. McCann, *International Business Ethics*,
DOI 10.1007/978-3-662-47434-1_1

1.2 Case Study: Can Football Be Fixed? Sportsmanship and the Culture of Corruption

1.2.1 Abstract

Football is a game that connects people from different backgrounds, languages, and countries. Like many other popular sports, it inspires youth to achieve greatness and men and women to seek excellence. Unfortunately, in recent years, football has been tainted with corruption. Match-fixing and illegal gambling have caused fans to lose confidence in the sport, which may have far-reaching social as well as economic consequences.

As recently as 2011, FIFA president, Sepp Blatter, chose to address the problem of corruption in football and eliminate match-fixing and illegal gambling. To do so, Blatter enlisted the help of Mark Pieth, anti-corruption specialist formerly from the World Bank. Together they challenged the corrupt culture of football and worked to enhance the transparency and integrity of the game. The question is whether their efforts are sufficient to achieve their goals or merely more cover-up for sports culture that cannot be reformed.

1.2.2 Keywords

FIFA, Football, Bribery, Corruption, Integrity, Match-fixing, Whistleblowing.

1.2.3 In the Name of the Game

Football, lovingly nicknamed "the beautiful game," has been described as a global language, second only to music (Best 2012). What makes football a universal leisure activity is its ability to appeal not only to sports enthusiasts but also to people with more commercial interests. Millions of fans gather every weekend to watch their favorite teams, as well as bask in the fashionable aura attached to the games. The football players themselves are often viewed as role models, because of their success in sports and their dedication to physical fitness. Their fans' involvement in the game is so deep that they often label their devotion to a club a true "faith," which justifies comparisons between football and a religious creed (Tomkins 2004). In the eyes of some observers, in the same way religion offers heroic role models and emotional release from our daily burdens, football also provides spectacles that allow us to identify with a cause that is greater than ourselves. The enthusiasm of football fans can ease anxieties, or at least attenuate them by means of healthy competition, as was the case in 2012 when the Union of European Football Associations' (UEFA) EURO Cup championship series provided some relief from the ongoing

Eurozone crisis (Diez 2012). Because football is a passion many share from youth, the game instills a sense of camaraderie and fairness among different groups of people. Notwithstanding football's global acclaim, however, an increasing number of episodes of widespread corruption have surfaced in the news media, jeopardizing both the game's credibility and that of the people involved.

1.2.4 Betting on "a Sure Thing"

Sports scandals have no nationality, but they often share a connection with illegal gambling activities. The amount of money moved by the whole gaming industry is enormous—annual estimates at the end of 2011 placed a €200 billion euros value on gaming revenue—a substantial part of which is due to football betting (Boniface et al. 2012). Some European countries like France and Italy have approved new regulations to offset fraudulent betting, but their efforts have not stopped illicit practices (Boniface et al. 2012). Instead, such moves may have generated the opposite effect. Instead of driving money away from illegal markets, the bulk of bets have been shifted to countries where gambling enjoys a lower degree of oversight by the relevant authorities, such as in Southeast Asia (Forrest 2012).

The recently disclosed "Asiagate" scandal, which revolved around the Zimbabwe Football Association (ZIFA) and its involvement with a Singaporean betting circle, is but one example of the new trend (Smith 2012). From 2007 to 2010, the Zimbabwean national team's world ranking collapsed due to a series of eleven defeats. It turned out that the players and several officials of ZIFA received up to US $5,000 dollars for each game lost, from Asian gaming syndicates conspiring to fix the outcomes of the matches (Sharuko 2012).

Match-fixing is a term heard repeatedly in conjunction with football scandals. It refers to attempts by individuals, clubs, or federations to alter the final results of the game by cheating. Criminal organizations fix football matches in order to ensure results consistent with their betting strategies (Boniface et al. 2012). This commonly occurs at the grassroots level where players and referees are approached. Bribed players and referees can exert a direct influence on the outcome of a game. Significantly, players most likely to betray their professional commitment to principles of fair play are footballers of less reputed teams, who often experience financial hardships that render them vulnerable to exploitation. The pressures generated by teammates, trainers, advisors, and relatives have an influence on players, too. In the 2012 Italian *Calcio scommesse* ("football scandal"), former footballers played a crucial role in identifying current players who were more likely to engage in illegal activities (Callow 2011).

The emotional strain experienced by referees is often similar to the pressure felt by players. Referees are scrutinized by authorities and must cope with the heated reactions of players, owners, and supporters when calls are made against their teams (Distaso et al. 2012). The scandals involving corrupt referees range from the Brazilian *Mafia do Apito* ("Whistle Mafia") of 2005 (Blakeley 2012) and Portugal's

Apito Dourado ("Golden Whistle") of 2004 (*WSC Daily* 2010) to the recent Chinese scandal of 2011involving 40 referees, club managers, and soccer officials in public trials. Among those exposed was Lu Jun, a prominent referee. Referee Lu was once acclaimed as the "Golden Whistle" of the Chinese football league, but after information surfaced about his acceptance of bribes, Lu was rechristened the "Black Whistle" (BBC 2012). The scandal surfaced through an investigation by Singaporean authorities confirming suspicions that members of the Chinese Football Association had been heavily involved in questionable activities for quite a while. The head of the Association, Nan Yong, for example, openly announced available positions on the national team for people willing to pay 100,000 RMB (The Economist 2011).

1.2.5 Attempts at Whistleblowing

The 2009 report of the International Federation of Football Professionals (FIFPro) claimed that 23.6 % of surveyed footballers were aware of specific instances of corruption, with greater frequencies reported in Eastern European countries. This figure is all the more troubling because footballers tend to observe a code of silence—known by its Italian name, *Omertà*—which instills a great reluctance to denounce misdeeds for fear of personal repercussions (FIFPro 2009). Nevertheless, Gubbio Sporting Club player, Simone Farina, attracted worldwide attention when he reported being offered a substantial amount of money in exchange for his help fixing a match in the Series B League. Farina's honesty led to national and international praise, as well as the arrest of 17 people. Farina's actions were the inspiration of the International Federation of Football Association's (FIFA's) September 2012 anti-corruption campaign. The initiative, designed with the assistance of Interpol, offered both a period of amnesty for the players and the establishment in different languages of a whistleblowing hotline (Dunbar 2012). Despite the need for such a program, it was soon halted when FIFA's Independent Governance Committee placed issues of gaming fraud under the regulatory oversight of its executive committee (Weir 2012).

1.2.6 Steps to Curb Corruption

The wave of corruption scandals in football provoked calls for a firm response. The UK Prime Minister, David Cameron, put it quite simply by stating that FIFA's reputation had reached an "all-time low" (Kuper 2012). External pressure by national and supranational organizations, as well as media and public opinion, all called for credible measures to combat corruption in the football associations. Such efforts reflect public concern for the consequences of football's increasingly negative image, particularly for the younger generations who still admire athletes as role models. The drop in football's popularity signals the likelihood of more worrisome financial problems that may come in the wake of declining advertising revenues.

A major obstacle to increased transparency is posed by common skepticism regarding the trustworthiness of FIFA's leadership. Recent allegations involving the misappropriation of funds for international tournaments and FIFA's opaque presidential nomination system have raised questions as to the organization's moral integrity. In response, FIFA president, Sepp Blatter, claimed he worked to "improve FIFA's governance since the beginning of last year [2011]. Not just [through] words, but [through] actions." In order to restore FIFA's tarnished reputation, Blatter appointed ex-World Bank advisor Mark Pieth[1] to establish an anti-corruption unit within the organization (Al Jazeera 2012).

Immediately following his appointment, Pieth became the focus of concern for FIFA's cynics and supporters. Sylvia Schenk from Transparency International promptly challenged him. Speaking to the Associated Sports Press, Schenk questioned the payment Pieth had received from FIFA when he submitted the preliminary results of his investigation: "We believe that someone paid by FIFA cannot be a member of the independent commission [overseeing reforms]" (BBC 2011b). Furthermore, she accused Pieth of focusing too much on future reforms, rather than looking back at the involvement of the Federation in past scandals. Pieth responded to the criticisms by stressing that the payment he received went directly to the Basel Institute of Governance, while expressing the urgency of taking concrete steps to improve the transparency of FIFA and its membership (Kuper 2012). In an interview with the *Financial Times*, Pieth declared, "I'm at the moment pretty optimistic. But it's very open. If it works out I'll be patted on the back. If it fails I'll be an idiot. I think we will know by mid-April whether they are serious" (*Financial Times* 2012).

In order to deliver on his promises, Pieth initiated a far-reaching reform program intended to challenge corruption and redefine transparency at all levels. The reform began with internal investigations of FIFA's alleged corruption. These investigations were meant to provide a sound basis for a new organizational outlook and to answer lingering suspicions around the legitimacy of FIFA's leadership. In his preliminary report, the newly appointed Pieth blamed FIFA for the way it handled accusations of misdeeds in the past. He said the Federation's action has been "insufficient, unconvincing, and unsatisfactory," especially in explaining Blatter's reelection and the bidding process for hosting World Cup matches in the years ahead (Bond 2012).

At the same time, several initiatives have begun at the grassroots level to combat corruption in football matches by establishing certain preventive measures. FIFA has collaborated with Interpol to establish an "Integrity in Sport Unit" that combines

[1] For almost 20 years, Pieth taught Criminal Law and Criminology at the University of Basel and served as head of the organized crime unit at the Swiss Federal Office of Justice (Ministry of Justice and Police). Previously, Pieth was a member of Switzerland's Financial Action Task Force (FATF) on money laundering and held a number of other posts in the OECD. In 2008, he was named a member of the World Bank's Integrity Advisory Board, which advises the Bank's President and the Audit Committee (Pieth.com 2012).

training and educational efforts to promote fair play among footballers. Over the past 10 years, this unit has promoted e-learning programs and national workshops to increase awareness of corruption among those who actually play the game (Boniface et al. 2012). Do you think that Pieth's proposals are sufficient to clean up FIFA football? What major obstacles must he overcome, if the reforms he's proposing are to be credible and effective?

In response to Pieth's challenge to "Do something really courageous [so that] generations of footballers and fans and stakeholders will thank you," Blatter pledged that "[FIFA] will stick to the road map and be ready in 2013." Although Blatter's road-map metaphor seems to welcome Pieth's reform agenda, his further remarks still leave room for skepticism. "Even if Professor Pieth will say we shall not cherry-pick," Blatter observed, "we cannot take the whole tree. It is impossible to take the tree and take all the cherries down" (Wharshaw 2012). His comment clearly suggests the likelihood FIFA will be selective in implementing the recommendations. This will come at the risk of undermining their overall effectiveness, as Pieth himself suggested: "I'm not saying you have to do everything, but these things are linked." (Wharshaw 2012). What do you think of Blatter's cherry-picking metaphor? Would you say he is serious about reforming FIFA, or is he only interested in avoiding further public scrutiny? If pruning the cherry tree means going no further than Pieth's "preventive measures"—including the cultivation of an ethic of "sportsmanship" among footballers and wannabe footballers—do you think that will be enough to save FIFA? What's wrong with taking down the whole cherry tree, if it really is rotten to the core?

1.2.7 But There's More to the Story

As it turned out, the FIFA cherry tree is still standing, though it may yet fall of its own deadweight. Mark Pieth didn't get much of a chance to cherry-pick, as Blatter and his allies blocked the reforms as soon as they began to challenge the practices of FIFA's executive committee, particularly its lack of transparency with regard to its members' compensation packages. Pieth had argued that full disclosure was essential to restore FIFA's credibility and seriousness about reform, warning that "This step would send a crucial message that [the directors] have nothing to hide . . . These may not be the most fundamental of reform issues but they send a symbolic message" (Radnedge 2013). After Pieth and other reformers quietly departed by the end of 2013, a new team led by Michael Garcia, Pieth's successor as head of FIFA's ethics committee, pressed on with the investigation of the executive committee members who had been accused of accepting substantial bribes and other cash payments in exchange for their votes in November 2010 selecting the future sites for the World Cup tournaments. After the meeting in May of 2011, in which Blatter was reelected President in a contest with Jack Warner, Trinidad's representative on the executive committee, there were further allegations of bribery and vote rigging (Hughes 2013; Conn 2013). At this writing, the latest news from FIFA indicates that an attempted coup to unseat Garcia by some members of the executive committee has been turned aside. While the investigations are ongoing, some observers try to balance criticisms of Blatter's "clumsy," if not corrupt, leadership style by conceding that there has been some progress, as is evident from the fact that the allegations of corruption are now out in the open. But others think that only the removal of FIFA's entire leadership team may help restore the hope that they had once placed in efforts to reform the organization internally.

1.2.8 Summary

Regardless of the outcome of these investigations for FIFA, bribery in football has clearly become an international concern. All too frequent corruption scandals seem to put at risk the survival of any spirit of "fair play" within the game. FIFA's poor transparency and its members' questionable business practices have provoked skepticism about the sincerity and effectiveness of its recent anti-corruption measures. The reform effort launched by Pieth was properly focused on restoring the Association's credibility with the public. This is seen as a necessary precondition for bringing back football's global status as "the beautiful game." Do you agree that football's popularity is decreasing as a result of all these allegations about corruption? Do you consider corruption in football a more pressing issue than corruption in other sports? Do those interested in international business ethics have anything to learn from the struggle against corruption in football? What do you think should be done to overcome corruption, either in the game of football or in other institutions that rule the game of business?

1.3 Case Study Discussion

We've all learned, perhaps the hard way, that there are some things in life that don't mix. How about oil and water? That's an easy one. What then about religion and politics or drinking and driving? Can you think of other pairs that don't mix well? Our case study on corruption in FIFA football presents us with another set of incompatibles, money and sports. It might even lead us to challenge the whole idea of professional sports, that is, games in which the players are paid to play. Are professional sports, like FIFA football, an oxymoron, that is, a contradiction in terms? One conclusion we might reach from reading this case study is that professional sports, where everyone—the players, the referees, the owners and managers of the teams, the stadium operators, and all the various vendors—has money on the table, should be either boycotted or banned altogether. Any time money is on the table, the game is likely to be corrupted by it. So let's "just say 'no'" to professional sports.

Some people, with no particular interest in professional sports, may find it easy simply to walk away from them. But then what about amateur sports? Do we think that corruption is impossible when none of the athletes are being paid a stipend or salary? If that were the case, then how do we account for the way that even amateur sporting events—like basketball games between university teams, as in the annual "March Madness" NCAA tournament in the USA—attract gamblers interested in sports betting, legal or otherwise? Match-fixing, alas, is not unheard of in amateur sports. Money is still on the table, even if precious little of it finds its way into the hands of the players.

Since there may be no easy answers for solving the problem of corruption in sports, we may need to back up a bit and ask ourselves why it matters. Why is it that people—who otherwise may turn a blind eye to corruption in politics or other activities—may still become outraged by corruption in sports? What is it about sports that make people think that athletes should exhibit high—even heroic—standards of morality, modeling an ethic of sportsmanship, when virtually all other human activities seem generally tainted by corruption? In a world where, seemingly, money talks and everything has its price, why should sports be any different? If it is true that money can buy everything else that anyone finds desirable, why shouldn't it also guarantee victories, or at least desired point spreads, in the games people play? Why did FIFA find it necessary to make a grand gesture of cleaning up the corruption in its games? Why not simply ignore the concerns expressed in the media, if not the voices of countless sports fans, and go on playing the games as if nothing untoward had ever happened? If FIFA's leadership didn't make a show of reforming football, they would lose their fans and the revenues generated from them. But that's only answering the question with another question. Why is there good reason to fear that the fans will turn away in disgust if the problem of corruption is not addressed convincingly and effectively? Why would sports fans abandon a game that they suspect has been fixed by the gambling syndicates? Does match-fixing make the game meaningless?

As we see from the case study, there are various levels of corruption that can be differentiated according to their proximity to the teams' performance on the field, as well as according to the amounts of money involved. At the high end on the money spectrum are the millions of dollars in bribes and kickbacks allegedly paid by local officials hoping to host a World Cup tournament in their city. At the low end are the payments made by gambling syndicates to players, coaches, and referees, seeking to determine the outcomes of the games. The estimated US$5000, for example, paid to some Zimbabwean players and officials for each game lost in the so-called "Asiagate" scandal may seem trivial compared to the money paid to get a FIFA tournament bid, but when compared to their monthly salaries (Zimbabwe Independent 2013), the bribes may have seemed like "an offer you can't refuse."

To be sure, there is no strict correlation between poverty and greed. If there were, then it would be impossible to explain why wealthy people—such as FIFA's executive leadership—would betray the trust placed in their hands in order to fatten their personal accounts with bribes. Greed is not an inevitable response to economic deprivation, as witnessed by the lives of the overwhelming majority of poor people whose basic decency and honesty cannot be explained away as due to a lack of opportunities to lie, cheat, and steal. The greed that motivates players to cheat—

hoping to pick up a few thousand dollars for going along with a match-fixing scheme—rests on a deep-seated cynicism about themselves and their sport. How does one become cynical about the profession for which one has trained for years, in which one had hoped to make one's mark? A good place to begin looking for answers is in the organization's leadership and its practices. If FIFA's top management stands accused of covering up the corruption they've tolerated in the process for selecting World Cup tournament sites, what conclusions are the players likely to draw from their example?

One might argue that the two forms of corruption in sports ought to be kept separate. The allegations against FIFA's executive committee concern business deals, within an organization headquartered in a country where until very recently commercial bribery was not a criminal offense (Loetscsher 2013). The irregularities in FIFA's executive committee are just business as usual, and no one should be surprised by what goes on there or upset about it. The focus of reform in football should concentrate on preserving the integrity of the game on the field. The fans are right to be outraged by match-fixing, and FIFA should do all it can to eliminate it. But there's no need to take reform efforts any further. If Mark Pieth and his successors can provide a credible deterrent to players who may be thinking of cheating, they need go no further than that.

This, of course, appears to have been the thinking of FIFA's executive committee, when they tried to water down Pieth's reform efforts and put a stop altogether to those of his successor, Michael Garcia. Once exposed, their plots collapsed, as it became apparent to all observers including the fans that they were interested only in avoiding further sanctions against their corrupt and immoral acts. It seems reasonable, then, to recognize the intrinsic connection between the two forms of corruption in football. The corruption in FIFA's boardrooms may not have caused the corruption that surfaced on the playing field. But it clearly stands as an obstacle to any credible and effective attempt to reform the way the game is played. Why would players, who stand to lose a significant opportunity to earn some extra money, cooperate with FIFA's ethics committee, when they have reason to suspect that Blatter's cronies have no intention of having their own practices investigated and reformed? Pieth was right to press FIFA toward comprehensive reform, though it is not yet clear that the efforts he initiated will succeed.

When it comes to moral reform within an organization like FIFA, the old maxim still applies: "Practice what you preach!" FIFA's executive leadership must realize that you cannot expect to reform what goes on between the white lines in the game of football, while turning back any serious effort to reform what goes on in the boardroom. Corruption in either of these settings is interrelated, but so is any serious effort to restore integrity to professional football or any other game. Where to begin? The key to preserving or enhancing an ethic of sportsmanship is not by prohibiting professional sports. Neither in sports nor in business is it true that money is the root of all evils. That assumption would mean that anything and everything in which money changes hands are tainted, which arguably is not true. Besides, this is not what the Bible says. It is the love of money that is the root of all evils (1 Timothy 6:10). It is useful to know that this proverb is invoked in the context of warning a novice Christian minister about the risk of corruption even in church work. A corrupt mind robs ministers of the truth, leading them to consider "godliness as a means to financial gain" (1 Timothy 6:5). The love of money or greed, in other words, is a sure sign of a corrupt mind. The love of money is not the same thing as valuing money or appreciating its usefulness in helping us to manage our affairs in the marketplace. The love of money, referred to in this Biblical proverb, means loving money above all else. Once our desires have been twisted by a corrupt mind, money is no longer their servant, but their master. We will stop at nothing to gain money. It is no longer a means but our only end in itself.

Confucius had his own way of warning against an unrestrained love of money. He observed that "wealth and high station are what men desire, but unless I got them in the right way I would not remain in them" (Analects 4:5). There is a right way to regard money and pursue wealth and a wrong way. Confucius clearly disapproves of acquiring them in the wrong way. Further on in the *Analects*, he says: "Riches and honors acquired by unrighteousness, are to me as a floating cloud" (Analects 7:16). A floating cloud is as insubstantial as an illusion. No one should sacrifice all other values in the vain hope of acquiring it. Just as a floating cloud is impossible to possess, so riches and honors acquired through unrighteous activities will soon pass away, leaving their devotee more impoverished and isolated than before he or she took up their pursuit. What is it, then, that makes some ways of acquiring riches and honors unrighteous? As in all other areas of human activity, the answer depends on knowing which ways are consistent with the appropriate rules and which are not. Accepting a stipend or a salary for joining the team and playing the game as well as one can is righteous and consistent with the rules; violating one's pledge of loyalty to the team, in order to accept a bribe for throwing the game or lowering its score, is not only unrighteous but also clearly inconsistent with the rules that make the game a game.

On this point, the wisdom traditions of China represented by both the Bible and the Confucian classics agree: Faithfully observing the appropriate rules (*Li*, 禮) governing specific forms of human interaction is the key not only to preserving righteousness (*Yi*, 義), also for cultivating a benevolent or humane spirit (*Rén*, 仁). The same point is made in the teachings of Jesus: "If you love Me, you will keep My commandments" (John 14:15). The commandments Jesus was referring to are the "Ten Commandments" that God revealed to Moses on Mount Sinai (Exodus 20:1–17; Deuteronomy 30:15–16) that are affirmed throughout the wisdom literature in Biblical tradition (Proverbs 19:16; Ecclesiastes 12:13) and specifically reaffirmed in Jesus' own teaching (Matthew 19:16–22). In subsequent chapters of this book, we will explore how these rules or commandments have shaped international business ethics. Here we note simply that observing the rules of propriety—taking them to heart and guiding one's actions by them—will set us on the path toward righteousness. What we know from these rules—as instructed by both Confucian and Biblical traditions as well as our own conscience, if we are willing to listen—is that some, but not all, forms of money making are both immoral and counterproductive, whether one is playing the game or not.

We see, then, that Pieth and his associates were right to emphasize the need for transforming FIFA's corporate culture, through educational efforts intended to restore a commitment to observing the rules governing the game of football. For education to be an effective means for reforming FIFA, it must go beyond disseminating information on the technical aspects of playing soccer, that is, how to organize teams and matches, how to score points, what referees are for, and what constitutes a foul and the various penalties imposed for misconduct, that is, the various areas covered in "The Laws of the Game" (FIFA 2013a). Yet even these seemingly technical rules challenge players and fans to raise their aspirations beyond simply winning the game at all costs. Among the Laws of the Game, "Law 12: Fouls and Misconduct" is particularly instructive for it specifies various penalties for on-the-field conduct "considered by the referee to be careless, reckless, or using excessive force." Of course, each of these terms—"careless," "reckless," and "using excessive force"—is morally significant, for they seek to distinguish a spirited football game from a street brawl or gang warfare. FIFA's rules on fouls and penalties, and the provision of competent referees to enforce them, are a constant reminder that what constitutes winning and losing a game can only be decided within a commitment by everyone involved to follow the rules of the game. However intense the play may be on the field, the point is to win the game, not eliminate the opposition through fair means or foul.

One section of Law 12 is particularly relevant. It explains the penalties for receiving either a yellow card for a "cautionable" offense or a red card for a "sending-off" offense. If a player receives a second yellow card in a single game, he or she is ejected from the game. As the color code suggests, the two offenses are distinguishable primarily in their seriousness. The first of these "cautionable" offenses is "unsporting behavior." The official interpretation of Law 12 makes it clear that unsporting behavior includes any form of cheating that involves deception or violence intended to overthrow the rules, including a comprehensive prohibition against any acts "which show a lack of respect for the game" (FIFA 2013b). As tedious as reading the rules may be, their intent is clear. The integrity of the game must be preserved, however intensely the outcome of any specific match may be contested. The Laws of the Game, however, do not specifically proscribe match-fixing or other corrupt practices, presumably because they assume that anyone playing the game is committed to the sport and its integrity, regardless of the outcome. The Laws of the Game, in short, are meant to instruct participants who sincerely desire to become top-notch players. Playing the game well, or observing a well-played game, teaches everyone to value the rules, without which neither righteousness nor benevolence can be cultivated through sports.

1.4 Ethical Reflection

Had FIFA been as effective in following the rules that ought to govern its business affairs as it is in disseminating the rules that ought to govern what happens on the playing field, there would be little or no need of reform. But if business is itself a game, what might top-notch players in business learn from the way people think about the games we play? While playing games may be universal in virtually all cultures, there is remarkable diversity not only in the kinds of games preferred from one place to another but also in their social and cultural importance. In ancient Greece, for example, the intellectual traditions that gave rise to Western philosophy were deeply committed to a model of sportsmanship inspired by the Olympic Games. First organized in 776 BCE, the Games continued for over a thousand years until they were suppressed in 394 CE by the Emperor Theodosius, as part of his campaign to impose Christianity as the state religion of the Roman Empire. Theodosius was not wrong in his assessment of their religious significance. They had become not only a primary expression of the cosmopolitan values championed by Alexander the Great (356–321 BCE) but also were inextricably linked to the worship of Zeus, the ruler of the Hellenistic pantheon. The divine origin of the Games may have helped sustain their role in promoting peace among the city-states of ancient Greece. The Games marked a truce in their seemingly incessant wars, during which athletic competitions were organized to honor their common allegiance to the Olympian deities. However intense those competitions may have been, they represented an alternative to war and not its continuation by other means.

Such peaceful competition could not have been sustained apart from a common commitment to an ethic of sportsmanship.[2] The Games were a sacred ritual, and as in all rituals, violations against the rules that constitute them were taboo. In addition to the Olympic truce, one concrete indication of their peaceful intent is the fact that in the boxing matches—which went on until one or the other of the contenders either surrendered or died—the dead boxer was automatically declared the winner. If the match were simply an exhibition of the skills required for victory in war, this practice would make no sense. When the movement to establish the modern Olympic Games was organized in the late nineteenth century, its founder Pierre de Coubertin projected an ideal of sportsmanship that remains central to the Olympian "creed":

> The most important thing in the Olympic Games is not to win but to take part, just as the most important thing in life is not the triumph but the struggle. The essential thing is not to have conquered but to have fought well. (The Olympic Museum 2007)

The most telling indication of the Olympic spirit of sportsmanship is to play by the rules, upholding them in all one's preparations and performance, allowing them to determine whose is the victory or the defeat.

To be sure, the Olympic ideal of sportsmanship, however familiar, may seem like a foreign import in China and East Asian cultures. The Confucian classics have precious little to say about games, perhaps for the same reason that Confucius did not

[2] *Wikipedia* defines "sportsmanship" as "an aspiration or ethos that a sport or activity will be enjoyed for its own sake, with proper consideration for fairness, ethics, respect, and a sense of fellowship with one's competitors. A sore loser refers to one who does not take defeat well, whereas a good sport means being a 'good winner' as well as being a 'good loser.'" Sportsmanship as the basis for a moral code emphasizes "virtues such as fairness, self-control, courage, and persistence, and has been associated with interpersonal concepts of treating others and being treated fairly, maintaining self-control if dealing with others, and respect for both authority and opponents" (*Wikipedia* 2014).

speak of "prodigies, force, disorder and gods" (Analects 6: 21). At most, there are only two games mentioned in the Analects, *liù bó* (六博) a dice game and *yì* (弈) known in China today as *wéiqí* (圍棋) or in Japan as *Go*, the "encirclement board game." Confucius is quoted as dismissing both as unworthy of a *junzi* (君子) or person of exemplary moral character:

> The Master said, 'Hard is it to deal with him who will stuff himself with food the whole day without applying his mind to anything good. Are there not gamesters and go players? To be one of these would still be better than doing nothing at all.' (Analects, 18:22)[3]

Playing these games may be better than the sheer idleness of a person given over to gluttony, but that surely isn't much of a compliment. In the book of Mencius, the game of *yi* is discussed twice. The first passage lists five things regarded as "unfilial"—that is, the neglect of one's duties toward one's parents—and among them are "gambling and go-playing, and being fond of wine, without attending to the nourishment of his parents"[4] (Book IV, Part B, chapter 30). By contrast, Mencius' second passage recognizes that *yi* is not a form of gambling, but a game that elicits the cultivation of skills closely connected with positive moral development:

> Now go-playing is but a small art, but without his whole mind being given and his will bent to it, a man cannot succeed at it. Go Ch'iu is the best go player in all the kingdom. Suppose that he is teaching two men to play. The one gives to the subject his whole mind and bends to it all his will, doing nothing but listening to Go Ch'iu. The other, though he seems to be listening to him, has his whole mind running on a swan which he thinks is approaching, and wishes to bend his bow, adjust the string to the arrow, and shoot it. Although he is learning along with the other, he does not come up to him. Why?—Because his intelligence is not equal? Not so" (Book VI, Part A, chapter 9).

Mencius' appreciation for Go-Ch'iu's achievement and the game's potential as an art of self-cultivation enable subsequent Confucian tradition to honor it among the "four accomplishments" of a *junzi*. The other three are excellence in "poetry, painting, and music" (Pinckard, n.d.).

Those who know the game of *Go* are unstinting in their praise of its moral and spiritual significance. Donald Potter, for example, claims that the Emperor Song Taizhong associated the game with the first three of the five classic Confucian virtues, namely, "*li* (propriety), *zhi* (wisdom), *ren* (human heartedness), *i* (righteousness), and *hsin* (sincerity)." His teacher, Potter recalls, explained the way playing *Go* naturally stimulates the cultivation of these virtues:

---

[3] This translation is James Legge's (citation). D. C. Lau's translation removes any lingering confusion that traditionally assumed that they referred to one game, known as *po-yi*: "The Master said, 'It is no easy matter for a man who always has a full stomach to put his mind to some use. Are there not such things as *po* and *yi*? Even playing these games is better than being idle" (Lau 1979: 147).

[4] This translation, also by James Legge, appears to assume mistakenly that "*po*" and "*yi*" both involve gambling, and indicate a dissolute lifestyle in which being "fond of wine" is typical. Mencius' list is significant in that the five categories of moral weakness—the next of which is "being fond of goods and money, and selfishly attached to his wife and children"—are each understood as symptoms of lack of respect and care for one's parents, clearly the core value in traditional Chinese morality. D. C. Lau's translation makes the connection even clearer by describing each of the five failings as contributing to "the neglect of one's parents" (Lau 1979: 135).

> *Go* is a gentleman's exercise for the cultivation of the mind. Without employing our minds in thinking about our moves we are offending against one of the four ethical principles as set forth by Mencius. Furthermore, to consider one's move expresses modesty; suggests the strategy of the opponent merits consideration.

Of the three virtues whose Chinese characters are displayed in East Asian "go clubs"—propriety (*li*), intelligence (*zhi*), and kindness (*ren*)—it is the commitment to propriety that "explains the spirit of dignity and consideration that guides participants in what is a competitive game" (Potter, n.d.).

An examination of this one game discussed in the Confucian classics, then, takes us to the same point that emerged in a consideration of the Olympic ideal of sportsmanship. Such games demonstrate that sportsmanship or "the spirit of dignity and consideration that guides participants" rests concretely upon the strict observance of the rules (or, if you will, the rituals of propriety) that make the game a game and not simply an act of warfare conducted by other means. If, for example, FIFA's commitment to playing by the rules on the field is also to be extended to the boardroom, we must go beyond what can be learned from the Olympic ceremonies and the *Go* clubs and toward a consideration of whether business is legitimately considered a game, and if so, what kind of a game is it? Our next step therefore must take us into the relationship between game theory and ethics.

Becoming a top-notch player in business requires us to determine how business is to be understood as a game. Game theory is useful at this point because it provides a game taxonomy in which, among other things, it is possible to locate the activities characteristic of business. Second, game theory is meant to clarify the meaning of rationality, particularly in situations—or "games"—in which the human interaction is "strategic," that is, when "interactions among economic agents produce outcomes with respect to the preferences (or utilities) of those agents, where the outcomes in question might have been intended by none of the agents" (SEP 2010). Game theory attempts to provide both normative models of the logic of strategic interactions and criteria for testing these models through empirical or descriptive analysis of what can be observed in such interactions. Though game theory emerged as a focus of philosophical inquiry more than 50 years ago, its success in creating mathematical models of various strategic games, such as the familiar "prisoners' dilemma," has not been matched with similar success in mapping actual interactions or predicting what rational actors or "players" are likely to do in them (Gruene-Yanoff 2014). Thus, game theory's relevance to international business ethics, though limited, does provide tools for interpreting the kinds of interactions that routinely occur in business.

The most important of these is a philosophical concept of "Game." Metaphors guide the way we think about our activities, including their moral limits and possibilities. When people think of what business is like, there are several metaphors that often come up, including "war" and "game." If business is like warfare—as many seem to think, given the popularity of Sunzi's *The Art of War* (孫子兵法; pinyin: *Sunzi bingfa*) as a guide to business strategy—then there are no rules, other than achieving victory as efficiently as possible. If, on the other hand, business is like a game, it also requires careful attention to strategy, but there are rules that not only specify what kind of game it is but also what constitutes winning or losing within it. Our discussion of the FIFA case study ought to have convinced us that business is more like a game than it is like warfare. As in all games, there are rules, and in order to play the game, you must learn the rules and the strategies that are permitted and forbidden within them. If we recognize that business is a game, we're not saying that winning isn't important; of course it is important, but what counts as winning can only be determined by knowing the rules and playing by them consistently.

The taxonomy of games developed in game theory allows us to explore the question of what kind of game business is. Games are classed as "static" and "dynamic" based on whether the moves are simultaneous or sequential; as "games of perfect information" and "games of incomplete information" based on whether the players do or do not have full or equal information; as single play and "repeated" games, based on whether the game is one shot only or to be played more than once with the same or different players; and as "zero-sum" and "nonzero-sum games" based on whether the players' interests always conflict or sometimes enable them to cooperate. Games may also be classified on how the "subgame" or actual playing rules are selected, whether these are fixed and immutable or open to negotiation. Finally, there is a question of whether agreements to cooperate that result from such negotiations are enforceable; if agreements can be enforced, the games are "cooperative" and if not, "noncooperative" (Dixit et al. 2009).

In light of this basic taxonomy, we can begin to see how ordinary business transactions might be understood as strategic games. Since most business transactions, except for, say, sealed bids on contracts, are sequential, business is a "dynamic game." Since the very nature of marketplace transactions means that buyers and sellers almost always lack perfect information, business is a game of "incomplete information." Since the purpose of a business is—in the memorable words of Peter Drucker—"to create a customer," the intention of the players is to repeat the game as frequently as possible. Their game is "repeated" and thus is one in which the players' reputations are very relevant to their choice of strategies. Since the legitimacy of the marketplace depends on creating and sustaining conditions under which both buyers and sellers make each other better off through their interactions, the game of business in general is "nonzero-sum." Situations will arise in business in which there is only one winner and all other players are losers, such as in a competition between two employees for a specific promotion. Though their individual competition may be "zero-sum," a rational decision over which to promote, from the business' point of view, is "nonzero-sum." All the firm's employees, as well as their other stakeholders, will benefit from management's making the right choice for the right reasons. Businesses clearly negotiate agreements and will normally sign contracts that spell out the negotiated rules governing their interactions. Finally, the agreements or rules governing business transactions are usually enforceable. The market itself normally enforces the rules, and if that is not sufficient in some situations, the rules are enforced by various regulatory agencies, established either by the government or by private NGOs with a stake in promoting good business.

Even this preliminary review of the game theory's taxonomy will suggest just how complex routine business decisions usually are. That is one reason why it is so very difficult to predict the outcomes of the various games of business. What we know is that business transactions are strategic for all players involved in them, buyers or customers, as well as sellers and the firms they represent. As surveys of game theory often remind us, "strategic" is not a euphemism for "cutthroat" competition or unrestrained selfishness. Strategic means that the players are acting rationally upon their understanding of their own preferences or self-interest. In business, as in other human interactions, such preferences may, and usually do, include the players' desire to do well while doing good, that is, to cultivate a reputation for honesty, fair dealing, and other moral virtues that enable lasting success in the marketplace. Game theory enables business students and practitioners to focus less on the question whether business is a game—it is, once "games" are properly understood—and more on the question of what kind of a game business is and how to play it well.

Those familiar with the modern history of business ethics will recall the impact of Albert Z. Carr's essay, "Is Business Bluffing Ethical?" (Carr 1968), which became one of the *Harvard Business Review's* classics. Carr's ethical argument that defended bluffing and other strategic deceptions in business negotiations was premised on the idea that not only is business a game, but the game it is most like is poker. The American game of poker involves betting or gambling, insofar as players wager on their assessment of the strength of the hands they've been dealt, with their wagers strategically calculated on the basis of what they think is the strength of the hands dealt to their opponents, as well as their opponents' capabilities as poker players. Carr is correct in observing that bluffing—that is, a player's strategy designed to deceive his or her opponents regarding the strength of his or her hand or intentions for playing it—is "ethical" in poker. It neither violates the rules of the game nor would opposing players consider it unsportsmanlike or cheating. To be sure, even Carr admits that there is a difference between bluffing and bold-faced lying, but within either poker or the game of business, such lying is wrong not for moral reasons, but because strategically it may provoke "dangerous hostility" among the other players or stakeholders. Nevertheless, Carr's description of poker is reminiscent of Sunzi's assumptions about warfare:

> Poker's own brand of ethics is different from the ethical ideals of civilized human relationships. The game calls for distrust of the other fellow. It ignores the claim of friendship. Cunning deception and concealment of one's strength and intentions, not kindness and openheartedness, are vital in poker. No one thinks any the worse of poker on that account. And no one should think any the worse of the game of business because its standards of right and wrong differ from the prevailing traditions of morality in our society. (Carr 1968: 3)

Carr may be right about bluffing in the game of poker, but is he also right in regarding the game of business as simply an elaborate version of its assumptions, rules, and acceptable strategies? Perhaps Carr himself is bluffing when he says that "no one should think any the worse of the game of business," assuming that in playing, it requires abandoning "the ethical ideals of civilized human relationships." The major differences between the games of poker and business appear as soon as we place poker in the taxonomy provided by game theory. Poker is a zero-sum game, in which there is only one winner for each hand; it is a game of "incomplete information," since the players cannot see all their opponents' cards; the rules of poker are rigid and enforceable, and it is repeated from one poker hand to the next. By contrast, the game of business is "nonzero-sum," insofar as cooperation is not only permitted but sometimes also encouraged as the key to success. While some of the rules of business are negotiable, once they are acknowledged in a contract, they are not only legally binding but also enforceable. Creating customers means playing what game theory terms a "repeated" game, in which the players' reputations—for example, in the cultivation of consumer loyalty to various brand names—usually increase the game's payoffs, and playing with less than "perfect information" is a constant challenge to all players, buyers, and sellers alike. The more realistic one's description of business transactions, the less plausible is Carr's equation of business with "zero-sum" games like poker.

1.5 Conclusion

The best answer to the question, what kind of game is business, may be the cryptic, "business is just business." Business is not like warfare, though like warfare, it does require strategic thinking and acting, if one is to be successful or victorious. Business is not like poker, though like poker, it is governed by rules that determine what it means to win or lose. Also like poker, it involves repeated play among players sometimes the same and sometimes different, none of whom has perfect information about either the situation in which the play is made or the capabilities of the other players. Though business requires players to sharpen their strategic skills, there are limits—both moral and legal—to what can be done strategically, if one is to stay in the game and have a chance of winning it. The fact that perfect information is impossible in business does not mean that its players will stop trying to obtain it by hook or by crook. Mistakenly applying lessons drawn from Sunzi's *The Art of War*, some players have learned the hard way that trading stocks and other financial instruments on the basis of insider information, for example, or trying to secure a strategic advantage through industrial espionage is against the rules whose violation may be severely punished. Such players apparently don't know what game they are playing, as if it were acceptable to play football on the basis of a rulebook governing some other game, say, wrestling or boxing.

If business is unlike any other game, then becoming a top-notch player requires learning its rules and committing oneself to play fair by them. Of course, in the real world where money is on the table, not only in business but also in many other games, we must confront the fact that corruption occurs all too frequently and that learning to resist corruption is and ought to be part of learning the rules and becoming a top-notch player. Reexamining the scandals that have recently plagued FIFA, as we have done in this our opening chapter, is meant to alert us to the need for vigilance in confronting the challenges of improving international business ethics. FIFA's problems should provide us with food for thought. You are not likely to be able to enforce the rules against cheating on the football field, if you turn a blind eye to the corruption emanating from the way FIFA does business. Sportsmanship is a lofty ideal that may lead us to a deeper appreciation for the virtues that can be learned and taught through participation in sports. But that ideal loses its credibility, when those who promote it are caught cheating in their business affairs. In order to restore the relevance of sportsmanship for becoming a top-notch player, we need to learn more about the virtues embodied in this ideal and their connection with the universal challenge of living a good life. Our next chapter, then, will introduce us to someone whose exemplary moral character is recognized by all who know him. Is it just coincidental that in his youth he was a star athlete for his high school team?

References

Aljazeera. (2012, March 29). *FIFA prepare for anti-corruption report*. Retrieved on June 20, 2012 from http://www.aljazeera.com/sport/football/2012/03/2012329183134582846.html

Basel Institute on Governance. (2012, March). *First report of IGC to FIFA's executive committee*.

Bauer, F. (2013, May 29). *The FIFA-Reform-Farce*. Deutsche-Welle (DW). Retrieved on April 2, 2014 from http://www.dw.de/the-fifa-reform-farce/a-16845472

BBC. (2011a, June 25). *Dozens named in Greece football 'scandal'*. Retrieved on April 4, 2012 from http://www.bbc.co.uk/news/world-europe-13914118

BBC. (2011b, December 2). *Transparency International cuts ties with Fifa*. Retrieved on June 29, 2012 from http://www.bbc.co.uk/news/world-europe-15996806

BBC. (2012, February 16). *China morning round-up: Football scandal sentences*. Retrieved on March 23, 2012 from http://www.bbc.co.uk/news/world-asia-china-17071073

Best, C. (2012, February 24). 'Beautiful Game' can transcend society's ills. *CNN Opinion*. Retrieved on June 24, 2012 from http://articles.cnn.com/2012-02-24/opinion/opinion_opinion-clyde-best-racism-football_1_global-appeal-discipline-beautiful-game?_s=PM:OPINION

Blakeley, R. (2012, March 20). Teixeira resignation implications for CBF. *The Rio Times*. http://riotimesonline.com/brazil-news/rio-sports/2014worldcup/teixeira-resignation-implications-for-cbf/

Bond, D. (2012, March 30). Fifa embraces new ethics drive, but questions remain. *BBC Sport*. Retrieved on April 5, 2012 from http://www.bbc.co.uk/blogs/davidbond/2012/03/will_fifa_welcome_change.html?postId=112133675

Boniface, P., et al. (2012, February). *Sports betting and corruption*. White Paper by IRIS Network, University of Salford, Cabinet Praxes-Advocats, University of Beijing. Translation supported by Sportaccord.

Callow, J. (2011, June 2). Italian football rocked by fresh match-fixing scandal. *The Guardian*. Retrieved on April 7, 2012 from http://www.guardian.co.uk/football/2011/jun/02/italy-football-corruption-match-fixing

Carr, A. Z. (1968). Is business bluffing ethical? *Harvard Business Review*. Retrieved on 7 March 2014 from http://hbr.org/1968/01/is-business-bluffing-ethical

Conn, D. (2013, October 3). World Cup 2022: Only a rerun of votes by Fifa will achieve credibility. *The Guardian*. Retrieved on March 28, 2014 from http://www.theguardian.com/football/blog/2013/oct/03/world-cup-2022-fifa-qatar

Diez, P. (2012, June 15). The economic and financial crisis is keeping the Euro 2012 joy at bay. *The Beginner*. Retrieved on June 22, 2012 from http://www.thebeginner.eu/europe/842-curbing-footballs-enthusiasm

Distaso, W., et al. (2012, February). *Corruption and referee bias in Football: The case of Calciopoli*. University of Navarra.

Dixit, A. K., Reiley, D. H., Jr., & Skeath, S. (2009). *Games of strategy* (3rd ed.). New York: W. W. Norton.

Dunbar, G. (2012, January 10). FIFA pledges to protect match-fixing witnesses. *The Washington Times*. Retrieved on April 15, 2012 from http://www.washingtontimes.com/news/2012/jan/10/fifa-pledges-to-protect-match-fixing-witnesses/?page=all

FATF-GAFI. (2009, July). *Money laundering through the football sector*. White paper.

FIFA. (2013a). *Tech support: The laws of the game*. Retrieved April 2, 2014 from http://www.fifa.com/aboutfifa/footballdevelopment/technicalsupport/refereeing/laws-of-the-game/index.html

FIFA. (2013b). *Tech support: Teaching material: Interpretation of the laws of the game: Law 12 – Fouls and misconduct*. Retrieved April 2, 2014 from http://www.fifa.com/mm/document/worldfootball/clubfootball/01/37/04/28/law12-en.pdf

Forrest, B. (2012, May 18). All the world is staged. *ESPN Magazine*. Retrieved on July 13, 2012 fromhttp://espn.go.com/sports/soccer/story/_/id/7927946/soccer-wilson-raj-perumal-world-most-prolific-criminal-match-fixer-espn-magazine

Gruene-Yanoff, T. (2014). *Game theory*. Internet Encyclopedia of Philosophy. Retrieved on April 8, 2014 from http://www.iep.utm.edu/game-th/

Hughes, R. (2013, May 7). One by one, those atop FIFA are falling. *The New York Times*. Retrieved on March 28, 2014 from http://www.nytimes.com/2013/05/08/sports/soccer/08iht-soccer08.html

Kuper, S. (2012, March 23). Can this man fix FIFA? *Financial Times*. Retrieved on June 29, 2012 from http://www.ft.com/cms/s/2/3762ca44-72ed-11e1-9be9-00144feab49a.html#axzz1zHWR62j2

Lau, D. C. (Ed. and Trans.) (1979). *Mencius* (Penguin classics). London: Penguin Books.

Loetscsher, B. (2013, September 9). *Switzerland to remedy deficiencies in combating corruption*. International Law Office. Retrieved on 28 March 2014 from http://www.internationallawoffice.com/Newsletters/Detail.aspx?g=79ff4e23-9851-4c9d-b507-0f38868c0418&redir=1

McKinstry, L. (2011, December 22). Corruption, greed, and moral squalor: The scandals of football that SHOULD be tackled. *The Daily Mail*. Retrieved on April 1, 2012 from http://www.dailymail.co.uk/debate/article-2077786/Corruption-greed-moral-squalor-The-scandals-football-SHOULD-tackled.html

Pieth, M. (2012). *About Mark Pieth*. Retrieved on June 22, 2012 from http://www.pieth.ch/about_mark_pieth/

Pinckard, W. (n.d.). *Go and the 'Three Games'*. Retrieved on April 5, 2014 from http://www.kiseido.com/three.htm

Potter, D. (n.d.). *The three virtues of 'Go'*. Retrieved on April 5, 2014 from http://www.kiseido.com/proper.htm

Radnedge, K. (2013, October 1). Frustrated pieth decides he has had enough of battle to reform FIFA. KeirRadnedge.com. Retrieved on June 15, 2015 from keirradnedge.com/2013/10/01/frustrated-pieth-decides-he-has-had-enough-of-battle-to-reform-fifa/

Roan, D. (2012, February 7). Report shows match-fixing rife in Southern and Eastern Europe. *BBC sport*. Retrieved on April 5, 2012 from http://www.bbc.co.uk/sport/0/football/16923742

Scott, M. (2011, November 30). Fifa needs new anti-corruption controls, warns head of governance *.The Guardian*. Retrieved on April 5, 2012 from http://www.guardian.co.uk/football/2011/nov/30/fifa-anti-corruption-head-governance

Scott, M. (2012, February 16). Ricardo Teixeira set to quit all football posts after allegations of new corruption scandal. *The Telegraph*. Retrieved on April 3, 2012 from http://www.telegraph.co.uk/sport/football/international/9087552/Ricardo-Teixeira-set-to-quit-all-football-posts-after-allegations-of-new-corruption-scandal.html

Sharuko, R. (2012, February 3). The Warriors and the ZIFA curse. *The Herald Online*. Retrieved on April 15, 2012 from http://www.herald.co.zw/index.php?option=com_content&view=article&id=33115

Smith, D. (2012, February 1). Zimbabwe suspends 80 footballers as part of 'Asiagate' match-fixing probe. *The Guardian*. Retrieved on April 16, 2012 from http://www.guardian.co.uk/world/2012/feb/01/zimbabwe-footballers-suspended-asiagate-match-fixing

Stanford Encyclopedia of Philosophy (SEP). (2010, May 5, 2010). *Game theory*. Retrieved on April 8, 2014 from http://plato.stanford.edu/entries/game-theory/

The Economist. (2011, December 17). *Little red card*. Retrieved on March 27, 2012 from http://www.economist.com/node/21541716

The Guardian. (2012, March 29). *Anti-corruption expert set to publish Fifa reform proposals*. Retrieved on April 6, 2012 from http://www.guardian.co.uk/football/2012/mar/29/anti-corruption-expert-fifa-reforms?INTCMP=ILCNETTXT3487

The Zimbabwe Independent. (2013, October 19). *The premier league of poverty*. Retrieved on March 28, 2014 from http://www.theindependent.co.zw/2013/10/18/premier-league-poverty/

Tomkins, S. (2004, June 22). Matches made in heaven. *BBC*. Retrieved on August 7, 2012 from http://news.bbc.co.uk/1/hi/3828767.stm

Weir, K. (2012, March 28). FIFA blows whistle on match-fixing hotline. *Reuters*. Retrieved on April 14, 2012 from http://af.reuters.com/article/sportsNews/idAFJOE82R0B420120328

Wharshaw, A. (2012, May 25). Have guts, do the right thing and back reforms, Pieth urges FIFA congress. *Inside the Game*. Retrieved on June 30, 2012 from http://www.insidethegames.biz/sports/summer/football/17068-have-guts-do-the-right-thing-and-back-reforms-pieth-urges-fifa-congress-

Wikipedia. (2014). *Sportsmanship*. Retrieved on April 10, 2014 from http://en.wikipedia.org/wiki/Sportsmanship

WSC Daily. (2010, January 26). *Tapping into Portugal's corruption scandal*. Retrieved on July 3, 2012 from http://www.wsc.co.uk/wsc-daily/979-January-2010/4486-tapping-into-portugals-corruption-scandal

Yin, P. (2012, January 9). Poised to strike. *The Beijing Review*. Retrieved on March 27, 2012 from http://www.bjreview.com/nation/txt/2012-01/09/content_419500.htm

Part I
Mapping the Field

Chapter 2
The Natural Priority of Moral Virtue

"To become a refined player, sharpen your discernment and cultivate good manners." (Stephan Rothlin, *Eighteen Rules for Becoming a Top Notch Player*, 2000)

2.1 Prelude

Chapter one provided a basic vision of what a person can reasonably hope to achieve by becoming a "top-notch player." Implicit in this use of the term, "player," is the idea that business is more like playing a game than like going to war. As economists would argue, war is a zero-sum game, in which there is but one winner for every loser. Business, however, is something else. It is a positive-sum game, that is, even when one side loses, everyone wins if the game is well played. Games, we soon learn in playing them, are competitions governed by rules, which themselves define the difference between winning and losing, as well as the value of the prizes awarded for playing well and the penalties imposed for cheating. Becoming a "top-notch player" inevitably demands not only the acquisition of technical skills but also a commitment to the integrity of the game itself—what we described in chapter one as "sportsmanship." Is there anything in business akin to sportsmanship? Leading role models in various sports exhibit a common characteristic, namely, a commitment to the integrity of the games they play. Moral leadership in business requires a similar commitment. But from where does such a commitment originate? This chapter tries to address this question concretely by starting with a case study on the life of Mr. Andrew So, who served as Hong Kong's second commissioner in the Office of the Ombudsman (1994–1999). His life demonstrates the natural priority of cultivating moral virtues, in business as in all other areas of human endeavor, as well as the inherently social nature of Asian valucs and virtues.

S. Rothlin, D. McCann, *International Business Ethics*,
DOI 10.1007/978-3-662-47434-1_2

2.2 Case Study: A *Junzi* Now Living in Hong Kong?

2.2.1 Abstract

Throughout his career as a teacher, community organizer, businessman, and public official, Andrew So has actively promoted values education, business ethics, and sustainable development in and for Hong Kong, China, and Asia. He has served in a number of leadership positions within the credit union movement, including the first managing director of the Credit Union League of Hong Kong and founding president of the Association of Asian Confederation of Credit Unions (ACCU), as well as a director and one term as treasurer of the World Council of Credit Unions (WOCCU). In 1994, he relinquished his position as the International Vice President for Asia and Africa of the CUNA Mutual Insurance Group after having served the group for over 20 years. Beyond his extraordinary achievements in guiding the development of credit unions in Asia, he accepted the appointment to the Hong Kong Legislative Council (LegCo) (1978–1985) and later served one term as the second commissioner in the Hong Kong Office of the Ombudsman (1994–1999). Since his retirement, he has remained unusually active in various community development projects promoting credit unions and values education. The case study is based on an interview that Mr. So granted us in May 2012, from which we've taken all the direct quotes attributed to him. His story allows readers to explore—following the sage advice of both Confucius and Aristotle—how virtue can be recognized in the lives of contemporaries, as well as ancients, and taught and learned from their example.

2.2.2 Keywords

Moral virtues, Values education, Confucian ethics, Catholic social teaching, Community organization, Office of the Ombudsman, Attitudinal change.

2.2.3 Can Virtue Be Taught Nowadays?

The histories of most human civilizations abound in stories commemorating the extraordinary virtues of the ancients, usually men, like the Athenian philosopher Socrates (469–399 BCE), the Stoic Roman Emperor Marcus Aurelius (121–180 CE), Siddhartha Gautama, known as the Buddha (fifth century BCE), or Confucius himself (551–479 BCE). But as much as the ancients are revered, there has always been a question of whether their virtues could actually be cultivated by our contemporaries, who must with us endure the temptations and moral ambiguities of living today. The loftier the ancient sage or moral exemplar, the greater the skepticism grows about the relevance of his moral teaching and example. If virtue ethics is to be given the serious consideration that we think it deserves, then we must be able to demonstrate the realism of living virtuously while fully engaged in life's challenges here and now. With that goal in mind, we invited Andrew to be interviewed by us, in order to explore with him the path that the pursuit of virtue had taken in his own life. We wanted him to explain the role of virtue in his activities as a top-notch player in business, education, and government administration and especially in the founding of NGOs, such as credit unions, dedicated to helping ordinary people help themselves and their families.

2.2.4 "A Sense of Sharing Displaces the Effects of Selfishness and Materialism"

In preparation for the interview, which occurred at his beloved alma mater, Wah Yan College in Kowloon, Andrew was asked to give us his motto. He offered this quote from Confucius: "A sense of sharing displaces the effects of selfishness and materialism." Although it surely reflects Confucius' teaching, it is not to be found in the *Analects* (*Lún Yǔ*: 論語). We found it in *The Record of Rites* (*Lǐjì*: 禮記), in Book IX on *The Conveyance of Rites* (*Lǐ Yun*: 禮運), where it is embedded in a description of the ideal commonwealth state or Grand Union (*dàtóng*: 大同),[1] whose contrast with current social conditions demonstrates the need for observing *Lǐ* (禮) or cultivating a virtuous life.

While a "sense of sharing" is described in the *Lǐ Yun* as the natural consequence of living in an ideal commonwealth, Andrew's initiation into it occurred in Hong Kong, at that time a British colony and hardly a commonwealth that any Chinese would have considered ideal:

[1] Here is the full text of the passage from the *Lǐ Yun*, describing the Grand Union: "When the perfect order prevails, the world is like a home shared by all. Virtuous and worthy people are elected to public office, and capable persons hold posts of gainful employment in society; peace and trust among all people are the maxims of living. All people love and respect their own parents and children, as well as the parents and children of others. There is caring for the old; there are jobs for the adults; there are nourishment and education for the children. There is a means of support for the widows, and the widowers; for all who find themselves alone in the world; and for the disabled. Every man and woman has an appropriate role to play in the family and society. A sense of sharing displaces the effects of selfishness and materialism. A devotion to public duty leaves no room for idleness. Intrigues and conniving for ill gain are unknown. Villains such as thieves and robbers do not exist. The door to every home need never be locked and bolted by day or night. These are the characteristics of an ideal world, the commonwealth state." The full text of the *Lǐ Yun* (Book IX of the *Lǐjì*: 禮記), in Chinese characters, with James Legge's original translation of it (Legge 1885) is available at http://ctext.org/liji/li-yun. (The translation quoted here (Confucius Publishing Co. n.d.) is less literal than Legge's, but we quote it as the source from which Andrew So has taken his motto.) Later on in this chapter, we will provide an analysis of the importance of this passage for understanding the nature of true virtue in Confucian ethics. Here, we cite it in full in order to provide context for understanding Andrew So's experience in seeking to live by it in today's world.

> There were ten younger brothers and sisters. I was born during the Japanese war, and we suffered much during the occupation. With a big family you have to share: how can you learn a sense of sharing with 'one child per family' policies? As my father taught me, with so many children, you have to share. The food bowl didn't belong to me; it belongs to my brothers and sisters, too. A sense of sharing came to me very naturally.

Lacking the support of an ideal commonwealth, where the practice of virtue would be its own reward, Andrew grew up in a Chinese family for whom "a sense of sharing" was the key to survival. His parents had migrated from Guangdong Province in order to overcome their rural poverty and in Hong Kong had opened a small store selling sundry items, though his father had hoped to become a tailor. Their small retail operation was like so many others in Kowloon, with the family living in rooms directly behind the storefront. Eventually, an uncle came from China to help out. Though the store was a modest success as Andrew remembers it, everyone had to work to make ends meet: "Were we middle class? Well not really, but we had enough rice to eat and all of us went to school. We were very contented."

By the mid-1950s, when Andrew was ready for high school, he was enrolled in Wah Yan College, a prestigious Jesuit institution in Kowloon, where he covered himself in glory as the captain of the football team that won three trophies in competition with its Hong Kong rivals. He also performed in several plays and served as a scoutmaster. Like other lads whose time was taken up by extracurricular activities, Andrew admits that he didn't study too much. Whatever his academic shortcomings, his days with the Jesuits occasioned another momentous change in his life: "While my grandmother and auntie were very fervent Catholics, my parents were atheists. I only became a Catholic when I went to Wah Yan College, and was baptized there at 13 years of age." Hardly one to leave it at that, he later became a leading member—the "prefect"—of an important Catholic student organization on campus, the Sodality of Mary, later known as the Christian Life Committee.

What Andrew learned by having to share the family food bowl seems to have been reinforced by his teen-aged commitment to Catholic faith and practice. Together they influenced other decisions he was to make with regard to the choice of a career. Though he had hoped to study literature, Andrew enrolled in the Teachers' Training College—now flourishing within the Hong Kong Institute of Education (HKIEd)—so that he could find employment quickly and thus could provide support for the education of his brothers and sisters. After completing his training, he taught for 2 years at the government's Adult Education Center in Tsuen Wan, with courses in English designed primarily for industrial workers. During this time, he remained in contact with the Jesuits and became particularly interested in one recently formed group, the Committee for the Development of Socio-Economic Life in Asia (SELA),[2] which promoted credit unions, labor unions, and adult education programs. In 1963, Fr. John Collins, SJ, invited Andrew to participate in a 1-month training seminar in Bangkok, where—in addition to receiving an in-depth orientation to the theory and practice of establishing credit unions—he

[2] For further information on SELA and its work promoting social and economic development, see the report by Ando Isamu, SJ, "Social Involvement of Jesuits in the East Asian Region" (n.d.).

was first introduced to the social teachings of the Catholic Church. As Andrew recalls, "Fr. Collins decided to promote credit unions in Hong Kong and asked me to help, and so I helped start the Credit Union Center here. I quit my government job, to go full time on credit unions."

2.2.5 *Organizing Credit Unions in Hong Kong*

When asked why he was willing to give up a secure government job as a teacher, in order to start up this new, unusual venture, Andrew admitted that he was not satisfied at the government school, because of an apparent lack of dedication on the part of his colleagues. Inspired by what he had seen and heard in Bangkok, he could readily embrace the credit union movement as a force enabling ordinary people to overcome poverty and other social problems, a motive that had also animated his work in adult education. What he and Fr. Collins started soon began to bear fruit. In 1964, they founded the St. Francis Credit Union in Hong Kong. Two years later, nine credit unions had been organized, and these agreed to form the Credit Union League of Hong Kong, with Fr. Collins named as the permanent adviser and Andrew appointed the league's first managing director.[3] Their efforts soon expanded internationally as in 1971 he became the founding president of the Asian Confederation of Credit Unions (ACCU) and served as a member of the board of directors of the World Council of Credit Unions (WOCCU).[4] For over 20 years, he also served as the International Vice President for Asia and Africa of the CUNA Mutual Group,[5] which provides financial services and insurance products for the international credit union system.

When Andrew began organizing credit unions in Hong Kong, he and Fr. Collins made a strategic decision that would shape the movement from that time on. Though their personal commitment to the movement had been inspired by the social teachings of the Catholic Church, the credit unions they established were not oriented to the needs of the church and its members. Since Roman Catholics in Hong Kong accounted for only 5 % of the population, limiting credit union membership to the Catholic parishes and institutions would have been counterproductive. Instead, the credit unions founded by Andrew and Fr. Collins were designed to serve various occupational groups, for example, teachers or industrial workers. As Andrew insisted in his interview, "We stick to the principle that we should not be identified as a church group." So it is that the biggest credit union they started was organized among the Hong Kong police, currently with 35,000 members.

---

[3] For the complete chronology, see "A Brief History of Credit Union Movement in Hong Kong" (Credit Union League of Hong Kong 2013).

[4] For more information on the activities of the ACCU and the WOCCU, see their websites listed in the References section of this chapter.

[5] For more information on the CUNA Mutual Group and its past and present activities, see their website listed in the References section of this chapter.

2.2.6 Guiding Principles

Although the credit unions' organizational strategy and service mission are emphatically secular, their roots in virtues and values promoted by Catholic social teaching should also be clear. When Andrew was asked to explain the principles animating his leadership in the credit union movement, he made two major points. Taken together, they define the essence of Catholic social teaching, in its practical intent. The first is taken from Walter Hogan, SJ, the second general secretary of SELA, whose words Andrew apparently absorbed at the training seminar in Bangkok in 1963:

> I believe the economy—the organization of men into farming, manufacturing, transportation, banking and other services—should be a conspiracy among brothers to bring forth good things from the earth, make them more useful to men and distribute them equitably with at least a decent family living as the minimum share of each. Work, labour of one kind or another, is the means God gave men to sustain family life.

The second consists of Andrew's own understanding of what such a vision would mean in and for Asia:

> If we take a searching look we must admit that we Christians in general and Christians in Asia have not been distinguished in the more profound expressions of love of the people, which proceeds beyond the building of hospitals and beyond the building of orphanages and goes on to the building of a society that will be a proper place for the human family to live. A society of justice, of love, of freedom, of peace, where the children of God can really lead the kind of life that will prepare them for full and eternal life with God in heaven.

While listening to these words, it occurred to us that what Andrew had absorbed from Catholic social teaching was itself a variation on the ideals that animated his motto taken from Confucius' *Lǐ Yun* (禮運). When asked to make a comparison between the two, with typical modesty, Andrew indicated that only recently has he taken up the "hobby" of reflecting philosophically on such things. Nevertheless, this novice summarized his reflections so far in these terms: "My belief has always been that in the West the mission of life is to acquire a place in Heaven, while among us Chinese, the mission of life is to acquire Virtue. I try to acquire both." Acquiring both—judging from Andrew's example—means harmonizing in a single way of life both the ancient wisdom of Confucius, as expressed in the *Lǐ Yun* (禮運), and the modern aspirations of Catholic social teaching.

2.2.7 Leading Practices

Andrew's concrete reflections on organizing and managing credit unions illustrate the nature of this synthesis. He cited four basic practices that distinguish credit unions not only from other microfinance projects but also from other community organization activities: "Credit unions are designed to promote self help, mutual help, democratic control, and democratic ownership,[6] each of which is meant to resist the kind of economic exploitation you see in loan sharking," for example, or the various forms of societal marginalization imposed by politically oppressive regimes. With regard to "self-help" and the other objectives, Andrew explained:

> We distinguish ourselves from microfinancing in that savings is the most important part, we teach people to save in order to finance their own good goals. In the credit union the assets are democratically controlled through the cooperative, that is, its members, and are used to promote mutual help, self help. Member owned, member controlled, self-help, mutual help. These goals are not necessarily shared by all microfinancing schemes.

"Self-help," then, means that the cooperative "never seeks outside seed money." When asked whether that meant the credit unions could only make loans consistent with the rate of savings among their members, he acknowledged that since this might create an obstacle to actually serving the needs of the poor, they could receive start-up funds from agencies that were sponsoring them, for example, the Casa Ricci in Macau. He does not count these as "outside seed money," apparently since the funds come from the sponsoring agency and not from commercial banks.

The discipline imposed by acting consistently with the notion of "self-help" carries over into the ways that "mutual help" is realized. Andrew gave an important concrete example of "mutual help" when discussing how the credit unions make loans: "Each loan has to be judged on its own merits. Based on the character of the person, we even make loans to people who have no assets beyond membership." Making loans based upon an assessment of personal character, rather than a person's current net worth, of course, presupposes that the members authorizing loans have some familiarity with the members applying for loans. When the credit union's members democratically elect the loan officers and other administrators, the loan application process becomes more like a peer review. As Andrew reminded us, typically, the credit union is making small loans. While its review process cannot provide financial planning services, because it is based in the community, it is sufficient to secure mutual accountability for the loans, verifying that they are made for the purpose stated and that those receiving loans are capable of paying them back. He also observed that there are basically two types of loans, "one for providential purposes, for example, to pay for emergency surgery or a hospital stay for your wife, the other for productive purposes, that is, to provide capital for business." The process by which loans are made is designed to guarantee that the help is mutual. Above all, in Andrew's mind, it is a practical extension of the processes of adult education with which he had begun his career. When families join the credit union, apply for loans, and try to increase their savings, "we provide them with financial counseling, and, for example, show them how to make a family budget, or encourage them to quit smoking in order to save money, whatever it takes to make a wise use of money."

---

[6] How these practices have been adapted to the needs of specific communities may be explored in more detail in the case study on ACCU credit unions in the Philippines, which is featured in the final chapter of this book.

Given his wide-ranging experiences in business, credit union organization, and government service, Andrew remains a realist about the necessity of vigilance against corruption, in any situation where money changes hands. Though credit unions provide an alternative to the practice of "loan sharking"—making small, short-term loans at exorbitant rates of interest—so prevalent in communities afflicted with poverty, he knows that there are other abuses that must also be prevented. One of these is "money laundering"—the practice of using legitimate financial institutions to conceal the origins of funds generated through criminal activity. When asked how the credit union guards against such abuses, Andrew noted that although they are unable to verify where each deposit comes from, "we do have a limit on how much you can deposit with the credit union. Each member is allowed to deposit not more than 10 % of the total assets of the credit union. So we do not have big shareholders. It is very rare that you would have such depositors." The restriction on deposits, of course, also demonstrates the credit unions' commitment to democratic ownership and control. No single shareholder is in a position to use his or her assets to preempt its governance structures or evade accountability to them.

2.2.8 "Devotion to Public Duty Leaves No Room for Idleness…"

The ACCU, which in 1971 started out with credit unions in only eight Asian countries, by 2012 was operating in twenty countries, serving the needs of 37.5 million members—6.3 million of them still struggling with poverty, as measured in their own regions—in 21,900 credit unions, with an aggregate staff of at least 330,000 volunteers and approximately 20,000 paid professional employees. If the ACCU cannot be credited with eliminating poverty throughout Asia, it has certainly enabled millions of families to find their own ways out of poverty or, at least, to cope with it more effectively than they had ever done before. As Andrew pointed out, since the causes of poverty are multiple and complex, the strategies for overcoming poverty must be responsive to local needs, opportunities, and constraints. Since corruption, particularly among public service personnel, had been a major problem in Hong Kong, it is only natural that the next phase of Andrew's career should unfold in government service.

In recalling his work in public life, Andrew reflected primarily on his 5-year appointment as the commissioner for Hong Kong's Office of the Ombudsman (1994–1999). Among other things, Andrew's service as ombudsman came during the years when the Hong Kong government made the transition from British colonial rule to the restoration of China's sovereignty in the HKSAR. Newspaper accounts in the *South China Morning Post* suggest that this was a particularly challenging time for an ombudsman, since the people's confidence in the new government greatly depended on how well it responded to their inquiries and complaints:

> In an executive-led administration, the Ombudsman's post fills a gap that exists in the absence of a fully democratic system. It provides an essential outlet for the public to

> have grievances set to rights. It is an important curb on the powers of bureaucracy, but can only be effective if the office is seen as separate from official channels. (SCMP, December 24, 1998)

Andrew was acutely aware of his role in maintaining the public's confidence in government during this period and worked diligently to expand the investigative powers of the office and citizen's access to it. Not only were the procedures for filing and handling complaints opened up during his tenure as commissioner, but in 1996, the ombudsman's office also organized a complaint management workshop for public officers. Andrew recalled for us how at that time he hoped to improve the government's responsiveness to the people's concerns:

> The Ombudsman is there to administer the Law of the Ombudsman. If you have a good system, you can find good people to do it. When I was appointed I was the second to hold that post, three years before the Handover and two years after it. Before me, a very prestigious judge held the position. When I was appointed, people asked, is he a lawyer? Is he a judge? My defenders said that he is neither but he has common sense.

When asked to explain what they meant by common sense, Andrew emphasized the kinds of character required to carry out the ombudsman's duties:

> When I retired from credit union work to become the Ombudsman, I considered it a mission, and I had a five year plan. I wanted to see a smooth transition to China in 1997. The government enlarged the powers of my office, as the number of complaints increased from 100 to 4000 a month during the transition. My job was to listen to the complaints of citizens, and sort out which were justifiable and needed to be pursued.

The sorting out, of course, is precisely what calls for common sense, shaped by the virtues that make for good public service. "The law is quite good. But you need moral courage to be a moral leader. You need courage to say No when you must say No, courage to stand up and be counted." The moral courage needed in a good ombudsman, then, is simply a commitment to carry out your responsibilities impartially. "The office calls for exercising good judgment, which requires prudence and the other virtues. A judge or lawyer might not take values or ethics into consideration. But sometimes I needed to." For Andrew, then, values or ethics is a matter of common sense, something that remains alive in the common people, if not always perfectly embodied in the policies and procedures of governments that are supposed to serve them.

Ever the teacher, however, Andrew did attempt to communicate these expectations to the government officials whose work he had to review as ombudsman. Even before he organized the workshop on complaint management, he sent around certain checklists meant to stimulate individual efforts to become more responsive to citizens' concerns:

> When I started the job, I made a list, a Fairness Checklist, and a list detailing what Good Governance is. I distributed these lists to all government agencies, with their approximately 280,000 civil servants. These allowed everyone to know on what basis I made decisions on what to investigate.

At the time when the government was in transition and when citizens' expectations, then as now, seem to be rising, particularly with regard to transparency and accountability demanded of government officials, Andrew was trying to minimize the need for complaints, investigations, and sanctions of various kinds. His checklists may have been no more than common sense, but they reminded civil servants how they should conduct themselves in order to avoid creating problems for themselves and the government.

Acutely aware that people expect government officials "nowadays on ethical issues [to] be whiter than white," Andrew prepared himself as ombudsman to lead by example. In assuming the office, he went to great lengths to anticipate problems and eliminate them before they arose:

> I resigned from the credit union work and the insurance company I was working for, in order to avoid conflict of interest. I was chairman of the Board of Education and various commissions, etc., and I resigned them all. But I did get permission to retain two jobs: one, to set up the values education/leadership institute at HKIIEd, which we had started in 1991, and also to retain my post in the Discharged Prisoner's Aid Society in Hong Kong. Though I didn't receive any compensation from either of these—and I didn't have to resign them—I did want to maintain my impartiality. But later when I was Ombudsman if any case were to come up involving these agencies, I had to declare my involvement so my impartiality would be clear.

Since impartiality in judgment was indispensable for discharging the duties of his office, he had to make his interests completely transparent. How could he expect civil servants to meet the public's increasingly rigorous expectations if he were to exempt himself from similar scrutiny?

2.2.9 "When the Perfect Order Prevails, the World Is Like a Home Shared by All..."

Upon his retirement from the Office of the Ombudsman in 1999, Andrew was awarded the prestigious Silver Bauhinia Star, which is presented to "persons who have taken a leading part in public affairs or voluntary work over a long period." Far from signaling the end of his efforts to promote the values envisioned in the *Lǐ Yun* (禮運) and Catholic social teaching, the award merely marked one more change of venue. In recent years, Andrew has returned to his earlier activities promoting moral education—particularly in business ethics—and organizing credit unions. One story he told us nicely captures the harmony between the two:

> In 1985, one of the Jesuits, Fr. Luis Ruiz, in Macau, was asked by the Chinese government to work with lepers. The government's policy on lepers was OK, but Fr. Ruiz saw that one thing was lacking: LOVE. So he employed Catholic sisters from India, Italy, and Argentina, to wash and care for the lepers, and later on to help children with AIDS. But 5 years ago, when at age 92 Fr. Ruiz passed away, I was asked by Casa Ricci to institutionalize what he had done. So we set up a foundation, and I was instrumental in changing its mission to help all the marginalized and poor through self-help, so they can become masters of their own destiny and make a contribution to the general good of the nation as a whole. So once again I started to convince the Jesuits in Macau: We need to go beyond building hospitals and orphanages. Our mission must be to build a society that would be a proper place for the

> human family. So my job with them is to promote human development, starting with credit unions, which were illegal in China at the time. Credit unions promote democracy from grass roots, which is where you have to start if there is to be democracy in China. Two years later we are teaching values education. We teach values, spirituality, but not Catholic doctrine as such. We teach resource management.

Andrew then recalled once more the words of Fr. Walter Hogan, who had inspired him at that fateful training seminar in Bangkok in 1963. Fr. Hogan had called for a "conspiracy among brothers to bring forth good things from the earth, make them more useful to men and distribute them equitably." Conspiracy, in Andrew's understanding, is a good word, one that emphasizes how persons sharing a common vision of the good life can work together to achieve it. Throughout his career, Andrew had done whatever he can to expand the circle of conspirators working for the common good. His actions make sense, when understood in light of his frequently reiterated belief in the dignity of every human being: "Each person is unique, has unique talents and a contribution to make: so we mean to draw the best out of a person, as in adult education, so in the credit union's activities." Are the values enshrined in Confucius' ideal commonwealth and its expression in other traditions, such as Catholic social teaching, obsolete in today's world of business and public affairs? Not as long as we continue to find people like Andrew So determined to make this world a home shared by all. What else would a *junzi* be doing in Hong Kong nowadays?

2.3 Case Study Discussion

One of the most important lessons to be learned from Andrew So is that the practice of virtue cannot be restricted to the cultivation of personal qualities, as important as these may be. The virtuous person or—in Confucian terms—the *junzi* is involved in public life, accepting public responsibilities whether in government service or in business and the professions, in order to advance the common good of society as a whole. Too often the practice of virtue has been reduced to self-cultivation, as if the point of the virtuous life is to remove oneself from all the temptations, the corruption, and the injustice that all too often accompany public affairs. No wonder that so many people consider the practice of virtue irrelevant, if not an obstacle to success, for anyone seeking to take an active role in government service or in business and the professions. The perennial philosophical question of whether virtue can be taught actually should be redirected: the real question is whether virtue can be taught well. Can we learn to see the deep connection between the practice of virtue and the acceptance of public responsibilities?

Andrew So answers this question not by giving us a lecture but by embodying an example. Yes, we can learn how to make the connection in our own lives, for we have the experience of teachers like Andrew who can still show us the way. So what questions occur to you, as you have listened to Andrew's story? If you were raised in a large family struggling for survival, would it make sense to cultivate a sense of sharing? What did your parents teach you about sharing? Would they have agreed with Andrew's parents? Do you agree with Andrew? If you are an older brother or sister, what do you think of the way he sacrificed his desire to study literature in order to get a job that would help pay for his younger brothers' and sisters' education? Or later on, when Andrew joins the credit union movement, would it occur to you that organizing such cooperatives might be an effective way of helping people overcome poverty while also cultivating the virtues—like thrift and honesty—that often lead to prosperity? Do you think Andrew's choice is relevant only to social workers and community organizers?

What, if anything, can Andrew teach you about doing business? After all, thanks to the administrative skills and the excellent reputation he acquired in the credit union movement, he was invited to join the management team of a major insurance firm. And then there's his tenure as Hong Kong's ombudsman. What stands out in your mind about the way he approached his duties as a public official? He spoke of the need for common sense and moral courage and more specifically about impartiality in administering the duties of his office. What do these mean to you? Does it surprise you that he values them so highly? Finally, do you see the underlying continuity in the way Andrew approached the various responsibilities that he has undertaken throughout his life? How would you put into words what you have learned about virtue by studying Andrew's story? While the ancient sages of China and the West all described cultivating the virtues as following the way, you may wonder whether the way is something known only to the ancient sages. A deeper look at people's lives clearly shows that there are many among us who still follow the way. Andrew is not alone; but once we have learned to recognize one example, we will soon discover many others.

2.4 Ethical Reflection

Inquiry into the nature of true virtue is as old as philosophy itself, both in China and in the Hellenistic traditions that shaped Western civilization. For various reasons, alas, the cultivation of virtue has been neglected and often despised as obsolete, in societies undergoing rapid changes in social and economic development, modernization, and now globalization. But we are convinced that this neglect can be reversed and must be reversed if business ethics is to flourish in China, along with other hallmarks of genuine reform and social progress. In order to understand the natural priority of virtue in business ethics, we have to set aside, if only for a moment, the standard account of business ethics.

Conceived as a region of applied ethics, that is, as a specific field in the application of philosophically validated moral norms, the standard account of business ethics seeks to expand the calculations that seem routine in any business decision-making by factoring in the ethical imperatives emergent from a formal analysis of the categories of moral judgment. Typically, these are two in number, namely, the famous pairings of good and bad, on the one hand, and right and wrong on the other.

Logical analysis of the way ordinary people use words like good and bad indicates that these express judgments about the consequences of our actions, while right and wrong have a similar function with regard to our duties and obligations. We will explore these in more detail in a later chapter. Here, the point is that broadening the list of considerations for managers to weigh in their calculations, while a step in the right direction, is not likely to be effective, unless managers make a personal commitment to good business ethics. In our view, moral clarity about the priority of right and wrong, good and bad, and other paired ethical categories occurs only in people who already are well grounded in the cultivation of moral virtue. In other words, business ethics must first be about moral character and the cultivation of those habits of the heart that enable a person to make personal integrity the hallmark of all their actions in business.

Each of us has discovered the priority of virtue in business ethics more or less through trial and error. With more than 50 years of experience between us in teaching and writing about business ethics, we have seen just how pedagogically ineffective the standard account offered by applied ethics is for training students and business practitioners to become "top-notch players." Those who learn business ethics as just another level to be added to the calculus of business decision-making, once faced with opportunities to make real decisions, soon realize that this level can easily be ignored or bypassed when the bottom line dictates quicker or dirtier ways to fix pressing problems short term. Honoring the priority of virtue in business practice makes it harder to ignore or set aside ethical considerations. Honoring the priority of virtue deliberately moves students and business practitioners away from the temptation to manipulate the rules of ethical abstractions and toward an existential encounter with everyone's basic human nature. If this shift seems like a return to the teachings of the ancient sages, both Confucian and Christian, undeniably, it is. For the superiority of their insights ought to be evident to anyone who has ever truly struggled to maintain their integrity while exercising managerial responsibilities.

Understanding the priority of virtue is not simply a teaching of the ancient sages. In her important book, *Good Intentions Aside: A Manager's Guide to Resolving Ethical Problems* (1993), Laura Nash usefully distinguishes two types of ethical problems, Type A and Type B. Type A problems are situations properly regarded as "moral dilemmas" in which a person doesn't know—or is in doubt—as to what the right thing to do is, while Type B problems are situations in which a person knows what the right thing to do is, but will not or cannot bring themselves to do it. Of the two, it is Type B problems that led us to rediscover the priority of virtue. While students and business people facing Type A problems may be helped significantly by the kind of analyses and managerial decision-making models offered in applied ethics, even the clarity achieved thereby will make no practical difference, so long as any underlying Type B problems remain unresolved. We will return in later chapters to Nash's distinction, because it not only allows us to highlight the priority of virtue, but in defining the limits of various approaches to business ethics, it also suggests how these might be integrated effectively, as we hope to show further on.

Reflection on Type B problems illuminates the natural priority of virtue by allowing us to see the contrast between weakness and strength. Virtue, in its Latin origins, means strength or the qualities of personal character (*virtus*) indicative of manliness (*vir*, a Latin word, provides the root for English terms like "virility" and "virile"). Not surprisingly, the manliness of the ancient Romans was conceived primarily in terms of prowess demonstrated on the battlefield. As Roman traditions were filtered through Hellenistic philosophy, virtue later became synonymous with the Greek word of "excellence" (*arête*); the qualities of demonstrated wisdom and courage made a man an ideal civic leader. Both traditions tended to conceive of virtue as a skill set, the result of cultivating a personal capacity for self-control. Weakness of character meant a lack of self-control, as is evident from the Greek term *akrasia*, which conveniently summarizes the underlying root of Type B problems.

While their respective explanations for such weakness of character may differ, both Chinese and Western traditions of moral philosophy agree that it can be overcome, at least to some extent. The cultivation of virtue, in both traditions, is an open-ended process, culminating either in becoming fully human, as in Confucian and Hellenistic thought, or becoming "perfect as your heavenly Father is perfect" (Matthew 5:48) through the grace of God, as in Christianity. In each of these traditions, there is optimism not only that there is a way forward toward genuine humanity but also that making progress along the way involves cultivating the moral virtues. Though the worldviews presupposed in these traditions differ dramatically on several important issues, for example, the reality of God, the meaning of Heaven, the origin of the universe, the nature of the afterlife, etc., there is a remarkable degree of consensus about the natural priority of virtue.

2.4.1 Confucian Virtues

In the teachings of Confucius (551–479 BCE), each human being (Chinese: 人; pinyin *Rén*) has the opportunity to become genuinely humane (Chinese: 仁; pinyin *Rén*). *Rén* (仁) is usually translated as "benevolence" or more concretely as knowing and loving people. Goodness or happiness—the goal of humane living—cannot be achieved without practicing benevolence in one's relationships with other people. The Confucian notion of an ideal commonwealth or Grand Union (*dàtóng*: 大同) helps explain both the possibility and the necessity of becoming fully human. It contains a description of ordinary living within this ideal commonwealth—where not only is a "sense of sharing" spontaneous and universal, but also "a public and common spirit ruled all under the sky." In such a *dàtóng* (大同), "they chose men of talents, virtue, and ability; their words were sincere, and what they cultivated was harmony," as everyone fulfilled their role in life and the work assigned to them. Confucius admits to being sad when he thinks of the Grand Union, because he has never witnessed it. The world we actually live in, he later explains in the *Lǐ Yun* (禮運), is precariously poised between becoming either a "small tranquility" (*xiǎokāng*: 小康) or an "infirm state" (*cī guó*: 疵國).

The "small tranquility" is a state in which there is sufficient order to insure that everyone is "well-off," while, by contrast, an "infirm state" is one that is characterized by massive corruption and disorder. The consequence of cultivating the Confucian virtues—as embodied primarily in the rules of propriety (*Lǐ*: 禮) that are codified and explained in *The Record of Rites* (*Lǐjì*: 禮記)—is that the Chinese people are more likely to enjoy the blessings of living in a *xiǎokāng* (小康) rather than suffering further in a *cī guó* (疵國) where harmony is impossible. The social character of Confucian teaching about the virtues is thus clear: virtuous practices, however admirable, are not simply for self-cultivation in any narrow sense but are the means to a higher end, namely, the creation of a state in which the people may flourish, by actively participating in the pursuit of the common good. When the Grand Union is realized on earth—if it ever can be realized—the practice of virtue may be its own reward, but in the meantime, in the struggle to overcome the predatory chaos of an "infirm state," the practice of virtue is the indispensable means to secure enough of a "small tranquility" to allow ordinary people a chance to live in harmony with their neighbors.

While the *Lǐ Yun* (禮運) lays out the consequences of choosing to live virtuously, Confucian tradition in various ways describes how the virtues may be cultivated, beginning with the process known as the "rectification of names" (*Zhèngmíng*: 正名). The names refer to the five basic relationships in which each of us finds himself or herself in life: parent and child, elder sibling and younger sibling, husband and wife, elder friend and younger friend, and ruler and subject. Rectification in any of these relationships is understood as an extension of the filial piety (*xiào*: 孝) first learned in honoring one's parents. Guided by a general sense of benevolence that Confucians generally believed to be innate in human nature, a person could progress toward greater humanity by observing the rules of propriety (*Lǐ*: 禮) with the intention of achieving righteousness (*Yì*: 义/義) in every relationship. Successful rectification thus is the result of a process of self-cultivation that is meant to allow a person's inherently moral nature to become increasingly clear and effective. The cultivation of virtue is possible because humanity is inherently good; it becomes necessary because that goodness is fragile and vulnerable to corruption.

Confucius' disciple, Mengzi (372–289 BCE), taught that there were four basic virtues inherent in human nature. A famous passage in the *Book of Mencius* begins with an observation on the universality of compassion: "All men have a mind which cannot bear to see the sufferings of others" (2A6: 1). He then notes that this "commiserating mind" is the basis for the kind of exemplary government exercised by the ancient kings. In order to demonstrate the reality of the compassion naturally occurring in human beings, Mengzi tells a story about what happens when "men suddenly see a child about to fall into a well." They "without exception experience a feeling of alarm and distress." Without calculating any reward they might obtain for doing so, they rush to save the child (2A6: 3). From this observation, Mengzi infers that normal people contain within themselves the "sprouts" from which the four basic virtues grow:

> The heart of compassion is the sprout of benevolence [*ren*]. The heart of disdain is the sprout of righteousness [*yi*]. The heart of deference is the sprout of propriety [*li*]. The heart of approval and disapproval is the sprout of wisdom [*zhi*].... In general, having these four sprouts within oneself, if one knows to fill them out, it will be like a fire starting up, a spring

> breaking through! If one can merely fill them out, they will be sufficient to care for all within the Four Seas. If one merely fails to fill them out, they will be insufficient to serve one's parents. (2A6: 4–5)[7]

Some process of "filling out" defines the way (*Dào*: 道) of acquiring the four basic virtues: humanity (*ren*), righteousness (*yi*), ritual propriety (*li*), and wisdom (*zhi*).

Teaching and learning the way of the virtues must begin by identifying the "sprouts" within oneself and others and then nurturing these to full maturity. How might that be done? Mengzi's "sprout" metaphor leads us to consider the practice of self-cultivation. If a sprout or a seedling is to grow, it must be weeded, watered, and exposed to sunlight—and all of these in just the right amount. Weeding suggests the exercise of self-control, what Mengzi describes as lessening one's desires (7B: 35). Unruly desires, that is, seemingly uncontrollable impulses that threaten to upset the heart-mind's natural serenity, must not be allowed to dominate the self. Some form of yoga or meditation practice seems appropriate here. Watering suggests the need for nourishment, in this case, perhaps, establishing a regular program of reading texts designed to build up the heart-mind. Exposure to sunlight suggests public accountability. Even in the process of self-cultivation, it is always good to have a mentor or, if you will, a guru, spiritual director, or teacher (*shīfu*: 師父).

Obviously, teaching and learning the *Dào* of virtue involve far more than mastering concepts through conventional forms of study. One learns the virtues ultimately by interacting with a mentor who has clearly demonstrated significant progress in self-cultivation. In his study on *Virtue Ethics and Confucianism* (2003), Bryan Van Norden refers to such teachers as "connoisseurs," that is, people who have distinguished themselves for their excellence in practicing a particular art. One example is "the wine guide" who can assist beginners in developing their own sense of good taste or quality in judging and selecting wines. Here is Van Norden's analogy between teachers of virtue and wine guides:

> What is distinctive about connoisseurs in all of these areas is that they perceive clearly things the rest of us 'see darkly' (if at all), that there are no straightforward rules to follow in order to perceive these things (as Mencius observes, 'A carpenter or a wheel-wright can give another his compass or T-square, but he cannot make another skillful.' (7B: 5)), and that there are no definitive tests for the presence of the things they perceive. (2003: 115)

Nevertheless, this does not mean that in cultivating the virtues there are no standards, any more than would it be true that one opinion is as good as another when it comes to good taste in wines or any other judgment of quality. What Van Norden is explaining, of course, is the role of exemplary persons (Chinese: 君子, pinyin: *jūnzǐ*) or moral leaders in teaching the virtues. Such persons may not be as lofty as sages, but their success in exercising moral leadership through self-cultivation will inspire others to take up the *Dào* and follow it wherever it may lead.

---

[7] The translation is taken from Bryan Van Norden's excerpts from the *Mengzi (Mencius)* presented in the *Readings in Classical Chinese Philosophy* that he edited with Philip J. Ivanhoe (2005). Van Norden's comments on the meaning of Mengzi's "sprouts" (2005: 116) prompted our use of his translation. Other important translations are the pioneering effort by James Legge (1991), first published in 1861, and more recently D.C. Lau's *Mencius*, published by Penguin Books (1970).

2.4.2 Western Virtues

Comparisons with Western traditions of virtue ethics are quite striking, especially the further back in time we go. In his *Nicomachean Ethics*, Aristotle (384–322 BCE) initiates the study of virtue ethics by observing the goodness intended by every human action: "Every art and every inquiry, and similarly every action and pursuit, is thought to aim at some good" (1094a). The meaning of this generalization is readily seen in specific examples: as in the case of playing a musical instrument, what makes a person a good flute player is his or her ability to play the flute well. The specific example then illuminates the generalization: what makes one a good person is leading a truly human life. Aristotle goes on to argue that the distinctive feature of such a truly human life is happiness. The challenge, then, is to establish the relationship between happiness and virtue.

Though goodness as such is clearly the key to happiness, as Aristotle observes, opinions vary as to what makes people happy. He quickly dismisses any idea that happiness consists only in making oneself comfortable. Since pleasure itself is as much a state of mind as of the body, it cannot be reduced mistakenly to pleasant physical sensations but must include the enjoyment of activities that are by nature pleasant, such as finding pleasure in virtuous actions. We are pleased either when we see someone else demonstrating courage or fairness or wisdom or self-control in action or when we are praised by others for acting on these or other indications of personal integrity. While it may be natural for the lover of horses to find happiness in caring for horses, human nature is fully realized in its capacity for rationality, whose exercise consists in perfecting the virtues. Aristotle divides these into two basic kinds: intellectual virtues and moral virtues. The intellectual virtues, the highest of which is wisdom, result from developing a person's intellect. The moral virtues result from achieving self-control over a person's bodily appetites through the use of reason. Although bodily appetites are normal, they must be disciplined so that they harm neither one's self nor others. The genius of Aristotle, however, takes us beyond self-cultivation of the mind and body, explaining that we are not only rational beings but also social beings whose final happiness is found within society or exercising our assigned roles in the civic community (*polis*).

Compared with the Confucian classics, Aristotle's way of philosophizing about virtue is highly abstract and impersonal. Nevertheless, he clearly agrees with Confucius and Mencius on a number of substantive points. First, both traditions affirm the goodness of human nature, as evident in the fact that good is the intended goal of all our desires and actions. Second, both affirm the inherently social purpose of cultivating the virtues. Aristotle's *Nicomachean Ethics* is intimately related to Aristotle's *Politics*, since the proper ordering of the self, achieved through the cultivation of the virtues, is the presupposition for exercising leadership in a properly ordered civic community. The political constitutions governing the latter reflect—or at least should reflect, if the civic community assists all its members find happiness—the constitution proper to human nature as such. As we have seen in our brief analysis of the *Lǐ Yun* (禮運), Confucian classics exhibit a similar pattern. The process of self-cultivation described as the "rectification of names" (*Zhèngmíng*) begins within the family and by analogy extends through ever-expanding circles of social relationships ("subjects" and "ruler") to the state. Honoring the principles of right and wrong in all one's actions not only is personally virtuous but also contributes to the happiness of the human community as a whole, which in turn is the key to social harmony within which personal happiness may be realized on a secure basis.

As we have already noted, the Chinese classics treasure the relationship between the teacher (*shīfu*) and students seeking enlightenment. The student, in turn, becomes the master, just as the child eventually becomes a parent. But neither happens spontaneously since self-cultivation involves learning through imitation and personal association, over and above whatever may be communicated by studying texts. Aristotle agrees that virtuous people do not simply emerge as such. They are taught by example, by stories, and by exemplary models. People are not fated to exercise moral leadership, but by discovering themselves in a specific web of relationships—Book IX of the *Nicomachean Ethics* focuses explicitly on the role of friendship in moral development—through which he or she gradually reaches a level of awareness that makes moral leadership possible. Though both Chinese and the Hellenistic traditions thus emphasize the social nature of becoming a virtuous person, the primary relationship in which moral development occurs seems different. Students learn from teachers (*shīfu*) in an attitude of filial piety modeled, in Chinese tradition, on a child's relationship with its parents, whereas among the ancient Greeks, the virtues are cultivated in peer relationships among friends, as explained, for example, by Socrates in Plato's dialogues, the *Lysis* and the *Symposium* (Cooper 1997). The social context tends to be egalitarian in the Socratic tradition and hierarchical in Chinese tradition.

Though both traditions honor four basic virtues, the differences between the two lists indicate different emphases. The four basic virtues taught by Confucian moral philosophy—humanity (*ren*), righteousness (*yi*), ritual propriety (*li*), and wisdom (*zhi*)—identify both substantive moral ideals and ways to fulfill them. Foregrounded in each are the importance of social considerations and the achievement of social harmony through self-cultivation. In Hellenistic tradition, the four "cardinal virtues"—so named because they serve as hinges linked to all other moral ideals—are prudence, justice, fortitude, and temperance. Though the cardinal virtues foreground personal dispositions indispensable to the achievement of happiness, each is also social in character. The degree of overlap between the two lists is striking, particularly in the case of wisdom (*zhi*) and prudence, and righteousness (*yi*) and justice. Nevertheless, the differences between ritual propriety (*li*) and fortitude or courage and between humanity (*ren*) and temperance suggest that while Hellenistic ethics is more concerned with identifying the formal habit of mind that enables a person to act virtuously, Confucian ethics is more concerned with identifying the way (*Dào*) in which proper habits of mind are cultivated.

Aristotle's conception of justice is particularly important for understanding the diverging emphases in the two traditions, for justice indicates not only an intention to act righteously (*yi*) but also the norms by which to measure righteous action.

Book V of the *Nicomachean Ethics* (Ross 1925) observes that justice, in one sense, is the greatest of the virtues because its exercise comprehends all of them and includes not only one's own good but that of all other people (Book V: 1). What justice is may best be understood by examining our experience of its opposite, namely, injustice, which comprehends acts that are regarded as either unfair or unlawful. Fairness and lawfulness, however, are not mere tokens of personal satisfaction but measures of the equality appropriately realized in human relationships. Equality itself is not a simple term but can be divided into two types, (a) arithmetical and (b) proportional, corresponding roughly to outcomes of (a) private transactions, as between neighbors exchanging goods with each other, and (b) the allocation of goods distributed by the proper authorities. In the form of equality that is proportional, legislation may require that one individual receives more than another because of his role within the community, but in exchanges that occur between individuals buying and selling with each other, fairness requires that all transactions be treated equally, for example, that the price charged to one customer should be the same for all customers. As a virtue, then, justice concerns the ways a person conducts his or her social responsibilities, whether in politics—understood as the arena of civic responsibilities—or in the marketplace. Cultivating the virtue of justice draws on capacities nurtured in other virtues, for without these, a person will lack the prudence needed to distinguish the contexts in which justice must be done and the fortitude and temperance necessary to act consistently by the standards of equality appropriate to either lawfulness or fairness.

The strength inherent in Aristotle's complex conception of justice is that it specifies the appropriate standard for dealing fairly and lawfully with one's neighbors or fellow citizens in public life, that is, the life of the *polis*. Its impersonal character, profiled in the mathematical norms by which it is measured out, is clearly appropriate to the relatively impersonal relationships of public life. Neighbors are not owed the same kind of loving kindness that one owes to members of one's own household, that is, one's wife, one's children, and other dependents. But neighbors are owed the minimum expressed by fairness and lawfulness. The virtue of justice is not extrapolated from obligations honored within the family and then applied analogously to relationships with others outside the family. Aristotle defines justice in mathematical terms as the equality achieved by envisioning a "Golden Mean" between too much and too little. In some situations, that measure will require that a distribution of goods be proportional to each individual's public responsibilities; in other situations, it will require that each individual receives equal treatment regardless of their social status or degree of familial affinity.

The strength inherent in the Confucian virtues is that they embody a deep insight into the reciprocity necessary for social harmony, whether in one's own family or in the state. The extrapolation of Confucian virtues from a person's primordial experience of filial piety (Chinese: 孝; pinyin, *xiào*) ensures that reciprocity will be the moral imperative animating all social relationships, with the expectation that virtue consists primarily in adapting one's attitudes and behaviors to the requirements of social harmony. Though some observers identify this Confucian ideal with skepticism about democracy, either in theory or in practice, the traditional emphasis on social harmony deserves our respect, because of its role in preserving Chinese civilization over millennia. Nevertheless, Confucian filial piety may conflict with the demands of fairness and lawfulness. In the *Analects*, for example, Confucius memorably commends as "upright" fathers and sons who fail to report each other's misdeeds to the proper authorities (Analects 13: 18). Loyalty to one's own family members apparently may override one's civic responsibility to uphold the rule of law. To be sure, even in ancient China, such an interpretation of filial piety was challenged soon after Confucius.

2.4.3 Mozi's Unclaimed Legacy

What Mozi (470–391 BCE) taught may best be understood not as a total rejection of Confucianism but as an indispensable supplement that shows us the way to integrate both Confucian and Aristotelian perspectives on virtue. Like the other perspectives, Mozi's philosophy also teaches the importance of treating humankind with respect. All three seek to go beyond distorted views of self-cultivation, in order to become more and more open to the needs of other people and finally of the concerns of the whole society. Mozi's work is significant, because it seeks to go beyond a narrow-minded love that is limited to one's own family—the kind of error that occurs when a small-minded person (Chinese: 小人; pinyin: *xiǎorén*) misunderstands Confucius's teachings. Mozi is both criticized and celebrated as the Chinese advocate of "universal love" (Chinese: 兼愛; pinyin: *jian'ai*). But what he meant by this term is sufficiently ambiguous to have his teachings identified with both Christian ethics and the ideology of the Chinese Communist Party. Philip J. Ivanhoe has proposed a useful clarification of *jian'ai* by translating it as "impartial care." This translation reflects Ivanhoe's discovery that "in Mozi's view, the central ethical problem was excessive *partiality*, not a lack of *compassion*." (Ivanhoe and Van Norden 2005: 60). What prevented people from finding the right way to achieve social harmony was their failure to consider all things impartially.

Impartiality means cultivating the use of reason to judge the consequences of various courses of action. If a proposed course of action has positive consequences for obtaining the basic goods that all people want—namely, a sufficiency of resources and a harmonious society in which to enjoy them—then it should be implemented, regardless of the pressure for social change it might bring to bear on traditional customs and practices. Mozi, for example, used such an impartial calculus to criticize Confucius's teachings in support of traditional Chinese funeral rituals (Book VI: 25, Book IX), a cornerstone of the practice of filial piety. Mozi was particularly concerned about the partiality enshrined in practices that required a lengthier mourning period and more lavish rituals for immediate family members. His argument is not a rejection of filial piety as such but a reminder that it, too, must be judged by the standard of humanity or benevolence. All social practices therefore must be reformed according to whether they "enrich the poor, increase the population, [and] bring stability to precarious situations and order to chaos." If they don't, "then these things clearly are not benevolent and right or the proper task of filial children." (2005: 81)

Mozi's critique of Confucianism suggests that rationality ought to be the hallmark of a moral leader (Chinese: 君子; pinyin: *jūnzǐ*) intending to be benevolent. The good that Mozi seeks seems to resonate well with Confucian virtues, but the way that he pursues it involves a critical analysis of the means for achieving them. Benevolence thus is identified with "impartial care" rather than the partiality or familial favoritism enshrined in the Confucian way of achieving social harmony. The *Book of Mozi* shows how consistently he applied critical reasoning not only to traditional Chinese social practices but also to the ways Confucius' disciples were interpreting them. Mozi's teachings therefore should not be regarded as a rejection of the social virtues that Confucius and his disciples were upholding but a program of reform that called into question any traditional practices that were contrary to the ends properly honored in these virtues. The natural priority of virtue remains, as does the ideal of moral leadership, but exercising the virtues requires rational analysis as well as humane self-cultivation. The ethical sprouts must be exposed to sunlight and weeded, as well as watered and planted in good soil.

If Mozi's teachings reveal the point where Chinese virtue ethics converges with the rational analysis of justice outlined by Aristotle, it also suggests why and how ethics inspired by the *Nicomachean Ethics* needs to learn from Confucius. Rational analysis may be an indispensable tool for achieving the kind of impartiality that both Mozi and Aristotle advocate, but unless that impartiality grows like a lotus flower from a compassionate heart, it may create more social conflict than harmony. Both Aristotle and Mozi place their hopes in philosopher kings, like Philip of Macedon who appointed Aristotle to tutor his son who became Alexander the Great and like the sage-kings of ancient China, like Kings Wen and Wu. But their appeal to such authorities carries the risk that the reforms they advocate will be imposed coercively over the heads of ordinary people, who presumably lack the virtues necessary to comprehend rational arguments. Though the risk of elitism is also evident in Confucian ethics, Confucius and his disciples clearly believe that human nature gives everyone the capacity for becoming benevolent. The pedagogical strategy for teaching Confucian virtue ethics thus goes much deeper than the rational arguments that scholars may understand, appealing instead to the heart-mind of compassion (Chinese: 心学; pinyin: *xinxue*) and educating it through the cultivation of the rituals and social practices that are known to strengthen it. The point of Confucian pedagogy is to develop moral sentiments—or what is known in Western philosophy as "conscience"—without which any moral arguments, however valid logically, are likely to be either ignored or twisted to serve only one's personal convenience.

2.5 Conclusion: A Virtuous Life in Business?

Let us apply the principles of virtue, outlined by Confucius, Mencius, Mozi, and Aristotle, to the realm of business, in both its individual and its social dimensions. These sages converge in their vision that human nature is essentially good. This insight has far-reaching consequences for business ethics, which not only investigates fraud, malpractice, and the full range of corrupt business practices but also searches for ways to improve business management so that these corrupt practices are minimized, if not actually eliminated. Virtue ethics disagrees with the conclusion that these abuses must be tolerated as inevitable in a flourishing business culture. When trust in business has been damaged—as it clearly has in the wave of recent scandals both in China and internationally—it is important to find ways to restore that trust by reforming business management in accordance with sound ethical teachings, rooted in the moral wisdom traditions honored in the civilizations that converge in our world today.

Nevertheless, we must move past the theoretical level. In the Greek tradition, the philosopher Socrates is the model of a wise and humble man. He acted toward his disciples and everyone he met in a way that embodied the principles he preached. Like Socrates, we must cultivate and train a set of virtues that will allow us to put our good intentions to work and to take courageous action, based on our considered moral convictions. Business ethics must inspire all actors of a society to build an ethical culture. No one can be an isolated hero. Individual convictions count for little when habits of corruption or the drive for the quick buck overwhelms them. Ethics must demonstrate that corrupt practices imply corrupt relationships among the people involved and cause friendships to deteriorate into immoral complicity.

An ethical culture does not stem from a set of prohibitive rules. It treasures a practical wisdom that rediscovers the original goal of ethics—to satisfy the human drive for happiness. An ethical culture is the soul of business ethics. Methods of analysis and a short list of basic principles will never be enough to inspire fair dealing and mutual trust. As we saw earlier in this chapter, ethical problems in business are usefully categorized as Type A and Type B problems, with Type A including situations where there is genuine confusion over what the right thing to do and Type B including situations where the right thing to do may be clear but those responsible lack the power or personal character necessary for actually doing it. In this chapter, we have attempted to show—following the good example of Andrew So—that virtue ethics is the key to cultivating one's personal capacities for moral leadership. Type B problems in business can be successfully overcome, but only if we are willing to rediscover the wisdom yet to be exhausted in the converging traditions of virtue ethics.

References

Association of Asian Confederation of Credit Unions. (n.d.). *Forty-two years of dedicated service to Asian Credit Unions*. Accessed online on November 16, 2013 at http://www.aaccu.coop/index.php

Confucius Publishing Co. (n.d.). *The record of rites, book IX: The commonwealth state*. Accessed online November 13, 2013 at http://www.confucius.org/lunyu/edcommon.htm

Cooper J. (1997). *Plato: Complete works*. In John M. Cooper (Ed.). Indianapolis: Hackett Publishing Company.

Credit Union League of Hong Kong. (2013). *Brief history of credit union movement in Hong Kong*. Accessed online November 15, 2013 at http://home.culhk.org/index.php?option=com_cobalt&view=record&cat_id=23&id=31&Itemid=111&lang=en

CUNA Mutual Group. (2015). *Home*. Accessed online on February 17, 2015 at http://www.cunamutual.com/portal/server.pt?open=512&objID=351&mode=2

Isamu, A. (n.d.). *Social involvement of Jesuits in the East Asian region*. Jesuit social justice and ecology secretariat. Accessed online November 15, 2013 at http://www.sjweb.info/sjs/pjold/pj_show.cfm?PubTextID=2435

Ivanhoe, P. J., & Van Norden, B. W. (2005). *Readings in classical Chinese philosophy* (2nd ed.). Indianapolis: Hackett Publishing Company.

Lau, D. C. (Ed.). (1970). *Mencius*. London: Penguin Classics.

Legge, J. (1885). *Lǐ Yun* (Book IX of the *Lǐjì*: 禮記). Accessed online 10 Nov 2013 at http://ctext.org/liji/li-yun

Legge, J. (1991). *The Chinese classics: Vol. II: The works of Mencius*. Taipei: SMC Publishing.

Nash, L. N. (1993). *Good intentions aside: A manager's guide to resolving ethical problems*. Boston: Harvard Business School Press.

Ross, W. D., (1925). *Nicomachean ethics Aristotle* (Reprinted by Veritatis Splendor Publications, 2012).

South China Morning Post. (1998, December 24). Wrong choice. Accessed online on 2 Sept 2013 at http://www.scmp.com/article/267084/wrong-choice

Van Norden, B. (2003). *Virtue ethics and confucianism*. Retrieved on June 15, 2014 from http://faculty.vassar.edu/brvannor/Mypapers/virtueethics.pdf

World Council of Credit Unions. (n.d.). *Home*. Accessed online 6 Nov 2013 at http://www.woccu.org/

Chapter 3
Business Ethics and the Sciences

"Analyze the facts and you will realize that honesty and reliability benefit you." (Stephan Rothlin, *Eighteen Rules for Becoming a Top Notch Player*, 2004)

3.1 Prelude

The exercise of moral leadership in business requires more than demonstrating an exemplary sense of personal integrity. Cultivating what Adam Smith called the "moral sentiments" is indispensable, but becoming a "top notch player" does not stop there. In today's business environment, managers must have sufficient understanding of the sciences warranting the technical specifications of the products they develop, in order to fulfill those specifications. As the Sanlu melamine contamination case makes clear, failure to observe those specifications—even in China—may result in serious harm not only to the firm's customers but also to the firm itself and its negligent managers. Just as management in today's international business environment requires a high degree of rational analysis, so, too, does business ethics. The chapter proceeds from the specific lessons to be learned from the disaster at Sanlu to explore the ways in which international business ethics itself has developed scientifically.

3.2 Case Study: Sanlu's Tainted Infant Formula

3.2.1 Abstract

The Sanlu Group led the Chinese dairy market in quality standards and market share in 2006. The Group was praised and rewarded for its consistency and lack of scandal. However, when quality regulations were relaxed as a reward for Sanlu's achievements, the company's management was tested, and ethical decision-making was forgotten. In 2008, Sanlu admitted to selling milk tainted with melamine, which resulted in four infant deaths and thousands of poisoning cases. The actions of

S. Rothlin, D. McCann, *International Business Ethics*,
DOI 10.1007/978-3-662-47434-1_3

senior members of Sanlu Group illustrate the moral issues involved in corruption, as well as relations with its joint venture partner. Questions regarding the ethics of public relations, corruption, and social responsibility are highlighted by this case that provoked worldwide concern about product safety issues in China.

3.2.2 Keywords

Sanlu, Melamine, Tian Wenhua, Product safety

3.2.3 Sanlu

The Sanlu Group was officially registered in 1996 in Hebei Province, following a series of acquisitions carried out by Shijiazhuang Dairy. Thanks to the relentless efforts of Tian Wenhua, a former veterinarian who rose quickly in Sanlu's corporate hierarchy, the company maintained leadership in the powder milk industry for over a decade. The prestige of the Group was such that Tian was eventually named deputy chairman of the China Dairy Industry Association and elected to the National Committee of the Chinese People's Political Consultative Conference. So impressive was Tian's impact that senior employees created this slogan to celebrate her achievement: "No Tian, no Sanlu" (Chinaview 2009).

The completion of a joint venture agreement with the New Zealand-based dairy cooperative, Fonterra, was a pivotal moment in Sanlu's history. Fonterra acquired a 43 % equity stake in the Chinese dairy firm and the joint venture started trading in Hong Kong in 2006, promising investors that it would fulfill its ambitious growth plans in the following 3 years. A new regional plant in Tangshan (Hebei Province) increased milk powder production capacity, increasing the company's total market share to 18 %. Sanlu thus became one of the largest employers in the area with close to 10,000 people on its payroll. At the same time investments in facilities in Weifang (Shandong Province) and Xinxiang (Hebei Province) allowed the firm to diversify by expanding its liquid milk and yogurt production (Sun and Chen 2009).

Throughout the years, Sanlu earned a reputation for being uncompromising on quality by priding itself on its strict control procedures and rigorous tests. Tian Wenhua put the pursuit of the highest standards at the core of her management style, as is evident in the motto she created for Sanlu: "Manufacture Quality Dairy to Serve the People!" (Ng 2009). This attitude enabled the company to win second prize at the 2007 National Scientific Techniques Awards in the category of "Innovative infant formula research and other related techniques." As allowed by law to reward companies for achieving consistency in passing such quality checks, the government exempted many of Sanlu's products from otherwise mandatory inspection.

3.2.4 The 2008 Milk Scandal

Nevertheless, on September 12, 2008, the Sanlu Group publicly acknowledged that its infant formula milk powder contained harmful amounts of the toxic chemical melamine. Ingesting melamine is associated with kidney disease. World Health Organization (WHO) regulations concerning its use in the food sector indicate it should be banned in any products that contain more than the trace amounts determined to be safe (Langman 2009). An industry-wide investigation by China's national inspection agency further revealed the extent to which adding melamine to enhance the apparent protein content of milk products had become commonplace. By the time action was taken, four infant deaths and over 56,000 cases of poisoning among infants had already occurred in the area of Shijiazhuang, where most of Sanlu's business was concentrated.

Sanlu's general manager Tian Wenhua apologized to the public after the inspection revealed its infant formula contained more than four times the amount of melamine traced in other analyzed brands. Alleging as an excuse that she had relied on a European Union "provisional statement" on health effects of melamine received from a representative of Fonterra, Tian waited 4 months before admitting the risks Sanlu was imposing on its consumers. Instead of acknowledging the problem, she tried to cover up the news until the same Fonterra alerted the New Zealand government, upon discovery of its partner's dangerous conduct (Lee 2008; Spears 2008). The fact that the EU provisional statement referred to by Tian set a 20 mg/k melamine margin of tolerance, whereas Sanlu's milk contained 2563 mg/k (Yuan Yuan 2011), suggests that Tian deliberately used Fonterra to cover the problem.

In the midst of a public relations catastrophe, Fonterra had to take drastic measures to explain its ignorance of what was going on at Sanlu, given the fact that it had three representatives on the board of the joint venture. Eventually, the New Zealand partner totally withdrew its investment in Sanlu. Fonterra's decision contributed to Sanlu's bankruptcy, since the dairy Group was struggling with the dramatic fall in its share price, as well as liabilities for damages owed to those harmed by the tainted product (Corporate Counsel 2012).

3.2.5 Cover-Up Allegations

According to a State Council investigation, Sanlu's management received the first complaints about product safety at the end of 2007. However, the company did not address the problem until June of the following year. In addition to this, the report held government officials in Shijiazhuang City accountable for the delay in warning provincial and state authorities. There is some speculation that Tian Wenhua delayed informing the Shijiazhuang City government until August 2, 2008, in order to avoid risking a major scandal during the Olympics. She justified her conduct as an attempt to reduce the risk of a social emergency that would have had detrimental consequences on the local economy.

Cover-up measures were not limited to the involvement of the authorities, but extended to health officials and media channels who feared that heated reactions from Chinese bloggers and netizens would spread panic throughout the country. Evidence found that the public relations agency, Teller International, advised Sanlu to persuade the major search engines to censor any suspect allegations of its shortcomings (France 24 2008). A scanned copy of a letter appeared on the web, which stated that Teller submitted a ¥3 million (US $440,000) budget to silence all potential sources of negative information. Chinese Internet giant Baidu, which was also mentioned in the memo, distanced itself from the affair with a public notice on September 13, 2008. Baidu's PR manager Yang Zi denied any involvement and argued it would have been easy to verify that all information about the case was accessible from their website. He further accused Teller and the whole PR industry of inappropriately using Baidu's name to advertise their censorship services to clients for their own private purposes (ChinaSmack 2010).

3.2.6 A Debated Trial

By the end of December 2008, 17 people accused of the deliberate production, sale, acquisition, and addition of melamine to raw milk went on trial. Tian Wenhua admitted her faults in front of the court. She confirmed the receipt of the first warnings in 2007 and her initial reluctance to refer the danger to the relevant government authorities. Tian's establishment of a working team to handle the problem was accepted as an extenuating circumstance, but this was not enough to save her from conviction on serious charges. On January 22, 2009, the Intermediate People's Court in Shijiazhuang handed down its final verdict. Two of Sanlu's managers, Zhang Yujun and Geng Jinping, who acted as middlemen in producing and selling melamine, were sentenced to death, whereas Tian was condemned to life imprisonment (Zhu and Cui 2009). Three other managers were recognized as culpable in varying degrees and sent to jail from 5 to 18 years. One of them, Wang Yuliang, was in a wheelchair after an attempted suicide (Chang 2009).

Relatives of the victims were kept at a distance of 100 yards from the court to contain their anger and desperation. Among the parents waiving signs saying "Return my child" and "Justice for people" (Chang 2009), Zheng Shuzhen's cry expressed everybody's sorrow. A grandmother from Henan Province, Zheng, called for revenge "My granddaughter died. She [Tian] should die too. She should be shot. She has brought such harm to the public, to children" (Daily Mail 2009). Nevertheless, Li Fangping and Liang Zikan, lawyers representing the families' and Tian's interests, respectively, agreed it was not a case to be judged merely on the basis of individual responsibilities. They contended that the convicted people had been scapegoats in a flawed system and that Tian's sentence to lifelong imprisonment was excessive. In an interview to *Renwu Zhoukan*, Liang held Sanlu only partly responsible for the incident, which was instead caused by problems at the industry level. He pointed to the lack of an established regulatory system and to the difficulty of monitoring the high number of small suppliers.

Indeed, Sanlu was not the sole tainted brand, although it was the one most exposed in the incident. In his opinion, rather than emerging from an objective evaluation, Tian's sentence was deeply influenced by public opinion. From a legal standpoint, according to Liang, she should have been jailed for less than 10 years, as in a normal case involving food safety (Renwu Zhoukan 2009). Sanlu's former joint venture partner, however, did not share this view. Andrew Ferrier, the CEO of Fonterra, made a press release soon after the court's decisions were communicated: "Fonterra deeply regret[s] the harm and pain this tragedy has caused to so many Chinese families," which were in need of the most serious responses by the Chinese government. Nevertheless, he made clear that "Fonterra support[s] the New Zealand Government's position on the death penalty," thus distancing himself and the firm from those who sought Tian's execution (Fonterra 2009).

As Sanlu was becoming the focus of national outrage in China, inhabitants of Nangang, Tian's hometown, could not believe the news. They could not believe the old lady now accused of having traded kids' health for profitability was the same Tian Wenhua they used to know. Everybody still remembered her last visit to the town on the occasion of her father's death a few years before. A neighbor Zhang Xuezhen recalled her modesty, notwithstanding the high status she had achieved in her lifetime (Cui 2008). Tian came from a disgraced family labeled as "pro-capitalist rightists" during the Cultural Revolution of the late 1960s and early 1970s. Having been herself vilified as a "capitalist dog," she had dedicated her life to restoring her family's reputation (Ng 2009). It took her years of efforts, studies, and impeccable conduct to earn people's respect and eventually make Nangang people proud. Nobody could explain how she could have thrown it all away for Sanlu's sake.

3.2.7 Uncompensated Claims

The value of Sanlu's shares dropped as an immediate consequence of the scandal. In addition, Fonterra's decision to withdraw its investment further aggravated the financial difficulties faced by the company, which was under obligation to pay debts totaling 700 million RMB (Shanghai Daily 2008). On December 25, 2008, the Chinese Dairy Group was officially declared bankrupt and its assets seized for settlement.

As mandated by the Chinese bankruptcy law, the first to get compensated with the liquidation of a company are the creditors, thus leaving almost nothing to injured parties. Nevertheless, the 21 brands revealed to have tainted products in the 2008 industry-wide inspection set up a fund for compensating the victims of the incident. The China Dairy Association became the mediator of this fund, which was formally operated by China Life Insurance. The parents of the affected children were confronted with the alternative of signing "A Letter to Parents of the Baby Patients" or the "Registration Form to Refuse Compensation." With the former, they accepted 2000 RMB in compensation, whereas the latter indicated their protest against the small amount of the proposed settlements (Xie 2011). The majority opted for the money, since they could either not afford to fight any further or did not understand the complexity of the legal procedures involved, and by the end of 2011, over 12 million RMB had been paid through the fund (China Daily 2012). In the end, 271,869 families chose to compromise, whereas 30,000 stood up for their rights to just compensation, consequently initiating new trials, none of which have been successful thus far (Xie 2011).

Zhang Xiuwen, the father of the first victim in Guangdong Province, sued Sanlu and the China Dairy Association in the Guangzhou Intermediate People's Court. He was asking for 900,000 RMB to cover his family's medical expenses as well as to compensate them for the psychological strain. The rejection of the suit by the court forced Zhang to pay the 40,000 RMB needed for the first operation to remove his son's kidney stones with money borrowed from a circle of friends. The critical condition of the baby required his presence all day long, forcing his family to rely solely on his wife's 1000 RMB monthly salary (CRI 2008). The voice of Zhang, as of many others, remains unheard leaving him without assurances or any future hope.

3.3 Case Study Discussion

The tainted milk scandal decreased consumers' confidence in the dairy industry. The Chinese people's demand for stricter quality monitoring grew steadily, and many resolved switching to imported brands. Public opinion about Sanlu boss Tian Wenhua's condemnation to life imprisonment was divided. If on the one hand she could count on support from her hometown, on the other, relatives of the victims called for the death penalty. The proceeds from Sanlu's bankruptcy were mainly used to pay suppliers, instead of contributing to the treatments needed by the survivors. A compensation fund for the victims was established at an industry level, but many of the families harmed by the tainted infant formula regarded it as insufficient and held out for a fair settlement determined in a court of law. Their apparent failure in court leaves a taint of injustice for all concerned.

The ethical issues involved in this case are many, and we want to leave you with enough room to think about them and discuss them on your own. There are, however, certain key points in the case study that you should consider. Like the people in Tian Wenhua's home village, you well may wonder why she was willing to sacrifice her hard-earned reputation as a moral business leader in order to cover up Sanlu's problem. If you had been in her shoes, what would you have done? Was she right in allegedly trying to prevent a food industry scandal from breaking out during the Beijing Olympics? Would you have done the same, even knowing that such a delay would put many more babies at risk of being harmed by the tainted infant formula? Is it reasonable to assume that she should have known the consequences of delaying her report to the relevant government agencies? Should she have known that there was a connection between the repeated indications that children were becoming ill and problems in the firm's supply chain regarding product quality? What did she know, and when did she know it?

Ascertaining Tian Wenhua's moral responsibilities as Sanlu's general manager is not the same as determining her guilt in a court of law (Xinhua 2009). The case study informs us of the remarkable convergence in opinions between the lawyers representing both Tian and the parents of the children victimized by Sanlu's infant formula. They claimed that those convicted of crimes in connection with this incident were "scapegoats in a flawed system and that Tian's sentence to lifelong imprisonment was excessive." The incident, they agreed, was caused by problems at the industry level, including the lack of an established regulatory system and the inherent difficulty of monitoring Sanlu's large network of small suppliers. Though such arguments might be useful in arguing for increased compensation for the victims or challenging the alleged harshness of Tian's punishment, are they relevant for understanding her moral responsibility? After all, Sanlu's problems with its suppliers began after it was awarded an exemption from the normal supervision that the government enforced upon the dairy industry. Was the problem of monitoring its suppliers any different once Sanlu was granted that exemption? If you were managing a company subject to such inspections, would you assume that you didn't need to monitor your suppliers once the government agents were no longer visiting your plants? Or would you assume that precisely because the government trusts you to regulate your own activities, you bear even greater responsibility to protect the health and safety of your customers?

Another moral issue is the alleged cover-up. If the allegations made against Sanlu's management are true, then the firm clearly conspired with a public relations agency to prevent information from reaching the public about the problems with its infant formula. Money was paid to the agency in order to silence critics and deflect criticism that might surface on the Internet and other news media. What do you think of such a conspiracy? Do you consider it moral or immoral to engage in a cover-up of embarrassing or potentially damaging facts? Would you do it out of loyalty to your employers? Would you do it to help either yourself or them to save face? Is there any limit to what you might do to avoid disclosure of inconvenient or embarrassing facts? Should there be? Does it matter to you that infants' lives were put at risk by the delay caused by the cover-up? Do you think that fear of causing a scandal is ever a good reason to engage in a cover-up? Do you think that the public has a right to know about problems that may cause harm to them? Or is it true, as the old saying goes, that what you don't know won't hurt you?

There are other questions besides these focused on what did they know, when did they know it, and what did they do or fail to do about what they knew, but we are raising these now in order to open this chapter's discussion of business ethics and the sciences. For the Sanlu case implies a number of concerns over what, if any, moral responsibilities arise from the presence or absence of scientific facts. Some of the things we know are based on common sense and thus may require no support from scientific argument. For example, to deliberately endanger a defenseless infant is completely contrary to Mencius' teaching about the heart of compassion that he believed was present in every human being. Common sense tells us to give babies special protection and never to deliberately put them in harm's way. Must we assume, then, that Tian Wenhua and the others found guilty in the Sanlu case were monsters, totally depraved because totally lacking in that heart of compassion? Or does this case require more than common sense to sort through the situation facing these managers? If you are unsure of what you would have done, when faced with this or similar challenges, it may not mean that you are a moral monster or totally lacking in common sense. But it may mean that you need to think some more about how you learn from facts and where they come from.

In this case, as in many others involving the products of modern industrialized processes, determining a manager's specific moral responsibilities depends on understanding the science and technology operative in the production he or she is supposed to be managing. The first principle of business ethics may be "do no harm," but it cannot be applied responsibly without knowing the facts and understanding the complex processes that shape the problem a manager may be addressing. Most people would not recognize melamine unless it was named on a warning label. Neither would common sense alone nor casual observation tell them whether melamine is harmful, or how it causes harm, or whether it can be totally eliminated from industrialized food production. To know these things, a manager must depend on science and the institutions—usually government agencies—that specialize in establishing standards for various products.

The problem, of course, is just how credible the standards set by the regulatory agencies are perceived to be, in the eyes of the producers whom they regulate, their subcontractors, as well as the public at large. If managers within the supply chain don't understand the science warranting the regulations or if they feel that the regulations are an arbitrary imposition that can be ignored whenever the regulators are not monitoring them, then they may be tempted to disregard the standards, especially when it is profitable to do so. Responsible managers must have not only sufficient knowledge of the science warranting the regulations but also sufficient capacity to enforce the regulations upon those whom he or she manages. In the Sanlu case, Tian Wenhua was accused of acting irresponsibly because she knew that (a) children who had been fed Sanlu's infant formula were becoming ill, that (b) Sanlu and its suppliers were increasing profits by "improving" the quality of milk powder used in infant formula by adding melamine, and that (c) the amounts of melamine adulterating the milk powder were well in excess of the standards set by the relevant regulatory agencies, both in China and abroad. Instead of acknowledging the problem caused by the tainted milk powder and taking immediate steps to curtail its production by Sanlu's suppliers, she decided to cover up or otherwise create confusion about the problem, as if it would somehow go away simply by taking evasive action.

Of course, the assured findings of science cannot be evaded. If the science is correct, the outcomes of an industrial process will remain the same, whether they are acknowledged or not. Any attempt at a cover-up will fail because the problem only gets worse the longer its existence is denied. Tian's obfuscations—particularly that inept attempt to use the European Union's provisional guidelines to defend her failure to take action against using melamine as an additive—indicate that she had a general understanding of the science involved and the appropriateness of the regulations based on it, but failed to act decisively on what she knew or should have known.

3.4 Ethical Reflections

3.4.1 The Role of Science in Business Ethics

The Sanlu case study, then, allows us to offer some generalizations about the role of science in business ethics, especially in a globalizing economy in which the processes organized and managed by businesses are industrial, that is, based on the systematic application of modern science and technology. *Since science is reality based, businesses must also be reality based*, if they are to succeed in the long run; they cannot be based on either wishful thinking or any willful practice of deception. As some economists have noted, the marketplace is best thought of as a very large and pervasive information processor. For markets to create genuine wealth, buyers and sellers must conduct their exchanges on the basis of rational calculations of mutual benefit. In various ways the sciences provide the information and insights necessary for making such rational calculations. If the calculations are not based on reality, as known through science-based exchanges of information, marketplace transactions will not yield the positive results expected from them. *The reality-based nature of market exchanges means that all participants in them have a vested interest in assuring that the information used by both buyers and sellers is truthful and accurate and thus reliable.* If the information available is inadequate, rational agents, precisely because they are rational, will not make a transaction, until they can be assured that the information they have is reliable.

Markets cannot exist, or at least they cannot flourish, unless everyone involved is committed to truthfulness and accuracy, if not full transparency. Every buyer and seller, therefore, in one way or another relies upon science to warrant the information upon which they act. Of course, as in all other aspects of life, there are those who seek to get ahead by cheating. They may lie in order to mislead people about what they are thinking and doing. They may commit fraud in order to profit, not with but at the expense of others. But *just as lying destroys the trust upon which our relationships with others are built, so fraud undermines the trust that people previously had in a business that goes that way.* Nevertheless, cheating in the form of ordinary lies or fraudulent activity in business is necessarily the exception rather than the rule. Cheating is rational only when it can safely be assumed that most everyone else is playing by the rules. *If everyone cheats, then there is no advantage to be gained by cheating.* Everything, every relationship or every transaction, is rendered meaningless by cheating.

This observation, which is really only a matter of logic, should help clarify why everyone in business has a vested interest in making sure that the information available to buyers and sellers is truthful and accurate. It should also tell us why everyone in business has a vested interested in the integrity of science, in order to assure respect for the validity of market regulations based on the assured conclusions of scientific analysis. An industrial firm must comply with valid standards for product quality—or guidelines for a product's safe use and a host of other matters essential to protect consumers from harm—whether the government regulators are conducting routine inspections or not. Just because a firm has been exempted from government inspection does not mean that the firm is allowed to relax its adherence to these standards. The standards must be internalized, monitored, and enforced by the firm's managers, if it is to achieve and maintain a good reputation for product quality. *The only way to ensure compliance with the relevant standards is to develop a corporate culture that encourages accountability and transparency at all levels of management and in all the firm's relationships with its various stakeholders.* Such a culture can only be developed by cultivating a proper understanding of the role of science in business ethics.

One of the hard lessons to be learned from the Sanlu case is that the global marketplace punishes firms whose actions and policies fail to recognize the importance of complying with science-based regulations. Sanlu's laxity in compromising its quality standards for the milk power used in making infant formula caused serious harm to its consumers. Even in China, that harm could not be successfully covered up. But, given the fact that Sanlu's milk powder was also being exported for use by its joint venture partner, Fonterra, and other international firms, the idea that a cover-up would succeed borders on insanity. Even if it wanted to, Fonterra could not lie in order to protect Sanlu, especially when Sanlu's failure placed Fonterra's own reputation at risk. In the immediate aftermath, Fonterra exited from the joint venture, sacrificing the investment that it had already made in Sanlu, and Sanlu went bankrupt. The consequences of Sanlu's failure are still being felt in China and even in Hong Kong where there is now a severe shortage of infant formula reported because so much of the products sold in Hong Kong are purchased for resale across the border in a "gray market," catering to the fears of local families who no longer trust the Chinese dairy industry to protect them from harm. It may take years to rebuild the trust that has been lost because of Sanlu's extraordinary disregard of science-based standards of product quality. Chinese consumers deserve better.

3.4.2 Business Ethics as "Science"

In Chap. 2, we introduced Laura Nash's helpful distinction between Type A and Type B problems in business ethics. Type A problems, it will be remembered, are situations properly regarded as "moral dilemmas" in which a person doesn't know—or is in doubt—as to what the right thing to do is, while Type B problems are situations in which a person knows what the right thing to do is, but will not or cannot bring themselves to do it. If, as we have seen in the previous chapter, Type B problems led us to rediscover the priority of virtue ethics for cultivating moral leadership in business, confronting Type A problems helps us to appreciate the significance of science in business ethics. *If there is genuine confusion about what the right thing to do is, there are two interrelated sources of this confusion: lack of understanding of the scientific basis of various managerial imperatives and conflicts of values inherent in the role of management.* Developing business ethics scientifically is meant to provide the conceptual resources necessary for settling these conflicts. Analytic moral philosophy is the chief tool used in this development.

Not surprisingly, ethics gets a lot more complicated when the focus shifts from self-cultivation to the various roles that people seek to fulfill in public life. Business management is but one of these roles. There are several points developed in analytic moral philosophy that are useful for understanding conflicts of values or ethical dilemmas in the role of management. These become apparent as soon as we make the effort—as modern moral philosophers do—to raise ethics or the study of morality to a scientific or theoretical level. *Ethical theory is divided into three basic divisions: descriptive ethics, normative ethics, and metaethics.* When we think of ethics, generally, we usually have only normative ethics in mind, that is, what happens when a specific moral judgment is rendered, determining whether an act is right or wrong, good or bad, and appropriate or inappropriate. Normative ethics thus provides theoretical grounds for judging the validity of the moral argument or rational justification that warrants such determinations. But analyses of what is involved in making such judgments—which all of us have had plenty of practice doing ever since early childhood—indicate our responses usually presuppose the answers to other important questions as well. Sorting out these questions and the way we answer them is what leads philosophers to distinguish descriptive ethics, normative ethics, and metaethics.

3.4.2.1 What Is Descriptive Ethics?

Descriptive ethics seeks to determine the basic facts about what people actually believe about morality and whether and how they act consistent with those beliefs. Descriptive ethics focuses on specific cultures and societies and how basic moral considerations are regarded in those cultures and societies. The information developed in descriptive ethics allows us to understand the context of moral decision-making in specific cases. Since ethics must fairly consider all the facts of a case study, our judgments are more likely to be reliable when they have been tested against the relevant facts known through descriptive ethics. This is why *descriptive ethics relies on sociology, anthropology, psychology, economics, law, and political science* to examine cases. To dwell purely in normative ethics is insufficient. We use the research of other fields to critique our own unexamined assumptions about how the principles of normative ethics ought to be applied in all cases.

In international business transactions, the cultural differences analyzed in the study of descriptive ethics should not be ignored. Commercial bribery, for example, is considered morally wrong in international business ethics, because it is a fundamental violation of the principle of justice as it normally applies in the marketplace. Commercial bribery is a form of cheating that completely undercuts the competition between buyers and sellers that economists tell us make market transactions efficient, fair, and beneficial to all concerned. For this reason, bribery is also illegal and severely punished at least in most modern economies. Nevertheless, it is often very difficult, without the aid of descriptive ethics, to determine whether a specific transaction involves a bribe or a gift or some other customary inducement.

It turns out that the criteria used to distinguish a bribe from a gift differ from one culture to another.

While most foreign businesses identify a bribe on the basis of the cost or actual amount of money involved in a gift, traditional Chinese culture is more concerned with the occasion of the gift and the sincerity of those giving and receiving it. Though bribery is strictly illegal in Hong Kong, for example, the agency charged with enforcing the law—the Independent Commission Against Corruption (ICAC)—has specifically ruled that the exchange of red packet envelopes filled with money between firms doing business with each other is not a bribe when done as part of the customary celebrations of Chinese New Year. *A simple act, that is, giving or receiving an envelope filled with money, may look entirely the same in two different settings, but their meaning in morality and law may be very different depending on how they are understood within a specific culture or performed within a specific social context.* While this may seem obvious to Chinese people, foreigners might have difficulty understanding what is going on and whether what they are observing is unethical, apart from the study of descriptive ethics.

One of the general lessons learned from descriptive ethics is how easily people from different cultures may misunderstand each other. The complexity of the Chinese language, of which only a few foreigners have a glimpse, is a major obstacle to making mutually beneficial business deals. Foreigners must carefully check the meaning of their Chinese partners' English, which may not be well understood apart from its underlying Chinese meaning. By the same token, Chinese who mean to do business with foreigners need to develop a better understanding not only of their languages but also of their cultures and what they value morally and spiritually. It is important for both groups to grow in appreciation of their common humanity. This requires setting aside inherited fears and prejudices and enlarging mutual understanding by describing the morality and customs of the cultures involved, comparing their moral systems, practices, and principles. While descriptive ethics is never perfect, it can play an important role in enabling us to compete successfully in an evolving global marketplace.

The practical goal of descriptive ethics is to enable us to see the situations in which we exercise moral responsibility as objectively as possible. Descriptive ethics, however, can itself become an obstacle to moral clarity, when it is misunderstood. *The diversity of human cultures and societies may tempt us to conclude that ethical relativism is true. Ethical relativists deny the possibility of objectivity, arguing that since biases inevitably arise from the subjective perspective of each person, no one is in a position to determine whether any one of them is true or false, right or wrong.* While relativists are correct in alerting us to the problems of prejudice or cultural bias, they are mistaken in dismissing the effort to achieve objectivity or moral consensus, over and above our subjective differences. When confronted with the facts of cultural diversity, a relativist takes the easy way out by jumping to the conclusion that either one opinion is as good as another or there is no telling how to resolve conflicts among conflicting perspectives on rational grounds. If ethical relativism is true, then the only way to resolve a conflict over morality is through brute force. Might would make right.

3.4.2.2 What Good Is Normative Ethics?

Normative ethics demonstrates its worth by providing a rational—and thus inherently peaceful—way of resolving differences among conflicting moral perspectives. *Based on the facts unearthed by a descriptive approach, normative ethics strives to make a balanced judgment.* Normative ethics refutes ethical relativism, by showing us the proper way to make decisive judgments about right and wrong. Norms spell out what actions we should take. They are based on generally acknowledged rules, such as not to kill, steal, or lie. The normative approach establishes a logical link between facts and the corresponding actions that can remedy a situation.

The relationship between norms is often complex. Recall the first principle of business ethics that apparently was violated by Sanlu's mismanagement of its infant formula crisis, namely, "do no harm." If we analyze the situation facing Tian Wenhua, we may discover a moral dilemma: "I don't want to harm anyone, but in order to deal with this situation, either I harm the firm and its investors, by making a prompt disclosure of the problem to the regulatory authorities and taking quick action against our suppliers, or I harm our customers, the families who buy our infant formula as well as their children who innocently consume it. Since I don't want to harm anyone, perhaps I should simply do nothing and hope for the best?" But how irresponsible is that? By her failure to act decisively and promptly, Tian harmed more infants and eventually harmed the firm by precipitating its bankruptcy. Could normative ethics have helped her make a good decision that not only would have saved lives but might have saved the firm? Had Tian studied normative ethics, she would have learned the ethical logic that stands behind the idea of "do no harm." When there is a conflict between preventing harm to people—especially to innocent children—and preventing harm to property, that is, the financial interests of the firm, the clear priority must be on preventing harm to people.

The next chapter will help us to understand why more clearly, but the point is already evident from the teachings of the Chinese sages, especially Mencius, who believed that the heart of compassion presumed in all of us places a clear priority on caring for others especially when they cannot care for themselves. We may have accepted Mencius' account of the origins of morality out of reverence for his authority among the ancients, but normative ethics can help us find good reasons not only to support Mencius' teaching but also to apply it to situations in our own experience. There are many different ways to elaborate on Mencius' basic point. We may want to consider the case for human rights and how they may be derived from a Confucian understanding of humanity or human dignity. But however we develop these, we see that the human right to life must always take priority over other rights that may conflict with it, such as the right to private property or wealth. Guided by normative ethics, Tian should have recognized that the only way to minimize the losses to her firm, its joint venture partner, and their investors would have been to prevent further harm to Sanlu's customers, by sending out an immediate warning not to buy or use its infant formula until all of the tainted product had been removed from its supply chain. *Normative ethics may involve a lot of abstractions, but these are abstractions with very practical consequences.*

3.4.2.3 A Role for Metaethics?

Metaethics is the broadest and most complex of the three disciplines in ethics. It moves to an even more abstract or philosophical level by exploring whether the norms that aim to resolve an ethical dilemma are geared to economic, legal, and political realities, based on further analysis of what people mean when they use moral terms—as in praising moral virtues and condemning moral vices or in making rules to encourage some forms of behavior and prohibit others. *One deep question that gives rise to metaethics is understanding why, in specific situations, people have failed to act ethically.* As we have already seen, the practical aspect of this question takes us back to Laura Nash's analysis of Type B problems and what resources virtue ethics can provide for overcoming them. But beyond the practical, inevitably, there is also a theoretical challenge to be confronted: What is human nature that it is so easily led astray from doing the right thing? And if our nature is warped in some way, is it reasonable to search for a remedy? If we are inclined to obscure the original goodness inherent in human nature and allow ourselves to become, like *xiaoren*, morally stunted in ways that actually run contrary to our own best interests, must we conclude that goodness is an illusion and that the attempt to cultivate a genuine humanity in ourselves is meaningless?

Answering the questions raised by metaethics, as the word implies, takes us far beyond morality, into the broader existential concerns that animate the religious and spiritual traditions, of not only China but also the entire world. Though the visions animating them differ in details, the traditions of Daoism, Buddhism, Catholicism, Christianity, and Islam—just to mention the religions of China—all provide deep answers to the theoretical questions raised by metaethics, questions that each of us, when the time is right, must confront for ourselves. In the meantime, we content ourselves here with a more modest level of questioning. We note that one reason ethics often fails is because people reject norms as straightjackets designed to hinder businesses from making profits. But a person can always go further asking why this is so. Similarly, others attribute the failure of ethics to a growing obsession with one's own prosperity. But what is it about prosperity—which after all is related to the pursuit of happiness—that so easily turns it into an obsession? Can we learn to enjoy prosperity without becoming addicted to it? While such questions are not easily answered, this book is meant to demonstrate that there are answers that give us reasons to hope. The sages were not wrong in observing that there is a way (*dao*)—or perhaps several good ways—to overcome the discrepancy between reality and our aspirations toward goodness and happiness, to narrow the gap between what is the case and what ought to be the case. Metaethics makes us aware of this discrepancy and provides positive orientation to managing that gap in our own lives.

3.5 Conclusion: Between Ethics and Morality

Critical reflection on the role of science in business ethics helps us understand the difference between morality and ethics, a difference that, as we have seen, depends on the context. Sometimes, they are the same. However, strictly speaking, they must be distinguished. *Morality refers to a range of practices, customs, and activities in a culture and the values that underlie them. Ethics is the study of morality. It is a systematic attempt to make sense of morality.* We speak, therefore, about business ethics, computer ethics, and marketing ethics, but not about computer morality or marketing morality, for morality is one, but the forms of ethics, as we have seen, are many.

In the Sanlu case study, we observed many things, among them, the moral sympathy of ordinary people in Tian Wenhua's village. They were inclined to defend her because she had been a source of pride and hope among villagers. Their expressions of sympathy were as far as their morality could take them in comprehending what had happened to Tian and why. Ethics informed by the sciences, however, enabled us to form a bigger and better picture of what was going on. Those who sentenced her to prison were not envious of her success. She had deliberately violated her responsibilities as CEO, and in her failure to act upon technical information whose practical consequences she should have understood, she endangered the health of thousands of innocent children and in a few instances contributed to their deaths. *The point of ethics is to bring clarity to cases where morality or common sense may only lead to confusion.*

It is not always easy to identify a wrongdoing or the actions that responsible managers might have taken to rectify the situation. Business activities usually occur in large organizations and involve many players. Given the pressures of a workplace, dilemmas continually emerge which must be solved in a limited amount of time. Ethics has to take into account many complex elements of a case and attempt to understand the dynamics inside specific groups before making any judgment. Nevertheless, the failure to act responsibly on the technical information available to managers and business leaders, as in the Sanlu case, has led to the collapse of many well-respected companies and has caused an enormous breakdown of trust in the marketplace. It is not yet clear what must be done to prevent similar tragedies. Regulation and laws alone will not bring change. We believe that honesty and decency must not be pushed aside in the drive to maximize profits. International business ethics uses perspectives from all cultures to increase trust in the marketplace.

References

Chang, A. (2009, January 22). China milk scandal: 2 get death penalty for their role. *The Huffington Post*. Retrieved on June 5, 2012 from http://www.huffingtonpost.com/2009/01/22/china-milk-scandal-2-get-_n_159908.html

Corporate Counsel. (2012, May 1). China market report: Food for thought. Retrieved on May 31, 2012 from http://www.law.com/jsp/cc/PubArticleCC.jsp?id=1202549129707&thepage=3

CRI. (2008, November 25). Sanlu urged to 'do the right thing'. Retrieved on June 1, 2012 from http://www.china.org.cn/environment/news/2008-11/25/content_16821904.htm

Cui, X. (2008, December 12). Sanlu boss stands trial for role in milk scandal. *China Daily*. Retrieved on June 4, 2012 from http://www.chinadaily.com.cn/regional/2008-12/31/content_7356693.htm

Field, M., &, Janes, A. (2008, September 2004). Fonterra takes 69pc Sanlu writedown. *Business Day*. Retrieved on May 2, 2012 from http://www.businessday.co.nz/industries/4704082

Fonterra Corporate Website. (2009, January 24). *Sanlu judgement*. Retrieved on July 12, 2012 from http://staging.fonterra.com/wps/wcm/connect/fonterracom/fonterra.com/our+business/news/media+releases/san+lu+judgement

France 24. (2008, September 17). *Tainted milk scandal—web users investigate*. Retrieved on June 1, 2012 from http://observers.france24.com/content/20080917-tainted-milk-scandal-webusers-investigate-china

Hutzler, C. (2008, November 16). Deaths uncounted in China's tainted milk scandal. *Associated Press (Google)*. Retrieved on June 16, 2015 from https://chinaview.wordpress.com/2008/11/18/deaths-uncounted-in-chinas-tainted-milk-scandal/

Langman, C. (2009, March 12). Melamine, powdered milk, and Nephrolithiasis in Chinese Infants. *New England Journal of Medicine*.

Lee, K. (2008, September 16). NZ alerted China to tainted milk, PM says. *South China Morning Post*, p. A1

Mc Donald, S. (2008, September 24). Fonterra posts $139 million impairment charge on Sanlu stake. *New Zealand National Business Review*. Retrieved on May 2, 2012 from http://www.nbr.co.nz/article/fonterra-posts-139-million-impairment-charge-san-lu-stake-3562

Mc Donald, M. (2009, January 22). Death sentences in China milk case. *International Herald Tribune*. Retrieved on May 5, 2012 from http://www.iht.com/articles/2009/01/22/news/23MILK.php

New Zealand National Business Review. (2008, November 19). *Sanlu asset sales plan taking shape*. Retrieved on May 3, 2012 from http://www.nbr.co.nz/article/sanlu-asset-sales-plan-taking-shape-37990

Ng, G. (2009, January 5). Ex-Sanlu boss clawed her way to the top. Asiaone. *The Straits Times*. Retrieved on June 4, 2012 from http://news.asiaone.com/News/Latest%2BNews/Asia/Story/A1Story20090105-112478.html

Renwu Zhoukan. (2009, March 3). Dairy scandal scapegoat Tian Wenhua's lawyer speaks out. Translated and edited by *Echinacities*. Retrieved on June 5, 2012 from http://www.echinacities.com/china-media/dairy-scandal-scapegoat-tian-wenhua-s-lawyer-speaks-out_1.html

Shanghai Daily. (2008, October 17). Dairy firms meet on possible Sanlu takeover. Retrieved on June 6, 2012 from http://www.china.org.cn/business/2008-10/17/content_16626191.htm

Spears, L. (2008, September 18). China revokes 'inspection free' right as milk scandal spreads. *Bloomberg*. Retrieved on May 5, 2012 from http://www.bloomberg.com/apps/news?pid=20601080&sid=a1rfKvOp3xwc&refer=asia

Sun, F., &, Chen, S. (2009). *Sanlu group and the tainted milk crisis*. The University of Western Ontario. Richard Ivey School of Business.

The New York Times. (2008, October 1). *China milk scandal firm asked for a cover up*. Retrieved on May 4, 2012 from http://www.nytimes.com/reuters/world/international-us-china-milk.html

Wang, Q., &, Shan, J. (2012, May 17). Millions paid to milk scandal victims. *China Daily*. Retrieved on May 31, 2012 from http://www.chinadaily.com.cn/china/2012-05/17/content_15314388.htm

Xie, L. (2011, August 12). The forgotten Sanlu babies. *The Economic Observer*. Retrieved on May 6, 2012 from http://www.eeo.com.cn/ens/2011/0812/208628.shtml

Xinhua. (2009, January 22). *Tian Wenhua, industry leader to disgraced prisoner*. Retrieved on June 3, 2012 from http://news.xinhuanet.com/english/2009-01/22/content_10704519.htm

Yuan Yuan. (2011, March 31). Food, food, safe food. *Beijing Review*. Retrieved on June 5, 2012 from http://www.bjreview.com.cn/quotes/txt/2011-03/27/content_370786_2.htm

Zhu, Z., &, Cui, X. (2009, January 22). Sanlu ex-boss gets life for milk scandal. *China Daily*. Retrieved on June 4, 2012 from http://www.chinadaily.com.cn/business/2009-01/22/content_7422528.htm

Chapter 4
Moral Decision-Making in Business

"If you analyze facts from different angles, you will discover the benefits of fair play." (Stephan Rothlin, *Eighteen Rules for Becoming a Top Notch Player*, 2004)

4.1 Prelude

The complexity of a manager's responsibilities to the firm's various stakeholders requires an approach to moral decision-making which respects that complexity. The failure of the Pepsi Sichuan JV in China should open the readers' eyes to the specific complexities involved in attempting to manage cross-culturally. When an opportunity for cross-cultural collaboration breaks down, as when Pepsi's international management discovered that their joint venture had been sabotaged by their partner in order to achieve his own business goals, how should managers respond? In order to learn all that one can from such disasters, a managerial decision-making model derived from Peter Drucker's early work is presented with some modifications that allow the concerns of international business ethics to be well integrated into the decision-making process. International business ethics, then, takes one further into the heart of managerial responsibility and not away from it.

4.2 Case Study: Pepsi Sichuan, "A Marriage too Good to be True"?

4.2.1 Abstract

When the joint venture (JV) between PepsiCo and its local partner in Sichuan broke down, many observers compared their relationship to an ill-fated marriage passing through various stages toward an inevitable failure. Initially described as a *marriage of convenience* or an *arranged marriage*, it brought together two most unlikely partners—with apparently asymmetrical ambitions. One was a major symbol of American capitalism and globalization, the beverage giant Pepsi-Cola. The other was the Sichuan Administration of Film, Radio and Television (SAFRT), a division

S. Rothlin, D. McCann, *International Business Ethics*,
DOI 10.1007/978-3-662-47434-1_4

of the provincial government that had previously sought to protect its local beverage industry against foreign competition.

Unlikely as the partners were, the more remarkable was the venture's early commercial success: soon after the marriage was consummated, it must have seemed like an ideal match, a *marriage made in heaven.* Nevertheless, a mere 8 years after its founding, the JV had become a burden that allegedly hindered both partners' businesses. By 2001, Pepsi China felt it had been "trapped in a *painful marriage* with its local partner in Sichuan" (Liu 2006). The Sichuan partner, in turn, criticized Pepsi for its *polygamous attitude* evident, it seems, in Pepsi's intent to treat the JV as merely one more addition to its list of more than 30 others all over China. In the course of their increasingly bitter dispute, both parties appealed to the local government not so much to counsel but more often to coerce the other side. Once it became clear that the government would refuse to take sides against its Chinese partner, Pepsi decided that it stood to lose more from being tied up in a dysfunctional marriage than from obtaining a divorce, which it eventually did through the international arbitration tribunal in Stockholm.

As we shall see, the ultimate collapse of Pepsi Sichuan was not a direct result of poor economic performance, but increasing frustration on both sides with their partners' unrealistic expectations and indifference, if not contempt, toward each party's perceived grievances. In what follows, our focus must be on what can be learned to avoid such an unhappy outcome. Could this marriage have been saved with a little more forethought based on a greater commitment to common standards of business ethics? In the 1990s and even today, many joint ventures in China have faced unexpected frustrations and challenges: what distinguishes the still successful JVs from those where the foreign party has long left China is not necessarily a better initial business plan but a better way of dealing with conflict once it erupts, as it almost inevitably will.

4.2.2 Keywords

Joint venture (JV), Carbonated soft drink (CSD), Franchise businesses, Contracts, Compromise.

4.2.3 How and Why Pepsi First Came to China

In 1993, PepsiCo[1] and SAFRT signed a contract of association creating a joint venture named "Pepsi Sichuan." The new enterprise was integrated into the global Pepsi family and supply network through the trademark and concentrate contracts signed in 1994. According to the original agreement, PepsiCo got a 27 % ownership

[1]After 1995, PepsiCo is represented through Pepsi Investment (China) Limited (which will be referred to hereafter as Pepsi China).

stake and 17 % dividend [profit] rights (Hsu 2007). By mid-1995, Pepsi China's initial investments (including noninterest-bearing loans to Pepsi Sichuan) are estimated to have totaled around USD $20 million. The contracts providing the concentrate supply also gave the JV access to the patents used in producing and bottling Pepsi beverages and allowed it to use Pepsi's global trademark. In return, the Sichuan government agreed to invest two million RMB by mid-1995 and authorized the newly formed Sichuan Radio and Television Co. to appoint Pepsi Sichuan's general manager, chairman of the board of directors, and three members of the board (Liu 2006). The nature and terms of this deal were unprecedented in Pepsi's history in China and even highly unusual when compared to most JVs set up in China at the time: for one, the Chinese partner was a government agency and had no relevant expertise in the beverage industry. For another, although Pepsi China contributed most of the equity (money, patents, brand, machinery), it only got a minority share of ownership and dividend rights.

In order to understand the terms of this arranged marriage, it is important to recognize the challenges Pepsi faced, as well as the interests of the Sichuan government and the *mei bo*—the Chinese "aunt" who traditionally arranges marriages—who became the big boss at Pepsi Sichuan, Mr. Hu Fengxian. Expanding in China was of strategic importance for Pepsi, for it could be decisive in its global rivalry with Coke. But even in China, Coke had the advantage of being the first mover and already dominated the carbonated soft drink (CSD) market in the southern coastal provinces that were the most advanced economically. Pepsi was thus forced to play catch-up. Key to its strategy was to go where Coke had not yet been active and win first-mover advantage for itself. Thus, when serendipity happened and a Sichuan government official—Mr. Hu—approached Pepsi, it saw a great opportunity opening. If Pepsi wanted to challenge Coke's overall market dominance in China, it couldn't afford to let this one go by. Pepsi thus came to the negotiating table with an urgent need to succeed and a willingness to pay a high price.

The CSD market in Sichuan, as well as the government that regulated it, proved to be a hard nut for Pepsi to crack. Though clearly desiring economic development and innovation, the Sichuan government was also keen to protect the small local producers of soft drinks, as well as larger enterprises like Tianfu Cola. The government then would let Pepsi in only if it could retain effective control over it. At this point the services on offer from Mr. Hu seemed indispensable. He could bring together both sides in a deal that would give Pepsi's strategy a chance to succeed while promoting local business development in unprecedented ways. Indeed, as a gesture of goodwill, Pepsi promised to help the Sichuan government to develop various unrelated industries—silk production, for example, printing and dyeing industries, as well as farm products, processing, and trade, enterprises that had little or no connection to CSD marketing and production. Pepsi China even agreed to let the JV eventually develop a national soft drink brand of its own, though it stipulated that any such product development could not be allowed to grow beyond 15 % of the market share/sales volume of the leading Pepsi brands.

Commonly regarded as a major coup for both parties at the time, these agreements would become the source of grievances that dogged the further course of the JV partners' relationship. In order to understand what happened and whether the grievances could have been addressed constructively, it is useful to distinguish two threads as the conflict unfolds: first, the cultural, economic, and structural issues involved in Pepsi Sichuan's resistance to Pepsi China's global business model and, second, the specific actions and attitudes of Mr. Hu, whose responses may be regarded as either a flagrant violation of universal standards of business ethics or a heroic attempt to live by Chinese cultural values in an environment increasingly dominated by globalizing MNCs.

4.2.4 "The Hu Factor" in the JV's Initial Success and Early Signs of Trouble

The most controversial figure in this story is Hu Fengxian, whose initial role as a *mei bo* was soon cast off in order to become the groom in this arranged marriage. In 1987, while still a radio program manager at SAFRT, Mr. Hu first approached Pepsi about its possible entry into the tightly regulated Sichuan market (Hsu 2007: 13). In Hu's estimation, the success of Pepsi Sichuan was largely his own, and later, he frequently referred to the company as his son. In three short years after its launch, the JV had achieved an average annual sales growth of 110 % while profits and taxable income rose by 88.2 % (Liu 2006: 288). This growth reflected the JV's market position—it quickly earned a 47 % market share in Sichuan and was recognized as the top beverage brand by a clear majority of the local population (Du 2002). Pepsi was forging ahead of Coke in Sichuan—a rare achievement that led one commentator to declare, "Pepsi Sichuan … had created history" (Liu 2006: 288). While there's no denying that this success was largely "thanks to Hu and his team's connections and business acumen" (Fernandez and Liu 2011: 70), it is also important to recognize the synergy between the product's distinctive taste and the way it was marketed in Sichuan. Pepsi earned a reputation for being more compatible than Coke with the hot pot dishes preferred by the local population. Pepsi Sichuan thus made great strides by promoting its drinks in hotels and restaurants. An A.C. Nielsen survey confirmed Pepsi's popularity among young Chinese consumers, who identified it as "the choice of a new generation," with a taste that stimulated their "spirit of limitless aspiration."

With such initial success, why did the relationship between the partners sour so quickly? Signs that something was wrong appeared as early as 1995—after the JV had been operating for barely more than a year. At that point Hu Fengxian abruptly reduced SAFRT's pledged investment in the JV from RMB 2 million to a mere RMB 11,000. Apart from provoking outrage within the Sichuan government when it was discovered, this move left Pepsi significantly puzzled and wary. Though Hu had been involved in the JV from the beginning, in Pepsi's perspective, its partner was the Sichuan government, not an individual entrepreneur. This incident alerted Pepsi to be on guard for further irregularities, as they watched Hu seek to extend his personal control over Pepsi Sichuan. During the following year when the provincial government ordered Hu to restore SAFRT's investment of RMB 2 million, Pepsi's fears were calmed, since the government's action encouraged them to think that it would help them discipline Hu should the need arise in the future.

Pepsi soon had more serious reasons for worry. After committing another USD $2.5 million to acquire another 5 % of the dividend rights in the JV, Pepsi demanded a more rigorous scrutiny of Pepsi Sichuan's accounting. According to Chinese law and the JV contract, Pepsi Sichuan should have reported regularly on its financial position to all of its investors. Nevertheless, Pepsi Sichuan's management, headed by Mr. Hu, blithely ignored this legal obligation, believing that his noteworthy economic success, and the timely distribution of the profits he did claim, should suffice to satisfy Pepsi. Left in the dark about the true financial results at Pepsi Sichuan and lacking much insight into Chinese accounting practices, Pepsi sought to enforce its presumed right to total transparency regarding the financial status of its JV. Contrary to Hu's expectations, due diligence and accurate accounting were just as important to Pepsi as economic success.

4.2.5 The "Factory Gate" Incident

Eventually, the tensions over transparency and accounting practices erupted into the first major clash between Pepsi and Hu: as stipulated in the JV contracts, Pepsi had agreed to reimburse many of the JV's expenses, especially for local marketing campaigns. However, Pepsi's standard procedure for reimbursements involved having the JV partner submit receipts for expenses. In the normal course of reviewing these, Pepsi accountants noticed major inconsistencies: the figures claimed by Pepsi Sichuan for construction expenses were often not documented with real invoices, and there seemed to be a suspicious pattern of double counting, that is, counting the same expense twice in different expense bundles. Hoping to verify the overall financial status of Pepsi Sichuan, as well as seeking documentation for the expense claims, in 1996, Pepsi's board of directors sent a team of auditors to Pepsi Sichuan's headquarters in order to inspect bank accounts and to verify the expenses actually claimed. Much to the auditors' surprise, their visit marked a turning point in the relationship between the JV partners: the auditors were refused entry at the factory gate and were not given access to any of Pepsi Sichuan's account books (Hsu 2007: 23).

Hu and his local managers simply refused to comply with the board's instructions, with the apparent intent of showing Pepsi how little real control it had over the JV. Such action, to be sure, only intensified Pepsi's suspicions that the funds allocated to Pepsi Sichuan had been misappropriated in order to pay for personal expenses (e.g., luxury cars, travel to Europe and New York, etc.) incurred by Mr. Hu and other members of his management team.[2] Once alerted to these irregularities, Pepsi made a further discovery about Hu's conduct that eroded what was left of its trust in him. Pepsi discovered that in 1996 Hu and his team had faked two board

[2] This was officially recognized in an auditing report from the Sichuan Auditing Bureau: Auditing Report, Sichuan Auditing Bureau, 2002, Statement of Claim, exhibit 38, Pepsi Co (Hsu 2007: 44).

meetings and produced corresponding minutes, in which they alleged that the board had authorized Pepsi Sichuan to extend its sales and distribution region into territories that had clearly been allocated to another JV partner. Faced with such apparently egregious violations of basic business ethics, not to mention the terms of the contracts that had founded the JV, Pepsi asked the provincial government to conduct a thorough investigation.

4.2.6 *Pepsi's Response: What to Do with Mr. Hu?*

During the next 2 years, Pepsi watched in horror as Mr. Hu tried to usurp all executive authority within its increasingly successful JV. How then should Pepsi have responded? Given that Hu displayed what appeared to be astonishing ignorance of, if not actual contempt for, standard Western management practices, he seemed more and more ill suited for the position of general manager. Nevertheless, while such arbitrary behavior may seem typical of a strong Chinese leader in the minds of some, it hardly fits well within the worldview of today's Western business corporations. From Pepsi's perspective, the JV was much bigger than any one individual or the relationship the firm had cultivated with any one individual. Pepsi followed the conventional view according to which the JV was founded on a relationship between two legal persons (i.e., companies), of which the managers appointed were to be judged solely on the basis of their performance and thus were easily removable. Judging Mr. Hu as primarily responsible for the irregularities now emerging in an otherwise highly successful JV and considering any individual as replaceable for the sake of the corporation's greater good, Pepsi regarded what to do about "the Hu factor" as both inevitable and straightforwardly obvious: Pepsi came to the conclusion that it must ask the Sichuan government to remove Mr. Hu from his management positions in Pepsi Sichuan.

However inevitable and obvious it may have seemed at Pepsi's headquarters, this decision was bound to be controversial in China. One observer, who was employed by Pepsi Sichuan at the time, made this comment on how Mr. Hu and many other Chinese viewed his situation:

> Neither Pepsi Co people nor Mr. Hu were ready to work together culturally and ethically. Mr. Hu privately commented that he and his team had [made] some errors in the management including accounting keeping, however, they made profit and distributed the dividend to Pepsi Co in time.... What he did not understand at the start was the fact that his outstanding performance in terms of output and quality of Pepsi drinks could not offset the blunders he had by faking some invoices and violating the financial rules. (Hsu 2007: 30)

Hu's mistakes, in short, were relatively minor and should have been overlooked in light of Pepsi Sichuan's dramatic success under his personal leadership. Hu apparently felt that both Chinese culture and common sense would support his preferred self-understanding as a leader in the mold of the Great Helmsman—none other than Chairman Mao himself—whose bold initiatives were designed primarily to achieve China's ambitious goals for economic and social development, while protecting the Chinese people from foreign domination. His success, in short, not only gave a good "face" to all patriotic Chinese, but it also conformed to the post-revolutionary model of leadership that would do whatever it takes to succeed, especially in dealings with foreign partners. However self-serving Hu's reasoning may have appeared to Pepsi's executives, it clearly had significant appeal among Hu's former colleagues in the Sichuan provincial government for for whom there were clear limits to what they would or could do in response to Pepsi's grievances against him.

4.2.7 *Pepsi's Business Model at the Core of the Conflict*

The conflict that sealed the fate of this "marriage of convenience," however, cannot be reduced to a clash of incompatible personalities. Equally important are the accountability structures mandated by Pepsi's universal business model and how these were perceived in China. Though it had enabled Pepsi's global success, many including some of Pepsi's Chinese partners felt that Pepsi's so-called principles gave it unfair, monopoly-like advantages which it exploited extensively—so they feared—to control the operations of any one of its JVs and reserve the lion's share of the profits for itself. Thus, many of the challenges Pepsi saw arising as early as 1996 were directly linked to its business model—which, of course, provided the ultimate standard by which Pepsi judged and responded to its Sichuan partner.

In essence, Pepsi is a franchise business that relies on highly localized partnerships in order to produce and market its global brands. While local collaboration is indispensable for Pepsi's global success, this leads to the immensely difficult challenge of maintaining discipline and retaining control over all of Pepsi's global operations or licensed partners. If only one of its local partners fails to meet the high quality standards (even producing an output just vaguely "different"), the repercussions for Pepsi are not confined to the country where it occurred but are potentially devastating on a global scale. Similarly, any local marketing strategy needs to conform to the core Pepsi brand identity. Thus, when sharing its two core assets—the ability to produce and bottle a beverage with the unique Pepsi taste and the use of its global trademarks—with hundreds of organizations worldwide, Pepsi needs to ensure that none of its partners can suddenly break away and start producing "Pepsi" on its own.

The Pepsi business model is thus designed so that Pepsi's control over its independent and semi-independent partners increases wherever its business is most vulnerable. Pepsi protects its secret formula, for example, by producing Pepsi concentrate in local factories that it wholly owns and exclusively controls. Local franchisees bottling Pepsi products must buy the concentrate from Pepsi and mix it in a standardized process designed to guarantee uniform quality and taste. Given the need to ensure high quality and consistency in its products, Pepsi provides bottlers with detailed instructions and technical specifications, mandating everything from the proper water-sugar-concentrate mix, to the machines to be used in mixing and bottling operations, to the designs and specific suppliers of the bottles and cans. In each of these areas, Pepsi understandably must maintain strict compliance among all its franchisees. It is also important to note that as Pepsi generally sets up many bottlers, it must prevent these different local partners from competing with each other. Thus, Pepsi generally assigns specific sales regions in each country and strictly enforces the agreements made by its local partners to refrain from encroaching in territories assigned to others.

Given Pepsi's business model, it should be clear why the unsettling events of 1996 seemed to require more than just Hu's removal. Indeed, when first alerted to the full extent of Hu's misconduct, Pepsi not only complained to the local government but also threatened to stop supplying concentrate to Pepsi Sichuan. That same year, Hu ordered Pepsi Sichuan to expand beyond its designated sales region, a violation of the JV contracts that could not be ignored by Pepsi's other partners in China. While none of them dared to be as openly defiant as Hu, there was a group of four so-called rebellious bottlers (including Pepsi Sichuan) among the 14 Pepsi bottlers in China. While Pepsi held a controlling stake of 50 % or more in each of the three other "rebels" (Shanghai, Nanjing, and Wuhan), in none of them did it exercise full and effective operational control (Liu 2006: 288). Even among the remaining ten bottlers, clandestine efforts to encroach upon the other bottlers' sales regions began to surface. Over and above the challenge of finding a better way of disciplining Hu (after withholding concentrate had proven ineffective), Pepsi had to come up with a standardized response to various malpractices among its bottlers in order to protect its business model.

Pepsi therefore set up a so-called Bottler's Association (PCBA) in 1996, with all 14 bottlers joining voluntarily. These agreed—under Pepsi's direction—not to transship into each other's territories. If such behavior occurred, it would be reported to the Bottler's Association, which would determine a compensation for the bottler whose business was hurt, payable as punishment by the bottler who had broken the agreement. Pepsi's participation was crucial, since the payment balances between bottlers were settled through increases and decreases in its concentrate prices. In the following years, Pepsi Sichuan kept breaking the promises it had given Pepsi and the other bottlers and thus saw the price it had to pay for the concentrate rise accordingly.

Mr. Hu regarded the PCBA as an unwarranted interference into his and the other bottlers' operations. Soon, he was rallying the other "rebellious bottlers" within the PCBA in opposition to the Pepsi business model. This may have come as a surprise to Pepsi, since the PCBA was intended as a vehicle for "self-disciplining" the bottlers. Pepsi believed it would relieve it of the vastly unpopular task of disciplining each bottler individually. Mr. Hu, however, exploited the bottlers' uneasiness about the PCBA in order to denounce Pepsi's "unfair monopoly advantages." By resigning unilaterally from the association on April 30, 1999, while continuing cooperation with Pepsi in bottling and distributing its products, Hu showed the other bottlers that Pepsi's exploitation of its alleged monopoly position could be challenged. Later, in 2001, Hu and Pepsi Sichuan arranged a secret meeting attended by all 14 bottlers in order to coordinate resistance against what he regarded as the unfair advantages of

Pepsi's business model, in particular its power to increase concentrate prices unilaterally.

Confirming Hu's success in rallying the different bottlers, in 2002, they complained collectively to the government that the BA was an illegal, coercive organization and successfully requested that it be outlawed. Although Pepsi China in response set up an alternative, legal organization that same month, the potential threat was considered serious. The bottlers' dissatisfaction with Pepsi's business principles and practices focused on two main points: Pepsi's power to interfere in the operations of the bottlers and the perception that Pepsi, accordingly, could unilaterally determine its own and the bottlers' profits as well. An incident that intensified both these grievances was Pepsi's directive in 2000 that bottlers must use bottles from the one supplier that it would designate for China as a whole. Pepsi Sichuan claimed that not being able to use an alternative supplier increased its production costs by RMB 7.7 million (Liu 2006: 48). Understandably, Pepsi's decision reinforced the feeling that its bottlers had little freedom to make independent entrepreneurial decisions in their own markets.

4.2.8 Hopes Dashed for Saving Pepsi Sichuan

In August 2000, Pepsi learned that the ownership of the Sichuan stake in the JV had been changed once again. At that time the Sichuan State Asset Management Bureau designated Sichuan Yunlv as the appropriate holding company for its ownership stake. Far from diluting Mr. Hu's control over Pepsi Sichuan, this move gave Hu more independence to act (Liu 2006: 293). Any hopes that Pepsi harbored that the Sichuan government might reign him in were dashed, when it realized that Hu would not only not be removed but, now firmly entrenched in Sichuan Yunlv, was likely to step up his resistance. Predictably, in 2001, Hu rejected out of hand Pepsi's proposal to acquire a 50 % ownership stake in the JV, giving it direct control over its operations.

Hu's own expectations centered primarily on one important promise that PepsiCo had made in the initial agreement, namely, to assist Pepsi Sichuan in developing and marketing a new drink, in addition to Pepsi's existing brands. Hu's ambition was understandable—submitting himself to Pepsi's principles only made sense to him in order to acquire the technical expertise necessary to develop his own national brand. Once the honeymoon was over between the JV partners, it became ever more apparent why this project was unacceptable to Pepsi, even as it remained essential for Hu. Enabling Pepsi Sichuan to develop its own brand would have required significant trust, yet Pepsi had learned not to trust Hu. Given the many breaches in the agreements establishing the JV, how could Pepsi make sure that he wouldn't use—without authorization—Pepsi's proprietary designs and trademarks? It was already clear that Hu intended to use the production facilities and infrastructure that had been funded by Pepsi's initial investment. So how could Pepsi be sure that Hu's new drink wouldn't compete directly with the Pepsi brands?

When pressed for the expected reassurances, Hu openly admitted why Pepsi would be put off by such a project: "Compared with Cola [that is, Pepsi Cola], the new beverage can fully utilize local resources to reduce costs. It will be more profitable than Cola. However, Pepsi China will be unhappy in that we needn't purchase concentrate from Guangzhou Pepsi for the new beverage" (Liu 2006: 294). Nevertheless, from Hu's perspective, the new drink project would liberate Sichuan Yunlv from its vulnerability to Pepsi's alleged monopoly. As with the other grievances, the parties continued to struggle without finding a mutually acceptable resolution. Every year since 1997, Pepsi routinely turned down Hu's proposals, claiming it was inopportune for one reason or another. Understandably, Hu must have felt that the marriage he had contracted with Pepsi had not only turned out to be painful, but also unfruitful.[3] From his perspective, Pepsi was consistently using the principles of its business model to further its own narrow interests. Returning from a board meeting with Pepsi executives on August 3, 2001, where he had for the fourth time been told to wait for Pepsi's approval, he told reporters that the Pepsi Sichuan would go ahead with introducing its own national brand, pointing out that the objections raised by Pepsi executives represented only the JV's minority stakeholder's opinion.

At this stage, Pepsi China was preparing to take unilateral action of its own, entering an arbitration process that was the equivalent of filing for divorce. What hindered Pepsi from seeking a divorce much earlier was its realization of the dilemma it faced in Sichuan and China. Here is how one analyst described it:

> A break-up with its partner was bound to undermine its advantage over Coke in Sichuan, but a continuation of this relationship could have dire consequences. Not only that, the internal conflict could also affect Pepsi's overall image in China. Another concern was the reaction of other bottlers. A new round of negotiations with the bottlers could create a dent in Pepsi's potential profits. Pepsi China had only two options: to terminate its cooperation with Sichuan Yunlv and find another partner or go alone. However, neither of the options seemed promising. It was quite challenging to find a trustworthy partner; a weak partner could endanger Pepsi's long-term advantage in Sichuan, while a strong partner could prove to pose another problem. If Pepsi chose to go alone, it would definitely need to build the sales networks from scratch and that will require huge investments. (Liu 2006: 298)

Sichuan Yunlv, on the other hand, apparently remained blind to the impact that its actions would have upon its JV partner. It seems to have considered its escalating quarrels with Pepsi as nothing more than a form of business bluffing that both sides would ultimately set aside at the negotiation table. From Yunlv's perspective, the financial benefits of cooperation were too good to give up over matters of principle. Indeed, after giving Pepsi every indication that Hu would not comply with Pepsi's business principles, Qu Zhidi, vice general manager of Sichuan Yunlv, announced, "We [Sichuan Yunlv] hope the cooperation will survive and develop. We hope they

---

[3] Hu's frustrations were often well founded. Previously, he had correctly predicted the market potential of a bottled water beverage. But with his proposals for exploiting this opportunity routinely rejected, he had to watch from the sidelines as such a product enjoyed explosive growth, becoming by 2000 the best-selling beverage in China with a 37 % overall market share. By 2001, the sales of bottled water had overtaken the combined market share of all CSDs in China (Liu 2006: 283).

[PepsiCo] will come back to the negotiating table and help the joint venture survive" (Taipei Times 2002: 2).

Assuming that both parties would somehow muddle through, Hu continued to take actions that could only provoke Pepsi China still further. In a final move demonstrating that Pepsi had lost control over the JV's operations entirely, Pepsi Sichuan chose not to honor the original contractual agreement that called for its management to resign on January 31, 2001, and the partners to reappoint jointly a new management team. Pepsi insisted that this agreement be honored and, when it was not, claimed that the incumbent management was illegal as of February 1. Pepsi's protest was simply ignored by Pepsi Sichuan and Yunlv.

Having long lost any trust in its JV partner and having little hope that the Sichuan provincial government would protect its interests, in 2003, Pepsi filed for arbitration with the intention of dissolving the joint venture. During November 2004, the two sides met with arbitrators in Stockholm, bringing to light much of the "dirty laundry" marring their 10-year marriage, while failing to acknowledge their own wrongdoing and any legitimacy to the other partner's grievances. Given the seemingly irreparable state of the relationship, the arbitration committee granted Pepsi's request in 2005 for the corporate equivalent of divorce. This, however, was not to be the last chapter in the Pepsi Sichuan story: the implementation in the Chinese courts of the Stockholm arbitration settlement dragged on for a while longer, as Mr. Hu sought to use his influence to extract more favorable terms. In the end, both partners lost out financially. Coke achieved a higher market share in Chengdu than Pepsi and seemed well on the way to winning the "Cola Wars" throughout China.

4.2.9 Conclusion

In retrospect, the breakdown of Pepsi Sichuan occurred because Pepsi's business model turned out to be completely contrary to Hu Fengxian's ideas regarding what it meant to own and operate a business. Hu was particularly irritated by the fact that Pepsi could at any time enforce its intentions by withholding concentrate or withdrawing trademarks, the lifelines of any franchisee. The mere possibility of such retaliation Hu considered an act of blackmail, arguing that Pepsi's monopoly over its own products and trademark was contrary to fair competition laws and principles. According to Hu, Pepsi was "playing both athlete and judge" (Liu 2006: 297) in what he came to regard as a game that had been rigged against him. In typical producer-supplier relationships, he argued, the supplier has no privileged access to its customer's financial status and profit margins. Yet Pepsi demanded a full accounting of Pepsi Sichuan's finances. Hu assumed that Pepsi would use this information to extract as much revenue as possible from its JV partner. Beyond his seemingly zero-sum attitude toward the distribution of the JV's profits, Hu accused Pepsi of acting unfairly, and contrary to their agreements, by seeking to undermine his managerial authority wherever possible.

At the core of all of Mr. Hu's grievances, then, was his feeling that Pepsi was deliberately seeking to deprive him of the rewards of his extraordinarily successful entrepreneurship. Once frustrated by Pepsi's business model, he felt justified in acting unilaterally—and in breach of his previous agreements—in order to achieve his goals. Pepsi, on the other hand, had made many promises to Hu and the Sichuan government that it could not fulfill—it should have realized—without jeopardizing its global business model. Even if the necessities of running a global franchise business did not allow room for modifying its business model, could Pepsi have done a better job of explaining its business model and honestly disclosing its many practical implications, positive as well as negative?

The failure to establish and maintain transparency and mutual trust in the management of their JV eventually led to corporate divorce and the negative economic consequences that usually follow a divorce. In order to learn from their failure as it unfolded, we investigated the terms of their association and each side's interpretation of what had been promised by the other. Their mutual regret over a marriage "too good to be true" could only have been avoided had both parties been able to understand their cultural differences and the resulting differences in their ambitions and ideas about how to do business. Apparently unwilling or unable to reflect on such matters, both partners silently and surreptitiously reached for greater control over both the decision-making and the profits from the JV. Both partners became increasingly strident in asserting their claims to what they considered their fair share, culminating finally in serious accusations that could only be resolved through a bitter divorce. As with all such marital breakdowns, we are left to wonder: could it have been different? What can we learn from the failure of the Pepsi Sichuan JV?

4.3 Case Study Discussion

Characterizing Pepsi Sichuan as an "arranged marriage" or "marriage of convenience" may help to shed light on the cultural differences that separated the expectations of its two partners. But since such descriptions may not resonate very well with romantic Western notions about marriage—as an exclusive, monogamous relationship of virtually eternal significance, based on mutual love—it may be useful to recall that Pepsi Sichuan was just a business. As one observer tersely summarized the situation, "The joint venture owned by Pepsi Co and the Sichuan TV Bureau, seemingly very different organizations in nature, was set up in Chengdu, as an exchange of interest" (Hsu 2007: 12). It wasn't really a marriage in any sense of the word. Nevertheless, the marriage metaphor allows us to explore the emotional intensity that informed their responses to each other's actions. The clash of cultures that was played out in their relationship apparently reveals very different attitudes toward honoring moral and contractual obligations, toward anticipating the needs of one's partner and responding to them on a good faith basis, and finally toward the vexing question of what one or the other partner should or shouldn't do when these expectations are either ignored or unilaterally repudiated. We are left to consider whether there is a role for international business ethics in addressing these revelations and whether a shared commitment to ethical principles might have helped restore the partners' capacity for mutual understanding and accommodation. However you regard the JV, either as a marriage or simply as a business proposition, could adhering to the basic principles of international business ethics have saved their relationship?

Attempting to step back from their messy divorce in order to find a teachable moment in it, we think it clear that the JV partners both hoped for a very big success. Both wanted their JV to become a top-notch player in the Chinese CSD market. Hu and his backers in Sichuan wanted to develop a new national brand that would dominate China's markets, while Pepsi hoped to use its opportunity in Sichuan to undermine Coke's dominance worldwide. In signing the contracts that brought Pepsi Sichuan into existence, both sides should have not only been aware of each others' goals but also agreed on how they were to achieve them. But as we have seen, in their rush to get into bed together, both parties seemed blind to each other's real desires. By establishing a JV intended to be its distributor for Sichuan, Pepsi thought it was entering into its standard franchise agreement with a local bottler. Hu, on the other hand, apparently thought he was using both Pepsi and the Sichuan government to set himself up as one of the great entrepreneurs of China. Not only was Pepsi not to be respected as the groom in this arranged marriage; it wasn't even to be honored as an equal business partner. When asked to justify his aggressive actions resisting Pepsi's business plan, Hu usually dismissed Pepsi as, at best, a minority shareholder or merely a supplier of raw materials to his beverage company. From his perspective, Pepsi was interfering with his entrepreneurship, trying to deprive him of his fair share—the lion's share—of the profits, while restricting his freedom to expand his operations in response to new opportunities.

Hu's assumptions, however, ran entirely contrary not only to Pepsi's business plan for its local franchisees but also to the contracts that he had signed with Pepsi. Hu felt justified in violating these, because in his view Pepsi had already reneged on key promises made to his company. One manager sympathetic to Pepsi's growing frustration—which reached its peak in response to Pepsi Sichuan's decision to launch its own national brand unilaterally—characterized Hu's actions as aggravated adultery: "How," he complained on Pepsi's behalf, "can a husband allow his wife to find a new lover?" (Liu 2006: 295). Such moralistic rhetoric inevitably reveals an ethical undercurrent to the grievances harbored on both sides. The tensions between the JV partners had become not only polarized but also personalized. Each accused the other of breaching the promises upon which the JV was founded. The only real question in their morality play was who was guilty of committing adultery first? Who was more flagrant in violating the promises they had made to each other?

Neither international business ethics nor classical Confucian culture is much interested in trying to determine who is the worst offender in this "painful marriage." Moralistic rhetoric may occasionally comfort those who consider themselves the injured or offended party, but "playing blame game" could neither save the JV nor provide observers like ourselves with useful lessons for the future. In terms of the categories outlined in previous chapters in this book, we see both parties accusing each other of creating Type B problems, that is, each was convinced that the other deliberately engaged in actions that were flagrantly immoral. Of course, in order to verify their accusations, we would have to ask, by what standards were they acting immorally?

Judged by the standards of international business ethics, Pepsi's refusal to follow through promptly on its promise to assist Pepsi Sichuan in developing a national brand of its own is surely questionable. For even in Western moral philosophy, it is commonly recognized that "justice delayed is justice denied." If Pepsi's top management routinely refused to implement his request, it is understandable that Hu would conclude that Pepsi had no intention of keeping its promises—surely a major Type B problem, by standards of international business ethics. On the other hand, Hu's various refusals to honor the terms of the original JV contracts, his defiant responses to Pepsi's various demands for transparency in financial matters big and small, and his attempts to organize a nationwide revolt against Pepsi within the PCBA, judged by the standards of Western moral philosophy, were clearly symptomatic of a Type B problem even larger than Pepsi's own. Viewing his conduct from their own perspective, Pepsi could only have concluded that Hu, alas, was incapable of recognizing any moral obligations in the relationship with this JV partner.

At the beginning of this chapter, we quoted one of Rothlin's rules for becoming a top-notch player, namely, "If you analyze facts from different angles, you will discover the benefits of fair play." In light of what happened to Pepsi Sichuan, perhaps now we can appreciate the need for investigating all the angles. If Western moral philosophy provides one angle for determining the ethical issues in the Pepsi Sichuan case, are there other angles? Would Chinese moral philosophy lend support to Hu's way of doing business with Pepsi? By now we should be prepared to admit that the answer to this question is complicated. There are some observers who think that classical Confucian and Daoist teachings recognize "no ethical duties… beyond the familial context other than to maintain social harmony" (Humphrey 2008: 25; Haley et al. 2004). If this were true, then any foreign business seeking to establish a JV in China would have to be prepared to cope with a cultural environment in which relying on mutually acknowledged ethical responsibilities is not only unrealistic but counterproductive as well. Absent any guarantee that the rule of law will be impartially enforced by the government, and enjoying at best only the weak form of *guanxi* that may result from participating in the drinking rituals that usually occur in Chinese banquets, foreign businesses would be well advised to forego any hopes of creating mutually profitable JVs with prospective partners in China.

We do not subscribe to this "once burnt, twice sorry" view of doing business in China. As the discussion in a previous chapter on Chinese virtue ethics should make clear, the teachings of Confucius, Mencius, and Mozi identify moral excellence with a universal respect for moral obligations. Even if the history of modern China—particularly after the campaign against "the Four Olds" (四舊; pinyin: *sì jiù*), during the Cultural Revolution (1966–1969)—served to undermine if not obliterate these traditions, the fact is that significant efforts are underway to restore their moral authority and extend their meaning to address the challenges arising in China's current era of economic and social reform (Cheng and Liu 2010). Though an entrepreneur like Hu Fengxian may be excused for lacking an appreciation of Chinese virtue ethics, it would be a mistake to assume that his actions are an authentic expression of Chinese culture, rather than symptomatic of its weakened condition. From whatever angle we view the fate of Pepsi Sichuan, it appears that both partners were involved in serious Type B moral problems. Our task, then, is not to vindicate one or the other side, but to address the Type A problem that is apparent in their mutual disregard. When both parties are in the wrong, how can we move on to make anything right?

4.4 Ethical Reflection

4.4.1 From Role Models to Moral Decision-Making Models

Whatever his merits as a *mei bo* or even as an entrepreneur, Hu Fengxian is not likely to be honored as a role model for moral excellence among Chinese business men and women. We know nothing of Hu's personal life, whether his family would regard him as a filial son, faithful husband, loving father, or trusted friend. But even if he were exemplary in all of these and were generous with his wealth, a true disciple of Confucius would have to admit that when it came to his business dealings with his JV partner, Hu was just another *xiǎorén*. In Confucian tradition, an exemplary moral leader, a *jūnzǐ* (君子), must keep his promises and strive to achieve results that demonstrate benevolence to all concerned. The four basic Confucian virtues—humanity (*ren*), righteousness (*yi*), ritual propriety (*li*), and wisdom (*zhi*)—are all implicitly universal. Only a *xiǎorén* would assume that benevolence applies only to family members and others with whom one has personal relationships (Chinese, 关系; pinyin, *guanxi*). The teachings of Mozi, as we have seen, are even more explicit. As we learned in Chapter 2, his ideal of impartial care (*jiān ài*) proscribes bad behavior toward any human being. All are to be treated with the same degree of care, regardless of personal relationships or lack thereof.

Nevertheless, in the protracted struggle for survival that continues to shape contemporary Chinese morality, some may regard Hu as a great leader, precisely because he refuses to accept the limits unfairly imposed upon him by his foreign partner. When, in Hu's view, that partner has already broken its promises to him, it is entirely appropriate for him to respond in kind. When their relationship has deteriorated into the corporate equivalent of war, Hu felt entirely justified to treat Pepsi as the enemy, using anything he could to defeat it. But does Hu have a correct understanding of his relationship with Pepsi? By the same token, if you were part of Pepsi's management team, how would you have interpreted Hu's behavior and responded to it? Would you allow your firm to be drawn into a war with your recalcitrant JV partner? At what point, if any, would you have demanded the same kind of arbitration process in Stockholm that Pepsi demanded in order to extricate itself from its failed marriage? Could anything have been done to prevent a divorce, or would any other policy have merely delayed the inevitable? Would you have done any differently?

Answering such questions shifts our focus from the Type B problems involved in willful and complete moral failure to Type A problems where what to do is uncertain. If we follow Rothlin's rule and analyze the facts from many angles, our level of uncertainty about what to do is likely to increase, at least temporarily. We learn to exercise caution, because our moral passions may prompt us to become one sided in our views and thus less able to arrive at a solution that achieves the benefits of fair play for all concerned. But fair play for all concerned requires us to deepen our understanding of the ways in which moral considerations can be integrated into good managerial practices. Shifting our focus from role models to models of moral decision-making in business, we will introduce a comprehensive framework for managerial decision-making that has demonstrated its effectiveness for practicing business ethics over many years, and then we will go further into three interrelated methods of deepening our understanding of how ethical analysis may improve our capacities for understanding moral issues from many different angles.

Peter Drucker's 1954 classic, *The Practice of Management*, identifies "five distinct phases" to managerial decision-making: "Defining the problem; analyzing the problem; developing alternate solutions; deciding upon the best solution; converting the decision into effective action" (Drucker 1986: 353). While these five phases may seem to be merely a systematization of common sense, it is Drucker's specific comments on each that open the way toward managerial effectiveness. Step 1, defining the problem, for example, means finding "the critical factor"—that is, "the element (or elements) in the situation that has to be changed before anything else can be changed"—and not merely reacting to various "symptoms" of it (Ibid: 354). Step 2, analyzing the problem may require several attempts to discover what the real problem is, and the analysis must identify not only the critical factor but also the conditions and objectives for its solution (Ibid: 356). Analyzing the problem thus means identifying the resources for a solution. The point is not necessarily to gather all possible facts about the problem, but to ask, "What information do I need for this particular decision?" (Ibid: 358). In the real world, as Drucker observes, "most decisions have to be based on incomplete knowledge—either because the information is not available or because it would cost too much in time and money to get it" (Ibid: 359). The point is to "know what information is lacking in order to judge how much of a risk the decision involves" as well as to judge how much flexibility may be needed once the decision is implemented. Drucker thus is recommending a trial-and-error approach, adapted from the canons of "scientific method" (Ibid: 361), which may require repeated experiment with the first two phases until an analysis that actually opens a path toward a solution is achieved.

Drucker's Step 3, developing alternative solutions, highlights the role of imagination in managerial decision-making. Deliberately exploring a full range of alternatives enables managers to avoid "falling into the trap of a false 'either-or'" (Ibid: 359). One alternative that must always be considered is "taking no action at all" (Ibid: 361). Because all alternative solutions involve interventions of one sort or another, Step 4 focuses on choosing the best solution. The best solution is the one that is consistent with the business' objectives, the available resources, time constraints, and other factors. Step 5 is making the decision effective. While this involves effective communication, Drucker warns against "selling" the solution, as if the task were merely to persuade the others involved to "buy" it. Instead, they must be led to "make it their own" (Ibid: 364). His reasoning bears repeating:

> The manager who 'makes' the decision…defines the problem. He sets the objectives and spells out the rules. He classifies the decision and assembles the information. He finds the alternative solutions, exercises judgment and picks the best. But for the solution to become a decision, action is needed. And that the decision-making manager cannot supply. He can only communicate to others what they ought to be doing and motivate them to do it. And only as they take the right action is the decision actually made. (Ibid: 364)

At the core of managerial decision-making, then, is the challenge of getting others to take the right action. But how do ethical considerations surface in the five steps of Drucker's decision-making process?

While business ethics is relevant for understanding each of the Drucker's phases, let us observe some specific points where moral considerations should be made explicit without distorting Drucker's model or losing its focus on business management. One aspect of "defining the problem" is to ask whether it is, at first sight, an ethical problem. Not all managerial problems involve violations of the basic norms of business ethics or conflicts among various moral beliefs, priorities, and values. But if a reasonable person detects either a Type A or a Type B problem in the situation, then recognizing it as such is an important step toward identifying the critical factor that must be changed in order to create an effective solution. If an ethical problem is indicated, "analyzing the problem" ought to include making an inventory of ethical resources for resolving it, including structures of corporate and personal accountability. An inventory of these, as a part of any managerial decision-making process, will highlight the significance of relevant business law, government regulations, corporate codes of ethics, company policy manuals with ethical implications, and public opinion, as well as the manager's personal moral convictions and the moral common sense of the people who must take action in this situation. "Analyzing the problem" will not only inventory these resources but also make an assessment of which ones are likely to create the most effective leverage for making the right decision.

As an exercise in imagination, "developing alternative solutions" involves brainstorming the broadest possible range of solutions, including the alternative of doing nothing. Moral and immoral, legal and illegal, and serious as well as silly solutions ought to be represented in this range. Examining all of them will help bring moral clarity not only to understanding the problem but also point toward the best solution. We suggest, therefore, adding a step to Drucker's model, by which moral clarity can be assured: "eliminate the sleaze." Sleaze is Chicago-style street slang for anything that is low or underhanded and dishonest or immoral. In our context, "sleaze" is the category used to identify any of the alternative solutions that fall below the standards highlighted in the inventory of ethical resources produced in response to this problem. If everything sleazy is eliminated in this phase, then the manager can proceed with confidence to choose from among the remaining alternatives the solution that makes the most business sense. Once an ethical moment has been integrated into the decision-making process, the manager can be confident that his or her business judgment on the best solution will also be a moral decision preserving or enhancing the ethical integrity of the firm. He or she won't be in the awkward position of trying to "sell" business ethics to his or her colleagues and subordinates, because the best solution will already be consistent with the relevant standards of business ethics.

Of course, there will be unusual situations when there are no good solutions and when acting consistently with the ethical norms identified in "analyzing the problem" may seem impossible for one reason or another. We believe that even in business, such situations are the exception rather than the rule. Nevertheless, moral philosophers have pointed out various ways of acting responsibly in these exceptional circumstances. There are maxims such as "choose the lesser of two evils" or "always err on the side of safety." In order to understand such advice and how it may further the integration of business ethics into managerial decision-making, we must now dig a little deeper into the practical implications of analytic moral philosophy. In Chapter 3, we learned that ethical theory is divided into three parts: descriptive ethics, normative ethics, and metaethics. In order to clarify what ought to be done in a particular situation, as in normative ethics, analytic moral philosophy has developed three methods of analysis: the deontological method, the utilitarian method, and the method of applying justice. While both Chinese and Western traditions highly value the insights underlying all of these three methods, their formal elaboration has occurred primarily in the context of modern post-Enlightenment European philosophy.

4.4.2 The Deontological, or Duty-Based, Method

This approach reflects the conclusions of the German philosopher Immanuel Kant (1704–1804 CE) whose *Critique of Practical Reason* (1788) explains why human actions must basically have a universal character and should respect people as ends and not only as means. Respect for persons, as understood by Kant, echoes Mozi's notion of impartial care (*jiān ài*), while also identifying it as a moral imperative that is universally obligatory on all human beings. Respecting the norms that are derived from this categorical imperative helps to clarify and strengthen our respect for persons. Mozi himself associates this imperative with the will of Heaven: "To accord with Heaven's will is to take right as the governing standard. To oppose Heaven's will is to take force as the governing standard" (Ivanhoe and Van Norden 2001: 93). He also compares the will of Heaven to a geometrical instrument, in contrast to a balance: "I hold to the will of Heaven as a wheelwright holds to his compass and a carpenter to his square.... I measure them with the clearest standard in the world" (Ibid.: 93–94). The sense of moral duty, recognized in a well-formed conscience capable of caring for others impartially, provides the basis for deontological ethics. We suggest that this standard can be applied to the challenges faced by business managers by following these steps:

Steps of the Deontological Method

1. Clearly state the action to be evaluated, making sure that all the relevant perspectives are taken into account.
2. Determine whether the action can be linked with some generally acknowledged attitude such as not to kill, lie, or steal.
3. Study the morality of the action with two criteria:
   (a) Does the action respect people as ends and not just as means only? If so, on first sight the action is moral; if not, then the action is immoral.
   (b) Does this action mean that all rational people would approve of it and recommend that all others act similarly, in similar situations? If so, on first sight the action is moral; if not, then the action is immoral.
4. If the action is considered moral, decide whether it conflicts with other duties or obligations and whether the conflicting duties or obligations can all be fulfilled. If all can be fulfilled and then all things considered, the action is moral. If the conflicts cannot be resolved, proceed to the method of applying justice.

4.4.3 The Utilitarian Method

The second approach derives from utilitarianism, a moral philosophy proposed by John Stuart Mill (1806–1873 CE) and other British philosophers. Utilitarianism is an ethical theory that holds that an action is right if it produces the greatest amount of good for the greatest number of people. This theory should be distinguished from cost-benefit analysis, a conventional method of managerial decision-making derived from a narrowly economic account of utility. They differ primarily in the perspective from which the analysis is done. Cost-benefit analysis calculates the good and bad consequences of performing a certain action usually with reference to its impact on the firm's bottom line or its impact on shareholder value. Good or bad consequences count only from the perspective of the one who is calculating them. Utilitarian analysis, by contrast, is a genuinely ethical theory that weighs the good and bad consequences of an action from their foreseeable impact on all the people concerned. Therefore, all the stakeholders are taken into consideration. Utilitarian analysis, in short, converges with the ideal of social harmony honored by all traditions of Chinese moral philosophy. With its emphasis on rational calculation, utilitarian analysis is very similar to Mozi's typical way of inferring and explaining the specific requirements of impartial care (*jiān ài*). We suggest that this method can be applied to the challenges faced by business managers by following the following steps:

Steps for Using the Utilitarian Method

1. Clearly state the action to be evaluated, considering it from every relevant perspective.
2. Identify the "stakeholders," i.e., all those who are directly and indirectly affected by the action.
3. Specify all the good and bad consequences of the action for all concerned, and in complex situations, imagine different scenarios to weigh the probabilities of various outcomes.
4. Make a moral judgment: if the action produces more good than bad, then the action is moral. If it produces more bad than good, then it is immoral.
5. Imagine other alternatives, and go through the same steps of analysis for each of the other alternative actions.
6. Compare the results of the above scenarios. The action that on the whole produces the most good, or the least harm (in Latin *minus malum*), is the most appropriate choice.

4.4.4 The Method of Applying Justice

Some business ethics manuals favor the utilitarian method over the deontological method, while others favor the opposite. But rather than force a choice between the two, we see both methods as necessary for achieving truly either justice or social harmony. Justice, in the teachings of Western moral philosophy, means treating equals equally. Justice as fairness, in Aristotle's account of it, involves a firm and consistent intention to "give each person his or her due." What moral philosophers believe is due to each person, of course, differs from one culture to another and from one epoch to another. The American philosopher John Rawls, for example, formulated an influential theory of distributive justice based on two principles:

1. "First: each person is to have an equal right to the most extensive basic liberty compatible with a similar liberty for others."
2. "Social and economic inequalities are to be arranged so that they are both reasonably accounted for every person's advantage and attached to positions and offices open to all" (Rawls 1971: 60).

Rawls' understanding of justice clearly defines what each person is due in terms of universal human rights and equal liberties for all and envisions a situation in which the burden of proof is upon anyone who would justify or perpetuate social and economic inequalities.

Such an approach to justice, however, differs substantially from the teachings of both Confucius and Mozi. Understandably, it may provoke a high degree of skepticism among Chinese philosophers and may seem unimaginable to ordinary Chinese people. For when, if ever, do we encounter persons and situations that are truly equal? Chinese moral philosophy presupposes a world of reciprocal relationships that are organized hierarchically. Confucian teaching regarding "The Rectification of Names" (正名; pinyin: *Zhèngmíng*) clearly recognizes their morally obligatory character, as in the paradigmatic relationships of parent-child, husband-wife, and older sibling-younger sibling. But the obligations play out asymmetrically and rarely, if ever, on the basis of acknowledged equality. Given the social world of the ancient Mediterranean empires, Aristotle would have understood Chinese reservations about Rawls' theory, however much he also may have applauded Rawls' effort to restore justice to its rightful position in moral philosophy.

Setting aside whatever opinions we may have either for or against Rawls, we must insist that the principle of justice is crucial to any serious account of international business ethics. Its relevance is best appreciated when addressing the frequent problem of conflicting moral claims. If analytic moral philosophy is correct, we are not free to choose between deontological and utilitarian methods simply on the basis of personal taste or preference. When people express their moral concerns about things that matter to them, they use terms like right and wrong as well as good and bad. Cross-cultural studies of the way these terms are used indicate that there is a logic to the relationship of deontological and utilitarian considerations that must be understood and observed in making good moral decisions. The method of justice, then, applies first of all to situations where there is a conflict between the results of deontological and utilitarian analyses. The following steps are meant to address such conflicts not only among individuals but also those that occur between and within groups, companies, and institutions.

Steps of Applying Justice

1. State clearly the moral issue that needs to be resolved and its conclusions from the utilitarian and deontological points of view. Identify the priorities that naturally arise in each view.
2. If basic duties are clearly evident from the deontological analysis, these should take priority over any calculation of good consequences. Make sure these basic duties are fulfilled regardless of whatever other good may be achievable in the situation. This rule we will call "the deontological override."
3. If there is a conflict among the basic duties identified, try to prioritize these. If they are unequal, fulfill those duties that are weightier or more imperative. If they are equal, with no real priority emerging, then fulfill the duties identified on the basis of achieving the greatest good for the greatest number. This rule we will call "utilitarianism of the last resort."
4. Although justice is never perfectly realized, nevertheless, we strive to approximate it. Aristotle's notion of fairness and Mozi's impartial care converge in recognizing the role of rational analysis in applying justice. In the end, we must determine whether and how our human nature is best realized in the way we decide to resolve particular moral issues.

4.5 Conclusion: Moral Decision-Making in the Pepsi Sichuan Case

If we adopt the angle of either of the partners in the Pepsi Sichuan JV, the moral problem seems typically Type B, and the ethical arguments about it are open and shut. The grievances that each side held against the other concern serious breaches of basic morality whether the standard appealed to is either Western or Chinese moral philosophy. If we adopt the Rawlsian method of applying justice, for example, Hu's claims appealing to a basic equality between the partners, in order to repudiate the restrictions imposed by Pepsi's standard business model, at first glance seems to make sense. On the other hand, Pepsi's ongoing demand for transparency and financial accountability plausibly rests on the same assumption of equality. Similarly, applying deontological ethics will highlight the promises that were broken on both sides, but without shedding much light on where the path of justice is likely to be found. Under such circumstances, when deontological rights and obligations appear to conflict and the path of justice remains uncertain, the utilitarian approach may be the most promising way to restore social harmony between the JV partners and for the sake of all their stakeholders.

In Western moral philosophy, utilitarian ethics is typically the path of compromise. Though as a matter of logic fulfilling deontological obligations ought to be the first priority, in a situation where both parties have failed to do so, seeking the greatest good for the greatest number may give both a way forward that allows them to set aside their grievances without either losing face or forfeiting their moral integrity. What sort of compromise might have been worked out to save Pepsi Sichuan? If discovering a basis for compromise were the first priority for both sides, how might the situation have played out differently? A serious and fully developed answer to this question, of course, might require us to reexamine all the angles evident in it, using the six-step decision-making model inspired by Drucker's work. Here, however, we will only make a few suggestions.

What, then, is the real problem that, if it had been solved, might have prevented the breakup of Pepsi Sichuan? There were many problems, as we have seen, so the challenge is how to identify the true problem of which the other problems were symptomatic. One problem is that though Pepsi had already operated in China for some time, its management apparently lacked any deep appreciation of Chinese history and culture or, more likely, it chose to ignore what it could have learned from its Chinese employees and consultants. Pepsi's initial negotiations with Hu and his backers apparently assumed that the objective was to get their signatures on contracts that would bind both parties as the JV developed. This predictably Western assumption about the sanctity of contracts is alien to Chinese business practices. Contracts cannot insure the Chinese partner's future compliance; only the careful cultivation of trust and loyalty through *guanxixue*, however enacted, can create a relationship in which two parties will act reciprocally to insure each other's benefit. So one problem is that Pepsi relied on the letter of its contracts and expected to use the Chinese government and its legal system to achieve compliance. Pepsi should have known that appealing to the Sichuan government to enforce its contractual rights against its JV partner at best might have only limited success and at worst could be interpreted by Hu and his backers as an act of war. Another problem, in hindsight, is Pepsi's apparent failure to educate its Chinese partner on the nature of Pepsi's franchise business. It is not clear how much effort Pepsi put into communicating with Hu, but his responses suggest either that he did not understand the kind of JV he had agreed to manage or that he deliberately ignored what he had agreed to, in order to justify his actions and save face with his Chinese stakeholders. In either case, Pepsi might have been able to generate more sympathy for its grievances against Hu's management of Pepsi Sichuan had it done a better job of educating all the JV's stakeholders to the nature of its business.

Ultimately, if Pepsi Sichuan were to be saved, its JV partners would have to compromise by conducting themselves, not in strict adherence to the "principles" that had made Pepsi successful elsewhere but in ways that were sufficiently flexible to be accommodated to Chinese cultural values. Given the importance of cultivating good personal relationships with its Chinese partners, Pepsi should have been more careful in its initial decision to work with Hu Fengxian. Instead of focusing on the strategic significance of Hu's connections with the Sichuan government and how these could be used to Pepsi's advantage, the firm might have spent more time getting to know him personally. What could they have observed as to his personal character? Was he worthy of the trust they were about to place in him? Did he exhibit respect for traditional Chinese notions of moral leadership? Was he more of a *xiǎorén* (小人) than a *jūnzǐ* (君子)? If doing business in China depends on cultivating personal relationships, then finding answers to such questions is crucially important, especially when operating in a social environment such as Sichuan proved to be, where Western assumptions about the rule of law are either weak or nonexistent.

The problem, however, is what to do now that the JV had been launched and its partners no longer trusted each other. How could sufficient trust be restored, so that the parties could work together to make a success of Pepsi Sichuan? That healing their relationship might still have been possible, even after so many mutual disappointments, apparently seemed realistic to at least one insider, Qu Zhidi, vice general manager of Sichuan Yunlv. As late as August 2002, Qu expressed the hope that both parties would put aside their grievances and "come back to the negotiating table" (Taipei Times 2002). Had they done so, what might they have worked out? Pepsi could have offered wholehearted support in developing and launching Hu's new national brand. This seems to be the one thing Hu wanted above all else. They might also have helped Hu set up an entirely new firm, independent of Pepsi Sichuan, to produce the new national brand. In exchange for their assistance, both technical and financial, Pepsi might have gained full control over the management of Pepsi Sichuan or at least some plan for reintegrating Pepsi Sichuan into the rules and procedures of its Bottler's Association in China (PCBA).

Some such set of concrete proposals, reaffirming and implementing the top priorities of both JV partners, might have provided a pathway forward together. But as it happened, Pepsi had already filed for arbitration in Stockholm, and the divorce proceedings were underway. Once it had obtained its divorce from Sichuan Yunlv, Pepsi expressed the hope of finding "a new joint venture partner committed to 'observing law and order, mutual trust and transparent decision-making'" (Taipei Times 2002). As is often the case in the USA, while one marriage may have failed, that's no reason to give up on marriage altogether. As in personal relationships, so also in business, divorce often sets the stage for finding another partner, one who understands his or her spouse better and is willing to build a life together based on a greater appreciation of their shared cultural values. As painful as the first marriage may have been and as messy as the divorce proceedings may prove to be, one is always better off trying to act responsibly, as one moves through the vicissitudes of relationships, whether in personal life or in business. Acting with integrity often means acknowledging one's mistakes and learning from them as one continues to search for a pathway forward. Learning to play fair, we eventually come to realize, will see us through our failures as well as successes, as in personal life, so also in business.

References

Ambler, T., Witzel, M., et al. (2008). *Doing business in China*. London\New York: Routledge.

Anderlini, J. (2013). *Xi vows to protect foreign businesses*. London: Financial Times.

Bremmer, I. (2013). Soft (Drink) power. *Foreign Policy – The Power Issue*. Retrieved April 30, 2013, from http://www.foreignpolicy.com/articles/2013/04/29/soft_drink_power?wp_login_redirect=0

Chen Derong. (1999). Three dimensional rationales in Chinese negotiation. In D. M. Kolb (Ed.), *Negotiation eclectics: Essays in memory of Jeffrey Z. Rubin*. Cambridge, MA: PON Books.

Cheng, Y., & Liu, B (2010) *China explores cultural therapy to cure social ills*. Retrieved July 16, 2013, from http://news.xinhuanet.com/english2010/china/2011-10/25/c_131212258.htm

Drucker, P. (1986). Making decisions. In *The practice of management*. New York: HarperCollins, Perennial Library.

Du, F. (2002). Will Pepsi faction end in Stockholm. *Law Service Times*.

Fei Xiaotong. (1992): *From the soil: The foundations of Chinese society* (Xiangtu Zhongguo). Berkeley: University of California Press.

Fernandez, J. A., & Liu, S. (2011). *China CEO: A case guide for business leaders in China*. Hoboken: Wiley.

Flannery, R. (2003). Pepsi's Chinese Torture. *Forbes Magazine*. Retrieved April 25, 2013, from www.forbes.com/forbes/2003/1222/086sidebar.html

Haley, G. T., Haley, U. C., et al. (2004). *The Chinese Tao of business: The logic of successful business strategy*. Hoboken: Wiley.

Hsu, J. (2007). Ethical Implication of the Business Strategy of Pepsi Co in its dispute with the local partner: Master thesis. In S. Rothlin (Ed.), *Master thesis for the 2006/7 Master of Business Administration program at the Sino-French School of International Management (IFCM)* (p. 66). Beijing: Sino-French School of International Management (IFCM).

Humphrey, R. (2008). Cultural literacy and sound due diligence: Two imperatives for business success in China. *Journal of the North American Management Society, 3*(1), 200824.

IBS Case Development Centre. (2009). Business environment in China. In MS Raju & X Dominique (Eds.), *Marketing management: International perspectives*. New Delhi: Tata McGraw-Holl.

Ivanhoe, P. J., & Van Norden, B. (2001). *Readings in classical Chinese philosophy*. New York: Seven Bridges Press.

Julia Ching. (1993). *Chinese religions*. New York: Orbis Books.

Liu, S. (2006). Pepsi's 'painful marriage' in Sichuan. *Asian Case Research Journal, 10*(02), 281–302.

Rawls, J. (1971). *A theory of justice*. Cambridge, MA: Harvard University Press.

TaipeiTimes. (2002, August 26). PepsiCo dumps its Chinese partner. *Taipei Times*, 12. Retrieved July 17, 2013 from http://www.taipeitimes.com/News/worldbiz/archives/2002/08/26/0000165685

The Economist. (2004, March 18). *A disorderly heaven*. Retrieved on June 16, 2015 from http://www.economist.com/node/2495184

Yallapragada, R. R., Sardessai, R. M., et al. (2012). Doing business in China: Investor beware. *Southwestern Economic Proceedings, 32*(3), 27–30.

Yu, C. S., & Xiaosheng (2002). The worst end might be the best start. *Xinhua News*. Beijing: Xinhua News Agency.

Chapter 5
Free and Fair Competition in Business

> *"Your Public Relations strategy will only secure your Reputation if it witnesses your drive for Quality and Excellence."* (Stephan Rothlin, *Eighteen Rules for Becoming a Top Notch Player,* 2004)

5.1 Prelude

Many of the most basic lessons in international business ethics depend upon the consensus view of modern economics that free and fair competition in the marketplace is the means for achieving the social—as well as personal—benefits of business activity. The basic lesson that we learned in Chap. 1, namely, that all "top-notch players" must be committed—win or lose—to respecting and enhancing the integrity of the game, here is carried over into a view of businesses' responsibilities to maintaining the integrity of marketplace competition. Centuries ago, Aristotle and his medieval disciple Thomas Aquinas developed a realistic moral theory of market transactions under the heading of "commutative justice." In this chapter, we reference their teachings in order to explain how business competition ought to work, if society is to achieve the benefits expected from ordinary business activity.

The case study with which we begin this chapter is the tale of two Mongolian dairy firms—bitter competitors for dominance in the Chinese dairy industry—who apparently thought that the only way they could win in their competition was by destroying each other's reputation for quality and reliability. The ensuing PR campaign by which Mengniu launched its attack against Yili provoked a panic among Chinese consumers who had already been shaken by the earlier melamine scandal that ruined the Sanlu Group. As the case study leads us to explore what happened to these firms and their managers, we see that the government and people of China clearly expect the difference between marketplace competition and predatory behavior to be observed in both law and morality. The case study, then, allows us to conclude section one of this book by reinforcing the lesson from our first chapter, namely, that it is a serious mistake to confuse business with war by other means.

S. Rothlin, D. McCann, *International Business Ethics*,
DOI 10.1007/978-3-662-47434-1_5

5.2 Case Study: Mengniu vs. Yili, What to Do with Unfair Competition?

5.2.1 Abstract

With the outbreak in 2008 of the melamine-tainted milk scandal, the Chinese dairy industry suffered a serious blow to its reputation. Since then Chinese consumers have become ever more sensitive to the issue of "product safety." Mengniu and Yili are among the top Chinese dairy brands. Adversely affected by the economic downturn and the melamine scandal, they began an all-out effort to dominate their markets. Competition reached its zenith when Mengniu hired a PR firm to manage its campaign. Aided by a few collaborators, Mengniu's manager, An Yong, directed Bosse PR Consulting to spread rumors about the alleged health hazards of using Yili's infant formula milk powder. The fear of a new melamine scandal led to an immediate boycott of the Yili brand.

Subsequent investigation revealed that Mengniu deliberately fabricated the rumors, which were proven to be entirely false. While Mengniu apologized to Yili and undertook several efforts to restore public confidence in its brand and the Chinese dairy industry nationally, the managers involved had to face criminal prosecution.

The case raises a number of issues from public accountability to unfair competition. In particular, it highlights the consequences involved in unethical business conduct, even when market competition becomes very intense.

5.2.2 Keywords

Mengniu, Yili, Bosse PR Consulting, Chinese dairy industry, Infant formula production, Brand management, Unfair competition.

5.2.3 Bitter Rivalry in the China Dairy Market

The recent history of China's dairy market begins with the privatization of state-owned enterprises. Once these became involved in subsequent mergers and acquisitions, the market was reduced from many local producers to just a few big players. The market itself attracted unwanted attention in 2008, when Sanlu and other producers were accused of using melamine as an additive in milk products intended for human consumption, particularly in milk powder adapted for use in infant formula. As we saw in Chap. 3's case study on Sanlu, the impact on the industry, both domestically and internationally, was devastating. Regaining consumer confidence has been the major goal of dairy producers and industry associations ever since. While low demand and the global economic crisis kept prices of raw materials down in 2009, the negative trends were later reversed as the global recovery began to take hold (Beijing Orient Agribusiness Consultant Ltd. 2011).

Within this history, the dramatic struggle between Mengniu and Yili unfolded. Mengniu's story cannot be detached from that of its iconic founder, Niu Gen-sheng, who recently retired from managing the firm in order to devote himself full time to philanthropy (China CSR 2011). A self-made man, Niu first entered Yili, the giant Inner Mongolian dairy producer, as a bottle washer and rose through the ranks to become a member of Yili's board of directors. His hard work and meteoric rise were nevertheless not fully appreciated by his senior colleagues who stalled his promotion for 1 year, during which he attended an MBA program at Beijing University (Zhang 2006).

The expertise and connections he acquired in Beijing served as a springboard for Niu to establish Mengniu Dairy Co. Ltd. in 1999, immediately following his resignation along with 50 subordinates from Yili. Despite having neither factories, nor an established brand, Mengniu became the fastest growing Chinese start-up ever. Niu began by successfully organizing a network of contractors—an arrangement that earned him 43 million RMB in 1 year and provided a sufficient base to begin the construction of the company's own production plants. The pivotal moment for the company occurred in 2002 when it accepted foreign investors and then in 2004 was listed on the Hong Kong stock exchange. Niu's innovative leadership was evident in his concern to reward those who had made the biggest contributions to the company's development. He had promised "Mengniu's people" that he would set aside his family's own stock in a fund for them, and he kept this promise 2 years later.

The longer history of the Yili Dairy Group began in 1992, after its reorganization from a state-owned enterprise in Inner Mongolia, first as the Hohhot Red Flag Dairy Factory, then as the Muslim Dairy Factory, and finally as Yili. Listed in 1996 and establishing itself in the market on par with the likes of Sanyuan and Bright (the reorganized Beijing and Shanghai state dairy enterprises), Yili's success under the leadership of Zheng Jun-huai proceeded smoothly until 2004, when Zheng was arrested for bribery. Along with six collaborators, Zheng was found guilty of embezzling public funds in order to finance a management buyout that appeared, in the view of many, to be a response to the perceived threat from the stronger ties Mengniu reportedly was developing with Morgan Stanley, in order to finance further expansion (Peverelli 2006).

Since Mengniu's founding by a former Yili employee, characterizing the relationship between the two companies as a "bitter rivalry" for once is more than just a cliché (Xinmin Weekly 2010). Competition to secure raw milk supplies and establish plants in the same geographical area and high investments in advertising, promotions, and price wars, all were characteristic of the new Mongolian dairy industry where the two companies were competing. Thus, in 2004 when defamatory rumors were spread about Mengniu, Yili was immediately suspected, though no evidence ever confirmed its involvement (Jiang 2004). Eventually, the two enterprises managed to divide the market amicably and thus avoided direct confrontation for about 7 years. If on the one hand Mengniu was directing its efforts toward dominating the liquid milk business, on the other, Yili focused on keeping its predominance as a supplier of milk powder, thus allowing both to grow and profit. In 2006, however, the conflict between the two erupted once more when they found themselves competing in a new arena: China's growing market for infant formula products (Lan 2010).

5.2.4 *Mengniu vs. Yili: A War of Words?*

Already shaken by new reports involving tainted and potentially harmful dairy products and subsequent cover-ups, consumers dependent on the Chinese dairy industry were thrown into panic once again in July 2010. Rumors spread claiming that Yili and the less famous dairy group, Synutra, were using harmful additives causing premature sexual development in children. Market reactions were fast and furious, leading to product boycotts and a drop in share prices for the firms accused in the rumors (China Daily 2010a). The Ministry of Health immediately stepped in fearing a new melamine scandal, but found no poisonous ingredients during numerous tests conducted across the country (China Daily 2010b). As soon as the focus shifted to the way these rumors had been spread, suspicions fell once again on Mengniu.

At the root of the scandal, investigators unearthed a predatory marketing strategy designed by Bosse PR Consulting, of which An Yong, the manager in charge of the Mengniu Child Division, was well aware. The PR Agency's CEO, Yang Zaifei, had close ties to Mengniu's top management, and company documents were found referring to the defamation campaign as "Plan 731" (Epstein 2010b). Both the charges and the evidence supporting them were flatly denied by Mengniu's CEO who fired An. Niu asserted that An alone bore "personal responsibility" in the affair and tried to immunize Mengniu from further suspicion by quoting the warning posted at the entrance of the company's Beijing yoghurt factory: "It takes 20 years to set up a good reputation and 5 min to break it" (Epstein 2010a).

The affair ended with the arrest, trial, and conviction of managers from both Mengniu and Bosse, with suspended jail sentences and fines for the six accused, including An Yong from Mengniu, as well as Xiao Xuemei and four others who worked for Bosse (Gu and Wang 2011). A public statement from Mengniu apologized to Yili, while also reminding everyone that proceedings concerning similar behavior from Yili in 2004 were still open (Shanghai Daily 2010). Consumer confidence was partially restored, but the public anxiety over the safety of China's milk products remains high.

Questionable behavior, on the frontier between clever marketing and unfair competition in the use of information, is not new to the Chinese dairy industry. Both Mengniu and Yili have occasionally indulged in unfair practices such as fabricating consumers' reports and publishing them on social networks and microblogs (Meihua 2010).

In this case, false information was deliberately spread—messages were posted on the Internet, for example—in order to mislead unwitting readers, thus undermining their confidence in Mengniu's major competitor. Consumers were not presented with any objective data to verify the arguments, and the impact of the false information was magnified due to the high sensitivity of consumers to product safety in the dairy industry in the wake of the earlier melamine scare. Having planted the false information, Mengniu was the only firm that stood to gain from the damage inflicted on its competitor's reputation. The damage caused by this deliberate attempt to exploit certain information asymmetries opened up by the Internet could only be rectified by the intervention of public authority, namely, the Ministry of Health. No benefit accrued to society at large since consumers' uncertainty rose, companies' reputations were impaired, and the Chinese dairy industry suffered another serious setback.

5.2.5 *Clever Marketing Strategy or Predatory Behavior?*

The Mengniu vs. Yili case is about the morality of deliberately misleading the public by spreading false information in order to damage a competitor's reputation. From the point of view of business ethics, were Mengniu and Bosse PR wrong to try defeating their competition in this way? Does it matter that these were Chinese companies? Would you view what they did differently if they were firms registered in the USA or EU? In China Mengniu was found guilty of spreading false claims on the Internet about Yili's product, thereby exploiting for their own gain customers' understandable anxieties over the issue of product safety. The strategy worked out by Bosse PR came at a time when the dairy industry as a whole was just recovering from the product safety scandal of 2008. Should that make a difference in your judgment of their business ethics? As it turned out, Bosse' strategy caused more collateral damage than may have been intended. Those who conspired against Yili were punished to the full extent of the law. While you may want to consider whether the law courts were too harsh, or perhaps too lenient, we should focus our discussion on the question of business ethics raised by this incident. Are there moral limits to what can and cannot be done when the competition among firms gets rough and tumble? Should there be? Can international business ethics indicate why and how businesses should think twice before engaging in similar behavior in the future?

5.3 Case Study Discussion

There are multiple moral issues in this story. How many did you identify in your reading of it? Let's check your list against the following considerations:

- Early in the story, we learned of the bribery conviction involving the Yili CEO. What does this tell us? Besides the question of whether we ought to consider commercial bribery immoral as well as illegal, there is the reason given for it, namely, the need to get financing to become more competitive with Mengniu. Fierce competition in business may help explain Yili's motives, but does it justify them? We will try to answer this question further on, in light of our analysis of the specific nature of competition in business.

- In the meantime, here's another issue: Mengniu and Yili were competing in a market still recovering from the melamine scandal. Should they have tried to soft pedal their competition in order to strengthen the public's overall confidence in the dairy industry? Should they have done so for the sake of social harmony, or out of respect for the common good, or in the interests of national security? Should any of these considerations lead them to refrain from spreading false rumors about their competitor's products?
- Going negative against one's competitors may seem like a clever marketing strategy, but it is also a moral issue, our third one. We must ask ourselves: Are there moral rules for marketplace competition? Should there be? There is also a metaethical issue implicit in this question, namely, whether competition is regarded differently in different cultures. Is business competition an act of war, and should Sunzi's *The Art of War* (孫子兵法, pinyin: *Sūnzǐ Bīngfǎ*) be our guide to marketplace competition? There's an old saying: "All's fair in love and war." Is that true in your view? If it is, and you mean to apply it strictly to business, then there's no point in discussing "fair" competition.
- A fourth moral issue is involved in Mengniu's lame attempt to defend itself, once it had been caught. The unproven suspicion that Yili was also spreading false rumors about Mengniu is used to justify Mengniu's using the PR firm to spread false rumors about Yili's products. Another old saying goes like this: "Two wrongs don't make a right." Can Yili's immoral behavior (assuming it is a fact) be used as valid excuse to justify Mengniu's immoral behavior? Does that saying hold cross-culturally, or do Chinese people think differently about this question than people from other cultures? Is there any guidance on what to do with conflicting moral intuitions in international business ethics?
- You may find yourself worrying about the way in which the CEO, Niu Gensheng, who previously had been praised by the media for his outstanding business acumen and exemplary moral leadership, washed his hands of the whole affair and blamed it all on the director of Mengniu's Child Division, An Yong, who was alleged to have conspired with Bosse PR. The fifth moral issue, then, is what are we to think of Niu's disavowal of An. Was he telling the truth about An? Or was he lying to save face for himself and the company? How would Niu's character be judged, when compared to the ideal of moral leadership developed in Chap. 2, from the classics of Western philosophers and Chinese sages?
- Finally, a sixth issue emerges, the ethics of PR firms in China, focused on what, if any, moral standards and legal guidelines are already in place, to regulate their activities. Should we explore the codes of ethics that have been enacted by some PR firms doing business in China? Are there ethical standards for firms like Bosse PR, and should they be adhered to when the competition gets rough?

Though such codes reflect standards generally advocated in international business ethics, is there any reason why they should not also apply to Chinese PR firms operating in China?

If you were able to identify more than three of the six moral issues in this case, congratulations! You are already on your way to becoming a top-notch player!

Though each of these six moral issues deserves extended discussion, perhaps the most useful one to pursue here is the ethics of business competition. Where would business ethics draw the line between fair and unfair competition as in the Mengniu vs. Yili case, between a clever marketing strategy and predatory behavior? This question will illuminate most of the other issues as well. It takes us to the heart of what it means to be in business, that is, what it means to compete in a marketplace. What, then, is a business? What is its purpose? Peter Drucker memorably observed, "The purpose of a business is to create a customer" (1954). This definition may surprise you. Perhaps you were thinking, "The purpose of a business? That's easy—to make as much money as you can as fast as you can." OK. Everyone in business wants to make as much money as they can. But Drucker's point is to make you think about how that is done. No business can make money unless it continually creates customers.

If you open a restaurant, for example, or even just a noodle shop, you will soon go broke if you don't have any customers. But how do you create customers? The short answer is that you compete for them. Yes. Businesses compete with one another in whatever market(s) are available to them. Your restaurant isn't competing for customers with the beauty salon next door, but it is competing with the other restaurants, fast-food joints, and street vendors in the neighborhood. The restaurant owner's objective is to attract customers who, in turn, are looking for a nice place to have a meal or a snack—that is, people who are in the market for food that is ready to eat. So he or she doesn't care about the beauty salon's customers, unless they are hungry. But as Drucker points out, a customer is someone who comes back for more. In order to create a customer, the restaurant owner must convince people to come back again and again because, having sampled his menu, they are sufficiently impressed by the quality of the food and service that they are eager to visit his restaurant again. A customer is someone with whom he or she has established a relationship. A customer comes back again because it is easier than starting all over again to find a place where he or she can get as much. He or she is not likely to stop coming simply because the restaurant down the street is having a sale this week.

Simple observation of how people behave, even in unregulated markets, demonstrates the importance of creating customers. In growing up we've watched how our parents shop. We know they will go out of their way to do business with someone they trust, sometimes a relative, or someone with whom they have some other kind of *guanxi*. Once the relationship has been established, they will continue to do business there, until or unless their trust is betrayed. If a restaurant serves food that is rotten or tainted, and it either disgusts them or makes them ill, it will be very hard to persuade them to give it a second chance, even if the restaurant owner has good *guanxi* with these customers. They will take their business elsewhere, if they have a chance to do so. Wouldn't you?

So how do I get customers to flock to my business? I create customers by serving their needs for a price that they consider fair. If the price they are willing to pay for my products exceeds the cost of producing them, then I make a profit. If I succeed in doing this repeatedly, as more and more people become my customers, I make a larger and larger profit. There is no magic to doing this. But it does involve a lot of hard thinking about who my customers are, what their needs are, and how I can meet those needs well enough to keep them coming back for more. A market emerges when there is a sufficient number of buyers and sellers interacting with one another in a free exchange of goods, in order to enable all participants to make their choices freely, that is, based on rational self-interest. Buyers and sellers, of course, are not simply atoms interacting in a chemistry experiment. They are people competing for each other's business, seeking to enter into or sustain relationships that will allow them more easily and more profitably fulfill their self-interest, in the form of either increased sales revenues, and thus profits, or increased satisfaction in the goods or services they have purchased.

Understood in light of Drucker's remarks on the purpose of a business, it is easy to see how and why "Plan 731" developed by Bosse PR failed to create customers for Mengniu. Instead of focusing, as one of Rothlin's rules advises, on promoting the firm's reputation for quality and excellence, it tried to undermine its competitor by spreading false and dangerous rumors, in a market that had already been hurt by the melamine scandal. Assuming they are competent in marketing, the managers at Bosse PR should have known that "Plan 731" was an act of terror that could only frighten customers away. Even if it succeeded in destroying Yili's reputation, how would that have secured Mengniu's reputation? As it turned out, Chinese customers in the market for infant formula feared for the safety of their children and whenever possible began to look for alternatives to either Mengniu or Yili. If anyone gained an advantage, it was only the foreign suppliers of infant formula, whom customers regarded as more trustworthy than the Chinese producers.

All this should have been readily predictable to anyone who understands what a customer is. If there is a genuine market, those who buy and sell in it do so freely, that is, they have choices, and they are not likely to be manipulated by those whose only claim on their loyalty and interest is fear. If marketers and public relations strategists in China don't already know this, surely as consumer markets continue to develop there, they will learn it the hard way. Competing for customers in a market, then, follows logic different from that of warfare, in which the competition between two armies is strictly "win-lose." Tactics that may have some plausibility on the battlefield—in which the civilian population is there to be captured or otherwise exploited by whichever army is victorious—are not only irrelevant but also counterproductive when businesses compete for the loyalties of their customers, as they must in a genuine marketplace. We will return to the discussion of the morality of market competition after we have explored what the sages and philosophers have said about the ethics of buying and selling.

5.4 Ethical Reflection

In theory, a market is an institution for facilitating "win-win" transactions or the fair exchange of money for goods and services. Businesses create customers when they treat fairly the individuals or entities with whom they hope to develop exchange relationships. But what does it mean for businesses to treat people fairly? The moral and spiritual traditions of both Chinese and European civilizations are quite explicit in their answers to this question. Chinese answers can be inferred from the kind of social practices regulating behavior in the marketplace that ancient sages, like Mencius and Mozi, advocated. European answers are evident in the theories of philosophers and theologians, like Aristotle and Aquinas that sought to define the nature of justice in market exchanges. St. Thomas Aquinas (1225–1274 CE) had a name for it, "commutative justice" (ST II-II, q. 61), and it is his observations that must inform our ethical reflections.

5.4.1 What Is Commutative Justice?

Aristotle introduced the notion of "commutative justice"—or the justice that occurs in successful private transactions—in his treatise, the *Nicomachean Ethics*, where he offered an explanation of the virtue of justice. As in many other philosophical inquiries, he begins by deriving a preliminary definition of the unknown from the known, and what people commonly know is the experience of injustice. He infers from the various examples people give of injustice that "the just, then, is the lawful and fair, the unjust the unlawful and unfair" (Book V, No. 1). Yet when one examines the acts that people regard as lawful and fair, Aristotle argues that within the virtue of justice, different kinds of justice must be understood, of which there are two principals, namely, the justice recognized in the distribution of public goods (known subsequently as "distributive justice") and the justice that "plays a rectifying part in [private] transactions between a man and a man" (known subsequently as "commutative justice)." Since human actions can be categorized as "voluntary" and "involuntary," Aristotle uses this distinction to note the difference between voluntary transactions that typically occur in the marketplace, in which property is acquired through mutual consent, and involuntary exchanges in which property is acquired through various forms of theft and violence (Book V, No. 2).

In order to distinguish the justice that is usually obtained in a lawful market transaction from the injustice involved in theft and robbery, Aristotle focuses on the purpose of such transactions, which in his view is to achieve "a sort of equality" between the two parties, conceived as an arithmetical mean between paying too much and paying too little (Book V, No. 4). In order to explain how this actually works in the marketplace, he observes the role of money prices in facilitating exchanges: money makes all things that can be exchanged "commensurate" insofar as each item has its price, without which our transactions would be confined to bartering, and most of our energies spent trying to determine on an ad hoc basis the worth of things to be exchanged. While prices may be determined through collective agreement among participants in a market, they are hardly arbitrary. Money prices, precisely because they represent such collective agreements, are subject to considerations of justice and injustice. As Aristotle observes, they are based on "demand":

> All goods must therefore be measured by some one thing, as we said before. Now this unit is in truth demand, which holds all things together (for if men did not need one another's goods at all, or did not need them equally, there would be either no exchange or not the same exchange); but money has become by convention a sort of representative of demand; and this is why it has the name 'money' (nomisma)-because it exists not by nature but by law (nomos) and it is in our power to change it and make it useless. There will, then, be reciprocity when the terms have been equated.... (Book V, No. 5)

In Aristotle's view, the justice of market transactions thus depends on their voluntary nature. But since no one would agree to a market exchange that he or she knew was unfair, the prices agreed to must make both parties "equal," at least in the rough sense that both parties can recognize that they have gotten their money's worth.

Aristotle's theory of commutative justice as a process of rectifying or insuring this kind of transactional "equality" may be puzzling since clearly "gain" and "loss" commonly occur in any marketplace. It may seem at first nearly impossible to reconcile the reality of "gain" and "loss" or the obvious role that "profit" plays in market transactions with Aristotle's notion of equality and his theoretical explanation of the kinds of justice—"distributive" and "commutative"—by analogy with the distinction between geometrical and arithmetical proportions. Nevertheless, his basic point should be clear: in any successful market transaction, when both parties regard themselves as equally satisfied in the exchange they are making, neither party regards himself or herself as having been cheated or abused by the other. Such a transaction is readily recognized as "lawful" and "fair" or—as today's terminology might describe it—as "win-win" since both parties regard themselves as better off for having agreed to the exchange than either party would have been if no transaction had occurred. Markets exist in order to facilitate such "win-win" transactions; money was invented as a means to facilitate the proper functioning of markets and their expansion, or institutionalization, through space and time.

Over 1500 years later, Aristotle's disciple, the Italian friar, Thomas Aquinas (1225–1274 CE), systematized the meaning of Aristotle's theory of "commutative justice" and outlined its meaning for business ethics. He did so as part of his comprehensive work on Christian theology, the *Summa Theologica* (1265–1274 CE), in which the Hellenistic tradition of virtue ethics was subsumed within the worldview of medieval Christianity. In the Summa's "Treatise on the Cardinal Virtues" (IIa-IIae, QQ 47–170), Aquinas reaffirms Aristotle's teaching on the virtue of justice, the suitability of distinguishing distributive and commutative justice, the significance of the "arithmetical mean" to establish fairness or "equality" between the parties to a marketplace transaction (Aquinas, IIa-IIae, Q. 61, Art. 2), and the indispensable role of freedom or "voluntary" agreement in determining justice in the marketplace. He further clarifies the difference between market transactions and gifts, for while both may be voluntary exchanges between two persons, the market transaction becomes a matter of justice "insofar as it includes the notion of debt." For example, in buying and selling, the transaction involves both parties' promise to pay the agreed upon price—either in money or in the goods or services exchanged for it—a promise that creates an obligation or a debt until the payment is made in full (Ibid., Q. 61, Art. 4).

Aquinas, however, not only clarifies Aristotle's teaching, but he also applies it to the ethics of buying and selling, what today is recognized as business ethics. Since justice, like all the virtues, is commonly recognized by its absence, commutative justice in marketplace transactions becomes clear by considering the forms "Of Cheating, which is Committed in Buying and Selling" (IIa-IIae, Q.77). Acts of buying and selling, or sales, are unjust when the "equality" to be achieved through the mutual agreement of buyers and sellers fails, with reference to price or some serious defect on the part of the thing sold. Aquinas takes up four questions in his explanation of cheating in the marketplace:

The first, "whether it is lawful to sell a thing for more than it is worth," explains the basic moral norm of equality, that is, what makes for a "win-win" transaction. Aquinas answers that, in principle, it is never lawful to sell a thing for more than it's worth, because such an "unequal" outcome can only be achieved through deceit or fraud. Since "buying and selling seem to be established for the common advantage of both parties… the common advantage should not be more of a burden to one party than to another." The transaction should be equally "fair" to both parties, if the exchange is to be based on the real worth of the items to be exchanged. If I have agreed, for example, to buy a flat in a housing project at a certain price on the basis of false information communicated to me by the seller, then I have been induced to pay more than the property is worth, and if the deception was deliberate, then I have been cheated. It is important to recognize what Aquinas is asserting here. He is not forbidding any attempts to make a profit on a sale, but he is clearly drawing the line between just and unjust or fraudulent transactions.

The second question, "whether a sale is rendered unlawful through a fault in the thing sold," shifts the focus from the intention of committing a fraud to questions concerning defects in the goods for sale (IIa-IIae, Q. 77, Art. 2). Following Aristotle's categories, he discusses defects with regard to substance (e.g., diluting wine with water), quantity (e.g., using false weights and measures), and quality (e.g., selling an unhealthy animal as if it were healthy). In each of these examples, a seller who offers a defective product for sale with the intent of deceiving the buyer is guilty of fraud and is bound to compensate the buyer for his or her loss in purchasing it for more than it is worth. If the seller offers a defective product for sale, while not knowing of the defect, he or she is not guilty of fraud, but he or she is bound to compensate the buyer when the defect becomes known.

Aquinas' third question, "whether the seller is bound to state the defects of the thing sold," continues to explore the moral obligations of merchants to their customers. He answers that the seller is bound to reveal any hidden defects, since "it is always unlawful to give anyone an occasion of danger or loss" (IIa-IIae, Q. 77,

Art. 3). He then describes examples of the loss or danger incurred by any customer who unwittingly buys defective goods. But Aquinas also recognizes the difference between hidden defects and those that are obvious. Selling a horse that has but one eye, for example, is not unlawful, since the defect should be apparent to both buyer and seller, and is likely to be reflected in the discounted sale price for the animal. Aquinas, apparently, would have no difficulty with the practice common in food supermarkets, of discounting the price of certain perishables—for example, packages of meat, fruit, or vegetables—as they approach the expiry date after which they cannot lawfully be sold. Nothing further needs to be said to the customers, since the price has already been adjusted to compensate those who will buy such merchandise.

If by this time the reader may be wondering how any merchant could ever make a profit if Aquinas' rules were generally followed in the marketplace, the answer becomes clear in his response in the fourth and final question, "whether, in trading, it is lawful to sell a thing at a higher price than what was paid for it." It is important to note that this question has not already been answered in his reply to the first question. The higher prices charged by those who are engaging in trade or going into business in principle are lawful and fair because the worth of the items sold may have changed in bringing them to market. Since trading usually involves obtaining goods in one market in order to sell them in another, "the value of the thing [may have] changed, with the change of place or time, or on account of the danger he [the merchant] incurs in transferring the thing from one place to another, or again in having it carried by another. In this sense neither buying nor selling is unjust" (IIa-IIae, Q. 77, Art. 4). Since the value or worth of the goods offered for sale has been enhanced by the merchant who has undertaken the risks and overcome the obstacles involved in bringing them to market, charging a higher price than was paid for them is only just compensation for his efforts.

Aquinas uses the occasion provided by this question to defend the legitimacy of trading or going into business, contrary to the views of many of his predecessors among Hellenistic philosophers and Christian theologians, whose condemnations of merchants as essentially greedy and dishonest are uncannily similar to the negative opinions expressed by many of Confucius' disciples. Both Aquinas and Confucius himself, however, recognize that the vices commonly attributed to merchants are "accidental" and not essential to either their nature or their occupation. As Confucius observed in the *Analects* (論語, pinyin: *Lún Yǔ*), "Wealth and high station are what men desire but unless I got them in the right way I would not remain in them" (Book IV, Number 5). Wealth earned through trading, Aquinas agrees, can be ethical: "Nothing prevents gain from being directed to some necessary or even virtuous end… [such as] for the upkeep of his household, or for the assistance of the needy: or again, a man may take to trade for some public advantage, for instance, lest his country lack the necessaries of life, and seek gain, not as an end, but as payment for his labors" (IIa-IIae, Q. 77, Art. 4).

5.4.2 Commutative Justice and Fair Competition in Business

Commutative justice, then, is the ethical principle specific to marketplace transactions. It seeks to clarify the nature of "win-win" exchanges, which are by definition voluntary, from certain "win-lose" transfers, such as theft and robbery, that are involuntary because either they involve deception, as in a theft when something is stolen without you being aware of it, or violence, as in a robbery when you are forced to hand over your goods or suffer bodily harm. Fraud, however, is the most common marketplace violation of the principle of commutative justice, inasmuch as it masquerades as a voluntary transaction, but in fact is based on a deliberate attempt to secure the sales agreement by deception. Fraudulent acts may appear to be voluntary, but in fact, the buyer's agreement is obtained only by the seller's withholding or distorting the information relied upon to arrive at a common estimate of a thing's real worth. Ready access to accurate information is essential for the proper functioning of the marketplace, since the economic benefits of free and fair competition cannot be realized if buyers and sellers lack the information needed to make a rational choice among competing bids. If buyers and sellers are deprived of what they require in order to make a rational choice among competitors, then the marketplace cannot operate efficiently.

Markets where prices are the outcome of various forms of manipulation, rather than a free exchange of information as to the true value of the goods for sale, are markets in name only, since the distortions introduced are meant to prevent free and fair competition, rather than facilitate it. A review of Hong Kong's recent enactment of a Competition Ordinance (2012), and the ongoing controversies surrounding its implementation, indicates that free and fair competition cannot be assumed as the natural outcome of the countless transactions that occur everyday in the marketplace. Free markets—that is, "free" in the sense of unregulated—do not automatically guarantee free and fair competition. Since markets will always attract some greedy participants—Confucius' *xiaoren* or Aquinas' cheaters—who seek to gain by eliminating their competitors, some form of rectification or commutative justice will always be a practical necessity. Since buyers and sellers in the marketplace rarely have the power to deter such anticompetitive behavior—given the inevitable asymmetries between buyers and sellers and between customers and merchants, all seeking to achieve their own goals—a strong case can be made for government regulation in order to preserve and enhance market competition.

Hong Kong's Competition Ordinance, for example, monitors and punishes three forms of anticompetitive behavior, namely, "agreements between undertakings [that is, businesses]… that have the 'object or effect of preventing, restricting or distorting competition' in Hong Kong", the operations of "single undertakings" [that is, businesses] that abuse their "substantial market power" in order to prevent competition, and "direct and indirect mergers (meaning an acquisition, joint venture or change of control) involving telecommunications [firms]… that have, or are likely to have, the effect of substantially lessening competition in Hong Kong" (Connolly 2013). Besides identifying the violations covered by this law, the Competition Ordinance establishes a Competition Commission and a Competition Tribunal with powers to investigate allegations and levy fines and other punishments, when violations have been proven in the proceedings established by the law. Hong Kong's Competition Ordinance, which is broadly similar to laws enacted in the EU, England, Canada, and Singapore, continues the tradition of market regulation consistent with the principle of commutative justice handed down from Hellenistic antiquity.

The principle of commutative justice is also evident in the codes of ethics by which public relations firms govern themselves. The code of ethics (Professional Charter) for the Council of Public Relations Firms in Hong Kong (CPRFHK 2002), for example, specifies the general duties that a member firm must honor, with specific attention to its stakeholder obligations. It makes clear that PR firms do not regard themselves and are not to be regarded by others as "hired guns" capable of saying or doing whatever it takes to advance their clients' gain at the expense of others. As in all other aspects of business, there are moral limits to what legitimate PR firms will do with and for their clients. In the CPRFHK code, each member firm "has the responsibility at all times to deal fairly and honestly with clients, past and present, fellow members and professionals, the public relations profession, other professions, suppliers, intermediaries, the government, political parties or people in the public service, the media of communication, employees, and above all else the public." Dealing fairly and honestly means, among other things, that the firm has "a positive duty at all times to respect the truth and shall not disseminate false and misleading information knowingly or recklessly, and to use proper care to avoid doing so inadvertently." In a subsequent document on "social media standards," the CPRFHK stated the positive values that support its code: truthfulness, transparency, personal and organizational responsibility, confidentiality, legality, play by the rules, and respect (CPRFHK 2011). It shows how these values must continue to be honored as its member firms address the opportunities and challenges afforded by the development of social media as an important vehicle for PR communications.

If you ask why the CPRFHK and other relevant codes emphasize basic honesty and truthfulness so strongly, the answer, of course, is that PR firms provide an important public service and not just to clients facing stiff competition. A legitimate PR firm is also a custodian of the public good—or social benefit—to be achieved through the development of true markets. Modern economic theory offers an essentially utilitarian argument for allowing market forces—or the aggregate of transactions occurring between buyers and sellers—to answer the great economic questions: what is to be produced, how much is to be produced, and for whom will it be produced? What an economist may describe as "allocative efficiency" is achieved when all participants in the marketplace are competing freely and fairly, and market prices reflect the true worth (or market value) of the goods and services on offer. When allocative efficiency is achieved, the social benefit of marketplace activity is maximized. The promise that markets make of achieving outcomes that on the whole are "win-win" depends on optimizing allocative efficiency. All participants in the marketplace—customers and merchants as well as the businesses like legitimate PR firms that facilitate their interactions—all, have a stake in preserving and enhancing the markets' attempt to optimize allocative efficiency. This, in short, is the social benefit of free and fair competition. Marketplace competition can achieve "win-win" results not only for the buyer and seller involved in any specific transaction but also for the public at large, if commutative justice is routinely observed.

5.5 Conclusion

We introduced this chapter with an acknowledgement of one of Rothlin's rules that seemed especially relevant to our featured case study on Mengniu vs. Yili: "Your public relations strategy will only secure your reputation if it witnesses your drive for quality and excellence." This rule encapsulates the main lesson to be learned from Bosse PR's misguided attempt to better Mengniu's competitive position against Yili. But instead of developing a public relations strategy that would secure Mengniu's reputation, Bosse PR devised a strategy—"Plan 731"—designed to destroy its rival's reputation by planting false rumors about Yili's products in China's new social media. It is hard to imagine how or why the managers involved at Mengniu and Bosse PR thought that such a predatory move would secure Mengniu's reputation or guarantee it a larger market share. Instead, once discovered—thanks to the panic that it induced among China's long-suffering consumers—"Plan 731" placed both firms in serious jeopardy, with government investigations leading to criminal trials and convictions. Had Rothlin's rule been observed—or if Bosse PR had lived by a code of ethics similar to that mandated by the CPRFHK—the firms involved would have realized that ethically responsible PR seeks to facilitate communication between its client and the public or markets in which the client is competing. Such facilitation is hardly compatible with deliberately spreading false rumors about the client's competitors; it must be focused instead on truthfully relating the client's own best efforts to achieve, as Rothlin observes, both quality and excellence.

In this chapter, we have introduced the principle of commutative justice in order to explain how market competition should unfold, if it is to remain "win-win" for all participants and stakeholders. Honoring the principle of commutative justice in all your market transactions, of course, will not guarantee profits on every single sale. But, as in sports, in contrast to engaging in warfare, the results will be "win-win" even when you lose. There is a public good to be realized in free and fair competition, and the promised social benefits of free market capitalism—increased prosperity for all of us—cannot be realized unless we are generally committed to playing by the rules that govern competition in the marketplace.

References

Beijing Orient Agribusiness Consultant Ltd. (2011). *China dairy market review & outlook proposal 2010–2011*. Beijing: BOABC.

China CSR. (2011, June 20). *Mengniu's founder leaves corporate role for philanthropy in China*. Retrieved on November 17, 2011 from http://www.chinacsr.com/en/2011/06/20/8301-mengnius-founder-leaves-corporate-role-for-philanthropy-in-china/

China Daily. (2010a, October 21). *Dairy giant Mengniu in smear scandal*. Retrieved on November 19, 2011 from http://www.chinadaily.com.cn/china/2010-10/21/content_11437735.htm

China Daily. (2010b, October 21). *Ministry clears milk of causing early puberty*. Retrieved on November 20, 2011 from http://www.chinadaily.com.cn/imqq/bizchina/2010-08/16/content_11156838.htm

Connolly, J. (2013, March 6). *An overview of the Hong Kong Competition Ordinance*. Briefing from Freshfields, Bruckhaus, and Deringer. Retrieved on July 23, 2013 from http://www.freshfields.com/en/knowledge/An_overview_of_the_Hong_Kong_Competition_Ordinance/

CPRFHK. (2002, September). *The code of ethics (Professional Charter) for the Council of Public Relations Firms Hong Kong*. Retrieved on July 23, 2013 from http://www.cprfhk.org/files/Ethics.pdf

CRPRFHK. (2011, February). *Council of public relations firms of Hong Kong: Social media standards*. Retrieved on July 24, 2013 from http://www.cprfhk.org/files/cPRFhk%20-%20social%20media%20guidelines.pdf

Epstein, G. (2010a, September 17). *Golden cow*. Forbes. Retrieved on November 20, 2011 from http://www.forbes.com/global/2010/0927/fab-50-10-china-mengniu-dairy-milk-golden-cow_3.html

Epstein, G. (2010b, October 21). *Creating a scandal for a fee: the dark arts of Chinese PR. Forbes*. Retrieved on November 20, 2011 from http://www.forbes.com/sites/gadyepstein/2010/10/21/creating-a-scandal-for-a-fee-the-dark-arts-of-chinese-pr/

Gu Yongqiang, & Wang Shanshan (2011, March 16). *Mengniu vicious word-of-mouth marketing case first instance verdict*. Caixin. Retrieved on April 25, 2013 from http://companies.caixin.com/2011-03-16/100237284.html

Jiang, J. J. (2004, April 27). Yili, Mengniu fighting for No 1. *China Business Weekly*. Retrieved on November 19, 2011 from http://www.chinadaily.com.cn/english/doc/2004-04/27/content_326794.htm

Lan, X. Z. (2010, November 1). A sour milk rivalry. *Beijing Review*. Retrieved on November 19, 2011 from http://www.bjreview.com.cn/business/txt/2010-11/01/content_308595.htm

Lerbinger, O., & Sullivan, A. J. (1964). *Information, influence and communication: A reader in public relations*. New York: Basic Books.

Li, J. (2010, October). Yili reported to the police, and Mengniu was involved in "Defamation scandal". *Beijing News*. Retrieved on November 21, 2011 fromhttp://news.xinhuanet.com/2010-10/21/c_13567352_3.htm

Meihua. info. (2010, October 21). *Dairy industry emergency: Online public relation fight between Mengniu and Yili*. Retrieved on November 28, 2011 from http://www.meihua.info/today/post/post_12d90f88-8788-4a57-82b4-94f21f778f26.aspx

China Mengniu Dairy Company Limited. (2011). *Ten years of Mengniu*. Retrieved on November 28, 2011 from http://www.mengniu.com.cn/mn10/

Peverelli, P. (2006). *Mengniu the follower: A case of intertwined identity. Chinese corporate identity: 127–156*. London: Routledge.

Shanghai Daily. (2010, October 23). *Mengniu says sorry, and accuses*. Retrieved on November 20, 2011 from http://www.china.org.cn/business/2010-10/23/content_21185174.htm

Sina Finance. (2010, October). *Statement about the An Yong scandal and defamation from Mengniu Group*. Retrieved on November 30, 2011, from http://finance.sina.com.cn/chanjing/cyxw/20101022/07528824194.shtml

The Times Weekly. (2010, October). *YangZaifei, the key person of Mengniu Scandal was interviewed and denied to discredit Synutra*. Retrieved on November 11, 2011 from http://news.sohu.com/20101021/n276121625.shtml

Xinmin Weekly. (2010, October). *Commercial war between Yili and Mengniu*. Retrieved on November 28, 2011 from http://news.sina.com.cn/c/sd/2010-10-27/161721363589.shtml

Yili Group. (2011). *Corporate profile*. Retrieved on November 28, 2011, from http://www.yili.com/about_yili/background.shtml

Yue, Y.(2010, October). Mengniu exposed the old act: Yili spent 5.92 million RMB to "Beat the cow (Mengniu)?" *New Express*. Retrieved on November 21st, 2011 from http://news.sohu.com/20101022/n276206877.shtml

Zhang, Z. G. (2006). *Inside story of Mengniu*. Beijing: Peking University Press.

Zhejiang Online. (2010, October 27). Commercial competition, where is the baseline? Retrieved on November 30, 2011 from http://society.zjol.com.cn/05society/system/2010/10/27/017038779.shtml

Part II
Areas of Stakeholder Responsibility

Chapter 6
Customers: Consumer Rights and Responsibilities

"To inspire trust, make your performance transparent."
(Stephan Rothlin, *Eighteen Rules for Becoming a Top Notch Player*, 2004)

6.1 Prelude

As we learned in the previous chapter, "the purpose of a business," according to Peter Drucker, "is to create a customer." There, we followed Drucker's insight for the light it casts on the nature of competition in business. We observed how the ethics of free and fair competition is reflected in the principle of commutative justice, as outlined by Aristotle and systematized by Aquinas. In this chapter, the first of our explorations of how international business ethics addresses the concerns of specific stakeholders, we will explain the ethical expectations that can and ought to govern the relationships between a business and its customers. While creating a customer means creating a relationship, it is hardly "a one-night stand." People become customers when the goods or service for sale by a business satisfy them to such an extent that they will continue the relationship, returning for more when the need arises.

In this chapter, we will explain the moral obligations that businesses and customers ordinarily assume toward each other as they develop their relationship. Consistent with the assumptions of virtue ethics that have inspired our approach to international business ethics, we will focus on what it takes to build "win-win" relationships rather than to rely on the legal rights and liabilities of either party. Our case study on Mattel will examine a situation in which problems involving subcontractors in the firm's Chinese supply chain allowed the production and sale of toys that could harm the children for whom they were intended. The discussion of the case will attempt to determine what steps management ought to take in order to minimize the risk of such harms occurring in the future, especially when managing the supply chain involves the challenges of cross-cultural transparency and accountability characteristic of an era of globalization.

S. Rothlin, D. McCann, *International Business Ethics*,
DOI 10.1007/978-3-662-47434-1_6

6.2 Case Study: Mattel—"An Ounce of Prevention Is Worth a Pound of Cure"

6.2.1 *Abstract*

Mattel is one of the world's largest and most famous toy manufacturers. It can count on a loyal customer base, whose trust has been earned throughout its 60 years of business. Notwithstanding the immense goodwill of its brand, a major supply chain scandal in 2007 put the company's reputation at great risk. The discovery of lead paint and easy-to-swallow magnets in its toys manufactured in China caused Mattel to launch three global recalls, resulting in the firm's taking extensive measures to resolve the crisis, rebuild its image, and, especially, increase the level of transparency and accountability in the management of its supply chain.

6.2.2 *Keywords*

Mattel, product safety, consumers' rights, brand impairment, supply chain management, globalization, transparency and responsibility.

6.2.3 *Mattel's Own Globalization*

Mattel's undisputed achievement in the toy industry rests principally on the popularity of its blonde Barbie dolls and preschooler toys marketed under the Fisher-Price brand. The tipping point in the company's rapid growth occurred through major acquisitions made between 1986 and 1999. Several competing manufacturers like Tyco Toy Inc. (Match Box cars), Pleasant Company (American Girl dolls), Bluebird Toys PLC (Poly Pockets), and The Learning Company became an integral part of Mattel's increasingly international business. These acquisitions allowed the firm to consolidate its leadership position as the world's largest toy company with earnings in 2010 hitting $684.9 million and sales of up to $5.856 billion (Mattel 2010a). With its headquarters in El Segundo, California, the company sells products in over 150 countries worldwide that account for 46 % of its gross sales. However, actual production is spread throughout 43 countries, including China, Malaysia, Indonesia, and Mexico. Because of cost advantages and improvements in infrastructure, Mattel has established a total of five branches in China (PRC), a venue that today accounts for over 80 % of Mattel's production (Mattel 2010a).

6.2.4 The Supply Chain at Mattel

Successful supply chain management has played a crucial role in product development at Mattel. In an industry characterized by cost-based competition and high seasonality, outsourcing production to foreign companies had been the best course of action since 1959, when the first Barbie doll was produced by a Japanese subsidiary of the company (Mattel 2010b). In a standard product life cycle, the bulk of Mattel's operations are conducted at offshore plants, which in turn rely on first-tier contractors and subcontractors resulting in a complex network of organizations. While such networks may be economically competitive, they may also hinder transparency and accountability, even within the supply chain itself (Biggemann 2008).

In order to manage the risks involved in such extended networks, especially in faraway countries, Mattel established a set of internal standards called Global Manufacturing Principles (GMP) and authorized the Mattel Independent Monitoring Council (MIMCO) to conduct audits (MIMCO 2000). In spite of these initiatives, a MIMCO audit found an imbalance between the company's proud emphasis on quality control and its apparent indifference to working conditions at its factories. Despite this imbalance, it was not problems with its labor force but product quality and safety issues that led to what can be considered the biggest scandal ever to hit the company.

6.2.5 2007 Product Safety Scandal

A long history of success coupled with Mattel's intimate association with memories of childhood made it easy for customers worldwide to have complete faith in the quality and safety of its products. Nobody would ever have questioned its trustworthiness, which is the reason why, when the first of a series of three global recalls was announced to an incredulous public in August 2007, there were harsh reactions causing the company's shares to decline by as much as 45 % (Biggemann 2008). The first recall involved a million and a half toys manufactured in China—including Dora the Explorer and Sesame Street dolls (Yidaba 2007a). In a matter of weeks, another 18.2 million toys (Story and Barboza 2007)—including 7.1 million pieces of Doggie Daycare, Shonen Tump's One Piece and tens of thousands of items in the Batman action-figure series—were taken off the shelves, followed by a third and final recall of 11 additional types of toys within the Barbie and Fisher-Price product lines, bringing the total number of individual toy units recalled to 20 million (Marshall and Kelley 2007). While the first and third recalls were because lead paint had been applied to the toys, contrary to Mattel's specifications, the second recall involved the presence of small magnets that could easily have been swallowed by children. The toys recalled because of the magnets—the vast majority of the items recalled, over 85 %—were the result of Mattel's own flawed designs (Story and Barboza 2007).

At the root of the lead paint problem was the Lee Der Industrial Co, Ltd., the Chinese subcontractor producing a number of the Fisher-Price toys. Lee Der had purchased paint from a nonauthorized third-party supplier, Mingdai, and had not verified its compliance with US safety standards on toxicity, which were substantially more rigorous than those for China's domestic market. When Mattel reported the lead paint problem, Lee Der was banned from exporting toys. This catastrophe prompted the suicide of its boss, Zhang Shuhong, who was found hanged at his factory. According to one observer, "Zhang was distraught over feeling he had been 'hurt' by the supplier of the suspect paint, whom he had counted as a good friend. '[He] was so evil-hearted to have sold the fake paint to our boss … our boss was ruined by his best friend'" (Taipei Times 2007). Though the story of Zhang's suicide was widely reported as if it confirmed the responsibility of Mattel's Chinese subcontractors, one must remember that suicide in China carries different meanings than it does in the West. Rather than an admission of guilt, Zhang's self-destruction may have been a protest proclaiming his innocence. Despite Zhang's apparent reputation as a morally exemplary businessman, what remained unexplained is how the lead paint went undetected, despite Lee Der's normal testing procedures (Barboza 2007).

At the point when public concern over the toxic lead paint was reaching its peak, Mattel announced the much larger recall of toys with potentially harmful magnets. Following the timing of Mattel's release of information, American news media tended to conflate the three recalls, creating the impression that failures in Mattel's Chinese supply chain were primarily responsible for all the defective toys. As a result, there was plenty of online chatter proposing a boycott of toys made in China (Yahoo! Answers 2007), but the boycott never materialized. One American mother who tried it explained why: "First off, about 90 percent of toys in the United States are made China. I realized early on that the big-box toy stores were going to turn up little for me, so I opted to go to small, mom-and- pop retailers… but overall the small stores were little better than the megaretailers. What has kept me going until now has been the thought that in light of all the recalls, U.S. retailers and producers would start to shift more of their sourcing back home or to other destinations. No dice. Only 15 percent of the nation's retailers have any plans to change their supply chains…." (Tahmincloglu 2007).

The Chinese government, to be sure, was painfully aware of the damage to China's reputation that the recalls and other manufacturing scandals were causing. After China denounced what it claimed was a "foreign media…campaign to discredit its reputation as an exporter," Thomas Debrowski, Mattel's VP for worldwide operations met in Beijing with Li Changjiang, chief of China's General Administration of Quality Supervision, Inspection and Quarantine of the People's Republic of China (AQSIQ). At that meeting, after being lectured by Li on how to conduct a product recall—"You cannot recall 10,000 products just because one is substandard… This is unacceptable."—Debrowski, conceding that the lead paint problem was only a small percentage of the recalls, apologized to China: "Mattel takes full responsibility for these recalls and apologizes personally to you, the Chinese people and all of our customers who received the toys…. We understand and appreciate deeply the issues that this has caused for the reputation of Chinese manufacturers" (The New York Times 2007). Li accepted the apology, saying,

"I appreciate your objective and responsible attitude towards the recalls and your sincere attitude towards our future cooperation." He also informed Debrowski that four Chinese nationals had been detained on charges of supplying Lee Der with the substandard paint that had triggered the first recall.

While Debrowski's apology provoked a brief but intense controversy in the USA—"It's like a bank robber apologizing to his accomplice instead of to the person who was robbed," Senator Charles E. Schumer of New York said in an interview. "They're playing politics in China rather than doing what matters." (Story 2007)—it also paved the way for more effective cooperation in monitoring Chinese exporters on product quality and safety issues. In October of 2007, Mattel announced the development of a three-point check system with the aim of strengthening the oversight of and increasing transparency in operations, alongside a corporate responsibility program charged with monitoring product quality, labor standards, and sustainability. From an organizational standpoint, the supply chain was simplified, forbidding first-tier suppliers from subcontracting to third parties, and the company launched a recall-dedicated website, which was immediately recognized as a model of excellence (Manufacturing.net, 2007).

When their worst fears of facing an "anti-China Christmas" that year did not materialize (Fetterman 2007), the Chinese agencies worked quietly in 2008 to close down subcontractors who could not or would not meet required product safety and quality standards. According to Xinhua, "following the Mattel recall, China launched a four-month special campaign on product safety led by then-Vice Premier Wu Yi. Altogether 3,540 toy makers were investigated and more than 700 were deprived of exporting licenses" (Wang 2008). By the end of the year, the number of registered toy exporters in Guangdong Province declined by nearly a third (China View 2009).

But in the meantime, what, if anything, was Mattel doing to address the fears of its customers? What should it have done to convince the millions of moms, like Eve Tahmincloglu, that their children were safe playing with toys made in China? Simultaneously with the announcement of the toy recalls, Mattel launched a public relations campaign designed to calm their fears. At the height of public concern, Mattel published a full-page advertisement in the *New York Times*, the *Wall Street Journal,* and other newspapers that began, "Because your children are our children too…," addressed "Dear Fellow Parents," and signed by Mattel CEO, Bob Eckert, who identified himself as "a father of four." In his letter, Eckert pledged his "personal commitment that we are working extremely hard to address your concerns and continue creating safe, entertaining toys for you and your children" (Story and Barboza 2007). The letter also invited readers to visit the firm's website for additional details on the steps Mattel was taking to solve the safety problems.

A visit to Mattel's website confirms that although the company has initiated 15 voluntary recalls since 2007, none of these came in response to incidents involving lead paint (Mattel Corporate Website 2013). The recalls, both before and after 2007, follow a consistent procedure in which a joint declaration from the firm and the U.S. government's Consumer Product Safety Commission (CPSC) is issued, listing the toys affected and their serial numbers, the nature of the hazard that caused the recall, any reported injuries that children may have sustained using the toys, and the place of origin where the toys were manufactured. The declaration also prescribes a specific remedy for consumers participating in the recall. Generally, they are advised to return the toys to Mattel in exchange for a "free replacement toy" (CPSC 2007). The recall declaration also contains a statement from the CPSC indicating the overall success of this cooperative program involving both government and industry. Since "deaths, injuries and property damage from consumer product incidents cost the nation more than $700 billion annually," the Commission monitors the safety of "more than 15,000 types of consumer products, …such as toys, cribs, power tools, cigarette lighters, and household chemicals." As a result, over the past 30 years, there has been a "30 percent decline in the rate of deaths and injuries associated with consumer products" (CPSC 2007).

While the CPSC's voluntary recall program seems to be working reasonably well, it cannot guarantee that there will be no further incidents involving the kinds of issues that surfaced in the Mattel recall. As Prakash Sethi, a noted business ethicist who monitored working conditions in Mattel's Chinese factories, observed, "If Mattel, with all of its emphasis on quality and testing, found such a widespread problem, what do you think is happening in the rest of the toy industry, in the apparel industry and even in the low-end electronics industry? Everyone is going to be found with lots of dirty laundry." But he also noted that MNCs like Mattel bear some responsibility for the conditions he's observed: "There is something to be said about the pressure that American and European and multinational companies put on Chinese companies to supply cheap products. The operating margins are razor thin, so you really should not be surprised that there is pressure to cut corners" (Story and Barboza 2007). Mattel's CEO Bob Eckert summed up the situation this way. While he could not guarantee that there would never be another recall, he admitted that "no business enterprise is perfect." The implementation of new monitoring systems that Mattel was now committed to was "evolutionary, not revolutionary." In his view, an important lesson seems to have been learned the hard way: "If you'd have asked me 10 years ago, I'd have said our role … is to earn a return on capital to make money…. Today I've become evangelical about the fact that making money and doing good are complementary, not conflicting. It's a responsibility" (Konrad 2007).

What do you think of Eckert's realization? Do you think his determination to restore the trust of his customers through increased transparency and accountability is sincere? Is it consistent with the ways Mattel handled the toy recalls, once they had gotten beyond trying to shift the blame for their defective products exclusively on the shoulders of their Chinese subcontractors? What do you think of the Chinese government's response to the crisis? Were they too quick to save face, in their demand for an apology? What sort of "dirty laundry" is Prakash Sethi likely referring to in Chinese manufacturing? What would you advise Mattel's customers to do? Should they continue to trust Mattel, because they've never had a problem with them? Should they start a consumer boycott? Should they lobby politicians like Senator Schumer to increase the pressure on China to adhere to basic standards of international business ethics? If you had a child who wanted a Mattel toy for Christmas, what would you do?

6.3 Case Study Discussion

The issues involved in the Mattel toy recall and the controversy surrounding it suggest that this is not an open-and-shut case (Kavilanz 2007). If it were, it would be a "no-brainer," perhaps even a multiplicity of "no-brainers," as Mattel's customers in their outrage against the risks to which their children were exposed learn to distrust the "Made in China" label, while Mattel itself scrambles to regain the trust their poor supply chain management seems to have broken. With some American politicians calling for protective tariffs against Chinese goods, and others threatening to organize a consumer boycott, we saw how readily the issues involved in the toy recall could become politicized. The toy recall contributed to another round of "China bashing," prompting Mattel's face-saving apology to the Chinese government, and further controversy over what the apology did and didn't mean. Amazingly enough, these awkward moments of cross-cultural misunderstanding did not lead to the collapse of Mattel's sales and earnings. The "anti-China Christmas" that some had expected simply did not happen, and after the season had passed both Mattel and the Chinese government moved quietly but firmly to weed out subcontractors who could not or would not comply with their mutually agreed-upon safety standards. Nevertheless, the toy recall cost Mattel at least USD $30 million and for a time did create an opportunity for smaller USA-based toy manufacturers to begin to recover some market share from the firms like Mattel that had globalized their supply chain.

When product safety recalls are properly managed, of course, they provide a remedy for customers put at risk of potential harm from items already purchased. They seek to minimize the hazard while offering compensation to those put at risk, while also preventing others from unwittingly taking similar risks. But where is the ounce of prevention that is worth a pound of cure? If the toy recall is a pound of cure, what might be the ounce of prevention? Is the recall alone enough to retain the loyalty of one's customers? If, as Rothlin's Rule suggests, trust between a firm and its stakeholders, especially its customers, is best secured through greater transparency, what more should Mattel have been doing with and for its customers? In order to answer this question, we must deepen our understanding of what it means to become a customer.

First of all, notice that the word is "customer" and not "consumer." They are not the same. The term "consumer" tends to be abstract and involves an objectification that is passive and depersonalizing. A consumer is one who purchases goods and services for individual use, rather than for use in further production. Consumers respond to market signals put out by producers and their intermediaries, with producers assigned the active role and consumers regarded as passive objects. Though producers study consumer behavior in order to gain their loyalty and trust, responsibility and control are generally understood as characteristic of producers, who may have legal and moral obligations while consumers have rights and entitlements.

"Customers," by contrast, actively enter into a relationship with the businesses that serve them. The choice of this term tends to shift the focus from an objectified understanding of economic transactions toward concern for the interpersonal, interactive, and relational dimensions of what goes on between businesses and their customers. Customers have choices. They choose to enter into a relationship with a particular business, when they see that the firm has kept its promises to them, responding to their needs and desires at prices they can afford to pay. The difference between customers and consumers may be subtle, but it is equivalent to the difference between marketing, properly understood, and selling (Levitt 1960). When a firm's priority is selling, its focus remains on its own need to make the sale, doing whatever it takes to find buyers for its products. When a firm has truly understood marketing, its focus begins and ends with the needs of its customers, which influence the design and development of the firm's products as well as all other aspects of its supply chain.

A firm that manufactures and sells toys, as Mattel does, must be aware that its customers—primarily parents and relatives hoping to delight the children whom they care for—will want toys that not only entertain children but that are also safe for them to use. Mattel's Bob Eckert apparently understands this. But in order to meet both expectations while also showing a profit for his enterprise, Mattel must become more rigorous in designing its toys. A proper understanding of marketing based on the needs and desires of its customers will prompt the firm—if it's not doing so already—to consult with child psychologists and conduct controlled experiments to learn what children at various stages of childhood development are likely to do with their toys, what features will delight them, which may unduly frustrate them, what may happen when the toy is broken—as inevitably it will be—in the course of children's play. The level of care involved in anticipating safety issues will vary according to the different stages of childhood development typical of the children for whom the toy is designed. In short, the level of care required will be determined by a proper understanding of its customers, an understanding that is not likely to occur apart from cultivating mutual relationships with them.

Anyone who has ever observed children at play knows, for example, that at a certain stage of development children explore literally everything with their mouths. That being the case, toys must be designed to minimize the risk of children swallowing anything toxic or harmful—such as magnets, or other small parts, too easily dislodged from the toy, or paints and other surface coatings too readily dissolved, chipped, or chewed. While toy designers and manufacturers may excuse themselves by insisting that their products were never intended for oral use, there's no way that children will be deterred from pursuing their oral pleasures simply by pasting warning labels, or assuming that their parents or caregivers will make sure that the toys are used properly.

Clearly, neither Mattel nor the vast majority of its Chinese subcontractors meant to profit by endangering their customers' children. Mattel's recall of toys containing hazardous magnets was the result of a flaw in the design of the toy and not of any failure within the firm's Chinese supply chain. For the most part, the detection of unacceptable levels of lead paint in certain toys depended upon which standard was used to determine the toxicity level. Except in a few instances, the paint used on Mattel's toys—according to China's General Administration of Quality Supervision, Inspection and Quarantine (GAQSIQ)—met the customary standard used in Europe and China, but not the more rigorous standard required for toys sold in the USA (China View 2007). Nevertheless, alleged confusion over the proper standard of measurement cannot absolve either Mattel or its subcontractors of responsibility for monitoring their manufacturing processes to ensure that they meet its customers' need for safe toys.

Prior to the acknowledgment of the problems that triggered the recall, Mattel's primary concern seems focused on its bottom line. What else can we conclude from CEO Bob Eckert's admission that "10 years ago, I'd have said our role …is to earn a return on capital to make money…."? How else can we explain the way Mattel globalized its supply chain than in order to maximize profits? What the company apparently failed to realize is that the lower labor costs that it hoped to achieve from outsourcing production must be offset by incurring certain increased costs involved either in operating its own factories in China or in rigorously monitoring the performance of its subcontractors. It would have been negligent or unconscionably naïve for Mattel or any other MNC outsourcing production in China to leave compliance with its standards exclusively in the hands of either its Chinese subcontractors or government inspectors. This is especially true in a situation such as Mattel's, where its Chinese subcontractors' own profit margins were under significant pressure. Add to these factors Mattel's own insistence—in the name of economic efficiency—that its subcontractors continually lower their costs, and the result is a situation in which, according to Guangdong Toy Association executive vice president, Li Zhuoming, "some producers had to use cheap raw materials, resulting in product quality problems" (Yidaba 2007b). Had Mattel been more careful in understanding its customers, it might have realized that there must be limits to what can be done to lower its production costs. Customers, of course, want attractive toys at affordable prices, but not if the price reductions result from flawed designs and cutting corners in manufacturing that significantly increase the risk of harm to their children.

6.4 Ethical Reflection

The same tradition of Hellenistic antiquity that developed the principle of commutative justice has also handed down two diverging moral maxims that remain important for guiding our discussion of the mutual rights and obligations of businesses and their customers. They are *Caveat Emptor* ("Let the Buyer Beware") and *Primum Non Nocere* ("Above all, do no harm"). While both are consistent with the principle of commutative justice, each has a distinctive history that we should note. "Do no harm" is rooted in the Oath attributed to Hipocrates of Kos, the famous physician who flourished in the early fourth century BCE. To this day, some version of the Hippocratic Oath is administered to physicians in the West upon completion of their training. It commits them as medical doctors to doing good for their patients while refraining from doing harm to them. Its extension to businesses, their owners, and managers reflects the recent trend to think of business ethics in terms analogous to the high moral standards expected of other professions. The origin of "Let the buyer beware" appears to be equally ancient, though harder to pinpoint. In modern times, it surfaces as a legal principle in cases involving commodities, and later real estate, where it limits the duties of buyers and sellers to disclose information that may affect the value of properties bought and sold. Consistent with Aquinas' interpretation of commutative justice, while the seller is bound to disclose any hidden defects in goods for sale, neither side is bound to reveal information that may change their resale value. *Caveat emptor* thus is prudent advice warning the buyer to exercise due diligence in negotiating the price to be paid for goods. Its complement may be found in the notion of *Caveat venditor* ("Let the seller beware"), which recognizes that sellers can also be cheated in market transactions.

Taken together, the two maxims—"Let the buyer beware" and "Do no harm"—imply that the relationships of buyers and sellers are normally asymmetrical. Though sellers may sometimes be victimized by buyers, in today's marketplace where businesses compete for customers, the typical situation is one in which customers are dependent upon businesses to anticipate their needs and provide products that actually meet these needs, as well as sufficient information to enable customers not only to use their products properly but also to earn their loyalty. Because businesses usually cannot anticipate every possible way in which their products may cause harm to customers engaged in risky or careless behavior, the maxim "Let the buyer beware" reminds customers that ultimately they, too, must exercise due diligence in using the goods and services that they have agreed to buy. We see, then, that there is reciprocity in the relationship of businesses and the customers they hope to attract, but it is asymmetrical, with businesses inevitably assuming responsibility for the ways their products are designed and produced as well as marketed.

6.4.1 Transparency for Accountability

The asymmetrical reciprocity characteristic of the relationship between businesses and their customers helps explain the relevance of Rothlin's Rule: "To inspire trust, make your performance transparent." The relationship requires the creation of trust, since consumers having choices in a competitive marketplace will choose to become customers of those businesses that they learn to regard as trustworthy. But how does a business prove itself to be trustworthy? Rothlin observes that it happens when businesses make their performance transparent. Linking trust with transparency, however, may seem foreign to anyone experienced in Asian business. Traditionally, secrecy—the idea that security depends on remaining as inscrutable as possible in one's dealings, especially with anyone outside the network of mutually recognized *guanxi* relationships—was thought to be indispensable for success, in business as in warfare or any other competitive venture. While trust may have been possible within one's *guanxi* network, it was not necessarily related to transparency but was achieved through observing the rituals that established one's role(s) within the network. Such a system may have been functional in the past, but along with many other things globalization may be rendering it obsolete. For globalization inevitably involves working closely with foreigners, that is, strangers with whom one enjoys only the weakest forms of *guanxi*, perhaps, alas, only the experience of getting drunk together at a Chinese banquet.

No doubt, then, earning trust through transparency involves a cultural transformation, in which not only the meaning of trust but also the means to achieve it may be shifting. If in the past, for example, trust meant that you did not monitor the performance of the people you trusted, now monitoring is indispensable, if trust—and not just among strangers—is to be achieved. This is the significance of another new term closely linked to transparency, namely, *accountability*. Accountability means that at any point in our relationship, if asked, I can explain truthfully what I am doing and why I am doing it. Accountability does not require blind obedience, but it does mean that one's reasons for doing things in a certain way are open to inspection. I can demonstrate my accountability precisely because my actions are transparent. This involves a major shift away from deals based purely on *guanxi* and their hierarchical order and toward a professionalism that ensures that all parties understand all that they need to consent to the deal, rationally and voluntarily. As Chinese and other East Asian companies increasingly work with foreign companies, they must learn that oral agreements may no longer be sufficient to fulfill these expectations.

One reason for this shift is that the main players in your firm or the one you are dealing with are likely to change, and without much time for rituals marking the transitions. The person you make a deal with on Monday can disappear by Tuesday. With such sudden changes, the accuracy of the figures that stipulate the *quid pro quos*—the various promises made regarding payments and performances—become even more important. It is still important to make deals based on trust and mutual friendship. However, old boy networks tend to degenerate into complicity, corruption, and sometimes engage in criminal activity. It is in the interest of all the company's stakeholders to have written statements and contracts that detail precisely what has been agreed upon. Many conflicts stem from business partners who hastily assume what is agreed upon instead of spelling out their mutual understanding point by point in a contract.

Here are some methods that successful firms have already adopted to help implement the shift in creating trust through transparency and accountability:

- Companies must preserve clear records of memos from official meetings. At the beginning of each meeting, everyone must have the information from previous meetings and a list of issues to be discussed.
- Meetings must avoid becoming like court rituals where no one dares to express an opinion because of an unwritten rule that final decisions have already been made from above.

- Companies must communicate annual reports, and if possible quarterly reports, to shareholders and stockholders in a timely and orderly way with all relevant information disclosed.
- The company must focus all efforts on its core business and clearly communicate to its stakeholders the key values that inspire it in its industry.
- Companies must develop standardized statistical reporting procedures in order to document their performance over time, and from one market to another.
- Voluntary disclosures must not only praise good news but also report the most urgent problems, as well as the setbacks encountered by the company.
- A company must communicate its plans to innovate and reach out to new customers.
- Companies must develop moral leaders who inspire confidence and trust by acting according to their duties.

Although this shift toward trust achieved through transparency and accountability represents a challenge to firms operating in China and East Asia, it is a crucial move both from an economic and an ethical perspective. The goal is to build, or after a crisis to restore, public trust, the vital link between a company and its stakeholders.

Such steps toward building or restoring trust through transparency and accountability are especially valuable in creating and retaining customers. In an era of globalization, when virtually everyone has access to the Internet through various devices including smartphones, it is becoming increasingly difficult to deceive one's customers or any other stakeholders. Even governments—judging by the success of "Wikileaks" and more recently the unauthorized exposure of the USA's National Security Agency (NSA) surveillance programs—are less and less able to operate behind a veil of secrecy. Still less so are businesses of whatever size or complexity, especially if they are competing internationally. Customers not only have more and more choices as markets develop, they are also better informed and throughout the world, especially in Asia, are reaching levels of education which enable them to make rational choices in the marketplace. Under such circumstances, businesses have little choice but to extend their pledge of transparency and accountability to all their stakeholders, especially their customers.

6.4.2 Hong Kong's "Guide to Consumer Rights and Responsibilities"

Various agencies, both local and international, both governmental and nongovernmental, have focused a lot of energy on developing guidelines increasing transparency and accountability specifically toward customers. One of the most successful of these is Hong Kong's Consumer Council, an independent civic agency first established in 1974 at a time of rapid inflation and public concern over price gouging. In 1977 its mission and objectives were clarified by the Consumer Council Ordinance, and since that time it has sought to become "the trusted voice in striving… towards safe and sustainable consumption in a fair and just market." The Council therefore is "committed to enhancing consumer welfare and empowering consumers to protect themselves," according to which "it acts as advocate for consumer interests; it facilitates constructive discussion and promulgation of pro-consumer policies; it seeks to empower consumers to help themselves." In fulfilling these promises, the Council has assumed ten main duties, including mediating disputes between consumers and businesses testing consumer products to determine their quality and safety; engaging in market research in order to promote best practices among businesses; disseminating information to consumers and empowering them through educational programs; networking with national, regional, and international groups promoting consumer interests; and collaborating with the government to improve legal protection of consumers (Consumer Council of Hong Kong 2013). The Consumer Council's website provides a model of transparency and accountability in action, inasmuch as it gives access to detailed information on its various efforts to fulfill these duties since its founding.

As part of its campaign to empower consumers, the Council has issued a "Guide to Consumer Rights and Responsibilities." The guide puts forward "eight basic consumer rights…commonly accepted…worldwide":

- The right to satisfaction of basic needs—To have access to basic, essential goods and services: adequate food, clothing, shelter, health care, education, public utilities, clean water, and sanitation.
- The right to safety—To be protected against products, production processes, and services which are hazardous to health or life. Personal data and privacy should be respected and protected.
- The right to be informed—To be given the facts needed to make an informed choice, and to be protected against dishonest or misleading advertising and labeling. Information to consumers such as product specification, place of origin, safety warnings, price, mode of payment, date of quality assurance, description of after-sale services, warranty, ingredients, nutritional facts, etc.
- The right to choose—To be able to select from a range of products and services, offered at competitive prices with an assurance of satisfactory quality.
- The right to be heard—To have consumer interests represented in the policymaking process of government, trade, and professional and industry associations, where the making and execution of those policies will have an impact on the supply of goods and services to consumers.
- The right to redress—To receive a fair settlement of just claims, including compensation for misrepresentation, shoddy goods, or unsatisfactory services.
- The right to consumer education—To acquire knowledge and skills needed to make informed, confident choices about goods and services, while being aware of basic consumer rights and responsibilities and how to act on them.
- The right to a healthy and sustainable environment—To live and work in an environment which is nonthreatening and sustainable to the well-being of present and future generations (Consumer Council of Hong Kong 2006).

Since the Council is aware that rights are not simply entitlements, it includes a list of four responsibilities that are incumbent upon all consumers:

- Keep yourselves informed as best as possible.
- Exercise due care when making decisions in the marketplace.
- Consider the detrimental consequences that may arise from ill-considered decisions.
- Honour reasonable obligations arising from your decisions (Consumer Council of Hong Kong 2006).

The Guidelines conclude with several pages of advice to consumers on how specifically to exercise these responsibilities, before and after they've purchased anything.

Parallel to its "Guide to Consumer Rights and Responsibilities" the Consumer Council also issued a "Good Corporate Citizen's Guide" (Consumer Council of Hong Kong 2005a) that urged businesses to adopt 12 principles animating good business practices, especially in their relationships with their customers. The 12 principles, covering "advertising and marketing, price indication, contracts, quality of goods and services, safety of goods and services, sustainable development, electronic commerce, privacy, equal opportunity, anti-corruption, fair competition, and complaints handling" (Ibid.), are comprehensive. They provide a framework of ethical expectations in which to understand the Council's approach to consumer protection, incumbent upon both businesses and their customers. At the time that the Guide was issued, the Council announced that it had been endorsed by 22 different chambers of commerce, trade associations, and professional bodies, representing a variety of industries catering to the needs of consumers in Hong Kong (Consumer Council of Hong Kong 2005b).

In urging the widespread adoption of the Consumer Council's "Good Corporate Citizen's Guide," Hong Kong's Secretary for Economic Development and Labour, Stephen Ip Shu-kwan, emphasized the "win-win" nature of corporate citizenship. Adhering to the high standards promoted in the Guide, "not only will the business succeed in its endeavours, but also that the community as a whole will benefit from the positive effect this has on maintaining dynamism in the economy." He also observed that the aspirations of both consumers and businesses are "not incompatible but interconnected" (Consumer Council of Hong Kong 2005b). The overall approach taken by the Consumer Council, then, seeks to achieve a harmonious balance between legal rights and ethical responsibilities, incumbent upon both businesses and their customers. Consistent with the principle of commutative justice, the Consumer Council's statements recognize that efforts to preserve free and fair competition in the marketplace as well as to deter cheating on the part of either buyers or sellers must be based on the kind of mutual trust that inspires genuine collaboration. Both businesses and their customers need to be reminded that their interests are best served by doing justice toward each other.

Similarly comprehensive efforts to protect consumers' rights have taken root in Chinese (PRC) law as well. First established in 1984 with the approval of the State Council, the China Consumers' Association (CCA) has been empowered "to supervise commodities and services; to protect consumers' rights and interests; to provide reasonable and scientific guidance on consumers' activities; and to promote a healthy development of the socialist market economy" (China CSR Map 2013). In carrying out those responsibilities, the CCA helped enact the "'Law of the People's Republic of China on Protecting Consumers' Rights and Interests' adopted by the fourth meeting of the eighth National People's Congress Standing Committee on 31st October 1993" (China Consumers' Association 2003). This law not only provides legal support for the CCA's activities, but it also spells out nine consumer rights that for the most part are very similar to the rights recognized in Hong Kong.[1]

In addition to consumer rights, China's law spells out the obligations of business operators, including obligations to observe the relevant laws (Article 16); to listen to the views of consumers (Article 17); to ensure that the goods and services they provide "are in conformity with the personal and property safety requirements," and if they are hazardous, to "make truthful presentations and give clear warnings to consumers" (Article 18); to provide truthful information, especially about prices, and refrain from making "misleading or false propaganda" (Article 19); to provide the "true names and signs" of the businesses and their operators (Article 20); to issue sales receipts or service certificates, especially when consumers make requests for such (Article 21); to certify "the expected quality, capability and usefulness prior to the expiration date" of the goods for sale, and ensure that the goods they sell are consistent with what's been advertised (Article 22); to provide a timely and effective procedure for the return and repair of defective goods (Article 23); to refrain from using the details of contracts to avoid responsibility for fulfilling their legal obligations to consumers (Article 24); and finally, to respect the personal dignity of their consumers; specifically, they "must not insult and slander consumers, must not search the body of consumers and the goods they carry and must not infringe upon the personal freedom of consumers" (Article 25).

The remainder of the law spells out the role of the State, as well as agencies like the CCA, in protecting consumers' rights and interests; formal procedures for resolving disputes between consumers and business operators; and sanctions, including penalties for failures in compliance. As in so many other examples of contemporary law in China, this law on protecting consumers' rights and interests is well informed, comprehensive, and consistent with the standards upheld by international business ethics. The challenge, of course, is enforcement. On the 10th anniversary of the law's enactment, Prof. Liu Junhai of the Chinese Academy of Social Sciences offered a positive survey of its effectiveness (Liu 2004). He reviewed the rationale for the law, its basic provisions, and proposed a number of initiatives

[1] The Hong Kong statement recognizes eight consumer rights, while Chinese law recognizes nine. The additional right concerns respect for the consumers' ethnicity: "In purchasing and using commodities and receiving service, consumers enjoy the right to demand respect of their personal dignity and national customs and habits." This right, of course, reflects the fact that China is a multiethnic nation. While over 91 % of China's population is Han Chinese, the remaining 8.5 % consists of 55 recognized national minorities, whose interactions with the Han in the marketplace have occasionally precipitated group conflict and violence, as in recent disturbances in Xinjiang Province.

to strengthen it. In particular, Liu noted the CCA's expanding role in doing comparative tests on products, especially those with "high-tech content," and informing the public of their results. Broadening its responsibilities in this area means that the CCA is now functioning in ways that are similar to the scope of the Consumer Council's activity in Hong Kong.

6.5 Conclusion

The development of NGOs like the Consumer Council in Hong Kong and the CCA in China, and their close collaboration with both the HKSAR and the PRC governments, should put the whole world on notice that consumer rights and responsibilities are advancing in China's new era of economic and social reform. Though compliance with the guidelines and laws for consumer protection leaves much room for improvement, their very existence ought to strengthen the resolve not only of consumers but also of ethically responsible business owners and managers. Nevertheless, casual observers, such as Mattel's customers in the EU and the USA, usually hear stories about catastrophes in Chinese manufacturing with little or no focus on Chinese efforts to correct their problems and enforce appropriate standards to protect consumers, not just in their export industries but also in their domestic markets. The very fact that, once the lead paint problem surfaced, Mattel and its subcontractors were able to address it quickly and effectively is indirect testimony to the progress already made in respecting consumer rights and concerns. At this point, there seems to be a growing international consensus, officially recognized by the PRC government and the CCA, as to the basic morality of creating customers by cultivating their trust through increased transparency and accountability. Despite the US$30 million price tag attached to the toy recalls, Mattel and its subcontractors did not suffer irreversible losses, because they already had started down the road toward transparency and accountability and thus were credible when they assured their customers that they were doing everything possible to correct the problem rather than cover it up.

There were, however, some bumps along the road that indicate just how much is yet to be done. It is clear in retrospect that Mattel—whether deliberately or not—mishandled the announcement of the toy recalls, by making it seem that the fault was mostly on the part of their Chinese subcontractors. This turned out to be false, as Mattel was forced to admit that the vast majority of items recalled—that is, the toys that had small magnets embedded in them—were dangerous because of a flaw in their original design, and not because of any product defects attributable to its subcontractors. The lead paint problem—a very serious one, to be sure, which the Chinese subcontractors were primarily responsible for—represented less than 15 % of the toys actually recalled. Even in their case, Mattel could hardly pose as an innocent victim, since it clearly failed to do as much rigorous testing of its products shipped from China as might reasonably have been expected and since the subcontractors using substandard lead paint were subject to enormous pressures from

Mattel to lower costs, irrespective of changes then underway in the Chinese markets for labor and raw materials. Is it any wonder, then, that the PRC government demanded and received an apology from Mattel for the way in which the recalls were announced and explained to the public at large?

Once Debrowski made the apology on behalf of Mattel, the way was opened for a more cooperative relationship, in which the surviving Chinese toy manufacturers began developing "a new business model." As Huang Chunman, general manager of Bright Spring Trading Ltd., a toy manufacturer based in Guangdong Province, observed, "Quality and design are now the top priority of our production, it surpasses all other issues like soaring material and labor costs" (China View 2008). No less would be expected, if everyone involved were to focus on creating and retaining the loyalties of their customers. A commitment to achieving continuous improvements in product quality and design may not always be transparent to one's customers, but when a crisis comes, and questions are raised, such a commitment does demonstrate the kind of accountability that makes it easier to maintain their trust, without which a business will perish.

References

AQSIQ China. (2007, September 12). *The toys recalled for the third time was qualified about lead release, News network of Guangxi*. Retrieved on November 28, 2011 from http://news.qq.com/a/20070912/003169.htm

Barboza, D. (2007, August 23). Scandal and suicide in China: A dark sof toys. *New York Times*. Retrieved on July 24, 2013 from http://www.nytimes.com/2007/08/23/business/worldbusiness/23suicide.html?pagewanted=all&_r=0

Biggemann, S. (2008). The Mattel affairs: Dealing in the complexity of extended networks. In A. Waluszewski & A. Hadjikhani (Eds.), *Proceedings of the IMP 2008 conference: Studies on business interaction – Consequences for business in theory and business in practice*. Uppsala: Sweden. Retrieved on November 28, 2011 from http://www.impgroup.org/uploads/papers/6874.pdf

China Consumers' Association. (2003). *Law of the people's Republic of China on protecting consumers' rights and interests*. Retrieved on August 4, 2013 from http://www.cca.org.cn/english/EnNewsShow.jsp?id=38

China CSR Map. (2013). *Organizations: China consumers' association*. Retrieved on August 4, 2013 from http://www.chinacsrmap.org/Org_Show_EN.asp?ID=63

China View. (2007, September 12). *China: Toys recalled by Mattel safe*. Retrieved on July 26, 2013 from http://news.xinhuanet.com/english/2007-09/12/content_6714314.htm

China View. (2008, February 5). *It's time to toy with a new business model*. Retrieved on August 6, 2013 from http://news.xinhuanet.com/english/2008-02/05/content_7573114.htm

China View. (2009, January 17). *Nearly 1,000 toy exporters shut down in S China in 2008*. Retrieved on August 6, 2013 from http://news.xinhuanet.com/english/2009-01/17/content_10673996.htm

Consumer Council of Hong Kong. (2005a, March 15). *Good corporate citizen's guide*. Retrieved on August 4, 2013 from http://www.consumer.org.hk/website/ws_en/competition_issues/model_code/2005031501.html

Consumer Council of Hong Kong. (2005b, March 15). *Businesses pledge support for Good Corporate Citizenship*. Retrieved on August 4, 2013 from http://www.consumer.org.hk/website/ws_en/news/press_releases/2005031502.html

Consumer Council of Hong Kong. (2006). *Guide to consumer rights and responsibilities*. Retrieved on August 4, 2013 from http://www.consumer.org.hk/website/ws_en/competition_issues/Consumer_Rights_Responsibilities/2006100401.pdf

Consumer Council of Hong Kong. (2013). *Mission*. Retrieved on August 4, 2013 from http://www.consumer.org.hk/website/ws_en/profile/mission/mission.html

Consumer Products Safety Commission (CPSC). (2007, August 14). *Mattel recalls Batman™ and One Piece™ magnetic action figure sets due to magnets coming loose*. Retrieved on July 25, 2013 from http://service.mattel.com/us/recall/J1944CPSC.pdf

Fetterman, M. (2007, December 23). Traditional toys sales skirt China recalls. *USA Today*. Retrieved on July 23, 2013 from http://usatoday30.usatoday.com/money/industries/retail/2007-12-23-toys_N.htm

Kavilanz, P. (2007, August 14). Blame U.S. companies for bad Chinese goods: Industry experts say U.S. companies need to monitor overseas factories more closely to prevent product safety lapses. *CNNMoney*. Retrieved on August 6, 2013 from http://money.cnn.com/2007/08/14/news/companies/china_recalls/index.htm?postversion=2007081413

Konrad, R. (2007, October 25). Mattel chief outlines 3-point system for toy safety. *Manufacturing.net*. Retrieved on November 28, 2011 from http://www.manufacturing.net/news/2007/10/mattel-chief-outlines-3-point-system-for-toy-safety

Levitt, T. (1960, July–August). Marketing Myopia. *Harvard Business Review*, 45–56. Retrieved on August 7, 2013 from http://academy.clevelandclinic.org/Portals/40/LHC%202012-13/Marketing%20Myopia.pdf

Liu, J. (2004). *Commemorating the 10th anniversary of the promulgation of the law on protection of consumers' rights and interests: Advancing the undertaking of the protection of consumers' rights actively*. Retrieved on August 6, 2013 from http://www.cca.org.cn/english/EnNewsShow.jsp?id=24&cid=982

Marshall, K., & Kelley, R. (2007, September 5). Mattel announces third toy recall. *CNNMoney*. Retrieved on November 28, 2011 from http://money.cnn.com/2007/09/05/news/companies/mattel_recall/index.htm

Mattel Corporate Website. (2010a). *2010 annual report*. Retrieved on November 28, 2011 from http://corporate.mattel.com/annualreport2010/pdfs/2010%20Mattel%20Annual%20Report(Bookmarked).pdf

Mattel Corporate Website. (2010b). *Barbie's doll makes her debut*. Retrieved on November 28, 2011 from http://corporate.mattel.com/about-us/history/default.aspx

Mattel Corporate Website. (2013). *Recall and safety alerts*. Retrieved on August 4, 2013 from http://service.mattel.com/us/recall.aspx

MIMCO. (2000, November 14). *Mattel independent monitoring council for global manufacturing principles*. Retrieved on November 28, 2011 from http://corporate.mattel.com/pdfs/MIMCO_MONTOI_FOLLOW-UP_AUDIT.pdf

MIMCO. (n.d.). *Audits find plants in overall compliance with company's global manufacturing principles*. Retrieved on November 28, 2011 from http://www.prnewswire.com/news-releases/independent-monitoring-council-completes-audits-of-mattel-manufacturing-facilities-in-indonesia-malaysia-and-thailand-76850522.html

Story, L. (2007, September 22). Mattel official delivers an apology in China. *The New York Times*. Retrieved on July 26, 2013 from http://www.nytimes.com/2007/09/22/business/worldbusiness/22toys.html

Story, L., & Barboza, D. (2007, August 15). Mattel recalls 19 million toys sent from China. *The New York Times*. Retrieved on November 28, 2011 from http://www.nytimes.com/2007/08/15/business/worldbusiness/15imports.html?pagewanted=all

Tahmincloglu, E. (2007, November 21). One mom's fruitless quest to boycott China Reporter struggles in attempt to protect family from unsafe products. *NBCNews*. Retrieved on August 7, 2013 from http://www.nbcnews.com/id/21825517/ns/business-holiday_retail/t/one-moms-fruitless-quest-boycott-china/#.UgGoDhaFnKA

Taipei Times. (2007, August 14). *Lee Der chief dies in apparent suicide after toy recall*. Retrieved on July 24, 2013 from http://www.taipeitimes.com/News/worldbiz/archives/2007/08/14/2003374217

The New York Times. (2007, September 21). *Mattel apologizes to China for recall*. Retrieved on November 28, 2011 from http://www.nytimes.com/2007/09/21/business/worldbusiness/21iht-mattel.3.7597386.html

Thottam, J. (2007, September 21). Why Mattel apologized to China. *Time*. Retrieved on July 23, 2013 from http://www.time.com/time/business/article/0,8599,1664428,00.html

Wang, X. (2008, June 10). EU new directive tougher, more cases of "substandard" Chinese toys. *China View*. Retrieved on August 6, 2013 from http://news.xinhuanet.com/english/2008-06/10/content_8341803.htm

Yahoo! Answers. (2007, November 8). *Boycott China toys*?!. Retrieved on August 7, 2013 from http://answers.yahoo.com/question/index?qid=20071108081752AAFFmlT

Yidaba. (2007a, September 5). *Shadow recall of toys*. Retrieved on November 28, 2011 from http://toys.yidaba.com/wanjuzhaohui/

Yidaba. (2007b, September 9). *Toys made in China were recalled, manufacturer struggled for small margins*. Retrieved on November 28, 2011 from http://toys.yidaba.com/hygc/294766.shtml

Chapter 7
Customers: Marketing Ethics

"To establish your brand name, act as a fair competitor."
(Stephan Rothlin, *Eighteen Rules for Becoming a Top Notch Player*, 2004)

7.1 Prelude

Properly understood, "creating a customer" might be expanded to cover the whole topic of marketing ethics. But a focus on customers is incomplete without examining the diversity of customers and the complexity of relationships that may develop in today's global markets. The case study we have chosen to introduce marketing ethics is taken from "ground zero" in the worldwide financial crisis in 2008, namely, the collapse of Bear Stearns, an investment firm that pioneered the securitization of risky mortgage loans classified as "subprime." The case study focuses on the breaches of fiduciary responsibility that occurred when Bear Stearns placed its own interests above those of its investor clients or customers. Our point in retelling this story is not to sponsor another round of "the blame game" but to encourage reflection on what ethical principles should guide marketers in their relationships with clients and customers. The basic moral assumptions that ought to be reflected in the simple and straightforward transactions of buying and selling should also guide more complex transactions even, or especially when, the buyers and sellers are major investment banks and the investors who rely on their advice and services. We may not be able here to answer the question whether good business ethics could have prevented the breakdown in financial markets, but we can shed light on what investment bankers and brokers owe their clients when they market financial products and services to them. As we learned in the previous chapter, customers and clients ultimately bear primary responsibility for protecting their own economic interests: "*Caveat emptor*!" ("Let the buyer beware"). But in no way does such sound advice absolve sellers who engage in various forms of fraud in order to make a sale or maximize profits. Even if buyers must protect their own interests, sellers are still bound by the basic principle of good business ethics, "*Primum non nocere*!" ("First, do no harm"). How, precisely, to balance both these principles in today's global marketplace is what we hope to accomplish in this chapter.

S. Rothlin, D. McCann, *International Business Ethics*,
DOI 10.1007/978-3-662-47434-1_7

7.2 Case Study: Financial Marketing the Bear Stearns Way

7.2.1 Abstract

The collapse of Bear Stearns, at that time a major investment bank on Wall Street, is commonly regarded as the prelude to the global financial crisis. It will long be regarded as a major milestone in the history of corporate moral failure. While millions of customers undoubtedly were hurt—among them homeowners and pensioners, as well as investors, big and small—Wall Street had created a culture of predatory lending that was indifferent to the consequences for its customers. At the end of the day, both subprime borrowers and institutional investors (e.g., retirement funds) were the ultimate victims, while Wall Street principals made billions. Our interest in the Bear Stearns collapse concerns the ethics of fiduciary responsibility or what the investment industry owes its clients and customers in managing their money. Beyond all the complexity and technical innovations involved in the creation of markets for investment products consisting of collateralized debt obligations (CDOs), especially mortgage-backed securities (MBSs), the question is whether markets, even at that abstract level, remain markets in which certain basic assumptions about mutual trust, transparency and accountability, still must be honored if business is to be conducted fairly and benevolently. In order to open this question up to useful discussion, our case study not only recounts Bear Stearns' involvement in the creation of a market for MBSs but also focuses on the specific actions of two of its hedge fund managers in that market, Ralph Cioffi and Matthew Tannin. When the market they had helped to create in MBSs fell apart, how did they respond? Would you have done any differently?

7.2.2 Keywords

Fixed income asset management, Collateralized debt obligation, Mortgages, Mortgage-backed securities, Hedge funds, Risk assessment, Fiduciary responsibility, Marketing, Customers, Investors, Stakeholders.

7.2.3 Bear Stearns: Victim or Perpetrator in the Financial Crisis?

In retrospect, the scene is heavy with irony. Sometime in March 2007 during office hours, Bear Stearns hedge fund managers Ralph Cioffi and Matthew Tannin were toasting each other with "very expensive" vodka in paper cups. They were still projecting a bright future for their hedge fund, even as a financial tsunami was about to wash it all away (Comstock 2010). Cioffi and Tannin managed investments—their own, Bear Stearns' own, as well as Bear Stearns clients and customers—trading in mortgage-backed securities (MBSs). As the market for these securities began to dry up in 2007, and their prices began to tumble, the two became more and more concerned about the hedge funds' stability. But as the vodka in paper cups may suggest, they were determined to carry on as if everything were normal, while encouraging their clients to invest even more in the hedge funds. Although they sensed that danger was imminent, they apparently had no idea that their decision to "wait and see" would lead not only to the loss of well over a billion dollars of their clients' money but also to the collapse of Bear Stearns and its forced sale to JPMorgan Chase.

In the months following Cioffi's and Tannin's office party, after a successful run of 85 years, and just after having received Fortune Magazine's accolade as among the top three most admired securities firm for 3 years in a row (BusinessWire 2005; CNN Money 2006, 2007),[1] Bear Stearns' demise would come fast and furious. In order to understand how troubles in a hedge fund invested in subprime mortgages could help precipitate a global financial crisis, as well as acrimonious charges that Bear Stearns had systematically defrauded its investors, we must step back a moment to review the nature of the subprime mortgage market and the firm's role in developing it.

7.2.4 *Bear Stearns and the Securitization of Home Ownership*

While the history of the dramatic expansion in the market for collateralized debt obligations (CDOs) and, specifically, mortgage-backed securities (MBSs) will remain controversial for a long time to come, it is only fair to note that this development was shaped by broader trends in the economy, in the financial markets, as well as in American politics. Despite all the abuses that later were revealed, the market for CDOs and MBSs could not have been created were it not for the US government's ill-considered experiment in banking deregulation and subsequent demands placed on the banks by various stakeholders. In 1999 Congress passed legislation that effectively repealed the Glass-Steagall Act, which in response to Crash of 1929 had created a firewall separating commercial and investment banking. Deregulating

---

[1] Fortune Magazine's ratings of "America's most admired companies" could easily be challenged on several grounds. Bear Stearns' high rankings for those years are only in the category of "securities firms," and in none of those years did the number one securities firm—Bear Stearns in 2005, and the ill-fated Lehman Brothers in 2006 and 2007—rank among the top 20 companies overall. The write-ups publicizing Bear Stearns' rankings never mention one key benchmark that supposedly is meant to be typical of "America's most admired companies," namely, their leadership in the practice of corporate social responsibility (CSR). Had CSR been an important element in Bear Stearns' corporate profile, could it have avoided the excesses that led to its sudden downfall? Who's to say? But the fact remains that the accolades that Bear Stearns received apparently were not related to any CSR activities, but were based exclusively on its bold innovations in financial marketing and egregious success in maximizing profits for its investors. Bear Stearns may have been among the most admired, but was it ever loved, and if so, by whom, and for what reasons?

their relationship removed the linchpin that prevented the banks from risking the funds of their customers and clients—both savers and investors—in order to make unprecedented profits from speculative trading at little or no risk to themselves (Sanati 2009). Later on, after the Al-Qaeda attack upon the World Trade Center known as "9-11," the deregulated banking system played a key role in the expansion of consumer credit that was meant to avert an economic recession. Incentivized by the Fed's anti-recessionary policies, the banks and other financial services began to market home mortgages even to clienteles who previously would have been considered too risky to be creditworthy or at least incapable of handling mortgages beyond a certain size. Such mortgages, which under other circumstances might have been questioned as instances of "predatory lending," were labeled as "subprime," a term with which the world would acquire painful familiarity in the coming years.

Thus despite all the political uproar later, most observers at the time regarded the rise of the subprime mortgage market as both politically desirable and economically viable.[2] As a result of the Fed's expansionary policies, Bear Stearns' customers and clients, and the markets generally, were awash in a sea of excess liquidity. Investors literally had more money than they knew what to do with. Following the collapse in 2001 of the so-called Dotcom Bubble, understandably they were reluctant to put their money in the stock market. At the same time, they continued to demand high returns and thus were open to innovative proposals for investing in high-return, high-risk bonds, especially if they could be persuaded that the risks were more apparent than real.

In response to their demands, leading investment bankers began to develop a MBS/CDO production chain, in which such debts were to be packaged, bought, and sold, as if they were mere commodities. At one end of the packaging process were potential homeowners, including for the first time many applicants who previously would have been considered too "high risk" to be granted a mortgage. Serving the needs and desires of such a dramatically expanded pool of potential customers represented an unprecedented opportunity for those who financed mortgages. Traditionally, savings and loan institutions—the so-called mortgage thrifts—had dominated this industry, by using their own capital during the whole life cycle of a mortgage. But now that the mortgage origination business had been decoupled from

[2] The politics of subprime mortgage lending was premised upon certain characteristics of American culture, primarily, the identification of "the American dream" with home ownership. The need for macroeconomic stimulus, in the immediate aftermath of "9-11," thus coincided with long-term trends—supported by key leadership elements in both major American political parties—toward deregulating the financial markets, including the fateful repeal of the Glass-Steagall Act (1933). It was the repeal of Glass-Steagall that enabled the merger of commercial and investment banking interests. A shadow banking phenomenon was created where investment bankers could raise funding outside of regulatory scrutiny, which could be used to buy and sell structured finance vehicles like securitized CDOs and MBSs. Within this system, managers like Cioffi and Tannin received enormous commissions while retaining, theoretically, no risk—unless, of course, they had invested their own money in the financial products they were also marketing to others. Had the Glass-Steagall Act still been enforced, the process of "securitization" by which the MBSs were created—along with the opportunities for abuse by unscrupulous managers and brokers—may have been, if not prevented, at least severely inhibited.

providing and servicing the mortgage loans, the thrifts confined themselves to processing mortgage applications as well as interacting with and advising potential homeowners. The capital invested in the mortgage loans however came from much bigger financial institutions—such as investment banks like Bear Stearns. Although the risks involved in mortgage lending had previously been managed by local thrifts with a good understanding of local conditions and a cautious approach to money management, lending decisions were now made by investment banks with a freshly whetted appetite for risk, which awarded mortgage originators for recruiting clients consistent with the kind of risks they desired to undertake. Since their risk appetite had increased dramatically due to financial market conditions and the general political climate, it was no surprise that mortgage lending expanded significantly to wider levels of society.

7.2.5 *Mortgage Loans Become a Commodity to be Traded like Pork Bellies*

No more than the mortgage originators did the investment banks that financed these mortgages intend to hold them on their balance sheets for long. Rather, the mortgages were the raw materials, a key ingredient in making commodities of structured-debt products, such as the CDOs that the investment banks went on to trade like pork bellies. These new financial packages were supposed to serve the customers' demand for securities with a high return but, paradoxically, limited risk. As more and more money had poured into classic fixed income instruments—for example, government bonds—the yields in these segments became increasingly less attractive. Credit card and auto loan receivables, as well as subprime mortgages, offered significantly more attractive returns, but these were not easily available to the average (institutional) investor. Lending to individual borrowers would have been impractical and extremely risky. The financial institutions that traditionally served the needs of individual borrowers were happy to sell the loans they had made in packages. However, such packages were too big—bundling several thousand debts—and far too unbalanced for all but the biggest investors. The CDO pioneers, including Bear Stearns, came up with a financial product that seemingly solved these problems: they claimed that by combining and structuring debts in innovative ways, they could minimize risk significantly. Thus, although some of the collateralized debts underlying the securities would produce very attractive rates because of their inherent risk, mixing them with other less risky debts was supposed to make them safe.[3]

[3]The process of mixing these CDOs in a structured investment product is known as "credit enhancement" (Investopedia.com 2014c). A "cash flow waterfall" was thus created that directed the first rights to cash flow from the mortgage pool to the investment grade tranches based on very sophisticated mathematical models that allowed the rating agencies, collaborating with the investment bankers, to create the illusion of safety (investment grade tranches). For more on the

Demand for these securities then was potentially high. However, the challenge of structuring so many different types of securities—often even mixing different types of CDOs—meant that their value would be difficult to assess. This would have limited their attractiveness to investors and impaired the investment banks' ability to sell them but for the role of investment rating agencies. Financial markets all over the world relied on such agencies—like Standard and Poors—to provide an independent and expert assessment of just how safe a specific investment is. Throughout the process of securitization, investment bankers structuring CDOs worked closely with these agencies to ensure that their products would attain a high, very frequently the highest, credit rating available. The rating agencies that were paid directly by the issuers of these securities (i.e., the investment bankers) had an enormous conflict of interest. They earned their fees only if they assigned an investment grade rating (i.e., "AAA") to securities whose value could only be assessed on the basis of unverified mortgage pool performance information supplied by the investment bankers. Securitization was immensely profitable: although a bank may have bought the subprime mortgages at a much lower price—the debts were cheap because they were considered risky—once the "subordinated" tranches were packaged with safer "senior" tranches, thanks to the overall ratings they received, they could be sold at a much higher price (Lambert 2012).

Once structured and labeled, such CDOs were sold to an ever-growing number of clients. From there on, however, the CDO took on a life of its own. Financial institutions packaging CDOs, very notably Bear Stearns itself, became actively involved in trading them, even offering opportunities to buy insurance against any possible failure—hence the marketing of "credit default swaps"[4] (CDSs). As the CDO/MBS frenzy accelerated, investment banks—with Bear Stearns at the forefront—began to intervene more directly in the mortgage origination stage. Driven by the ever-growing demand for MBSs—the CDO type is preferred because of its profitability—in October 2006 Bear Stearns bought a mortgage originator, Encore Credit Corp., a step that was common among investment banks at the time. Not only were such firms profitable in themselves, but they also afforded the bank direct access to the raw materials needed to maintain the scale and profitability of their MBS operations. Correspondingly, firms like Encore—that once may have been

mathematical models and their role in facilitating the process of credit enhancement, see Stewart (2012).

[4]A credit default swap (CDS), simply put, is an insurance against the default of a security. The person purchasing the CDO will pay its issuer an "insurance premium" until the security matures. If the security defaults, the issuer will compensate the purchaser of the CDS (Investopedia.com (2014b). Bond insurers like AIG sold credit default swap insurance that allowed the investment bankers like Bear Stearns to book "fairy dust" profits when the CDOs were created. Using discounted cash flow techniques, the investment bankers showed phantom net present value profits upon which investment banker executives based their bonuses. Bond insurers like AIG, who were not required to put up collateral, ultimately went bankrupt when the subprime mortgage market imploded in 2007–2008 and the CDOs dropped dramatically in value. The credit default swaps supporting the trading of CDOs thus enabled vast sums to be won and lost among investment bankers and their insurers, with only the US government's bailout capable of preventing a total collapse of the financial system worldwide.

more responsive to the credit worthiness of their customers—were now incentivized to "engineer" the mortgages according to their new owners' need for profitable CDOs. The higher fees that mortgage originators received from investment banks for issuing subprime mortgages in fact led some of them to discourage potential homeowners from even specifying their incomes in the application process. Given the voracious appetite of investment banks and their clients for high-yield MBSs, it was as if the borrowers' credit worthiness were no longer a significant factor in qualifying for a mortgage.

In light of this brief account of the development of the MBS/CDO product chain, we may begin to consider the ethical questions raised by the Bear Stearns debacle. Everyone now knows that the CDOs weren't as safe as they had been made out to be by their promoters. The mathematical models that were used to reassure investors assumed that mortgage defaults would never affect the entire US housing market across all states and social strata (Stewart 2012). This proved to be dangerously in error as the entire housing market slowed in 2007 and ever more borrowers defaulted. The ethical question, of course, is what did the investment banks know, and when did they know it? Were their miscalculations honest mistakes or did they involve calculated deception, a fraud of unprecedented proportions? Before reaching a verdict, we should proceed cautiously: Is fraud the only way to explain the actions of Bear Stearns toward their markets and clients? Or does the scope and scale of a bank "too big to fail" allow us to see how the Bear Stearns sales teams could be selling MBSs in good faith that colleagues packaging them knew were made of hazardous materials? How we judge what they were up to may depend on whether the individuals involved sincerely believed in the risk assessment algorithms and their promise, like alchemy, of turning inferior metals into gold!

As the slowdown in the overheated US housing market became apparent, it appears that the banks, rating agencies, and other financial institutions were very aware of the imminent danger, yet chose to carry on with business as usual.[5] In the wake of the global financial crisis, several investigations have shown that although key protagonists recognized the disaster when it came into sight, many chose not to share these insights with their clients. A particularly revolting example is that of the rating agencies whose main job was to provide the wider investment public with revised assessments as soon as they knew that a security previously rated by them was deteriorating in outlook. Publicized email conversations, for example, from Standard and Poors, reveal that its analysts considered the subprime-backed CDOs

[5]As the American novelist, Upton Sinclair, memorably observed, "It is difficult to get a man to understand something, when his salary depends upon his not understanding it!" Remember that like other investment bankers, the Bear Stearns executives received the lion's share of their compensation through stock options. Therefore, they had every incentive to manipulate the firm's accounting practices to show short-term profits that would drive stock prices higher. This put enormous pressure on their allegedly "independent" auditors to acquiesce in various questionable schemes that maximized (and exaggerated) short-term profitability, by masking the precariousness of their financial position. Under the circumstances, carrying on with "business as usual" is hardly an innocent choice.

to be no better than "junk,"[6] yet continued to give them an "AAA" rating for fear of losing the business of the investment banks who were paying for their services.[7] All of which takes us full circle back to Cioffi and Tannin and the hedge funds they managed for Bear Stearns. Whose problems were these meant to solve? Were unwary investors being lured into some kind of Ponzi scheme[8] that, in addition to protecting the bank's capital, might save some investors but only by betraying the interests of others?

7.2.6 *Bear Stearns' Corporate Culture: Root of the Crisis?*

While some might consider Bear Stearns' overexposure to the risks involved in the MBS market and the firm's subsequent failure as nothing more than a bet gone sour, a closer look at the corporate culture might explain what went wrong and why. Bear Stearns' failure appears to be a prime example of how an entire firm can become addicted to increasingly risky investment schemes and the profits that they promise. This was an addiction that spread to all of Bear Stearns' banking operations, from structuring financial instruments, to trading, and to wealth management—overruling all notions of prudence, self control, or, most importantly, the firm's fiduciary responsibilities to its clients and other stakeholders.

Once disaster struck, clues to the pathological nature of the Bear Stearns culture became obvious. If you were to travel back in time to visit the Bear Stearns trading floor, however, you would have seen a big, overbearing sign stating: "Lets Make Nothing but Money" (Wayne 1983). Similar clues might have been gathered by sitting in on a Bear Stearns board meeting. Regardless of when in the firm's 85-year existence you alighted from your time machine, you would have encountered a culture, starting at the top, in which one's say, one's influence over strategic

---

[6] "Junk," or more precisely "junk bonds" describe bonds with the lowest ratings. They are considered to be very risky, but often yield very attractive returns if they don't default (Investopedia.com 2014e).

[7] S&P was sued by the Justice Department over abuses that occurred in this practice (Eaglesham et al. 2013). It is known as the "Issuer Pays" model, in which the ratings agency does not get paid unless an investment grade rating is achieved (Frankel 2013). For a fuller explanation of role of the credit rating agencies in the financial crisis, see "The Council on Foreign Relations' 'Backgrounder: The Credit Rating Controversy'" (Allessi et al. 2013).

[8] Investopedia defines "Ponzi scheme" as "a fraudulent investing scam promising high rates of return with little risk to investors. The Ponzi scheme generates returns for older investors by acquiring new investors. This scam actually yields the promised returns to earlier investors, as long as there are more new investors. These schemes usually collapse on themselves when the new investments stop" (Investopedia.com 2014f). The Bear Stearns hedge funds probably were not intended as a Ponzi scheme, since the investments were CDOs meant to leverage the real value of mortgages and related financial products. On the other hand, in retrospect, at least, the promised yields to investors seem to have depended entirely on the hedge fund managers' ability to continue recruiting new investors. When the market for MBSs softened, the hedge funds collapsed, much like a failed Ponzi scheme.

decision-making, depended on one's past record of making money for the firm. After its collapse, Bear Stearns executives admitted as much: "If you didn't make money for the firm, you could have all the thoughts you wanted and they may or may not listen.... This haphazard strategy is key to understanding what happened in 2008" (Cohan 2009: 196).

This culture did not go unnoticed on Wall Street, where it shaped Bear Stearns' ambiguous public image for both admirers and critics. Thirty years ago, Leslie Wayne had already identified the basic ethical challenge implicit in the firm's relentless focus on making nothing but money. Was there a conflict of interest at the heart of the "Bear Stearns' identity: Whether it acts as an agent for clients by providing service for a fee or whether it is simply a trading vehicle for its partners or both" (Wayne 1983). Most likely the firm's admirers would have insisted that it was doing both—which completely ignores the potential conflicts involved, even if they were doing both better than anyone else. Nevertheless, this culture also had its attractions: Bear Stearns was willing to invest where more conservative firms were cautious. Investing in bankrupt or troubled companies, for example, or representing dissident shareholders in uphill takeover battles, Bear Stearns was aggressive and innovative, to the point of serving less financially secure clients whom other Wall Street firms regarded as beneath their notice.

Regardless of such positive outcomes, the controversial nature of Bear Stearns' corporate image seems to have been pretty clear. Samuel L. Hayes, of the Harvard Business School, also observed in 1983 that: "Bear Stearns is seen as a firm of bright, sharp entrepreneurs who are more self-motivated or motivated for the individual gain of the firm rather than building a corporate entity for the long run " (Hayes et al. 1983: 75). George L. Ball, president and CEO of Prudential-Bache Securities, went even further by saying that "Most firms will, at times, forgo profit for reasons of perception. But Bear Stearns has the idea that a legitimate transaction is one that earns a dollar—even if you don't want to bring it home for dinner with mother" (Cohan 2009: 201).[9] Given the high visibility of the firm's corporate image, it may well be asked how this culture is reflected in Bear Stearns' leadership role in marketing CDOs and MBSs and finally the hedge funds whose risks were fast becoming all too evident. Were Cioffi's and Tannin's funds the kind of investment schemes that no one would want to bring home to dinner with mother?

---

[9] Ball's comment hearkens back to a time when predatory behavior on Wall Street could still be restrained by a shared culture of shame, perpetuated by "the good ol' boy" network that persisted among seasoned investment bankers. Just as you might be ashamed to bring some of your pals home for dinner, because you knew that your parents wouldn't approve of them, so there may be some business deals that are so questionable—for one reason or another—that you wouldn't want your family to know how far you are willing to compromise yourself just in order to make more money. Shortly after Ball made this comment, it became clear that the Wall Street culture of shame that had been enforced by Wall Street's "good ol' boys"—however selectively—was fast eroding, as we learned from Michael Lewis' brilliant cultural analysis, *Liar's Poker: Rising through the Wreckage on Wall Street* (New York: W.W. Norton, 1989).

7.2.7 BSAM's Hedge Funds: A Cautionary Tale

The hedge funded managed by Cioffi and Tannin was labeled the "Bear Stearns High-Grade Structured Credit Fund."[10] As the name suggests, it invested its clients' money into what were billed as "high-grade" structured credit instruments. The fund's "investment philosophy," printed on the back of the summary report that investors received every month, was to "generate total annual returns through 'cash and carry' transactions and capital markets arbitrage." The prospectus was quite specific on how these returns were to be earned: "The Fund generally invests in high quality floating rate structured finance securities. Typically, 90 % of the Fund's gross assets are invested in AAA or AA structured finance assets" (Cohan 2009: 305). Potential and current clients were told that this meant that the fund would use leverage to generate returns by borrowing money in low-cost, short-term credit markets (called repo markets) in order to invest in long-term CDOs that had a substantially higher return (Ibid: 283). Although it later turned out that many investors did not understand the nature of the CDOs in which the firm was investing their money, the fund was very successful and thus popular. For 40 months in a row, the fund produced profits, netting 9.46 % on a yearly average, and 16.88 % (after expenses and fees) in 2004—extraordinary results for a fund that investors assumed was invested primarily in safe, low-risk investment classes.

But it was not just investors that were rejoicing in the success of this fund. Bear Stearns and its Asset Management affiliate were also jubilant. In 2004–2005, the high-grade fund accounted for 75 % of BSAM's total revenues, indicating that the fund was a major factor in BSAM's success. The good news at BSAM redounded to the credit of Cioffi and Tannin, who were hired to boost an Asset Management division that had been underperforming. When Bear Stearns hired them, top management may not have understood the risks involved in the hedge funds or, for that matter, the set of new financial products that promised such high returns (Burrough 2008). What's more, Bear Stearns' top management seems not to have given much thought to the question of whether they were involved in a conflict of interest by setting up funds that were mostly trading and investing in financial products for which Bear Stearns was the main producer and marketer. The firm's desire to "Make Nothing but Money" apparently obscured any fiduciary duty it may have owed to its clients and customers, who expected the firm to offer sound financial advice based on a critical assessment of their individual tolerance for risk.

But if the firm's own stake in the ABSs bought and sold by BSAM was not fully transparent, how could its customers accurately judge the value of the products that the firm was so aggressively promoting? In Bear Stearns' defense, one may point out that it is easy to criticize in hindsight. In the early 2000s, its role in creating a market for ABSs and CDOs was something for which the firm was envied and admired. At that point, it may have seemed only natural to use its expertise and

[10] It was later split into two, and the additional fund was called "Bear Stearns High-Grade Structured Credit Enhanced Leverage Fund."

strong market position to offer its BSAM customers and clients a unique advantage while boosting its own business. The prospect of high returns, as well as Cioffi's impressive track record in making enormous amounts of money, seemed to have dispelled any doubts that senior management at BSAM might have had. Before becoming the BSAM hedge fund's manager, Cioffi was described by one senior manager at the firm as "the top fixed-income (FI) salesman in a firm where FI was king." According to Paul Friedman, the COO of BSAM, Cioffi was "absolutely the best salesman I ever met … he was incredibly personable, smart, creative and got things done" (Cohan 2009: 281).

Critics, however, pointed out that Cioffi had previously failed when he was appointed manager of institutional sales. This role had offered a different challenge beyond his past experience as a salesman, but it was similar to his future role as a hedge fund manager. What he lacked in both was an attention span sufficient to address management problems and a knack for communicating well with his colleagues. As Friedman quipped, "he had adult ADD (attention deficit disorder)" (Cohan 2009: 281). Many at Bear Stearns were thus surprised that Cioffi was tapped to manage the BSAM hedge funds. According to Friedman, "There was a fair number of skeptics internally who could not figure out how this guy—who was bright but had never managed money—was now going to run money. He knew nothing about risk management, and had never written a ticket in his life that wasn't someone else's money. I sure as hell would not have given him my money. But he sets out and he is reasonably successful" (Cohan 2009: 281).

Cioffi's success at BSAM—as well as the risk of failure carried with it—rested upon his unique access to his former colleagues and their work in packaging the structured financial products. A major architect of Bear Stearns' MBS CDO product chain, he now would become the major "sell-side face" of the market. According to the Securities and Exchange Commission (SEC), "He was involved in the creation of the structured credit effort at Bear Stearns and a principal force behind [their success] as a leading underwriter and secondary trader of structured finance securities, specifically CDOs and ABS" (Cohan 2009: 280). But in assuming the post as hedge fund manager, Cioffi should have undergone a significant reorientation in his attitude toward these securities. No longer a salesperson focused primarily on promoting MBS CDOs, he was now in charge of a fund with much broader investment goals of which these should have been but a fraction. Rather than selling for Bear Stearns, he was now supposed to be buying for his clients according to investment strategies tailored to their specific needs. In all fairness there is evidence that he acknowledged that reality or at least paid lip service to it (Cohan 2009: 312). At various points during the funds' life, he made statements to reassure investors that he was implementing a conservative strategy when it came to the products that he had previously specialized in.

But were his reassuring words only an empty gesture, designed to calm the nerves of wary investors by camouflaging the reality of a faltering housing market? When the MBS CDOs started to tumble the façade of fiduciary responsibility began to crumble. Since investors had been widely left in the dark about what kinds of securities they were invested in, they now began to request more specific information about the assets they had been sold.[11] Step by step, investors and senior managers at Bear Stearns alike discovered with shock that even in the months leading up to the crisis, Cioffi had promised one thing (the right thing) and done another (quite objectively, a fatal thing).[12]

By June 2007, BSAM's staff was struggling with how to answer clients' specific questions about the nature of their investments. Typically, "I thought I was invested in a high-grade fund but it sounds now like the funds may have been invested in a fair amount of assets in subprime?" (Cohan 2009: 349). The prepared response was finally revelatory (and truthful), but—because of that—also earthshaking[13]:

> As of May 31st, 2007, over 90 % of the [Enhanced Leverage Fund's] assets are invested in securities rated AA or AAA.... The press has referred to this portfolio as a subprime fund. Based on our management's analysis, the percentage of underlying collateral in our investment grade structures collateralized by "subprime" mortgages is approximately 60 %. (Cohan 2009: 359)

This figure was ten times more of what had previously been disclosed regarding the portion of subprime mortgages packaged in the average MBS CDO.

The disclosure was bound to accelerate the flow of redemptions by investors frantic to get their money back, as well as a predictable increase in the number of lawsuits when they could not. One scene may best represent the shock experienced on all sides as Bear Stearns' staff began to come to grips with BSAM's crisis. In the early months of the subprime mortgage crash, Douglas Sharon (a star broker of the firm), Daniel Taub (its head of litigation), and Michael Solender (general counsel of the firm) met to discuss the moral and legal problems that had been unfolding in the wake of Cioffi's handling of the fund. Apart from angering some of the firm's most important clients by promising to invest only in instruments "as safe as a bank," Cioffe's specific comments that had been issued from month to month were particularly damning. As Sharon put it, "this guy has been predicting Armageddon in print, telling you he has been avoiding the 2006 vintage...and as it turns out [he] jumped straight into the volcano" (Cohan 2009: 355). Instead of protecting the interests of BSAM's investors, Cioffi had become one of the main customers for Bear Stearns'

---

[11] Previously BSAM hedge fund investors had only been given notification about the asset/security class, which was remarkably vague. With only bare information about the CDO's category, one must rely on the assessment of the ratings agency, which proved to be unconscionably unreliable. Subsequent lawsuits, most still unresolved, testify to the difficulty investors had in attempting to obtain sufficient information about the assets they had purchased (cf. Eaglesham et al. 2013).

[12] The allegation of Cioffi's deliberate malpractice is evident from comparing the monthly commentary he issued to BSAM's investors in March 2007, outlining the steps he had taken to protect them from increasing turbulence in the MBS market, with what the trades he was actually making on their behalf. As William D. Cohan explained, "The problem was that none of it was true. Cioffi had not avoided residential mortgage backed securities, as he had suggested to his investors on their monthly statements. Actually he had done precisely the opposite and had started to load up on these toxic securities at exactly the wrong moment. Since he was no longer trading with Bear Stearns, the firm had no idea of what he was doing" (Cohan 2009: 312).

[13] The importance of this statement can hardly be exaggerated. As William D. Cohan explained, "Here, for perhaps the first time in black and white, was the admission – varnished repeatedly with gibberish – that all had not been what it seemed in the funds" (Cohan 2009: 350).

products and was reliant on Bear Stearns to trade these and support BSAM's activities in the repo market.

The breach of BSAM's fiduciary responsibility is evident in the details of Cioffi's repeated technical violations of Bear Stearns' compliance rules. Prior to any major transaction with its parent firm, BSAM was required to seek approval from the hedge fund's independent—without Bear Stearns affiliation—directors. Not only did Cioffi violate this rule in 70 % of his transactions,[14] he also willfully ignored numerous requests from Bear Stearns' compliance department to bring his practices into line with its stated policies. Once fully understood by Bear Stearns' top management, these violations forced the firm to impose a trading moratorium on the fund and Cioffi—a decision that was certainly not easily made because it meant that the fund would lose its major trading partner and repo lender, thus hurting its trading position substantially.

7.2.8 The Everquest IPO: Robbing Peter to Pay Paul?

As the subprime mortgage market deteriorated, Cioffi's efforts to dispose of some of the MBS CDOs became increasingly problematic. How was BSAM to dispose of its holdings without causing a landslide in the markets? Instead of selling these toxic assets to the same, small circle of institutional investors, he came up with a daring plan to sell them to a new group of customers with an appetite for risk, who previously had had no access to this product: retail investors. Cioffi planned to unload the funds' CDOs priced at US$700 million dollars, by transferring them to a separate company and selling its shares in an IPO (Cohan 2009: 307). Although it was definitely a key element in Cioffi's strategy to avoid disaster, ultimately the plan did not achieve its intended results. Underwritten by Bear Stearns, the IPO would have been known as "Everquest." While it would have offered unwary retail investors securities not valued "at arm's length" (Investopedia.com 2014a), had it succeeded it would have taken off BSAM's books some of its most illiquid (and dangerous) CDOs (Goldstein 2007).

The boldness of this plan did not go unnoticed. *Businessweek* commented that one should "never underestimate the ability of Wall Street Investment Firms to find a new way to pawn off risky assets onto retail investors" (Goldstein 2007). Indeed, the moral questions arising were far from negligible. As BSAM's COO, Friedman, who surprisingly knew nothing about it until the day the IPO was canceled, put it: "The notion of packaging the most opaque and complicated securities into a complicated structure and selling them by IPO to the widows and orphans of this world

[14]The allegation and the evidence in support of it are detailed in the "Administrative Complaint, in the matter of Bear Stearns Asset Management, Docket E2007-0264" issued by the Commonwealth of Massachusetts on November 14, 2007. Retrieved on 2 February 2014 from the Archives of the Massachusetts Secretary of State, http://www.sec.state.ma.us/sec/sct/archived/sctbear/bear_complaint.pdf.

was one of the most bizarre ideas I ever heard" (Cohan 2009: 340). It seemed as though Everquest was "really nothing more than a landfill for increasingly toxic mortgage securities" (Goldstein 2007). Although Cioffi might have undertaken this step to protect his hedge fund clients' interest, the moral question remains: Wasn't Cioffi merely robbing Peter in order to pay Paul? Didn't he have the same fiduciary responsibilities to the trusting novice investors whom he hoped to recruit for his IPO as he had to his similarly trusting, yet more powerful and experienced hedge fund clients?

Of course, managing a hedge fund may require those involved to be very discrete in their communications. After all, one disaffected client may trigger a panic in which the remaining investors also try to pull out, leaving everyone worse off. But does that justify deliberately making false statements, even if they are motivated by a desire to minimize the harm that may be done to everyone involved? If you were in Cioffi and Tannin's shoes, how far would you go to calm the fears of nervous investors? Would you go beyond the kind of bluff that Cioffi was overheard making: "I want to be very clear about the way in which subprime risk is embedded within the structures that we own. We are not believers in the world-is-coming-to-an-end housing bubble scenario" (Cohan 2009: 306)? Would you continue to make bullish statements about your hedge funds, as Cioffi did in April 2007, while knowing that the subprime market was rapidly deteriorating, thus making your promise of a 14 % and 11 % return (Cohan 2009: 333) wildly misleading, to say the least? What these hedge fund managers knew and when they knew it is important for understanding their actions: "On March 23, Cioffi… initiated the process of removing US$2 million of the US$6 million that he personally invested in the Enhanced Leverage Fund" (Cohan 2009: 325). What do you make of such a move? Was Cioffi still interested primarily in protecting his hedge fund clients or had he decided just to save himself?

Cioffi's defenders later pointed out that the removal of his US$2 million investment was simply a transfer to another BSAM hedge fund. Since he was expected to be investing his own money in funds he was comanaging, this might have been a plausible explanation. Nevertheless, his transaction was sufficiently questionable to form a separate count in the four count criminal indictment issued against Cioffi and Tannin in 2008 (United States District Court 2008). The various stratagems meant to reassure BSAM's investors and persuade them not to withdraw their money from the funds merited indictments on charges of securities fraud. The Grand Jury was convinced that Cioffi and Tannin were guilty of repeated and deliberate misrepresentations of the actual state of the BSAM hedge funds, a criminal offense since investors relied on such assessments to guide their investment decisions. Cioffi's transfer of US$2 million to another Bear Stearns hedge fund merited him an indictment for insider trading, since he withdrew his personal stake in the Enhanced Leverage Fund at a time when other investors were unable to do so.

7.2.9 *Conclusion: Bear Stearns' Demise*

As it turned out, Cioffi and Tannin were judged "Not Guilty" of the financial crimes for which they had been indicted (Hurtado et al. 2009), and eventually the SEC's charges against them were quietly set aside (Lattman 2012). Bear Stearns, alas, was not so fortunate. The turbulence in the MBS market that had prompted Cioffi and Tannin's questionable activities only grew worse, as anxious investors demanding to redeem their shares lent credence to rumors that not only BSAM but also Bear Stearns itself were faced with serious liquidity problems. Simply put, investors and their advisors became increasingly worried that the firm didn't have the money—or any realistic hope of obtaining it—necessary to cash out their holdings. Bear Stearns' crisis turned out to be terminal when, in March 2008, rather than be forced into bankruptcy the firm was sold to J. P. Morgan Chase for only a fraction of its former value. Cioffi and Tannin in no way should be held responsible for either the demise of Bear Stearns or the global financial crisis that ensued from it. Wall Street observers suspect that short-sellers, who stood to gain from any dramatic drop in Bear Stearns' share price, had orchestrated a remarkably effective campaign of rumor mongering and unprofessional financial reporting that eventuated in a full-blown financial panic (Burrough 2008). Nevertheless, though they were acquitted of any criminal charges, Cioffi and Tannin still present for us a range of troubling moral issues. What do businesses owe their customers and clients? If businesses, like Bear Stearns, are advising customers and clients on their investment decisions, what is an appropriate standard of care for them and their interests? Does fiduciary responsibility have any meaning after the financial tsunami hit Wall Street in 2008? Are you satisfied that if Cioffi and Tannin were not found guilty of anything criminal, there is no further need to reflect on the morality of their actions?

7.3 Case Study Discussion

Traditionally, in the West as in China and elsewhere in Eastern Asia, law and morality are distinct, though also related in various ways. Though Cioffi and Tannin were acquitted when their court case went to trial, and while no one as yet has been convicted of a crime related to the collapse of Bear Stearns, the court's verdict hardly settles all issues regarding their ethical responsibilities. In Chap. 5, we explored the notion of commutative justice, which should be acknowledged as the first principle of business ethics. Following the teachings of Aristotle in the *Nicomachean Ethics*, we observed that the essence of all legitimate business transactions lies in their voluntary character. Buyers and sellers seek to make a deal—or, if you will, reach a mutual agreement—on the basis of a common estimate of the value of the goods or services they are paying for. Their voluntary character, however, depends on more than the fact that no one is coercing or threatening the use of force in order to close the deal. The use of force, no doubt, would mean that the exchange is really a form of robbery or extortion. A legitimate business transaction is regarded as voluntary when both buyers and sellers have sufficient information to make a rational decision on whether the deal is in their best interests. When one party helps the other party to make a rational decision, by providing a full disclosure of any relevant facts about the goods or services to be bought or sold, the decision to go ahead with the deal is both free and fair, with both parties conforming to the principle of commutative justice.

In Chap. 6, however, we began to explore the normal situation in today's global business world, where the relationship between a business firm and its customers is asymmetrical. They are rarely in a position to deal with each other symmetrically, with equal access to relevant information about the goods or services to be bought or sold, with equal opportunity to take their business elsewhere, if a free and fair agreement as to the value of these for one reason or another cannot be realized. We observed in Chap. 6 that in the normally asymmetrical relationship between a business firm (like Mattel, Inc.) and its customers (the parents and other caregivers who buy toys for their children), commutative justice requires that businesses meet a higher standard of care, anticipating the needs and protecting the interests of their customers even when, or especially when, their customers lack the knowledge or the power to do so themselves. Within the asymmetrical relationships that in today's global economy are characteristic of a business and its customers, the first principle of business ethics becomes clearer: "*Primum non nocere*" or "Above all, do no harm." The question raised for marketing ethics, in light of the Bear Stearns case, is whether investment bankers ought to be held to the same standard of care that other businesses must observe when dealing with their clients and customers.

There are, of course, plausible reasons for assuming that the traditional principles of business ethics simply do not—and should not—apply to investment bankers like Bear Stearns. It could be argued that the clients and customers with whom they typically are dealing are institutional investors—fellow members of the Wall Street fraternity—who ought to have sufficient access to the information needed to estimate the value of the CDOs and other financial instruments that Bear Stearns was selling. If they failed to exercise due diligence in protecting their own interests and those of their clients, they have no one to blame but themselves. To be sure, throughout the history of the financial bubble created around subprime mortgages, there were analysts who tried to warn anyone who would listen about the enormous risks involved.[15] But these Cassandras were generally ignored until the market teetered on the brink of disaster. Nevertheless, the idea that anyone who sustained heavy losses in the collapse of the subprime mortgage market deserved it is hard to square with the facts. As we have just seen, BSAM's hedge fund managers, Cioffi and Tannin, weren't simply bluffing as they tried to persuade investors not to cash in their holdings in CDOs. The indictments brought against them accuse them of fraud, that is, of deliberately deceiving investors, their clients, and customers, in

[15] See, for example, Michael Lewis' account of how money was made and lost in the collapse of the subprime mortgage market, *The Big Short* (Lewis 2010).

order not only to keep BSAM afloat but also to protect their own investments in the hedge funds. In the eyes of the Grand Jury that indicted them, Cioffi and Tannin apparently were willing to harm some investors in order to protect others, including themselves.

When Albert Z. Carr wrote his groundbreaking article, "Is Business Bluffing Ethical?" (Carr 1968), as we saw in chapter one, he argued that ethical standards in business are legitimately different from those presupposed in our interpersonal relationships. If one were to follow Carr's argument in the Bear Stearns case, we might conclude that since Cioffi and Tannin were only playing the game of business, they were no more obliged to inform their customers and clients about the actual risks involved in the investments they promoted than is a poker player obliged to show his hand to his adversaries. On this account, various stakeholders who were victimized by the creation of the subprime mortgage market, its dramatic expansion, and its catastrophic collapse—namely, the homeowners, legitimate savings and loan associations, and investors, not only in that market but also in anything impacted by it—have no moral claim against Bear Stearns and its hedge fund managers.

In laying out his argument, Carr recalled the comment from his former boss, President Harry F. Truman, who observed in another context, "If you can't stand the heat, stay out of the kitchen" (1968: 3). If you can't stand to lose a hand at poker, don't sit down to play. If you can't stand to take a big risk, don't invest in MBSs. Cioffi and Tannin, no doubt, were bluffing when they reassured their investors—even on the brink of disaster—that the BSAM hedge funds were "as safe as a bank." Someone persuaded by Carr's argument might justify their bluff by observing that the investors should have known they were bluffing and made their bets accordingly. But they made the wrong bets, and they lost big, as often happens in high stakes poker games.

Even if we concede that bluffing may not always be unethical, the question remains whether at some point Cioffi and Tannin crossed the line between bluffing and lying, between making glib reassurances to their customers and clients and conspiring to commit fraud. The government agencies that even Carr relies on to set and enforce the rules of the business game certainly thought they had crossed the line, but for one reason or another were unable to get a criminal conviction against them, thus leaving the ethical questions unanswered. Just because Cioffi and Tannin were acquitted of any crimes, are we to assume that everything they did was moral? Consider the systematic violation of Bear Stearns' compliance rules governing transactions between its departments and the BSAM hedge funds. We learned that 70 % of Cioffi's BSAM transactions violated these rules. Is that merely a technical issue, manifestly irrelevant for understanding the ethical implications of this case? Perhaps, it all depends on what the compliance rules were intended to do. They were meant to create an artificial barrier—a "Chinese wall," if you will—between BSAM and its parent company, in order to protect the hedge fund's clients and customers from any conflict of interest on the part of the firms involved. An independent director was to sign off on each transaction, so that some oversight would be exercised in order to minimize the risk of fraudulent activity. It would appear that

Cioffi and Tannin regarded the compliance rules as just another bluff, a pure formality designed to reassure nervous investors.

Consider also the Everquest IPO that even BSAM's COO, Paul Friedman, described as "really nothing more than a landfill for increasingly toxic mortgage securities." Had the Everquest IPO not been withdrawn, it would have repackaged these toxic assets as securities to be sold to retail investors, the group whom Friedman described as "the widows and orphans of this world." Carr might well wonder whether Cioffi and Tannin were still playing poker when they tried to offload BSAM's MBSs to such newbies. If BSAM's customers and clients were primarily institutional investors, the game they played with them just might bear some resemblance to poker; but the retail investors targeted in the Everquest IPO were likely to lack both the experience and skills needed to spot a bluff and respond to it strategically. The Everquest IPO and related strategies for postponing or avoiding the collapse of BSAM's hedge funds were meant to protect the interests of some investors at the expense of others. Cioffi and Tannin were using whatever bluffs and stratagems they could devise to buy time, so that at least some of their clients and customers could unwind their positions, while unwary others were induced to take on greater risks, buying even more toxic assets. Carr, however, admits that it is possible to cheat at poker and that such cheating may be severely punished. Wouldn't even Carr have to concede that Cioffi and Tannin crossed the line between bluffing and cheating, when they tried to open up the game to inexperienced players who stood no chance of winning?

When BSAM's hedge funds collapsed, even experienced players howled that they had been cheated in a game that had been rigged against them. They demanded that the appropriate regulatory agencies prosecute Cioffi and Tannin for conspiring to defraud them by misrepresenting the risks involved in the MBSs they had been persuaded to buy. Were they wrong to accuse Cioffi and Tannin of cheating? Was their outrage over sustaining such large losses merely the sour grapes of players who should have known better, who lost big because they failed to spot the bluff and respond to it skillfully? The facts presented in the Bear Stearns case suggest that dismissing the concerns of BSAM's investors as mere sour grapes is highly inappropriate and morally obtuse. Blaming the victims of Cioffi and Tannin's breathtaking irresponsibility undercuts the ethical legitimacy of capitalism and the utilitarian case to be made for identifying the common good with free but regulated markets.

7.4 Ethical Reflection

At several points in the Bear Stearns case, we considered the fiduciary responsibilities of Cioffi and Tannin, in particular, as well as their supervisors and mentors at BSAM and Bear Stearns. If the game of business is just another form of high stakes poker, then the notion of fiduciary responsibility is just another bluff, a piece of strategic fiction designed to mask the true nature of the game and how it is played.

But what if no one is bluffing? What if fiduciary responsibility is itself part of the rules of the game of international business? How, then, might it unlock for us the basic assumptions about ethics in marketing?

In legal terms, a "fiduciary" is "a person legally appointed and authorized to hold assets in trust for another person" (Investopedia 2014d). While traditionally a fiduciary serves to protect the interests of children and the elderly who have lost or not yet acquired the capacity to act in their own self-interest, the concept of fiduciary responsibility has been extended to include the duties assumed by anyone who manages assets for the benefit of another person rather than for his or her own profit. While many people assume that anyone providing investment advice or financial services would have fiduciary responsibilities to their customers and clients, it is reported that in the USA "approximately 85 % of financial advisers do not," the vast majority of whom are "stockbrokers, insurance agents, or simple sales representatives" (Paragon Wealth 2014). One major difference between investment advisers who exercise fiduciary responsibility and those who do not is the basis of their compensation. Fiduciaries receive set fees for their services and are expected to focus exclusively on their customers' or clients' best interests. Non-fiduciary financial advisers, on the other hand, earn commissions based on the sales they make. Human nature being what it is, the incentives offered non-fiduciary advisers mean that they are selling financial products that will benefit them—and not necessarily their customers and clients—the most.

7.4.1 Fiduciary Responsibility

Any investment broker or adviser who claims to be exercising fiduciary responsibilities must meet certain behavioral benchmarks. First of all, fiduciaries are licensed, usually as Registered Investment Advisers (RIA's) or Investment Advisor Representatives. In the USA, they register with the Securities and Exchange Commission (SEC) or the state security division and thus are acknowledged as qualified to exercise fiduciary responsibilities. Second, they are expected to uphold higher standards of professional ethics that, among other things, requires them not only to disclose their own financial interests but also to manage on behalf of their customers and clients "a prudent investment process." According to Investopedia's Jerry and Melissa Sais, such a process typically consists in four steps, "1) Organize, 2) Formalize, 3) Implement, and 4) Monitor" (Sais and Sais 2013). "Organize" means knowing the relevant laws and regulations—such as the Employees Retirement and Income Security Act—and structuring one's consultation with each customer or client accordingly. "Formalize" involves creating an investment strategy for each customer or client that responds to his or her specific needs, as typically indicated by his or her "investment horizon," "acceptable level of risk, and expected return." These indicators will help the adviser to identify "appropriate asset classes" from which to create a diversified portfolio of investments. The results of this consultation with one's customer or client should be detailed in a written "investment policy statement." "Implement" means doing "due diligence" on possible investments or investment management proposals consistent with the customer or client's policy statement. "Monitor"—perhaps "the most time consuming and also the most neglected part of the process"—entails keeping track of the investments' performance over time to determine whether the goals and objectives outlined in the investment policy statement are being met.

Finally, Jerry and Melissa Sais insist that fiduciary responsibility includes taking care that the fees charged for managing the customer or client's investments remain "fair and reasonable." Their message to fiduciaries clearly reflects our own view of becoming a top-notch player in business. Here is their advice:

> Fiduciaries should embrace their responsibilities and understand that they will not be judged on the returns of their portfolio, but on the prudence employed in the creation of the returns. If fiduciaries get the process right, they should be able to achieve admirable returns for their organizations. In the end, it's not whether you win or lose, it's how you play the game.

Albert Carr may have been correct in describing business as a game, but his misunderstanding of the kind of game being played in business completely undercuts the ideal of sportsmanship that implicitly underpins an ethic of fiduciary responsibility.

One consequence of 2008s financial crisis was an attempt to enact legislation that would impose fiduciary duties upon virtually all broker-dealers and investment advisers. Section 913 of the Dodd-Frank Act authorized the SEC to revise its rules so that any broker-dealers providing personalized investment services to retail customers meet the same duty of care imposed by existing law upon investment advisers. The SEC's Investor Advisory Committee (IAC) responded by investigating the effectiveness of current regulatory standards, while also exploring various frameworks for implementing the Dodd-Frank proposal. The result, so far, has been an indefinite postponement of the SEC's promulgation of new rules for exercising fiduciary responsibility (Quiñones 2014). Meanwhile, confusion reigns regarding the specific standard of care to be exercised by broker-dealers and investment advisers. The USA's Financial Industry Regulatory Authority (FINRA), a nongovernmental organization that seeks to regulate the business practices of member brokerage firms and exchange markets, seems to have moved toward constructive engagement in support of the fiduciary responsibilities proposed in the Dodd-Frank Act.

Prior to the Dodd-Frank Act, broker-dealers were minimally regulated by "the suitability rule" that required them to have "a reasonable basis" for their investment recommendations but did not require them to monitor the performance of the customer or client's portfolio or to provide ongoing advice to them regarding the investments under their management. By contrast, registered investment advisers already were expected to exercise a fiduciary duty that required them to act in the best interests of their clients and appropriately manage and fully disclose conflicts of interest (Quiñones 2014). FINRA's new suitability rule (Regulatory Notice 12–25), however, tends to collapse the previous distinction between broker-dealers and investment advisers by imposing upon all members "the requirement to act in the best interests of the client." In spelling out FINRA's expectations regarding the suitability of financial advice, regardless of whomever may be offering it, its president, Richard G. Ketchum, urged members to adopt the new standard without waiting any further for the SEC to act:

> Finally, before any complex product is offered to a retail client, your financial adviser should be able to write down on a single page why this investment is in the best interests of your client. This does not have to wait until you find out the details of any fiduciary rule-making the SEC may make. Being able to articulate why an investment is in the best interests of your client is fundamental to what the securities industry must be about if it is to deserve the trust of investors. The time to do it is now. (Ketchum 2012)

Not surprisingly, 85 % of financial service advisers not currently held to the higher standard of fiduciary responsibility have put up stiff resistance to implementing the Dodd-Frank legislation, and so far, their lobbying efforts appear to have been successful. The USA's National Association of Insurance and Financial Advisors (NAIFA), for example, alleged that "the likely result will be that professional investment guidance for retirement savings will become more expensive or not available at all for small accounts or individual plan participants." Instead of protecting retail investors, the legislation is likely to harm them, since they may be either unwilling or unable to pay the fees that registered investment advisers charge their clients and customers. Universalizing fiduciary responsibility, in NAIFA's view, may come at a cost that is unacceptable to most retain investors. In a recent survey of investment advisers, whose regulations already require the higher standard of fiduciary responsibility, better than two-thirds of the respondents rejected arguments like NAIFA's. As reported in *Forbes* (Wasik 2013), Kathleen McBride, a founder of two groups supporting the Dodd-Frank changes, explained their conflicting positions:

> [T]here is fear at brokerage firms and insurance companies that if they have to put investors' interests ahead of their own they won't be able to sell the high commission, high fee securities they routinely do now – securities or alternatives that are in the firm's interest but not the investor's. And it is likely that not all that they are permitted to sell to investors would be appropriate if they had to put investors' interests ahead of their own.

Though brokerage firms and insurance companies may become less profitable in the short term, in the long term adhering to the higher standard may lead toward higher profits. Brokerages and other financial service firms that commit themselves to rigorous enforcement of fiduciary duties—argues McBride—will benefit from increased "credibility and investor confidence, and of course, client retention is a lot less expensive than client acquisition." Peter Drucker himself couldn't have said it better: If the purpose of a business, including businesses providing financial services, is to create a customer, then consistently and transparently, fulfilling one's fiduciary responsibilities remains the best way to fulfill that purpose.

7.4.2 Fiduciary Duties in China's Companies Law of 2005

Even several years after 2008s financial crisis, the debate over the scale and scope of fiduciary responsibility continues unabated on Wall Street. Nevertheless, the rest of the world appears to be making sincere efforts to integrate this principle into the laws and policies regulating business corporations. One notable example is China's experience since the promulgation of its Companies Law in 2005 (CSRC 2005). In Article 148, the Companies Law specifically recognizes fiduciary duties—namely, "the duties of loyalty and diligence to the company," which must guide the conduct of a company's "directors, supervisors, and senior managers." While the Companies Law does not define these duties, it does stipulate eight prohibited acts, all of which concern the misappropriation of company funds, unauthorized disclosure of privileged information, as well as a catch-all prohibition against "other acts committed in violation of the duty of loyalty." Both Chinese and foreign observers, mostly representing various law firms operating in China, have responded favorably to the inclusion of these duties, but they also note the difficulties involved in implementing them or initiating lawsuits in order to force a specific company to adhere to them (Zhang 2009; Cheng 2014; Siu and Zou 2013). It is also clear that the relevant articles in China's Companies Law stipulate "the duties of diligence and loyalty" primarily with reference to the company as a whole and not with reference to various stakeholder groups, beyond the shareholders. The company's investors thus may have some recourse against violations of these fiduciary duties on the part of its "directors, supervisors, and senior managers," but its customers, clients, and other stakeholders apparently are not similarly protected. This does not mean that Chinese firms providing brokerage services or investment advice are free to defraud their customers with impunity, but that such crimes are not likely to be prosecuted directly on the basis of the Companies Law.

Under such circumstances, the wisdom of Rothlin's rule for marketing ethics, "To establish your brand name, act as a fair competitor," should be obvious. Fair competition is possible only if all participants make a steady and sincere commitment to play by the rules of the game. This is no less true in the game of business than in any other game. Cheating, by definition, involves deliberately breaking the rules in order to win at all costs. When that happens, the competitors are no longer playing a game, but are engaged in a struggle in which there are no rules and where, ultimately, neither victory nor defeat has any meaning. The disappearance of brand names, like that of Bear Stearns, or Lehman Brothers, or the many other banks, insurance firms, and real estate agencies, that did not survive the financial crisis of 2008, signal the massive collapse of trust that occurred when investors, homeowners, and other stakeholders realized that these firms were no longer playing the game of business. Instead they were out to use the game as a cover for predatory practices—against each other, as well as against their customers and clients, and other stakeholders—designed to commit fraud on an unprecedented scale. Business is no longer a game, when marketing becomes a bluff meant to cover the hard realities of making a killing.

7.5 Conclusion: Overcoming "Marketing Myopia" in Investment Banking

There are no special ethics for the investment or financial services industry that would justify Wall Street's recklessness with other peoples' money as "fair competition." Perhaps Carr himself was bluffing when he argued that ethics in business—like ethics in poker—is and ought to be different from "the ethical ideals of civilized human relationships" (Carr 1968: 3). Apparently, his view of human relationships—civilized or not—is significantly lacking in either imagination or experience. Doing business is a human activity, as are all the other games that people play, for fun or profit. Regardless of their motive or the complexity of the actions involved, all of them involve human understanding and human choices. In various ways, all of them exhibit the basic characteristics of human responsibility—or if you will, moral agency—even if only in attempting to deny or evade it. If there is no legitimate reason to distinguish ethics in business from ethics in other areas of human responsibility, then all the more should we reject the idea that the ethics of marketing financial services or managing investments should be any different from the ethics of marketing children's toys or infant formula or any other goods and services that respond to genuine human needs.

Several years before Albert Z. Carr published "Is Business Bluffing Ethical?" Theodore Levitt wrote an equally provocative piece for the Harvard Business Review, titled "Marketing Myopia" (Levitt 1960). There he distinguished a genuine idea of "marketing" with the more common and entirely problematic notion of "selling." While he does not make reference to Drucker's earlier work, *The Practice of Management* (1954), Levitt persuasively argues for a systematic rethinking of marketing centered on the needs of a business' targeted customers and clients. He rejects a narrow focus on selling as "Product Provincialism" (Levitt 1960: 52) and demonstrates from American business history (e.g., the rise and fall of the USA's railroad system), how and why such shortsightedness inevitably leads to the decline of businesses once considered too big—too secure and too successful—to fail. Marketing, by contrast, focuses on the customer:

> An industry begins with the customer and his needs, not with a patent, a raw material, or a selling skill. Given the customer's needs, the industry develops backwards, first concerning itself with the physical delivery of customer satisfactions. Then it moves back further to create the things by which these satisfactions are in part achieved. How these materials are created is a matter of indifference to the customer, hence the particular form of manufacturing, processing, or what-have-you cannot be considered as a vital aspect of the industry. Finally, the industry moves back still further to finding the raw materials necessary for making its products. (Ibid: 55)

In ways similar to Drucker's argument advocating the practice of "management by objectives," Levitt claims that a focus on the needs of customers and a business' capacity for satisfying them is actually more consistent with "scientific method"—"being aware of and defining their companies' problems, and then developing testable hypotheses about solving them"—than any narrow focus on the technologies of production and sales.

Any genuinely scientific approach to customer satisfaction inevitably must consider a business' fiduciary responsibilities, not just to its shareholders, but also in various ways to all its stakeholders, especially its customers and clients. If the basic principles of commutative justice, embodied in free and fair market competition, must still be honored in business, if marketing itself presupposes creating and sustaining a level of trust in which the pledge above all to "Do No Harm" is respected by everyone involved, then the asymmetries in the relationships between businesses and their stakeholders, however arcane and complex, must be understood and respected. When the subprime mortgage market blew up in 2008, creating a "Black Hole" that nearly swallowed the global financial system, the prophetic nature of Levitt's warning about the destructive consequences of narrowing a business' focus to selling instead of genuine marketing should have been obvious to all concerned. Marketing, whether the product is infant formula or collateralized debt obligations, is one crucial area where high ethical standards and sound business practices largely coincide with one another.

References

Abelson, M. (2010, August 18). Ralph Cioffi, after the fall. *The New York Observer*. Retrieved on November 5, 2013, from http://observer.com/2010/08/ralph-cioffi-after-the-fall/#axzz2szvplA1X

Allessi, C., Wolverson, R., & Sergie, M. A., (2013, October 22). *Backgrounder: The credit rating controversy*. The Council on Foreign Relations. Retrieved on 8 February 2014 from http://www.cfr.org/financial-crises/credit-rating-controversy/p22328

Burrough, B., (2008, April). Bringing down bear stearns. *Vanity Fair*. Retrieved on October 10, 2013, from http://www.vanityfair.com/politics/features/2008/08/bear_stearns200808

Business Wire. (2005). *FORTUNE magazine names bear stearns 'Most Admired' securities firm*. Retrieved on January 22, 2014, from http://www.businesswire.com/news/home/20050225005422/en/FORTUNE-Magazine-Names-Bear-Stearns-Admired-Securities#.Ut_1jRCIWM8

Carr, A. Z. (1968). Is business bluffing ethical? *Harvard Business Review*. Retrieved on March 7, 2014 from http://hbr.org/1968/01/is-business-bluffing-ethical

Cheng, J. C. (2014, January). *Challenges surrounding directors' duty of care in Chinese Corporate Law*. Indiana University Research Center for Chinese Politics and Business, RCCPB Working Paper #34. Retrieved March 11, 2014 from http://www.indiana.edu/~rccpb/pdf/Jui-Chien_Cheng_oct_2013_34.pdf

CNN Money. (2006). *America's most admired companies 2006*. Retrieved on January 22, 2014 from http://money.cnn.com/magazines/fortune/mostadmired/snapshots/1341.html; http://money.cnn.com/magazines/fortune/mostadmired/2006/industries/industry_49.html

CNN Money. (2007). *America's most admired companies 2007*. Retrieved on January 22, 2014 from http://money.cnn.com/magazines/fortune/mostadmired/2007/snapshots/2835.html; http://money.cnn.com/magazines/fortune/mostadmired/2007/industries/industry_52.html

Cohan, W. D. (2009). *House of cards – A tale of hubris and wretched excess on wall street* (1st ed.). New York: Doubleday.

Comstock, C. (2010, November). Bear Stearns' Cioffi and Tannin toasted to bankruptcy with vodka in paper cups. *Business Insider 16*. Retrieved August 23, 2013, from http://www.businessinsider.com/ralph-cioffi-and-matt-tannin-toasted-to-the-future-with-vodka-in-paper-cups-2010-11

CSRC. (2005). *Companies law of the People's Republic of China*. China securities regulatory commission. Retrieved on June 17, 2015 from http://www.csrc.gov.cn/pub/csrc_en/laws/rfdm/statelaws/200904/t20090428_102712.html

Durden, T. (2011). JP Morgan sold MBS covered by 'Sack of shit' loans… then shorted all those with exposure: A Goldman-AIG Redux. *Zerohedge Magazine*. Retrieved October 10, 2013 fromhttp://www.zerohedge.com/article/jp-morgan-sold-investors-mbs-covered-sack-shit-loans-goldman-aig-redux

Eaglesham, J., Neumann, J., & Perez, E. (2013. February 6). U.S., S&P Settle in for bitter combat. *The Wall Street Journal Online*. Retrieved February 6, 2014 from http://online.wsj.com/news/articles/SB10001424127887324445904578285802822704578

Frankel, A. (2013, February 5). Can we now admit it's time to end issuer-pays credit rating model? *Reuters*. Retrieved on February 9, 2014 from http://blogs.reuters.com/alison-frankel/2013/02/05/can-we-now-admit-its-time-to-end-issuer-pays credit-rating-model/

Gasparino, C. (2009, September 16). Prosecutors fumble wall street probes. *The Daily Beast*. Retrieved on February 9, 2014 from http://www.thedailybeast.com/articles/2009/09/17/no-more-wall-street-arrests.html

Goldman, D. (2009). *Former bear stearns execs not guilty*. Retrieved September 09, 2013, from http://money.cnn.com/2009/11/10/news/companies/bear_stearns_case/

Goldstein, M. (2007, May 11). Bear Stearns Subprime IPO. *Bloomberg Business Week*. Retrieved on February 10, 2014 from http://www.businessweek.com/stories/2007-05-11/bear-stearns-subprime-ipobusinessweek-business-news-stock-market-and-financial-advice

Gopal, P., Shenn, J., & Hurtado, P. (2011). *Ambac says JPMorgan refused mortgage repurchases it also sought*. Retrieved on November 1, 2013 from http://www.bloomberg.com/news/2011-01-25/jpmorgan-refused-mortgage-repurchases-it-also-sought-ambac-assurance-says.html

Hayes, S. L., Spence, A. M., & Marks, D. V. P. (1983). *Competition in the investment banking industry*. Cambridge, MA: Harvard University Press.

Hurtado, P., Van Voris, B., & Sandler, L., (2009, November 11). Bear managers' acquittal may hamper U.S. Fraud prosecutions. *Bloomberg News*. Retrieved on February 11, 2014 from http://www.bloomberg.com/apps/news?pid=newsarchive&sid=alBcul0c3hPk

Investopedia.com. (2014a). *Arms length transaction*. Retrieved on February 10, 2014 from http://www.investopedia.com/terms/a/armslength.asp

Investopedia.com. (2014b). *Credit default swaps – CDS*. Retrieved on January 22, 2014 from http://www.investopedia.com/terms/c/creditdefaultswap.asp

Investopedia.com. (2014c). *Credit enhancement*. Retrieved on 06.02.2014 from http://www.investopedia.com/terms/c/creditenhancement.asp

Investopedia.com. (2014d). *Fiduciary*. Retrieved on March 18, 2014 from http://www.investopedia.com/terms/f/fiduciary.asp

Investopedia.com. (2014e). *Junk bonds*. Retrieved on January 22, 2014 from http://www.investopedia.com/terms/j/junkbond.asp

Investopedia.com. (2014f). *Ponzi scheme*. Retrieved on February 6, 2014 from http://www.investopedia.com/terms/p/ponzischeme.asp

Ketchum, R. G. (2012, May 21). *Remarks by Richard Ketchum at the FINRA annual conference*. Retrieved 12 March 2014 from http://www.finra.org/Newsroom/Speeches/Ketchum/P126481

Lambert, G. D. (2012, December 09). *Profit from Mortgage debt with MBS*. Retrieved February 6, 2014 from http://www.investopedia.com/articles/06/mortgagebackedsecurities.asp

Lattman, P. (2012, February 9). *S.E.C. reaches settlement in Bear Stearns fraud case*. Retrieved October 20, 2013, from http://dealbook.nytimes.com/2012/02/09/s-e-c-reaches-settlement-in-bear-stearns-fraud-case

Levitt, T. (1960, July–August). Marketing Myopia. *Harvard Business Review*, 45–56.

Lewis, M. (1989). *Liar's Poker: Rising through the Wreckage on Wall Street*. New York: W.W. Norton.

Lewis, M. (2010). *The big short: Inside the doomsday machine*. New York: W.W.Norton.

Paragon Wealth. (2014). *What is fiduciary responsibility?* Retrieved on March 11, 2014 from http://www.paragonwealth.com/about_paragon/fiduciary_advisor.php

Quiñones, J. (2014, March 4). *Uniform fiduciary standard for broker-dealers: An update the securities edge*. Retrieved on June 17, 2015 from http://www.thesecuritiesedge.com/2014/03/uniform-fiduciary-standard-for-broker-dealers-an-update/

Sais, J., & Sais M. (2013). *Meeting your fiduciary responsibilities*. Investopedia. Retrieved on June 17, 2015 from http://www.investopedia.com/articles/08/fiduciary-responsiblity.asp

Sanati, C. (2009, November 12). 10 years later, looking at repeal of Glass-Steagall. *New York Times Dealbook*. From: http://dealbook.nytimes.com/2009/11/12/10-years-later-looking-at-repeal-of-glass-steagall/

Siu, W.W., & Zou, J. (2013, October 31). *Advisory: China business series: Directors and supervisors*. Pillsbury Winthrop Shaw Pittman LLP. Retrieved online March 10, 2014 from http://www.pillsburylaw.com/publications/china-business-series-directors-and-supervisors

Stewart, I. (2012, February 12). The mathematical equation that caused the banks to crash: The Black-Scholes equation was the mathematical justification for the trading that plunged the world's banks into catastrophe. *The Observer (The Guardian)*. Retrieved on 6 February 2014 from http://www.theguardian.com/science/2012/feb/12/black-scholes-equation-credit-crunch

United States District Court, Eastern District of New York, Criminal Division. (2008, June 18). *The United States of America against Ralph Cioffi and Matthew Tannin, Defendants*. Retrieved on February 11, 2014 from http://online.wsj.com/public/resources/documents/bearindictment.pdf

Wasik, J. (August 23, 2013). *Why Wall Street, insurers don't want Fiduciary duty. Forbes*. Retrieved on March 15, 2014 from http://www.forbes.com/sites/johnwasik/2013/08/23/why-wall-street-insurers-dont-want-fiduciary-duty

Wayne, L. (1983, June 12). A daring dealmaker piles up profits. *New York Times*. Retrieved on February 6, 2014 from http://www.nytimes.com/1983/06/12/business/a-daring-dealmaker-piles-up-profits.html

Williams Walsh, M., & Nixon, R. (2013, February 5). S&P emails on mortgage crisis show alarm and gallows humor. *New York Times Dealbook*. Retrieved on February 6, 2014 from http://dealbook.nytimes.com/2013/02/05/case-details-internal-tension-at-s-p-amid-subprime-problems/?_php=true&_type=blogs&_r=0

Zhang, W. (2009). *Fiduciary duties: Preconditions for enforcement*. Retrieved on March 11, 2014 from http://www.oecd.org/daf/ca/corporategovernanceprinciples/42205277.pdf

Chapter 8
Employees: Dignity and Workers' Rights

"To increase productivity, provide safe and healthy working conditions." (Stephan Rothlin, *Eighteen Rules for ecoming a Top Notch Player,* 2004)

8.1 Prelude

Expectations regarding how businesses treat their employees seem to vary significantly from one culture to another. Is it possible for international business ethics to approach the question of fair and humane treatment of workers without creating a pretext for another rambling discussion of the evils of globalization? We believe that a genuinely cross-cultural approach to the treatment of workers is possible, based, first, on a deeper appreciation of the indigenous moral and spiritual traditions encoded in "Asian values"; and second, on a more accurate perspective on the ways local Asian firms and foreign multinational corporations can collaborate in addressing the specific problems of Asian workers. Thus this chapter will, on the one hand, summarize Asian discussions of human dignity as they relate to employment conditions in an industrial economy, and on the other hand, examine the ways in which Apple and its Asian subcontractor, Foxconn, attempted to respond to allegations that they were running a sweatshop in China. Our point is neither to praise nor to blame Apple and Foxconn, but to determine what businesses owe to their employees by way of demonstrating proper care for their basic dignity and human rights. The case study, we hope, will help shift discussions away from the abstract ideological posturing for and against globalization and multinational enterprises, and toward the challenges that workers and those who manage them actually face in any industrial economy.

S. Rothlin, D. McCann, *International Business Ethics*,
DOI 10.1007/978-3-662-47434-1_8

8.2 Case Study: Who Cares About Foxconn and Its Employees' Health and Safety?

8.2.1 Abstract

In June 2006, a story appeared in the British tabloid, *Mail on Sunday*, accusing Foxconn of running a "sweatshop" where it produced Apple iPods. The story immediately stirred up a controversy in which the stakes were particularly immense for Apple because such an accusation could seriously tarnish its reputation particularly in the USA and the EU. After the initial wave of outraged denials, both Foxconn and Apple agreed to open the alleged sweatshops to investigation and urged that their operations be judged by the standards already established in Apple's Supplier Code of Conduct. When the investigative report was released later that summer, it found no evidence that Foxconn used either child labor or forced labor, and while admitting that the average weekly hours of Foxconn employees exceeded the legal limit in China of 60 h, it denied that these employees had been coerced into overtime work. A few years after the controversy appeared to have died down, it burst open again with news in 2010 regarding a wave of suicides—14 deaths in all—among mostly younger Foxconn employees. What more compelling evidence could there be for confirming that Foxconn was, indeed, running a sweatshop? Why would employees be committing suicide, if not in protest against the inhumane working conditions there?

A moralistic response to this story would have been to play the blame game, and use it to shame China into living up to the promises of Communist ideology, while demanding that Apple cut off its business with any subcontractors, Chinese or otherwise, who fail to make drastic changes in the way workers are treated in their factories. But while such a response might soothe the moral outrage of those who assume that everything made in China must be produced under sweatshop conditions, at best it reflects only part of the story. In what follows we attempt to present a fresh and unbiased study of Apple-Foxconn that raises important questions about what any company owes its workers, starting with a commitment to respect their human dignity and honor their human rights. Our intent is to move the discussion away from playing the blame game, and toward a better understanding of how and why it is in the interests of all stakeholders to monitor working conditions and improve them whenever possible.

8.2.2 Keywords

Foxconn, OEM, ICT, outsourcing, sweatshop, Apple's Supplier Code of Conduct, overtime regulations, NGOs.

8.2.3 *Introducing Foxconn*

A member of the Taiwanese Honghai Group, Foxconn is a high-tech company manufacturing electronic products for the world's top businesses specializing in the "6C" industry: computer appliances, communication devices, consumer electronics, digital contents, automobile components, and circuits. The Group was established in 1974 as a small business, Honghai Plastic Enterprise Co. Ltd., specializing in the production of knobs for black and-white television sets. Three years after becoming profitable, Honghai had achieved a solid base for the rapid development that characterized the years that followed (Xu 2007).

The Foxconn brand dates back to 1985, when the company established its American branch. China's economic reforms allowed this Taiwanese company to build its first offshore plant in Shenzhen in 1988. Foxconn reached an important milestone in 1996, when a large investment in Longhua Science and Technology Park established the company's leadership position in the Chinese original equipment manufacturing (OEM) market (Xu 2007). Since then, the enterprise has grown rapidly as exports have increased from US$2.4 billion in 2001 to US$82.3 billion in 2010 with its workforce increasing to 900,000 during that period (Wei 2010).

At the same time, Foxconn leveraged its growing success in China to expand worldwide. Hundreds of subsidiaries and representative offices were set up in the Chinese mainland, Taiwan, Japan, Southeast Asia, America, and Europe to fulfill its global "3T" strategy—time to market, time to volume, and time to money—meaning manufacturing the right products in the right time according to customers' orders to meet the market demand (Wei 2010).

Under this strategy, top brand companies such as Apple, Motorola, Nokia, IBM, Sony, Hewlett Packard, and Cisco Systems have made Foxconn their foundry of choice because of its superior cost advantages and managerial efficiency. Foxconn's success led the American magazine, *Business Weekly*, to name the company's founder, Guo Taiming, "King of Outsourcing" (Zhang 2006a). However, on June 11, 2006, things took a different turn when the London tabloid, *Mail on Sunday*, ran an exposé on "the stark reality" lurking beneath Foxconn's shiny surface.

8.2.4 *The Sweatshop Scandal*

The *Mail on Sunday* story claimed that women workers at the Foxconn plant manufacturing Apple's most famous products earned approximately US $50 per month while averaging 15 h per workday (Klowden 2006). As the allegations spread from Britain to the rest of the world, they elicited condemnation from international nonprofit organizations. In response, these organizations called for a boycott against Apple as well as its supplier network. Foxconn's senior management was outraged by the claims that their plant was a sweatshop and called a press conference in order to refute each allegation in detail (Chen and Liu 2006). Senior VP of Foxconn operations, Li Jinming, noted that Apple was sending a team of investigators to report on the general state of working conditions at the Shenzhen plant and verify any claims of employee abuse. He asserted that if the Chinese media had lingering doubts about Foxconn, they should consult Apple's Supplier Code of Conduct (Apple Inc. 2006) and wait for the results of Apple's investigation.

When the *First Financial Daily* published a follow-up story alleging retaliation against the Foxconn employee who had blown the whistle on working conditions at the plant, the firm filed a lawsuit against the reporters in the Shenzhen Intermediate People's Court. The article's authors, Wang You and Weng Bao, would be liable for substantial penalties had they been convicted of defamation (Liu and Yang 2006). By the end of the summer, the result of Apple's on-site investigation was released. While it exonerated Foxconn of accusations involving either child labor or forced labor, Apple acknowledged that a substantial number of employees admitted to working more than 60 h a week, thus exceeding the standard set in the company's Supplier Code of Conduct. By then, Foxconn had reduced the damage claim against reporters Wang and Weng from 30 million RMB to a symbolic one RMB. Once presented with the evidence supporting Apple's findings, Wang and Weng's employer, the *First Financial Daily*, helped negotiate an agreement that included Foxconn's commitment to improve factory management and increase levels of transparency (*Information Times*, 2006). Apple's investigation had also reported that Foxconn promised to make other improvements consistent with the standards set in Apple's Supplier Code of Conduct (McNulty 2006). Though this may have appeared to be the most desirable outcome for all concerned, a new series of scandals further tarnished Foxconn's already damaged reputation.

8.2.5 The Foxconn Suicides (2010–2011)

After a relatively quiet period during which some multinationals severed ties with Foxconn in order to avoid risking their own reputations, 2010 opened with a wave of suicides by younger employees—fourteen deaths in all—that reignited the worldwide controversy over working conditions at the plant. On the one hand, some reports assumed that the rash of suicides confirmed just how inhumane the working conditions must be at Foxconn; on the other hand, some pointed out that the suicide rate among Foxconn employees was dramatically lower than the national average for China indicated by the World Health Organization (Mattimore 2010). Even if Foxconn was not directly to blame for the suicides, how if at all should the company have responded to them?

On the heels of the fourth suicide of an employee who jumped out of an office window, Foxconn finally addressed its shortcomings. The company admitted to poor management of new staff, and expressed a willingness to improve internal policies and engage in efforts to strengthen its corporate culture. At first dismissed as isolated events, ultimately the suicides demanded attention as a systemic problem requiring a comprehensive solution. In addition to announcing some welcome salary increases, Foxconn outlined policies designed to demonstrate greater care for the psychological state and physical health of its employees. It also unveiled plans to transfer some production plants inland in order to allow employees more frequent visits to their hometowns.

The notoriety of the case attracted the attention of the Chinese government. Official inquiry suggested that suicides were a response to a complex combination of individual, corporate, and social factors related to the rapid industrialization, urbanization, and modernization of China over the last 20 years. In order to avoid further tragedies, different departments in the municipal government of Shenzhen began to offer assistance to young employees considered most at risk. Thus the Public Security Bureau took over the training of Foxconn security personnel at the factory; the Women's Federation and the Communist Youth League's Culture and Physical departments sponsored social activities at the plant; and the Departments of Labor and Social Security thoroughly scrutinized employment contracts, wages, and overtime regulations and ordered a stop to certain illegal practices (Wang and Zhan 2010).

Thanks to the help of academia and the international NGOs that had been monitoring working conditions in Chinese factories since 2006, the issue was brought to the attention of the world. Responsibility for the poor relationship between employers and employees was primarily pinned on the necessity of meeting the tight deadlines and strict demands of their foreign customers. Foxconn's defenders alleged that such constraints made the monitoring of working conditions nearly impossible and exacerbated the neglect of the employees' basic needs. Fearing negative publicity, the information and communication technology (ICT) industry as a whole took measures to prevent or at least reduce the likelihood of similar problems. The major players and stakeholders of Foxconn, such as Apple, HP, and Dell, publicly promised closer monitoring of their suppliers' factories and, in particular, to aid in Foxconn's efforts to improve working conditions. In February 2011, when Apple released its annual *Supplier Responsibility Progress Report*, the improved conditions achieved at Foxconn were given high praise (Apple Inc. 2011).

Nevertheless, 6 months later the sudden death of 23-year-old Chen Long, a worker at Foxconn's Guanlan plant in Shenzhen, was attributed to overwork. The Foxconn ordeal had yet to run its course (Jina 2011).

8.2.6 Summary

Despite its high standing in China's OEM market, Foxconn became embroiled in controversy over the harsh conditions to which its workforce allegedly was exposed in order to serve the demands of a rapidly globalizing ICT industry. Even with growing pressure at the national and international levels to improve the situation, 2010 saw a wave of suicides by younger employees. Foxconn's response to these events was firm, motivated by a strict sense of urgency, and involved municipal entities, nongovernmental organizations, and foreign stakeholders of the company.

If the question of who cares about Foxconn and the health and safety of its workers is to be anything more than a face-saving exercise, we have to ask ourselves what, if any, are the responsibilities of OEM managers serving the global marketplace. Suicides especially evoke the full range of moral passions. They are not just another kind of industrial accident. Upon learning of such things, we all feel the urge to blame somebody, to do something, anything that might stop the senseless waste of human life. Surely there must be a moral issue here, when we all feel so upset by what happened. But what is the moral issue? What can we do to achieve moral clarity about the proper way for a company like Foxconn to care for its employees?

8.3 Case Study Discussion

There is a false moral clarity in the accusation that Foxconn, with Apple's complicity, was running a "sweatshop." It presupposes a moral judgment, namely, that working conditions in a plant described as a "sweatshop" fall below the minimum standards of care or respect for human dignity that are expected in all human activities. It accuses Foxconn's owners, investors, and managers of deliberately abusing their employees. If proven to be true, that raises serious moral issues. It is not surprising that Foxconn's management reacted defensively when the accusation was made in the local and international media.

So the first question is whether Foxconn was running a sweatshop. Is there sufficient evidence to justify this charge? The answer seems inconclusive, since for all its problems Foxconn was the employer of choice for hundreds of thousands of Chinese migrant workers. By contrast, everyone will agree that the Rana Plaza garment factory in Dhaka, Bangladesh, which collapsed in 2013, killing 1135 workers, was indeed a sweatshop (Burke 2013). Not only was the building itself catastrophically unsafe, but it was also overcrowded with workers, materials, and the machinery involved in producing clothing. It was also not properly ventilated, among its many other violations. On the day of the disaster, when workers tried to warn their bosses about the new and dangerous cracks that had appeared in the walls and ceilings, they were ordered into the building and back to work. Because of their negligence, the owner and his staff will face murder charges. Not all working conditions in Asian factories are as bad as they were at Rana Plaza. But just how different were they in the Foxconn plants?

The evidence that Foxconn was running a sweatshop included references to the average wages and working hours of their employees. The *Mail on Sunday* tabloid article stated that in 2006 Foxconn workers received an average wage of US$50 a month, and worked an average of over 15 h day. While such hours and wages may seem unconscionable in the UK, the EU, and the USA, the relevant issue is whether they are immoral and illegal in China. The working hours average clearly implies that Foxconn employees were working overtime, and the case study reminds us that the legal limit on hours worked per week is 60. Since Foxconn's workers are mostly migrants who are seeking to make as much money as they can in as short a time as possible, Apple's report that they were not coerced into overtime work seems credible.

So what about the wages at Foxconn? Are they morally unjust? What is a fair wage, morally considered? If it happens that Foxconn wages are better than most other factories in the area, does that make them fair? Conversely, if Foxconn wages are just a fraction of what factories in the UK or the USA would pay for similar work, does that make them unfair? If it happens that Foxconn's workers freely agreed to these wages, and were not coerced into working overtime, does that make them fair? If workers demand overtime work in excess of the Chinese government's legal limit, is Foxconn morally justified in giving these workers what they want? While it may be difficult to determine precisely what a fair wage is for Chinese migrant workers, their choices surely count against any naïve assumption that Foxconn is running a sweatshop.

Because Foxconn is one of Apple's major subcontractors, Apple was quickly drawn into the controversy over working conditions at the Shenzhen plant. So the second question is whether it is fair to hold Apple responsible for the policies and practices of its subcontractor? Why should Apple be held responsible? If Apple does bear some share of the responsibility, what should be its role in responding to the problems at Foxconn? When the Foxconn exposé first surfaced in 2006, Apple sent investigators to the Shenzhen plant who then issued a report based on its Supplier Code of Conduct. The report refuted the most serious charges against Foxconn, but did admit that overtime work exceeding the legal limits in China was routine. It pledged to assist Foxconn in addressing this problem. Did Apple do enough to respect the freedom and human dignity of Foxconn workers? Should they have done more? If so, what should they have done, that would have been more caring than what they actually did or failed to do?

The third question should be focused on the suicides that occurred at the Foxconn plant in 2010–2011. Do these prove that the firm was indifferent to basic human values and minimum standards of good business ethics? If the suicides are regarded as personal tragedies that are primarily of personal significance, there may be little point in trying to connect them to basic standards of business ethics? On the other hand, if they are regarded as *prima facie* evidence that Foxconn indeed was exploiting its workers, they may be very relevant to our discussion. Was Foxconn in fact responsible for the wave of suicides among its employees? How did the firm respond to them? Was its response sufficient or should something more have been done? Similarly, what about Apple's response? In order to demonstrate its commitment to international business ethics, would you recommend that Apple simply wash its hands of Foxconn and find a new subcontractor whose policies and practices seem more consistent with its Supplier Code of Conduct? If not, and you think that Apple should maintain its relationship with Foxconn, what responsibilities do you think it has for improving working conditions at Foxconn's plant?

In Chap. 4, we introduced a basic distinction between "Type A" and "Type B" ethical problems in business, and a model that integrated ethical concerns into strategic management decision-making. We argued that if management's problem is "Type A"—that is, if we discover in it a situation that is complex, involving conflicting moral principles and priorities, and not an obvious failure to do the right thing, as in "Type B" problems—then a decision-making model may help to sort out the issues and establish priorities for responsible action. An unbiased reading of the Apple-Foxconn case study will support the conclusion that they were faced with a "Type A" problem. If we were convinced that Foxconn was running a sweatshop, then of course, their problem would have to be regarded as an example of "Type B." But the more that the relevant facts of the case are examined, and the better the labor market in the Pearl River Delta, as well as the challenges facing Chinese migrant workers, are understood, the less credible is the sweatshop accusation. Even if Foxconn were not running a sweatshop, there would be significant problems to be resolved in this case. Let us see how our decision-making model may help us to understand them.

There are six steps in our model, as we learned in Chap. 4. Peter Drucker identified five of these steps: "Defining the problem; analyzing the problem; developing alternate solutions; deciding upon the best solution; converting the decision into effective action" (Drucker 1986: 353). In order to clarify the role of moral considerations in his analysis, we expanded step two, "analyzing the problem," so that it includes an inventory of ethical resources implicit in the situation; and we divided step five, "deciding upon the best solution," so that it involved both a rejection of any solutions that failed to meet the ethical standards evident in step two, and then a positive choice—based on legitimate business considerations—from among the remaining solutions. Our belief is that by making explicit the role that moral considerations already play in managerial decision-making, we improve the chances that the decisions actually made will be both more ethical and more business like, than if the moral dimension had been left unexplored. So what happens when the decision-making model is applied in the Apple-Foxconn situation?

Step 1: What is the Problem? Here is one definition of the problem: In the context of ongoing controversy over working conditions at the Foxconn plant, a wave of suicides among younger workers has occurred. What should Apple and Foxconn do about them? Alternatively, defining the problem may revolve around responding to the negative publicity threatening to damage the reputations—and thus undermine various stakeholders' confidence in the brands—of both Apple and Foxconn. What sort of PR strategy should they adopt in order to defuse the negative publicity? Who are the various stakeholders involved in this case? How should Apple and Foxconn regard the ethical obligations that they have to each and all of them? If there are conflicts, which obligations should take priority? How might Apple and Foxconn respond to them?

Step 2: What are the Resources for a Solution? Considered strictly in terms of financial results, Apple and Foxconn are two of the most successful companies in the history of Asia Pacific business. They have more than sufficient material resources to address any problems that surface for them. In addition, both are pledged to follow Apple's Supplier Conduct Code. Their founders have been written up as exemplary moral leaders in business. China's labor laws are explicit on the question of the health and safety of workers, even to the specifics of wages and overtime work. In addition, the business press both in China and abroad has shown a keen willingness to press the moral issues involved in this case. All of these and more can be deployed in support of a solution that will optimize both ethical responsibility and sound business practice.

Step 3: Range of Possible Solutions? Here we brainstorm anything that might address the problem, moral or immoral, legal or illegal. Here are some options; as such they remain hypothetical: (1) Do nothing. Deny any responsibility for the suicides, but send condolences and a small severance package to each victim's family as a gift. (2) Immunize the firms from further problems by giving generous gifts to any judges and government regulators who might be involved in the investigation of possible future claims against Apple and Foxconn in China. (3) Develop an aggressive public relations campaign in China, directed at the editors and other opinion makers of prestigious business journals that will ensure that Apple and Foxconn will get favorable stories published whenever the need arises. (4) If there is a Human Relations (HR) department at Foxconn, fire the top managers, making an example of them, blaming them for failing to have adequate counseling programs and other measures in place to assist troubled employees. (5) Develop a consciousness-raising workshop for all managers in production operations, based on Chinese cultural values and contemporary realities, in order to improve employee morale at the factory. (6) Announce a dramatic increase in hourly wages for all factory workers at Foxconn. (7) Work through the HR department at Apple to implement Apple's Supplier Code of Conduct at all Foxconn operations. (8) Arrange a series of training workshops sponsored by Apple where the Foxconn managers will be given specific help in identifying and addressing the concerns of troubled employees, in order to prevent suicides and other destructive acts at Foxconn facilities. (9) Systematically reorganize the work units at Foxconn from the bottom up, so that workers can have a positive experience of being consulted about their work routines and how to improve them, in order to demonstrate Foxconn's commitment to respecting their human dignity.

Step 4: Eliminate the "sleaze," that is, anything that falls below the standards identified in Step 2. The second solution appears to be contrary to both Chinese law and basic morality. Numbers one, three, and four, arguably may be immoral, in the sense of being irresponsible, depending on how the facts of the case are understood.

Step 5: From the remaining options, choose the solution that makes the most business sense: Since five through nine have already been judged as morally acceptable, each should be examined for its practicality in achieving good business results. Some combination of seven, eight, and nine may be the best, but good business reasons would have to be given for this or any other choice that has met the ethical or "eliminate the sleaze" test.

Step 6: Implementation: The results of this exercise are meant to lead us through a thought experiment to integrate best moral practice with business decision-making by working out a plan of action (as detailed as realistically possible) for making appropriate changes in Foxconn's corporate culture. It must include recognizing the need for dialogue and personal appropriation of whatever code or statement of professional standards is to be honored from now on at Foxconn, with proper assistance from Apple. Drucker's own comments on implementation suggest that once we realize that this is where our decision-making will lead us, we will seek to enlist the support of everyone involved by enabling them to take ownership of the process of change that we are creating.

Once we have conducted the thought experiment, and in this case concluded that the best integration of ethics and business effectiveness would be for Apple and Foxconn to implement some of the proposals (seven, eight, and nine) considered in Step 3, it may be useful to update the case study to see what eventually did emerge as a solution to the problem of employee suicides at the Shenzhen facility. Two years after the wave of suicides, the cooperative effort to achieve compliance with Apple's Supplier Code of Conduct seems to have made substantial progress on all issues except excessive overtime work (Apple Inc. 2010). In 2012, Apple joined the Fair Labor Association (FLA), a nonprofit consortium of universities, civic associations, and businesses, which had already inspected over 1300 factories in Asia and Latin America (Greenhouse 2012). The FLA was hired to do audits of working conditions at the Foxconn plants, and after its initial report in 2012, Apple and Foxconn worked together and by December 2013 had "met 99 % of the conditions set out by the monitoring group" (James and Culpan 2013). The one area in which Foxconn's compliance was still deficient was in restrictions on working overtime hours, reported in three of its factories. Foxconn explained its failure as a result of labor shortages and employee turnover, at a time when the firm was striving to meet its production targets. Nevertheless, even here Foxconn made significant progress, reducing the average workweek to 52 or 53 h, while still exceeding the limit set in Chinese labor law that caps overtime hours at an average 36 h a month (Ibid).

The FLA report recommended that further steps be taken, including "closer monitoring of working hours on a weekly basis, revising policies and procedures, and better forecasting and production planning." These proposals follow up on the improvements that Foxconn instituted in the wake of the employee suicides: significant increases in wages, coupled with hiring counselors and stepped up planning for social activities for its employees, in close collaboration, as we reported in the case study, with various civic groups and governmental agencies in the Shenzhen area. As to the motives of employees who actively seek additional overtime work, the FLA observed: "Although the current starting wage is 20 % above the legal minimum wage, workers do not feel it is high enough to meet basic needs and provide discretionary income" (James and Culpan 2013). Clearly, Foxconn attempted to respond to the wave of suicides, on the assumption that these were not the result of some organized protest against poor wages and intolerable working conditions. Given the fact that the suicide rate among its employees was dramatically lower than the national average for China indicated by the World Health Organization (Mattimore 2010), Foxconn recognized that the problem at its plants was more subtle and pervasive than what the accusation of running a "sweatshop" would allow. Improving conditions at its plants would entail changing the culture, so that its workers—mostly migrants from poorer, rural areas in the western provinces of China—would come to understand that they were valued as partners and respected in their basic human dignity.

8.4 Ethical Reflection

It is very difficult, if not virtually impossible, to maintain one's basic human dignity when one is working at the kind of job that involves a lot of grime and sweat, breathing polluted air, enduring deafening noise from gargantuan machines and sheer exhaustion from trying to keep up with the incessant demands of bosses who seem to think of you as an expendable cog in a machine. Up until very recently, this is what most industrial workers had to face day in and day out across the planet. This is what it must have been like working in clothing factories like Rana Plaza in Bangladesh—or in China's coal mines, especially before the government began its campaign to improve health and safety conditions for mine workers.[1] The challenge of respecting human dignity under such conditions is immediate and obvious. It begins with showing care for the workers' basic physical needs, in a way that distinguishes them from animals or robots. Indeed, one way to describe the outrage of sweatshop conditions is to note how animals or robots—both of which may represent a greater investment than the wages paid to human beings—are better treated than the employees who tend them. If there is no difference between an employee and an animal or a machine used in production, then there is no human dignity.

As should be obvious from the case study, the challenge of respecting human dignity is far subtler at Foxconn, where at least a basic level of care for the workers' physical needs seems to have been met. But what of their other needs, which might be regarded as social or cultural, emotional or moral, and spiritual? In an enterprise

[1]When Stephan Rothlin published the predecessor to this book, namely, *Becoming a Top-Notch Player: Eighteen Rules of International Business Ethics*, in 2004, this chapter focused primarily on the working conditions in China's coal mines, where the country's growing need for energy had prompted a dramatic increase in coal mining, and an even more dramatic increase in mining accidents. Rothlin cited reports then available from government agencies in China documenting the tragic loss of life, and pleaded that the lives of mine workers and other dangerous occupations be shown an appropriate level of respect for their human dignity. As he asked at the time, "Why should a life extinguished in a mine in Muchongguo appear to be less worthy than a life destroyed in the deadly attacks of the World Trade Center in New York?" Since that time, there has been some progress in this area of mining safety, just as there has been in improved working conditions in Foxconn's plants. Nevertheless, much needs to be done. As Jill Joyce, senior policy and research advisor at the UK's Institution of Occupational Safety and Health, observed in a recent article, "China's appalling mining death rate—dealing with 'disorderly management'": "Profit is really important everywhere and we are always battling to say good health and safety can save you money. Try having an accident; that is expensive. If companies added it all up properly they would find its worth investing in safety" (Ibrahim 2012). But this is also precisely the point of Rothlin's rule for this chapter: "To increase productivity, provide safe and healthy working conditions." Respecting human dignity and workers' rights is not only virtuous, but it is also the key to productivity gains, good business practices, and increased profits.

so vast, with hundreds of thousands of employees devoting their working hours to high-tech manufacturing, what of their need for recognition, respect, and support in dealing with the unprecedented challenges of loneliness, and worry over the friends and relatives they had left behind, now so far from home? If we are to understand the responsibilities of employers to demonstrate proper care for their employees, we must examine more deeply the notion of human dignity, and the obligations that it imposes on each and every one of us.

8.4.1 On Human Dignity: Catholic Perspective

Like many key concepts in business ethics, the idea of "human dignity" at first may seem like another foreign import. It is easily dismissed as, at best, a reflection of the naïve idealism of foreign missionaries and, at worst, a subtle conspiracy to slow down China's economic development, by raising unrealistic expectations that are inconsistent with Asian values. There is no doubt about the religious origins of Western notions of human dignity. Both the Judaeo-Christian Bible and the traditions of Hellenistic philosophy assert a vision of human nature that is ultimately spiritual in character. The first chapter of the Book of Genesis, for example, presents a narrative of creation in which human beings—both men and women—are exalted as "made to the image and likeness of God" (Genesis 1:26). The Book of Psalms, the prayer book of the ancient Israelites' Temple in Jerusalem, contains this poetic expression, in a hymn of praise to the Creator:

> What is mankind that you are mindful of them, human beings that you care for them? You have made them a little lower than the angels and crowned them with glory and honor. You made them rulers over the works of your hands; you put everything under their feet… (Psalm 8: 4–6)

The Ten Commandments (Exodus 20:1–17), which the Bible honors as a summary of God's instructions for living together in harmony with Him and each other, spell out the obligations entailed by this God-given dignity. They are regarded as implicitly universal and meant for all human beings, insofar as all have but one Father and Lord.

Given the Israelites' experience of oppression in Egypt, the Bible is also very clear, as in Exodus 22: 22–24, on the obligations of the strong to protect the weak—usually symbolized in references to "the stranger, the widow, and the orphan in your midst." The prophet Malachi, for example, delivered this warning regarding the Day of Judgment:

> So I will come to put you on trial. I will be quick to testify against sorcerers, adulterers and perjurers, against those who defraud laborers of their wages, who oppress the widows and the fatherless, and deprive the foreigners among you of justice …says the Lord Almighty. (Malachi 3:5)

Further on, in the New Testament, Jesus describes the "Kingdom of Heaven" in a parable showing the King judging the nations, separating "the people one from another as a shepherd separates the sheep from the goats." The people who are invited to enjoy the blessings of his Kingdom are they who provided food to the hungry and drink to the thirsty, welcomed the stranger, clothed those in need, cared for the sick, and comforted those in prison. Each of these activities the King values as if they had been done to Himself: "Truly I tell you, whatever you did for one of the least of these brothers and sisters of mine, you did for me" (Matthew 25:40). Respecting the dignity of the weak—"the least of these brothers and sisters of mine"—is no different from showing respect for the King's own dignity. The obligation is incumbent upon all human beings in their dealings with one another, without regard to the status—high or low—of the people involved at any given moment.

In the nearly two millennia since the Bible reached its definitive form, words such as these have had a major impact on Western notions of human dignity and the basic respect that is due all persons. Since the nineteenth century, philosophers have identified this perspective as the tradition of "Personalism" and have witnessed its elaboration in Catholic social teaching. For more than a century, the Popes who have governed the Roman Catholic Church have written a series of letters outlining the meaning of human dignity in a world increasingly shaped by the forces of industrialization, modernization, and globalization. In their view, respecting human dignity naturally gives rise to a robust and comprehensive understanding of human rights (John XXIII, 1961 and 1963), as well as the political will required to implement them in all human institutions (Pius XI, 1931; Paul VI, 1967; John Paul II, 1991; Benedict XVI, 2005). What respecting human dignity means specifically in the relationship between businesses and their employees has been spelled out in detail (Leo XIII, 1891; John Paul II, 1981; Benedict XVI, 2005).

Laborem Exercens, John Paul II's systematic philosophical treatise on human labor, for example, reaffirms workers' right to employment, a right to a "just wage," that is, a single salary sufficient for maintaining a family, a right to adequate health care, a "right to rest," not just at regular intervals every Sunday, but also an annual vacation, a right to a pension and to "insurance for old age or in case of accidents at work" (1981, sections 18–19). The encyclical also endorses the trade union movement, as well as the workers' right to strike or other forms of collective action in defense of their rights, while also warning of the dangers of politicizing labor unions or using the strike weapon in ways that are contrary to the common good of society as a whole (1981, section 20). Each of these rights, however, is understood as enabling men and women to fulfill their basic "obligation" to work, in order to fulfill the Creator's purposes in this life (1981, section 16).

8.4.2 On Human Dignity: Confucian Perspective

Though Western notions of human dignity, and the natural rights entailed by it, do emerge from specifically European religious and philosophical traditions, similar concerns have been discovered and developed through a critical examination of other traditions, for example, Confucianism. "Although human dignity is explicitly a western concept," according to Zhang Qian, "it has a close Chinese correlate" (Zhang 2000). Zhang uses categories developed in Western moral philosophy to understand the interrelated Confucian notions of "*zun yan*" (尊严) and "*rén gé*" (人格), which taken together comprise both the descriptive and the prescriptive dimensions of the normative concept of human dignity. While both terms may be translated as "dignity," *rén gé* is descriptive and refers to the "possibilities" of human life, that is, the potential for moral excellence that is inherent in all human beings; "*zun yan*," on the other hand, is prescriptive insofar as everyone must strive to actualize these possibilities wherever they find themselves in life. The "*jūnzǐ*" (君子), as we learned in Chap. 2, represents the ideal convergence of these two dimensions. As Zhang points out, "a Confucian gentleman is a person who values his inborn virtues and takes care to preserve and develop what he believes to be noble in him," and in doing so he cultivates his dignity. But such cultivation is not, and cannot be reduced to a narrow preoccupation with one's own righteousness. "The gentleman's sense of justice presupposes his conscious recognition of the same basic worth in all other persons that command his respect. Respect for others is the natural extension of his self-respect…."

Understanding the fact of interdependence in human life naturally leads to a recognition of "the basic rule of reciprocity," or The Golden Rule, common to both Confucian (Analects 15: 24) and most other wisdom traditions, including the teachings of Jesus (Matthew 7:12). In Zhang's view, since "human dignity requires universal respect," the "*jūnzǐ*" (君子)—"recognizing the weaknesses and limitations in individual human beings"—will "concern himself with setting up proper laws and social institutions to secure such an end, that is, to prevent everyone from taking actions that would diminish anyone else's (and his/her own) dignity. These laws and institutions establish what are in nature private rights, because they protect the dignity of every citizen against private encroachment from others." "Although, historically, the Confucianists were not always conscious of the need for institutional balance of power," Zhang believes that developing "a constitution that can limit the powers of the state and social organizations, and provides basic rights to every individual against public encroachment" is implicit in the Confucian concept of dignity.

Since skeptics may object that Zhang's interpretation of the moral excellence embodied in the ideal of the "*jūnzǐ*" is out of touch with the basic needs and desires of ordinary people, for whom Confucian self-cultivation is an impossible dream, Zhang points out that Mencius well understood the dignity that even beggars try to maintain, "if someone throws food on the floor for him to pick up, as if the latter were feeding an animal" (Mencius, Book 6A: 10). Zhang drives home the relevance of this point in today's economy:

> As long as one has not lost the minimal sense of self-esteem, he would feel offended if his employer treats him merely as a machine for producing profit or government agents push him around rudely, as if they were taming a wild beast. In these situations one would feel humiliated because he thinks that he deserves better treatment than what a mere animal or machine receives. Although he may purport to ignore or even consciously reject the worth inherent in him, thereby degrading himself and inviting despises from others, his aversion

> against the maltreatment seems to imply that he still thinks himself to have some value. Thus, it can at least be argued that the sense of dignity is not limited to those cultivated persons; rather, it is universally found in every human being, even though the degree of such sentiment may vary. (Zhang 2000)

The cultivation of human dignity—our own and that of anyone else with whom we live and work—requires not just a personal commitment to the Golden Rule of reciprocity, but also a concern for the institutionalization of rights and obligations that will enable human dignity to be universally respected.

8.4.3 Human Dignity and the UN's Universal Declaration of Human Rights

One such attempt that continues to have global significance is the United Nations' Universal Declaration of Human Rights (UDHR), adopted by the UN General Assembly on December 10, 1948 (United Nations 2014). The Preamble of the UDHR begins with an assertion of "the inherent dignity and the equal and inalienable rights of all members of the human family" as "the foundation of freedom, justice and peace in the world." "Dignity" is specifically invoked twice in the Preamble and three times in the articles. In each instance it is paired with both human rights and the assumption, as in Article 1, that "all human beings are born free and equal in dignity and rights. They are endowed with reason and conscience and should act towards one another in a spirit of brotherhood." The other two articles in which "dignity" is explicit are Article 22, regarding economic, social, and cultural rights, and Article 23, which outlines the rights of workers:

> (1) Everyone has the right to work, to free choice of employment, to just and favorable conditions of work and to protection against unemployment.
> (2) Everyone, without any discrimination, has the right to equal pay for equal work.
> (3) Everyone who works has the right to just and favorable remuneration ensuring for himself and his family an existence worthy of human dignity, and supplemented, if necessary, by other means of social protection.
> (4) Everyone has the right to form and to join trade unions for the protection of his interests (UDHR, Article 23).

Not surprisingly, the rights of workers enshrined in the UDHR mirror those advocated by Catholic social teaching.

In order to understand China's posture toward the UDHR, we must begin with the fact that in the immediate aftermath of World War II, China was represented on UDHR drafting committee by Dr. Zhang Peng-chun (P. C. Chang) who served as the Vice-Chairman. As Chairman Eleanor Roosevelt recalled, Zhang insisted that UDHR must "reflect more than simply Western ideas" and should follow an "eclectic" approach that emphasized the practical consensus among its members in spite of their philosophical differences. Specifically, said Mrs. Roosevelt, Zhang "suggested that the Secretariat might well spend a few months studying the fundamentals of Confucianism" (United Nations 2014). Zhang's contribution in clarifying the

UDHR's underlying assumptions about human dignity has been widely recognized (Sun 2013). Zhang, for example, proposed including the word "conscience" in Article 1 of the Declaration, in order to reflect "the value of Confucian culture" (Luo 2011).

In a speech opening the 4th Beijing Forum on Human Rights, Luo Haocai further elaborated Zhang's perspective by outlining an inclusive approach to the world-views that converged toward practical consensus in the UDHR:

> Historically speaking, the spread and popularity of human rights concept has never been solely determined by a certain human rights culture but, on the contrary, reflected the exchange and integration of various cultures... [T]raditional Chinese culture has always stressed the coordination between one man and another and between man and society, advocated self-restraint and self-control and the philosophy 'don't do unto others what you don't want others do unto you'. It also emphasized collective awareness and social responsibility. It is the historical explanation and cultural roots why currently we stress the unity of rights and obligation in human rights protection and why we place great importance on collective human rights (Luo 2011).

Luo's point is to clarify the cultural basis for China's participation in the world's ongoing dialogue about dignity and human rights. The consequences of China's participation have become increasing clear since the Peoples' Republic (PRC) was admitted to membership in the UN in 1971. Beginning in 1981, China has ratified five of the major international conventions on human rights, and signed another one (Mo 2007).[2] In light of this historical background, the question for us is not whether the human rights of workers are recognized in China, but how they are reflected in China's labor laws.

8.4.4 China's Labor Contract Law

A review of the successive revisions of the Labor Contract Law of the PRC, especially of 2007 and 2013, indicate that workers' rights are well grounded in them, with an increasingly greater scope afforded for labor unions to work with both employers and the government toward more effective compliance. It is significant that labor contracts are the primary vehicle for fulfilling these rights, since the assumption is that the employer-employee relationship is voluntary and rational, that is, based on mutual self-interest. The reform of the Law is meant to extend the

[2] Mo Jihong, a Research Fellow at the Chinese Academy of the Social Sciences, reported that there are seven such major international conventions on human rights, starting with the "International Covenant on Economic, Social and Cultural Rights (ICESCR)," which China signed in 1998, and the "International Covenant on Civil and Political Rights (ICCPR)," which China ratified in 2001. Mo's report is especially useful in detailing the process by which such conventions inform the ongoing legislative process within the National Peoples' Congress and other government agencies. China, to be sure, is very concerned to protect its own national sovereignty and thus the process of implementing these conventions is complex, particularly when there are any apparent contradictions between existing Chinese law and rights detailed in the UN conventions. For further details, see Mo 2007.

use of labor contracts to as many workers as possible, so that the various ways in which workers have been abused in the past can be progressively reduced. The 98 Articles of the 2007 revision of the Law contain no references to human dignity or human rights as such; however, it does stipulate in detail the "legitimate rights and interests" (Article 1) of employees as well as employers that ought to be acknowledged in the contract. For example, Article 17 spells out the "mandatory terms" that must be contained in any valid contract including, among other things, "the term of the labor contract; the scope of work and place of work; working hours, rest and leave; labor compensation; social insurance; labor protection, working conditions and protection against occupational hazards," and any other provisions required by relevant Chinese laws (National People's Congress 2007).

The Law also stipulates the conditions that would invalidate a labor contract (Article 26—which highlights typical ways in which the voluntary character of employment is violated: "through fraud, coercion or exploitation of the other party's disadvantageous position"), and the employees' rights to terminate their contracts (Article 38—which stipulates the employees' legitimate grievances, among which are failure "to provide work protection or working conditions as stipulated in the labor contract"; failure "to pay labor compensation in full or on time"; and failure "to pay the social insurance premium for the employee in accordance with the law." Of course, the employers' rights are also listed (Article 39), but the main point of the law is clearly to protect workers from abuse:

> If an Employer uses violence, threats or unlawful restriction of personal freedom to force an employee to work, or if an Employer forces or instructs an employee to perform dangerous tasks which would endanger his personal safety in violation of rules or regulations, the employee may terminate his labor contract immediately without giving any prior notice to the Employer (Article 38).

The law also encourages the formation of labor unions and assumes that they will normally work with the government and businesses to "establish a tri-partite mechanism for the coordination of employment relationships" (Article 5), and will "assist and guide workers in the conclusion and performance of labor contracts" and "establish a collective consultations mechanism with the Employer in order to protect the lawful rights and interests of the workers" (Article 6).

The systematic acknowledgment of the role of labor unions in employment relationships made the revised Labor Contract Law highly controversial among both Chinese businesses and multinational corporations operating in China. Their unsuccessful efforts to persuade the National People's Congress to water down the legislation were premised on the idea that if the protection of workers' rights were extended with significant new compliance measures, that foreign companies would leave China and thus "reduce employment opportunities for PRC workers" and "negatively impact the PRC's competitiveness and appeal as a destination for foreign investment" (Brecher et al. 2006). But as Xiaoying Li documented in a study measuring the impact of the revised Labor Contract Law, "the new Law increased the percentage of workers with written contracts, raised social insurance coverage, reduced violations of workers rights and wage arrears, and was positively associated with the likelihood that a firm would be unionized, but had no discernible effect on wages." The Amendments attached in 2013 went even further to protect migrant workers who have been victimized by labor outsourcing arrangements that have the effect, if not the intent, of evading 2008's reform of the Labor Contract Law. By providing stricter limitations on outsourcing through local employment agencies, the Amendments mandate "equal pay for equal work" for outsourced workers, as well as require local agencies to operate within a regulated licensing system (Grams, Pan, and Goldner 2013). Here, too, the trend is to uphold workers' rights by bringing all Chinese workers into the new system of Labor Contract Law.

In light of these promising developments in China, no one can dismiss concerns for the dignity and rights of workers as if they were a foreign import, forced upon Chinese employers and employees by international agencies seeking to impose Western values and practices. China's ratification of the United Nations' human rights conventions has become the starting point for a legal reform that actually is making a difference in the lives of workers. The convergence of Confucian and Western values with regard to human dignity is a fact with genuine consequences not only for China's growing commitment to the rule of law, but also for international business ethics. Complying with China's laws, and cooperating fully with various agencies involved in their implementation, is the surest path toward meeting the standards of international business ethics.

8.5 Conclusion

Ten years ago, when Rothlin formulated the rule invoked in this chapter, the hope of making substantial progress in China toward recognizing workers' rights founded upon human dignity may have seemed like an impossible dream. How might business people operating in China be persuaded that it was not only morally right but also profitable to implement policies reflecting a concern to protect workers' rights? Rothlin's rule, "To increase productivity, provide safe and healthy working conditions," was meant to point out the practical consequences of such policies. Increased productivity is the only sure way to increase profits; and yet the failure to provide safe and healthy working conditions eventually imposes costs that can only diminish profits, as productivity decreases, as workers become discouraged by the deaths of their comrades, or sick and hobbled by injuries not properly attended to. Under such circumstances, work becomes a season in Hell, and eventually workers in their misery will retaliate in ways that are still more costly to those who victimize them. The case to be made for fulfilling workers' rights, then, is not ideological or political, but simply a matter of enlightened self-interest. If your business plan can succeed only by treating workers as if they were slaves or robots, then you had better come up with a better business plan. Those familiar with slavery, on the one hand, or high-tech automation, on the other, should know that complying with the legitimate rights of workers actually is cheaper than either alternative.

When we return from our ethical reflections to the problems faced by employees and managers at the Foxconn plant, we must be humble enough to admit that moral clarity alone will not be sufficient. An impartial observer is likely to conclude that neither human dignity nor workers rights were systematically and consistently violated at the plant. Especially, in light of the tragic suicides that occurred there in 2010, it appears that the challenge of addressing the cultural, psychological, and spiritual needs of Foxconn's migrant workforce is far more subtle than simply assuring that all the terms of their labor contracts are in order. However welcome and promising they may be, reforming China's Labor Contract Law provides no guarantee that such tragedies will never happen again. But what such reforms do contribute, nevertheless, is important. They are one more element in creating an economic culture in which the dignity of workers and their rights are respected as a matter of course. Absent such a culture, the obligation to respect everyone's human dignity is reduced to a matter of personal conscience, which all too often means that when genuine respect occurs it is an indication of exemplary moral leadership, which is all too rare in the world as we know it. The Law puts a floor under our moral aspirations. Though we may already be inclined to do the right thing, the Law reinforces our good motivation. We now know the price to be paid, if we fail to do it, and do it well.

References

Apple Inc. (2006). Report of iPod manufacturing. Retrieved on November 18, 2011 from http://www.apple.com/hotnews/ipodreport/

Apple Inc. (2010). Apple supplier conduct code. Retrieved on November 18, 2011 from http://images.apple.com/supplierresponsibility/pdf/Supplier_Code_of_Conduct_V3_3.pdf

Apple Inc. (2011). Apple supplier responsibility 2011 progress report. Retrieved on November 18, 2011 from http://images.apple.com/supplierresponsibility/pdf/Apple_SR_2011_Progress_Report.pdf

Brandon, M. (2006, June 21). Discrepancies in Apple supplier code of conduct. *Sustainable Log*. Retrieved February 25, 2012 from http://sustainablelog.blogspot.com/2006/06/discrepancies-in-apple-supplier-code.html

Brecher, J., Smith B., & Costello, T. (2006, November–December). Multinationals to China: No new labor rights. *Multinational Monitor, 27*(6). Retrieved on May 1, 2014 from http://www.multinationalmonitor.org/mm2006/112006/brecher.html

Burke, J. (2013, June 6). Bangladesh factory collapse leaves trail of shattered lives. *The Guardian*. Retrieved on December 30, 2014 from http://www.theguardian.com/world/2013/jun/06/bangladesh-factory-building-collapse-community

Chen, S., & Liu, H. (2006, June 17). Foxconn front responded to the report of sweatshop. *Shenzhen Economic Daily*. Retrieved November 21, 2011 from http://news.sznews.com/content/2006-06/17/content_156939.htm

China Economy. (2010, April 11). Foxconn firstly apologized for consecutive jumping-off-building. Retrieved on November 18, 2011 from http://www.ce.cn/xwzx/gnsz/gdxw/201004/11/t20100411_21258552.shtml

Drucker, P. (1986). Making decisions. In *The practice of management*. New York: HarperCollins/Perennial Library.

Duhigg, C., & Barboza, D. (2012, January 25). In China, human costs are built into an iPad. *New York Times*. Retrieved on April 17, 2014 from http://www.nytimes.com/2012/01/26/business/ieconomy-apples-ipad-and-the-human-costs-for-workers-in-china.html

Fengping. (2010). *The debate between the death of employees in Foxconn and the sweatshop*. Retrieved on November 21, 2011 from http://finance.ifeng.com/opinion/fengping/28.shtml

Foxconn Technology Group. (n.d.). *Group profile*. Retrieved on November 18, 2011 from http://www.foxconn.com.cn/GroupProfile.html

Grams, R., Pan, L., & Goldner, A. (2013, February 6). Amendments to China labor contract law will force employers to reevaluate their use of labor outsourcing. *Benesch Attorneys at Law: Resources: Client Bulletins*. Retrieved on April 30, 2014 from http://www.beneschlaw.com/Amendments-to-China-Labor-Contract-Law-will-Force-Employers-to-Re-evaluate-their-Use-of-Labor-Outsourcing-02-06-2013/

Greenhouse, Stephen. (2012, February 13). Critics question record of monitor selected by apple. *New York Times*. Retrieved on April 22, 2014 from http://www.nytimes.com/2012/02/14/technology/critics-question-record-of-fair-labor-association-apples-monitor.html

Ibrahim, O. (2012, October 31). *China's appalling mining death rate – dealing with 'disorderly' management*. Mining-technology.com. Retieved on April 22, 2014 from http://www.mining-technology.com/features/featurechina-mine-death-rate-coal-safety/

Information Times. (2006, August 31). *The compensation declined to 1 RMB, the freezing of two journalists' asset removed*. Retrieved November 21, 2011 from http://informationtimes.dayoo.com/html/2006-08/31/content_14885487.htm

James, S., & Culpan, T. (2013, December 13). Apple supplier Foxconn fails hours law amid improvement. *Bloomberg*. Retrieved on April 22, 2014 from http://www.bloomberg.com/news/2013-12-12/apple-supplier-foxconn-fails-china-labor-law-amid-99-compliance.html

Jina, G. (2011, June 30). Worker suddenly died when showering, the factory refused to supply the working record. *Orient Morning Post*. Retrieved on November 18, 2011 from http://www.dfdaily.com/html/33/2011/6/30/624564.shtml

Klowden, T. (2006, June 12). iPod city: Apple criticized for factory conditions. *Mail on Sunday*. Retrieved on November 21, 2011 from http://arstechnica.com/old/content/2006/06/7039.ars. The story on which Klowden based her report was originally published as "The stark reality of iPod's Chinese factories" in the *Mail on Sunday*, last updated August 18, 2006. Retrieved on February 23, 2012 from http://www.dailymail.co.uk/news/article-401234/The-stark-reality-iPods-Chinese-factories.html

Liu, Z., & Yang, J. (2006, August 31) The beginning and end of the case: Journalists were claimed for sky-high compensation. *Beijing News Online*. Retrieved on November 21, 2011 from http://news.thebeijingnews.com/0547/2006/0831/011@205698.htm

Luo, H. (2011, September 22). Different cultures show same respect for human dignity. *China Daily USA*. Retrieved on May 1, 2014 from http://usa.chinadaily.com.cn/opinion/2011-09/22/content_13764204.htm

Mattimore, Patrick. (2010, May 21). Media badly misplaying Foxconn suicides. *Peoples Daily Online*. Retrieved on February 23, 2012 from http://english.people.com.cn/90001/90780/91345/6994665.html

McNulty, S. (2006, August 17). *Apple issues report on iPod manufacturing*. [Web log comment]. Retrieved on November 18, 2011 from http://www.tuaw.com/2006/08/17/apple-issues-report-on-ipod-manufacturing/

Mo, J. (2007, December 10). International human rights conventions in China. *China Human Rights Magazine (China Society for Human Rights Studies), 7*(2), 2008. Retrieved on April 20, 2014 from http://www.chinahumanrights.org/CSHRS/Magazine/Text/t20080604_349282.htm

National Peoples Congress. (2007). Labor contract law of the Peoples Republic of China. Lehman, Lee & Xu Resource Center. Retrieved on April 30, 2014 from http://www.lehmanlaw.com/resource-centre/laws-and-regulations/labor/labor-contract-law-of-the-peoples-republic-of-china.html

Sun, P. (2013). *The contribution of P. C. Chang as typical Chinese wisdom to the declaration*. HR Stories (China Society for Human Rights Studies). Retrieved on May 1, 2014 from http://www.chinahumanrights.org/Messages/Hrpics/09/t20131217_1128321.htm

United Nations. (2014). *The Universal declaration of human rights*. Retrieved on April 25, 2014 from http://www.un.org/en/documents/udhr/

Wang, C., & Zhan, Y. (2010, May 25). 11 consecutive suicides in Foxconn, government got involved to investigate. *Xinhua News Online*. Retrieved on November 18, 2011 from http://news.xinhuanet.com/2010-05/25/c_12140632.htm

Wei, X. (2010). *Inside story of Foxconn*. Chongqing: Chongqing Press.

Xu, M. (2007). *Guo Taiming and Foxconn*. Beijing: China Citic Press.

Zhang, Q. (2000, September). The idea of human dignity in classical Chinese philosophy: A reconstruction of Confucianism II. *Journal of Chinese Philosophy 27*(3), 299–330. Retrieved on April 13, 2014 from http://article.chinalawinfo.com/Article_Detail.asp?ArticleID=32900

Zhang, D. (2006a, March 30). Guo Taiming: Legend of foundry king. *Sinafinance*. Retrieved on November 21, 2011 from http://finance.sina.com.cn/leadership/crz/20060330/15532461685.shtml

Zhang, H. (2006b, September 15). Foxconn case: The First Finance was still loser. *Boraid Online*. Retrieved on November 21, 2011 from http://www.boraid.com/DARTICLE3/list.asp?id=61600

Chapter 9
Employees: Discrimination and Sexual Harassment

"If you act against discrimination, you will increase your productivity and profitability" (Stephan Rothlin, *Eighteen Rules for Becoming a Top Notch Player*, 2004)

9.1 Prelude

The scandal involving Dominique Strauss-Kahn, at that time the director of the International Monetary Fund (IMF) and a possible candidate for the presidency of France, provides the basis for a case study on sexual harassment and discrimination in the workplace. As in the previous chapter, where considerations of human dignity prompted an investigation of workers' rights and obligations, the major issue here is whether incidents of sexual harassment and discrimination—starting with a recognition of their existence in the workplace, moral attitudes toward them, and whether management's responsibilities toward a firm's employees—should also be regarded as a violation of these standards. Given the diverging attitudes found in various cultures, should international business ethics be concerned about sexual harassment and discrimination in the workplace? We believe not only that they should be concerned but also that the concern is growing even in Asian businesses, NGOs, and government agencies. In order to situate this problem in an Asian setting, this chapter will present discussions of it Hong Kong and China. It turns out that the expectation that the workplace ought to be a safe space where employees—at whatever level of responsibility—should not be subjected to sexual harassment and discrimination is growing around the world and indeed is one sign of the positive consequences of globalization. It can no longer be dismissed as simply another American obsession.

S. Rothlin, D. McCann, *International Business Ethics*,
DOI 10.1007/978-3-662-47434-1_9

9.2 Case Study: A Rising Star Falls to Earth: Moral Leadership and Sexual Harassment

9.2.1 Abstract

In May 2011, Dominique Strauss-Kahn was arrested by New York City police for allegedly committing various criminal sexual acts against a maid at his hotel, including attempted rape, at a time when he was there on business for the IMF. The events brought Strauss-Kahn under intense scrutiny. Not only were his decisions at the IMF investigated, but his leadership capabilities and personal life were also opened to public dissection. However, the ethical issues presented in this case go beyond Strauss-Kahn's admitted "moral failure". The Strauss-Kahn case provides the opportunity to outline more specific organizational policies and procedures regarding sexual harassment as well as the need for moral leadership among business executives who must enforce such policies and procedures on their employees.

9.2.2 Keywords/Phrases

IMF, Strauss-Kahn, sexual harassment, moral leadership.

9.2.3 Icarus Soars at the IMF

Dominique Strauss-Kahn is a French lawyer, economist, and politician known for his persuasive personality and innovative thinking. He obtained a PhD in economics from the University of Paris and holds degrees in law, business administration, political studies, and statistics (IMF 2011). Strauss-Kahn formally began his political career in 1981 when he was appointed Deputy Commissioner of the Economic Planning Agency for the Socialist Party. He served in that role until he was first elected to parliament in 1986. Strauss-Kahn led France's Finance Commission (1988–1991), worked as Minister of Industry and International Trade (1991–1993), and was appointed Minister of Economy, Finance and Industry in 1997 (IMF 2011). In this position, Strauss-Kahn directed the introduction of the euro and represented France in a number of international financial institutions including the International Monetary Fund (IMF). Strauss-Kahn's impressive resume assisted his rapid rise in the ranks of French politicians, as he was reelected three times to the National Assembly between 2001 and 2007.

In November 2007, Strauss-Kahn became the tenth managing director of the International Monetary Fund (IMF 2011). In a statement upon his appointment, Strauss-Kahn maintained, "I am determined to pursue without delay the reforms needed for the IMF to make financial stability serve the international community while fostering growth and employment" (BBC 2007). In the wake of the global financial crisis, Strauss-Kahn was considered the Socialist Party's best chance for winning the 2012 presidential elections. Although never officially announced as the Socialist nominee, polls showed Strauss-Kahn leading the other Socialist candidate, Francois Hollande, as well as the incumbent, Nicolas Sarkozy (Pilkington and Chrisafis 2012).

9.2.4 *Icarus Falls from the Sky*

On the evening of May 13, 2011, Dominique Strauss-Kahn checked into a $3,000 per night suite at the Sofitel hotel in New York City as one of the world's most powerful men, but by the next afternoon, he was in custody as a common criminal suspect, arrested, and indicted for attempted rape, sexual abuse, and criminal sexual acts along with unlawful imprisonment of another (Pilkington 2011). On May 14, 2011, Nafissatou Diallo, a maid at Sofitel, entered Strauss-Kahn's suite to make up his room. Diallo alleges that when she entered, Strauss-Kahn sexually assaulted and attempted to rape her.

Nafissatou Diallo, an immigrant refugee from Guinea in West Africa, had worked at Sofitel for 3 years prior to her encounter with Strauss-Kahn (*Newsweek* 2011). When the media released her name, Diallo was portrayed as a hard working single mother and devout Muslim. However, as more facts came to light, Diallo's credibility came into question. It became known that Diallo had fabricated an alleged arrest as well as a gang rape in Guinea that allowed her to seek asylum in the USA (Melnick 2011).

Strauss-Kahn appeared in court on May 16, where Diallo gave a detailed account of the sexual assault. Strauss-Kahn pleaded not guilty on all counts. However, on May 24, the DNA test results found that the semen on Diallo's clothing matched the DNA sample supplied by Strauss-Kahn (Pilkington 2011). Even though the DNA gave irrefutable evidence that a sexual encounter had taken place in the Manhattan Sofitel, the prosecution chose not to risk going to trial given Diallo's complicated background, contradictory testimony, and potential lack of credibility before a jury, especially when weighed against the word of an international figure like Strauss-Kahn (*Newsweek* 2011). The criminal case against Strauss-Kahn was dismissed.

It was not until September 2011 that Strauss-Kahn admitted that his involvement with Diallo was a "moral failure" which cost him his chance at the French presidency (*New York Times* 2012). Nevertheless, as the furor over the alleged rape in New York had begun to dissipate, Strauss-Kahn became the focal point of a number of other accusations of sexual misconduct.

9.2.5 *Moral Leadership and Its Exercise at the IMF*

Leaders define the organizations they guide, in personality, purpose, and priorities. Good leaders often help to develop good companies, and moral leaders are expected to cultivate moral excellence in the companies they direct. Moral companies address stakeholder concerns like consumer safety, environmental protection, and positive conditions of employment. German philosopher Gerhold Becker defines moral leadership as a character trait "extending beyond individual selfishness… [in which a] commitment to ethics must not have merely instrumental value, but intrinsic value" (Becker 2009). As social creatures, we can only realize our full potential when we consider the interests of others as well as ourselves. Therefore, offering decent wages, providing safe equipment, and fostering respectful treatment of employees are essential components for judging the effectiveness of moral leadership in business. Becker also recommends that organizations must have a system of "checks and balances" so that leaders do not accumulate too much power without accountability (Becker 2009).

Toward the end of World War II, the IMF was created as part of the Bretton Woods system governing international financial and monetary affairs (US Department of State). The IMF's "fundamental mission is to help ensure stability in the international system" (IMF 2012b). Currently, the IMF serves the needs and interests of 188 member countries, constituting "an organization…working to foster global monetary cooperation, secure financial stability, facilitate international trade, promote high employment and sustainable economic growth, and reduce poverty" (IMF 2012b).

Various governing bodies carry out these lofty objectives. Governance at the IMF consists of two separate supervisory boards and the position of managing director. The board of governors is comprised of two representatives from each member country and is responsible for "approving quota increases, special drawing right allocations, the admittance of new members, compulsory withdrawal of members, and amendments to the Articles of Agreement and By-Laws," but in reality, most of its duties are delegated to the IMF's executive board (Independent Evaluation Office of the IMF 2012). While the executive board's 24 directors are collectively responsible for the daily management of the Fund, it is the managing director that leads the Fund in policy and precedent.

The Fund's legal status is complicated by the international character of its governance structure; although it is based in Washington DC, not all US laws apply to the organization. Furthermore, directors are appointed by their countries of origin and, therefore, must balance the loyalty they have toward their home governments with their loyalty to the IMF (Bowley 2011). A retired director, who sat on the executive board, told *The Washington Post* on condition of anonymity that the issue of loyalty is a "widespread concern. [Directors serving on the executive board] want a favorable report [for their countries]. Then they are supposed to oversee the managing director and the functioning of the institution. There is an inevitable tension. They are structurally dependent on the managing director" (Schneider 2011). Based on the IMF's stated mission, how would you prioritize the duties of the executive board and managing director toward their own countries and the IMF's membership as a whole? Will the IMF's leadership be credible and effective if they are known to be "balancing" their loyalties?

When Strauss-Kahn became managing director of the IMF in 2007, the Fund was an organization in search of relevance after being criticized for its ineffective economic policies. Strauss-Kahn helped restore the IMF's influence and prestige. In 2007, the outstanding loans to developing countries totaled US$10 billion, but by 2011 under Strauss-Kahn's leadership, outstanding loans amounted to US$84 billion. During those 5 years, the IMF's total capital quadrupled from US$250 billion to US$1 trillion (Weisbrot 2011). Furthermore, Strauss-Kahn played a leading role in attempts to improve Europe's crumbling economies, which made him a rising star on the global stage (*Newsweek* 2011). In fact, because of his preliminary efforts to restructure the Greek economy, Strauss-Kahn was named one of the world's 100 most influential people in 2010 (Elliott 2010). Strauss-Kahn's position at the IMF increased the momentum of several reforming initiatives in global financial markets. In 2009 during the midst of the financial crisis, for example, the IMF made US$283 billion worth of financing available to member countries, with no policy conditions attached.

However, as Strauss-Kahn attempted to lead the IMF into a new age of international economic development, a review of 41 IMF agreements during 2009 found that 31 of the policies were "pro-cyclical" (Weisbrot 2011). Pro-cyclical agreements are fiscal and monetary policies designed to have no impact one way or another on the cycle of economic activity. When economic activity is slowing, pro-cyclical policies do nothing to overcome the decline in economic growth, making it difficult for countries to lift themselves out of recession. Under Strauss-Kahn's reforms, countries still had to abide by IMF conditions such as deregulation and privatization. Critics point to the case of Latvia, where the IMF has been characterized as "overly harsh" for forcing the government to increase spending on IMF programs from 21 to 25 % of the budget (Andersen 2009). Economists who questioned the IMF's unwillingness to engage in "countercyclical" policy making denounced Strauss-Kahn for "applying the medieval economic medicine of 'bleeding the patient'" (Weisbrot 2011). What responsibility did Strauss-Kahn have to the international community because of the power given to him by the IMF to set policy? When his advisers and critics disagree over the most effective policy for stimulating economic growth, how is he to determine which way to proceed?

9.2.6 Institutional Failure at the IMF?

Strauss-Kahn's infamous arrest in New York brought unwanted publicity to the IMF in all its policies and not just on its management of international monetary and financial affairs. Despite Strauss-Kahn's resignation in the aftermath of the Sofitel incident, *The New York Times* published an article titled "At IMF, men on prowl and women on guard" that criticized the Fund's policies on sexual harassment and discrimination (Appelbaum and Stolberg 2011).

With new inquiries into IMF's organizational policies came the reemergence of a 2008 sexual harassment accusation against Strauss-Kahn, made by a former IMF economist, Piroska Nagy. Although the affair was determined to be consensual, Nagy claims she felt pressured because of Strauss-Kahn's high profile. Nagy describes the situation: "I was not prepared for the advances of the IMF director general. I didn't know what to do … I felt damned if I did, damned if I didn't" (Beattie 2011). Nagy broke off the relationship with Strauss-Kahn when her husband discovered the affair. Soon after, the IMF offered terminated employees an attractive severance package, and Nagy used the opportunity to leave the Fund.

The IMF's internal policy at the time stated, "Intimate personal relationships between supervisors and subordinates do not, in themselves, constitute harassment" (*World Watch* 2011). In this regard, the IMF's policy seemed to make allowances for a type of relationship that is usually not tolerated by organizations in the USA (*World Watch* 2011). By contrast, the World Bank—the IMF's sister organization—defines any relationship between superiors and subordinates "a de facto conflict of interest," which must be disclosed immediately (Schneider 2011). Nevertheless, as Masood Ahmed, a spokesman for the IMF, pointed out, if allegations of sexual harassment are made, "particularly relating to senior management, [they] need to be investigated" (Shipman 2008). Thus, the IMF hired a law firm, Morgan, Lewis & Bockius, to investigate Nagy's complaints and relationship with Strauss-Kahn.

The primary concern of the investigation was to establish whether Nagy received any promotions due to her relationship with Strauss-Kahn (Thomas 2011). The IMF executive board determined that Strauss-Kahn did not abuse his power by entering into an affair with Nagy, although his actions were deemed inappropriate. The results left the impression that senior management at the IMF was exempt from credible scrutiny of their actions, even when a complaint was reported. In a letter to the investigators, Nagy wrote that Strauss-Kahn was "a man with a problem that may make him ill-equipped to lead an institution where women work under his command" (Thomas 2011).

IMF employees acknowledge that personal relationships are bound to form in an organization where colleagues travel for weeks at a time and work in unsupervised environments (Appelbaum and Stolberg 2011). Susan Schadler spent 32 years at the IMF, rising to deputy director of the European Department before leaving in 2007. Schadler recounts her understanding of the situation: "There is this implicit culture that [sexual advances] weren't really seen as something that the fund is going to worry about…I think that's what bothered women" (Appelbaum and Stolberg 2011).

9.2.7 New Directions: Recovering the Right to Lead

When Frenchwoman Christine Lagarde replaced Strauss-Kahn as the managing director of IMF, she agreed as part of her contract to have one-on-one meetings with the IMF's ethics chief, Virginia Canter (Schneider 2011). Lagarde's contract also introduced new terminology to the description of managing director: "You shall strive to avoid even the appearance of impropriety in your conduct" (Schneider 2011) and promise to "observe the highest standards of ethical conduct, consistent with the values of integrity, impartiality, and discretion" (IMF 2011). The language of Lagarde's clause contrasts with that of Strauss-Kahn's 2007 contract, which stated that as managing director, he should "avoid any conflict of interest, or the appearance of such a conflict" (Wearden 2011).

A concern for the IMF as well as other multinational organizations is how to manage the cultural differences and implied meanings reflected in the formulation of policies covering issues such as sexual harassment. French law defines sexual harassment as an exploitation of hierarchical power (Saguy 2001), meaning that harassment occurs if and only if the sexual relationship involves an abuse of power, such as the superior's bestowing upon or withholding a promotion from the subordinate involved. This was the standard applied when Morgan, Lewis & Bockius investigated Strauss-Kahn's affair with Nagy. By contrast, in the USA, sexual harassment has a much broader meaning. The Equal Employment Opportunities Commission (EEOC) defined sexual harassment as any "unwelcome sexual advances, requests for sexual favors, and other verbal or physical conduct of sexual nature" (Saguy 2001), whether any abuse of hierarchical power is evident or not. Besides "quid pro quo" exploitative relationships, sexual harassment under EEOC guidelines also includes consensual activities that create a "hostile work environment" for third parties not directly involved in the relationship. The difference between French and American law is one of many examples of why organizations must form some kind of consensus on what constitutes sexual harassment.

In the wake of the Strauss-Kahn case, the IMF worked hard to mend its reputation by developing stricter guidelines for ethical conduct in the workplace. Coincidentally, an appraisal of ethical guidelines for IMF employees was in progress before Strauss-Kahn's resignation. An ethics committee had been established in 2000, but underwent a thorough restructuring after Strauss-Kahn's affair with Nagy surfaced. In fact, prior to April 2008, the ethics committee had not met to discuss a single case of ethical misconduct, and members of the ethics committee "did not receive training on how to conduct an effective investigation of alleged misconduct" (Chelsky 2008). These issues were raised in a report compiled at the request of the executive board to address loopholes in the IMF's governing system.

Since the release of the report, Canter—the IMF's new ethics chief—has addressed the issues raised by establishing a new program of ethics education internally and a formal written protocol for dealing with sexual harassment cases. In 2008, an integrity hotline was launched to encourage whistle-blowing among employees. The ethics office also publishes annual reports detailing employee complaints, in order to increase the Fund's transparency and accountability to its stakeholders (IMF 2012c).

By October 2011, Canter's mandatory ethics training program for staff was established, covering topics such as bullying, sexual harassment, and intimidation (Schneider 2011). The IMF's new Code of Conduct regards sexual harassment and discrimination with what the *Financial Times* says is a much tougher approach than before (Harding 2011). The new Code of Conduct and ethics training are company-wide devices used to support moral leadership throughout the organization. With the new Code in place, employees and management must disclose any relationship between a superior and subordinate, and anyone subjected to sexual harassment must report it.

All IMF staff are required to sign a contract that commits them to abide by the IMF's ethics guidelines and Code of Conduct. However, despite the progress made with the Code of Conduct, men and women sitting on the IMF's executive board are exempt from the regulations in place for monitoring employee misconduct. "There are a lot of controls in place when it comes to the staff [at the IMF], but not for the leadership" explained Katrina Campbell, a New York-based corporate ethics expert (Freedman, Freeman 2011). In fact, the newly developed ethical advisor is not at liberty to investigate members of the board. The IMF's Independent Evaluation Office (IEO) described the situation: "Neither the policies nor the structure of the Fund encourages any person to report misconduct by an executive director or managing director to any authority" (Walden 2011). Instead, the executive board is responsible for the conduct of its own members as well as the managing director. Its internal regulatory system works with the board's ethics committee, although what exactly they do is confidential (Bowley 2011). Do you believe Canter's program will be successful throughout the company? How can members of the executive board be held to the same level of accountability as employees, if they are not subject to the same rules?

As the furor over the Strauss-Kahn affair began to dissipate, critics resumed airing their concerns about IMF leadership, since Lagarde marked the 11th consecutive appointment of a European to the post of managing director, five of whom have been French nationals. European favoritism has become an increasingly controversial issue among IMF member countries, specifically the BRICS nations (Brazil, Russia, India, China, South Africa), which have the largest developing economies. In 2011, the BRICS nations released a statement demanding transparency in the appointment of managing directors. They called the tradition of appointing Europeans to the post "obsolete" and argued that it undermined the legitimacy of the Fund. Instead, appointment to the position should be based on merit (Handley 2011). The Fund, which was created so that wealthy nations could support the economies of developing nations, seems to be working in reverse, when executive leadership remains an exclusively European preserve. Is it reasonable that IMF relies on European countries, most recently France, as it guides developing economies? What aspects of moral leadership and transparency should be considered when electing new leaders? How, if at all, should country of origin be taken into consideration when assessing the merits of various candidates for the post of IMF managing director?

9.2.8 Summary

Genuine leadership is founded on moral principles. Therefore, Strauss-Kahn's alleged assault upon Diallo was not just a "moral failure" on his part, but also a reflection of his leadership. Strauss-Kahn's failure to control his apparent sexual addiction not only cost him the French presidency but also shed light on the IMF's lax sexual harassment policies and an organizational culture that allows its leadership to exempt itself from accountability to standards with which all other IMF employees must comply. Within the current IMF governance structure, members of the executive board are not held accountable for their sexual advances toward employees, unless they constitute a conflict of interest.

When a company's governance structure is supported by morals, leaders are held accountable for their decisions (Becker 2009). If subordinates are unable to address harassment concerns with their superiors, then the implicit moral culture of an organization is compromised. Organizations must employ ethical standards that are mandatory for every level of the organization.

Until the Sofitel scandal, the male-dominated professional sphere in which Strauss-Kahn traveled viewed his reputation with women as an amusing vice (*British Press* 2011). In fact, the executive board forgave Strauss-Kahn, asking for little more than an apology for his affair with Nagy. Given the chance, would you restructure IMF's executive board? How would you respond to the BRICS nations' demand for the transparent election of future managing directors? What aspects of institutional oversight would you add to its policy on sexual harassment and the handling of employee complaints? Should these be different for different countries?

9.3 Case Study Discussion

Making a connection between the scandals involving Dominique Strauss-Kahn and the challenge for businesses dealing with issues of sexual harassment and sexual discrimination is not straightforward. As discussed in international business ethics, sexual harassment and sexual discrimination are problems that occur within the employment relationship. They are to be distinguished from broader social concerns, on the one hand, over the incidence of sexual violence or, on the other hand, the persistence of sexist attitudes, which may or may not show up at work. Strauss-Kahn's alleged sexual assault on Nafissatou Diallo at the Sofitel hotel, however outrageous and criminal, does not come under the category of sexual harassment, since he is not her employer and she is not his employee. On the other hand, his affair with economist Piroska Nagy, when she worked for the IMF, would clearly qualify as a possible case of sexual harassment, even though both parties claimed it was "consensual."

From the perspective of international business ethics, the judgment of the IMF's executive board, which determined that Strauss-Kahn did not abuse his power by having an affair with Nagy, needs to be challenged. The executive board's decision is consistent with the IMF's internal policy at the time: "Intimate personal relationships between supervisors and subordinates do not, in themselves, constitute harassment." How the executive board reached that conclusion is puzzling in light of the fact that the World Bank's guidelines, for example, stipulate that any personal relationship between superiors and subordinates must be regarded as "de facto [a] conflict of interest" which must be disclosed immediately. The superiors involved in such a relationship cannot be absolved of conflict of interest simply because there is no evidence that the subordinates in question received a promotion or other professional advancement, as a result of their affair. Even in the case of Strauss-Kahn's relationship with Nagy, it seems odd that the executive board give him only the slightest slap on the wrists, in spite of the fact that soon thereafter she quietly left the IMF, as one of a group of employees who had completed their service, with a substantial severance package. Even the appearance of conflict of interest ought to have been a concern for the IMF's executive board.

In a world where moral concerns regarding fair treatment of women in the workplace are rapidly evolving, Strauss-Kahn's behavior coupled with his persisting attitude—"I don't think I have any kind of problem with women" (CNN 2013)[1]—made it impossible for him to continue on as the IMF's managing director. But given the many allegations that surfaced after the incident at the Sofitel hotel, one may wonder how it was that the IMF's executive board did not investigate these things when he was nominated and why, if they did know, they would still have gone forward with Strauss-Kahn's appointment. His problem, in short, is not just personal but also an institutional failure. In the apparently permissive culture of the IMF management, Strauss-Kahn could tell himself that his sexual addiction was not only normal but also merely a private matter, a hobby perhaps, of no particular interest to anyone but himself.

Strauss-Kahn's abrupt departure left the IMF in a shambles. His successor, Christine Lagarde, signed an employment contract far more explicit in outlining the IMF's expectations for moral leadership. "You shall strive to avoid even the appearance of impropriety in your conduct" (Schneider 2011) and promise to "observe the highest standards of ethical conduct, consistent with the values of integrity, impartiality, and discretion" (IMF 2011). The warning against "even the appearance of impropriety" contrasts with the warning against "conflict of interest" included in Strauss-Kahn's contract. The term, "impropriety," is significant in light of the fact that the executive board, in ruling out any abuse of power in Strauss-Kahn's affair with Nagy, nevertheless had found him guilty of acting "inappropriately," which prompted an apology from him. If the same finding were to be made against his successors, presumably more than an apology would now be demanded of them.

Clearly, in the wake of the Strauss-Kahn scandal, the IMF has taken steps to address the problem of sexual harassment, but will these steps be sufficient to change what had been characterized as "an institution whose sexual norms and customs are markedly different from those of Washington" (Appelbaum and Stolberg 2011)? Two years later, the IMF announced that, under the leadership of its newly appointed Ethics Advisor, it had issued "enhanced standards of conduct" designed to "strengthen the institution's ethical framework" (IMF 2013). The enhancements

[1] Strauss-Kahn went on to say that "I have a problem with understanding what is expected from politicians of the highest level. It's different from what [a] Mr. and Miss in the street [can do]." Of course, even by his account of what he did with Ms. Diallo, he would have been arrested, if caught doing it "in the street." Apparently, in his view, his sexual behavior is quite normal and becomes a problem only when one becomes a politician—or business executive—at the highest level. Whatever Strauss-Kahn's expertise in finance and economics may have been, his attitude betrays a remarkably naïve view of organizations and the demands of moral leadership within them.

include "a new policy on close personal relationships in the workplace," which requires staff to report "intimate" relationships to the "Ethics Advisor, his/her supervisor, or the Human Resources Department," in order to assess and resolve any "potential conflicts of interest and workplace fairness concerns." Those who fail to report will be judged guilty of misconduct and subject to disciplinary action. In addition, the revised standards define as misconduct any attempt to retaliate against staff who report misconduct or participate in the IMF's dispute resolution system. Also noted is greater emphasis on prevention and early resolution of cases involving harassment, including sexual harassment, the penalty for which may include termination of employment.

How effective are these new policies? Even before their formal adoption in 2013, the ethics office has been issuing annual reports in an effort to be transparent about the IMF's progress. The latest published report from 2012 provides detailed statistics on the kinds of issues reported to the IMF Ombudsperson and the recently established integrity hotline (IMF 2012d). In Ethics Advisor Virginia Canter's judgment, the statistics showing increased requests for ethical advice demonstrate the success of the in-house mandatory ethics training programs. As staff members increase their awareness of the IMF's renewed commitment to higher ethical standards, there likely will be more requests for advice. One interesting trend that surfaces in the annual report of 2012 is the decline in the number of overt cases of sexual harassment and increase in the number of cases involving other forms of harassment such as bullying. The ethics office means to eliminate all forms of harassment, in order to demonstrate the IMF's commitment to its "core values," namely, "integrity, respect, impartiality, and honesty."[2]

It would seem, then, that under its new leadership, with Christine Lagarde as managing director, and Virginia Canter in the ethics office, the IMF has indeed begun a process of cultural transformation similar to that which many other major institutions—including international businesses, government agencies, and NGOs—have had to undergo. Overcoming scandals such as the one involving Strauss-Kahn may have furnished the motivation for initiating this process, but the underlying need for it goes far deeper than the personal failures of prominent executive leaders. The historically unprecedented entry of women into the workforce—particularly their service as colleagues and partners, demonstrating competencies and achieving credentials that are equal or better than those possessed by the men they work with—has created a situation in which traditional "patriarchal" or "sexist" attitudes

[2] The IMF's core values statement contains this promising explanation of "what do we want to achieve together": "1) An intellectually open atmosphere that seeks diverse views to develop the best solution, 2) Best management practices that support all of us in making our best contribution, through opportunities for professional development and recognition of achievements. 3) A healthy work-life balance. 4) Fair, transparent rules, equitably applied and avenues to help us seek recourse, without stigma, if we are wrongly treated. 5) A workplace free of all types of discrimination." The most important of these five goals may be the third one, on cultivating a healthy work-life balance. The old IMF culture apparently turned a blind eye to sexual and other forms of harassment, assuming that such things were bound to occur in the organization's highly stressful work environment, fostering "a climate in which romances often flourish — and lines are sometimes crossed" (Appelbaum and Stolberg 2011).

and practices are simply obsolete and increasingly dysfunctional, from the point of view of the organizations in which they serve. As the struggle to overcome sexism in the workplace has proceeded, it becomes clear that related forms of bullying and discrimination involving sexual, religious, and racial minorities must also be challenged. The men and women who have stepped forward to challenge the abuses tolerated, if not perpetrated, by the traditional male hierarchy, are representing not just themselves, but members of all groups who have found their human dignity trampled in the workplace. We need to inquire more deeply into the ethical assumptions animating the struggle against sexual harassment and discrimination, particularly in order to understand its global significance. No one can dismiss this struggle, as if it were merely an odd manifestation of a Western culture now in its final stages of irreversible decadence.

9.4 Ethical Reflection

What, then, is sexual harassment and why is it a problem both morally and legally? The US government's Equal Employment Opportunity Commission (EEOC) provided this comprehensive description of sexual harassment. It has become the standard in virtually all jurisdictions where the UN Declaration of Human Rights is acknowledged:

> Unwelcome sexual advances, requests for sexual favors, and other verbal or physical conduct of sexual nature constitute sexual harassment when (1) submission to such conduct is made either explicitly or implicitly a term or condition of an individual's employment, (2) submission to or rejection of such conduct by an individual is used as the basis for employment decisions affecting such individual, or (3) such conduct has the purpose or effect of unreasonably interfering with an individual's work performance or creating an intimidating, hostile, or offensive working environment. (Boatright 2003)

A more recent statement from the EEOC tries to make the same points, but in language that is more concrete and practical:

> "Sexual Harassment:
>
> - It is unlawful to harass a person (an applicant or employee) because of that person's sex. Harassment can include "sexual harassment" or unwelcome sexual advances, requests for sexual favors, and other verbal or physical harassment of a sexual nature.
> - Harassment does not have to be of a sexual nature, however, and can include offensive remarks about a person's sex. For example, it is illegal to harass a woman by making offensive comments about women in general.
> - Both victim and the harasser can be either a woman or a man, and the victim and harasser can be the same sex.
> - Although the law doesn't prohibit simple teasing, offhand comments, or isolated incidents that are not very serious, harassment is illegal when it is so frequent or severe that it creates a hostile or offensive work environment or when it results in an adverse employment decision (such as the victim being fired or demoted).
> - The harasser can be the victim's supervisor, a supervisor in another area, a co-worker, or someone who is not an employee of the employer, such as a client or customer." (EEOC 2014a)

Sexual harassment, then, is clearly illegal in the USA, and the EEOC provides detailed instructions on how to file a formal complaint, if one has been a victim of this crime.

Because the EEOC was instituted to enforce Title VII of the Civil Rights Act of 1964 that prohibits all forms of discrimination in employment, sexual harassment, like harassment in general, is treated under that category. "Title VII prohibits employment discrimination based on race, color, religion, sex and national origin." Thus, in addition to prohibiting discrimination based on sex—which normally means "treating someone (an applicant or employee) unfavorably because of that person's sex" in any aspect of an employment relationship, "including hiring, firing, pay, job assignments, promotions, layoffs, training, fringe benefits, and any other term or condition of employment"—the guidelines consider sexual harassment to be "illegal when it is so frequent or severe that it creates a hostile or offensive work environment or when it results in an adverse employment decision (such as the victim being fired or demoted)" (EEOC 2014b).

9.4.1 An Assault Upon Human Rights and Dignity

The moral basis for the laws and regulations prohibiting sexual harassment and discrimination is the same as that supporting human rights legislation, as we saw in Chapter 8. The UN Declaration on Human Rights explicitly affirms that "the rights and freedoms" set forth in it admit of no distinction based, among other things, on sex (Article 2). Furthermore, "the right to work, to free choice of employment, to just and favorable conditions of work," as well as "equal pay for equal work" (Article 23) apply to "everyone" equally. While it is clear that the UDHR did not anticipate a world in which men and women work side by side in virtually every business and industry and thus does not explicitly prohibit sexual discrimination and harassment, its affirmation of everyone's aspiration toward "an existence worthy of human dignity" clearly implies that its provisions cannot be reconciled with any system of employment that supports sexual discrimination and condones sexual harassment. The obvious conclusion is that sexual harassment is simply another assault on human dignity, and as such it is included, at least in principle, in the universal moral consensus respecting human dignity and condemning any violations of it.

Since assaults upon human dignity usually involve some form of abuse of power and privilege, by analogy, we can recognize the immorality of sexual harassment as yet another abuse of power in the workplace, usually—but not always—perpetrated by superiors against subordinates. In short, sexual harassment is a form of bullying and in no way should be confused with amorousness or romantic passion. The most important word describing sexual harassment is the first word: "unwelcome." Sexually aggressive behavior, when it is known to be unwelcome, must be regarded as a form of bullying—or abuse of power—and not dismissed as merely an excess of amorous desire. Understanding sexual harassment as a form of bullying is clearly presupposed in the EEOC's description of "quid pro quo" relationships, in which "submission to such conduct is made either explicitly or implicitly a term or condition of an individual's employment" or "rejection of such conduct by an individual is used as the basis for employment decisions affecting such individual." The most acute assault upon human dignity occurs in these situations, since they involve coercing sexual relations on the basis of either promises of more favorable treatment or threats of retaliation. But what about consensual relationships—may these, too, involve sexual harassment?

Assuming that the consent is genuine and mutual, there are two typical cases for discussion: superior-subordinate relationships and peer-to-peer relationships. While some institutions, particularly universities, have declared that all superior-subordinate sexual relationships—for example, between a professor and a student or between a supervisor and an employee—are liable to treatment as cases of sexual harassment,[3] the possibility of genuine mutual consent is evident in controversies over "office romances." Confronted with the risk of sexual harassment lawsuits arising from affairs that have ended badly, some businesses in the USA have attempted to ban office romances entirely or, if not impose an absolute ban, at least require full disclosure of the existence of such liaisons to one's superiors and the Human Resources Department. Both measures, even in business, place the burden of proof upon the superiors involved and are deemed necessary in order to insulate the firm from any legal liability should the relationship turn sour. The IMF's "enhanced standards of conduct" is a useful example. While it no longer regards office romances as strictly a private matter, it does require staff to report "intimate" relationships to the "Ethics Advisor, his/her supervisor, or the Human Resources Department," in order to assess and resolve any "potential conflicts of interest and workplace fairness concerns." Those who fail to report will be judged guilty of misconduct and subject to disciplinary action. In that way, professional accountability is maintained, as well as transparency, without prohibiting office romances of either type.

As we have seen in the previous chapter, respecting human dignity involves a complex of rights and responsibilities that sometimes may conflict with one another. Protecting one's own dignity is first of all a personal responsibility. If you don't do it, no one else is likely to. There are obvious limits to what an institution can do to respect the dignity of its employees. Respecting human dignity usually is understood as requiring us to respect everyone's need for personal privacy. If an organization's policies go too far in compromising personal privacy, they are likely to be counterproductive. An organization that seeks to minimize its risk of lawsuits and other embarrassments stemming from incidents of sexual harassment may be

[3] Chosen at random, see the policy of St. Paul College in St. Paul, MN (St. Paul College 2014), which is provided as guidance to all students. The policy makes it clear that in any relationship "where a power differential exists between the involved parties," a violation of the college's ban on sexual harassment will be assumed, with "the burden of accountability" falling upon the more powerful party, making it "exceedingly difficult to use mutual consent as a defense." In such a situation, where an accusation of sexual harassment may lead to termination of employment, parties who exercise responsibility as teachers and supervisors are well advised to refrain from any romantic or sexual relationship with anyone on campus.

tempted to set aside its employees' rights to privacy. But if it does so, it can hardly invoke its concern for human dignity to justify its policies. An absolute ban on office romances, for example, is likely to cause more problems for the Human Resources Department than it solves. On the other hand, a policy that focuses on personal privacy to the exclusion of other concerns—as, apparently, was the IMF's policy before and during Strauss-Kahn's term as managing director—is likely to tolerate the development of a corporate culture in which sexual predators will flourish. Given the complexities of human interaction in the real world of organizational behavior, while the principle of human dignity—even as translated into the core values of, for example, the IMF—may be clear, the best ways of implementing it remain an open question.

9.4.2 Sexual Discrimination and Harassment in Hong Kong

When we turn then, beyond the discussion of sexual harassment and discrimination in the USA and the EU, to what is happening in East Asian settings, we see both substantial progress and many obstacles to further reform. The more involved an organization—be it a business, an NGO, or a government agency—is in the globalization process, the more likely it is to subscribe at least in principle to international standards regarding sexual harassment and discrimination. Consider the case of Hong Kong, which still stands as the gateway between China and the West, the venue where the globalization process is most advanced in Asia. Hong Kong's legislative response is contained in "Chapter 480: The Sex Discrimination Ordinance" (SDO) which not only declares "unlawful certain kinds of sex discrimination, discrimination on the ground of marital status or pregnancy, and sexual harassment" but also provides for "the establishment of a Commission with the functions of working towards the elimination of such discrimination and harassment and promoting equality of opportunity between men and women generally" (HKSAR Government 1996). The work of educating the public and supporting compliance efforts in government agencies, businesses, and NGOs is the work of the Equal Opportunities Commission (EOC). The Commission routinely conducts surveys and issues reports on Hong Kong's progress in confronting sexual harassment and discrimination.

The definition of sexual harassment adopted in Hong Kong's SDO is very similar to that of the USA's EEOC.

> For the purposes of this Ordinance, a person (howsoever described) sexually harasses a woman if-
>
> (a) the person- (i) makes an unwelcome sexual advance, or an unwelcome request for sexual favours, to her; or (ii) engages in other unwelcome conduct of a sexual nature in relation to her, in circumstances in which a reasonable person, having regard to all the circumstances, would have anticipated that she would be offended, humiliated or intimidated; or
>
> (b) the person, alone or together with other persons, engages in conduct of a sexual nature which creates a hostile or intimidating environment for her. (Section 2, 5)

A subsequent amendment (Sections 2 and 8) makes it clear that the description applies equally to men as well as to women who may be victims of harassment. One interesting difference between HK's SDO and the USA's EEOC guidelines is that sexual harassment is defined broadly and covers offenses that occur outside the workplace, but with a similar emphasis on "unwelcome conduct" that "creates a hostile or intimidating environment." Sexual harassment in the workplace, however, is specifically discussed as part of the SDO's comprehensive approach to "unlawful discrimination." It is clear that the intent of the SDO is to enforce equality of opportunities in, among other things, employment by prohibiting any unlawful discrimination based on sex, with sexual harassment understood as but one manifestation of conduct whose effect, if not intent, is to discriminate.

As the HK EOC itself reports, it has had only modest success in achieving the SDO's compliance goals. In its most recent "Sexual Harassment – Questionnaire Survey for Business Sector," the statistics indicate that while the percentage of complaints handled by the EOC involving sexual harassment is on the rise, the interest of businesses in formulating policy statements about it is modest, at best (EOC, 2012). Of the 6000 companies invited to participate in the survey, only 3 % responded, and of these, only 57 % (113 responses) reported that they already have a sexual harassment policy in place. Of those who do not (85 responses), the most common reason for not having a policy is that they see "no urgency" to do so, since they have not had any incidents to report so far. Only 17 % of these indicated a willingness to consider formulating a policy in the next 12 months. Going without a policy, of course, carries its own risks, since in Hong Kong as elsewhere, employers can be held vicariously liable if their employees are convicted of the crime, in the absence of specific guidelines and adequate staff training in their enforcement. Despite the apparent indifference of too many companies in Hong Kong, the EOC intends to launch a series of campaigns to promote "anti-sexual harassment" awareness and compliance with the law, working in cooperation with various business and professional associations.[4]

[4]In 2014, the EOC released another report, specifically focused on sexual harassment and employment discrimination among airline flight attendants. With a slightly higher response rate (4 %), the survey revealed that 27 % of the respondents had been sexually harassed in the past 12 months and that "the most common harassers were the customers." Although all international airlines serving Hong Kong have policy statements on sexual harassment, only 61 % the flight attendants were even aware of its existence, and only 11 % knew "the names and contacts of designated staff who handle complaints." In addition, "68 % of the respondents had not received any training courses on anti-sexual harassment." Of those who had been harassed in the past year, 50 % had either chosen to do nothing or merely mentioned it to colleagues and relatives. In the EOC's view, these findings suggest that compliance must go beyond merely having a policy and must provide effective training if the policy is to be credible. "To combat the feelings of fear and helplessness, a strong corporate culture of protecting employees from sexual harassment and discrimination should be promoted in the company." (EOC 2014)

9.4.3 Legal Protections for the Rights and Interests of Women in China

If compliance with existing laws, such as the Sexual Discrimination Ordinance, is still a struggle in Hong Kong, what can be said about other Asian venues, such as China? Most observers recognize that in the past decade, China has made enormous progress. "Outlawing sexual harassment against women via legislation by making it both a criminal offense as well as a civil wrong also indicates a remarkable change in attitude in China, which is still a male-dominated society" (Srivastava and Gu 2009). Sexual harassment and discrimination are prohibited by the "Law of the People's Republic of China on the Protection of Rights and Interests of Women" originally adopted by the Seventh National People's Congress (NPC) of 1992 and amended at the 10th NPC in 2005. The Law is "formulated to protect women's lawful rights and interests, promote the equality between men and women and allow full play to women's role in socialist modernization" (Article 1). Besides issuing an absolute prohibition against discrimination, maltreatment, abandonment, and physical abuse of women (Article 1), the law defines women's rights in six key areas of public life and "encourages women to cultivate a sense of self-respect, self-confidence, self-reliance and self-strengthening, and to safeguard their own lawful rights and interests by utilizing law" (Article 5). Chapter IV, on "Rights and Interests Relating to Work and Social Security," guarantees women equal rights in these areas (Article 22), as well as "equal pay for equal work" and equal "welfare benefits" (Article 24). Employment discrimination is specifically prohibited (Article 25), including any unilateral reduction in wages or benefits because of marriage, pregnancy, maternity leave, or breast-feeding. Women shall be guaranteed equal access to "social insurance, social relief, social welfare and health care services" (Article 28).

With regard to sexual harassment, the Law takes up this issue in Chapter VI, devoted to "Rights Relating to the Person." Besides affirming the inviolability of "women's freedom of the person," this chapter also specifically prohibits "trafficking" in women and commits the state and its various agencies to take "timely measures to rescue women who are abducted, trafficked or kidnapped" (Article 39). The article prohibiting sexual harassment also acknowledges "the right to file complaints with units where they work and the departments concerned" (Article 40). As the final article in this chapter makes clear, the protection of women's rights and interests reflects China's concern to respect the human dignity of women:

> Women's rights of personality, including their right of reputation, right of honor, right of privacy and right of portrait, shall be protected by law. Besmirching women's personal dignity by such means as humiliation and libel is prohibited. Decrying or besmirching women's personality through the mass media or by other means is prohibited. The use of a woman's portrait for profit-making purposes in advertisements, trademarks, window display, newspapers, magazines, books, audio-video products, electronic publications, internet, etc., without the women's personal consent, is prohibited (Article 42).

As in other areas of business ethics in China, we discover that the laws of China are quite impressive and consistent with relevant international standards. The unanswered questions, then, take us to the challenge of achieving full compliance with those standards.

Protecting the rights and interests of women, to be sure, requires more than the passing of legislation. A comprehensive review of judicial decisions involving sexual harassment in China argues that "the plight of women in China will not be resolved so long as judges still suffer from the hangover of China's traditional society, which accords women an inferior position to men" (Srivastava and Gu 2009: 45). In spite of a number of surveys demonstrating the prevalence of sexual harassment in China, women who are victims of it tend to "suffer in silence [rather than] use legal means to voice their grievances." In the ten court cases reviewed by Srivastava and Gu, ironically enough, "most of the successful cases were decided before the sexual harassment provision was formally adopted by the 2005 law" (2009: 49). One decision handed down in Beijing in 2004 "established four factors to consider in a sexual harassment case":

> First, the conduct of the defendant must be unwelcome to the claimant. Second, the harassment must be sexual in nature. Third, there must be some overt act, such as the use of sexual language, gestures, or other visual signals implying a demand for sexual favors. Fourth, the conduct must violate the claimant's dignity and freedom of her person. (Srivastava and Gu 2009: 50–51)

While these factors are consistent with legal definitions used in both China and Hong Kong, the majority of cases reviewed in which sexual harassment claims were dismissed indicate that these involve a formidable burden of proof. While Chinese Civil Procedure Law rightly stipulates that "the complaining party must provide evidence to substantiate its claim," in sexual harassment cases, this constitutes an "especially onerous" burden of proof when "a person in a position of power harasses a person in a position of lesser power" (2009: 56). Coupled with the psychological difficulties involved in making such claims in court, and the fact that the penalties for sexual harassment go no further than imposing compensatory damages, there are ample reasons why the legal remedies meant to safeguard women's rights and interests remain relatively ineffective.

Srivastava and Gu pinpoint two other factors in China's compliance challenge that differ from Hong Kong. First, "current Chinese law does not automatically impose vicarious liability on employers for sexual harassment perpetrated by their employees." Second, "there is no law in China providing for the establishment of an equal opportunity commission" (Srivastava and Gu 2009: 58). Beginning in 1998 in the USA, the threat of vicarious liability is widely believed to have prompted many employers to formulate policies and training programs on preventing sexual harassment in the workplace. Employers could immunize themselves from accusations that they were complicit in the violations perpetrated by their employees, if they could demonstrate that they had such policies and programs in place (Samson 2013). The legal sanction, in other words, promoted effective education and training in the workplace. Similarly, the establishment of an equal opportunity commission in both the USA, as part of Title VII of the Civil Rights Act of 1964, and Hong Kong, as part of the Sex Discrimination Ordinance of 1995, demonstrates institutional support for the long-term process of transforming cultures so that human dignity is respected and human rights are protected. In this, as in other matters, China would do well to learn from what has been accomplished in Hong Kong.

As this review of the progress made and challenges to be faced in implementing China's Law on the Protection of the Rights and Interests of Women suggests, legal reform is necessary but hardly sufficient. A change of heart is needed, one in which the spiritual and cultural resources of China's wisdom traditions may be mobilized to support appropriate forms of cultural change. Contrary to Srivastava and Gu, who tend to assume an excessively negative view of the role of women in traditional Chinese society (Srivastava and Gu 2009: 45–46), scholars have been reviewing Confucianism, Daoism, and other traditions for signs of hope supporting Chinese women's aspirations for change. One such groundbreaking study is Robin R. Wang's *Images of Women in Chinese Thought and Culture: Writings from the Pre-Qin Period through the Song Dynasty* (2003) which, among other things, featured the writings of female Chinese writers, such as the Han dynasty scholar, Ban Zhao, who argued that, if women are to fulfill their proper roles in Chinese society, they must receive a proper Confucian education (Wang 2003: 177–186). If one is serious about cultivating human dignity on the basis of moral and spiritual traditions indigenous to China, there are resources for defining Chinese cultural values no longer as resistant to recognizing the dignity of women, but as affirming and supporting a more humane view of their rights and responsibilities in public life. Just as Confucianism and other Chinese traditions cannot be used to ignore or set aside the basic rights of workers in general, so they cannot be used to justify sexual harassment and discrimination.

9.5 Conclusion

This chapter is meant to promote awareness of the progress that has been made in China and other East Asian venues in protecting the dignity and human rights of women and men, particularly with reference to the universal problems of sexual harassment and discrimination. Scandals like the affair that brought down IMF managing director, Dominique Strauss-Kahn, are a reminder of just how universal the problems are and how challenging the task of transforming organizational cultures so that sexism and other forms of predatory behavior become no more than a relic of a past well lost. While we have noted the diversity of approaches, not only in the West but also in China and Hong Kong, regarding the protection of basic dignity and human rights, particularly with reference to gender and sexuality, we have also attempted to show the underlying moral consensus, namely, that willful violations and predatory sexual behavior stand condemned and will no longer be ignored or tolerated in a globalizing civilization. Businesses and organizations that promote international trade and commerce are at "ground zero," so to speak, in the struggle against sexual harassment and discrimination. The struggle, as we have seen, provides an important opportunity to demonstrate moral leadership, particularly in China and other East Asian venues.

At the beginning of this chapter, we invoked one of Stephan Rothlin's 18 rules for becoming a "top-notch player" in business: "If you act against discrimination, you will increase your productivity and profitability." We have attempted in this chapter to highlight the moral reasons and legal considerations involved in acting against discrimination. But the fact remains, as Rothlin pointed out, that acting against discrimination—including transforming business cultures in which sexual harassment is tolerated—will also impact a firm's bottom line. Sexual harassment lowers morale among workers, which in turn can only lead to declining productivity. If you continue to tolerate sexual harassment, you are likely to alienate your best workers, undermining both their loyalty to the firm and their willingness to stay on with it. You can well imagine the cost of replacing them, when they finally get fed up with your indifference and decide to move on. Both productivity and profitability, therefore, are at stake. If you want a strictly business reason for doing the right thing, this is clearly it.

References

AFP. (2011, May 20). *IMF rejects report of widespread sexual harassment*. Retrieved on June 1, 2012, from http://www.google.com/hostednews/afp/article/ALeqM5jJpK8JMoTWl7zmigSFzYh3AHfx7A?docId=CNG.5449d35b30cae0a9c8d1371153c12502.81

Andersen, C. (2009, May 28). Latvia caught in vicious economic downturn. *IMF*. Retrieved on August 20, 2012, from http://www.imf.org/external/pubs/ft/survey/so/2009/car052809a.htm

Appelbaum, B., & Stolberg, S. (2011, May 19). At I.M.F., men on prowl and women on guard. *The New York Times*. Retrieved on June 1, 2012, from http://www.nytimes.com/2011/05/20/business/20fund.html

BBC. (2007, September 28). *Frenchman is named new IMF chief*. Retrieved on June 18, 2012, from http://news.bbc.co.uk/2/hi/business/7018756.stm

BBC. (2012, March 27). *Profile: Dominique Strauss-Kahn*. Retrieved on May 27, 2012, from http://www.bbc.co.uk/news/world-europe-13405268

Beattie, A. (2011, May 19). IMF chief's 2008 affair back in the spotlight. *The Financial Times*. Retrieved on June 6, 2012, from http://www.ft.com/cms/s/0/65ea7500-81b3-11e0-8a54-00144feabdc0.html#axzz1x0Cy7DBO

Becker, G. (2009). Moral leadership in business. *Journal of International Business Ethics, 2*(1), 7–21.

Blodget, H. (2011, May 16). France furious about Dominique Strauss-Kahn perp-walk. *Business Insider*. Retrieved on June 14, 2012, from http://www.businessinsider.com/france-furious-about-dominique-strauss-kahn-perp-walk-2011-5

Boatright, J. (2003). *Ethics and the conduct of business* (4th ed.). Upper Saddle NJ: Prentice Hall.

Bowley, G. (2011, May 29). At IMF, a strict ethics code doesn't apply to top officials. *The New York Times*. Retrieved on June 20, 2012, from http://www.nytimes.com/2011/05/30/business/global/30fund.html

British Press. (2011, May 17). *IMF woes reflect 'macho' French politics*. Retrieved on June 1, 2012, from http://www.asiaone.com/News/AsiaOne+News/World/Story/A1Story20110517-279204.html

Chelsky, J. (2008, April). The role and evolution of executive board standing committees in IMF corporate governance. *Independent Evaluation Office of the International Monetary Fund*. Retrieved on July 31, 2012, from http://www.ieo-imf.org/ieo/files/completedevaluations/052108CG_background7.pdf

CNN. (2013). *Exclusive: 'I don't think I have any kind of problem with women,' Strauss-Kahn says*. Retrieved on June 18, 2015 from http://www.cnn.com/2013/07/10/world/europe/france-dsk/index.html

EEOC. (2014a). Types of discrimination: Sexual harassment. Retrieved on June 18, 2015 from http://www.eeoc.gov/laws/types/sexual_harassment.cfm

EEOC. (2014b). *Title VII of the Civil Rights Act of 1964*. Retrieved on June 18, 2015 from http://www.eeoc.gov/laws/statutes/titlevii.cfm

EOC. (2012). *Sexual harassment – Questionnaire survey for business sector*. Retrieved on June 18, 2015 from http://www.eoc.org.hk/EOC/OtherProjects/survey/SHsurveyEF2.pdf

EOC. (2014). *Sexual harassment and discrimination in employment questionnaire survey for flight attendants*. Retrieved on June 18, 2015 from http://www.eoc.org.hk/EOC/Upload/ResearchReport/SHFlightAttendants_e.pdf

Elliott, M. (2010, April 29). The 2010 time 100. *Time*. Retrieved on June 20, 2012, from http://www.time.com/time/specials/packages/article/0,28804,1984685_1984864_1985437,00.html

Erlanger, S., &, Bennhold, K. (2012, May 16). As case unfolds, France speculates and steams. *The New York Times*. Retrieved on June 14, 2012, from http://www.nytimes.com/2011/05/17/world/europe/17france.html?pagewanted=1&_r=1

Fraser, C. (2011, November 28). 'Conspiracy' claims bolster DSK mystery. *BBC News*. Retrieved on June 6, 2012, from http://www.bbc.co.uk/news/world-europe-15917722

Freeman, M. (2011, May 31). IMF ethics controls "didn't apply" for top dogs on board of directors. *Business ETC*. Retrieved on July 31, 2012, from http://businessetc.thejournal.ie/imf-ethics-controls-didnt-apply-to-top-dogs-on-board-of-directors-146438-May2011/

Handley, P. (2011, May 25). Brics speaks strongly against European IMF leader. *Mail & Guardian*. Retrieved on August 1, 2012, from http://mg.co.za/article/2011-05-25-brics-speak-strongly-against-european-imf-leader

Harding, R. (2011, May 21). Scrutiny reveals fund with tighter ethics code. *The Financial Times*. Retrieved on July 31, 2012, from http://www.ft.com/intl/cms/s/0/285583bc-8337-11e0-a46f-00144feabdc0.html#axzz22AVhn9ot

HKSAR Government. (1996). *Cap 480 – Sex discrimination ordinance*. Retrieved on June 18, 2015 from http://www.eoc.org.hk/eoc/graphicsfolder/showcontent.aspx?content=ordinance_sdo

House, R., Hanges, P., Ruiz-Quintanilla, A., Dorfman, P., & Javidan, M. (1999). *Cultural influences on leadership and organizations*. Project Hope. Retrieved on June 18, 2015, from http://www.vnseameo.org/zakir/process.pdf

Hume, N. (2011, May 19). L'affaire DSK: French right to private lives on trial. *Spiked*. Retrieved on June 6, 2012, from http://www.spiked-online.com/index.php/site/article/10529/

Independent Evaluation Office of the IMF. (2012). *IMF Governance: Outline of current structures and practice*. Retrieved on August 1, 2012, from http://www.ieo-imf.org/ieo/files/completedevaluations/05212008CG_main6.pdf

International Monetary Fund. (2011). *Dominique Strauss-Kahn*. Retrieved on May 30, 2012, from http://www.imf.org/external/np/omd/bios/dsk.htm

International Monetary Fund. (2012a, April 19). *Factsheet: Poverty reduction strategy papers*. Retrieved on August 20, 2012, from http://www.imf.org/external/np/exr/facts/prsp.htm

International Monetary Fund. (2012b). *About the IMF*. Retrieved on August 1, 2012, from http://www.imf.org/external/about.htm

International Monetary Fund. (2012c). *Accountability*. Retrieved on July 31, 2012 from http://www.imf.org/external/about/govaccount.htm

International Monetary Fund. (2012d). The Ethics Office 2012 Annual Report: Embracing Ethical Values. Retrieved on May 12, 2014 from http://www.imf.org/external/hrd/eo/ar/2012/eoar2012.pdf

International Monetary Fund. (2013, August 5). *IMF updates standards for staff conduct*. Retrieved on May 12, 2014, from https://www.imf.org/external/hrd/conduct.htm

Mainiero, L. A. (2012, January 1) Sexual hubris and international norms regarding workplace romance: What can Europe learn from the US and vice versa? *European Journal of Management*. Retrieved on May 13, 2014, from http://www.freepatentsonline.com/article/European-Journal-Management/293812519.html

Melnick, M. (2011, July 26). No longer the perfect victim? Nafissatou Diallo defends herself. *Time*. Retrieved on June 7, from http://healthland.time.com/2011/07/26/no-longer-the-perfect-victim-nafissatou-diallo-defends-herself/

Newsweek. (2011, July 25). *The maid's tale*. Retrieved on June 6, 2012, from http://www.thedailybeast.com/newsweek/2011/07/24/dsk-maid-tells-of-her-alleged-rape-by-strauss-kahn-exclusive.html

Pilkington, E. (2011, May 24). Dominique Strauss-Kahn DNA 'found on maid's clothing'. *The Guardian*. Retrieved on June 7, from http://www.guardian.co.uk/world/2011/may/24/dominique-strauss-kahn-dna-claim

Pilkington, E., & Chrisafis, A. (2012, April 27). DSK: New York sex scandal orchestrated by political opponents. *The Guardian*. Retrieved on May 27, 2012, from http://www.guardian.co.uk/world/2012/apr/27/dsk-sex-scandal-political-opponents

Quinn, R. (2011, May 17). Strauss-Kahn lover felt coerced into having affair. *News FR*. Retrieved on June 28, 2012, from http://www.newser.com/story/118728/mistress-piroska-nagy-accused-imf-chief-dominique-strauss-kahn-of-abusing-power.html

Saguy, A. (2001). *Sexual harassment in France and the United States: Activists and public figures defend their definitions*. Princeton University. Retrieved on June 28, 2012, from http://educ.jmu.edu/~brysonbp/symbound/papers2001/Saguy.html

Samson, R. L. (2013, June 26). *Supreme court clarifies employer liability for supervisor harassment under title VII*. Iowa Employer Law Blog, Dickinson Law. Retrieved on May 15, 2014, from http://www.dickinsonlaw.com/2013/06/supreme-court-clarifies-employer-liability-for-supervisor-harassment-under-title-vii/

Samuel, H. (2011, May 16). Dominique Strauss-Kahn arrest: French privacy laws among strictest in Europe. *The Telegraph*. Retrieved on June 6, 2012, from http://www.telegraph.co.uk/finance/dominique-strauss-kahn/8517641/DominiqueStrauss-Kahn-arrest-French-privacy-laws-among-strictest-in-Europe.html

Schneider, H. (2011, May 21). IMF works to fortify new ethics rules amid tumult. *The Washington Post*. Retrieved on August 1, 2012, from https://www.lexisnexis.com.avoserv.library.fordham.edu/lnacui2api/results/docview/docview.do?docLinkInd=true&risb=21_T15240289999&format=GNBFI&sort=BOOLEAN&startDocNo=1&resultsUrlKey=29_T15240294603&cisb=22_T15240294602&treeMax=true&treeWidth=0&csi=8075&docNo=3

Shipman, T. (2008, October 8). Head of IMF investigated over 'improper behavior' with a subordinate. *Telegraph*. Retrieved on June 20, 2012, from http://www.telegraph.co.uk/news/worldnews/northamerica/usa/3224674/Head-of-IMF-investigated-over-improper-behaviour-with-subordinate.html

Srivastava, D. K., Gu, M. (2009). Law and policy issues on sexual harassment in China: Comparative perspectives. *Oregon Review of International Law, 11*(43) 43–69.

St. Paul College. (2014). *Sexual discrimination/harassment & violence*. Retrieved on May 13, 2014, from http://www.saintpaul.edu/currentstudents/Pages/SexDiscHarassViol.aspx

Stephens, B. (2011, July 5). The DSK lesson. *The Wall Street Journal*. Retrieved on May 30, 2012, from http://online.wsj.com/article/SB10001424052702304490004576422462548199624.html

The New York Times. (2012, May 15). *Dominique Strauss-Kahn*. Retrieved on June 7, 2012, from http://topics.nytimes.com/top/reference/timestopics/people/s/dominique_strauss kahn/index.html

The Whirled Bank Group. (2003). *Structural adjustment program*. Retrieved on August 21, 2012, from http://www.whirledbank.org/development/sap.html

Thomas, L. (2011, May 16). Woman in 2008 affair said to have accused IMF director of coercing her. *The New York Times*. Retrieved on June 20, 2012, from http://www.nytimes.com/2011/05/17/world/europe/17fund.html?_r=1

US Department of State: Office of the Historian. Milestones: 1937–1945, The Bretton Woods Conference, 1944. Retrieved on August 1, 2012 from http://history.state.gov/milestones/1937-1945/BrettonWoods

Walden, S. (2011, May 18). Why IMF whistleblowers were silent. *Government Accountability Office*. Retrieved on June 25, 2012, from http://www.whistleblower.org/blog/31/1123

Wang, R. R. (2003). *Images of women in Chinese thought and culture: Writings from the pre-qin period through the song dynasty*. Indianapolis: Hackett Publishing.

Wearden, G. (2011, July 5). IMF insists on ethics clause for Lagarde. *The Guardian*. Retrieved on July 31, 2012, from http://www.guardian.co.uk/business/2011/jul/05/christine-lagarde-ethics-clause

Weisbrot, M. (2011, May 19). *Strauss-Kahn's legacy at the IMF: Less than meets the eye?* Center for Economic and Policy Research. Retrieved on August 20, 2012, from http://www.cepr.net/index.php/op-eds-&-columns/op-eds-&-columns/strauss-kahns-legacy-at-the-imf-less-than-meets-the-eye

World Watch. (2011, May 20). *Office romance, sexual harassment rife at IMF*. Retrieved on June 20, 2012, from http://www.cbsnews.com/8301-503543_162-20064648-503543.html

Chapter 10
Employees: Whistle-Blowing

"Your loyal dissent can lead your institution in the right direction." (Stephan Rothlin, *Eighteen Rules for Becoming a Top Notch Player*, 2004)

10.1 Prelude

No management team should be blamed for natural disasters, like the earthquake and tsunami that hit Fukushima, Japan, in 2011. But they must be held responsible for the ways they respond to the crises triggered by such events. As the case study proceeds, we witness the unfolding of Tokyo Electric Power Company's (TEPCO) response to the Fukushima disaster. The early reports of heroism on the part of workers and managers at TEPCO's nuclear facilities soon gave way to allegations of a cover-up and a new narrative involving whistle-blowing against the firm, in order to alert the general public about what had actually happened. Rooted in the Fukushima disaster, this chapter revisits the ongoing controversy about whistle-blowing, distinguishing situations where it appears to be obligatory, and other situations in which it may be permissible, in contrast to situations where it would be irresponsible to engage in it. We believe that the issue must be approached from an appreciation of the loyalty that employees owe to their employers, a loyalty that must not be violated except in cases of genuine necessity. While the whistle-blowing at TEPCO may be morally justified, there are clearly other situations in which it may be inappropriate.

10.2 Case Study: Tokyo Electric Power Company and the Fukushima Disaster

10.2.1 Abstract

In a rare departure from civility, following the crisis at the Fukushima Daiichi nuclear power plant, Japanese Prime Minister Naoto Kan shouted "What the hell is going on?" to executives of the Tokyo Electric Power Company (TEPCO)

S. Rothlin, D. McCann, *International Business Ethics*,
DOI 10.1007/978-3-662-47434-1_10

(Goodspeed 2011). The prime minister seemed to be speaking for the entire nation, which had grown increasingly frustrated by the lack of reliable information in the days following the disaster, triggered by the Tohoku earthquake and tsunami, which struck the northeastern coast of Japan on March 11, 2011. As a result of the widespread perception that TEPCO was withholding the facts concerning the origins and magnitude of the crisis, on October 30, 2011, Japan's Diet or national parliament granted the Fukushima Nuclear Accident Independent Investigation Commission a mandate to report on the causes of the disaster. The nonpartisan panel concluded that the nuclear crisis was "profoundly man-made" (NAIIC, 9) and could have been prevented by a more transparent corporate and bureaucratic culture.

This case study highlights the moral agents involved in responding to the disaster and the ensuing scandal surrounding TEPCO, not to lay blame but to reflect on the lessons that the case offers for business leaders and their stakeholders. Should TEPCO and its subcontractors have taken more seriously the warnings of various whistle-blowers about the dangers of a nuclear accident? Did the disaster that occurred following the Tohoku earthquake justify the warnings of whistle-blowers like Mitsuhiko Tanaka, or did it demonstrate their irrelevance? Like all managers faced with a catastrophic event—particularly in the field of nuclear energy—the key players at TEPCO may have faced unprecedented levels of stress as they tried to balance the interests of their shareholders against national and international demands for public safety. How well have they done in managing this crisis? The Asian setting of this case offers additional food for thought questioning the moral limits to "saving face"—in light of the universal right to know the truth and to respect the human dignity of all stakeholders, especially the people directly affected by their actions.

10.2.2 Keywords

TEPCO, Fukushima disaster, Nuclear power, NAIIC, Amakudari.

10.2.3 Unforeseen Catastrophe, Disastrous Responses

A month after the Fukushima disaster, James Acton, associate of the Nuclear Policy Program at the Carnegie Endowment for International Peace, declared that it may not have been "the worst nuclear accident ever, but it is the most complicated and the most dramatic.... This was a crisis that played out in real time on TV. Chernobyl did not. This crisis just goes on and on" (International Business Times 2011). Alas, two and a half years later, the crisis remains unresolved as the Japanese government has stepped in to address "an 'emergency' that TEPCO was not containing on its own," namely, the flow of highly radioactive groundwater into the ocean, publicly acknowledged in August 2013 (Saito and Slodkowski 2013). TEPCO's failure to reveal the full extent of the hazards posed by the radioactive water is but the latest in a series of crises that began with the cascade of equipment failures, nuclear meltdowns, and radiation leakages that followed the earthquake and tsunami.

The damage initially sustained by the Fukushima Daiichi plant and the failure of TEPCO's emergency systems made it impossible to cool reactors 1, 2, and 3 adequately. With no effective cooling system still operable, it was only a matter of time before there was a full nuclear meltdown and further explosions in the containment buildings due to "an accumulation of hydrogen gas" (IAEA, 2011). Once the extent of the devastation was evident, the Japanese government ordered the evacuation of all nonemergency personnel from the area within a 20 km radius of the crippled plant (Reuters 2011a). As radiation was released into the atmosphere from the interior of the plant, the situation escalated from a local crisis to a potentially global environmental catastrophe. Upon discovery of the escaping radiation, the government raised the nuclear alert level to seven, the highest point on the scale and "on par with the 1986 Chernobyl warning" (McCurry 2011).

Unfortunately, a competent and comprehensive response from TEPCO and the government was not forthcoming. While the technical difficulties involved in calculating a reliable estimate on the total amount of radioactivity released contributed to the confusion, it should have been clear to all concerned that the health and safety risks related to exposure to excessive radiation extend years beyond the risk of immediate casualties (Muller 2012). As the crisis wore on, the government and TEPCO were both criticized heavily in the foreign press for poor communication with the public concerning its magnitude. Germany's leading news magazine, *Der Spiegel*, labeled the government's insularity, lack of transparency, and refusal to embrace foreign assistance "utterly hapless" (Hackenbroch et al. 2011). TEPCO's response to international calls for information concerning radiation levels released from the plant was worse than that, as it eventually was discovered that "staff may have been told to lie, and give false readings to try and cover up true levels of radiation" (Kyodo News 2012).

International media coverage of the disaster initially focused not only on the apparently negligent behavior of TEPCO and the Japanese government but also on the selfless deeds of individual technicians who put their lives in jeopardy in order to contain the radiation. The "Fukushima Fifty" were hailed as heroes by the international press, with some reports even going so far as to conclude that their willingness to make extraordinary personal sacrifices for the public welfare exemplified "the collectivist ethos of the Japanese people" (Axelrod 2011). Several workers died as a direct result of the explosions, whereas others were exposed to levels of radiation that greatly exceeded acceptable lifetime limits. As for the long-term effects of the disaster, new cancer deaths are forecast to range from a low of 100 (NPR 2012) to a high of 1,000 (von Hippel 2011), and an official Japanese government panel "has estimated that cleaning up the Fukushima disaster and compensating its victims could cost as much as 20 trillion yen (US$257 billion)" (Reuters 2011b). Besides the price paid in lives and yen for TEPCO's mistakes, the disaster inflicted immeasurable damage to the reputations of both the company and the Japanese government. The suspicion that the disaster could have been prevented was confirmed months later by the official findings of the Fukushima Nuclear Accident Independent Investigation Commission.

10.2.4 Blowing the Whistle on the Nuclear Power Industry

Many observers had predicted what happened at the Fukushima Daiichi plant. Long before the catastrophe, at least one engineer, Mitsuhiko Tanaka, who had supervised the construction of the containment vessel for Reactor No. 4, warned of a defect that he had helped cover up. In 1974, the walls of the "reactor pressure vessel" had been warped when it "was being treated one last time to remove welding stress" (Clenfield 2011b). Rather than scrap the defective vessel as required by law, Tanaka devised an ingenious way to smooth over the warp, which allowed the vessel to be installed at no further cost. At the time, Tanaka considered himself a "hero" for saving his employer, Babcock-Hitachi, from a possible bankruptcy, had they been forced to absorb the loss caused by the defect. But years later in 1986, after having embarked on a career as a science writer, Tanaka realized the serious risks involved in his Hitachi heroics. While working on a documentary on the Chernobyl nuclear disaster in the Soviet Union, "All of a sudden I was sobbing and I started to think about what I'd done…. I was thinking, 'I could be the father of a Japanese Chernobyl'" (Clenfield 2011b). Two years later he attempted to warn the Japanese government, by confessing his role in the cover-up to Ministry of Economy Trade and Industry (METI), the agency that, among other things, regulates the nuclear power industry. Hitachi simply denied his allegations and METI saw no reason to investigate further. Hoping to alert the public, Tanaka wrote a book in 1990 entitled, *Why Nuclear Power Is Dangerous*, which went out of print in 2000. Tanaka's effort, however, may not have been in vain. Two days after the Fukushima earthquake, his publisher called to inform him that his book would now be put back into print (Clenfield 2011b).

While Tanaka's revelations are just the tip of the iceberg, he appears to have been the first to blow the whistle on the shoddy record of Japan's nuclear power industry. It is hardly a coincidence that in 2011 he was appointed a member of NAIIC, and their report substantially confirms the stories that he and other insiders brought forward as evidence of TEPCO's malfeasance. Comprised of experts from the fields of nuclear science, law, medicine, and public administration, NAIIC compiled its report based on "900 hours of hearings and interviews with 1,167 people" (NAIIC 2012: 11). Foreign experts from the USA, France, and Russia were included in the investigation, and all hearings were open to public observation via Internet broadcast. In a moment of extreme crisis for Japan's nuclear power industry, its traditional culture accustomed to saving face through indirect, discreet communication was shattered by the blunt conclusion of the Commission:

> The TEPCO Fukushima Nuclear Power Plant Accident was the result of collusion between the government, the regulators, and TEPCO, and the lack of governance by said parties. They effectively betrayed the nation's right to be safe from nuclear accidents. Therefore, we conclude that the accident was clearly "manmade". We believe that the root causes were the organizational and regulatory systems that supported faulty rationales for decisions and actions, rather than issues relating to the competency of any specific individual. (NAIIC 2012: 16)

The NAIIC investigation, in short, encountered the same unconscionable indifference to public safety, bureaucratic insularity, and refusal to admit mistakes and take responsibility for correcting them that Tanaka had experienced when he tried to alert authorities to the problems at Fukushima over 20 years earlier.

10.2.5 A Man-Made Disaster?

Although the NAIIC report attributed blame to the nexus of interests linking TEPCO and the government, TEPCO was singled out for its own particular failures. First of all, the Commission concluded that TEPCO failed to develop voluntarily the most basic safety requirements, "such as assessing the probability of damage, preparing for containing collateral damage from such a disaster, and developing evacuation plans for the public in case of a serious radiation release" (NAIIC 2012: 16). Officials from TEPCO pleaded that the company has undertaken all necessary safety measures, as required by law. Although TEPCO's operations were technically in compliance with existing laws and regulations, NAIIC concluded that both TEPCO and the Nuclear and Industrial Safety Agency (NISA) "were aware of the need for structural reinforcement [but] rather than demanding their implementation, NISA stated that action should be taken autonomously by the operator" (NAIIC 2012: 16). Given NISA's suggestion that changes should be voluntary, TEPCO passed up every important opportunity to embrace more advanced preventive measures and more stringent safety standards. From its perspective, "new regulations would have interfered with plant operations and weakened their stance in potential lawsuits. That was enough motivation for TEPCO aggressively to oppose new safety regulations and draw out negotiations with regulators via the Federation of Electric Power Companies" (NAIIC 2012: 17). Since TEPCO's bottom line might be adversely affected by the costs of new regulations, that was sufficient reason to lobby strenuously against any changes.

TEPCO's culture of bureaucratic insularity was blamed for its failure to embrace American technologies, developed after the 9/11 attacks, which would have contained any radiation release caused by traumatic shock to rooms containing nuclear fuel rods. Moreover, NAIIC found TEPCO's emergency response preparations entirely inadequate: "Response manuals with detailed anti-severe accident measures were not up to date, and the diagrams and documents outlining the venting procedures were incomplete or missing. Even emergency drills and training had not been sufficiently prioritized. These were all symptomatic of TEPCO's institutional problems" (NAIIC 2012: 30). Just as TEPCO failed to embrace advanced safety technology before the disaster, the company later "rejected offers from France, the USA and Germany for specialized robots resistant to nuclear radiation" (NAIIC 2012: 31) that could have assisted the rescue personnel during the response. Even more disturbing, NAIIC ruled that "neither the Chairman nor the President of TEPCO were present or accessible at the time of the accident, an inconceivable situation for an operator of nuclear power plants. The Chairman and the President also had different understandings of the emergency response structure, a fact that very likely contributed to the delay in TEPCO's response to the accident" (NAIIC 2012: 33). Instead of conveying timely information to both the government and the public, TEPCO merely "insinuated what it thought the government wanted to hear and therefore failed to convey the reality on the ground" (NAIIC 2012: 33). In light of recent revelations concerning the ongoing release of severely radioactive water from the plant into the ocean and TEPCO's "lack of a sufficient sense of urgency" about it (Fackler 2013a), it appears that the NAIIC report has yet to bring about the changes needed to face the crisis head-on.

10.2.6 Playing Games with Japan's "Heavenly Descendants"

Understanding the gamesmanship characteristic of corporate governance at TEPCO provides important clues to why and how the disaster became "man-made." Massive corruption perpetrated by "fallen angels" (Takeda 2011) and colluding politicians facilitated a deliberate underestimation of nuclear power's risks to society. According to reports from the international press, the relationship between TEPCO and the Nuclear and Industrial Safety Agency (NISA) was analogous to a "revolving door" of careerism (Onishi and Belson 2011), in which "most senior officials went to work at TEPCO" upon retirement from NISA. In a context dominated by political lobbying by nuclear power advocates, NISA is the operating arm of the Ministry of Economy Trade and Industry (METI), Japan's main promoter of nuclear power. Shiokawa Tetsuya, a member of the Japanese Communist Party, observed that since the 1960s TEPCO had been reserving its vice-presidency for METI's retirees (Takeda 2011).

Having bureaucrats at the end of their tenure landing jobs at companies they used to oversee is routine in Japan. This practice takes the name of "*amakudari*," a term adapted from Shinto religion meaning "descent from heaven" (Onishi and Belson 2011). *Amakudari* is both a way to compensate government regulators for the low pay and harsh working conditions faced during their civil service and a "means of lubricating the machinery of public-private sector relations" (Ogawa 2011). Because of *amakudari,* TEPCO's former senior managers were the ones overseeing the enforcement of government policies and regulations. As a result of the revolving door policy, the company was left to regulate its own safety practices, resulting in flagrant examples of conflict of interest in which even problems that posed unacknowledged risks to the public at large were mostly ignored.

Attempts at reforming the *amakudari* system have been numerous, though largely unsuccessful (Ogawa 2011). Politicians who tried to legislate reform of the system have encountered administrative obstacles, resistance to which has been characterized by one nuclear safety advocate, Kusuo Oshima, as "political suicide" (Onishi and Belson 2011). When news of the Fukushima disaster first broke, Prime Minister Kan made severe statements against *amakudari.* He admitted the unacceptability of the practice and committed himself to take concrete measures to correct it.

But some questioned whether Kan would make the necessary reforms, given the 4,240 cases of *amakudari* he had failed to address since the Democratic Party's parliamentary victory the year before (Ogawa 2011).

10.2.7 Saving Face or Rebuilding Trust?

Reactions to the Commission's report were mixed. The facts were hard to justify. But predictably everyone involved in the systemic failure attempted to minimize his personal culpability. As a result of the Commission's scathing criticisms, Chairman Masataka Shimizu retired from TEPCO, with Senior Manager Tsunehisa Katsumata replacing him as CEO (*NBC*, 2011). Having disappeared for a few weeks at the height of the crisis, Shimizu resurfaced a month later, only to offer a lame apology to the public. Toshio Nishizawa was promoted as President at TEPCO, a post that some regarded as the most undesirable corporate leadership role in Japan. Though Nishizawa made various statements apparently intended to buy time to find a solution to the problems at TEPCO—for example, "I feel a massive weight of responsibility to assume the post when we are in an unprecedented crisis never experienced in the history of the company.... But I decided to take it because I believe it is my mission to challenge head-on this difficult situation" (Layne and Uranaka 2011)—little progress was made as TEPCO continued to obfuscate its responsibilities.

A year later, in July 2012, burdened with substantial compensation claims and clean up costs, TEPCO was nationalized (Japan Today 2012). The purpose was to prepare the company to make good use of a $12 billion capital injection from the government. Kazuhiko Shimokobe, a turnaround specialist and head of the Nuclear Damage Liability Facilitation Fund state bailout facility, replaced Katsumata as CEO in April (Forum on Energy 2012). Finding somebody to fill the uncomfortable position was not easy due to the poor relationships between the ruling Democratic Party and the business community (Obe 2012). Some potential candidates even questioned the actual willingness of the Japanese government to back reforms (Obe 2012) and curb *amakudari* and similar public-private arrangements perpetuating corruption. In replacing Katsumata, Shimokobe was given the task of coming up with a comprehensive restructuring plan. He resolved to promote a new president from within the company in order to avail of the experience of somebody having greater familiarity with its internal management issues. The managing director of the compensation fund, Naomi Hirose, agreed to take over the role and was formally appointed president of TEPCO in May 2012 (Forum on Energy 2012).

Once the new management team was formed, Shimokobe and Hirose initiated a double effort, on the one hand, to restore TEPCO's finances and, on the other, to reform the company's management and safety culture (*WNN* 2012). Two organizations were set up with the assistance of domestic and overseas external experts. The Nuclear Reform Monitoring Committee became responsible for monitoring the implementation of reforms; and the Investigation/Verification Project Team was instructed to follow up on the Fukushima reports. Their interplay is expected to ensure that corrective measures are implemented, wherever needed, especially in the areas of "governance, risk management, and information disclosure." Hirose also leads an internal Nuclear Reform Special Task Force. The task force will be supervised by TEPCO's Nuclear Reform Monitoring Committee and is responsible for the direct implementation of reforms. When these appointments were announced, TEPCO said that it was "determined to abandon our previously held overconfidence" in the existing safety culture and measures and to begin to implement management reforms. "We are determined to prevent the reoccurrence of another disastrous accident. To this end, present safety policies will be reformed from the ground up while taking into consideration domestic and overseas expert opinions," the statement said (WNN 2012).

As an indication of the changes it hoped to make, TEPCO's new leadership had promised to shed more light on the disaster. Thus in August 2012 the company released 150 hours of tapes recorded during the 5 days after the tsunami hit the power plant (BBC 2012). Showing the videos was an attempt to deflect at least partially the company's responsibility for the event and highlight the enormity of the natural calamity that triggered the crisis. The edited content from the videos focuses on the reactions of top managers and includes former Prime Minister Kan's rushing into TEPCO's headquarters, apparently, to urge the officials not to leave the plant—an explanation that cannot be confirmed since the scene where he appears has no sound (Tabuchi 2012b). In an interview subsequent to the state of emergency, Akio Komori, then plant manager at Fukushima, gave a different version of what happened during the prime minister's visit. He contended that TEPCO never saw withdrawal as an option for all the workers at the plant. He admitted, however, that once the radiation levels had become dangerously high, TEPCO considered the possibility of withdrawing workers not directly involved in stabilizing the plant's safety (Frontline 2012).

Komori's version has been criticized for several reasons, including his tendency to attribute the nuclear meltdown exclusively to the impact of the tsunami and not—as Mitsuo Tanaka and the NAIIC report indicated—on the earthquake's initial impact. Reaching a clear understanding of what actually occurred at Fukushima Daiichi, of course, is the first step toward acknowledging past mistakes and preventing them in the future. If the plant's systems for controlling temperatures in the nuclear reactors were initially rendered unworkable because of the earthquake that preceded the tsunami, then they indicate TEPCO's and METI's greater degree of responsibility for the disaster. Given the location of the Fukushima Daiichi plant, the containment structures and the safety systems should have anticipated the likelihood of a severe earthquake. If, on the other hand, the plant's safety was compromised only after the tsunami struck, then disaster could more plausibly be attributed to an unprecedented natural calamity, thus significantly diminishing TEPCO's and METI's degree of responsibility. The ongoing failure of transparency on the part of TEPCO and METI thus cannot be explained away simply as a matter of incompetence or the lingering effects of traditional Japanese culture. It may be a calculated attempt to deceive all their stakeholders in order to minimize their potential exposure to lawsuits. At this point, there is as yet no commonly recognized account of the sequence of events at the Fukushima plant.

10.2.8 Conclusion

After over a year of cleanup operations, TEPCO wanted the world to believe that the situation at the Daiichi plant has stabilized, a belief shaken once more by the recent reports of contaminated water leaking into the ocean and the Japanese government's decision to take over responsibility for the cleanup. As Eiichi Yamaguchi, a professor of science and technology policy at Doshisha University in Kyoto, declared, "This is an admission by the government that TEPCO has mismanaged the cleanup and misinformed the public…. The government has no choice but to end two years of TEPCO obfuscating the actual condition of the plant" (Fackler 2013b). It is now clear that TEPCO's focus has been on stabilizing its finances rather than searching for the kind of new energy technologies that critics hope will eventually substitute for nuclear power generation. Hirose has declared there are now no funds to support developments along that line, consistent with the expectation of restoring the company's financial standing (*Japan Today* 2012). Nevertheless, Hirose further maintained that, given the lessons to be learned from the Fukushima disaster, Japan's energy sources must be diversified. This is the only way to avoid detrimental effects to the supply in case of shortages of oil or gas or the increasing risks of relying on nuclear power. In fact, the price volatility of natural resources might seriously threaten the Japanese national economy (Seth 2012c). Such statements, however, have only prompted further controversy. Despite his declarations in favor of increased transparency, Hirose's unwillingness to admit faults in the past and his fierce skepticism about reducing nuclear energy production lower his credibility in the eyes of the public. Faced with the daunting challenge of restoring the public's trust, TEPCO's managers are now paying a price for their previous complacency.

Toshihiro Higuchi writing in *The Bulletin of the Atomic Scientists* expressed his perplexity concerning the "fundamental causes" of the disaster, which he sees primarily as reflecting "the ingrained conventions of Japanese culture: our reflexive obedience; our reluctance to question authority; our devotion to 'sticking with the program'; our groupism; and our insularity" (Higuchi 2012). His voice joins that of the many critics who pointed to cultural factors—like *amakudari*—that tend to smother individual accountability. Yet Higuchi recognizes the irony that the characteristics of the Japanese culture, now heavily criticized, had once been praised for underpinning Japan's previously sterling record for nuclear safety (Higuchi 2012). He argues that these cultural traits are but the downside of Japanese self-discipline, harmony, and professionalism.

As a result of the Fukushima disaster, the future of TEPCO and Japan's nuclear energy industry is uncertain. Reconciling safety concerns and financial considerations seems an impossible task for the managers involved. How would you approach the challenges they face? Do you believe policymakers will be able to regulate the nuclear industry and enable it to grow safely and economically? Or should policymakers abandon nuclear energy and focus on substantially reducing Japan's dependence on it? If the long-term solution to this dilemma involves reforming, if not eliminating, the *amakudari* system and related cultural practices, what is the next step to be taken? Those of us who may 1 day exercise managerial responsibilities should pause to consider what, if anything, would we have done when faced with a crisis of such cataclysmic proportions. Would we have tried to hide ourselves, as Shimizu did for a few weeks, in the hope that the storm will pass? Would we have done any better than Shimokobe and Hirose in using the opportunity afforded by the crisis to make significant progress toward transparency and accountability? Would we have been any less obfuscating than Komori had we been given the task of defending TEPCO's actions and policies?

Finally, what are we to make of Mitsuhiko Tanaka? If Japan seems wedded to the *amakudari* system and related cultural practices, how do you explain Tanaka's long struggle to warn his countrymen about the dangers of nuclear power? Is he a whistle-blower? Is whistle-blowing even conceivable in Japan? Was he right to violate his presumed loyalty to his former employer, Hitachi, in order to warn the public after Chernobyl? Are there limits to the loyalty we owe to our employers or to our families and the nation as a whole? What happens if and when these loyalties seem to conflict? Once he informed Hitachi's management of the problem, and they reassured him that there was no problem, should he have dropped the matter and forgotten about it? Do you think he was right to bring it all back up again when TEPCO was in crisis as a result of the disaster at Fukushima Daiichi? Was it right that a whistle-blower should have been given such a prominent role in developing the findings of the NAIIC report? If you had been in Tanaka's shoes, what would you have done?

10.3 Case Study Discussion

The story of Japan's response to the disaster that struck the Fukushima Daiichi nuclear power plant raises many ethical questions about accountability and transparency and the ethic of responsibility as it was exercised at various points by various people, acting both as individuals and as representatives of various corporate bodies. At one end of the spectrum we must consider the significance of heroes, like the employees at the plant and various first responders who did not abandon their posts when the disaster struck, but risked their lives in order to regain control of the nuclear plant. We need to consider the role of heroic virtue in shaping our ethical expectations. Shouldn't we demand moral heroism of everyone? Why were the responses of these people singled out for praise and gratitude? What made their actions heroic is that they demonstrated moral leadership above and beyond the call of duty. They volunteered to risk their lives in order to minimize the risks that others would have to face had they failed to respond. Had there been no plant employees and first responders trying to regain control of the damaged nuclear reactors, the scale of the disaster could have been far worse. We now know that several of these heroes were killed, and others were exposed to life-threatening doses of radiation. All moral and religious traditions honor as heroes those who knowingly sacrifice their own lives that others may live—or at least be taken out of harm's way.

At the other end of the spectrum, of course, we find those who in the face of disaster fail to perform their duties, by running away or other acts of cowardice. Such persons stand condemned, because they could have stayed at their posts with relatively little risk to their own safety. Had they performed their normal duties, the impact from the disaster might have been mitigated in various ways. The strange disappearance of TEPCO's Chairman Shimizu symbolizes the cowardly way out, and it seems fitting that he was forced to resign his office soon after he came out of hiding. Had Shimizu faced the same kind of personal risks encountered by the plant employees and first responders, his failure to perform his duties as CEO might have been forgiven as human—all-too-human. But the risks that he faced were mostly to his reputation, with any pretense of moral leadership—not to mention sound management practice—now washed out to sea, along with other detritus from the earthquake and tsunami.

Shimizu is not to be singled out as the only villain in this unfolding tale of man-made disaster. What of the other executives and managers at TEPCO, along with their peers at METI and NISA? What of the architects of Japan's nuclear power industry in the governing political parties, both the Liberal Democratic Party and the Democratic Party of Japan? Where on the spectrum of moral leadership, ranging from the heroic to the cowardly should we place the hundreds, if not thousands, of bureaucrats whose personal security within the system of *amakudari* apparently blinded them to the hazards of nuclear power specific to Japan? Should they be held responsible for their apparent indifference to the clear and present need for increased safety measures and adequate planning and training, in the wake of catastrophic events like the Fukushima earthquake and tsunami?

10.4 Ethical Reflection

Whatever verdict public opinion may render on the collective responsibility—or irresponsibility—of those executives and managers involved in the design, construction, regulation and management of Japan's nuclear power industry, it should be clear that the system that they administered created a situation in which whistle-blowing became both possible and necessary. Our case study identifies Mitsuhiko Tanaka as a whistle-blower because he attempted to alert senior management at Hitachi to the dangers involved in covering up a known defect in the containment vessel the firm had constructed for use at TEPCO's Fukushima Daiichi plant. Prompted by his understanding of the Chernobyl disaster, Tanaka had undergone a change of heart. Now a science writer, he went back to his former employers at Hitachi to warn them of the danger of a nuclear meltdown that was likely to occur when and if the containment vessel ruptured, as he thought it must eventually given its faulty construction. When Hitachi ignored Tanaka's warnings, he took them to the public at large, writing a book explaining the problems at Fukushima Daiichi in the context of the overall risks involved in Japan's nuclear power program. Tanaka's action, and his subsequent role in the NAIIC investigation, prompts us to consider the ethics of whistle-blowing, in order to determine whether it is ever appropriate and under what conditions.

10.4.1 The Ethics of Whistle-Blowing

In order to address the question whether Tanaka is to be praised as a moral hero or condemned for his treacherous disloyalty to his employers, we need to consider first what whistle-blowing is. While there is a range of activities that may be described in this way, essentially whistle-blowing occurs when someone within an organization, usually an employee, observes or participates in some form of wrongdoing—whether as an inadvertent mistake or the predictable result of some policy or practice—and tries to have it corrected (Boatright 2003, p. 106). This initiates a process that may evolve through several stages. First, the whistle-blower reports the observed wrongdoing to his or her supervisors, with the expectation that they will act to correct the problem reported. If they ignore the report, or otherwise fail to respond to it constructively, and if the situation seems serious enough to warrant it, the whistle-blower may take the report outside the organization, by informing the agencies to which the organization is routinely accountable, for example, government regulators, professional associations, or possibly the public at large through the news media. The point of taking the report outside the organization is to generate sufficient pressure to get it to change its policies or otherwise take action to correct the problem. Needless to say, most organizations discourage whistle-blowing for they consider any unauthorized report of their problems to outside agencies a serious breach of loyalty and trust and thus subject to severe punishment, ranging from termination of employment to loss of professional status or reputation and in the most extreme cases to some form of personal retaliation.

Ralph Nader, the activist who exposed the safety risks involved in American automobiles in his groundbreaking book, *Unsafe at Any Speed* (1965), is credited with being the first to identify whistle-blowing with moral leadership. Before Nader the term "whistle-blower" was "used to tar someone who breaks a code of silence and squeals to the authorities" (Zimmer 2013). But in 1971, at a Conference on Professional Responsibility that he had organized, Nader performed a "terminological salvage job," by calling for "civic-minded 'whistleblowers' in corporations and government to step forward and report fraud and other misdeeds" (Ibid.). If the ethic of responsibility in organizations requires both transparency and accountability, neither could be achieved without the help of whistle-blowers willing to disclose what they knew in order to prevent further harm to the organizations' various stakeholders, including the public at large.

Though it is unlikely that she was inspired by Nader's work, Karen Silkwood was among the first to blow the whistle in the USA's nuclear power industry. An employee at the Kerr-McGee's Cimarron Fuel Fabrication Site near Crescent, Oklahoma, Silkwood was involved in the manufacture of plutonium pellets for nuclear reactor fuel rods. Soon after beginning her employment, she joined the local Oil, Chemical, and Atomic Workers Union, in which she was charged with investigating and documenting health and safety violations, including the contamination that she had personally sustained because of allegedly faulty safety equipment and procedures at the plant. In 1974, Silkwood testified against Kerr-McGee before the Atomic Energy Commission (AEC), the US government agency charged with regulating the nuclear power industry. Later that year, after contacting a reporter from the *New York Times* with the intent of going public with her allegations, Silkwood died mysteriously in an automobile accident. While it was never proven in a court of law, her supporters then and now contend that Silkwood was murdered because she had blown the whistle on Kerr-McGee.

Silkwood's story remains an instructive basis for mapping the moral logic of whistle-blowing. She is not an antinuclear activist, but a wife and mother who worked at a plant producing nuclear fuel rods. She observes a problem, namely, the unsafe conditions under which she and her co-workers perform their assigned tasks. She asks questions and reaches out for assistance. The unsafe working conditions, of course, were obvious to all who had to endure them, but pointing them out to her supervisors apparently was an exercise in futility. So she joins the union, which was operating legally at the plant, in order to see whether anything can be done to correct the situation. She is given responsibility for investigating and documenting the safety violations. She works with the union to confront her supervisors with the safety problems at the plant. They ignore her concerns and accuse her of faking evidence of the problems and explain away specific evidence of plutonium contamination in her own body as a deliberate act of sabotage. Her effort to persuade her supervisors to address the plant's unsafe working conditions attracted the attention of the national news media. The automobile accident in which in she died occurred as she was on her way to hand over documents and be interviewed in order to warn the public at large of the hazards involved in nuclear energy.

Silkwood's story affords us an opportunity to examine certain basic moral assumptions about an employee's loyalty to his or her employer and vice-versa. In his effort to encourage "civic-minded 'whistle-blowers'" Ralph Nader was not rejecting the moral legitimacy of employee loyalty as such, but he was implying that there are clear limits to it. Often these limits surface in situations "when a boss asks for something unethical" (Chewning 1995). As we have seen previously, employees are human beings, with moral rights and responsibilities of their own. Their loyalty to their employers is morally significant, but not absolute. If their employer asks them to do something unethical, or if they observe something unethical occurring at work, they have a duty, as well as a right, to resist, at least to the extent of their own involvement in it. Silkwood's employers expected her to turn a blind eye to the safety problems at the plant, just as Tanaka's former employer, Hitachi, expected him to honor the code of silence and not disclose what he knew about the defective containment structure at the Fukushima Daiichi plant.

Unlike Tanaka, however, Silkwood's attempt to blow the whistle occurred while she was still employed by Kerr-McGee. She had all the more reason to think twice before going public with what she knew. While it may be appropriate for employers to demand that employees maintain confidentiality, and not reveal to outsiders any significant information about what goes on at work, no employer has a right to expect employees to keep quiet when the boss asks them for something unethical. Kerr-McGee refused to upgrade its plant safety procedures, even though it should have known that failure to do so might increase the risks of illness or even death to some of its employees. Hitachi refused to acknowledge Tanaka's warnings about the potential consequences of failing to replace the defective containment structure at TEPCO's plant. Failure to acknowledge these problems and take appropriate action to correct them carried risks sufficiently serious to override considerations of employee loyalty and justify going public with what they knew about them. But notice the conditions under which both Tanaka and Silkwood blew the whistle on their employers. Their going public came only after they had made a sincere effort to document the problems involved and have them corrected by their employers. They attempted to alert the public at large only after their employers had refused to act.

Without a doubt, whistle-blowing is dangerous and costly to all concerned. Employers will actively discourage it, because once outside regulatory agencies and the news media are involved, they can no longer control the story. Once the public at large hears of it and demands action, employers will have to correct the problem but no longer on their own terms, nor according to their own schedule. A loyal employee, of course, will not want to force his or her employer's hand in this way, except as a last resort. The problem must be serious enough to warrant public concern, and all other avenues for solving it must appear to have been exhausted.

Genuine loyalty never requires employees to ignore what they know to be true. The whistle-blower who acts with integrity is not only "civic-minded" but also demonstrates a higher loyalty to his or her employer, since the point is to pressure management into correcting the problem before it seriously damages or destroys the company. Enlightened employers therefore should adopt policies that promote the best interests of the company. Rather than trying to suppress whistle-blowers by threatening them with various forms of retaliation, they will attempt to open up appropriate channels of communication—for example, an internal ombudsman's office, or a credible and effective mentoring system, or even a "suggestion box"—so that employees who think they have identified problems, especially ethically serious problems, will have secure ways of bringing these to management's attention, without jeopardizing their jobs or their personal safety. Employers who encourage sincere communication between management and employees lessen the need or the moral justification for blowing the whistle outside the firm.

Because blowing the whistle by going outside the firm is an activity that is likely to be viewed by all concerned as adversarial, we may well ask under what conditions such a move is morally permissible, and when, if ever, is it morally obligatory. The two may be distinguished based on the seriousness of the hazards involved, especially to the public at large. Morally permissible means that problems, while not immediately life threatening, are serious enough to merit the public's attention, while morally obligatory means that failure to blow the whistle is likely to put innocent lives at risk. It would appear that the acts of whistle-blowing done by both Silkwood and Tanaka were morally obligatory, since ignoring the nuclear safety problems they identified was likely to result in recklessly endangering innocent lives. In both cases, the whistle-blowers were forced to become adversarial because of their employers' refusals to respond. In trying to alert the public at large, both Silkwood and Tanaka, in a sense, were forced to go to war against their employers. But are there any moral conventions or ethical principles governing a whistle-blower's engagement in the moral equivalent of war?

10.4.2 Whistle-Blowing and the Just War Tradition

Based on ancient Roman law, Medieval Christianity in Europe developed an ethical perspective that answered basic questions about the morality of warfare, when it was permissible, when it was obligatory, and what conduct within warfare could be regarded as legitimate. This perspective is known as the just war tradition and to this day it features prominently in Christian discussions of these questions (USCC, 1983). The theory of the just war attempts to state the ethical conditions that must be met, if the decision for a nation to go to war is to be regarded as morally justified: these are known as "*ius ad bellum*" (right to go to war) criteria. It also states two conditions governing ethically legitimate tactics in warfare, known as "*ius in bello*" (right conduct in war) criteria. Here are the seven *ius ad bellum* criteria: Just Cause, Competent Authority, Comparative Justice, Right Intention, Last Resort, Probability of Success, and Proportionality. There are also two *ius in bello* criteria: Proportionality and Discrimination.

Were we to review these criteria in detail, we would see immediately that the intent of the just war Tradition is neither to bless nor to glorify warfare but to restrict, insofar as possible, the harms done by resorting to using military force to resolve disputes among nations. The *ius in bello* criteria, for example, are meant to safeguard the rights—beginning with the right to life—of noncombatants or civilians, since they are regarded as having no direct involvement in the hostilities and should therefore be exempt from its ravages. The just war tradition retains its relevance mostly in situations where professionalized military forces, duly authorized by various states, are engaged in combat. Its relevance to contemporary forms of warfare, ranging from thermonuclear war to various forms of counterinsurgency warfare including antiterrorist campaigns, is highly debated and debatable, even among ethicists who recognize the relevance of just war principles to so-called conventional warfare.

If the activity of whistle-blowing eventually confronts an employee with the choice of going outside the firm in order to expose and correct problems occurring within the firm, how might the just war criteria help clarify the ethics involved in breaching the loyalty owed to his or her employer in order to do so? While an individual employee can hardly be compared to a sovereign state, like the state he or she is expected to act responsibly in carrying out the tasks or functions assigned to him or her. Just as warfare is a deliberate breach of the peace that is supposed to obtain among sovereign states, so whistle-blowing may involve a deliberate violation of the loyalty that an employee normally owes to his or her employer. When, if ever, is such a breach ethically justified?

All seven *ius ad bellum* criteria may help to address this question. When, then, is whistle-blowing morally justified in business? Let us review briefly each of the seven criteria: (1) Just Cause: The ethical problem is serious, and the firm's failure to address it creates significant potential for harm to various stakeholders. (2) Competent Authority: The employee disclosing the problem to outside regulatory agencies or the news media has already made a good faith effort to have the firm deal with the problem internally. (3) Comparative Justice: The evil to be confronted is worse than the evil that may be set in motion by resisting it. Since public disclosure is bound to have a negative impact on the business, at least short term, the positive consequences anticipated from disclosure must outweigh the negatives that can be identified. (4) Right Intention: The employee must be motivated by a higher loyalty to the firm's stated mission or purpose and not by personal motives of revenge or expected benefit. (5) Last Resort: All reasonable efforts to resolve the problem internally have failed. If the problem is to be solved, the external pressure resulting from public disclosure must be the only option. (6) Probability of Success: The employee's external exposure of the problem is likely to bring results; it is not likely to be ignored. (7) Proportionality: The employee acts to minimize damage to the firm's legitimate business interests; his or her response is proportional to the problem being addressed.

In evaluating Tanaka's decision to blow the whistle on Hitachi and TEPCO, we can see how all seven of these criteria may be applied.

(1) Just Cause: After Chernobyl, Tanaka realized the catastrophic harm that an explosion in the defective containment structure would cause to all living things in the vicinity of the Fukushima plant. Had he remained silent, he would have been partially responsible for such a catastrophe. When he failed to persuade his former bosses at Hitachi, he used his prominence as a science writer to alert the public to the potential disaster. Without a doubt, seeking to protect innocent lives is a just cause. Whether it justifies taking his case to the public at large depends on how serious the threat actually is. After Chernobyl, the risks of doing nothing ought to have been obvious to anyone involved.
(2) Competent Authority: Hitachi's managers ought to have recognized that Tanaka was the most competent person to judge the risks involved in the defective containment structure. After all, he had been the supervising engineer during its construction. His was not the warning of an ill-informed novice or a disgruntled employee. As an experienced engineer, he had the expertise to determine what might happen were the defect not corrected. Because of his unique competence, not only was it permissible for him to blow the whistle, but it also was obligatory.
(3) Comparative Justice: When Tanaka years earlier had tried to finesse the repair of the defective containment structure, he did so because he knew that replacing it might bankrupt the company. Thus he was aware of the potential financial harm to his employer. Later, he came to a vivid realization of the potential physical harm to the residents of the Fukushima district. Comparative justice, he now recognized, required him to act to protect their lives rather than the financial health of his employer.

(4) Right Intention: Tanaka was no longer employed by Hitachi when he blew the whistle on the Fukushima containment structure. Years earlier, he had resigned his position with them, in order to pursue a career as a science writer. His book on the dangers of nuclear energy was not his only achievement in his new career. While the book was written in order to make amends for his complicity in the Hitachi cover-up, the intention was not revenge against his former employers. He simply wanted to alert the Japanese public to the problems in nuclear safety that put all their lives at risk. Had his intention not been proper, it is hard to imagine how or why he would later be appointed to the NAIIC that investigated the disaster.
(5) Last Resort: Tanaka decided to write a book to alert the public to the dangers of nuclear energy, in the course of which he confessed his role in covering up the defect in the containment structure that was still online at the TEPCO plant. It is clear from the accounts of his actions and motivations that he went public only after failing to persuade Hitachi management to investigate the problem. What else could he have done with his story?
(6) Probability of Success: There was, of course, no guarantee that writing a book on nuclear safety would move Japanese public opinion to demand the appropriate actions be taken. Nevertheless, the book did serve as a benchmark precisely because of its author's expertise in the field. When finally the earthquake and tsunami demonstrated the severity of the problem and vindicated Tanaka's analysis of it, he was now in a position to advise the Japanese government on how best to prevent a reoccurrence of the disaster.
(7) Proportionality: Neither Tanaka nor NAIIC was attempting to put TEPCO out of business or promote a fundamental shift in Japanese government policy on nuclear energy. Their effort was to minimize the risk of future nuclear accidents, by mandating appropriate safety standards and technological upgrades sufficient to protect the people of Japan. The problem, as they see it, is not nuclear energy as such, but its responsible management within the existing structures of Japanese society and governance, private as well as public. They recommend specific reforms proportional to the problems they have identified and analyzed. They are not calling for the wholesale dismantling of Japan's nuclear power industry. Taken together each of the seven criteria reviewed here suggests that Tanaka was morally justified in blowing the whistle on Hitachi and TEPCO. His work ought to be regarded as a model for responsible whistle-blowing throughout eastern Asia.

10.5 Conclusion: Beyond Whistle-Blowing

The loyalty that employers expect from employees is rooted in traditional Confucian teaching on filial piety, which originates from the relationship between a son or a daughter and his or her parents and which extends to larger entities such as the clan, the village, the city, the company, or the government. The goal of filial piety is to preserve harmony and peace in these relationships. But as we have seen, not only in the TEPCO case, the harmony envisioned in this ideal often supports policies that discourage people from voicing legitimate dissent. Loyalty becomes identified with maintaining a strict hierarchical order—such as that fostered by the bureaucratic practice of *amakudari* in Japanese business and government—that promotes conformity over all other organizational values. Not surprisingly, this perverted sense of loyalty stifles debate and thus tends to create an organizational culture in which whistle-blowing becomes both possible and necessary. While it can benefit the public at large, from another perspective, it can harm both the individual and the organization. Both lessons need to be taken seriously, when judging the appropriateness of any particular case of whistle-blowing.

Cultivating harmonious relationships at the workplace remains an employee's first priority. Therefore, it is inappropriate to encourage suspicion and intrigue within the firm. Employees must keep confidentiality about a company's reports and ensure that rumors do not spread distorted information about the company. Whistle-blowing, therefore, should always be the last resort in voicing dissent. Especially in fields that affect public health, in which mistakes can cost lives, internal channels of communication must exist, but in establishing them, even outside Asia, care should be taken that no one loses face. Like an ombudsman to whom the public can voice complaints, a respected member of a company's board, trusted because of his or her experience, must be available to receive and scrutinize criticism. The lack of channels to process legitimate complaints has caused the self-destruction of many companies, and certainly TEPCO would have been better prepared to respond to the Fukushima disaster had they been developed at that plant.

Ethics argues for an environment where loyal dissent can be voiced within a company, thus minimizing the need for blowing the whistle outside the firm. Thus we acknowledge that the authority of the company's managerial hierarchy must be respected. While advocating whistle-blowing could be misunderstood as an endorsement of defiance against the management team and its direction of the company, a proper understanding of the ethics of whistle-blowing must avoid any form of fanaticism that would promote a workplace climate of mutual denunciation and suspicion. We believe that such an understanding can be inferred from a review of the moral limits in adversarial relationships, as enshrined in the just war tradition. But rather than focus exclusively on whistle-blowing, we further suggest that developing a culture of innovation and loyal dissent within a company will improve not only employee loyalty but also the firm's credibility in the markets that it seeks to serve. This requires the development of communication structures and open forums so that all members of a team feel encouraged to contribute their ideas. When emergencies arise, like the earthquake and tsunami that devastated the Fukushima Daiichi plant, companies that are candid in their communications, both internally and externally, will be better prepared to cope with them and move quickly onto the path of recovery.

References

Axelrod, J. (2011, March 16). Fukushima heroes: Not afraid to die. *CBS News*. Retrieved on September 12, 2012 from http://www.cbsnews.com/2100-18563_162-20043554.html

BBC. (2012, August 7). *TEPCO releases recordings of Fukushima nuclear crisis*. Retrieved on September 12, 2012 from http://www.bbc.co.uk/news/19159927

Black, R. (2011, March 15). Reactor breach worsens prospects. *BBC*. Retrieved on September 13, 2012 from http://www.bbc.co.uk/news/science-environment-12745186

Boatright, J. R. (2003). *Ethics and the conduct of business* (3rd ed.). New York: Prentice-Hall.

Cantoria, C. (2011, August 3). *Nuclear power plant accidents and their damaging effects*. Bright Hub. Retrieved on August 9, 2013 from http://www.brighthub.com/environment/science-environmental/articles/65993.aspx

Chewning, R. (1995). When a boss asks for something unethical. In M. Stackhouse, D. McCann, & S. Roels (Eds.), *On moral business: Classical and contemporary resources for ethics in economic life* (pp. 723–726). Grand Rapids: Wm. B. Eerdmans Publishing Co.

Clenfield, J. (2011a, March 18). Japan nuclear disaster caps decades of faked reports, accidents. Bloomberg. Retrieved on August 12, 2013 from http://www.bloomberg.com/news/2011-03-17/japan-s-nuclear-disaster-caps-decades-of-faked-safety-reports-accidents.html

Clenfield, J. (2011b, March 23). *Fukushima engineer says he helped cover up flaw at Dai-Ichi reactor No. 4*. Bloomberg. Retrieved on August 12, 2013 from http://www.bloomberg.com/news/2011-03-23/fukushima-engineer-says-he-covered-up-flaw-at-shut-reactor.html

DNA. (2012, March 11). *Japan marks first anniversary of quake-tsunami disaster*. Retrieved on September 12, 2012 from http://www.dnaindia.com/world/report_japan-marks-first-anniversary-of-quake-tsunami-disaster_1660956

Fackler, M. (2013a, August 6). New leaks into Pacific at Japan nuclear plant. *New York Times*. Retrieved on August 13, 2013 from http://www.nytimes.com/2013/08/07/world/asia/leaks-into-pacific-persist-at-japan-nuclear-plant.html

Fackler, M. (2013b, August 7). Japan stepping in to help clean up atomic plant. *New York Times*. Retrieved on August 8, 2013 from http://www.nytimes.com/2013/08/08/world/asia/fukushima-nuclear-plant-radiation-leaks.html

Forum on Energy. (2012, June 27). *Timeline of TEPCO ownership*. Retrieved on September 16, 2012 from http://forumonenergy.com/2012/06/27/timeline-of-TEPCO-ownership/

Frontline. (2012, February 28). *TEPCO's Akio Komori: 'The options we had available were rather limited'*. Retrieved on September 12, 2012 from http://www.pbs.org/wgbh/pages/frontline/health-science-technology/japans-nuclear-meltdown/TEPCOs-akio-komori-the-options-we-had-available-were-rather-limited/

Goodspeed, P. (2011, March 16). Livid Japanese PM takes personal control of crisis management. *The National Post*. Retrieved on August 28, 2012 from http://fullcomment.nationalpost.com/2011/03/16/peter-goodspeed-livid-japanese-pm-takes-personal-control-of-crisis-management/

Hackenbroch, V., Meyer, C., & Thielke, T. (2011, April 5). A hapless Fukushima clean-up effort. *Der Spiegel*. Retrieved on September 12, 2012 from http://www.spiegel.de/international/world/a-hapless-fukushima-clean-up-effort-we-need-every-piece-of-wisdom-we-can-get-a-754868.html

Higuchi, T. (2012, September 4). Japan's culture: Culprit of the nuclear accident. *Bulletin of Atomic Scientists*. Retrieved on September 22, 2012 from http://www.thebulletin.org/web-edition/op-eds/japan's-culture-culprit-of-the-nuclear-accident

International Atomic Energy Agency. (2011, March 15). *Fukushima nuclear accident update*. Retrieved on September 13, 2012 from http://www.iaea.org/newscenter/news/2011/fukushima150311.html

International Business Times. (April 9, 2011). *A month on, Japanese nuclear crisis still scarring*. Retrieved on September 13, 2012 from http://www.ibtimes.co.in/articles/132391/20110409/japan-nuclear-crisis-radiation.htm

Iwata, M. (2012, September 5). TEPCO head fears end of Nuclear in Japan. *The Wall Street Journal*. Retrieved on September 12, 2012 from http://online.wsj.com/article/SB10000872396390444273704577633393350192040.html?mod=googlenews_wsj

Japan News Today. (2011, September 19). *TEPCO President Toshio Nishizawa makes motivational speech at Fukushima Daiichi nuclear plant*. Retrieved on September 13, 2012 from http://www.youtube.com/watch?v=QMME5pk0JqA

Japan Today. (2012, September 10). *TEPCO says it has no money to develop renewables*. Retrieved on September 12, 2012 from http://www.japantoday.com/category/national/view/TEPCO-says-it-has-no-money-to-develop-renewables

Kyodo News. (2012, May 24). *TEPCO puts radiation release early in Fukushima crisis at 900,000 TBq*. Retrieved on September 13, 2012 from http://english.kyodonews.jp/news/2012/05/159960.html

Layne, N., & Uranaka, T. (2011, May 20). TEPCO chief quits after $15 billion loss on nuclear crisis. *Reuters*. Retrieved on September 12, 2012 from http://www.reuters.com/article/2011/05/20/us-TEPCO-idUSTRE74I89G20110520

Los Alamos Science. (1995). The Karen Silkwood story: What we know at Los Alamos. *Los Alamos Science, 23*. Retrieved on August 22, 2013 from http://www.fas.org/sgp/othergov/doe/lanl/pubs/00326645.pdf

McCurry, J. (2011, April 12). Japan raises nuclear alert level to seven. *The Guardian*. Retrieved on September 13, 2012 from http://www.guardian.co.uk/world/2011/apr/12/japan-nuclear-alert-level-seven

Mochizuki, I. (2012, September 11). Thyroid disease rate spiked to 43.7%, 'About 1 in 2 children have nodule or cyst in Fukushima city'. *Fukushima Daily Blog*. Retrieved on September 12, 2012fromhttp://fukushima-diary.com/2012/09/thyroid-disease-rate-spiked-from-35-8-to-43-7-about-one-in-two-children-have-nodule-or-cyst-in-fukushma-city/

Muller, R. (2012, August 18). The panic over Fukushima. *The Wall Street Journal*. Retrieved on September 21, 2012 from http://online.wsj.com/article/SB10000872396390444772404577589270444059332.html

Nader, R. (1965). *Unsafe at any speed: The designed-in dangers of The American automobile*. New York: Grossman Publishers.

NAIIC. (2012, July 5). *The National Diet of Japan*. Retrieved on September 12, 2012 from http://cryptome.org/2012/07/daiichi-naiic.pdf

NBC News. (2011, May 19). Report: President of Japan's troubled TEPCO resigning. Retrieved on September 13, 2012 from http://www.msnbc.msn.com/id/43101927/ns/business-world_business/t/report-president-japans-troubled-TEPCO-resigning/#.UFGSCc1DSTY

NEI. (2012, August 13). *TEPCO continues dismantling Fukushima Daiichi 4*. Retrieved on September 13, 2012 from http://safetyfirst.nei.org/japan/TEPCO-continues-dismantling-fukushima-daiichi-4/

NHK Documentary. (2012, July). *Fukushima the truth behind the chain of Meltdowns*. Retrieved onSeptember12,2012fromhttp://enenews.com/TEPCO-manager-thought-situation-could-ruining-country-reactor-2-start-burning-inside-cool-video

Obe, M. (2012, April 19). Japanese government finds new chairman for TEPCO. *The Wall Street Journal*. Retrieved on September 19, 2012 from http://online.wsj.com/article/SB10001424052702304331204577353302409041804.html.

OECD. (2011, June 17). *Status of National actions in response to the TEPCO Fukushima Daiichi accident*. Retrieved on September 13, 2012 from http://www.oecd-nea.org/nsd/docs/2012/sen-nra-wgoe2012-1.pdf

Ogawa, H. (2011, May 23). *The problem with Amakudari. The Diplomat*. Retrieved on September 22, 2012 from http://thediplomat.com/a-new-japan/2011/05/23/the-problem-with-amakudari/

Oi, M. (2012, June 4). TEPCO ex-executives get golden parachute. *BBC*. Retrieved on September 12, 2012 from http://www.bbc.co.uk/news/business-18550747

Onishi, N., & Belson, K. (2011, April 26). Culture of complicity tied to stricken nuclear plant. *New York Times*. Retrieved on June 19, 2015 from http://www.nytimes.com/2011/04/27/world/asia/27collusion.html

Rashke, R. L. (1981/2000). *The killing of Karen Silkwood: The story behind the Kerr-McGee Plutonium case* (2nd ed.). Ithaca: Cornell University Press.

Reuters. (2011a, April 21). Japan says 20 km Fukushima ring will be no-go zone. Retrieved on September 12, 2012 from http://www.reuters.com/article/2011/04/21/japan-fukushima-idUSL3E7FL0AQ20110421

Reuters. (2011b, December 6). Japan sees atomic power costs up by at least 50 percent by 2030. Retrieved on September 12, 2012 from http://www.reuters.com/article/2011/12/06/japan-nuclear-cost-idUSL3E7N60MR20111206

Saito, M. S., & Slodkowski, A. (2013, August 7). *Japan says Fukushima leak worse than thought, government joins clean-up*. Reuters. Retrieved on August 9, 2013 from http://www.reuters.com/article/2013/08/07/us-japan-fukushima-pm-idUSBRE97601K20130807

Schumaker-Matos, E. (2012, March 20). The cost of fear: the Framing of a Fukushima report. *NPR*. Retrieved on September 12, 2012 from http://www.npr.org/blogs/ombudsman/2012/03/15/148703963/the-cost-of-fear-the-framing-of-a-fukushima-report

Seth, R. (2012a, July 20). TEPCO befuddled by allegations against their role in the nuclear disaster. *The Japan Daily Press*. Retrieved on September 21, 2012 from http://japandailypress.com/TEPCO-befuddled-by-allegations-against-their-role-in-the-nuclear-disaster-207021

Seth, R. (2012b, August 15). TEPCO manager Masao Yoshida's video diary. *The Japan Daily Press*. Retrieved on September 12, 2012 from http://japandailypress.com/TEPCO-manager-masao-yoshidas-video-diary-159195

Seth, R. (2012c, September 6). TEPCO chief Naomi Hirose is skeptic about nuclear power in Japan. *The Japan Daily Press*. Retrieved on September 21, 2012 from http://japandailypress.com/TEPCO-chief-naomi-hirose-is-skeptic-about-nuclear-power-in-japan-0611325

Soble, J. (2011, April 13). TEPCO president's 'sorry' return to work. *The Financial Times*. Retrieved on September 12, 2012 from http://www.ft.com/intl/cms/s/0/35ea8424-65ef-11e0-9d40-00144feab49a.html#axzz26KnBkLWw

Tabuchi, H. (2012a, July 5). Inquiry declares Fukushima crisis a man-made disaster. *The New York Times*. Retrieved on September 12, 2012 from http://www.nytimes.com/2011/04/27/world/asia/27collusion.html?pagewanted=2&_r=4&src=me

Tabuchi, H. (2012b, August 6). Japan utility shows recordings of nuclear crisis. *The New York Times*. Retrieved on September 12, 2012 from http://www.nytimes.com/2012/08/07/world/asia/TEPCO-shows-video-from-japans-nuclear-crisis.html?_r=0

Takeda, N. (2011, August 8). Amakudari: Japan's fallen angel. *The Truman Factor*. Retrieved on September 22, 2012 from http://trumanfactor.com/2011/amakudari/

Tanaka Ryusaku Journal. (2012, June 16). The shareholder derivative action – TEPCO: "There was no mistake in our response after the accident". Retrieved on September 12, 2012 from http://dissensus-japan.blogspot.com/2012/06/shareholder-derivative-action-TEPCO.html

TEPCO. (2012, March 11). *A message from TEPCO president Toshio Nishizawa marking the first year since the Fukushima Daiichi Nuclear Power Accident*. Retrieved on September 13, 2012 from http://www.TEPCO.co.jp/en/press/corp-com/release/2012/12031103-e.html

The Asahi Shimbun. (2011, December 7). TEPCO president noncommittal on liability, rate hike. Retrieved on September 12, 2012 from http://ajw.asahi.com/article/0311disaster/fukushima/AJ201112070020

Uechi, K. (2012, September 12). TEPCO sets up 3rd-part panel to improve nuclear safety, win trust. *The Asahi Shimbun*. Retrieved on September 12, 2012 from http://ajw.asahi.com/article/0311disaster/fukushima/AJ201209120078

United States Catholic Conference (USCC). (1983). *The challenge of peace: God's promise and our response: A pastoral letter on war and peace by the National Conference of Catholic Bishops*. Retrieved on August 30, 2013 from http://old.usccb.org/sdwp/international/TheChallengeofPeace.pdf

von Hippel, F. (2011, September/October). The radiological and psychological consequences of the Fukushima Daiichi accident. *The Bulletin of the Atomic Scientists, 67*(5), 27–36.

Weisenthal, J. (2011, March 29). Hasn't been seen in weeks, and there are rumors he has fled or committed suicide. *Business Insider*. Retrieved on September 13, 2012 from http://articles.businessinsider.com/2011-03-29/news/30063469_1_rumors-suicide-politicians
Westlake, A. (2012, May 17). TEPCO's price increase proposal met with customer opposition. *The Japan Daily Press*. Retrieved on September 12, 2012 from http://japandailypress.com/TEPCOs-price-increase-proposal-met-with-customer-oppostition-172290
WNN. (2012, September 12). TEPCO launches reformation. Retrieved on September 29, 2012 http://www.world-nuclear-news.org/C-TEPCO_launches_reformation-1309127.html
Zimmer, B. (2013, July 12). Word on the street: The epithet nader made respectable. *Wall Street Journal*. Retrieved on August 27, 2013 from http://online.wsj.com/article/SB10001424127887323368704578596083294221030.html

Chapter 11
Investors: Ethics and Finance

> *"Respecting your colleagues is the smartest investment you can make."* (Stephan Rothlin, *Eighteen Rules for Becoming a Top Notch Player*, 2004)

11.1 Prelude

Among the consequences of the 2008, global financial crisis was the emergence of an international movement, centered on "Occupy Wall Street" and other protests, such as the squatters community that developed in Hong Kong in the public space under the headquarters of the HSBC. This movement has been roundly criticized by some for its lack of a coherent focus or objective and other aesthetic breaches of civil etiquette. But others have seen it as an ethical challenge against the actions of certain players in the global financial industry who, in order to maximize their own gains, have ignored their own fiduciary responsibilities toward investors as well as the public at large. One such defender of Occupy Wall Street is Tom Myers, whose firm specializes in the kind of forensic accounting that has helped expose the crimes and misdemeanors perpetrated in the financial crisis. Myer's "Open Letter" in defense of Occupy Wall Street is the point of departure for our exploration of proposals for an Investor Bill of Rights (IBOR) and other attempts at reform within the banking and investment communities, both in Asia and elsewhere. These efforts provide us with an opportunity to consider the case for a broader and more proactive understanding of the nature of fiduciary responsibility and what it ought to mean for those who take seriously the ethical principles inherent in the basic logic of financial transactions. They also may enable us to conceive a financial system which is better connected to the "real economy," for example, by creating and encouraging investment in small and middle sized companies which are the true motor of the economy. Since the financial system must serve the common good, and not simply the interests of the super rich, our focus is on those reforms, both public and private, that promise to benefit all stakeholders.

S. Rothlin, D. McCann, *International Business Ethics*,
DOI 10.1007/978-3-662-47434-1_11

11.2 Case Study: Investors and Bankers Respond to Calls for Financial Reform

11.2.1 Abstract

Once the collapse of Lehman Brothers in September, 2008, dramatized the scale and scope of the global financial crisis, the momentum already building for reform in the investment and banking industries achieved not only a sense of greater urgency through popular protests like Occupy Wall Street (OWS), but also a clearer focus on the role of investors and bankers in making reform a reality. Two important indications of their seriousness about reform are the renewed discussion of an Investor Bill of Rights (IBOR) and the success of innovative efforts to create and sustain ethical banking practices. In this case study, we will be exploring proposals for an IBOR, starting with an open letter that Tom Myers—a highly respected forensic accountant and CEO of the China Trade Institute—wrote in response to the OWS protests, and then the innovative practices of banking institutions that have made ethics central to their mission, such as *Banca Popolare Etica* in Italy, the Grameen Bank in Bangladesh, the E. Sun Bank of Taiwan, as well as the various efforts at banking reform undertaken in China by various banks in cooperation with the PRC government. While these promising efforts are no guarantee that the investment and banking industries will never again engage in the kind of reckless activities that provoked the global financial crisis, they do suggest that reform is sustainable, particularly if commercial banks, large and small, renew their efforts to serve the needs of all their stakeholders and that appropriate laws are developed.

11.2.2 Keywords

Investor Bill of Rights (IBOR), ethical banking, *banca popolare*, cooperative financial institution, microbanking, Association for Sustainable and Responsible Investment in Asia (ASrIA), Basel III reforms, social responsibility investments (SRIs).

11.2.3 Occupy Wall Street and the Prospects for Financial Reform

When the global financial crisis of 2008 revealed the extent of the abuses that had taken place, a resistance movement was born out of long smouldering frustrations provoked by the dysfunctions of the market, excessive pay for top managers, and a widespread feeling that the system was rigged against large segments of society. The movement known as Occupy Wall Street (OWS) began on September 17, 2011, in Zuccotti Park, located in New York City's Wall Street financial district. It raised issues such as social and economic inequality, greed, corruption and the undue influence of business on government—particularly corporations from the financial services sector. "We are the 99 %" was the slogan advanced by OWS, referring to the unequal distribution of income and wealth in the U.S. and throughout the world, separating the wealthiest 1 % from the rest of the population.

Eventually, the movement grew in numbers and "We are the 99 %" could be seen on placards in other cities around the United States and in other Western countries. Local groups often have different agendas, but how to change the global financial system that disproportionately benefits a tiny minority, undermines democracy, and generates financial instability were among its chief concerns. For nearly a year (October 15th, 2011 to September 11th, 2012), the Hong Kong chapter, Occupy Central, for example, created a makeshift community beneath the HSBC (Hong Kong Shanghai Banking Corporation) headquarters to dramatize its grievances.[1] While Occupy Central echoed the OWS movement's global protest against corporate greed and economic inequality, it sought to educate people to the role played specifically by the HSBC and other major Hong Kong banks. Before it was dismantled in 2012, the Occupy Central encampment attracted a commune of occupiers including students, young professionals, activists, the unemployed, and homeless (Reuters 2012). In London, the Occupy London movement protested not only against the injustices of the financial system, but also against oppression around the globe and the U.K.'s foreign policies (Occupy London 2011).

Critics dismissed the Occupy movement, labeling it and its supporters as "freeloaders" (Zernike 2011), "human debris" (Hixon 2011), and "anti-American" (Colley 2011). They predicted that the movement would have little impact on politics and public policies regulating the financial system. But there were others who praised it and supported it publicly. When asked about his views on OWS, Bill Clinton, former president of the United States, said he thought the movement was

[1] The Occupy Central movement of 2011–2012 is distinct from, but indirectly related to the Occupy Central movement now ongoing in Hong Kong. While both are dedicated to the cause of advancing social and economic justice for the citizens of Hong Kong, the relatively small encampment of 2011–2012 was focused on addressing alleged misconduct among the big banks in Hong Kong, especially in their dealings with small investors. By contrast, the 2014 Occupy Central is a mass movement focused on the struggle over the policies and procedures that will govern electoral reform, particularly, the requirements to be used to screen candidates for the office of the HKSAR Chief Executive. The struggle for economic justice remains a major concern in the 2014 movement since Hong Kong politicians of every stripe recognize that were the "One Man, One Vote" standard of democracy to be enforced, the expanded electorate would likely support economic and social reforms meant to assure greater prosperity and security for all of the HKSAR's citizens. For a reliable account of the Occupy Central 2014 movement, following all its vicissitudes since it began on September 26th, see the archive available at the South China Morning Post (SCMP 2015). Since the Occupy Central 2014 movement involves issues well beyond our focus on international business ethics and financial reform, we will make no further comment on it. All statements concerning Occupy Central and other efforts related to the OWS movement refer to the events of 2011–2012, and should not be misconstrued one way or another as referring to the 2014 movement in Hong Kong.

"great" and that "[it] has done more in the short time they've been out there than I've been able to do in more than the last 11 years trying to draw attention to some of the same problems we have to address" (Gilani 2011). Distinguished philosopher and activist, Noam Chomsky, expressed his support to the movement and called it "an unprecedented opportunity to overcome America's current hopelessness" (Chomsky 2011).

11.2.4 Ten Practical Proposals

Although the original OWS movement was forced to abandon Zucotti Park in November 2011, they did not occupy it in vain. The movement inspired many professionals to become more directly involved in efforts to reform the financial services industry. In 2012, for example, Thomas A. Myers, a certified public accountant, financial investigator, and the founder and president of T.A. Myers & Co., published an open letter to the people participating in the Occupy movement. In his letter, he defended the OWS activists as "steadfast examples of the fortitude and conviction that represent what is right, what is just, and what is fair" (Myers 2012). Based on what he had learned from his own investigations as a forensic accountant, he also provided a well-informed analysis of what went wrong on Wall Street, revealing how major financial institutions would bet against their own clients in order to obtain higher profits for themselves. Nevertheless, his intent was "not simply to point fingers at the wrongdoing, but also to suggest change in order to avoid such travesties in the future."

Myers advanced ten practical reforms that he felt would move the already existing financial system toward serving the common good.

> Collectively, an organization of pension funds and institutional investors could demand such proactive and enlightened measures as, e.g.:
>
> 1. Commitment to investment programs emphasizing social, governmental, and environmental responsibilities
> 2. Curbs on runaway corporate executive salaries
> 3. Monitoring the regulatory "reform" packages that have been already authorized by Congress including that the provisions of the Dodd-Frank bill and Sarbanes-Oxley are not watered down by Congressman who are lured by the lobby dollar and are counting on a public with a short memory
> 4. Independent oversight and other limitations on the powers of the Federal Reserve with requirements for representation from all stakeholders including especially, the interests of consumers and the middle class while, at the same time, enforcing strict conflict of interest provisions;
> 5. Shareholder rights to determine corporate board of directors;
> 6. Requirements for investment transparency, including that the Byzantine labyrinth of complex deal documents relating to enigmatic structured finance products such as synthetic CDOs and credit defaults swaps be translated into plain English
> 7. Laws to make it especially onerous to defraud a pension plan (e.g. triple damages provisions and mandatory criminal sentencing) with stringent standards for investment advisors to such plans

8. Investment in products that create sustainable jobs and provide value to society in sharp contrast to the opaque structured finance products engineered for the gambling casino that Wall Street promotes
9. Imposition of a financial transaction tax which discourages activity that is unhealthy for our financial markets and, at the same time, raises hundreds of billions of much-needed revenue for the U.S. Treasury
10. Progressive taxes on the wealthy as advocated by none other than Warren Buffett (Myers 2012)

Myers, of course, was under no illusion about the struggle involved in advancing even moderate reforms such as these. Invoking the memory of Dr. Martin Luther King, Jr., he exhorted concerned citizens to "stand in solidarity with the OWS brothers and sisters who …will not capitulate to a corrupt financial system that casually and systematically diminishes the working people that have always been the backbone of our great country." He knew that the forces aligned against reform would be ready with their counter slogan, "Don't blame big business – blame government regulation." But Myers recognized the problem could not be papered over by empty rhetoric:

> The aggressive *de*regulation which was steadfastly pursued by government in the decade before the financial crisis (most notably passage of the Private Securities Litigation Relief Act and the repeal of Glass Steagall) set the stage for the 2008 debacle. However, it was the avaricious Wall Street investment bankers and their entourage that took the ball and ran with the legislators' open invitation to conflict of interest and, ultimately, to steal, that was provided by indiscriminate deregulation (Myers 2012)

Any real reform of Wall Street will involve a package of external regulations and internal transformations—of personal attitudes and corporate cultures. For this reason, Myers advocates both the imposition of a "financial transaction tax"–the so-called "Tobin Tax"[2]–as well the universal recognition of the moral imperatives embedded in an "Investor Bill of Rights" (IBOR).

11.2.5 Toward an Investor Bill of Rights (IBOR)

An IBOR would enable investors, making common cause with other stakeholders, an opportunity to be heard and to better protect themselves and their own financial interests. According to Myers, if institutional investors—such as pension plans, and

[2] The so-called "Tobin Tax," named after the American economist James Tobin (1918–2002) who originally suggested it, "was developed with the intention of penalizing short-term currency speculation, and to place a tax on all spot conversions of currency. Rather than a consumption tax paid by consumers, the Tobin tax was meant to apply to financial sector participants as a means of controlling the stability of a given country's currency" (Investopedia 2014b). Tobin tax proposals remain controversial because, in the opinion of its opponents, "it would eliminate any profit potential for currency markets. Proponents state that the tax would help stabilize currency and interest rates" (Investopedia 2014b). A brief history of Tobin tax proposals is available from The Financial Times (Sandbu 2011), while further information on efforts to have it enacted into law is available from the Center for Environmental Economic Development (CEED)'s advocacy website on the "Tobin Tax Initiative" (CEED/IIRP n.d.).

endowment funds—were to acknowledge these rights, their clients and customers "would be in a position to dictate more appropriate behavior from the financial markets controlled by Wall Street." An IBOR would demand that investment banks actually perform their fiduciary duties, not only to their wealthy customers but to other stakeholders as well. Were an IBOR to be generally recognized as the basis for the reform of financial regulation, customers, and other stakeholders would have greater opportunity to work together for the common good, by requiring investment banks to finance projects that have a positive outcome on communal and social development.

Tom Myers is not the first person to advocate developing a truly transformative IBOR. The idea behind it has been around since the 1970s, when John G. Simon, Charles W. Powers, and Jon P. Gunnemann proposed a basic policy for institutional investors—in particular, universities and other educational institutions—seeking to acknowledge their social responsibilities (Simon et al. 1972). Later, in 2001, while addressing the U.S. Securities and Exchange Commission, its Chief Accountant at that time, Lynn E. Turner, described the possibility of an Investor's Bill of Rights as "A Commitment for the Ages." His proposal consisted of a 16-point Bill of Rights calling for honesty, transparency, independent audits, and protection of the shareholders and investors' right to equal and fair treatment, as well as the corresponding obligations incumbent upon investors (Turner 2001). However, this prototype of a Bill of Rights remained a dead letter until it resurfaced in the aftermath of the global financial crisis. In 2010, a year after testifying before the Senate Committee on Banking, Housing, and Urban Development,[3] J. W. Verret, at that time the Chief Economist and Senior Counsel at the House Committee on Financial Services, published his own version of an Investor's Bill of Rights, which included the following:

I. Investors have a right to invest with managers who treat the company with the same care that a reasonably prudent person would give their own investments. If governments become stockholders in private industry and gain control over a business, they should be held to the same standard of loyalty and care in maximizing returns for investors as any other person controlling a publicly traded company.
II. Investors have the right to disclosure designed to present an accurate representation of the risks they face and the impact of those risks on their investments. Investors have a right to a clear warning when a company is unable to gauge its exposure to potentially catastrophic risk.
III. Investors have a right to redress against managers and investment advisers who commit fraud, and receive just compensation for losses that directly result from that

[3] On July 29, 2009, Verret gave testimony, "The Misdirection of Current Corporate Governance Proposals," before the Senate hearing on "Protecting Shareholders and Enhancing Public Confidence by Improving Corporate Governance" (Verret 2009). It contains a concise statement of the six major factors contributing to the global financial crisis of 2008, used as a benchmark for assessing the merits of some proposals for corporate governance reform under consideration as part of the Dodd-Frank legislation, then pending before the U.S. Congress. Verret was particularly concerned to caution against proposed regulatory requirements that would actually "leave no room for investors to design corporate governance structures appropriate for their particular circumstances." His testimony is relevant here because it confirms that an IBOR should serve as a basis for more effective self-regulation in the banking and investment industry, rather than far-reaching and possibly excessive changes to the existing regulatory framework.

fraud. Investors have a right to rules that clearly define fraud. Investors should not be used as a foil for politically motivated prosecutions that purport to have their interests at heart.

IV. Investors have a right to know when investments are safe or insured and when they are not. Investors have a right not to be lulled into false confidence based on implicit government backing or empty regulation.

V. Investors have a right to permit their companies to craft executive compensation packages that promise to buy the best talent properly motivated to maximize profits at the company during good times and minimize losses in bad times.

VI. Investors have a right to participate in elections for corporate directors by methods they design themselves, free from the tyranny of a minority of investors who may seek to use a corporation toward purposes that might limit returns and free from "one size fits all" federal mandates.

VII. Debt and equity investors have the right to clear and consistent procedures for liquidation when their investment becomes insolvent, no matter how large or complex that business might be. They have a right to know precise criteria a government will use in providing bailouts, with vague references to systemic risk being insufficient justification, and companies should remain free from coerced acceptance of government backing against their wishes. Healthy institutions should not be forced to subsidize unhealthy institutions.

VIII. Investor's have a right to regulation protecting their rights only after the benefits of new regulation are strictly measured against compliance costs, so that investors don't pay for regulation generating the appearance of regulatory success merely because more regulations are issued. The sole fact that an industry is currently unregulated is insufficient justification for new regulation.

IX. Investors have a right to choose the analysts they trust to advise them in equity or debt investments free from regulatory pressure to favor select institutions or regulatory requirements that only select agencies may rate debt for regulatory purposes.

X. Sophisticated investors and institutions have the right to security in their property rights to privately negotiated agreements with other sophisticated investors and institutions. (Verret 2010)

Although still in a formative stage of development,[4] such proposals could transform the way investment banking is actually done, simply by holding the financial industry to the principles that it already claims to honor. The major challenge, of course, is to develop appropriate institutional settings for achieving compliance. Otherwise, an IBOR inevitably remains merely aspirational, since apparently it is difficult to convince bankers that abiding by their own rules will allow them to maximize profits. According to a survey released in 2012 by Labaton Sucharow, a whistleblower law firm, more than a fifth of the interviewed senior financial managers "believed that the rules may have to be broken in order to be successful" (Allen 2012), thus condoning their involvement in unethical or illegal activity. When the same firm conducted the same survey a year later, it found out that the situation was getting worse: of the 250 managers surveyed, the number who believed they needed to break the rules in order to be successful rose to 29 %, and 24 % of those surveyed admitted that they would trade on inside information if they could get away with it (Pavlo 2013). Not all financiers are so unscrupulous. Around the world we find

[4]There are other noteworthy discussions of the IBOR, for example, "Calling for an 'Investor Bill of Rights" (Zamansky 2008), and "Global Investors' Bill Of Rights May Prevent Economic Déjà vu" (Selengut 2008).

bankers challenging this amoral way of thinking, who not only abide by socially positive investment policies, but also have been able to produce profit from these. One example is Italy's *Banca Etica*.

11.2.6 Ethical Banks and Their Best Practices

The *Banca Popolare Etica* headquartered in Milan, Italy, gives us reason to hope that banks can decide to abide by socially responsible policies—they can refuse to participate in funding wars or violence, or environmental destruction, or human trafficking of various sorts—and still make a reasonable profit. *Banca Etica* was recently described by the *The Economist* as "a bank that takes its name seriously" (*The Economist* 2013). Relatively unknown even among Italians, *Banca Etica* made news after the Italian parliamentary elections in 2013, when an anti-establishment group, the Five Star Movement, opened accounts there. *Banca Etica* describes its mission as "creating a place where savers, driven by the common desire for more transparency and the responsible management of financial resources, may meet socio-economic initiatives, inspired by the values of a sustainable social and human development… *Banca Etica* does not set out to reject the basic rules of finance, but it rather seeks to reform its main values" (*Banca Popolare Etica* n.d.).

Within its Articles of Association, *Banca Etica* lists the principles of Ethical Finance that it will follow in developing its policies and practices:

- Ethically oriented finance is aware of non economic consequences of economic actions
- Access to finance, in all its forms, is a human right
- Efficiency and soberness are components of ethical responsibility
- Profit produced by the ownership and exchange of money must come from activities oriented towards common well-being and shall have to be equally distributed among all subjects which contribute to its realisation
- Maximum transparency of all operations is one of the main conditions of all ethical finance activities
- The active involvement of shareholders and savers in the company's decision making process must be encouraged
- Each organization which accepts and adheres to the principles of ethical finance undertakes to inspire its entire activity to such principles.

Note that the principles of ethical finance espoused by *Banca Etica* go well beyond the notion of fiduciary responsibility operative in Verret's IBOR proposal. *Banca Etica* is committed to serving the common good and not just safeguarding the immediate interests of depositors and borrowers. For this reason, it is registered in Italy as a *banca popolare* ("popular banking institute"), that is, a cooperative financial institution operating with "a high level of participation" by its shareholders in the bank's governance, consistent with the principle of shareholder supremacy." When actual voting occurs, "all shareholders have the same power, regardless of the number of shares owned, according to the principle 'one subject, one vote'" (Banca Etica n.d.). While still a small bank, with little more than 36,000 shareholder-members, among whom are less than 6,000 organizations, the savings deposited in it amount to nearly a billion euros while loans currently amount to around 819 million euros (*Banca Etica* 2015). At the 2013 annual shareholders' meeting, the bank disclosed that only 0.4 % of their loans were in default, and just 4.9 % of them were labeled as "problematic," thus meriting its reputation as one of Italy's best-run banks (*The Economist* 2013). In its 15 years of operation, the bank has focused mostly on providing loans to the non-profit sector and green businesses, while categorically rejecting investment opportunities in ethically questionable businesses promoting, for example, pornography, oil speculation, or arms manufacturing. Executive pay at the *Banca Etica* is not allowed to exceed six times the lowest wage paid to any of its full-time employees. Its impressive governance record suggests that banks can make better decisions regarding where and how to invest, without engaging in predatory practices that increase the risks of provoking a financial crisis.

11.2.7 Ethical Banking Practices in Asia

Although Wall Street banks might deny the relevance of cooperative financial institutions, dismissing them because of their relatively small scale, it is worth noting that sometimes practices originating in such innovative settings are actually integrated into global banking operations. One such example is the Grameen Bank's successful development of microbanking in Bangladesh. Originally conceived as a "Bank for the Poor," the Grameen Bank was begun by Muhammad Yunus with a personal loan, the equivalent of US$27. In the 35 years since its founding—as it reported in October, 2011—the Grameen Bank has disbursed US$11.35 billion in loans, of which US$10.11 billion has been repaid. Currently, the bank claims that its loan recovery rate is nearly 97 %. Given the fact that most of its borrowers are poor, this rate has been sufficiently impressive to provoke interest in micro-banking among major global banks. "A Billion to Gain?" (ING 2006), a survey sponsored by the ING Bank and the Ministry of Foreign Affairs of the Netherlands, confirmed substantial involvement by major international banks in micro-banking activities. HSBC, for example, reported that although "microfinance is to be viewed as a business, not as philanthropy, … the bank engages with the micro-finance sector on a commercially viable and sustainable basis, whilst not losing sight of its CSR dimension" (ING 2006: 61).[5]

[5]When a follow-up study of the same name was published in 2008, conspicuously absent was HSBC, which reportedly was involved in "completely restructuring its microfinance activities" (ING 2008: 11). A search of HSBC websites, however, reveals that in India HSBC, in addition to "a lending program for small MFIs …has started offering commercial loan products to Large Microfinance Institutions (MFIs)… In 2008, we have put in place a microfinance strategy, with the objective of increasing our presence in this segment and building around a lending portfolio, a host of services which can facilitate capacity building, improve operational efficiency and bring the best practices of a transactional banking business to the microfinance domain" (HSBC India 2014b).

The "CSR dimension" at HSBC, of course, refers to "corporate social responsibility," meaning that the bank uses "microfinance to advance their corporate citizenship policy." Involvement with microfinance institutions (MFIs) makes sense so long as it not only enhances the bank's public image, but also can be justified from a business point of view. Within a strictly business perspective, CSR activities remain what they've always been. They are merely a different means to the same end of profit-maximization. International commercial banks are getting involved in microbanking, precisely because they've learned that there are profits to be made there. The ING report frankly admits this: "HSBC is keen to operate in areas of high social impact; although prepared for lower commercial returns, in view of favourable delinquency rates it is clear that this should be a commercially viable venture" (Ibid: 61). The Grameen Bank's success has alerted major commercial banks to an overlooked business opportunity. The poor, especially poor women, are as likely as the rich—if not even more likely—to pay back loans made to them. The poor are "bankable," precisely because the risks involved in doing business with them turn out to have been greatly exaggerated. The potential contribution of commercial banks to microfinance remains huge, because MFIs need start-up capital and a range of support services that these banks are in a good position to fulfill.

Also in Asia, after the global financial crisis, some people have started to raise questions regarding the need for reform in their industry. As a result, according to the Association for Sustainable and Responsible Investment in Asia, there are now over 400 identified sustainable mutual funds investing in the region and a burgeoning private equity sector (ASrIA n.d.). In 2013, a global Forum for the Development of Banking Transparency was held in Beijing. Organized by the Chinese State Council Development Research Center, the Global Commercial Papers Union, and the Hong Kong Commercial Daily, the Forum released its first annual report, analyzing the practices of 29 different Asian banks over a 2-year period, in order to monitor progress in achieving greater transparency. Three different Chinese banks were acknowledged for their efforts: Industrial Commercial Bank of China (ICBC), Agricultural Bank of China (ABC), and Construction Bank of China (CBC) (Hexun.com 2013). The Forum also was meant to demonstrate the fact that transparency has become a critical point for developing the banking industry, and that the performance of participating banks will be reviewed in the run up to the next Forum (Guan 2013). ICBC, for example, has shown leadership by improving its own corporate governance and establishing an independent audit, in preparation for its privatization through an IPO. In order to recruit new investors, ICBC strengthened its objective of maximizing returns while also changing its service culture. By listing on the

---

The information about HSBC's microfinance involvement, interestingly enough, is presented as one of a series of initiatives—specifically, one focused on "financial inclusion"—illustrating its commitment to "corporate sustainability." Here is the bank's explanation: "At HSBC, sustainability means managing our business responsibly and sensitively, and ensuring we include social, economic and environmental factors in the decisions we make to ensure long-term business success. We believe it is our duty to our customers, investors and employees to foster an ethical, responsible and sustainable corporate philosophy. Our goal is to be one of the world's leading brands in corporate sustainability" (2014a).

stock exchanges of both Hong Kong (SEHK) and Shanghai (SSE), the bank was required to comply with international standards, which brought in international auditors, added compliance rules, and provided more protection for minority shareholders (Lu and Cossin 2013). Nevertheless, two of the Forum's award-winning banks stood accused of predatory practices this year, as both the ICBC and CBC were found to be selling trust fund products to people who were unfamiliar with the concept of trust funds, and convincing them that these were part of a risk-free, high return investment strategy (Bloomberg News 2014). After the scandal broke, both banks stopped offering these services.

Some Asian governments seem to be stepping up their regulatory efforts in order to promote a more transparent banking industry. On January 8th, 2014, the Central Bank of China (CBRC) announced the issue of the "Guidelines for Commercial Banks of Global Systematical Importance Evaluation Index Disclosure." These guidelines are meant to bring China into line with Basel III's regulations[6] for Systematically Important Financial Institutions (SFIS). SFISs are institutions that due to their crucial role in their local or global economy are labeled as "too big to fail," since their failure or bankruptcy would cause severe damage to the world's economy, as happened during 2008's global financial crisis. The guidelines require SFISs to constantly check their assets and disclose them to third-party regulators; it urges them to strengthen managerial accountability and improve transparency towards clients and society, and also forces SFISs to maintain an extra 1–2.5 % capital reserve above the minimum capital level required of other banks. In China, all banks that have assets over 16 billion RMB are to follow these guidelines. However minimal the impact of such guidelines may turn out to be, they are a step forward in the effort to change the values of the financial world, and thus respond to some of the demands of the movement supporting an Investor Bill of Rights and other reforms. How significant they will turn out to be will not be known until long after the SFISs begin making their reports in November 2014. However, there is reason to hope that Chinese banks are upping their game, by attempting to respond constructively to the new Basel III regulations. Experts see this move as a gesture of compliance, as well as a positive initiative that might be imitated by other local banks (Law 2014). Indeed, experts like Tom Myers—who is deeply involved in advising clients about international trade in China—have strong hope that China may provide a strong positive influence on the development of the global financial system, provided that they truly implement a new culture of transparency.

[6] Basel III refers to "a comprehensive set of reform measures designed to improve the regulation, supervision and risk management within the banking sector" (Investopedia 2014a). The Basel III reforms are to be phased in over five years, and are meant to address basic issues in banking and investment risk management, by "strengthen[ing] "microprudential regulation and supervision, and add[ing] a macroprudential overlay that includes capital buffers" (BIS 2011). For detailed descriptioins of Basel III provisions, consult the *Bank for International Settlements* website (BIS 2011); see also the constructive analysis provided by the international accounting firm, *Klynveld Peat Marwick Goerdeler* (KPMG 2011).

In addition to efforts at regulatory reform in China and other east Asian nations,[7] there are Asian banks actively seeking to improve the transparency of their operations, the ways they relate to their customers, while also demonstrating their commitment to socially responsible investment policies. One example is Taiwan's E-Sun Commercial Bank, founded in 1989 by a group of investors and professionals looking to create a bank that pursues excellence and sound corporate governance. E-Sun Bank looks to follow an old Taiwanese saying, "Pure as Jade, Stern as Mountain" (*E.SUN FHC* 2008), by becoming a role model for financial institutions and a benchmark for the financial services industry. Its goal is not only to be the best bank possible for their customers, but also to be the most respected publicly. It is a bank looking to honor traditional Asian values in their operations: The E-Sun team embraces the values of "reality, capability and responsibility," "teamwork, harmony and happiness," "leadership, excellence and honor," and "contentment, appreciation and gratitude," and intends to put them into practice confident that they will lead E-Sun to a prosperous future.

E-Sun Bank is one of the few banks in the Greater China region to have a fully developed Corporate Social Responsibility (CSR) program. On the one hand, the bank wishes to provide the best banking service possible to its customers, but on the other hand, it wishes to push its values beyond the business world, creating benefits that can be shared with the whole community. As the bank says, they "have long considered fulfilling its corporate social responsibility (CSR) and making social responsibility investment (SRI) both its mission and commitment." They do so by providing its employees very distinctive benefits and the community with free financial consulting services, as well as participating in the clean-up of the communities surrounding their banks and other environmentally conscious activities, including providing seed-capital to schools, educational resources to areas in need, and promoting sports and other activities. E-Sun also looks to protect its customers from any possible departures from its stated commitments and provides a very detailed legal framework against which the products they offer to their customers have been meticulously tested beforehand, as well as abiding by Taiwan's own Consumer Protection laws. The E-Sun Bank has won the Corporate Social Responsibility Award from Global Views Monthly for three consecutive years (2006–2008) and has received the "Best Corporate Social Responsibility" award, granted by the Taiwan Academy of Banking and Finance.

[7] In June 2013, to cite another example, the Singaporean government proposed a new regulatory framework for financial benchmarks (Monetary Authority of Singapore 2013) This proposal was in light of the MAS' recent investigations to Singapore's banking industry, having found 20 banks deficient in the governance, risk management, internal controls, and surveillance systems for their involvement in benchmark submissions. A total of 133 traders were also accused of engaging in several attempts to inappropriately influence the benchmarks. The MAS is looking to revise its framework and introduce specific criminal and civil sanctions for those engaging in illegal activities. Also, new regulations will be imposed on financial institutions regulated by the benchmarks, such as a tighter regulatory regime, better corporate governance, and a strict adherence to their Code of Conduct. These actions could be seen as a preventive measure enabling the financial industry in Singapore to learn from the mistakes that contributed to the Wall Street disaster in 2008.

11.2.8 Conclusion

As we can see from such examples, things are slowly, but steadily looking better for the banking industry in Asia. Though time will tell how far efforts at banking reform will succeed, it is clear that there is growing interest in pursuing a better world by "giving back," and providing customers with not only a world-class service, but a service that can provide more than sound financial advice and steady returns. While most of these efforts are independent of initiatives seeking to promote a universal Bill of Rights for Investors, they actually respond to the same heightened expectations regarding the need for ethical banking everywhere. The best practices that support ethical banking, as we have seen, are not simply a reflection of European priorities and aspirations, nor are they simply a reaction to the predatory and scandalous behavior tolerated until recently among Wall Street bankers. Ethical banking is a cause now embraced globally, in the financial centers of Asia as well, in order to create a sustainable future in which savers and borrowers, investors, and other stakeholders can meet each others' needs with trust and confidence.

11.3 Case Study Discussion

Previously in Chap. 7 we explored the collapse of Bear Stearns, as it was merged into JPMorgan Chase when it was sold at a tiny fraction of its value before the subprime mortgage crisis. It is estimated that shareholders, on paper at least, lost 95 % of the value of their investments prior to its collapse (Sloan 2012). These were real losses and they haven't been made up, either through the government bailouts or through subsequent lawsuits against JPMorgan Chase (Erwin 2013). Nor were the losses investors suffered from Bear Stearns an isolated example. Shareholder losses in the 5 years subsequent to the subprime mortgage crisis, for the "too big to fail" banks, insurance companies, and brokerages involved in it, ranged from 99 to 28 % (Sloan 2012). Is it any wonder, then, that reform in the banking and investment industry should make a priority of securing something as basic as an Investor Bill of Rights (IBOR)? Recall from Chap. 7 that while it is assumed that anyone providing investment advice or financial services would have fiduciary responsibilities to their customers and clients, in the USA "approximately 85 % of financial advisers do not," the vast majority of whom are "stockbrokers, insurance agents, or simple sales representatives". The proposals for an IBOR, if it were to be enacted into law and enshrined in the ethics of finance, would not only strengthen fiduciary responsibility requirements, but also make them mandatory for all financial advisers.

Why should something so simple and basic as IBOR have been ignored for so long? Some of the answer may lie in history: making markets in financial transactions, buying and selling debt as well as negotiable assets, has gone on for much longer than the current trend toward professionalization, with its heightened expectations of transparency and accountability. It is a history marred by fraud and all-too-many financial scandals (Lund 2014) as well as the inability of government to make appropriate interventions. As in so many other areas, improvements in business ethics are closely linked to the advent of professionalism. Professionalization means growing beyond the rough and tumble of winner-take-all competition, and toward mature markets in which goods and services are priced fairly, where customers and all other stakeholders are treated with respect, and where transparency and accountability are internalized as values by all participants. Within financial markets where buyers and sellers do more than pay lip service to professional standards, conducting one's business consistent with the norms of fiduciary responsibility becomes second nature. When transparency and accountability are genuinely honored, implementing and policing compliance with the relevant codes of conduct becomes part of best practices within an industry. Perhaps the greatest scandal exposed by the global financial crisis was the revelation of just how far the professional standards enshrined in such codes, reflecting such values, had been corrupted in a mad pursuit of maximizing profits.

How would the implementation of an IBOR restore the values enshrined in the principle of fiduciary responsibility? Rights entail responsibilities, or duties and obligations. If I have a right to something, then someone has a duty or obligation to see that I get what's coming to me. If you make me a promise, for example, then I have a right to expect that you will keep it, and you have a duty or obligation to keep it. If you have no intention of keeping your promise, or if you know that keeping such a promise is impossible for whatever reason, then you shouldn't make a promise. Why would anyone make a promise? Because they want the other party to accept their word and modify their behavior accordingly. If you make me a promise, you want me to rely on it, and I intend to rely on it, at least until you make a credible excuse for failing to keep it. Most business transactions, or exchanges involving buyers and sellers, follow this simple and straightforward logic of making and keeping promises. You have goods or services for sale and I want to buy them or hire them. We agree on a price. One or the other of us goes first. I pay you the money in exchange for your promise, and you keep your promise, delivering the goods or performing the services in a timely manner.

In a timely manner—this qualification not only suggests how promises are kept but also how they are broken. Rarely do buyers and sellers find themselves in a situation of perfect symmetry and simultaneity. If I write you a check to pay for the goods or services you are delivering to me now, you are accepting the check as a promissory note redeemable at my bank for the amount we agreed to. You are also probably taking it on trust that I will not call my bank and cancel the check the moment we've completed our business. The time factor in human interactions makes promise making and keeping both possible and necessary. Promising, among other things, is a ritual designed to create mutual trust, which is necessary if the time factor and other asymmetries that may inhibit trust are to be overcome. By making and keeping promises we come to rely on each other, we build up a relationship of trust because we know from past experience that we will do what we say we will do.

What sort of a promise then is "fiduciary responsibility"? First of all, it is a pledge or an assurance that if I agree to let you manage my savings and other negotiable assets, you will honor my own best interests in doing so. You will use your expertise as a financial adviser to select investments that are appropriate to my interests and tolerance for risk, whether or not these investments will bring you the most in commissions or other rewards. If there is a conflict between your self-interest and my priorities as an investor, I can assume that you will act faithfully to serve my interests first. Someone who undertakes a fiduciary responsibility promises to manage his or her client's funds as a trustee, that is, for the benefit of the one on whose behalf he or she is pledged to act. The IBOR, then, is a list of the rights granted in establishing the kind of trusteeship that exists between an investor and his or her financial adviser or whomever agrees to manage his or her investments. Why would anyone trust another to manage his or her investments? The answer should be obvious: I have the reasonable belief that if I trust you with this responsibility, my savings will earn a greater return—one more consistent with my financial goals—than if I were to attempt to manage it personally. I am relying on your expertise as a financial adviser to help me make the best decisions consistent with my goals as an investor.

The rights described in Verret's proposal follow naturally enough from a consideration of the nature of fiduciary responsibility: Among other things, he proposes that investors have a right to invest with managers capable of showing "the same care that a reasonably prudent person would give their own investments"; they have a "right to disclosure designed to present an accurate representation of the risks they face and the impact of those risks on their investments"; they have a "right to redress against managers and investment advisers who commit fraud, and receive just compensation for losses that directly result from that fraud." While such rights clearly reflect the expectations of fiduciary responsibility by defining investor rights against financial advisers, Verret goes on to formulate other rights intended to protect investors against excessive or misguided government regulation. Since government regulation is often proposed to correct a perceived lack of fiduciary responsibility, Verret's IBOR would minimize government regulation in order to restore a common commitment to fiduciary responsibility.

Furthermore, Verret's IBOR would limit government regulation on the basis of its cost-effectiveness. He apparently assumes that investors are as likely to be harmed by overregulation as they are by the predatory practices of some financial advisers and brokers. Thus, investors, in his view, have "a right to regulation protecting their rights only after the benefits of new regulation are strictly measured against compliance costs, so that investors don't pay for regulation generating the appearance of regulatory success merely because more regulations are issued"; or "a right not to be lulled into false confidence based on implicit government backing or empty regulation." Similarly, Verret's IBOR includes a right protecting investors against losses allegedly incurred when the government forces the liquidation of their investments, or conversely when the government forces a company to accept a bailout based on allegedly "systemic risks." Investors, therefore, have "a right to know precise criteria a government will use in providing bailouts, with vague references to systemic risk being insufficient justification, and companies should remain free from coerced acceptance of government backing against their wishes." Verret's IBOR, then, is a reassertion of the paramount value of freedom, as in his assertion of the investors' "right to choose the analysts they trust to advise them in equity or debt investments free from regulatory pressure," and as the ultimate owners of the enterprises in which they are invested, they have "a right to participate in elections for corporate directors by methods they design themselves."

Oddly, Verret's proposal concludes with an assertion of the right of "sophisticated investors and institutions… to security in their property rights to privately negotiated agreements with other sophisticated investors and institutions" (Verret 2010). One well may wonder how Verret would determine who or what qualifies as "sophisticated," and in what ways, if any, this right differentiates them from other investors who could not or would not make such a claim. You may recall from Chap. 7 that the primary victims of the irregularities exposed in the collapse of Bear Stearns' BSAM—not to mention the list of those seriously hurt in Bernard Madoff's Ponzi Scheme—were generally regarded as sophisticated. No doubt, Verret is attempting to distinguish this group of investors from the widows, pensioners, and small investors whose losses are often invoked in order to justify increased government regulation. Nevertheless, when attempting to define an IBOR, it may not be useful to make generalizations that will apply only to specific groups, especially groups so casually distinguished on the basis of their alleged sophistication.

Despite the arguable shortcomings in Verret's IBOR, his main point remains crucial. Government regulation alone does not and cannot provide a secure path to genuine reform in the financial industry. On the other hand, further deregulation or clinging to a *laissez-faire* ideology that refuses the help of regulatory agencies is surely a recipe for disaster. The middle ground, showing the path toward reform voluntarily embraced by various enlightened financial institutions that are willing to experiment with new rules, in service to a heightened sense of fiduciary responsibility, may be the most promising way forward. This is why the case study goes beyond an IBOR to examine what innovative banks and financial institutions are accomplishing as they define their own path toward excellence or moral leadership. The efforts of *Banca Etica* in Italy, the Grameen Bank in Bangladesh, and E-Sun Bank in Taiwan demonstrate the promise of strategies making service to the common good central to the ethics of fiduciary responsibility.

The achievements of these innovative ethical banks alert us to the fact that the best way to minimize the risk of global financial catastrophe may be to recognize that financial transactions are never merely private—that is, expressing only the interests of the parties directly involved—but inevitably include a social dimension—that is, some accountability for the so-called "ESG" issues highlighted in the United Nations-supported Principles for Responsible Investment (PRI) Initiative (*Financial Times* 2013). ESG is an acronym representing the convergence of "environmental, social, and corporate governance" concerns that stakeholders, including ultimately the public at large, increasingly hope to see bench marked in evaluating the investment decisions of all major institutions. The *Financial Times* reports that "as of February 2014, 1,064 asset owners and asset managers and 183 professional service partners, representing combined assets of more than $34 trillion, had committed themselves to the six principles of the PRI," each of which is intended to promote increased transparency and accountability for ESG issues. Furthermore, according to the *Financial Times*, the European Federation of Financial Analysts Societies (EFFAS) has identified nine topical areas that highlight ESG issues in all sectors and industries:

> "1) Energy efficiency; 2) Greenhouse gas (GHG) emissions; 3) Staff turnover; 4) Training & qualification; 5) Maturity of workforce; 6) Absenteeism rate; 7) Litigation risks; 8) Corruption; and 9) Revenues from new products." These provide an initial framework for developing "KPIs (key performance indicators)" specific to each sector or industry.

The point of the UN Initiative supporting Principles for Responsible Investment (PRI) and similar efforts is to make "the performance of investment and fund portfolios on environmental, social and governance criteria and the quality of their performance against measurable ESG factors" visible to shareholders and investors so that they might "find new market opportunities with companies that place the management of ESG factors at the core of the business." Financial reform, therefore, involves the judicious development of a "carrot and stick approach," with government regulation providing the sticks, that is, the threat of sanctions against those who fail to perform their fiduciary responsibilities, while voluntary global initiatives like the PRI point out the carrots, that is, the opportunities and potential rewards of becoming proactive in response to the ESG issues that have emerged in the wake of the global financial crisis. As we have seen, ethical banking institutions like *Banca Etica* and E-Sun have already shown that it is possible to embrace an ESG centered agenda for financial reform while also earning a reasonable profit for their investors.

11.4 Ethical Reflection

The positive comfort that we would like to take from the range of responses to the global financial crisis outlined in our case study presupposes that investment banking practices, in principle, are reformable. We assume that, like all inherently good human activities, while they are vulnerable to corruption and abuse, they are not so totally depraved as to merit absolute condemnation and universal suppression. But is our hope merely wishful thinking, or is it reasonably based on an accurate understanding of what financial markets are and ought to be? One way to approach this question is to ask whether investment banking is any different from casino gambling? What makes investment decisions different from rolling the dice or playing the slot machine? In the opening chapter to this book we argued that it is a category mistake to equate business with warfare. We argued that business is more like a game, with rules that define winning and losing, with penalties for violating the rules that often do affect the outcome of the game. But what about games of chance? Further on, we rejected Albert Carr's idea that business is like a game of poker, in which bluffing is often crucial to success. But poker is only one of the games conducted in a gambling casino. How does investment banking compare with the rest of these?

11.4.1 Financial Markets and Gambling Casinos: Is There a Difference?

Games of chance—that may be the most important clue to understanding the difference between financial markets and gambling casinos. In a casino, besides poker, there are many other games that involve a mixture of chance and skill. Think of dice games like craps, or card games like blackjack. Financial markets, of course, also involve such a mixture, but the proportions may be very different. Investing differs from gambling in that it is—or ought to be—based on reliable information and rational analysis that allows investors to minimize the risk of losses and maximize potential gains.[8] The information needed by investors is specific and involves various assessments of previous performance and likely outcomes. The information needed by gamblers is generic, and usually consists in little more than knowing how to play the game, how to make bets, and how to collect one's winnings. Making a bet at a roulette table or shooting craps requires no specific knowledge of previous outcomes, but simply an awareness of the chances involved in betting on one number or another. Gambling, in contrast to investing, remains highly impersonal. While a gambler may be aware that the odds generally favor the casino organizing the various games, he or she needs only a reassurance that the games are not rigged one way or another. Investing, on the other hand, is likely to involve a personal

[8] In an essay, "What is the Difference Between Gambling and Investing?," Thomas Murcko criticizes dichotomies contrasting the two, showing the ways in which they often overlap in reality. Nevertheless, in his view, there are systematic differences which he summarizes as follows: "*Investing*: 'Any activity in which money is put at risk for the purpose of making a profit, and which is characterized by some or most of the following (in approximately descending order of importance): sufficient research has been conducted; the odds are favorable; the behavior is risk-averse; a systematic approach is being taken; emotions such as greed and fear play no role; the activity is ongoing and done as part of a long-term plan; the activity is not motivated solely by entertainment or compulsion; ownership of something tangible is involved; a net positive economic effect results.' *Gambling*: 'Any activity in which money is put at risk for the purpose of making a profit, and which is characterized by some or most of the following (in approximately descending order of importance): little or no research has been conducted; the odds are unfavorable; the behavior is risk-seeking; an unsystematic approach is being taken; emotions such as greed and fear play a role; the activity is a discrete event or series of discrete events not done as part of a long-term plan; the activity is significantly motivated by entertainment or compulsion; ownership of something tangible is not involved; no net economic effect results'" (Murcko 2013). The difference, in short, consists in the way investment decisions are made. The closer they approximate rational analysis, based on reliable information and expertise, the less they resemble a gambler's betting strategies at a casino.

relationship between the investor and his or her financial advisers who have access to the knowledge and expertise needed to make responsible investment decisions.

The relevance of the ethic of fiduciary responsibility to managing investments is based on the assumption that knowledge and expertise, rather than dumb luck, are the key to success. If a financial adviser is to provide genuine assistance to an investor, his or her methods and motives must be totally transparent. If the assistance is to be genuine—and why would any investor pay for it if it were less than genuine?—the adviser must be prepared to resolve all conflicts of interest in favor of his clients. He or she must not only formulate a reasonable investment strategy for his clients, but also be capable of explaining it clearly in a way that enables clients to give their informed consent to it. The situation of a financial adviser thus is similar to that of other professionals, like doctors and lawyers, who provide not only advice—for example, diagnoses, prescriptions, and strategies for improving health care or overcoming legal difficulties—but also perform services that their clients cannot perform for themselves. The ethic of fiduciary responsibility spells out the expectations for anyone entrusted with the management of other people's money. Financial advisers have fiduciary responsibilities toward their clients, and these, as we have seen, find expression in various proposals for an Investor Bill of Rights (IBOR).

11.4.2 Private Transactions and Responsibility for the Common Good

A transaction between a financial adviser and his or her clients, however, is not limited to the two parties directly involved in it. There is no such thing as a strictly private transaction. Like all other forms of business or marketplace activity, there are other stakeholders with legitimate interests in what goes on between an adviser and his or her investors, just as there are whenever buyers and sellers agree to exchange goods and services for money in any market. Even a narrowly defined IBOR, such as the one proposed by Verret, recognizes the legitimate role of government agencies that must regulate the relations between financial advisers and investors. But as we have seen in other areas of business, the list of stakeholders is hardly exhausted by acknowledging the rights and responsibilities of buyers, sellers, and government regulators. In a situation involving investment decision-making, the full range of stakeholders is likely to be involved, including a business' employees, their customers and suppliers, as well as the public-at-large. In the activities of innovative ethical banks observed in our case study, we see a trend toward recognizing the moral imperative of accountability to the common good.

Concern for the common good can no longer be dismissed as a piece of obsolete rhetoric, a holdover from premodern civilizations. Many economists as well as visionary leaders in business and other international organizations have created a range of models and practical policies for bench marking performance in light of so-called "ESG"—environmental, social, and governance—issues. These issues effectively express the aspirations contained in the common good in the world as we know it. Formulated in various UN initiatives, such as the Millennium Development Goals, which are reflected in the UN's Principles of Responsible Investment (PRI), the common good is now recognized as a legitimate moral priority for consideration in all aspects of financial decision-making. Among other international financial institutions, the World Bank has responded by proposing an "Environmental and social framework: setting standards for sustainable development" (World Bank 2014), which identifies ten (10) environmental and social standards[9] that must be met by any agency, governmental or not, applying for a loan for its development projects. While the World Bank's proposal, for various reasons, has not yet received universal approval, it clearly stands as a model for the kind of financial reforms required in an enhanced ethic of fiduciary responsibility.

It is unlikely that there will ever emerge a global consensus on what is required if investment decision-making is to be held accountable to the common good, in any of its current formulations.[10] However commendable the efforts of various United Nations' agencies, or the initiatives proposed by NGOs like the World Bank, there will always be a need for moral leadership from bankers, financial advisers, and investors, addressing local problems through the development of innovative institutions like *Banca Etica*, the Grameen Bank, the E Sun Bank, and others too numerous to mention. Without their experimental efforts, the formulations of larger global institutions like the World Bank, the various agencies of the United Nations, or even the corporate reassessments of "too-big-to-fail" banks, like Barclays (Salz 2013), are likely to remain abstract and notional. By recognizing the common good as central to an ethic of fiduciary responsibility, we mean to show that achieving these goals will require everyone's participation. Investors and their financial advisers

[9]The World Bank's ten environmental and social standards cover the following concerns: (1) Assessment and Management of Environmental and Social Risks and Impacts; (2): Labor and Working Conditions; (3): Resource Efficiency and Pollution Prevention; (4): Community Health and Safety; (5): Land Acquisition, Restrictions on Land Use and Involuntary Resettlement; (6): Biodiversity Conservation and Sustainable Management of Living Natural Resources; (7): Indigenous Peoples; (8): Cultural Heritage; (9): Financial Intermediaries; and (10): Information Disclosure and Stakeholder Engagement. These standards go beyond the general specification of development goals and toward the determination of specific procedures for organizing the information to be reported and reviewed in any World Bank decision regarding the funding and assessment of the projects its supports. Since it was proposed for consultation, the document has been criticized for the relative weakness of its standard on "Labor and Working Conditions" (ITUC 2014) and for its comparative neglect of "governance" issues, the third element in the ESG formulary (Jarvis 2013).

[10]The challenges involved in achieving a broad consensus about the substantive meaning of the common good are analyzed in Dennis P. McCann's essay, "The Good to be Pursued in Common" (McCann 1987). Later on McCann examined the tradition of Catholic social teaching in order to trace the history of its diverse formulations of what, in practice, the common good requires, in an essay. "The Common Good in Catholic Social Teaching: A Case Study in Modernization" (McCann 2005). While it is unlikely that there will emerge any definitive consensus on what all is entailed in the common good, the term remains useful and relevant for categorizing and comparing various practical agendas, such as the "ESG" proposals reviewed in this chapter.

cannot afford to sit on the sidelines and wait for the architects of the global financial system to come up with a new Bretton Woods agreement.

11.5 Conclusion

This chapter on Ethics and Finance follows up on the discussion of the collapse of Bear Stearns during the global financial crisis that began in 2007. The Bear Stearns case study was featured in Chap. 7 on Marketing Ethics and was meant to demonstrate what can happen when creating customers—in Peter Drucker's sense—no longer serves as the purpose of a business. In that chapter we first discussed the notion of fiduciary responsibility and documented the consequences of failing to honor that principle. Why, then, is it necessary to have further discussion of it in this chapter? The global financial crisis, we believe, has had both negative and positive aspects. Since the Bear Stearns case study emphasized the negative side, namely the failure to adhere to the ethic of fiduciary responsibility, we thought that the positive side needed further explanation. The case study for this chapter, which surveyed a range of reform initiatives, beginning with proposals for an Investment Bill of Rights (IBOR), was meant to demonstrate that the financial services industry is now experimenting with a range of innovations that are clearly designed to institutionalize the ethic of fiduciary responsibility.

One of the most promising consequences of the financial reform efforts currently underway is the expansion of the notion of fiduciary responsibility to reflect its ethical anchoring in the common good. We believe that increased moral awareness of the common good reflected in, among other things, the emergence of "ESG" concerns in international banking practices and investment policies is more realistic than conventional notions of fiduciary responsibility that unfold as if financial transactions were essentially private matters, of concern only to the parties directly involved in them. Substantive efforts to identify and assess critically the environmental and social impacts of various investment proposals—for example, their likely impact on climate change or on local labor conditions—must be encouraged, if investors and their financial advisers are to help create solutions to our common problems, rather than additional obstacles to their solution.

At the beginning of this chapter, we provided a motto intended to establish the basic message of what would follow. Stephan Rothlin had formulated a rule that we meant to honor here: "Respecting your colleagues is the smartest investment you can make." In light of what has actually been presented in this chapter, this rule may seem somewhat oblique. At first glance, it only emphasizes the need for a healthy respect for Human Resources at all levels of business development, in all kinds of businesses. But is it relevant in a chapter devoted to ethics in the financial services industry? It all depends, of course, on whom we regard as colleagues. Establishing an IBOR demonstrates the need for a basic level of mutual respect between financial advisers and their clients: neither can succeed without respecting the other as colleagues. But as we moved beyond their interactions to a consideration of the role of investment in pursuing the common good, we became aware of the need to form collegial relationships with all our stakeholders. Investment decisions will not succeed in achieving everyone's legitimate interests until we learn to respect all stakeholders as colleagues in a common enterprise. This, it turns out, is no less true of investment banking and the financial services industry than it is of all other businesses. Therefore, it seems only logical to insist on the value of respect when we analyze innovative new ways to structure finance which will be beneficial to the larger society as it clearly indicates the priority of "human capital"[11] over financial capital.

References

Allen, F. (2012, July 10). Financial executives confess: Sure, we lie and cheat. *Forbes Magazine*. Retrieved August 12, 2014, from http://www.forbes.com/sites/frederickallen/2012/07/10/financial-executives-sure-we-lie-and-cheat/

ASrIA. (n.d.). About us – Association for sustainable & responsible investment in Asia. *Association for sustainable & responsible investment in Asia*. Retrieved August 12, 2014, from http://asria.org/about-us/

Banca Etica. (n.d.). *Idea and principles*. Retrieved August 12, 2014, from http://www.bancaetica.it/idea-and-principles

Banca Etica. (2015, May 31). *Statistical information*. Retrieved June 19, 2015, from http://www.bancaetica.it/statistical-information

BIS. (2011). Basel III: A global regulatory framework for more resilient banks and banking systems. *Bank for international settlements*. Retrieved from http://www.bis.org/publ/bcbs189.pdf

Bloomberg News. (2014, March 24). Chinese investors call for more transparency in trust products. *Bloomberg*. Retrieved from http://www.bloomberg.com/news/2014-03-23/trust-default-protesters-recall-zero-risk-pledges-china-credit.html

CEED/IIRP. (n.d.). *Tobin tax initiative*. Center for environmental economic development (CEED)/The International Innovative Revenue Project. Retrieved October 28, 2014, from http://www.ceedweb.org/iirp/

Chomsky, N. (2011, November 1). Occupy the future. *In These Times Magazine*. Retrieved August 12, 2014, from http://inthesetimes.com/article/12206/occupy_the_future

Colley, L. (2011, November 4). Why Britain needs a written constitution. *The Guardian*. Retrieved August 12, 2014, from http://www.theguardian.com/books/2011/nov/04/why-britain-needs-written-constitution

Erwin, N. (2013, November 19). Everything you need to know about JPMorgan's $13 billion settlement. *The Washington Post. Wonkblog*. Retrieved September 16, 2014, from http://www.washingtonpost.com/blogs/wonkblog/wp/2013/10/21/everything-you-need-to-know-about-jpmorgans-13-billion-settlement/

E.SUN FHC. (2008). *About E.SUN: Service network: E.SUN bank*. Retrieved August 12, 2014, from http://www.esunfhc.com.tw/about/about_bank.info

Financial Times. (2013). Financial times lexicon: Definition of ESG. Retrieved October 18, 2014, from http://lexicon.ft.com/Term?term=ESG

[11] Catholic Social Teaching offers an impressive defense of the priority of labor over capital, which has inspired our own efforts in international business ethics. The most comprehensive and rigorous analysis of this idea is to be found in Pope John Paul II's encyclical letter, "Laborem Exercens" (John Paul II 1981).

Gilani, S. (2011, December 6). The rumors about Bill Clinton are true. *Forbes*. Retrieved August 12, 2014, from http://www.forbes.com/sites/shahgilani/2011/12/06/the-rumors-about-bill-clinton-are-true/

Guan, C. Y. (2013, January 18). 国际金融透明度发展论坛在京举行 中国银行业透明度显著提升. 华语广播网 *(Chinese Radio International Online)*. Retrieved August 12, 2014, from http://gb.cri.cn/1321/2013/01/18/5791s3996063.htm

Hexun.com. (2013). 国际金融透明度发展论坛-专题." 和讯网. Retrieved August 12, 2014, from http://bank.hexun.com/2013/jrtmdlt/

Hixon, T. (2011, November 3). Occupy wall street: No whining! *Forbes*. Retrieved August 12, 2014, from http://www.forbes.com/sites/toddhixon/2011/11/03/occupy-wall-street-no-whining/

HSBC India. (2014a). *What we do: Microfinance*. Retrieved September 1, 2014, from http://www.hsbc.co.in/1/2/miscellaneous/about-hsbc/corporate-sustainability/what-we-do

HSBC India. (2014b). *Corporate sustainability*. Retrieved September 1, 2014, from http://www.hsbc.co.in/1/2/miscellaneous/about-hsbc/corporate-sustainability

ING. (2006). *A billion to gain? A study on global financial institutions and microfinance*. Retrieved August 31, 2014, from http://www.wbcsd.org/web/projects/sl/ing_a_billion_to_gain.pdf

ING. (2008, March). *A billion to gain? The next phase*. Retrieved September 2, 2014, from http://www.ing.com/ING-in-Society/Sustainability/Growing-into-a-sustainable-sector-A-Billion-to-Gain.htm

Investopedia. (2014a). Basel III Definition. *Investopedia*. Retrieved October 27, 2014, from http://www.investopedia.com/terms/b/basell-iii.asp

Investopedia. (2014b). Tobin tax definition. *Investopedia*. Retrieved October 27, 2014, from http://www.investopedia.com/terms/t/tobin-tax.asp

ITUC. (2014, October). *A Robust world bank labour safeguard and IFI support for a Wage-and Public Investment-Led Recovery*. Statement by global unions to the 2014 annual meetings of the IMF and world bank, Washington, 10–12 October 2014. Retrieved October 19, 2014, from http://www.ituc-csi.org/IMG/pdf/statement_imfwb_1014.pdf

Jarvis, M. (2013, July 22). *A missing 'G' in ESG? – An emerging case for integrated environmental, social and governance analysis*. World Bank Blog – Governance for Development. Retrieved October 19, 2014, from http://blogs.worldbank.org/governance/missing-g-esg-emerging-case-integrated-environmental-social-and-governance-analysis

John Paul II. (1981). *Laborem exercens* ("On Human Work"). Retrieved October 28, 2014, from http://www.vatican.va/holy_father/john_paul_ii/encyclicals/documents/hf_jp-ii_enc_14091981_laborem-exercens_en.html

KPMG. (2011). *Basel III: Issues and implications*. Retrieved October 28, 2014, from www.kpmg.com/global/en/issuesandinsights/articlespublications/documents/basell-iii-issues-implications.pdf

Law, F. (2014, August 4). China's ICBC sells riskier bonds. *The Wall Street Journal*. Retrieved August 12, 2014, from http://online.wsj.com/articles/chinas-icbc-sells-basel-iii-compliant-bonds-1407147380

Lu, A., & Cossin, D. (2013). The ICBC path to Chinese governance: Lessons for the western and emerging markets. *European Financial Review*. Retrieved August 12, 2014, from http://www.europeanfinancialreview.com/?p=1243

Lund, B. (2014, April 18). Top 10 financial scandals of all time. *Daily Finance Investor Center*. Retrieved September 17, 2014, from http://www.dailyfinance.com/2014/04/18/top-10-financial-scandals/

Mathiason, N. (2009, October 29). Cluster bomb trade funded by world's biggest banks. *The Guardian*. Retrieved August 29, 2014, from http://www.theguardian.com/business/2009/oct/29/banks-fund-cluster-bomb-trade

McCann, D. (1987). The good to be pursued in common. In O. F. Williams & J. W. Houck (Eds.), *The common good and U.S. capitalism* (pp. 158–178). Lanham: University Press of America.

McCann, D. (2005). The common good in catholic social teaching: A case study in modernization. In P. D. Miller & D. P. McCann (Eds.), *In search of the common good* (pp. 121–146). New York: T & T Clark.

Monetary Authority of Singapore. (2013, June 14). MAS proposes regulatory framework for financial benchmarks. *Monetary authority of Singapore*. Retrieved August 28, 2014, from http://www.mas.gov.sg/News-and-Publications/Media-Releases/2013/MAS-Proposes-Regulatory-Framework-for-Financial-Benchmarks.aspx

Murcko, T. (2013). What is the difference between gambling and investing?. InvestorGuide.com. Retrieved October 20, 2014, from http://www.investorguide.com/article/12525/what-is-the-difference-between-gambling-and-investing/

Myers, T. A. (2012) Open letter from Thomas A. Myers to occupy wall street. *Journal of International Business Ethics, 5*(1), 50–59. Retrieved August 12, 2014, from http://www.americanscholarspress.com/content/BusEth_Abstract/v5n112-art7.pdf

Occupy London. (2011, October 27). *About – Occupy London*. Retrieved August 12, 2014, from http://occupylondon.org.uk/about-2/

Pavlo, W. (2013, July 18) Survey says 'Wall street is facing an ethical crisis'. *Forbes Magazine*. Retrieved August 12, 2014, from http://www.forbes.com/sites/walterpavlo/2013/07/18/survey-says-wall-street-is-facing-an-ethical-crisis/

Reuters. (2012, September). Occupy Hong Kong activists camp out at HSBC headquarters. *The Straits Times*. Retrieved August 12, 2014, from http://www.straitstimes.com/breaking-news/asia/story/occupy-hong-kong-activists-camp-out-hsbc-headquarters-20120912

Salz, A. (2013). *Salz Review: An independent review of barclays' Business Practices*. Retrieved March 15, 2014, from http://online.wsj.com/public/resources/documents/SalzReview04032013.pdf

SCMP. (2015). *South China morning post topics: Occupy central*. Retrieved on June 18, 2015 from http://www.scmp.com/topics/occupy-central

Selengut, S. (2008). Global investors' bill of rights may prevent economic Déjà vu. *Nice Articles*. Retrieved August 12, 2014, from http://www.9articles.org/global-investors-bill-of-rights-may-prevent-economic-deja-vu/

Simon, J., Powers, C., & Gunnemann, J. (1972). *The ethical investor; universities and corporate responsibility*. New Haven: Yale University Press. Retrieved August 12, 2014, from http://acir.yale.edu/pdf/EthicalInvestor.pdf

Sloan, A. (2012, June 13). The 5 myths of the great financial meltdown. *Fortune Magazine*. Retrieved September 16, 2014, from http://fortune.com/2012/06/13/the-5-myths-of-the-great-financial-meltdown/

Straits-Times. (September 12, 2012). Occupy Hong Kong activists camp out at HSBC headquarters. *The Straits Times of Singapore*. Retrieved August 12, 2014, from http://www.straitstimes.com/breaking-news/asia/story/occupy-hong-kong-activists-camp-out-hsbc-headquarters-20120912

The Economist. (2013, June 1). Ethical banking in Italy; *Banca Etica. The Economist*. Retrieved August 12, 2014, from http://www.economist.com/news/finance-and-economics/21578691-bank-takes-its-name-seriously-ethical-banking-italy

Turner, L. (2001, June 18). *Speech by SEC staff: The investor's bill of rights: A commitment for the ages*. Retrieved from http://www.sec.gov/news/speech/spch505.htm

Verret, J. W. (2009, August 6). The misdirection of current corporate governance proposals. *Social Science Research Network: Tomorrow's Research Today*. Retrieved August 12, 2014, from http://papers.ssrn.com/sol3/papers.cfm?abstract_id=1444858

Verret, J. W. (2010, April 10). *Investor's bill of rights*. Retrieved August 12, 2014, from http://truthonthemarket.com/2010/04/19/investors-bill-of-rights/

World Bank. (2014). *Environmental and social framework: Setting standards for sustainable development*. Washington, DC: World Bank Group. Retrieved October 19, 2014, from http://documents.worldbank.org/curated/en/2014/07/19898916/environmental-social-framework-setting-standards-sustainable-development

Zamansky, J. (2008, May 9). Calling for an 'Investor bill of rights.' *Seeking Alpha*. Retrieved August 12, 2014, from http://seekingalpha.com/article/76477-calling-for-an-investor-bill-of-rights

Zernike, K. (2011, October 21). Wall St. Protest isn't like ours, tea party says. *The New York Times*. Retrieved August 12, 2014, from http://www.nytimes.com/2011/10/22/us/politics/wall-st-protest-isnt-like-ours-tea-party-says.html

Chapter 12
Investors: Investment, Ethics, and Corporate Responsibility

"Care for your Business by Caring for Society."
(Stephan Rothlin, *Eighteen Rules for Becoming a Top Notch Player,* 2004)

12.1 Prelude

This chapter begins with a case study on an Indian firm that has become a major player in the information technology sector, Infosys. This firm is important because its history allows us to expand the notion of investment beyond securing capital for business expansion to creating social capital by investing in corporate social responsibility (CSR). How CSR fits into Infosys's overall business development strategy, and with what success, will enable us to discuss CSR as an investment in a firm's sustainability and not simply as a charitable donation to be recognized as a business expense. Revisiting the meaning of CSR in Asian contexts, with an emphasis on the ways in which firms like Infosys are innovating in this area, will enrich the discussion of CSR for businesses worldwide. This chapter will make explicit the ethics of CSR, showing how it flows from a proper understanding of international business ethics generally, as well as examining some of the challenges of responding to the community's heightened ethical expectations, once a firm earns a reputation for CSR leadership.

12.2 Case Study: Infosys' Investment in Corporate Social Responsibility

12.2.1 Abstract

Because the concept of corporate social responsibility (CSR) began in countries like the USA and Great Britain, its detractors have criticized it for being culturally and economically insensitive to conditions in developing countries. In such venues, wealth creation, some contend, must precede the adoption of corporate practices that might reduce profits. Nevertheless, companies across the developing world are

S. Rothlin, D. McCann, *International Business Ethics*,
DOI 10.1007/978-3-662-47434-1_12

creating their own styles of CSR which are not only in accordance with best global practices but suited to the particular needs of their own cultures and societies. India's Infosys Technologies is a good example. Infosys' history cannot be detached from that of its founders, first and foremost Narayana Murthy and his wife Sudha. While this case study analyzes the role of Infosys in promoting community development and seeks to recognize an Indian understanding of CSR, it also provides an opportunity to discuss what happens when management makes mistakes that others judge as lapses in business ethics. Companies with sterling reputations for their CSR efforts are likely to be subject to close scrutiny by the news media. If mistakes occur and scandals surface, how should these be dealt with, so that the good being done by the firm's CSR efforts will not be undermined?

12.2.2 Keywords

Infosys, N. Murthy, CSR in India, Philanthropy, Sustainability, Transparency, Trusteeship, India's Companies Act of 2013, the Pyramid of CSR

12.2.3 The Beginning of the Infosys Saga

As in the best of fairy tales, few people would ever have expected the young Narayana Murthy to achieve his dream. Sudha, a brilliant engineer and Murthy's future wife, recalls: "Murthy was always broke. He always owed me money. We used to go for dinner and he would say, 'I don't have money with me, you pay my share and I will return it to you later.' For 3 years, I maintained a book of Murthy's debts to me. No, he never returned the money and I finally tore it up after our wedding" (*Rediff* 2006). Despite Narayana's straightened circumstances, Sudha saw in her husband something unique. She saw the face of India's software revolution (Thoppil 2012), from which Infosys would become a globally competitive enterprise.

Although there would be no Infosys without Narayana Murthy, the Infosys saga starts with seven founders. In his memories, the founding takes on a mystic aura, "It was a wintry morning in January 1981, when seven of us sat in my apartment, and created Infosys" (*Rediff* 2005). He is referring to his colleagues at Patni Computer Group: N. Nilekani, the friend of a lifetime; S. Gopalakrishnan, the global thought leader (*Forbes* 2011); S. D. Shibulal, the former Infosys CEO; K. Dinesh, the trusted problem solver (*Business Standard* 2012); N. S. Raghavan, today a thriving venture capitalist (Mishra 2009); and A. Arora, the highly regarded programmer who left the company in 1989 (*Teck.in* 2006). Murthy borrowed start-up capital of about US$ 250 dollars from his wife and registered the company in Mumbai on July 2, 1981. The Pune house on loan from the Murthys became Infosys' first office. Two years later, in 1983, the group moved to Bangalore (*Rediff* 2006). Murthy remembers the hardships of those first years. He describes the sacrifices made by his team as "unparalleled" (Mishra and Chandran 2011). When asked about the key to their success, he provides a simple answer: "We stuck with it, and God has been kind to us." That makes for a great story, but Murthy—like Charles Dickens' Mr. Micawber—already knew that a business can only grow if it remains profitable, which means that everyday "you spent less than what you earned, that's all" (BBC 2011).

The idea of setting up a software development business was clearly an ambitious one as "computers were not easily available in the market. It used to take at least 3 years to import a computer to India," says Murthy. At that time, entrepreneurship in India labored under significant constraints. While India's first Prime Minister Jawaharlal Nehru acknowledged the need for a strong private sector to complement the action of the state, as time went on the regulations imposed by India's government failed to address the needs of its most innovative sectors, such as software, media, or biotechnology (Khanna 2008). With the establishment of a populist regime under Indira Gandhi in 1967, the situation faced by entrepreneurs like Murthy actually worsened. Starting from the Monopolies and Restrictive Trade Practices Act of 1969, the State placed both conglomerates and small businesses under rigorous scrutiny. The "License Raj," however, did not stop Infosys' development (Khanna 2008), since the company's founders were determined to play by the rules, no matter what (Mishra and Chandran 2011).

The American Data Basics Corporation was the first client of the newborn enterprise (*Rediff* 2006). As Murthy recalls, "The first customer is the most important. They can make or break a start up" (BBC 2011). In Infosys' case, thanks to some unconventional support and a lot of trust from American Data Basics, they made it. Today Infosys Technologies Ltd. provides consulting and IT services to clients in more than 150 countries. It has offices in over 30 countries and employs over 160,000 people worldwide. With annual revenues of over USD$8 billion and a net profit of USD$1.75 billion for the fiscal year ending in 2014 (SEC 2014), Infosys has emerged as the fifth largest of India's publicly traded firms and has won recognition as one of the most innovative global companies. In the Forbes Innovation rankings for 2011, the company placed 15th worldwide, which was the highest ranking for both an Indian company and any firm in the IT sector (*Forbes* 2011).

12.2.4 An Indian Perspective on CSR

Yet over and above his entrepreneurial skills, Murthy's commitment to CSR is equally impressive. In an interview with BBC, he explained its origins in his personal conversion from "a confused leftist to a determined compassionate capitalist" (*BBC* 2011). Indeed, Murthy's sense of mission was evident when, after 3 years working in France, he became determined to bring back to India some good ideas on how to raise it from poverty. He therefore donated his assets to charity and started a journey across Europe in search of enlightenment (Khanna 2008). A "seminal experience" in a Bulgarian prison (*BBC* 2011) changed his mind-set, however, concerning pure socialism as the answer to mankind's problems (Khanna 2008). He awoke to the idea that wealth could not be redistributed without first creating it. "That's when I realized that the only way countries, like India, can solve the problem of poverty is by entrepreneurship" (*BBC* 2011).

The combination of a commitment to strong social values as well as entrepreneurship as a way out of poverty is typical of CSR thinking in India. Many other "enlightened" entrepreneurs, determined to contribute to more than merely the economic development of India, share this vision. Among these, the Tata family is certainly a champion and according to Sudha Murthy an inspiration for the sense of social responsibility animating Infosys. A former employee at Tata Motors Limited (TELCO), she recalls J. R. D. Tata's words to her as she announced her intention of leaving the firm to join her husband's new venture: "Gently, he said, 'So what are you doing, Mrs Kulkarni?' (That was the way he always addressed me.) 'Sir, I am leaving Telco.' 'Where are you going?' he asked. 'Pune, sir. My husband is starting a company called Infosys and I'm shifting to Pune.' 'Oh! And what will you do when you are successful?' 'Sir, I don't know whether we will be successful.' 'Never start with diffidence,' he advised me. 'Always start with confidence. When you are successful you must give back to society. Society gives us so much; we must reciprocate. I wish you all the best" (Murthy 2004).

12.2.5 Values at Infosys

What, then, did the Infosys founders intend to give back to society, and how would they translate the ideal of reciprocity into a corporate culture that would ensure both business success and social responsibility? The founders emphasize certain values, each usually expressed in a single word meant to guide the formation of Infosys policies and practices. Among these are "sustainability," "transparency," and "integrity." Here is what they have said:

> Sustainability is not a reaction to our risks. It is our core value. – S.D. Shibulal, Chief Operating Officer and Director (Infosys 2010)

> Our value system at Infosys can be captured in one sentence: 'The softest pillow is a clear conscience. – N. Murthy, Chairman Emeritus (Knowledge@Wharton 2001)

> Our values are to have a very high integrity and high transparency. We'd rather lose business and have a good night's sleep. – K. Dinesh (Khanna 2008)

Interpreting these and translating them into benchmarks for assessing corporate performance is no easy matter. A good night's sleep may be virtue's own reward, an indication of a conscience at peace with itself and the world. But how can getting a good night's sleep—a goal that every person inevitably must share—inform the expectations of a giant corporation that must manage the activities of tens of thousands of employees, the majority of whom are skilled professionals, operating in so many different venues across the globe? The founders' desire for "a good night's sleep," clearly, was meant to be symbolic, the natural reward for acting with "high integrity and high transparency." But there's more. Infosys' emblematic slogan "Powered by Intellect and Driven by Values" indicates a commitment to be the best both commercially and ethically (Fernando 2012). In order to make good on this commitment, Infosys developed the C-LIFE principle featuring the core values that it means to honor in all aspects of its corporate conduct. C LIFE is an acronym for "Customer Delight,"[1] "Lead by Example," "Integrity and Transparency," "Fairness," and "Excellence," aspirations that extend the C-LIFE principle into every aspect of the company's engagement with its stakeholders.

12.2.6 *Implementing C-LIFE Principles: Infosys' Social Contract*

The C-LIFE principles, as well as the company's commitment to managerial accountability, need to be explored further to determine how precisely they shape Infosys's corporate culture and its commitments to CSR. Clearly, a "Social Contract" stands at the heart of implementing the C-LIFE principle. Corporate governance, according to Infosys, is attuned to a vision of the role of business in society expressed in terms of a social contract. The business cannot exist without the consent of the societies in which it operates, constituted by the various groups of stakeholders with whom management must interact. A willingness to reciprocate, that is, to uphold the implied terms of the social contract presupposes an understanding that whatever success a firm may have is a direct result of the quality of its interactions with all its stakeholders.

Thus the C-LIFE core values constitute the "framework of corporate governance" at Infosys whose "dimensions" include (1) "transparency, fairness and accountability," which translates into policies requiring "the highest levels of disclosure with all our stakeholders," achieved through compliance with government-mandated forms of auditing and financial reporting; (2) strong "board governance," the majority of whose members are "independent," that is, not Infosys employees, in order to represent the interests of all the firm's stakeholders; (3) "enterprise risk management" procedures designed to protect the firm's sustainability; (4) "corporate

[1] The Indian blogger, Rahul Bemba, has noted that in its most recent reports Infosys has quietly changed the "C" in the "C-LIFE" acronym. No longer does it represent "Customer Delight," but now it is "Client Value" (KrRahul 2011). Rahul explains that the change actually indicates a deepening awareness of the significance of building business relationships, since "clients" normally have "long-term association with us," who are, "in some way or the other, under protection from you for some work or service." "Value" in contrast with "Delight" shifts expectations from subjective satisfaction to the quality of what is actually delivered as goods and services. In Rahul Bemba's view while the two terms are simply different sides of the same coin, the focus should be on "client value," which if it is achieved will also "automatically" bring delight to one's customers. Bemba's reflections suggest that Infosys' employees, indeed, take the C-LIFE principle seriously and find it worth discussing in the social media.

policies" reinforcing a commitment to following "all applicable laws and regulations," through routine "training and awareness programs" designed to achieve compliance with the corporate "Code of Conduct and Ethics" which, among other things, covers "anti-bribery" and "ethical handling of conflicts of interest" and a "Whistleblower Policy" for encouraging the identification of problems and finding constructive solutions to them, all of which are meant to "enable a culture of disclosure"; and (5) a "sustainability focus" intending to "achieve a fine balance of economic, environmental and social imperatives" in order to address "the needs and expectations of our internal as well as external stakeholders." The corporate governance framework now also includes an active "Corporate Social Responsibility Committee" in order to comply with the recent changes in India's Companies Act of 2013 (Infosys 2014a: 108).

As described in its Business Responsibility Report, this framework demonstrates that CSR is an expression of the social contract that Infosys believes will ensure the firm's sustainability. Given its crucial importance, CSR not surprisingly is comprehensive, involving initiatives that "strive for economic development that positively impacts the society at large with a minimal resource footprint" while focusing those impacts "through its activities on the environment, communities and stakeholders" (Infosys 2014a, b: 95):

> Over the years, we have been striving to achieve a fine balance of economic, environmental and social imperatives, while also paying attention to the needs and expectations of our internal as well as external stakeholders. Our corporate social responsibility is not limited to philanthropy, but encompasses holistic community development, institution building and sustainability-related initiatives. (Infosys 2014a: 13)

All the CSR activities at Infosys aim at enabling Indian people to prosper. Instead of onetime transfers, they focus on developing skills and resources. This approach to community development responds to the founders' beliefs about the "power of entrepreneurship" to make a difference.

An important question, of course, is whether such CSR activities, for all the good intentions inspiring them, actually meet the standards that Infosys has attempted to institutionalize throughout the firm. Pratap Bhanu Mehta, president of the Centre for Policy Research, waves a cautionary flag: "There is a real risk in India that CSR just creates a new kind of patronage network, where one politician runs an educational trust, or another politician wants something done in their constituency" (Crabtree 2012). The reforms mandated in the Companies Act of 2013 were meant not only to generate more funding for CSR activities; they were also intended to address an apparent lack of "transparency, fairness and accountability" in the way CSR programs have often been managed. Promulgated after much delay, the Companies Act of 2013, Section 135, mandates a CSR policy for "every company having a net worth of rupees five hundred crore or more, or turnover of rupees one thousand crore or more or a net profit of rupees five crore or more during any financial year." A crore, of course, is the equivalent of ten million rupees. The qualifying firms "shall constitute a Corporate Social Responsibility Committee of the Board consisting of three or more directors, out of which at least one director shall be an independent director."

Besides mandating a new structure of accountability, the Companies Act of 2013 requires the CSR Committee to "ensure that the company spends, in every financial year, at least two per cent of the average net profits[2] of the company made during the three immediately preceding financial years, in pursuance of its Corporate Social Responsibility Policy." The Companies Act of 2013 further stipulates "that the company shall give preference to the local area and areas around it where it operates, spending the amount earmarked for Corporate Social Responsibility activities." Failure to spend that amount will result in the board being required to file a report detailing the company's reason for not doing so. Further on, Schedule VII of the Companies Act lists the kinds of activities that qualify for CSR funding:

> Activities relating to:
> (*i*) eradicating extreme hunger and poverty;
> (*ii*) promotion of education;
> (*iii*) promoting gender equality and empowering women;
> (*iv*) reducing child mortality and improving maternal health;
> (*v*) combating human immunodeficiency virus, acquired immune deficiency syndrome, malaria and other diseases;
> (*vi*) ensuring environmental sustainability;
> (*vii*) employment enhancing vocational skills;
> (*viii*) social business projects;
> (*ix*) contribution to the Prime Minister's National Relief Fund or any other fund set up by the Central Government or the State Governments for socio-economic development and relief and funds for the welfare of the Scheduled Castes, the Scheduled Tribes, other backward classes, minorities and women; and
> (*x*) such other matters as may be prescribed (Ministry of Law and Justice 2013)

Since India is the first country to advance such a proposal (*Dezan Shira & Associates* 2012), its success in getting major businesses to comply with this law will be closely monitored by other countries seeking to promote proactive CSR policies. Not surprisingly, the list of activities approved in the Companies Act closely mirrors the projects already at one time or another undertaken by the Infosys Foundation.

[2]Apparently, there is a lack of transparency in determining whether Infosys itself is currently in compliance with the new law. While Infosys "profit" after "tax expenses" have been deducted, as reported in its March 2014 Directors Report 10,194 crore its reported contribution to the Infosys Foundation was 9 crore, as indicated in the same report (Infosys 2014a). If 2 % of Infosys' after tax profit were allocated for CSR activities, with a significant portion going to the Infosys Foundation, one might expect a much higher figure than 9 crore. Investors seeking more information on the Infosys Foundation are directed to the Infosys Sustainability Report (Infosys 2014b), which is very impressive for its descriptions of the firm's CSR activities and the Foundation's programs, but beyond confirming the 9 crore figure, remains rather opaque in financial details that would confirm Infosys' compliance with the CSR provisions of the Companies Act. Presumably, in years to come, Infosys will provide more transparent and more readily accessible reports on its total expenditures for CSR activities, including donations to the Infosys Foundation, and how these comply with the mandated 2 % contribution.

12.2.7 A Family Business Empowering India

Once Infosys began operating on a sustainable basis, the seven founders made a decision. Their wives would not be involved in running the company (*Rediff* 2006). Sudha Murthy especially found the decision hard to accept. She is a talented engineer, a charismatic woman, and the one who had financed her husband's dream of founding Infosys. Besides, given her role in helping to write the first software produced by the company, she had all the credentials needed to be chairman herself (Regatao 2000). Nevertheless, Sudha understood the founders' rationale and accepted her role as a devoted housewife and mother. Later when her children had grown up, Sudha and the "Infosys wives' team" turned to social concerns. While some of them chose to set up independent charities, Sudha Murthy and Sudha Gopalakrishnan linked their activity to Infosys, thus creating the Infosys Foundation.

Since its establishment in 1996, the Infosys Foundation has implemented numerous projects aimed at supporting the underprivileged in Indian society. Its activities began in Karnataka and have since expanded to Tamil Nadu, Andhra Pradesh, Maharashtra, Orissa, and Punjab. Infosys' annual contribution to the Foundation supports its initiatives in healthcare, education, culture, rural development, and aid to the elderly and destitute (Infosys Foundation 2012a). Such initiatives have taken the form of projects, direct aid grants to other grassroots organizations, and employment readiness programs. "Community Services" is the pillar of the Foundation's role in Infosys' CSR efforts, since it relates specifically to IT education for children and teachers in rural India. In a cooperative project with Microsoft called "Computers@Classrooms," for example, in the year 1998 alone, Infosys donated 744 computers to 272 institutions across the country (Infosys 1999). Consistent with its C-LIFE principle, Infosys actively encourages its employees to participate in community development activities as well. Engineers and IT experts work with local governments and schools in ways that promote the development of information technology education in underprivileged areas. Moreover, senior-level managers have been instrumental in influencing the government at both the national and state levels to allocate higher budgetary grants for primary education and the construction of broadband Internet in rural areas.

In 2009, Infosys established a second nonprofit trust, the Infosys Science Foundation. Since its inception, the Infosys Science Foundation has awarded an annual Infosys Prize to honor outstanding achievements in the fields of the social sciences, physical sciences, engineering and computer sciences, mathematical sciences, and life sciences. A jury, "comprising eminent leaders in each of these fields, evaluates the achievements of the nominees against the standards of international research" and rewards the finest Indian researcher in each field with a prize amounting to US$150,000 (PTI 2003). Domestically, the Infosys Prize is second only to the Nobel Prize in its level of prestige and makes instant celebrities out of its annual laureates. Since the Infosys Prize is meant to stimulate interest in research areas that are closest to the firm's core competencies, it is a telling example of how the Foundation addresses CSR concerns that are crucial to the firm's sustainability.

Alongside sponsoring CSR initiatives that will promote the firm's long-term development, Infosys also remains committed to pure philanthropy, that is, to funding activities beyond the scope of its CSR, considered as a business-related activity. The Infosys Foundation has contributed substantially to orphanages, hospices, and shelters for the destitute. Orphanages have been constructed across rural India by the Foundation, which has also worked to rehabilitate the most vulnerable members of Indian society, such as the blind and pariah peoples. In 2005, for example, the Foundation established the Bangalore Hospice Trust, which works to ease the suffering of terminally ill cancer patients. In another project, the Foundation donated about 340 sewing machines to destitute women in Karnataka and Tamil Nadu to help them secure a means of livelihood. The Foundation is also conducting social awareness and literacy campaigns in rural areas, thanks to Narayana Murthy's personal interest, provoked when he visited relatives in the countryside and was overwhelmed by the illiteracy of his cousins and nieces (*The Times of India* 2011). Aside from its ongoing program operations, the Infosys Foundation provides financial support and volunteers in response to human crises and natural disasters. Following the disastrous 2009 floods in Karnataka, for instance, the Foundation "contributed US$6.8 million towards relief, rehabilitation and reconstruction. Under the auspices of the state government's 'Aasare' scheme, Infosys partnered with local NGOs to construct homes across 18 villages in five districts" (Infosys Foundation 2012b). The director of the Indian Red Cross praised Infosys' participation in the Aasare scheme as a model for sustainable development.

12.2.8 An Uncertain Future

When S. D. Shibulal became Infosys' CEO in August 2011, he was "a man in a hurry with a plan" (Bernstein 2011), since he knew that retirement awaited him in 2015. He called his plan "Infosys 3.0 – Building Tomorrow's Enterprise," which was supposed to extend the founders' legacy to the next generation. Despite his high hopes, in the short term, Infosys' financial performance was disappointing. Compared to the performance of its greater rival—Tata Consultancy Services, whose shares increased in value by +5.6 % during the first half of 2012—Infosys' share price over the same period dropped a worrisome 18 % (Glekin 2012). The disappointment prompted Narayana Murthy to come out of retirement in June 2013 in order to take the helm once more (Einhorn 2013). Since that time, Infosys has recovered some of the lost ground, though the recovery has been less than spectacular (PHYS ORG 2014). It is useful to note, however, that none of Infosys' critics blame its lackluster performance on its CSR expenditures. Even if India's Companies Act were to allow it, cutting back on these is likely to shake investor confidence even more than a few quarters' disappointing returns (Lys et al. 2013).

However impressive Infosys' effort to earn a reputation as a global leader in CSR is, no system is ever foolproof. A firm that claims moral leadership, not only in CSR programming but also in its ethical Code of Conduct, will inevitably attract greater scrutiny, by admirers and adversaries alike. For instance, in 2003, Infosys had to settle a sexual harassment case out of court for US$3 million, involving one of its directors, a rising IT superstar, Phaneesh Murthy—no relation to Narayana Murthy—and his executive secretary. In 2002 Phaneesh's resignation was demanded when the company learned of his failure to disclose the relationship as well as the restraining order his executive secretary had filed against him. Though Infosys eventually severed its ties with Phaneesh, it could hardly avoid negative publicity. According to *The Hindu*, sexual harassment in India is generally discussed behind closed doors (Bhagat 2002), but Infosys' troubles were blown up by the Indian news media into the biggest scandal ever. In order to restore the firm's credibility, Narayana Murthy announced his determination to follow up on the matter: "The litigation is behind us. We have taken further steps to strengthen our internal processes and improve the checks and balances to handle similar situations" (IBS 2002). According to Mohandas Pai, former HR director at Infosys, the firm's failure to respond promptly and decisively arose from a communications gap between regular employees and heads of departments, rather than from the company's insensitivity toward abusive behavior (*CNBC-TV 18* 2011).

The Infosys Annual Report for 2001–2002 had already disclosed the formulation of a sexual harassment policy (Bhagat 2002). But in the wake of the Phaneesh Murthy scandal, Infosys announced new measures designed to demonstrate "zero tolerance" toward abusive behavior at the workplace. The incidents sparked a reappraisal of organizational practices and, among other things, led to the creation of a rigorous sexual harassment training program that has become mandatory for employees at every level of the organization. The Infosys HR department has also implemented a four-tier system of sanctions, in which the punishment of improper conduct varies not only by the degree of seriousness but also in relation to one's position at the company. Observed Mohandas Pai, "At the senior level, you have to have a tougher standard than at other levels because it is a question of leadership. In all such cases people in power have to have a higher degree of compliance" (*CNBC-TV 18* 2011). Most recently, Infosys' Business Responsibility Report for 2012–2013, "Relevance through Innovation," shows that the firm's commitment to the C-LIFE principle has resulted in a comprehensive approach to sexual harassment and other abuses, based on respect for human rights and reinforced by the firm's stated commitments in its Code of Conduct (Infosys 2013a, b).

Be that as it may, critics are growing more strident against Infosys' current management and its capacity to respond to a rapidly changing IT market (Lison 2012a). When Narayana Murthy came out of retirement in 2013, he met with skepticism: "Keeping margins fat is especially difficult now since the IT outsourcing business has become so commoditized…. The multinationals that outsource so much of their work to India know that, too, and are more price-sensitive than they were back during Murthy's tenure as Infosys boss. 'The buyers are a lot smarter now,'" says Bloomberg Industries analyst, Anurag Rana (Einhorn 2013). Even before Murthy's return, Peter Schumacher observed that "the CEO rotation strategy at Infosys has diluted the power of the office of the CEO and hurt performance." He explained: "When the CEO changes every few years critical issues don't get addressed […]

Eventually the organizational dynamics can get very messy and difficult to control" (Thoppil 2012). Murthy himself, however, appears confident that staying the course may be the best way to turn the company around: "Speaking on an analyst call, Murthy said that there was nothing wrong with their Infosys 3.0 strategy. 'We could have done better in executing the strategy,' he said" (ENS Economic Bureau 2014).

Investors' expectations were not the only problem that Murthy had to confront upon his return. Potentially far more damaging than the company's embarrassment over sexual harassment policy and its implementation are recent allegations that Infosys fraudulently used short-term visas to send Indian personnel to work in its operations in the USA (Tennant 2011). It's easier to obtain short-term visas (B-1) for specific projects, and the costs of procuring them are dramatically lower than the fees charged for long-term (H-1B) visas (Preston 2012). But in Alabama, USA, Jason Palmer filed a lawsuit against Infosys accusing his superiors of harassment after he had used the firm's internal whistle-blowing procedures to denounce the illegal visa practices. While the Alabama court dismissed Palmer's suit declaring there were no legitimate grounds for it in state law, eventually Infosys had to agree to pay US$34 million in fines to various US regulatory agencies, to settle all claims against its alleged abuse of the B-1 business visitor visa program (Preston 2013). Infosys' violations of US immigration laws could jeopardize the company's strategic plan going forward, since it faces increasing pressure to comply strictly with visa requirements that are being tightened in various countries where it operates. As a result, the firm is likely to employ more locals abroad—in this case, perhaps as many as 50 %—and will have to make adjustments in the pay scale of those Indians sent to the USA using the proper H-1B visa (Nambiar 2011). Lingering controversy arguably creates yet another problem for Infosys' public relations, since the company, as we have seen, has built its reputation on "transparency," "values," and "strict compliance with the law."

12.2.9 Conclusion

Since its establishment in 1981, Infosys Technologies has climbed the ladder of success. Thanks to the relentless efforts of its founders, it has presented to the world a fresh face for India. In accordance with Narayana Murthy's strong personal values, as we have seen, Infosys Technologies advocates and participates in a wide array of initiatives aimed at enhancing business-community relations. By creating the Infosys Foundation in 1996, Murthy's wife Sudha assumed a leadership role in much of this work, while the company itself has contributed more than just financial support. Employment policies, environmental concerns, and research partnerships serve to illustrate that the company's C-LIFE principle extends to every facet of the company's practices. However, critics of the "Indian CSR way" have questioned the transparency and accountability of Infosys' charitable activities and its trusts. How seriously should we take the warning signals regarding possible conflicts of interest arising from a strategic use of CSR, not only by Indian companies but also by companies elsewhere that may be involved in similar activities?

12.3 Case Study Discussion

These are challenging times for Infosys and other companies trying to compete in the rapidly changing IT industry. As the recent reassessments provoked by allegations of fraud involving visas for its Indian employees working in the USA have shown, Infosys' existing business model—dependent upon foreign firms' outsourcing of various IT services—may soon be obsolete, as the Internet and cloud computing converge toward the next big thing. Companies like Infosys must achieve a degree of flexibility in responding to the new challenges, one that will test whether it can remain faithful to its founders' vision and whether it can deliver consistently on its promise of being "powered by intellect, driven by values." Since Infosys is recognized globally as a leader in both IT innovation and CSR, the challenge is whether progress in either of these areas can be achieved without getting caught in a trade-off between the one and the other. Can Infosys continue to demonstrate that leadership in CSR needn't come at the expense of financial performance?

With the appointment of the new CEO, Vishal Sikka, Infosys is clearly making improved financial performance its first priority (Sheshadri and Toness 2014). As the first CEO not selected from Infosys' original group of seven founders, the question for Sikka is whether he will maintain the firm's tie to the Infosys Foundation or find some other vehicle to fulfill the firm's CSR commitments. The fact that the CSR requirements stipulated in India's new Companies Act of 2013 clearly apply to Infosys makes it likely that Sikka will do nothing to destabilize the firm's CSR programs. We should take a closer look at Infosys' CSR strategy and its contribution to the firm's overall sustainability. What is the payback that Infosys hopes to achieve from its CSR programs?

A recent Infosys "White Paper" on "Rethinking Corporate Social Responsibility (CSR) in Financial Services" (Infosys 2013c) highlights "The Sustainability Imperative of CSR." The paper explains that since "in today's business environment CSR programs are financed by shrinking budgets… CSR cannot be ad hoc and subject to tokenism…[but] must be as sustainable as its [the firm's] business model." In order to make CSR sustainable, financial institutions (FIs), for example, must respond to nine challenges in today's business environment. Among these are "the absence of a framework for benchmarking CSR" effectiveness, using the "right metrics," and the difficulties of attracting and incentivizing "employees who drive CSR programs." As the White Paper notes, since "Wall Street does not embed CSR in the valuation of a company," establishing a sustainable CSR program requires making a strong "business case" for it. The case that Infosys wants to make is, therefore, that CSR is "Good for Society, even Better for Business." "Responsible companies need to develop a framework that makes CSR sustainable seamlessly by leveraging capabilities and enhancing the competitive advantage of the company."

Formulating the business case in the context of the financial services industry—or in any other industry, for that matter—means identifying the "paybacks" from sustainable CSR. There are four that Infosys recommends: CSR "(1) enhances brand equity, (2) builds trust and confidence, (3) improves financial performance, and (4) increases business growth." Brand equity is enhanced because "responsible companies face far lesser scrutiny from regulatory authorities." Trust and confidence lost because of the global financial crisis can be rebuilt by cultivating "relationships with different stakeholders." Improved financial performance, according to a study commissioned by the Global Alliance for Banking on Values, can be measured "across financial indices such as return on assets, growth in loans and deposits, and capital strength" (GABV 2013). Finally, the prospects of business growth "increase when CSR is aligned with business."

How such alignment may be accomplished is outlined by Infosys in an analysis of "the DNA of sustainable CSR," which identifies the components of a "holistic CSR strategy," starting with a "forensic audit" of the environmental and social impact of the firm's current operations: adoption of a "3-P's" approach to CSR program development, with specific objectives involving "people, process, and products"; the institutionalization of a "CSR office"—a team of executives backed by the firm's top management—"to implement the CSR strategy and deliver results"; and finally making a routine of "sustainability reporting" through which all the firm's stakeholders are not only informed but also invited continually to "buy in" to its CSR programming. Given the remarkable convergence between what Infosys has learned in developing its own strategy for CSR and what it recommends to its clients, it is clear that Infosys hopes to attract new business from clients who will use its services to develop sustainable programs in CSR.

The evolution of CSR at Infosys may be understood as an innovative response to the general history of CSR in India. Tatjana Chahoud and her team at the German Development Institute in Bonn have provided a concise outline of that history, understanding it in terms of four phases. Here is her characterization of these:

> During the first phase (1850–1914) CSR activities were mainly undertaken outside companies and included donations to temples and various social welfare causes.
>
> The second phase (1914–1960) was largely influenced by Mahatma Ghandi's theory of trusteeship, the aim of which was to consolidate and amplify social development. The reform programmes included activities geared particularly to abolishing untouchability, empowering women and developing rural areas.
>
> The third phase (1960–1980) was dominated by the paradigm of the "mixed economy". In this context, CSR largely took the form of the legal regulation of business activities and/or the promotion of public-sector undertakings (PSUs).
>
> The fourth phase (1980 until the present) is characterized partly by traditional philanthropic engagement and partly by steps taken to integrate CSR into a sustainable business strategy. (Chahoud et al. 2007: 3–4)

Thus while the history of the Infosys Foundation clearly unfolds within the fourth phase, it may be understood as representing the legacy of the previous three, insofar as it reflects the personal commitments of the company's founders, who supported Gandhian efforts at community development, premised on making the "mixed economy" work for all people.

As Narayana Murthy's tale of enlightenment suggests, there clearly is a link between his understanding of entrepreneurship in service to the community and Mahatma Gandhi's notion of "trusteeship." Both doubted that state socialism, such as India adopted after independence, could solve the problem of poverty and inequality. India's "License Raj," as bitter experience proved, not only could not prevent the very rich and powerful from taking the lion's share of the nation's wealth but, by restricting all forms of entrepreneurship, also retarded the development of those actually trying to improve the lives of the poor and destitute. Given Sudha Murthy's connection with J. R. D. Tata, who pioneered the practice of Gandhian trusteeship in his own business, it is not surprising that the Infosys Foundation would seek to follow this same vision.

Narayana Murthy's distinctive contribution to Gandhian trusteeship is to create a model of entrepreneurship in which CSR plays an integral role in the development of a sustainable business strategy. As Infosys' pamphlet on advancing CSR in the financial services industry makes clear, such a model shifts the emphasis away from the traditional moral, religious, and cultural reasons supporting CSR activities and toward an understanding of their strategic importance in creating a sustainable business. The business case, of course, goes well beyond the challenge of securing legitimacy for the business by creating "goodwill" among all the firm's stakeholders by supporting good works—charitable activities like funding a homeless shelter or a soup kitchen, for example—within the community. The business case involves making a priority of CSR activities that will engage and enhance the firm's core competencies—such as the cooperative project with Microsoft called "Computers@ Classrooms," which in providing access to computers and enabling the development of computer skills is actually creating future customers, as well as prospective employees, for Infosys. In this way, the Infosys Foundation ensures that there will be significant "paybacks" to Infosys for the resources invested in CSR activities.

The integration of CSR activities into a sustainable business strategy, however, may require the firm to become more rigorous in assuring the firm's compliance with basic standards of business ethics. Ethical lapses can no longer be swept under the rug, by appealing to the firm's good works in the community. If anything, the fact that the firm's public relations strategy emphasizes its innovative leadership in CSR activities means that it will get more rigorous scrutiny whenever any ethical violations are alleged against it. Judging by the quality and comprehensiveness of its Code of Conduct and Ethics (Infosys 2013a)—which itself is intended to demonstrate the firm's compliance with regulatory requirements in the USA where a major portion of its business occurs—Infosys is acutely aware of this challenge. In this new phase of CSR development, in India as well as elsewhere, CSR activities will no longer earn a free pass exempting the firm from criticism. On the contrary, making CSR an integral element of the firm's sustainable business strategy will require that it adheres to the highest standards of business ethics in all its operations.

12.4 Ethical Reflection

Is there a right way for a business to exercise its corporate social responsibilities? What is the ethical basis for CSR? In order to address this question, it is important to distinguish CSR from charity and philanthropy. CSR activities should not be confused with random acts of kindness. They are distinguished not only in terms of their motive, the manner of their disclosure, as well as the way they are managed and organized within the firm. The key term in CSR is "responsibility," which inevitably signifies a concern for justice and the common good. CSR is premised on the idea that successful businesses actually owe their success to their stakeholders, especially their customers, as well as to the goodwill of the community, and therefore should reciprocate by participating in the advancement of the common good of society as a whole. If CSR is not to be confused with charity, neither should it be confused with simply complying with whatever the law requires. Paying fair and reasonable wages in a timely manner, showing concern for the health and safety of workers, cooperating with law enforcement and various regulatory agencies, and keeping one's promises to one's investors, customers, and suppliers—each of these is significant in fulfilling moral obligations that are routinely incurred in the course of doing business, but none of them should be confused with exercising CSR.

Social responsibilities typically address issues that are external to the firm. Once again, Infosys' "Computers@Classrooms" is a useful example. Infosys clearly did not create the problem of poverty in India or the woeful lack of access to quality education for so many of its citizens. By distributing computers to rural schools that lack them and providing training so that local teachers can learn to use them with their students, the firm in a small way is addressing a social problem by mobilizing its own resources—social networking and professional expertise, as well as a budget to support the purchase of computers—to open access to an education that may prepare students for a very different future. It might be odd were a company not involved in IT to initiate a "Computers@Classrooms" program, since it would lack the core competencies needed to make it work. By the same token, once other IT companies become aware of Infosys' initiative, they may become interested in replicating a project that provides real help at least cost to themselves.

The "Computers@Classrooms" program, by the way, allows us to make another important point. Quite often, the strategic deployment of expertise and equipment will have greater positive impact than cash grants. Encouraging one's own staff to provide training and supervision, as well as assistance in setting up the computers, is more likely to ensure success than simply providing the money for schools to try doing it themselves. The reciprocity that develops is a tangible benefit not only for the schools that receive Infosys' assistance but also for the firm's own sustainable future, as well as staff morale.

12.4.1 The Ethical Basis for CSR

The ethical basis for CSR, then, is analogous to what common sense requires of each of us as members of a human community. Recall from Chap. 2 the story told by Mengzi to show that all people "have a mind which cannot bear to see the sufferings of others," demonstrated by an example depicting what happens when "men suddenly see a child about to fall into a well." They "without exception experience a feeling of alarm and distress." Without calculating any reward they might obtain for doing so, they rush to save the child (2A6). Mengzi uses this story to illustrate the "sprouts" from which the four basic virtues grow: humanity (*ren*), righteousness (*yi*), ritual propriety (*li*), and wisdom (*zhi*). To assert that businesses are capable of exercising their CSRs is to understand that, since people establish businesses in order to achieve certain common human purposes, they must function analogously to the way people exercise their individual responsibilities. If people are held accountable for keeping the promises they make, then businesses can and ought to be held similarly accountable. The basic Confucian virtues—like the Golden Rule of reciprocity—are just as relevant for judging corporate behavior as they are for judging individual or personal behavior.

As Mengzi's example of the child about to fall into a well suggests, people can and ought to come to the aid of others, when they can do so at little cost to themselves. Their action may be praised as heroic, if they do so when the costs are high—as when a soldier sacrifices his life to save his comrades in arms—but failure to act when they could do so at little cost to themselves is commonly regarded as shameful and immoral. The case for businesses exercising their CSRs is analogous: if businesses can provide assistance to the community at little cost to themselves, they ought to do so simply as a token of our common humanity. In that sense, the moral argument is that businesses exist on the basis of a social contract. Infosys is surely right to recognize a social contract at the center of its C-LIFE strategy for creating a sustainable business. But a social contract implies real moral obligations. If a business fails to address the needs of the community, especially when they could provide assistance at little cost to themselves, they are rightly vulnerable to condemnation for their shameful indifference to others.

The ethical expectation that businesses ought to provide assistance to the community is enshrined in India's Companies Act of 2013. The stipulation that firms generating profits on a certain scale should reserve 2 % of those profits for funding CSR activities reflects the idea that they must help when they can do so at little cost to themselves. The assumption is that contributing 2 % of a firm's net profit is a fair estimate of what successful businesses can readily afford to do. Neither the Companies Act of 2013 nor the general argument about CSR requires businesses to make heroic sacrifices: no one is demanding that businesses bankrupt themselves or bust their budgets trying to meet unrealistic CSR goals. If a business were to try demonstrating exemplary moral leadership, thus becoming, say, the institutional equivalent of a *jūnzǐ* (君子), it might consider contributing more than the 2 % minimum required by law. It might—as we shall see in Chap. 17—earmark a substantial portion of its profits for philanthropic purposes, as the Tata Group does by allocating the bulk of its shares to the Tata Trusts. But even in such cases where the commitment is far beyond the 2 % mandated by the Companies Act, there is no obligation to fund CSR activities at levels that would actually jeopardize a business' sustainability.

12.4.2 Milton Friedman's Critique of CSR

As the protracted struggle over India's Companies Act clearly indicated, even modest proposals requiring firms to support CSR programs will meet with stiff resistance. Beyond controversies over how to pay for such programs, there is a philosophical objection frequently raised at this point. An American pundit identified with the Chicago school of economics, Milton Friedman (1912–2006), for example, rejected the very idea of CSR, arguing that "there is one and only one social responsibility of business--to use its resources and engage in activities designed to increase its profits so long as it stays within the rules of the game, which is to say, engages in open and free competition without deception or fraud" (Friedman 1970). As a zealous defender of individual freedom, Friedman did not reject the idea of charity or philanthropy, but in his view it was only legitimate as a personal choice of individuals. For a business or its executive leadership to allocate resources for CSR, in his view, is to impose a tax upon the owners or investors, depriving them of their fair share of its profits. For this reason, he described CSR as pursuing "collectivist ends… without collectivist means."

Friedman's point, however wrongheaded, illuminates the vulnerability of companies like Infosys that are investor owned and publicly traded. In his view, a firm's management must maximize profits for its investors; if they are so inclined, they can take their dividends and donate them to whatever charities they like. Friedman, no doubt, would join the chorus of those demanding that Infosys should increase its dividends to its shareholders. If defunding CSR activities and the Infosys Foundation will increase their dividends, then by all means they should do so.[3] The flaw in Friedman's argument, as we see it, is twofold. First, he equates CSR with philanthropy and then dismisses the idea that the resources invested in CSR are spent to achieve a business purpose.

Pure philanthropy, as the term implies, is related to a business purpose only indirectly. If it is pure, it is gratuitous, in the sense that it is done out of compassion and not for any hidden business motive. Some of the activities of the Infosys Foundation clearly qualify as pure philanthropy, for example, its contribution in 2005 to the Bangalore Hospice Trust, which works to ease the suffering of terminally ill cancer patients, or its response to human crises and natural disasters, such as the disastrous 2009 floods in Karnataka. Neither of these relates directly to a business purpose in the way that "Computers@Classrooms" does, both in intent and in effect. The

[3] Given the fact that Infosys' reported contribution to the Infosys Foundation (Infosys 2014b) was a surprisingly modest 9 crore (US$1.48 million), it would appear that investors would not enjoy a windfall, where the firm's commitment to the Foundation is to be withdrawn. It is also unclear what Friedman's response to India's Companies Act of 2013 would be. He strongly recommends that businesses compete within "the rules of the game," which would surely mean obeying whatever is required of them by law; nevertheless, he would also strongly criticize the law as another example of trying to achieve "collectivist ends [indeed with]… collectivist means." If Indian businesses were to follow Friedman's philosophy, they would do everything in their power to undermine, if not actually repeal, the Companies Act and the 2 % tax that it imposes under the guise of mandated CSR programming.

statements made in the firm's annual sustainability reports provide ample evidence that Infosys' CSR activities were organized and managed in order to fulfill a business purpose, one that directly represents the C-LIFE principle that defines Infosys operations as a whole.

Yet Friedman rules out the business case made by companies like Infosys, contending that "in practice the doctrine of social responsibility is frequently a cloak for actions that are justified on other grounds rather than a reason for those actions." Hardheaded business executives, in his view, should resist the "strong temptation to rationalize these actions as an exercise of 'social responsibility.'" While there may be short-term advantages to cloaking one's strategic business decisions in the mantel of CSR, the price of such "hypocritical" posturing is to "strengthen the already too prevalent view that the pursuit of profits is wicked and immoral and must be curbed and controlled by external forces. Once this view is adopted, the external forces that curb the market will not be the social consciences, however highly developed, of the pontificating executives; it will be the iron fist of Government bureaucrats" (Friedman 1970). One can well imagine what Narayana Murthy and his colleagues might have to say in response to Friedman's overheated rhetoric. While they might sympathize with his grievances against government bureaucrats, they would also insist that there's nothing "hypocritical" about linking CSR to the overall sustainability of one's business. If anything, Infosys not only succeeds in making CSR part of its strategic business plan but also has done innovative work in documenting precisely how CSR performance can be measured in its contribution to the firm's success. Friedman's objections to CSR, therefore, should be regarded as obsolete.

12.4.3 A CSR Pyramid

What then is CSR, considered systematically? In a seminal attempt to conceptualize CSR as a whole, Archie Carroll proposed that a genuine CSR agenda operates on four levels simultaneously, each of which can be understood as components in a "CSR pyramid" (Carroll 1991). At the base of the pyramid is the economic component, based on a recognition that the underlying motive of business activity is to make a profit. Carroll makes a moral distinction between the profit motive and the goal of profit maximization, since without making a profit it is impossible to fulfill any of a business' goals, while profit maximization may wrongly sacrifice all other goals in order to enhance a business' bottom line. Closely related to the economic component are a firm's legal responsibilities, which form the second step in the pyramid. A legal "business is expected to comply with the laws and regulations promulgated by federal, state, and local governments as ground rules under which business must operate" (Carroll 1991: 5). Carroll describes this expectation as a "social contract," in which the law is regarded as a system of "codified ethics" that are binding on all members of society.

The component of "ethical responsibilities embrace those activities and practices that are expected or prohibited by societal members even though they are not codified into law." This third step in the pyramid "precedes the establishment of law because they become the driving force behind the very creation of laws or regulations" (Carroll 1991: 6). As "expectations emanating from societal groups," these require "levels of ethical performance…[based on] such principles as justice, rights, and utilitarianism." In Carroll's view, the discipline of business ethics "has firmly established an ethical responsibility as a legitimate CSR component." Finally, at the pyramid's vertex are a firm's "philanthropic responsibilities" that address "society's expectations that businesses be good corporate citizens." The difference between philanthropy and the ethical responsibilities represented in the third step is that philanthropy "is not expected in an ethical or moral sense"—meaning that it is not obligatory in the way that obeying the law and the basic ethical principles that undergird it is. "Therefore, philanthropy is more discretionary or voluntary on the part of businesses even through there is always the societal expectation that businesses provide it" (Carroll 1991: 7). Philanthropy, as Carroll suggests, is "icing on the cake—or on the pyramid, using our metaphor."

Viewed systematically, then, a firm that embraces a CSR agenda must "strive to make a profit, obey the law, be ethical, and be a good corporate citizen." All four of these are necessary, but no one of these is sufficient, if a firm is to make a credible claim of exercising its CSRs. Carroll specifically contrasts his view of CSR with Friedman's perspective:

> Economist Milton Friedman…has argued that social matters are not the concern of business people and that these problems should be resolved by the unfettered workings of the free market system. Friedman's argument loses some of its punch, however, when you consider his assertion in its totality. Friedman posited that management is "to make as much money as possible while conforming to the basic rules of society, both those embodied in the law and those embodied in ethical custom" (Friedman 1970). Most people focus on the first part of Friedman's quote but not the second part. It seems clear from this statement that profits, conformity to the law, and ethical custom embrace three components of the CSR pyramid—economic, legal, and ethical. That only leaves the philanthropic component for Friedman to reject. Although it may be appropriate for an economist to take this view, one would not encounter many business executives today who exclude philanthropic programs from their firms' range of activities. It seems the role of corporate citizenship is one that business has no significant problem embracing. Undoubtedly this perspective is rationalized under the rubric of enlightened self-interest. (Carroll 1991: 8–9)

While Carroll's perspective was "made in the USA" and intended simply as a reflection on the development of CSR in that country and the managerial challenges involved in implementing it there, it should be clear that his CSR pyramid coheres rather well with the rationale for CSR developed within Infosys. What becomes clear both in India and elsewhere is that CSR is not an afterthought but an integral dimension of corporate governance, playing an indispensable role in any firm's struggle toward sustainability. Visualizing Infosys' commitments to CSR in terms of Carroll's pyramid allows us to see that philanthropy is neither credible nor effective unless it rests on a base of a firm's consistent performance of its economic, legal, and ethical responsibilities. No one component of CSR can be put in the foreground in order to cover up deficiencies in the other components.

12.5 Conclusion

In this chapter we have examined the experience of one leading Asian business, Infosys, seeking to integrate its CSR commitments into a sustainable business model. The Infosys case is noteworthy because it demonstrates how CSR thinking has evolved in India, to the point where the Companies Act of 2013 now requires businesses over a certain size to organize a CSR committee and set aside 2 % of the firm's net profits to fund CSR activities. Infosys' early leadership in CSR has enabled it to market its skills and experience in developing such programs for its various clients. The intimate connection that can and should obtain between CSR and a firm's core competencies is well illustrated by the role CSR plays in generating new business for Infosys.

The case also allowed us an opportunity to explore what happens when a firm showing leadership in CSR is accused of engaging in unethical business practices. It is clear that cultivating a reputation for moral leadership through CSR activities will inevitably attract attention focusing on the firm's policies and business practices generally. This fact should not deter businesses from seeking to earn an outstanding reputation for moral leadership in business, but it should make them aware that, if they seek to distinguish themselves on ethical grounds, their operations must be consistent with the firm's stated ideals in all aspects of its business.

Stephan Rothlin gave us the slogan introducing this chapter in his previous work, *Becoming a Top Notch Player: Eighteen Rules of International Business Ethics* (2004): "Care for your Business by Caring for Society." His point would be well understood by Narayana Murthy and his colleagues who founded Infosys. If you build "caring for society" into your way of doing business, you are more likely to create a sustainable business. That being the case, whatever is allocated for CSR activities—whether in the form of an annual grant or in some other structure—should not be regarded as another tax imposed from on high or some form of political extortion nor simply as a cost that yields no benefits to the firm. Instead, CSR must truthfully be regarded as an investment: those businesses that invest in CSR activities will find that society reciprocates their efforts in various ways, including some that actually make a difference on the firm's bottom line.

References

Advani, S. (2008, February 15). S.D. Shibulal and S. Gopalakrishnan | Geek gods. *Wall Street Journal*. Retrieved September 7, 2012, from http://www.livemint.com/2008/02/14231142/SD-Shibulal-and-S-Gopalakri.html

Arakali, H. (2012, August 21). Infosys shares rise after US visa lawsuit dismissed. *Reuters*. Retrieved September 6, 2012, from http://in.reuters.com/article/2012/08/21/infosys-shares-rise-lawsuit-idINDEE87K01T20120821

BBC. (2011, April 4). Start-up stories: NR Narayana Murthy, Infosys. Retrieved September 6, 2012, from http://www.bbc.co.uk/news/business-12957104

Bernstein, J. (2011, August 12). SD Shibulal: Man in a hurry. CBR. Retrieved September 6, 2012, from http://outsourcingbpo.cbronline.com/features/sd-shibulal-man-in-a-hurry-infosys-120811

Bhagat, R. (2002, July 26). Harassment blues to the fore. *The Hindu*. Retrieved September 8, 2012, from http://www.thehindubusinessline.in/2002/07/26/stories/2002072600091100.htm

Business Standard. (2012). Mohandas Pai, K Dinesh quit Infosys board. Retrieved September 7, 2012, from http://www.business-standard.com/india/news/update-mohandas-pai-k-dinesh-quit infy board/132182/on

Carroll, A.B. (July-August, 1991). *The pyramid of corporate social responsibility: Toward the moral management of organizational stakeholders*. Business Horizons. Retrieved September 12, 2014, from http://www-rohan.sdsu.edu/faculty/dunnweb/rprnts.pyramidofcsr.pdf

Chahoud, T., Emmerling, J., Kolb, D., Kubina, I., Repinski, & Schläger, C. Corporate social and environmental responsibility in India – Assessing the UN global compact's role. Studies 26. *German Development Institute/Deutsches Institut für Entwicklungspolitik (DIE)* (Bonn: 2007). Retrieved June 13, 2014, from http://www.die-gdi.de/uploads/media/Studies_26.pdf

Choudhury, U. (2012, August 21). Infosys wins 'visa case' in US court, but faces criminal probe. *Firstpost World*. Retrieved September 6, 2012, from http://www.firstpost.com/world/infosys-wins-visa-case-in-us-court-but-still-faces-criminal-probe-423959.html

CNBC TV 18. (2011, August 28). Sexual harassment redefined. Retrieved September 8, 2012 http://thefirm.moneycontrol.com/news_details.php?autono=481526

Crabtree, J. (2012, March 30). Blighted benevolence. *The Financial Times*. Retrieved September 9, 2012, from http://www.ft.com/intl/cms/s/0/0241c678-77e1-11e1-b437-00144feab49a.html#axzz25z1YZJ7r

Dezan Shira & Associates. (2012, July 10). Corporate social responsibility in India. *India Briefing*. Retrieved September 9, 2012, from http://www.india-briefing.com/news/corporate-social-responsibility-india-5511.html/

Einhorn, B. (2013, June). Infosys founder Murthy returns—and Faces U.S. Visa Shock. *Bloomberg Businessweek*. Retrieved May 22, 2014, from http://www.businessweek.com/printer/articles/121700-infosys-founder-murthy-returns-and-faces-u-dot-s-dot-visa-shock

ENS Economic Bureau. (2014, March 13). Infosys' economic performance worries Murthy. *The New Indian Express*. Retrieved May 22, 2014, from http://www.newindianexpress.com/business/news/Infosys-Performance-Worries-Murthy/2014/03/13/article2105780.ece

Fernando, A. C. (2012). *Business ethics and corporate governance* (2nd ed.). Chennai: Pearson Education.

Forbes. (2011). S. Gopalakrishnan. Retrieved September 7, 2012, from http://www.forbes.com/profile/s-gopalakrishnan-1/

Forbes. (2012). The world's most innovative companies. Retrieved September 5, 2012, from http://www.forbes.com/special-features/innovative-companies.html

Friedman, M. (1970, September 13). The social responsibility of business is to increase its profits. *The New York Times Magazine*. Retrieved June 16, 2014, from http://www.umich.edu/~thecore/doc/Friedman.pdf

Glekin, J. (2012, July 12). Founders playing musical chairs has hurt Infosys. *Firstpost*. Retrieved September 8, 2012, from http://www.firstpost.com/politics/founders-playing-musical-chairs-has-hurt-infosys-375896.html

GABV (2013, October). Real banking for the real economy: Comparing sustainable bank performance with the largest banks in the world. *Global Alliance for Banking on Values*. Retrieved June 13, 2014, from http://www.gabv.org/wp-content/uploads/New-13-5923_GABV_report_Washington_07mvd1.pdf

IBS. (2002). Sexual harassment at Infosys case study. Retrieved September 9, 2012, from http://www.icmrindia.org/casestudies/catalogue/Business%20Ethics/Sexual%20Harassment%20at%20Infosys%20-%20Business%20Ethics.htm

Infosys Foundation. (2012a). About us. Retrieved September 5, 2012, from http://www.infosys.com/infosys_foundation/about-infosys-foundation/mission.asp

Infosys Foundation. (2012b). A model village emerges from a trail of devastation. Retrieved September 5, 2012, from http://www.infosys.com/sustainability/Documents/key-sustainability-drivers. pdf

Infosys. (1999, January 19). Infosys and microsoft launch "Computers@Classrooms" program. Retrieved September 5, 2012, from http://www.infosys.com/newsroom/press-releases/Documents/1999/pcdonation.pdf

Infosys. (2010). Materiality and our key drivers. Infosys sustainability report 2009–2010. Retrieved June 19, 2015 from http://www.infosys.com/sustainability/Documents/infosys-sustainability-report-2009-10.pdf

Infosys. (2013a). Infosys code of conduct and ethics. Amended version adopted by the Board of Directors, 07 May 2013. Retrieved June 7, 2014, from http://www.infosys.com/investors/corporate-governance/Documents/CodeofConduct.pdf

Infosys. (2013b). Relevance through innovation. Business responsibility report, 2012–2013. Retrieved June 7, 2014, from http://www.infosys.com/sustainability/Documents/business-responsibility-report-2012-2013.pdf

Infosys. (2013c). Rethinking corporate social responsibility (CSR) in financial services. Retrieved June 13, 2014, from http://www.infosys.com/industries/financial-services/white-papers/Documents/corporate-social-responsibility.pdf

Infosys. (2014a). Directors report, March 2014. Retrieved September 11, 2014, from http://www.moneycontrol.com/annual-report/infosys/directors-report/IT#IT

Infosys. (2014b). Evolving with changing times. Business sustainability report, 2013–2014. Retrieved June 13, 2014, from http://www.infosys.com/sustainability/documents/infosys-sustainability-report-2013-14.pdf

Jayashankar, M. (2010, July 1). Nandan Nilekani: Governtrepreneur. *Forbes*. Retrieved September 7, 2012, from http://www.forbes.com/2010/01/07/forbes-india-nandan-nilekani-governtrepreneur.html

Kelkar, R., ed. (1960, April). *M. K. Gandhi on Trusteeship*, Published by Jitendra T. Desai Navajivan Mudranalaya, Ahemadabad-380014 India. Retrieved June 14, 1914, from http://www.mkgandhi.org/ebks/trusteeship.pdf

Khanna, T. (2008). *Billions of entrepreneurs: How China and India are reshaping their futures—And yours*. Cambridge, MA: Harvard Business Review Press.

Knowledge@Wharton. (2001, May 23). Infosys' Murthy: Sharing a "simple yet powerful vision". Retrieved September 6, 2012, from http://knowledge.wharton.upenn.edu/article.cfm?articleid=364

KrRahul. (2011, August 5). C-LIFE discussion: Customer delight or client value? Rahul's. Retrieved September 10, 2014, from http://rahulbemba.blogspot.com/2011/08/c-life-discussion-customer-delight-or.html

Lane, R. (2013, February 19). The giving pledge goes global—Warren buffet details America's latest 'export'. *Forbes*. Retrieved June 19, 2014, from http://www.forbes.com/sites/randalllane/2013/02/19/the-giving-pledge-goes-global-warren-buffett-details-americas-latest-export/

Lison, J. (2012a, May 15). Infosys' growth pangs: Founders need to let go of their continuing influence? *The Economic Times of India*. Retrieved September 7, 2012, from http://articles.economictimes.indiatimes.com/2012-05-15/news/31711431_1_shibulal-infosys-management-infosys-executive

Lison, J. (2012b, June 12). Rs 20,000 crore cash pile: Analysts call for Infosys to return cash to shareholders through share buy-back. *The Economic Times of India*. Retrieved September 6, 2012, from http://articles.economictimes.indiatimes.com/2012-06-12/news/32270156_1_buyback-program-infosys-shares-crore-cash-pile

Lys T., Naughton, J., & Wang C. (2013, March 4). Pinpointing the value in CSR: The unexpected link between CSR spending and financial performance. Kellogg Insight. Retrieved May 22, 2014, from http://insight.kellogg.northwestern.edu/article/pinpointing_the_value_in_csr/

Mahajan, &, Ives. (2003, October). Enhancing business-community relations – Infosys Technologies Ltd Case Study. *UN Volunteers – New Academy of Business*. Retrieved September 6, 2012, from http://www.worldvolunteerweb.org/fileadmin/docs/old/pdf/2003/031201_EBCR_IND_infosys.pdf

Ministry of Law and Justice. (August 30, 2013). The companies act of 2013. Retrieved June 5, 2014, from http://www.mca.gov.in/Ministry/pdf/CompaniesAct2013.pdf

Mishra, B.R. (2009, July 6). There's life after Infosys. *Business Standard*. Retrieved September 7, 2012, from http://www.business-standard.com/india/news/theres-life-after-infosys/363038/

Mishra & Chandran. (2011, May 19). History revisited: The initial years at Infosys. *Business Standard*. Retrieved September 6, 2012, from http://www.business-standard.com/india/news/history-revisitedinitial-years-at-infosys/436090/

Murthy, S. (2004, August). Appro JRD. Retrieved September 9, 2012, from http://www.tata.com/aboutus/articles/inside.aspx?artid=UxG8Uwjyiks=

Nambiar, P. (2011, September 14). Infosys targets 50% local staff overseas in onsite locations. *The Economic Times of India*. Retrieved September 6, 2012, from http://articles.economictimes.indiatimes.com/2011-09-14/news/30154460_1_infosys-targets-infosys-technologies-nandita-gurjar

PHYS ORG. (2014, January 10). Infosys shares surge on stronger revenue forecast. Retrieved May 22, 2014, from http://phys.org/news/2014-01-infosys-surge-stronger-revenue.html

Preston, J. (2012, August 20). Judge dismiss whistle-blower suit against Infosys. *The New York Times*. Retrieved September 6, 2012, from http://www.nytimes.com/2012/08/21/us/alabama-judge-dismisses-infosys-whistle-blower-suit.html

Preston, J. (2013, October 29). Deal reached in inquiry into visa fraud at Tech Giant. *The New York Times*. Retrieved June 12, 2014, from http://www.nytimes.com/2013/10/30/us/indian-tech-giant-infosys-sai…ach-settlement-on-us-visa-fraud-claims.html

PTI. (2003, May 11). If we react Phaneesh will be embarrassed: Infosys. *The Economic Times of India*. Retrieved September 8, 2012, from http://articles.economictimes.indiatimes.com/2003-05-11/news/27562456_1_phaneesh-murthy-infosys-sexual-harassment-lawsuit

Rai, S. (2003, May 13). Technology Briefing|Software: Infosys settles sexual harassment case. *The New York Times*. Retrieved September 5, 2012, from http://www.nytimes.com/2003/05/13/business/technology-briefing-software-infosys-settles-sexual-harassment-case.html

Rai, A. (2005, April 3). The women who run Infosys. *The Economic Times of India*. Retrieved September 6, 2012, from http://articles.economictimes.indiatimes.com/2005-04-03/news/27493622_1_sudha-murty-narayana-murthy-dollar-bahu

Rediff. (2005, August 12). *Narayana Murthy's dream for the future*. Retrieved on June 18, 2015 from http://www.rediff.com/money/2005/aug/12bspec.htm

Rediff. (2006, July 11). The amazing Infosys story. Retrieved September 7, 2012, from http://www.rediff.com/money/2006/jul/11sld2.htm

Rediff. (2007, June 12). Sudha Murthy on Infosys and life's values. Retrieved September 9, 2012, from http://www.rediff.com/money/2007/jun/12sudha.htm

Regatao, G. (2000, August 10). First ladies of IT. *Rediff*. Retrieved September 10, 2012, from http://www.rediff.com/money/2000/aug/10bang.htm

Securities and Exchange Commission (SEC). (2014, April 15). IFRS USD PRESS RELEASE. Retrieved September 9, 2014, from http://www.sec.gov/Archives/edgar/data/1067491/000106749114000022/exv99w01.htm

Sheshadri, S., & Toness, B. V. (2014, June 12). Infosys Hires Ex-SAP Executive as CEO to Revive Margins. Bloomberg News. Retrieved June 12, 2014, from http://www.bloomberg.com/news/2014-06-12/infosys-names-sikka-ceo-after-four-years-of-tight-margins.html

Sirisha, D. (2003). Narayana Murthy and Infosys. *ICFAI Center for Management Research*. Retrieved September 6, 2012, from http://www.asec-sldi.org/dotAsset/292791.pdf

Teck.in. (2006, May 3). Infosys birthday and the seven founders. Retrieved September 6, 2012, from http://teck.in/infosys-birthday-and-seven-founders.html

Tennant, D. (2011, March 29). Infosys tries to thwart public hearing of visa fraud case. *IT Business Edge*. Retrieved September 6, 2012, from http://www.itbusinessedge.com/cm/blogs/tennant/infosys-tries-to-thwart-public-hearing-of-visa-fraud-case/?cs=46201

The Economist. (2008, January 17). Going global. Retrieved September 5, 2012, from http://www.economist.com/node/10491136

The Hindu. (2003, October 5). Another sexual harassment suit filed in California – Phaneesh says allegations are 'garbage'. Retrieved September 8, 2012, from http://www.thehindubusinessline.in/2003/10/06/stories/2003100601650100.htm

The Hindu. (2004, November 24). Phaneesh settles harassment law suit out-of-court: Infosys. Retrieved September 8, 2012, from http://www.thehindubusinessline.in/2004/11/25/stories/2004112502760600.htm

The Hindu. (2012, May 27). Infosys delivers 279 houses in flood-hit regions. Retrieved September 5, 2012, from http://www.thehindubusinessline.com/industry-and-economy/info-tech/article2054885.ece

The Telegraph. (2011, April 20). Pai takes a dig at Infosys founders. Retrieved September 7, 2012, from http://www.telegraphindia.com/1110420/jsp/business/story_13877276.jsp

The Times of India. (2007, August 21). Infosys to fund USD 150,000 annual award. Retrieved September 5, 2012 http://articles.timesofindia.indiatimes.com/2007-08-21/india-business/27987795_1_infosys-statement-annual-award-innovation

The Times of India. (2011, August 3). Infosys gesture to orphanage. Retrieved September 5, 2012, from http://articles.timesofindia.indiatimes.com/2001-08-03/bangalore/27253818_1_narayana-murthy-infosys-orphanage

Thoppil, D. A. (2012, September 4). Infosys founders talk succession. *WSJ India Real Time*. Retrieved September 6, 2012, from http://blogs.wsj.com/indiarealtime/2012/09/04/the-founding-fathers-of-infosys-talk-succession/

UN. (2007, February). CSR and developing countries: What scope for government action? Sustainable development innovation briefs. Retrieved September 5, 2012, from http://www.un.org/esa/sustdev/publications/innovationbriefs/no1.pdf

Chapter 13
Competitors: Intellectual Property Rights

> *"If you protect intellectual property, all stakeholders will receive their due share."* (Stephan Rothlin, *Eighteen Rules for Becoming a Top Notch Player,* 2004)

13.1 Prelude

The concept of intellectual property rights (IPRs), and a firm's ethical obligations toward observing these rights, may be difficult to implement anywhere, but especially so in Asia. Traditional cultures in Asia—particularly those that have emerged in the shadow of China—assume that imitation is the sincerest form of flattery. One learns by imitating perfect exemplars, an attitude no less true of technological innovations as it is of moral leadership. Nevertheless, globalization has brought increased awareness of the legal and moral necessity of observing IPR. The challenges that IPR present to Asian cultural values are highlighted by our case study from Thailand, in which the government of Thailand allowed its Ministry of Health to violate the IPRs of foreign drug manufacturers in order to provide needed medicines for AIDS patients at lower prices. The Thai government's initiative raises some questions about the moral legitimacy of IPRs and their enforcement. Was Thailand right to violate its WTO agreements on drug patents (TRIPS)? Were there other, more effective ways to achieve its goal of providing medicine to indigent AIDS patients? Did the major MNCs involved in developing the much needed medicine show enough flexibility in responding to the problem in Thailand? How should such firms relate to their local competitors? Are there effective ways for them to work together to meet local needs? What, then, is an IPR? If an IPR is truly a right, under what circumstances might other human rights override it? If other rights are more pressing, what might be a morally responsible way to manage such cases?

S. Rothlin, D. McCann, *International Business Ethics*,
DOI 10.1007/978-3-662-47434-1_13

13.2 Case Study: TRIPS and AIDS Medicine: Compulsory Licensing in Thailand

13.2.1 Abstract

In November 2006, Thailand's Government Pharmaceutical Organization (GPO) announced the compulsory licensing of the HIV drug efavirenz, which enabled the Thai government to import generic versions of it from India without the patent holder's (Merck's) consent. The GPO was able to do this because Merck held a patent in Thailand, but not India. This case raises ethical issues concerning intellectual property rights (IPRs) and their protection (or lack thereof) internationally. Ethical challenges in this case involve observing the conflicting rights of various stakeholders, including government, pharmaceutical companies, shareholders, and HIV patients worldwide. Discussing how pharmaceutical companies like Merck balance such stakeholder claims with their legitimate business objectives may be useful for anyone planning to participate in the global marketplace.

13.2.2 Keywords

Intellectual property, Compulsory license, TRIPS, Doha Declaration, World Trade Organization, HIV/AIDS

13.2.3 Merck

Merck & Co., Inc. is a pharmaceutical giant, the second largest healthcare company in the world. Merck has led the healthcare industry with discoveries such as vitamin B1 and the first measles vaccine. In the fight against HIV/AIDS, Merck also developed a leading antiretroviral drug, efavirenz. Considered one of the most effective first-line therapies for treating HIV/AIDS, efavirenz enables patients to resist diseases that often accompany HIV/AIDS such as tuberculosis or liver infections. It also has fewer side effects than alternative antiretrovirals (Ling 2006).

Merck and other pharmaceutical companies spend an average of US$802 million on research and development (R&D) for each new drug that wins approval by the Food and Drug Administration (Bate 2007). Even though the business of pharmaceuticals is lucrative,[1] the R&D invested in many potential drugs often ends in failure (with sunk costs incorporated into the US$802 million figure for successful drugs). The science behind developing new drugs such as efavirenz is often

[1] Although R&D for new drugs is extremely expensive, the marginal cost of producing the drug is relatively low.

quite complex, with the process possibly taking up to 15 years with no promise of success even after discovery. The R&D costs of efavirenz were approximately US$550 million.

As declared in the firm's mission statement, Merck's company values include the aspiration to "improve the health and wellness of people around the world by expanding access to our medicines" (Merck 2012). Consistent with this pledge, Merck established a new pricing strategy in 2001 designed to make drugs more affordable to more countries by differentiating prices according to the three income tiers specified by the World Bank.[2] The new pricing strategy set a precedent by making wealthy countries fund the majority of R&D costs, enabling Merck to balance the high costs of R&D with the low marginal cost of production while increasing accessibility. As of 2006, in the USA, a high-income country, efavirenz cost $6,000 per adult/year. In middle-income countries, such as Thailand, Merck was making minimal profits at the price of $500 per adult/year (Cervini and Prabhu 2012). In 72 low-income countries, Merck sold efavirenz for a price at or below the cost of production. The new pricing strategy increased accessibility in accordance with Merck's mission by offering significantly reduced drug prices in more than 130 countries (Bate 2007).

13.2.4 TRIPS

The Trade-Related Aspects of Intellectual Property Rights (TRIPS) Agreement was promulgated in 1994 in conjunction with the formation of the World Trade Organization (WTO). TRIPS defined the minimum criteria for the international intellectual property (IP) regulations governing trademarks, copyrights, and patents.

Patents are government-issued assurances that give inventors sole rights over their products. For pharmaceutical companies, patents provide exclusive rights to new drugs for a set time period, typically 20 years. For the duration of the patent, companies can charge high prices in order to recuperate the costs of R&D. While patents are essential for the development of new drugs, they give rise to pricing policies that inadvertently limit the access poor societies have to essential medicines. In order to overcome this restriction, in 2001, TRIPS was modified with the Doha Declaration. The Doha Declaration bolstered the power of governments to break patents in public health emergencies by issuing compulsory licenses (T'Hoen 2010). As a result of the Doha Declaration, the competition between pharmaceutical conglomerates and generic drug manufacturers intensified as they fought for the same market share in low- and middle-income countries.

---

[2] The three tiers are based on measures of gross national income (GNI) per person in a given country. The breakdown is as follows: low income, $1,005 or less; middle income, $1,006–$12,275; and high income, $12,276 or more (World Bank 2012).

13.2.5 Thailand, Compulsory Licenses

In 2006, there were approximately 580,000 Thai citizens diagnosed with HIV/AIDS, due mostly to Thailand's notorious and ill-advised promotion of sex tourism (Bate 2007).[3] In 2003, the Thai government began reducing the health budget, so that by 2006, the government could no longer maintain the former level of HIV/AIDS treatment, supplying the needed medicines to only 82,000 of the country's nearly 600,000 HIV/AIDS patients.

In response to the perceived public health emergency, the head of the Ministry of Health's Department of Disease, Thawat Suntrajarn, demanded lower-priced medicines from pharmaceutical companies (Bate 2007), accusing them of selling drugs at "very high" prices, "making it a big hurdle for patients to access [HIV/AIDS drugs] and the government cannot afford them" (Fraser 2006).[4] The Ministry's demand carried with it the threat of compulsory licensing as delineated in the Doha Declaration.

The text of the Doha Declaration states that generic forms of patented drugs can be produced in "public health crises, including those relating to HIV/AIDS, tuberculosis, malaria and other epidemics" (WTO 2001). If companies choose not to relinquish their patents voluntarily or negotiate lower prices, countries can issue compulsory licenses to manufacture or purchase generic versions of patented drugs. The procedure usually begins with negotiations between countries and drug companies.

Thailand's Minister of Public Health, Mongkol Na Songkhla, never negotiated with Merck prior to announcing the compulsory licensing of efavirenz on November 26, 2006 (Steinbrook 2007). The compulsory license allowed the Government Pharmaceutical Organization (GPO) to import generic versions of efavirenz from India, where the drug was not patented, despite Merck holding its patent in Thailand (Steinbrook 2007). The GPO was also authorized to produce generic efavirenz in Thailand, as soon as the country developed appropriate infrastructure (Gerhardsen 2006). The compulsory license for efavirenz would last 5 years and provide medication for 200,000 of the 580,000 Thais with HIV/AIDS. Patients who could afford Merck's efavirenz would not be given the generic version of the drug.

Three days after the announcement of the compulsory license for efavirenz, on November 29, 2006, just 1 day before World AIDS Day, Thailand's Ministry of Health began talks with the managing director of Merck Thailand. Douglas Cheung agreed to adjust Merck's pricing strategy to satisfy the need for efavirenz if Mongkol

---

[3] Khun Chantawipa Apisu, founder of EMPOWER, a forum that provides community and education to Thailand's sex workers, comments on the economics of the sex industry: "Much of the tourist industry is dependent on sex workers and it makes up around 7 % of the GDP – more than rice exports" (Short 2010).

[4] In 2006, Thailand's GDP per capita was $9,100, the second highest in Southeast Asia (Bate 2007). On that basis, Thailand was entitled to purchase pharmaceutical drugs at a mid-tier range. As a middle-income country, Thailand paid substantially less than the USA and European countries, but more than countries in Africa that lack Thailand's economic resources.

refrained from issuing the compulsory license. To make efavirenz more accessible to middle-income countries—like Thailand—with more than 1 % of the adult population affected by HIV, Merck lowered the price from $500 to $277 per adult/year, the same as the cost of efavirenz in least developed countries (Cervini and Prabhu 2012). Cheung maintained that no profits would be made on the sale of efavirenz in Thailand.

Despite the apparent agreement, on January 25, 2007, Mongkol issued the compulsory license of efavirenz, citing Merck's supposedly unreliable shipments as the main reason for the action. Production in India was scheduled to begin immediately and continue until Thailand developed appropriate facilities to begin domestic production (Bate 2007). The cost of importing generic efavirenz was $264 per person/year, a fraction less than the price Merck was offering (Ling 2006).

Thailand was able to import generic drugs from India because of India's long history of resisting international patent regulations. The Indian Patent Act of 1970 protected patented processes but not products, which allowed the generic pharmaceutical industry to develop the skills and technology needed to reverse engineer existing drugs (Matthews 2006).

When the WTO adopted the TRIPS regulations on patents, India was required to conform to the new criteria, providing patent protection for 20 years from the date of filing for both products and processes (WTO 2012). Accordingly, in 2005, India amended its Patent Act to include product patents. Nevertheless, since efavirenz had received FDA approval in 1998, 7 years prior to the amended Patent Act of 2005, generic drug manufacturers in India had enough time to reverse engineer and generically produce efavirenz successfully. Later, when Thailand issued its compulsory license, Merck had yet to register efavirenz for a patent under India's new laws. Thus, India did not violate TRIPS by allowing Thailand to purchase its generic versions of efavirenz. In 2006 at Thailand's announcement of the compulsory license, six Indian generic drug manufacturers had the technology to produce efavirenz (Coriat 2008).

13.2.6 Humanitarianism or Opportunism?

As a doctor and a politician, Thai Minister of Health, Mongkol Na Songkhla, aggressively pursued compulsory licensing. When asked about compulsory licenses, he responded, "We can't give in. There are patients' lives at stake" (*The Nation* 2007). AIDS activists praised him, while patent supporters vilified him.

According to Paul Cawthorne, head of *Médecins Sans Frontières* in Bangkok, Mongkol was under huge pressure from the pharmaceutical industry and other ministries to abandon his AIDS relief initiative (Silverman 2007). Barbara Whitesell, the US Trade Representative in Asia and Pacific Region, and Peter Mandelson, the EU's Commissioner for External Trade, criticized Mongkol's actions, emphasizing that compulsory licenses were to be used only as a last resort (Health Info 2009). However, Mongkol did not break any international regulations mandated by the

WTO. Nor was he legally required to disclose to Merck the GPO's plans prior to the public announcement of the compulsory license.

Yet controversy surrounds not only the sincerity of Mongkol's humanitarian rhetoric but also the internal business practices of the GPO under Mongkol's direction. In 2002, Jaruvan Maintaka, the Thai Auditor General, reported "the GPO sold about 60 % of its medical products to government agencies at above market prices. In some cases, products were marked up 1,000 %" (Bate 2007). Other reports suggest that the GPO was uninterested in developing new drugs in Thailand. Although the GPO earned profits over US$35 million in 2005, only 2 % of these were reinvested in R&D (Bate 2007).

While Merck was negotiating with the Thai government, the company simultaneously pressured the US government to take a stand against the compulsory licensing of efavirenz, claiming that Thailand had yet to officially declare a public health emergency (Ford et al. 2007). In early 2007, the US government responded to Merck' s request by commissioning the Coalition Against Counterfeiting and Piracy (CACAP) to compile a Report on the Criteria and Methodology for Determining the Eligibility of Candidate Countries for Millennium Challenge Account Assistance (Washington College of Law 2008). The CACAP fights for the protection and enforcement of intellectual property rights. The report from January 2007 named Thailand as a country with escalating counterfeiting problems—that is, the unauthorized production and sale of generic substitutes—and identified AIDS drugs as the primary product counterfeited.

Compulsory licensing and price constraints, of course, may have a negative impact on the pharmaceutical companies' "bottom line." Although limiting profits seems contrary to the logic of business economics, companies often sacrifice profits when competing for market share (Malhotra 2010). Theoretically, pharmaceutical companies can maximize profits by adjusting prices to meet demand in mid-tier countries, when such price reductions lead to increased market share (Frank 2001). However, selling drugs at prices below their production costs in the long run becomes profitless and pointless. Therefore, when a firm anticipates reductions in revenue, it usually means less incentive for a business to invest in R&D. Ed Kelley, a Bangkok-based intellectual property lawyer, underscored the concerns of investors: "What investors need is some idea that when they come into a market like this with world-class technology, they won't lose control of it to… government policy [determined] to nationalize foreign assets" (Schuettler 2007). However, investors in the pharmaceutical industry usually are aware of such risks. Forcing lower drug prices translates into lower cash flows, which are essential for R&D funding. Rates of return cannot remain lower than the opportunity cost of capital without undermining the drug industry's capacity for innovation.

In a paper released by the Thai Ministry of Public Health, Mongkol argued on the contrary that issuing the compulsory license did not cut into Merck's profits. The government supplied generic medicine only to people who could not afford it. Those who could afford efavirenz continued to purchase the drug from Merck.

Furthermore, as part of the stipulations outlined in Article 31 of TRIPS, the Thai government was required to pay adequate remuneration to Merck for using its formula through the compulsory licensing scheme (T'Hoen 2010). The royalties paid to Merck were 0.5 % of the total sales in Thailand (Steinbrook 2007), a figure that many would view as hardly adequate.

13.2.7 International Perception of Thai TRIPS Case

A survey conducted by the World Bank on the Thai drug program reiterated that the government took a major risk by issuing the compulsory license. Margaret Chan, WHO director general, advised Thailand: "I'd like to underline that we have to find a right balance for compulsory licensing. We can't be naïve about this. There is no perfect solution for accessing drugs in both quality and quantity" (Bate 2007). Although the Doha Declaration permits countries to issue compulsory licenses, Thailand could still face trade repercussions. Nevertheless, supporters of generic manufacturing were optimistic, claiming that this action may strengthen Thailand's ability to negotiate lower drug prices with other pharmaceuticals in the future (Fraser 2006).

Various AIDS groups have publicly supported Thailand throughout the controversy over compulsory licensing. *Médecins Sans Frontières* released a statement praising the license: "Thailand is demonstrating that the lives of patients have to come before the patents of drug companies" (Bate 2007). The Clinton Foundation also endorsed Mongkol's actions. Former United States president, Bill Clinton, spoke on the subject: "No company will ever die because of the high price premium for AIDS drugs in middle-income countries – but patients may. I believe in intellectual property … but that need not prevent us from getting essential life-saving medicines to those who need them in low- and middle-income countries alike" (CPA Global 2007).

However, drug companies will not invest in R&D when there is no financial incentive to do so. One commentator compared compulsory licensing to a license to steal (Alsegard 2004). The position of the pharmaceutical industry appears to agree with this observation. The Doha Declaration does not in itself create a barrier to profits. However, when countries force prices below a company's profit line, through negotiations or compulsory licensing, R&D suffers. Merck released a statement in which the company implies that the long-term benefits of R&D outweigh the immediate benefits to patients receiving generic medications. One spokesman claims, "This expropriation of intellectual property sends a chilling signal to research-based companies about the attractiveness of undertaking risky research on diseases that affect the developing world, potentially hurting patients who may require new and innovative life-saving therapies" (Hunter et al. 2009).

13.2.8 Industry Reaction

When Thailand's Ministry of Public Health chose to import the generic efavirenz from India despite Merck's lowered price, pharmaceutical companies began reevaluating their pricing strategies in middle-income countries. Abbott Laboratories undertook the most drastic step in response to what it perceived as the threat of compulsory licenses. Abbott chose to give discounts to every middle-income country except Thailand and removed Thailand's registration for its HIV drug, Aluvia. Abbott's response showed the company's displeasure at Thailand's disregard for intellectual property. Dirk van Eeden, director of public affairs at Abbott, commented, "This is a consequence, directly, of the Thai government's decision not to support innovation by breaking patents…" (Kazmin and Jack 2007).

Both Bristol-Myers Squibb and Sanofi-Aventis, two leading drug companies, went the opposite route. The companies agreed to lower their prices marginally, although grudgingly. A spokesperson from Bristol-Myers Squibb stated that Thailand's compulsory licensing of efavirenz creates huge concern for the future of research-based drug companies (Zamiska 2007). The importance of R&D is particularly urgent with HIV/AIDS medications, because new innovations will be needed as current drugs become ineffective.

Merck's Douglas Cheung, for one, was blindsided by the announcement of the GPO's compulsory license. "Imagine my shock when I picked up my newspaper and saw [Mongkol] had issued a compulsory license for our drug," Cheung told reporters after the announcement (Schuettler 2007). Despite Mongkol's allegation that Merck overpriced efavirenz, Cheung defended his company's position. He asserted, "Merck and its subsidiaries across the world have implemented a policy to offer [Efavirenz]… at nonprofit prices to developing countries …and that includes Thailand. I assure you that our corporate goals and policies regarding pricing of [Efavirenz]…in Thailand are in line with providing optimal ARV access to HIV patients" (Bate 2007). Do you agree with this statement and Merck's overall pricing strategy and subsequent responses? What do you think about Abbott's approach? Or Bristol-Myers'?

13.2.9 Summary

The case of efavirenz in Thailand focuses on the rights of intellectual property and the price of human wellness. Thailand successfully issued a compulsory license to provide generic HIV/AIDS medication to some Thais living with these diseases. Although TRIPS and the Doha Declaration were built with provisions restricting compulsory licensing for public health emergencies, Thailand's actions remain controversial. As we have seen, Cheung was willing to lower the cost of efavirenz in Thailand to retain Merck's patent. Abbott responded differently by lowering the cost of drugs in every middle-income country except Thailand.

When countries break patents, pharmaceutical companies have little incentive to spend on R&D for diseases within those countries. Therefore, the WTO encourages countries to negotiate lower prices directly with pharmaceutical companies prior to issuing compulsory licenses. There is colossal demand for access to less expensive generic medications especially in the developing world, and in extreme cases, compulsory licensing may provide a solution. However, in Thailand, it seems to have created as many problems as it solved. What recommendations would you make to Merck and other pharmaceutical companies in regard to their patentable products? Does your perspective change when the intellectual property at issue is a copyrighted song, movie, or software program rather than a life-saving drug? How and why?

13.3 Case Study Discussion

There are several issues concerning IPRs in this case study, but one of them is not whether IPRs exist and in principle, like other property rights, ought to be respected. Further on, we will revisit this basic theoretical question, but for now, our focus is on how Thailand's Government Pharmaceutical Organization (GPO) dealt with Merck's IPR claim on a new drug, efavirenz, proven effective in improving substantially the quality of life of people suffering from AIDS. By signing the Trade-Related Aspects of Intellectual Property Rights (TRIPS) Agreement, as well as its modification in the Doha Declaration, the Thai government acknowledged not only the reality of the IPRs involved in pharmaceutical manufacturing but also the procedures under which those rights could be modified. The compulsory license that the GPO issued withdrawing Thailand's recognition of Merck's patent on efavirenz was intended as a last resort, to be enacted only in an emergency and only after the failure of negotiations over distribution and pricing policy. Apparently, Thailand's Minister of Public Health, Mongkol Na Songkhla, regarded the compulsory license as a bargaining chip for bringing Merck to the negotiating table, for the license was issued 3 days before he contacted the managing director of Merck Thailand, Douglas Cheung. Even after Cheung proposed significant price cuts in order to avoid compulsory licensing, Mongkol issued it anyway. One question for discussion is whether Mongkol acted responsibly in the way he handled the compulsory licensing of efavirenz.

Is there any moral justification for Mongkol's actions? In his own defense, he declared, "We can't give in. There are patients' lives at stake." From a moral point of view, while he broke promises made not only to Merck but also to the agencies regulating the manufacture and sale of drugs internationally, he did so in order to save lives. Thus, there are moral arguments to be made on both counts. Promise keeping, as we have seen, is a basic paradigm of ethical integrity. We must keep the promises we freely make, unless there are very serious reasons requiring us to break those promises. Promise keeping is central to the theory and practice of respecting deontological obligations. Nevertheless, Mongkol's reason for deliberately breaking the Ministry of Public Health's promise to Merck appears to be serious. He was trying to mitigate the sufferings of those AIDS patients in Thailand who could not afford to purchase the efavirenz they needed to treat their diseases. Since the Thai government had decided that it could no longer afford to subsidize drug prescriptions at the same level that it had done before, some way had to be found to bring down the price of efavirenz to the point where it was affordable. By issuing a compulsory license, Mongkol acted unilaterally and dramatically to bring the price down.

If forced to justify his actions ethically, Mongkol could appeal to the utilitarian principle, "the greatest good for the greatest number." The relief of hundreds of thousands of AIDS patients would surely count as a greater good than whatever financial loss Merck and its shareholders may have suffered. This argument, or something very like it, underlies the praise offered by *Médecins sans Frontières*: "Thailand is demonstrating that the lives of patients have to come before the patents of drug companies." But there may be more to it than that. As the case study revealed, Mongkol's management of the GPO raised questions for some regarding the purity of his motives and the nature of his relationship with the Indian manufacturers from whom he would purchase a generic substitute for Merck's efavirenz. The good that he actually intended may have been more for his own benefit, as a politician and entrepreneur, than for Thailand's impoverished masses of AIDS sufferers. So how do you weigh Mongkol's actions? Is he to be praised as a moral leader, or is he just another politician posturing as one?

Equally difficult questions may be asked regarding the conduct of Merck and the other pharmaceutical manufacturers. They claim to have been operating in Thailand in accordance with the rules mutually agreed upon with the Thai government, namely, the TRIPS agreement and the Doha Declaration. These rules protect their patents on essential drugs like efavirenz, while also setting out a framework for negotiating price adjustments in specific circumstances. But some AIDS activists regard these rules as unfairly favorable to the interests of the pharmaceutical industry. Why should any business claim a patent on drugs that are essential for treating serious diseases like AIDS? Indeed, as a humanitarian gesture, or an exemplary demonstration of corporate social responsibility, shouldn't such drugs be distributed freely at or below the costs of manufacturing them?

The pharmaceutical industry's answer, of course, is that, however well intended, such proposals will only make investors reluctant to risk their capital on R&D and will thus inevitably slow the process of innovation and eventually reduce the supply of essential drugs. As we heard in the case study, "This expropriation of intellectual property sends a chilling signal to research-based companies about the attractiveness of undertaking risky research on diseases that affect the developing world, potentially hurting patients who may require new and innovative life-saving therapies" (Hunter et al. 2009). Any realistic appraisal of the cost of providing, for example, efavirenz to AIDS patients must include the costs of R&D involved not only in producing this drug but the costs of other experiments that failed to yield new drug formulas. Merck estimated that bringing efavirenz to market cost the firm US$550 million, even before a single dose was distributed. Is it realistic, let alone fair and just, to demand that Merck—or any other pharmaceutical manufacturer—simply write off such expenses as a charitable contribution without either going bankrupt or substantially changing its marketing strategies?

Merck is not insisting that low- or middle-income countries pay the full costs of the essential drugs they need. As we have seen, in 2001—the same year as the Doha Declaration—Merck agreed to a pricing scheme differentiating prices according to the three income tiers specified by the World Bank. Though Thailand is considered a middle-income country, in response to the threat of compulsory licensing, Merck cut its price for efavirenz even further, to a little more than half what the scheme called for, namely, US$277 per adult/per year, a price equivalent to what it was charging in low-income countries. Though the Thai government still complained that the price was too high, Merck contended that it could not recoup the R&D costs of producing efavirenz at that price level. By making such an adjustment, Merck appears to have attempted a humanitarian gesture that would also serve to protect its IPR on a drug deemed essential for alleviating the symptoms of AIDS. But was it enough? Should Merck have done more? Was theirs a reasonable and appropriate response to the Thai government's pleas on behalf of its citizens suffering from AIDS?

It is useful to recall the responses of other pharmaceutical companies involved in Thailand. We learned that when Thailand issued its compulsory license on efavirenz, Abbott Laboratories reacted by giving discounts to every middle-income country except Thailand and removing Thailand's registration for its HIV drug, Aluvia, in retaliation for what it considered "the Thai government's decision not to support innovation by breaking patents…." Two other companies, Bristol-Myers Squibb and Sanofi-Aventis, lowered their prices, while warning that compulsory licensing raises concern over the future of research-based drug companies operating in Thailand. The latter's reaction mirrors Merck's attempt to work out an accommodation that would preserve their patent rights to innovative drugs. If you had been advising pharmaceutical companies, which response would you favor, the path of retaliation set out by Abbott Laboratories or the path of accommodation set out by Merck and the others? Do you think justice or the greatest good for the greatest number is more likely to be achieved by the one or the other? How so?

13.4 Ethical Reflection

The complexity of the moral issues involved in the TRIPS and AIDS medicine in Thailand case is well summarized in the comment from Margaret Chan, WHO director general, who observed: "I'd like to underline that we have to find a right balance for compulsory licensing. We can't be naïve about this. There is no perfect solution for accessing drugs in both quality and quantity" (Bate 2007). Being forewarned that there is no perfect solution, let us recall the distinction introduced earlier in Chap. 2 regarding the two types of problems encountered in international business ethics. There we adopted Laura Nash's proposal distinguishing type A and type B ethical problems. Type A problems are situations, properly regarded as "moral dilemmas" in which a person doesn't know—or is in doubt—as to what the right thing to do is, while type B problems are situations in which a person knows what the right thing to do is, but will not or cannot bring themselves to do it. Of the two, the ethical challenge facing decision-makers in not only Thailand's Ministry of Health but also the pharmaceutical companies is that they are confronted by competing moral claims that do not readily lend themselves to prioritization. These are type A problems, requiring those involved to balance the pharmaceutical companies' IPRs—that is, their right to profit from the sale of drugs for which they hold an internationally recognized patent—on the one hand, against the right to life, or at least the right of access to affordable healthcare, that is regarded, on the other hand, as a basic human right. Since it appears to be impossible to do justice equally to both of these rights simultaneously, the type A "moral dilemma" is, as WHO's Chan has observed, how to achieve "the right balance" between them.

We may need to pause a moment to consider why finding the right balance is necessary. What if the challenge was exclusively focused on providing universal access to the drugs that contribute to affordable healthcare? What if IPRs were not rights at all and that patents protecting such alleged rights were only an arbitrary imposition of rents by MNCs with the power to do so? Is there a valid moral argument for IPRs in general and the protection of patents like Merck's on efavirenz—or Abbott Laboratories' on Aluvia—in particular? Here an exploration of long-standing cultural assumptions—both East and West—may be relevant.

13.4.1 The Concept of Intellectual Property

The concept of intellectual property assumed in international business ethics is primarily an extension of the traditional Western—or at least, Anglo-American—concept of private property. So, then, what is private property? Property may be described as a bundle of rights (Becker 1977). The Scottish philosopher John Locke suggested this definition when he observed, "Where there is no property, there is no injustice" (Locke 1690a). He might have achieved a greater degree of clarity had he said, "Where there is no property, there is neither justice nor injustice." Justice, in the classic sense of rendering to each his or her own (*suum cuique*), in his view, depends upon a prior recognition of each person's right of ownership, first of all, over his or her own body and whatever he or she may acquire through his or her own bodily labors (Locke 1690b). It is unjust to take from another what another has a right to, namely, his or her property. Locke believed that this basic moral idea is as certain and demonstrable as any axiom of mathematics (Locke 1690a). Civil government—the result of a social contract by which free persons seek to go beyond the presumably barbarous and chaotic state of nature—exists to secure justice for all, mainly through the protection of their individual property rights (Locke 1690b).

Property refers, then, to anything acquired by mixing one's labor with the free (that is, unclaimed) goods of this earth. Property is of various kinds, such as tangible property, for example, real estate, as well as intangible property, for example, stocks, bonds, and other financial securities. Intellectual property consists of a bundle of rights governing products of the intellect. By analogy with the moral and legal assumptions governing other forms of property, recognizing some idea or artistic creation or invention as intellectual property implies that someone has labored to produce it, that is, an idea or artistic creation or invention whose ownership has not been claimed by anyone else. As with other forms of property, the assumption is that a person's successful claim to ownership—be it individual or corporate—entitles him or her with the right to exercise control over it, that is, to decide whether to possess it or to share it or to exchange it for some other good, in all the different ways in which property can be shared or exchanged or simply given away.

The claim of ownership, once successfully made and recognized, raises the question of what proofs the producer of some new idea, artistic creation, or invention can use to validate his or her right. This, too, is analogous to the ways in which other forms of property ownership are successfully validated, through documentation ranging from wills and deeds to sales receipts. Since civil government, according to Locke, is formed in order to secure justice for all those participating in the social contract, it is hardly surprising that the state would find it appropriate to protect intellectual property rights along with the other property rights. In addition to the state's basic function as the ultimate "night watchman" guarding the security of each person's life, liberty, and property, the specific protections afforded toward intellectual property are a result of the state's interest in encouraging innovation by allowing producers to control the distribution of—or make a profit from—the new ideas, inventions, and discoveries that they validly claim to have produced.

13.4.2 Forms of Intellectual Property and Their Claims to Protection

There are three ways to ethically and legally protect intellectual property, so that everyone who can validly claim a contribution to the development of a new idea or intellectual product will have their claim respected and enforced: copyright, patent, and trade secrets.

Copyright: The goal of copyright is to protect the written expression of ideas. Although formulated to protect the written word, copyrighting now extends to a variety of creative products, such as tape recordings, films, videotapes, video compact disks, computer programs, and virtually all forms of digitalized information, as well as works of art. Copyright laws in the USA originally protected copyrighted material for 28 years and could be renewed for an additional 28 years (De George: 1999, 297). The US laws, however, were weaker than those in Europe and elsewhere. Eventually, the USA conformed to international copyright agreements, which protect copyrighted material for the life of the author plus 70 years and protect corporations that successfully claim authorship for 95 years. Under certain restricted conditions (usually involving personal use or some educational purpose), one is allowed to copy some or all of a copyrighted work.

Patent: A patent prohibits direct copying, but does not prevent learning from a new product or developing a competing product, for example, through so-called reverse engineering. Both patents and copyrights require that intellectual products be made available to the public so that they can become socially useful, which occurs when they are priced and distributed through a marketplace. Patents are specifically intended to protect inventions. Since society has an interest in encouraging innovation and new product development, patent laws not only extend but also limit protection because every invention builds upon the ideas of others. The Latin saying *liber ex libro* expresses this idea symbolically, by observing how every new book builds upon insights found in other books. Progress in knowledge is always social and belongs to society, which must protect its own interest in it for the sake of the common good, while also regulating the property rights—including intellectual property rights—of the individuals or corporations that have acquired them.

Trade Secrets: Trade secrets are often the key to a company's survival under conditions of fierce competition. Businesses will spend large amounts of money to keep their innovations and strategies secret. They may validly claim a right to protect their investment because the unauthorized disclosure of trade secrets—usually in the form of industrial espionage—in effect is a form of stealing. Competitors who use spies to learn trade secrets are trying to steal market share. Unlike copyrighted and patented products, trade secrets are not to be revealed at any time. It is therefore reasonable for a company to restrict access to confidential information and to seek compensation as determined in a court of law from those individuals or groups caught spying on them. Companies often define in their ethical codes how employees are to treat confidential information and sometimes require employees to sign an agreement not to divulge such information, even after they have quit their jobs for whatever reason.

13.4.3 Intellectual Property in Chinese Moral Philosophy

Western thinking about IPRs and their enforcement, however, is only part of the range of concerns that ought to inform international business ethics. Skepticism about the fairness of enforcing the IPRs, especially of foreign businesses, and their frequent disregard by East Asian producers and consumers no doubt do complicate the challenges involved in understanding their moral and legal basis. Nevertheless, Asian resistance to IPRs and their enforcement should not be misunderstood as simply a reflection of alleged contemporary trends toward cynicism, cultural decadence, and moral irresponsibility. Nor should the problem be explained away as the reflection of deep-seated cultural assumptions that have existed, for example, in China for centuries. Western attempts to identify a traditional Chinese cultural barrier to the acceptance of IPR regulation usually appeal to William P. Alford's groundbreaking study, *To Steal a Book Is an Elegant Offense: Intellectual Property*

Law in Chinese Civilization (Alford 1995). Alford's broad survey of the history of IPRs in East Asia creates the impression that concern over IPRs and their enforcement was extremely rare until various Western imperialisms forced China to open itself for trade in the nineteenth century. Whatever the laws were to regulate publishing during the dynastic history of Imperial China, they existed not to enforce an author's private property rights, but to promote social harmony by preserving the integrity of the Chinese classics and other important books or protecting the state from subversive ideas. Imperial censorship policies informed the development of laws regarding intellectual property even after the Maoist revolution, while only very recently, and under pressure from foreign entities, has China begun to accommodate itself to the allegedly international consensus on IPRs and their enforcement. Given their apparently foreign origins, is it any wonder that Chinese entrepreneurs and consumers seem so indifferent to them?

As the title of Alford's book—*To Steal a Book Is an Elegant Offense*—is meant to dramatize, IPRs and their enforcement allegedly were unheard of in premodern Chinese culture. And yet, this familiar Chinese proverb—indirect testimony to Alford's popularity in the West—cannot be traced back to Confucius, but to the early twentieth century literary master Lu Xun, who created the comic figure Kong Yiji, a shabby copyist with a fondness for alcohol, who failed his exams in the Classics, and "who sometimes stole books to trade for wine" (Yu 2012; quoting Shi Wei 2006). Much to the delight of his companions at the Universal Prosperity bar, Kong defends himself by claiming lamely that stealing a book is hardly a crime—at least not for a scholar like himself (Lu Xun, "Kong Yiji," 1919; in *The Real Story of Ah-Q and Other Tales of China*, 2009). Lu Xun's attitude toward Kong Yiji is wonderfully complex, as if this buffoon symbolizes the dead end of a Confucian civilization that by the time of the May 4th Movement had turned out to be laughably irrelevant to the needs of Chinese people. Adamantly delusional about his gentlemanly pretensions, while inventing Confucian proverbs to cover up his petty thievery, Kong Yiji is hardly a fair representative of premodern Chinese attitudes toward IPRs. Nevertheless, this poor defender of *rujia* (儒家) and a *junzi*'s (君子) moral dignity does highlight certain traditional attitudes that, as Alford argues, do suggest divergences between typically Western and typically East Asian attitudes toward IPRs.

One common example is the copying of artistic works of others. As Alford points out, upon discovering that his calligraphy or a scroll painting had been judged so perfectly executed that forgers were copying it, a *junzi* would not attempt to stop them. As the famed song artist Mi Fu (1051–1107 CE) observed, "In matters of calligraphy and painting, one is not to discuss price. The gentleman is hard to capture by money" (Alford 1995: 28). The ideal Confucian would realize that those capable of making intellectual contributions already know that their work is but a reflection or but another stage in the transmission of a tradition that is rooted in the nature of things. Intellectual creations, in theory, should be shared freely so that they can improve the condition of society as a whole. "On what basis," then asks Alford, "could anyone exclude others from the common heritage of all civilized persons?" (Ibid: 29). But such lofty ideals apparently coexisted in premodern China with the reality of exemplary scholars like Zhu Xi (1130–1200 CE), who, as Ken Shao has observed, "was very active in seeking copyright protection for his new books" (Shao 2012: 107). Contrary to Alford, Shao argues persuasively that, once the technologies allowing for commercial printing were developed, Chinese intellectuals were concerned to protect their works against unauthorized publication that not only threatened their livelihood but also failed to preserve the integrity of their texts and other intellectual creations.

A major difference in Chinese attitudes toward IPRs, as Shao argues, is reflected in the state's reluctance to grant monopolies to various private persons and groups (Shao 2012: 110). The creators of intellectual property should not use the law to enforce private interests—such as monopolies—that conflict with the interests of the state and the people.[5] Since the Emperor's legitimacy depended on his fulfilling the Mandate of Heaven (Chinese, 天命; pinyin, *tiānmìng*), which is informed by the traditional expectation that "people are the root" (Chinese, 民本; pinyin, *minben*), the government's first priority is to secure the prosperity of the Chinese people as a whole (Nuyen 2000). Property rights, and by extension IPRs, will be regulated in light of the principle of *minben.* This principle, of course, cannot be used to warrant the wholesale denial of IPRs, any more than the Confucian ideal of the *junzi* can be used to justify violating them. But it does mean that IPRs can never be regarded as absolute, in the sense of being enforceable against all other legitimate claims, especially the state's overriding concern for preserving social harmony.

How precisely IPRs are respected, therefore, involves the complex interaction among all the various methods of governance operative in both traditional and contemporary China. As Alford observed, "traditional Chinese thought arrayed the various instruments through which the state might be administered and social harmony maintained into a hierarchy ranging downward in desirability from heavenly reason (*tianli*), the way (*dao*), morality (*de*), ritual propriety (*li*), custom (*xixu*), community compacts (*xiang yue*), and family rules (*jia cheng*) to the formal written law of the state" (Alford 1995:10). The result is that positive law—civil or criminal—is likely to be invoked as a last resort, only after the other administrative "instruments" have failed. If there were a dispute, for example, over the unauthorized reproduction of copyrighted material, the state would prefer to have it resolved informally by the parties availing themselves of the various ways in which disputes are customarily resolved and social harmony restored. Of course, with the encroachment of various forms of Western imperialism in the nineteenth and twentieth

[5] Explaining this difference may also require a critical comparison of the role of the state, understood as a construct emerging from a Lockean social contract, contrasting with the traditional Chinese view of the state as ultimately the natural expression and embodiment of the Chinese family. Analogous to the family, the Chinese state's first priority is preserving social harmony so that all family members may flourish. The Lockean social contract assumes no such analogy, since the contractors are individuals who agree to forego the liberty they exercise in the state of nature in order to secure protections that cannot be obtained in the state of nature. The first of these protections concerns their rights to life, liberty, and property. Individual property rights therefore are central to the role of the state in a Lockean social contract, in ways that they simply cannot be in Chinese social philosophy.

centuries, China has undergone modernization, sometimes embracing it, sometimes resisting it, but usually attempting to adapt to it in ways that will preserve the political and cultural integrity of China for the benefit of the Chinese people. The PRC government's approach to IPRs reflects the processes of adaptation, consistent with China's overall posture toward modernization and now globalization.

13.4.4 IPR Regulation in Today's China

China thus has implemented extensive laws and regulations to protect intellectual property rights (SIPO 2013), among them, the Trademark Law, the Patent Law, the Copyright Law, the Law Against Unfair Competition, the Computer Software Protection Rules, the Regulations on the Protection of Intellectual Property by Customs, the Civil Law, the Contract Law, and the Regulations Governing the Registration of Enterprise Names. China has also entered into a number of international agreements regarding intellectual property rights: the Paris Convention on the Protection of Industrial Property, the Madrid Agreement on International Registration of Trademarks, the Berne Convention for the Protection of Literary and Artistic Works, the Universal Copyright Convention, the Geneva Convention for the Protection of Producers of Phonograms, and the Patent Cooperation Treaty.

Since 1980, China has been a member of the World Intellectual Property Organization (WIPO), an NGO dedicated to promoting the use and protection of intellectual property. With their headquarters in Geneva, Switzerland, the WIPO is one of 16 specialized agencies in the UN's system of organizations. It administers 21 international treaties dealing with different aspects of intellectual property. In 1996, the WIPO expanded its role and further demonstrated the importance of intellectual property rights in the management of global trade by entering into cooperation with the WTO. Although it is beyond the scope of this chapter to explain the complicated legal framework of intellectual property rights, it is important to know that China has not only signed these international agreements, but in the eyes of WIPO, has made substantial progress in implementing them (WIPO 2010). China must also receive credit for increasing its effort to comply with these agreements since joining the WTO in November 2001. While a large gap still exists between the enactment of these laws and their actual enforcement, their very existence suggests that China's continued identification with its classic moral and spiritual traditions, such as Confucianism, simply has not proved to be an insurmountable obstacle to the recognition of IPRs and their legal enforcement.

As Peter Yu points out, the challenge of enforcing a fair regime of IPR laws and regulations in China today, as elsewhere in East Asia, is not primarily cultural or developmental. Nor is it any less severe in technologically advanced societies, such as the USA. Nor, finally, is indifference to IPR regulation a necessary by-product of authoritarian rule (Yu 2003). In the absence of any convincing evidence that culture or, if you will, "Asian values" explain local reluctance to embrace international IPR standards, Yu argues that each country must concentrate instead on developing IPR stakeholders who will recognize their own self-interest in abiding by fair and relevant regulations. Since most East Asian countries have adequate IPR legislation in place, the challenge is one of compliance, which Yu analyzes in terms of the "divide" separating IPR stakeholders from "nonstakeholders." He proposes four comprehensive policies that could reduce this divide: First, educate the nonstakeholders about the IPR system, so that they understand not only what it is but how it might be made to work to protect their own interests. Second, take steps to help nonstakeholders develop their own stake in the system.[6] Third, collaborate with local governments to develop effective enforcement methods. Fourth, and finally, create products that are priced affordably for local markets[7] (Yu 2003: 11–14). In short, once entrepreneurs recognize that they can make more money by complying with IPR laws than by flaunting them, the problem of enforcing them will begin to take care of itself.

13.5 Conclusion

Yu's plea for patience, flexibility, and mutual understanding confirms our own inclination to support ethical rather than legal approaches to IPRs and their enforcement. As Rothlin has previously stated among his *Eighteen Rules for Becoming a Top Notch Player*, "If you protect intellectual property, all stakeholders will receive their due share." The analyses offered by Yu as well as Shao and others take us one step further by recognizing that progress in respecting IPRs will depend on how well we all learn to convert "nonstakeholders" into stakeholders. Doing whatever we can to expand the circle of inclusion is an indispensable prerequisite for exercising moral leadership and responsibility. If you are convinced that respecting IPRs may be an important dimension of doing justice and promoting social harmony, then our efforts must focus, as Yu pointed out, on promoting awareness regarding the moral basis for IPRs. Such initiatives are likely to succeed, not when they are brought in

[6] Yu cites an example from China that concerns a dispute between joint venture partners over "design fees" that mirrors issues we explored in the Pepsi Sichuan case study in chapter four: "A case in point is a U.S.-China joint venture whose Chinese partner was unwilling to allocate a portion of the joint venture profits to the foreign partner for design fees. The reaction of the Chinese partner was natural and understandable; it understood neither intellectual property protection nor the intentions behind the foreign partner's action. However, once the foreign partner explained to the Chinese manufacturer that it could charge separately for its design work and helped the manufacturer determine the cost of its own design processes, the Chinese partner became receptive to the idea of allocating profits for intellectual property. It even actively lobbied local regulators for the right to design fees" (Yu 2003: 13). While Yu's example has an ending far happier than what Pepsi and its Sichuan partner were able to achieve, it represents a promising alternative, provided that the joint venture partners can still trust each other.

[7] This last point is illustrated by the motion picture industry's successful effort in China to market VCD copies of commercial films, either dubbed in Putonghua or imprinted with Chinese subtitles, that are sold for somewhere between 10 and 25 % of the price of an imported DVD copy. As one music recording company observed, "We think the best way to stop piracy is to make music so cheap it isn't worth copying" (Yu 2003: 14).

as a last resort once disputes have arisen, but when they emerge naturally as part of a person's basic moral education.

One such initiative, launched a few years ago and still ongoing, is Hong Kong's Youth Ambassadors Against Internet Piracy campaign in which youth groups, ranging in age from 9 to 25, were recruited to help monitor IPR issues on the Internet (IPRPA 2013). The program, which is a result of cooperation between the HKSAR government's Customs and Excise Department (C&ED) and businesses supporting the Intellectual Property Rights Protection Alliance, seeks to educate youth on the significance of IPRs, while also recruiting them to monitor illegal Internet activities, for example, the pirating of music and videos through the use of bit torrent technology. The campaign received international attention in 2005 and 2006, when it was subject to much scorn (Vance 2005) and some skepticism (Bradsher 2006). While Western accounts tended to focus on the inappropriateness of recruiting youth as spies to do the bidding of IP industry giants like the Motion Picture Association, they seem to ignore the fact that such innovative educational initiatives are precisely what may be most effective in East Asia, assuming that there is a legitimate moral basis for protecting IPRs. At any rate, the critics ought to realize that, in the absence of such educational campaigns, the only alternative is more and more punitive law enforcement. The success reported for the Hong Kong Youth Ambassadors Against Internet Piracy, which along with other educational campaigns seems to have substantially improved the HKSAR's record on a full range of IPR indicators (WIPO 2012), may not be replicable in Western societies faced with similar challenges, but it remains a promising development for other Asian venues.

The first task of reason in ethics is to clarify the principles that protect the public interest or the common good. International business ethics participates in this work by entering into dialogue with business people and experts in various fields to determine solutions and compromises that respect the interests of all of society. Ethical insights are not artifacts to be venerated in a museum and invoked only for chiding gullible youth and other onlookers. They are to be freshly examined for their capacity to bring together insights from other fields, such as economics, law, and sociology. Ethics also urges the revision of legislation when it becomes clear, for example, that intellectual property rights regulations act against the public interest. As we have seen in the TRIPS case study featured in this chapter, the focus of moral concern cannot simply be on compliance but must also address the fact that the prices of certain products, such as pharmaceuticals, books, and compact disks, which are standard products in the developed world, are too expensive for the average citizen in a developing country. Arguably, the prices charged for these products are unjust, when they are calculated not to protect legitimate property rights, but to achieve windfall profits for small, privileged groups of monopolists.

We must face up to the fact that applying strict IPR rules without further concern to meet the legitimate needs of all stakeholders can become a form of oppression. If we are critical, for example, of Mongkol's decision to breach Merck's IPR through compulsory licensing, it is because this may not have been the most effective way to achieve fairness for all concerned. Nevertheless, we can only applaud his apparent determination to do something for Thailand's AIDS-infected people who cannot afford to buy the medicine they urgently need. Ethics, at its best, does not contradict the law, but improves it. It articulates the voices of people whose rights are violated, but who cannot afford lawyers to defend themselves. By considering every stakeholder's interest, ethics intends to find a proper balance that will do justice to the many conflicting claims involving intellectual property rights.

References

Alcorn, K. (2006, November 29). Thailand to issue compulsory license for efavirenz. *AidsMap*. Retrieved May 21, 2012, from http://www.aidsmap.com/Thailand-to-issue-compulsory-license-for-efavirenz/page/1425713/

Alford, W. P. (1995). *To steal a book is an elegant offense: Intellectual property law in Chinese civilization*. Stanford: Stanford University Press.

Alsegard, E. (2004). Global pharmaceutical patents after the Doha declaration: What lies in the future? *Scripted*. Retrieved May 31, 2012, from http://www.law.ed.ac.uk/ahrc/script-d/docs/doha.asp#Proposals

AVERT. (2009). HIV & AIDS in Thailand. Retrieved May 27, 2012, from http://www.avert.org/thailand-aids-hiv.htm#contentTable1

Bate, R. (2007, April 4). Thailand and the drug patent wars. *American Enterprise Institute*. Retrieved June 8, 2012, from http://www.aei.org/article/health/thailand-and-the-drug-patent-wars/

Bate, R., & Boateng, K. (2007, August 9). Drug pricing and its discontents. *American Enterprise Institute*. Retrieved June 8, 2012, from http://www.aei.org/article/health/drug-pricing-and-its-discontents/

Becker, L. C. (1977). *Property rights: Philosophic foundations*. Boston: Routledge & Kegan Paul.

Bradsher, K. (2006, July 18). Dare violate a copyright in Hong Kong? A boy Scout may be watching online. *New York Times*. Retrieved on September 18, 2013, from http://www.nytimes.com/2006/07/18/arts/18pira.html?pagewanted=1&_r=1&ei=5090&en=e1558dc44194c9d4&ex=1310875200

Cervini, E., & Prabhu, K. (2012). *Compulsory Licensing*. Cambridge, MA: Harvard University, Harvard Model Congress Asia.

Coriat, B. (2008). *The political economy of HIV/AIDS in developing economies*. Cambridge, MA: Edward Elgar Publishing, Inc. Retrieved on September 19, 2013, from http://books.google.com.hk/books?id=HQpvZ6xs1C8C&pg=PA101&source=gbs_toc_r&cad=4#v=onepage&q&f=false

CPA Global. (2007, May 11). Clinton foundation backs Thai patent policy. Retrieved July 10, 2012, from http://www.cpaglobal.com/newlegalreview/2480/clinton_foundation_backs_thai_patent_policy

Deazley, R., Kretschmer, M., & Bently, L., (Eds.). (2010). *Privilege and property: Essays on the history of copyright*. Cambridge: Open Book Publishers. Retrieved September 10, 2010, from http://digital-rights.net/wp-content/uploads/books/Privilege&Property-Deazley.pdf

De George, R. T. (1999). *Business ethics* (5th ed.). Upper Saddle River: Prentice Hall.

Ford, N., Wilson, D., Chaves, G. C., Lotrowska, M., & Kijiwatchakula, K. (2007, July). Sustaining access to antiretroviral therapy in the less-developed world: Lessons from Brazil and Thailand. *AIDS*. S21–S29.

Fox News. (2007, May 9). Clinton backs Thailand's move to break patents on AIDS drugs. Retrieved June 26, 2012, from http://www.foxnews.com/story/0,2933,270955,00.html

Frank, R. (2001, March). Prescription drug prices: Why do some pay more than others do? *Health Affairs, 20*(2), 115–128. Retrieved June 26, 2012, from http://content.healthaffairs.org/content/20/2/115.long

Fraser, J. (2006, December 4). Thailand issues license to issue generic form of Efavirenz; Snubs Merck AIDS drug monopoly. *Natural News*. Retrived May 31, 2012, from http://www.naturalnews.com/021232.html

Gerhardsen, T. (2006, December 22). Thailand compulsory license on AIDS drug prompts policy debate. *Intellectual Property Watch*. Retrieved May 27, 2012, from http://www.ip-watch.org/2006/12/22/thailand-compulsory-license-on-aids-drug-prompts-policy-debate/?res=800_ff&print=0

Gosain, R. (2007, September 3). Strict public health policy threatens pharmaceutical patents. *International Law Office*. Retrieved May 30, 2012, from http://www.internationallawoffice.com/newsletters/detail.aspx?g=263aef08-eed1-41c1-93d5-e920b6a4679c

Health Info. (2009). Life versus vested interest: The government introduces compulsory licensing based on the right to life. Retrieved June 13, 2012, from http://www.hiso.or.th/hiso/picture/reportHealth/ThaiHealth2009/eng2009_17.pdf

Hunter, R., Lozada, H., Giarratano, F., & Jenkins, D. (2009). Compulsory licensing: A major issue in international business today? *European Journal of Social Sciences, 11*(3), 370–377.

IPRPA. (2013). Youth Ambassador against internet piracy. Hong Kong intellectual property rights protection alliance. Retrieved September 19, 2013, from http://www.iprpa.org/eng/anti_campaign.php

Kazmin, A., & Jack, A. (2006, November 30). Merck to cut AIDS drug cost in Thailand. *Financial Times*. Retrieved May 22, 2012, from http://www.ft.com/intl/cms/s/0/04455f9e-80b0-11db-9096-0000779e2340.html#axzz1vYozy8Ab

Kazmin, A., & Jack, A. (2007, March 14). Abbott pulls HIV drug in Thai patent protest. *Financial Times*. Retrieved June 13, 2012, from http://www.ft.com/intl/cms/s/0/a2e81cc8-d1d1-11db-b921-000b5df10621.html#axzz1xdVHXI5p

Ling, C. Y. (2006, December 6). Thailand uses compulsory license for cheaper AIDS drug. *Third World Network*. Retrieved May 31, 2012, from www.twnside.org.sg/title2/resurgence/196/cover5.doc

Locke, J. (1690a). An essay concerning human understanding (Vol. II, 2nd ed.). Chapter III: Of the extent of human knowledge. Paragraph 18: Morality capable of demonstration. Retrieved September 10, 2013, from http://www.gutenberg.org/cache/epub/10616/pg10616.html

Locke, J. (1690b). Second treatise of government. Chapter V: Of property. The project Gutenberg edition of the second treatise of government. Retrieved September 10, 2013, from http://www.gutenberg.org/files/7370/7370-h/7370-h.htm

Lu, X. (1919). "Kong Yiji". In *The real story of Ah-Q and other tales of China. The complete fiction of Lu Xun*. Translated with an Introduction by Julia Lovell, with an Afterword by Yiyun Li. New York: Penguin Books, 2009, pp. 32–37.

Malhotra, G. (2010, July 21). Pharmaceutical reverse payments and lower drug costs: An interesting dilemma. *PharmaPro*. Retrieved June 26, 2012, from http://www.pharmpro.com/blogs/2010/07/Pharmaceutical-Reverse-Payments-and-Lower-Drug-Costs/

Mayne, R. (2005). *Regionalism, bilateralism, and "TRIP Plus" agreements: The threat to developing countries*. New York: Human Development Report Office. Retrieved June 21, 2015, from http://hdr.undp.org/en/content/regionalism-bilateralism-and-%E2%80%9Ctrip-plus%E2%80%9D-agreements

Matthews, D. (2006, December 22). Patent Reform in India: The Campaign to protect public health. *Queen Mary School of Law*. Retrieved June 8, 2012, from http://www.ipngos.org/NGO%20Briefings/Patents%20Act%20amendment.pdf

Medecins Sans Frontieres. (2007). MSF welcomes move to overcome patent on AIDS drug in Thailand. Retrieved May 30, 2012, from http://www.doctorswithoutborders.org/press/release.cfm?id=1905

Merck. (2011, September). Public policy statement: Intellectual property and access to medicines in the developing world. Retrieved May 30, 2012, from http://www.merck.com/about/views-and-positions/public-policy-statement-ip-2011.pdf

Merck. (2012). Our company. Retrieved May 24, 2012, from http://www.merck.com/about/our-history/home.html

Montlake, S. (2007, January 31). Thailand widens the scope of generic drugs. *The Christian Science Monitor*. Retrieved May 27, 2012, from http://www.csmonitor.com/2007/0131/p07s02-woap.html

Nuyen, A. T. (2000). Confucianism, the idea of min-pen, and democracy. *Copenhagen Journal of Asian Studies*, *14*, 130–151. Retrieved September 14, 2013, from http://rauli.cbs.dk/index.php/cjas/article/download/2154/2151

Schuettler, D. (2007, February 16). Thai drug move stirs patent debate. *Reuters*. Retrieved June 25, 2012, from http://www.reuters.com/article/2007/02/16/us-thailand-drugs-patents-idUSBKK7253920070216

Seidenberg, S. (2008, February 1). Patent abuse. *Inside Counsel*. Retrieved May 22, 2012, from http://www.insidecounsel.com/2008/02/01/patent-abuse

Shao, K. (2012). Chinese culture and intellectual property: Let's realise we have been misguided. *The WIPO Journal*, *4* W.I.P.O.J. 00, 103–110. Retrieved September 10, 2013, from http://www.wipo.int/export/sites/www/freepublications/en/intproperty/wipo_journal/wipo_journal_4_1.pdf

Short, P. (2010, August 3). 25 Years in Thailand's sex industry. *CNN*. Retrieved June 13, 2012, from http://www.cnngo.com/bangkok/life/25-years-thailands-sex-industry-233135

Shi, W. (2006). Cultural perplexity in intellectual property: Is stealing a book an elegant offense? *32* N.C. J. Int'l L. & Com. Reg. 1, 11.

Silverman, E. (2007, November 23). Thailand's health minister leaves next month; will compulsory licensing come to an end? *Pharmalot*. Retrieved May 31, 2012, from http://www.pharmalot.com/2007/11/thailands-health-minister-leaves-next-month-will-compulsory-licensing-come-to-an-end/

SIPO. (2013). Laws and policy. State intellectual property office of the PRC. Retrieved September 18, 2013, from http://english.sipo.gov.cn/laws/

Steinbrook, R. (2007). Thailand and the compulsory licensing of Efavirenz. *New England Journal of Medicine, 356*(6), 544–546.

T'Hoen, E. F. M. (2010). TRIPS, Pharmaceutical patents and access to essential medicines: Seattle, doha and beyond. In H. Murphy (Ed.), *The making of international trade policy: NGOs, Agenda-setting, and the WTO* (pp. 39–68). Northampton: Edward Elgar Publishing, Inc.

The Nation. (2007, May 8). Compulsory licenses, Mongkol: 'We can't give in with lives at stake.' Retrieved June 13, 2012, from http://www.nationmultimedia.com/2007/05/05/national/national_30033438.php

Vance, A. (2005, May 5). Hong Kong scouts gain IP proficiency badge: Dib, dib, dib MPA Style. *The Register*. Retrieved September 19, 2013, from http://www.theregister.co.uk/2005/05/05/scout_ip_badge/

Washington College of Law. (2008, March). Timeline for Thailand's compulsory licenses. Retrieved May 31, 2012, from http://www.wcl.american.edu/pijip/documents/timeline.pdf

WIPO. (2012). *World intellectual property indicators – 2012* (WIPO economics and statistics series). Retrieved September 18, 2013, from http://www.wipo.int/export/sites/www/freepublications/en/intproperty/941/wipo_pub_941_2012.pdf

WIPO Magazine. (2010). China's IP journey. *WIPO Magazine*, Number 6, December 2010, pp. 25–28. Retrieved September 17, 2013, from http://www.wipo.int/export/sites/www/wipo_magazine/en/pdf/2010/wipo_pub_121_2010_06.pdf

The World Bank. (2000). Thailand social monitor: Thailand's response to AIDS, building on success, confronting the future. Retrieved May 27, 2012, from http://www-wds.worldbank.org/external/default/WDSContentServer/WDSP/IB/2002/03/29/000094946_02031904060482/Rendered/PDF/multi0page.pdf

The World Bank. (2012). How we classify countries. Retrieved May 24, 2012, from http://data.worldbank.org/about/country-classifications

World Trade Organization. (2001, November 14). *Declaration on the TRIPS agreement and public health*. Retrieved on June 20, 2015, from https://www.wto.org/english/thewto_e/minist_e/min01_e/mindecl_trips_e.htm

World Trade Organization. (2012). Overview: The TRIPS agreement. Retrieved June 11, 2012, from http://www.wto.org/english/tratop_e/trips_e/intel2_e.htm

Yu, P. K. (2000). From pirates to partners: Protecting intellectual property in China in the twenty-first century. *American University Law* (Vol. 50, Cardozo legal studies research paper no. 34). Retrieved September 10, 2013, from http://papers.ssrn.com/sol3/papers.cfm?abstract_id=245548

Yu, P. K. (2003). *Four common misconceptions about copyright policy* (MSU-DCL Public Law research paper no. 01-16). Retrieved September 12, 2013, from http://papers.ssrn.com/sol3/papers.cfm?abstract_id=443160

Yu, P. K. (2006). TRIPs and its discontents. *Marquette Intellectual Property Law Review, 10,* 369–410. Milwaukee, WI: Marquette University Law School. Retrieved on June 21, 2015 from http://scholarship.law.marquette.edu/iplr/vol10/iss2/7/

Yu, P. K. (2012). International intellectual property scholars series: Intellectual property and Asian values, 16 intellectual property L. Rev. 329 (2012). Retrieved September 10, 2013, from http://scholarship.law.marquette.edu/cgi/viewcontent.cgi?article=1195&context=iplr

Zamiska, N. (2007, February 8). Thai move to lower drug costs highlights growing patent rifts. *Yale Global.* Retrieved May 31, 2012, from http://yaleglobal.yale.edu/content/thai-move-trim-drug-costs-highlights-growing-patent-rift

Chapter 14
Competitors: Fighting Corruption in the Marketplace

"Your economic achievements will only stand on firm ground if you diminish corruption." (Stephan Rothlin, *Eighteen Rules for Becoming a Top Notch Player*, 2004)

14.1 Prelude

What is corruption in the marketplace? As the word implies, corruption means deliberately ruining some good in order to achieve a purely private benefit. The good of the marketplace consists in the integrity of the business transactions that are facilitated within it. Good transactions are those that are freely entered into, based on sufficient information and meeting commonly recognized standards of fairness—the theoretical basis of which was presented in Chap. 5. Commercial bribery—including kickbacks and other questionable payments—is a fundamental form of corruption in the marketplace. It corrupts the competition that is assumed as an integral part of the process leading toward a successful business transaction. When one firm gains an unfair advantage through bribery, its competitors are harmed precisely because they are effectively blocked from competing. To illustrate these points and their significance in the context of current trends in Asian economic development, we will begin this chapter with a case study on the practice of bribery undertaken by Siemens China. The case study will allow readers to come to grips with the actual reality of competition in Chinese markets and the seeming inevitability of bribing in order to maintain and expand one's business there. But what is the ethics of bribery? Is bribery OK when "everyone else is doing it"? Do "two wrongs make a right"? Readers will be led through the entire process, beginning with Siemens' decision to make a policy of bribery, through its detection, the criminal conviction of the executives involved, and the steps Siemens China has taken since the incident to change its policies and show leadership in the fight against corruption.

S. Rothlin, D. McCann, *International Business Ethics*,
DOI 10.1007/978-3-662-47434-1_14

14.2 Case Study: The High Cost of Corruption, Siemens Bribery Scandal

14.2.1 Abstract

What do offshore bank accounts, money smuggling, and shell companies have in common? They were all part of two decades of rampant bribery initiated by the German company, Siemens AG. Siemens, a multinational electronics company known for innovation and quality, admitted to bribing governments for contracts. Siemens faced accusations of bribery and other corporate corruption in 20 countries, including Argentina, Bangladesh, Greece, and Nigeria, making the Siemens case the largest bribery scandal in modern corporate history.

China Mobile executive Shi Wanzhong received bribes totaling US $5.1 million in exchange for equipment contracts with Siemens. After the scandal was revealed, Shi was tried for economic crimes and given the death penalty, while the middleman who facilitated the bribes was given a 15-year prison sentence.

The Siemens case forces us to address the issues of bribery, corruption, and unfair competition, as well as certain philosophical questions about moral relativism and universal moral values in the context of a globalizing economy.

14.2.2 Keywords

Siemens AG, Bribes, Foreign Corrupt Practices Act (FCPA), Securities and Exchange Commission (SEC), Unfair competition, Moral relativism, The universalizability of ethical principles

14.2.3 An Unexpected Monster

The beginning of the Siemens scandal reads like the opening scenes of a thriller novel. Reinhard Siekaczek, a middle-aged Siemens accountant, awoke early on the morning of November 15, 2006. Waiting at the front door of his Munich home were a prosecutor and six police officers, each eager to arrest him.

In hindsight, Siekaczek acknowledged he knew the authorities would come for him eventually. At the time, he was a midlevel executive at Siemens AG, the German-based global electronics powerhouse, whose slogan challenged employees to “Be Inspired” (*The Economist* 2008). Unremarkable in appearance, Siekaczek in reality played a key role in the largest bribery case in modern corporate history. On behalf of Siemens, Siekaczek managed an annual budget specifically earmarked for the payment of bribes, which ranged between US $40 and $50 million (Millker and Schubert 2009). A system of offshore accounts and slush funds was meant to disguise the money trail.

The result was reminiscent of horror movies in which the Frankenstein monster comes to life. Did Siemens executives realize what they had created? Did they ever imagine that this monster could possibly carry an agenda of its own? They did not—at least not until it was too late.

14.2.4 Institutionalized Corruption

Siekaczek, who would later be charged with 58 counts of breach of trust, was just the tip of the iceberg. German prosecutors began investigating Siemens in 2005 after reports of bribery, tax evasion, and embezzlement were filed in Lichtenstein, Switzerland, and Austria (Steptoe 2009). In November 2006, over 200 German police, prosecutors, and inspectors raided 30 Siemens offices in Germany, including that of the CEO Klaus Kleinfeld. Law enforcement officers also arrested eight executives who, like Siekaczek, were accused of offering bribes in over ten countries. The countries that were paid the heftiest bribes were China, Russia, Argentina, Israel, and Venezuela (Millker and Schubert 2009).

Payments were conveyed to corrupt foreign officials via cash-filled suitcases. Siemens managers in the telecommunications industry could apply for up to €1 million euros at a time for bribes. In what *The Economist* mockingly described as an "honor system," managers were allowed to approve their own funding requests (2008). The lack of documentation allowed the practice to thrive. The US Department of Justice (DoJ) estimates that approximately US $67 million in cash was carried out of the Siemens' offices in order to make the illegal payments (*The Economist* 2008).

The practice of corporate bribery began at Siemens in 1989 shortly after the company was restructured. The new structure gave division heads much greater freedom to pursue business in less developed countries. In an ill-advised attempt to increase market share in these areas, general payment funds were earmarked for paying foreign bribes. At this time, bribes were tax deductible under the German tax code and were referred to by Siemens as "NA," an abbreviation for *nützliche Aufwendungen* or useful expenditures (Millker and Schubert 2009). However, when Germany outlawed the bribing of foreign officials and civil servants in 1999, Siemens set up a "paper program" to mask the budget for bribery overseen by Siekaczek (Millker and Schubert 2009).

Siekaczek concedes his actions were illegal, but defended them as necessary in order to maintain the competitiveness of Siemens' overseas units. "It was about keeping the business unit alive and not jeopardizing thousands of jobs overnight," Siekaczek explained (Millker and Schubert 2009). "It had nothing to do with being law-abiding, because we all knew what we did was unlawful. What mattered here was that the person put in charge was stable and wouldn't go astray" (Millker and Schubert 2009). Siekaczek further reflected, "I would never have thought I'd go to jail for my company. Sure, we joked about it, but we thought if our actions ever came to light, we'd all go together and there would be enough people to play a game of cards" (Millker and Schubert 2009). What do you think about Siekaczek's excuse? Would you be willing to pay bribes to ensure the health of your company and protect your coworkers' jobs? What does Siekaczek's facetious tone suggest about his motives? Note that Siemens' major ethical concern was that the managers carrying out the bribery policy would not themselves be stealing from the firm.

To facilitate the relationships Siemens established through its web of bribes, the management changed tactics and began writing checks made out to cash that could be deposited in "off the record" accounts (*The Economist* 2008). Furthermore, managers would authorize payments by signing on removable paper notes, so as to "peel off" any sense of accountability (*The Economist* 2010). In this way, Siemens gradually lost control over its clandestine operations, never realizing the potential of the creature it had brought to life. In retrospect, it was negligent ethics and minimal accountability that created the monster.

14.2.5 The High Cost of Bribery

The German prosecutor ended Siemens' legal proceedings in 2008 after establishing the failure of the former managing board to fulfill its supervisory responsibilities. As a result of the trial, the company was fined €395 million euros (Siemens 2008). But that was hardly the end of the affair. In 2006, the United States Securities and Exchange Commission (SEC), under the authority of the Foreign Corrupt Practices Act (FCPA), had also begun its own Siemens investigation. The FCPA explicitly states that it is illegal for domestic companies to give or receive bribes in any form. Foreign companies whose securities are listed in the USA are required to follow the same anti-bribery provisions as American companies (FCPA 2012). The US regulatory agencies were forced to look into the bribery allegations because Siemens trades shares on the New York Stock Exchange. It was therefore subject to US law and jurisdiction.

On December 15, 2008, the SEC reported that it had reached a settlement with Siemens to the tune of US$1.6 billion (Scarboro 2011), almost 20 times larger than any other fine imposed by the FCPA (Lichtblau 2008). According to David Gao of *The Guardian*, Siemens was fearful it would have to pay fines as high as US$5 billion. However, the cooperation between Siemens and the US DoJ, especially when the firm promised to honor its pledge of amnesty for the whistle-blowers involved in the case, led to a reduced fine (Gao 2008). In an interview with *National Public Radio*, Peter Solmssen, general counsel at Siemens, spoke about the whistle-blowing amnesty program: "We had about 130 people who came in and told us where the money had gone and what their role had been" (Shapiro 2008).

White-collar crime expert, Ellen Podgor, believes that confessing to paying bribes had less to do with minimizing Siemens' settlement fines than the threat of being excluded from business in the USA. "The amount of money being paid is not the crucial factor. The crucial factor is not being doomed," Podgor explained (*The Economist* 2008). With the settlement, Siemens also released information to Chinese authorities about mainland involvement in the bribery scandal.

14.2.6 *Culturally Corrupt?*

Germany's *Economic Weekly Magazine* quoted an unnamed Siemens employee claiming that "up to half of Siemens' business in China was involved in bribery," thus prompting further investigation into Siemens' activities in China, where approximately 90 % of its business was carried out through third parties or middlemen (*China Tech News* 2007).

Siemens used middlemen to facilitate contracts in two ways. The first was by employing a sales agent, who was responsible for business in a particular area and was given commissions based on sales volume. The second method was by "signing business consultancy agreements with shell companies." Explained one executive, "[The] agreement stands for a sum of kickback and the shell company simply acts as a channel for money laundering" (Jieqi 2011).

According to the US Department of Justice, three groups under the umbrella organization Siemens China were implicated in the bribery scandal: Siemens Medical Solutions Group, Siemens Power Transmission and Distribution, and Siemens Transportation Systems. Among these three companies, US$61.4 million in bribes was paid to Chinese officials in the telecommunications, construction, and medical care industries. The contracts obtained by Siemens through these bribes totaled RMB¥2.1 billion (US$328 million) (*People's Daily* 2011).

Bernd Eitel, director of media and public relations of Siemens China, said after the scandal went public that the firm "has begun to monitor all consulting companies, namely, third parties that are engaged in providing sales-related consulting and guidance to Siemens" (*China CSR* 2007). Siemens moved to minimize future suspicions of third party consultants by having each consultant approved by the corporate Standard Conformity Office and the CEO (*China CSR* 2007).

Twenty Siemens employees were terminated for inappropriate conduct during the scandal. When questioned about their dismissal, Eitel wrote, they "didn't comply with the compliance guidelines of the company" (Liu 2007)—a response that may be suspect for trying to render the firm's internal procedures as opaque as possible.

The SEC specifically identified Shi Wanzhong, head of human resources for China Mobile Group, as accepting Siemens bribes between 2001 and 2006 during his time as president and general manager at China Mobile Anhui (*People's Daily* 2011). In his capacity as general manager, Shi was responsible for equipment procurement in China Mobile's Anhui Province operations. China Mobile is a state-owned enterprise that is traded on both the New York and Hong Kong stock exchanges. It is the leading mobile telecommunications provider in China with 70 % of the total market share (*Freebase* 2009).

In what some mistakenly assume is an unspoken rule for doing business in China, bribes are condoned and may seem to be encouraged. Siemens misunderstood the way the Chinese business environment is changing and therefore did not hesitate to approach Shi through one of his longtime friends, Tian Qu. Siemens persuaded Tian to serve as a middleman, a conduit through whom Shi was persuaded to accept bribes (Jieqi 2011). Tian worked to broker equipment sales between China Mobile and Siemens in his capacity as a middleman. In exchange for their cooperation, Shi and Tian received a total of US$5.1 million in kickbacks (Lopez 2011) from Siemens through an Anhui-based consulting company that channeled funds to Tian's personal bank account (Jieqi 2011). Content with this arrangement, neither Shi nor Tian had reason to challenge the system or look for alternative sources of moral and legal guidance. Shi and Tian were caught up in what they took to be the prevailing culture of corruption and thus acted both recklessly and contrary to Chinese law.

The Intermediate Court of Hebi City, Henan Province, tried Shi and Tian, but in criminal court proceedings that were closed to the public, as they contained "state secrets" (*People's Daily* 2011). The Chinese Criminal Law outlines levels of criminal liability for individuals, companies, and officials engaged in bribery. With regard to the case at hand, Article 386 of the Criminal Law states, "Whoever has committed the crime of acceptance of bribes shall, on the basis of the amount of money or property accepted and the seriousness of the circumstances, be punished in accordance with the provisions of Article 383," which includes sentences of "fixed-term imprisonment of not less than 10 years or life imprisonment… if the circumstances are especially serious, he shall be sentenced to death" (Criminal Law 1997). The culmination of the trial on June 21, 2011, found Shi guilty of accepting bribes and sentenced him to death with a 2-year reprieve (Jieqi 2011), while Tian received 15 years in prison for facilitating the bribes (*Shanghai Daily* 2011).

14.2.7 The Economics of Crime

Despite its competitive advantages in international business, Siemens found it difficult to meet its profit expectations, according to an article published in *The Economist*. The company's large budget for bribery hampered its revenue growth, as the contracts involved were not sizeable enough to offset the cost of the bribes. The investigations and trials exposed "a stunning level of deception and corruption," said US assistant attorney general, Lanny A. Breuer. "Business should be won or lost on the merits of a company's products and services, not the amount of bribes paid to government officials" (Wyatt 2011). In fact, had Siemens complied with Brewer's understanding of business ethics, the company might have been more profitable both before and after the scandal.

Nevertheless, having been caught in a scandal, Siemens incurred even more expenses. The direct costs of the scandal amounted to US$2.6 billion, including fines and internal fees for lawyers, investigations, etc. Costs that were not directly financial included the loss of CEO Klaus Kleinfeld and a member of the board both of whom left as a result of the incident, but were neither charged nor implicated in it. As for Siemens' stock value, investors lost substantially as both its market value and its reputation were tarnished. The company ended the 2009 fiscal year with a startling 60 % drop in net income, significantly more than the loss competitors endured during the global financial crisis that year (Racanelli 2012). American stockbroker, Nicholas Heymann, commented on the state of Siemens: "They were caught using steroids to win…Then suddenly they had to start trying to do it the old-fashioned way" (*The Economist* 2010). Heymann's comment stresses that if you are caught cheating in a game, you are penalized with losses. The same is true in business.

14.2.8 Recovery

CEO Kleinfeld resigned his post after the bribery scandal became public. When the Siemens board selected Peter Loescher as Kleinfield's replacement, it did so with every intention of revamping the company's corporate culture. Austrian born, Loescher was the first "outsider" to lead the German company since its founding 165 years ago (Racanelli 2012). He was praised as a pragmatist and understood his first task as CEO was to institute damage control. Loescher said his job was "to clean up this whole situation as quickly as possible," and he was repeatedly heard saying, "Siemens needs to get faster, less complex and more focused" (Racanelli 2012).

Loescher was saddled with the difficult task of instilling confidence in a company that had been overrun by scandal. He responded by appointing a task force focused on specifying job descriptions and regulating employees. The task force quickly identified "two layers of top management that effectively had no operational accountability in the previous organizational structure" (Racanelli 2012). Half of the top 100 managers were replaced. The task force also investigated €420 million euros of suspect expenditures made between 1999 and 2006.

Loescher went beyond the legal requirements to realign Siemens' company culture with a moral core; he appointed Michael Hershman, an anti-corruption expert and cofounder of Transparency International, to review anti-corruption controls and ethics training at Siemens (*The Christian Science Monitor* 2008). The new policies included the appointment of an ombudsman to encourage whistle-blowing and prevent future scandals. During a 2010 interview with *USA Today*, Loescher commented on the current situation saying, "Today, Siemens is a role model. Dow Jones has ranked us in its sustainability world index. We went from a compliance ranking of zero out of 100 to 100 out of 100. Siemens stands for clean business always and everywhere" (Jones 2010). In an interview with *The Economist*, Loescher expanded on his confidence in Siemens and his way of challenging its employees. "It is about aligning accountability and responsibility. At the end of the day I look into [their] eyes and say: you are responsible" (*The Economist* 2010). What is your opinion of Loescher's steps to transform Siemens' culture? Do you think his efforts sincerely reflect his personal beliefs, or are they merely window dressing intended to lure back alienated investors?

14.2.9 Summary

The global bribery scandal at Siemens AG was not just a monster that took on a life of its own. Not only were jobs and money lost but also confidence, reputation, and freedom. Siemens' use of criminal-like stratagems, including money-filled suitcases, shell companies, and offshore bank accounts, can all be attributed to a misguided attempt to beat out the competition.

The Chinese angle in the Siemens scandal has a particularly discouraging conclusion. Siekaczek and other Siemens executives approached business in China with a false understanding that bribery was the only way to achieve success. The Chinese government, however, took a severe approach to those convicted of accepting bribes. The result was the sentencing to death of Shi and 15 years imprisonment for Tian. Do you think that Siemens bears any responsibility for the fate of its Chinese collaborators? How could Siemens have been so indifferent to the risks involved for the people who carried out its blatantly immoral and illegal schemes?

The Siemens story shocked the world as a reputable multinational was discovered to have institutionalized corruption. What began as an attempt to get ahead created a monster with the potential to destroy the company. Seasoned executives like Siekaczek enabled the proliferation of bribery by doing their best to carry out this misguided policy. But once the scheme was exposed, Loescher worked equally hard to revitalize Siemens' ethics and corporate culture. Under his leadership, consumers are once again confident in the Siemens name. In 2010, Loescher proudly declared, "We increased growth targets at the same moment that we were cleaning the whole thing up" (*The Economist* 2010). His success appears to have transformed Siemens from a company on the brink of collapse after an experiment gone awry to a company that once again has discovered a firm moral core.

14.3 Case Study Discussion

The comment by Nicholas Heymann on Siemens' challenge may be a good place to start the discussion: "They were caught using steroids to win…. Then suddenly they had to start trying to do it the old-fashioned way" (*The Economist* 2010). It assumes what we have attempted to show in various ways throughout this book, namely, that business is more like a game than it is like warfare. Nobody asks soldiers on a battlefield whether they are using steroids or any other illegal substances in order to make them more competitive. But players in various games can be penalized or disbarred from further competition altogether if they are caught using steroids or willfully violating the rules in other ways. Players who cheat at competitive sports often use steroids in the hope that these will enhance their performance and increase their chances of winning. Companies that pay bribes and kickbacks in order to gain a marketing advantage over their competitors are doing the same thing. Bribery and other questionable payments are generally regarded as illegal—and contrary to the standards of international business ethics because they preempt the competition that is supposed to guarantee that markets will yield their promised economic benefits to all.

As Heymann pointed out, once Siemens was convicted and had hired a new CEO, Peter Loescher, to turn the company around, "they had to start trying to do it the old-fashioned way." Siemens would have to learn how to play the game of business without cheating, that is, its sales force would have to relearn how to market its products and close the deals for them, without paying bribes and kickbacks. Our interest in the Siemens case, then, ought to be focused on how they recovered their capacity to play "the old-fashioned way." Did Loescher succeed in turning the company around? If so, how did he do it? In November of 2012, Loescher published an essay in the Harvard Business Review, "On Using a Scandal to Drive Change" (Loescher 2012). A major factor was restructuring Siemens management: "Within months of my taking over, we replaced about 80 % of the top level of executives, 70 % of the next level down, and 40 % of the level below that. I fundamentally changed how our managing board made decisions. We also worked to streamline and simplify our global operating units." The restructuring of the managing board reduced it to eight members: "the heads of three operational units—energy, industry, and health care— plus the HR head, the CFO, the new head of supply chain management and sustainability, me, and a new position for legal counsel and compliance." The new position, Loescher reasoned, had to represent an independent perspective that could actually challenge the managing board on its policies: "In the wake of the bribery scandal, it was very clear that legal counsel and compliance had to be at the table and had to be somebody from the outside."

One lesson from the Siemens case is that corruption entrenched in a corporate culture can be rooted out, if the top leadership is willing and able to remove those managers who allowed it to flourish. Wholesale restructuring of Siemens management, plus the appointment of an independent watchdog to the managing board, showed what Loescher was capable of. As he said, "In the beginning it was 'Oh, he is just talking.' I'm not just talking. Now, when I make a statement, people know I will follow through." The turnaround had to come from the top, Loescher concluded, since rank-and-file Siemens employees "felt that the corruption scandal represented a failure of leadership. They were shocked and ashamed, because they are very proud to be part of Siemens." When counting the costs of corruption, one must not underestimate its negative impact on employee morale. Compliance with legal guidelines and moral norms is not simply an accommodation to external pressures; it must also be understood as a reflection of most employees' desire for security and peace of mind, their need to work for a company they can be proud of—which, of course, usually pays off in terms of increased productivity.

Loescher and the new management team at Siemens must have sensed the psychological and moral hazards involved, had they been content to produce a public relations response that only masked a deeper resistance to change. The corporate restructuring was quickly followed by the publication of a revised set of "Siemens

Business Conduct Guidelines" (Siemens 2009). In his "Foreword" to this document, Loescher showed his complete support for them:

> These Business Conduct Guidelines have been adapted in line with new legal requirements and are based on international treaties on human rights, anti-corruption and sustainability. They are intended to strengthen awareness of the law and moral standards as an integral part of our entrepreneurial actions. The key message is that only clean business is Siemens business. I call on all employees to live and breathe the Business Conduct Guidelines.

The Guidelines are comprehensive and detailed. They clarify Siemens' expectations in six key areas: (A) Basic Behavioral Requirements, (B) Treatment of Business Partners and Third Parties, (C) Avoiding Conflicts of Interest, (D) Handling of Company Property, (E) Handling of Information, and (F) Environment, Safety, and Health. The first two of these address issues that emerged in the bribery scandal. The Basic Behavioral Requirements begin with "observing the law and the legal system in every country where we do business…in addition to applicable Siemens policies." Siemens pledges to honor the values of "mutual respect, honesty, and integrity" in all its business dealings both internally and externally. Preserving and enhancing Siemens good reputation are the responsibility of each and every employee.

In that same section on Basic Behavioral Requirements, Siemens spells out its expectations of managers, not only for their instruction but also "to give employees an idea of the leadership and support they should expect from their superiors":

> All managers bear responsibility for all employees entrusted to them. All managers must earn respect by exemplary personal behavior, performance, openness, and social competence. This means, among other things, that each manager must emphasize the importance of ethical conduct and compliance, make them regular topics of everyday business and promote them through personal leadership and training. (Siemens 2009: 5)

The Guidelines list the duties that Siemens managers must perform in exercising "responsibility for all employees entrusted to them," each of which is understood as a dimension of their "duty of due care": a "duty of selection" requiring them to "carefully select employees based on their personal and professional qualifications and suitability"; a "duty to give instructions" requiring them to "give precise, complete and binding instructions to employees, especially with regard to compliance with the law"; a "duty of monitoring" to "ensure compliance with the law is continuously monitored"; and a "duty of communication" informing employees of "the importance of integrity and compliance in everyday business" and the consequences of "violations of the law."

The other five areas, then, provide greater detail on how these Basic Behavioral Requirements are to be met in Siemens business practice. Section B, "Treatment of Business Partners and Third Parties," details the specific policies that the firm has adopted to eliminate corruption. It begins with an affirmation of the ideal of "fair competition": "Fair competition permits markets to develop freely – with attendant social benefits. Accordingly, the principle of fairness also applies to competition for market share." It then goes on to benchmark practices that either promote fair competition or undermine it, starting with strict compliance with "antitrust laws."

Industrial espionage, as well as "bribery, theft, or electronic eavesdropping," or communicating "knowingly false information about a competitor or its products or services" is forbidden. In prefacing its section on anti-corruption policies, the Guidelines offer the following description of Siemens' intentions:

> We compete fairly for orders with the quality and the price of our innovative products and services, not by offering improper benefits to others. As a result, no employee may directly or indirectly offer, promise, grant or authorize the giving of money or anything else of value to a government official to influence official action or obtain an improper advantage. The same applies to a private commercial counterparty in a business transaction in consideration for an improper advantage. (Siemens 2009: 7)

In order to ensure that the anti-corruption policy is crystal clear, the Guidelines provide detailed instruction on what constitutes an "improper benefit" as well as what potential recipients are covered, namely, "government officials" broadly understood, as well as their representatives "(for example, a consultant, agent, intermediary, business partner or other third party)," as well as "private commercial counterparties in a business transaction."

With one section of the anti-corruption Guidelines focused on "offering and granting advantages," the other concentrates on Siemens' employees "demanding and accepting advantages." This section, however, also defines the permissible limits of accepting or giving token gifts as in the case of closing a business deal: "This does not apply to the acceptance of occasional gifts of purely symbolic value or meals or entertainment reasonable in value that are consistent with local customs and practices and Siemens policies. Any other gifts, meals or entertainment must be refused." Similarly, though the Guidelines prohibit making "political contributions (donations to politicians, political parties or political organizations)," it goes on to define permissible donations to support activities conventionally identified with corporate social responsibility (CSR): "As a responsible member of society, Siemens makes monetary or product donations for education and science, art and culture, and social and humanitarian projects." The chief concern expressed in this area is to ensure that "all donations must be transparent," meaning, "among other things, that the recipient's identity and planned use of the donation must be clear and the reason and purpose for the donation must be justifiable and documented" (Siemens 2009: 8). Equally rigorous Guidelines are spelled out in each of the remaining sections, particularly on the meaning of "conflict of interest" and how to avoid it: "Employees must inform their supervisor of any personal interest they could possibly have in connection with the execution of their professional duties."

The ideal of a "clean business," as defined by Loescher and Siemens' new compliance staff, then, is a business in which both transparency and accountability have been integrated into the reward system for managers and employees at all levels of the corporation. The Guidelines are comprehensive and detailed and backed up with the promise or threat of penalties up to and including termination of employment. "Compliance with the law and observance of the Business Conduct Guidelines shall be monitored worldwide in all Siemens companies on a regular basis. This shall be done in accordance with applicable national procedures and legal provisions" (Siemens 2009: 21). Clearly, Siemens expects the Guidelines to be as rigorously enforced in China and its other East Asian operations as they are in the EU or the USA. While the firm recognizes the diversity of its workforce—"We work together with individuals of various ethnic backgrounds, cultures, religions, ages, disabilities, races, sexual identity, world view and gender."—such diversity will not serve as an excuse for ignoring or evading the duties incumbent on all Siemens employees worldwide.

Have the Guidelines been followed since their adoption in 2009? A recent Internet search suggests that they have, for there are no new scandals reported since Loescher and his team restructured Siemens' management. But this is more than an instance of the dog not barking. Loescher's effort was not simply to do penance for the sins of the past, but to restore public trust by making Siemens a globally recognized leader in compliance and ethics. By 2010, Siemens was already receiving high praise from Transparency International (TI), an important NGO working to fight corruption globally.[1] Indeed, based on the evidence of its effectiveness in the years since Loescher's appointment; the firm's compliance program, including its Business Conduct Guidelines; the various training programs based on them; as well as its attempt to establish partnerships with NGOs like TI and its affiliates in order to sustain the anti-corruption campaign globally—taken together—these initiatives suggest that not only is the corporate turnaround genuine, but that the Siemens story deserves to be studied as a model for developing effective compliance policies (Dietz and Gillespie 2012).

---

[1] One perspective expressing skepticism about Siemens' turnaround and Transparency International's praise for it appeared on the website of the *Corporate Crime Reporter*, which recently published a piece, "Transparency International and the Greenwashing of Siemens" (Corporate Crime Reporter 2014), claiming that TI was absolving Siemens of its involvement in corruption because it had applied for funding from the Siemens Integrity Initiative, established as part of the firm's settlement with the World Bank which required it to put US$100 million into civil society fighting corruption. Our own review of the *Corporate Crime Reporter*'s evidence suggests that the case alleging an improper relationship between TI and Siemens is highly doubtful, since the allegations of ongoing corruption at Siemens are taken from Siemens' own "Annual Report" (Siemens 2013), filed, as required by law, with the US Securities and Exchange Commission. The evidence cited by the *Corporate Crime Reporter* is taken from a list of legal proceedings disclosed by Siemens involving past cases of bribery and other corrupt practices. A careful review of the list, however, will show that none of these cases allege violations happening after Loescher and his team began the turnaround at Siemens. They consistently indicate that Siemens has cooperated with regulatory and other governmental authorities in the investigation and settlement of all previous allegations, some of which are still pending. It seems unfair to accuse Siemens of ongoing involvement in corruption, when the evidence clearly refers to ongoing attempts to settle previous claims against the firm. Similarly, if the charges against Siemens are without foundation, so is the charge that TI failed to do "due diligence" in reaching its decision to apply for a grant from the Siemens Integrity Initiative. The wisdom of TI's decision to apply for such a grant may be questioned, but in no way should it be distorted into the serious and unsubstantiated charge of "greenwashing."

14.4 Ethical Reflection

Previously in Chap. 5, we defined the ethics of free and fair competition in business in reference to the principle of commutative justice, which explains the role of both freedom and fairness in buying and selling. While the principle has its roots in the moral philosophy of Hellenistic antiquity, primarily Aristotle's *Nicomachean Ethics*, its premodern development in the thought of St. Thomas Aquinas presupposes a marketplace where most buying and selling occur between individuals and not either between customers and business corporations or between governments and corporations. The differences between these types of transactions mean that the rough equality between buyers and sellers presupposed in the classical understanding of commutative justice rarely, if ever, occurs in today's marketplace. Instead of the rough equality presupposed when—to recall Aquinas' example discussed in Chap. 5—one farmer sells his neighbor a horse that is blind in one eye, in today's marketplace, the relationships of buyers and sellers are characterized by complex asymmetries that make the task of achieving a free and fair outcome that is mutually beneficial far more challenging than simply invoking the wisdom of *caveat emptor* ("let the buyer beware") and *caveat venditor* ("let the seller beware").

14.4.1 What's Wrong with Commercial Bribery?

It is in the context of these asymmetries—in access to resources, knowledge, and power—that we must ask what's wrong with commercial bribery? As we shall see further on, it's generally illegal, but is it immoral? Why? Siemens' *Business Conduct Guidelines* provide an important clue. "Fair competition permits markets to develop freely – with attendant social benefits." Since Adam Smith's *The Wealth of Nations* (1776), neoclassical economics has explained the market's promise of social benefits in terms of "allocative efficiency." When there is genuine competition in the markets, resources are directed to their most efficient uses through the discipline imposed by prices, freely and fairly arrived at by mutual agreement among buyers and sellers.[2] Any distortion in the flow of information, or the impact of extraneous factors that may undermine the markets' ability to set prices, will result in "market failures" which in turn will undermine the expected social benefits. Monopolies, monopsonies, and externalities, including price controls and taxation, will distort market prices, along with various forms of corruption. A bribe or a kickback, for example, paid by one firm in order to obtain the business of another firm corrupts

[2] The social benefits resulting from allocational efficiency depend upon a number of conditions that roughly correspond to the assumptions operative in the principle of commutative justice. The outcomes of market activity may be regarded as optimizing not only justice but also efficiency so long as these conditions are generally respected. For example, the prices for various goods and services cannot be dictated by any entity exercising monopoly power and, among other things, must be both "informationally efficient" and "transactionally or operationally efficient" (Investopedia 2014).

the market, by ensuring that the decisions of buyers and sellers no longer are based on a rational analysis of competitive bids for goods and services.

The Siemens Guidelines pledge the firm to preserve the integrity of the markets in which the firm competes: "We compete fairly for orders with the quality and the price of our innovative products and services, not by offering improper benefits to others." Bribery and other forms of corruption are immoral because they are meant to secure improper advantages in these markets. The free and fair competition, by which social benefits in the form of continuous innovation, lower cost curves, and greater consumer choices are obtained, is suspended in order to induce one or the other party to the transaction to make their decision on noneconomic grounds. Ironically, when a firm like Siemens engages in a policy of paying bribes and kickbacks in order to obtain contracts, they unwittingly reveal a lack of confidence in their own products and services. If the price and quality of what they had to offer for sale were competitive, paying bribes and kickbacks would not be necessary. They would not need to corrupt the marketplace in order to do business.

A willingness to engage in commercial bribery, then, is indicative not only of market failure but also a basic violation of the spirit of entrepreneurship. Entrepreneurship should never be confused with greed, as if the point were to make as much money as possible by whatever means necessary. Genuine entrepreneurs are—or ought to be—people who believe that they have a better idea and a better way to provide some product or service, at a better price, than their competitors. They welcome free and fair competition and, win or lose, try to learn from whatever signals the market sends their way. They do not try to distort or suppress the results of free and fair competition in the marketplace, since without those signals they cannot continue to improve their products and services. Corruption in the marketplace is their greatest enemy, since it means that market outcomes cannot be relied upon to tell them where they and their products stand relative to their competitors. Free and fair competition attracts entrepreneurs; corrupted competition can only repel them.

A proper understanding of how markets create the social benefits they promise suggests that all buyers and sellers have a moral duty to preserve the integrity of the markets in which they compete. We believe this is yet another dimension of the principle of corporate social responsibility (CSR). If corruption contributes to market failure—which guarantees that only the corrupt participants will benefit from corrupt transactions—then the various regulatory agencies, national as well as international, public as well as private, must intervene to restore the integrity of the marketplace. Siemens deserved the sizable fines and penalties that it received, for it had collaborated in the corruption of emerging markets on an unprecedented scale. Those individuals who were caught and punished with termination of employment or convicted of economic crimes deserved what they got, even if they did not benefit directly and personally from their actions. Paying bribes and kickbacks on behalf of one's employer is no less reprehensible than receiving bribes and kickback for one's personal advantage. Whatever the motive, the individuals involved failed in their duty to preserve the integrity of the marketplace.

14.4.2 An Emerging Global Consensus

The ethical case against bribery and corruption seems more compelling and more universally recognized now than it did a decade or so ago. Although bribery and extortion involving transactions with government officials have been condemned for countless generations—we see, for example, indications of its disapproval not only in the Hebrew Bible (Amos 5:12–15) but also in the Confucian classics (Mencius Book 2B: 3)—until recently, commercial bribery, not involving government officials, seems to have been widely accepted as common practice. China is a good example of how attitudes toward bribery and other forms of corruption in the marketplace have been changing. In the past the practice of paying bribes or kickbacks in order to attract more customers was widespread, as if these were the only way to facilitate business. The excuse for such practices was that everybody else is doing it. Refraining will mean losing out, like ceding a competitive edge to a rival company. It was common then for Chinese business people to tell outsiders who questioned the practice of bribery to adapt to the unspoken rules of the local game or go home.

The shortsighted realism of this advice presumes that corrupt practices have always been part of the game throughout Asia and that they were the most practical approach to securing mutually beneficial business relationships, otherwise known as a form of "guanxixue" (关系学). The goal of bribery, as we have seen, is to attain privileged advantages that increase one's wealth, influence, and power. Many people assumed that the positive results of corruption outweighed its disadvantages. Those defending this approach to building business relationships might tell themselves, "I am only following the rules, and society tacitly approves this practice." The assumption that bribery and kickbacks are inherent in a culture, and required by its tacit rules for success, overlooks the fact that only a limited number of people ultimately profit from such deals.

In China, there has been progress, slow and steady at first, but with increasing momentum, thanks to the anti-corruption campaigns stepped up with the prosecution of Bo Xilai, in rejecting this perverse tolerance of bribery and other forms of corruption. Recent scandals have increased public awareness of the negative effects of bribery. The practice of bribing doctors as well as government officials in China, of which GlaxoSmithKline (GSK), for example, stands accused, is believed to have "resulted in higher drug prices and illegal revenues of more than US$150 million" (Barboza and Thomas 2014). GSK's "massive bribery network" thus was meant to create a market failure that eliminated competition among pharmaceutical firms in order to increase prices and maximize profits. As a result, GSK's top manager in China, Mark Reilly, a British citizen, not only will face trial for economic crimes in China but also is under criminal investigation by the Serious Fraud Office in the UK (Kollewe 2014). These scandals indicate that tolerating bribes because "every other business is doing it" not only disregards the needs of the public, but demonstrates just how out of touch the firms involved are with shifting opinion in China.

An editorial for *China Today*, "Multinationals in China Must Operate According to Law," made the case for government intervention in this way:

> No market economy can tolerate commercial bribery, and such practices will be resolutely checked and cracked down upon. China is no exception…Commercial bribery not only undermines the rule of law and fair trade, but also erodes a country's economy. The GSK investigation was the first bold move against commercial bribery by the new generation of Chinese leadership. Multinationals in China need to understand that the Chinese government's campaign against commercial bribery is not intended to suppress foreign capital but rather is a rigorous effort to create a healthy and orderly market through fair competition. (Jin 2013)

While criminal prosecution is not the only way in which governments can act to restore the integrity of markets within their jurisdictions, it is a necessary first step, since corruption "cannot germinate and proliferate without a supportive, or at least tolerant, environment. Therefore, to eradicate this vice, we must simultaneously punish corruption and promote reforms."

Other organizations, like Transparency International (TI), have their own indispensable role to play in supporting governments and businesses in their efforts to transform cultures that once tolerated bribery and corruption. TI is the most competent voice and internationally acknowledged institution working to educate the public globally to the dangers of corruption. TI publishes regular reports with reliable data concerning corruption. Since its first publication in 1995, TI's annual Corruption Perception Index (CPI) has changed perceptions about corruption worldwide. The CPI methodology has been continuously improved since its inception, drawing data from various institutions, in order to document the scale of public sector corruption. The CPI's definition of public sector corruption is the misuse of public power for private benefit, which includes bribery of public officials, kickbacks in public procurement, and embezzlement of public funds. The CPI's measurement of corruption assesses two aspects: the frequency of corruption and the total value of bribes paid. These two elements go hand in hand.

According to the CPI of 2001 (Transparency International 2001), China ranked 57th on the list of least corrupt out of a total of 91 countries. In that year, East Asian countries—despite family resemblances indicated by the pervasive influence of Chinese, primarily Confucian, values—achieved widely disparate results: Among the 91 countries surveyed, Singapore ranked 4th; Hong Kong, 14th; Japan, 21st; Taiwan, 27th; Malaysia, 36th; South Korea, 42nd; Thailand, 61st; Philippines, 65th; Vietnam, 75th; and Indonesia, 88th. Clearly, corruption is not an inevitable consequence of sharing Chinese values. A comparison with the latest CPI, from 2013 (Transparency International 2013), suggests the possibility that changes may occur over time, even as the overall pattern remains remarkably stable. China ranks 80th on the list of 177 countries included in the 2013 survey, with Singapore ranked 5th; Hong Kong, 15th; Japan, 18th; Taiwan, 36th; South Korea, 45th; Malaysia, 53rd; Mongolia, 83rd; Philippines, 94th; Thailand, 102nd; Indonesia, 114th; Vietnam, 116th; Laos, 140th; Myanmar, 157th; Cambodia, 160th; and North Korea, 175th. While these results may appear roughly similar, in light of the fact that the number of countries surveyed has nearly doubled, we can see that most of the East Asian nations have improved their rankings with the greatest improvements shown in Indonesia, South Korea, Philippines, China, and Vietnam. On the other hand, given that the CPI scores are calculated on a scale of 0–100, with 0 being the most corrupt and 100 the least, only Singapore (86), Hong Kong (75), Japan (74), Taiwan (61), South Korea (55), and Malaysia (50) managed to rank in the top half of the nations surveyed. Clearly, there is much more work to be done in publicizing the problem of public sector corruption and actually transforming the attitudes that support it.

Another useful measurement of the struggle against corruption is TI's "Bribe Payers' Index" (BPI). The most recent BPI report (Transparency International 2011) prefaced its findings with a statement reflecting the growing consensus internationally that bribery and other forms of corruption are—and ought to be—regarded as both illegal and immoral:

> Foreign bribery has significant adverse effects on public well-being around the world. It distorts the fair awarding of contracts, reduces the quality of basic public services, limits opportunities to develop a competitive private sector and undermines trust in public institutions. Engaging in bribery also creates instability for companies themselves and presents ever-growing reputational and financial risks. This is particularly relevant in light of recent anti-bribery reforms in a number of key countries around the world, such as in China and the United Kingdom.

Unlike the CPI, which is measured annually, capturing one dimension of the international corruption equation—the demand side—the BPI is published every 3 years. It measures the supply side of the equation—"the perceived likelihood of companies from the countries surveyed to pay bribes abroad." The results of the interviews of 3016 private sector leaders from the 30 countries surveyed indicated that Russian and Chinese companies were thought to bribe most frequently, while Dutch and Swiss companies were thought to bribe least frequently. While several countries got good scores (8.0 or better on a ten-point scale) for infrequency of bribery, including Japan and Singapore, none were regarded as completely free of corruption.

For the first time, the BPI of 2011 included measurements of bribery between private companies and found that it is regarded by the business executives interviewed as "just as common as bribery between firms and public officials." Although the 2011 survey showed no overall improvement since the last BPI in 2008, it confirmed the following trends: First, "the perceived likelihood of companies from a given country to bribe abroad is closely related to views on the level of business integrity at home." Second, government policy in the home country, particularly the credibility of its own efforts to achieve compliance with anti-corruption reforms, is "closely related" to perceptions of its companies' willingness to bribe abroad. Third, given their growing impact in "international trade and investment flows," the noticeably "weak performance" registered for China and Russia indicates the urgent "need for them to address foreign bribery and corruption globally." Finally, BPI 2011 reported that "bribery is perceived to occur in all business sectors, but is seen as most common in the public works contracts and construction sector." On the other hand, "agriculture and light manufacturing are perceived to be the least bribery-prone sectors, followed by civilian aerospace and information technology."

14.4.3 How Can Corruption Be Diminished?

When fighting corruption globally, it is more useful to try to diminish it rather than to eradicate it entirely. Given how deeply corruption is rooted in many countries, simply eradicating it presents an impossible goal that tends only to encourage inaction. To diminish corruption, however, implies an ongoing struggle to reduce corrupt practices. Legislative measures are necessary, but not sufficient to diminish corruption. The USA set a benchmark in 1977 by passing the Foreign Corrupt Practices Act (FCPA 2012), which made it illegal for American companies to pay bribes to government officials in foreign countries. Since these companies were exposed to significant penalties at home, eventually, they received fewer and fewer requests for bribes from their business partners abroad. The law attempted to establish a model for other countries to follow. In 1999, the USA's FCPA led to the formulation of the Anti-Bribery Convention of the Organization for Economic Cooperation and Development (OECD), requiring its signatories to enact legislation that will criminalize the act of bribing foreign public officials (OECD 2011). The OECD, of course, has no legislative authority of its own, but it does monitor implementation by participating countries. As of 2013, the only East Asian countries to sign the OECD convention are Japan and Korea, though China, Indonesia, and Malaysia have participated as observers in the OECD's Working Group on Bribery in International Business Transactions.

Another important resource for combating corruption is the United Nations' Convention against Corruption (UNCAC), adopted by the UN General Assembly in 2003. The Convention contributed a 10th Principle to the UN Global Compact (UNGC), already begun in 2000, as "a strategic policy initiative for businesses that are committed to aligning their operations and strategies with ten universally accepted principles in the areas of human rights, labor, environment and anti-corruption" (UNGC 2013a). The 10th Principle reads as follows: "Businesses should work against corruption in all its forms, including extortion and bribery" (UNGC 2013b). The specific point of the 10th Principle is to send a "strong worldwide signal that the private sector shares responsibility for the challenges of eliminating corruption" (UNGC 2013c). While governments must play a lead role in diminishing corruption, the cooperation and active support of international businesses are indispensable if such policies are to be effective. In addition to the basic moral argument against corruption, the UNGC provides a list of seven considerations that constitute "the business case" against it. Each of these is meant to demonstrate that the costs of tolerating or engaging in corrupt practices far outweigh any benefits. If "the ethical case" that condemns corruption as "a misuse of power and position and has a disproportionate impact on the poor and disadvantaged" isn't persuasive, then the UNGC's attempt to educate business' managers, investors, and other stakeholders to the nature of their own self-interest in a rapidly globalizing economy should gain a serious response.

As already noted, China's own efforts to combat corruption are anxiously monitored by TI and other international agencies. The rankings just reported for

China—namely, its 80th place finish among 177 nations surveyed in the 2012 CPI and its poor showing on the 2011 BPI, where only Russia was considered more likely to bribe—created some controversy in the Chinese blogosphere, where the results met with cynical disbelief as "too good to be true" (Caragliano 2012). Nevertheless, the "Xi administration's emerging policy platform… appears to have anti-corruption and clean government at its core" and cannot be dismissed as simply a "pretext to purge political enemies," as previous campaigns apparently have turned out to be. One distinguishing note of the Xi administration's campaign is its active encouragement of social media exposés of corruption. The big question, of course, is what besides opening up the blogosphere may be needed to create a culture in which corruption is widely discredited and vulnerable to criminal prosecution?

14.4.4 Hong Kong's Independent Commission Against Corruption (ICAC)

One possible model for further progress in China's struggle against corruption is Hong Kong's Independent Commission Against Corruption (ICAC). In Hong Kong, where the ICAC has operated for 40 years, corruption has been reduced dramatically from what it was in the 1960s and 1970s (ICAC 2014a). Had TI been conducting its surveys at that time, Hong Kong no doubt would have ranked among the most corrupt venues in East Asia. Public corruption was rampant, especially in the police force, in a city where "many people had to take the 'backdoor route' simply to earn a living and secure other than basic services. 'Tea money', 'black money', 'hell money' – whatever its name – became not only familiar to many Hong Kong people, but accepted with resignation as a necessary way of life" (ICAC 2014a). The understandable resentments of ordinary citizens reached their boiling point in 1973, when a chief police inspector, Peter Godber, was accused of amassing a retirement nest egg of over HK$4.3 million. When the attorney general demanded that he explain the source of his fortune, Godber "managed to slip out of the territory undetected, which unleashed an unprecedented public outcry… Protesters with slogans like, 'Fight Corruption, Arrest Godber' insisted that he be extradited to stand trial," which he did in 1975 and was convicted and imprisoned for 4 years. The Commission that investigated Godber's alleged crimes and his escape also issued a Second Report recommending the establishment of an anti-corruption agency that would be separate from any department of government, including the police.

Once set in motion, the ICAC has been dedicated to fighting corruption "using a three-pronged approach of law enforcement, prevention and education." The three factors accounting for the ICAC's success each make a distinctive contribution. The Operations Department is the arm of the ICAC that investigates any "alleged or suspected offences against the ICAC Ordinance, the Prevention of Bribery Ordinance, and the Elections (Corrupt and Illegal Conduct) Ordinance" (ICAC 2012). These ordinances not only authorize the establishment of the ICAC and define its broad powers of investigation and prosecution, but also the nature of the offenses that are within the scope of its operations. The specific details of these Ordinances (HK Department of Justice 2003; HK Department of Justice 2014a; HK Department of Justice 2014b) are important, for they clearly indicate the risks that anyone violating them are likely to face and thus are relevant for assessing the deterrent value of the ICAC's operations.

Besides the Operations Department, the ICAC's two other branches, the Corruption Prevention Department and the Community Relations Department, may be equally responsible for the success of the ICAC's work in Hong Kong. The Corruption Prevention Department analyzes the administrative practices of government departments and public bodies in order to reform any of these that are especially vulnerable to corruption. It also offers consultations to the managers of such agencies, when asked to advise them on anti-corruption policies and best practices. By contrast with the short-term and focused assistance provided by the Corruption Prevention Department, the Community Relations Department represents a strategy that is long term and focused on popular education at all levels, including innovative projects using various media involving the Internet, TV, and radio, as well as moral education packages for use in primary and secondary school curricula. Under the auspices of the Community Relations Department, the Hong Kong Ethics Development Centre (HKEDC) was established in 1995 in order to facilitate the participation of businesses—six major Hong Kong chambers of commerce form its steering committee—in the promotion of moral education, especially in business ethics. Among the resources offered to educators by the HKEDC is a library of case studies available online for use in training students to understand the most effective ways to combat corruption in various industries (HKEDC 2013). Anyone concerned to develop strategies for long-term efforts to transform cultures in which corruption is tolerated, if not actually encouraged, would do well to explore these resources.

While the ICAC has hardly eliminated corruption in Hong Kong, its success in substantially reducing corruption deserves serious study as a model for similar efforts in other Asian venues, if not elsewhere in the world. Its three-pronged approach allows for close coordination among departments focused on law enforcement, collaborative support for businesses serious about compliance with the law, and an effort at popular education that is innovative in its use of various media to reach out especially to the youth. TI has been monitoring Hong Kong since it began reporting its annual Corruption Perception Index in 1995. That year, it was 17th in the world. Since 1998, the first year after Hong Kong had been repatriated into China, its rating has fluctuated between 16th and 12th worldwide, with only Singapore receiving a higher score among Asian nations (Transparency International 2014). A review of these results over time, as well as comparisons with the scores of nations ranked among the top 20, will suggest two points: one, that the results are remarkably stable over time and, two, that Hong Kong's return to China in 1997 under the formula "One Country, Two Systems" has not resulted in any dramatic change in perceptions of corruption there. While dramatic change apparently established itself in the 20 years that the ICAC operated in Hong Kong prior to TI's development of a CPI, the subsequent CPI ratings detect no substantial slackening in the city's struggle against corruption. There have been significant changes at the ICAC over time, but most of these involve a laudable expansion of its focus from corruption involving government officials to corruption in business deals involving private enterprises. Unless there is significant deterioration in Hong Kong's commitment to the rule of law, the independence of its judiciary, and the integrity of its investigative journalism, the hope that the ICAC will continue to operate effectively seems a reasonable one.

14.5 Conclusion

In this chapter, we have attempted to show that corruption is a cancer destroying the free and fair competition among businesses that is believed to be the source of the social benefits promised in a market economy. If the economic analysis of how those social benefits are realized is correct, then all businesses—as well as all stakeholders, including the government and the people whom it is meant to serve—have a stake in preserving the integrity of market competition. Put simply, businesses owe each other a competitive market that is free and fair. Corruption occurs whenever anyone conspires with others to destroy competition, in order to secure improper advantages either for themselves or for the firms or agencies that employ them. When corruption occurs, we all have a moral obligation to expose it and do whatever we can to either reduce or eliminate it. Our case study in this chapter gives us reason to hope that businesses can change their corporate cultures, in order to combat corruption. There is much to learn from the changes in policy and business practices that Siemens put in place in order to turn away from corruption and restore its own sense of integrity. We also learned that businesses can hardly be expected to make such changes unless they are prevailed upon to do so by the pressure of public opinion, the threat of legal sanctions, or the cooperation of various government agencies and NGOs, each of which must contribute their own expertise and resources to fighting corruption. Finally, we tried to identify resources in Asia, such as the 40-year experience of the ICAC in Hong Kong, as well as NGOs like Transparency International, that are willing and able to support businesses that are ready to renounce all forms of corruption and renew their own commitment, as Siemens did, to "clean business." Businesses owe it to each other to compete with integrity and to do what is necessary to ensure that their competitors do the same.

References

Abrams, S. (2011, June 30). Siemens bribery case and the anti-corruption new world-order. *Business Insider*. Retrieved July 16, 2012, from http://articles.businessinsider.com/2011-06-30/wall_street/30012545_1_siemens-ag-chinese-court-sec-charges

Barboza, D., & Thomas, K. (2014, May 13). Former head of Glaxo in China is accused of Bribery. *The New York Times*. Retrieved June 26, 2014, from http://www.nytimes.com/2014/05/15/business/international/glaxosmithkline-china.html

Caragliano, D. (2012, December 12). Is China really the 80th-most-corrupt country on earth? *The Atlantic*. Retrieved June 27, 2014, from http://www.theatlantic.com/international/archive/2012/12/is-china-really-the-80th-most-corrupt-country-on-earth/266172/

China CSR. (2007, September 19). Siemens China investigating business consultants. Retrieved August 14, 2012, from http://www.chinacsr.com/en/2007/09/19/1695-siemens-china-investigating-business-consultants/

China CSR. (2008, December 16). Siemens concludes bribery proceedings for dealings in China and other countries. Retrieved June 20, 2015, from http://www.chinacsr.com/en/2008/12/16/3898-siemens-concludes-bribery-proceedings-for-dealings-in-china-and-other-countries/

China Tech News. (2007, August 22). Siemens China business under investigation. Retrieved July 16, 2012, from http://www.chinatechnews.com/2007/08/22/5784-siemens-china-business-under-investigation

Corporate Crime Reporter. (2014, April 2). Transparency international and the greenwashing of Siemens. Retrieved June 23, 2014, from http://www.corporatecrimereporter.com/news/200/siemens-and-the-greenwashing-of-transparency-international/

Criminal Law. (1997). *Criminal law of the People's Republic of China*. Retrieved on June 21, 2015 from http://www.fmprc.gov.cn/ce/cgvienna/eng/dbtyw/jdwt/crimelaw/t209043.htm

Dietz, G., & Gillespie, N. (2012, March 26). Rebuilding trust: How Siemens atoned for its sins. *The Guardian: Guardian Sustainable Business*. Retrieved June 23, 2014, from http://www.theguardian.com/sustainable-business/recovering-business-trust-siemens

FCPA. (2012). Foreign corrupt practices act. Retrieved July 17, 2012, from http://www.justice.gov/criminal/fraud/fcpa/

Freebase. (2009). China mobile. Retrieved August 13, 2012, from http://www.freebase.com/view/en/china_mobile

Gao, D. (2008, December 15). Record US fine ends Siemens bribery scandal. *The Guardian*. Retrieved August 14, 2012, from http://www.guardian.co.uk/business/2008/dec/16/regulation-siemens-scandal-bribery

HK Department of Justice. (2003). Chapter 204. Independent commission against corruption ordinance. Retrieved June 28, from http://www.legislation.gov.hk/blis_pdf.nsf/6799165D2FEE3FA94825755E0033E532/A3E9ED78744D8631482575EE004CB37D/$FILE/CAP_204_e_b5.pdf

HK Department of Justice. (2014a). Chapter 201. Prevention of bribery ordinance. Retrieved June 28, 2014, from http://www.legislation.gov.hk/blis_pdf.nsf/6799165D2FEE3FA94825755E0033E532/660A25EA15B8C9D6482575EE004C5BF1/$FILE/CAP_201_e_b5.pdf

HK Department of Justice. (2014b). Chapter 554. Elections (Corrupt and illegal conduct) Ordinance. Retrieved June 28, 2014, from http://www.legislation.gov.hk/blis_pdf.nsf/4f0db701c6c25d4a4825755c00352e35/4F5BE2F0A9A7AE91482575EF0019E514/$FILE/CAP_554_e_b5.pdf

HKEDC. (2013). Publications and Resources: Case Studies. Hong Kong Ethics Development Centre. Retrieved June 28, 2014, from http://www.hkedc.icac.hk/english/publications/case_studies.php

ICAC. (2014a). Brief history. Retrieved June 27, 2014, from http://www.icac.org.hk/en/about_icac/bh/index.html

ICAC. (2012). Operations department: Statutory duty. Retrieved June 27, 2014, from http://www.icac.org.hk/en/operations_department/sd/index.html

Investopedia. (2014). Allocational efficiency. Retrieved June 24, 2014, from http://www.investopedia.com/terms/a/allocationalefficiency.asp

Jieqi, L. (2011, June 30). Siemens bribery scandal ends in death sentence. *Caixin Online*. Retrieved July 16, 2012, from http://english.caixin.com/2011-06-30/100274546.html

Jin, S. (2013, September 25). Multinationals in China must operate according to law. *China Today*. Retrieved June 25, 2014, from http://www.chinatoday.com.cn/english/economy/2013-09/25/content_569718.htm

Jones, D. (2010, February 15). CEO Loescher uses his moral compass to steer Siemens. *USA Today*. Retrieved July 24, 2012, from http://www.usatoday.com/money/companies/management/advice/2010-02-14-siemens-CEO-advice_N.htm

Kollewe, J. (2014, May 28). GlaxoSmithKline faces criminal investigation by Serious Fraud Office. *The Guardian*. Retrieved June 26, 2014, from http://www.theguardian.com/business/2014/may/28/serious-fraud-office-investigates-glaxosmithkline

Lichtblau, E. (2008, December 15). Siemens pays 1.34 billion in fines. *The New York Times*. Retrieved July 16, 2012, from http://www.nytimes.com/2008/12/16/business/worldbusiness/16siemens.html?_r=1&ref=technology

Liu, J. (2007, August 23). Siemens fired 20 employees in China last year for misconduct. *Bloomberg*. Retrieved August 14, 2012, from http://www.bloomberg.com/apps/news?pid=newsarchive&sid=agDA.ZGHGw3I&refer=germany

Loescher, P. (2012, November). How I Did It…The CEO of Siemens on using a scandal to drive change. *Harvard Business Review*. Retrieved June 20, 2014, from http://hbr.org/2012/11/the-ceo-of-siemens-on-using-a-scandal-to-drive-change/ar/1

Lopez, L. (2011, June 21). China Mobile executive gets death penalty for taking bribes from Siemens. *Business Insider*. Retrieved July 16, from http://articles.businessinsider.com/2011-06-21/news/29974810_1_siemens-bribes-death-sentence

Millker, C., &, Schubert, S. (2009, February 13). At Siemens, bribery was just a line item. *PBS*. Retrieved July 12, 2012, from http://www.pbs.org/frontlineworld/stories/bribe/2009/02/at-siemens-bribery-was-just-a-line-item.html

Moral Relativism. (2002). Moral relativism: What's it all about? Retrieved July 17, 2012, from http://www.moral-relativism.com/

OECD. (2011). Convention on combating bribery of foreign public officials in international business transactions and related documents. Retrived on June 27, 2014, from http://www.oecd.org/daf/anti-bribery/ConvCombatBribery_ENG.pdf

People's Daily. (2011, June 22). China court gives verdict in Siemens bribery case. Retrieved July 17, 2012, from http://english.people.com.cn/90001/90776/90882/7417043.html

Racanelli, V. (2012, March 10). The culture changer. *Barrons*. Retrieved August 13, 2012, from http://online.barrons.com/article/SB50001424052748704759704577265510752521758.html#articleTabs_article%3D1

Roberts, D. (2010, July 8). The higher costs of bribery in China. *Bloomberg Businessweek*. Retrieved July 16, 2012, from http://www.businessweek.com/magazine/content /10_29/b4187011931530.htm

Scarboro, C. (2011, June 21). SEC charges Siemens AG for engaging in worldwide bribery. *Securities and Exchange Commission*. Retrieved July 16, 2012, from http://www.sec.gov/news/press/2008/2008-294.htm

Shanghai Daily. (2011, June 21). China Mobile gets death in bribery case. Retrieved July 16, 2012, from http://www.china.org.cn/china/2011106/21/content_22831176.htm

Shapiro, A. (2008, December 16). Siemens hit with $1.6 billion fine in bribery case. NPR. Retrieved July 19, 2012, from http://www.npr.org/templates/story/story.php?storyId=98317332

Siemens AG. (2008, December 15). Siemens AG reaches a resolution with German and U.S. authorities. Retrieved July 24, 2012, from http://www.siemens.com/press/en/pressrelease/?press=/en/pressrelease/2008/corporate_communication/axx20081219.htm

Siemens AG. (2009, January). Siemens business conduct guidelines. Corporate Compliance Office. Retrieved June 20, 2014, from https://www.siemens.ca/web/portal/en/AboutUs/Documents/BusinessConductGuidelines.pdf

Siemens AG. (2013, November 27). Annual report pursuant to section 13 or 15(d) of the securities and exchange act of 1934, for the fiscal year ended September 30, 2013. Retrieved June 23, 2014, from http://www.siemens.com/investor/pool/en/investor_relations/financial_publications/sec_filings/2013/20_f.pdf

Steptoe. (2009, January 8). International law advisory: Record US and German settlements of the Siemens case reflect new realities of corruption cases. Retrieved July 17, 2012, from http://www.steptoe.com/publications-5819.html

The Christian Science Monitor. (2008, December 17). Big victory against global bribery. Retrieved July 16, 2012, from http://www.csmonitor.com/Commentary/the-monitors-view/2008/1217/p08s01-comv.html

The Economist. (2008, December 17). The Siemens scandal: Bavarian Baksheesh. Retrieved July 17, 2012, from http://www.economist.com/node/12800474

The Economist. (2010, September 9). A giant awakens. Retrieved July 17, 2012, from http://www.economist.com/node/16990709

Transparency International. (2001). Corruption perceptions index 2001. Retrieved June 27, 2014, from http://archive.transparency.org/policy_research/surveys_indices/cpi/2001

Transparency International. (2011). Bribe payers index 2011. Retrieved June 27, 2014, from http://issuu.com/transparencyinternational/docs/bribe_payers_index_2011?e=2496456/2293452

Transparency International. (2013). 2013 corruption perceptions index. Retrieved June 27, from http://cpi.transparency.org/cpi2013/

Transparency International. (2014) Corruption perceptions index: Overview. Retrieved June 28, 2014, from http://www.transparency.org/research/cpi/overview

UNGC. (2013a). Overview of the UN global compact. Retrieved June 27, 2014, from http://www.unglobalcompact.org/AboutTheGC/index.html

UNGC. (2013b). Global compact principle 10. Retrieved June 27, 2014, from http://www.unglobalcompact.org/AboutTheGC/TheTenPrinciples/principle10.html

UNGC. (2013c). Transparency and anti-corruption. Retrieved June 27, 2014, from http://www.unglobalcompact.org/AboutTheGC/TheTenPrinciples/anti-corruption.html

Wyatt, E. (2011, December 13). Former Siemens executives are charged with bribery. *The New York Times*. Retrieved July 18, 2012, from http://www.nytimes.com/2011/12/14/business/global/former-siemens-executives-charged-with-bribery.html

Chapter 15
The Social Environment: Business Etiquette and Cultural Sensitivity

"If you strive to understand the value of different cultures, you will find common points." (Stephan Rothlin, *Eighteen Rules for Becoming a Top Notch Player*, 2004)

15.1 Prelude

For international businesses, managing the social environment requires becoming increasingly skillful in responding to the cultural sensitivities of stakeholders in local communities where the firm is active. The case study takes the reader through a tragedy—a boy was killed because of a malfunctioning elevator in the apartment complex where he and his family lived—and the process by which the firm that had manufactured and installed the elevator responded and failed to respond to the moral expectations honored within the local Japanese culture. Schindler's failure to apologize to the local Japanese community may have been dictated by lawyers concerned that the firm make no admission of guilt that might adversely affect them in future lawsuits, but it was a disaster from the perspective of Schindler's ability to remain a viable business there. In light of this case study, can international business ethics help firms avoid such fiascos? Where is the line to be drawn, if at all between observing business etiquette and complying with international business ethics? The chapter will emphasize the indispensable role that training in cross-cultural awareness should play in managerial decision-making if businesses are to succeed in social environments away from their original homes.

15.2 Case Study: Schindler's Apology

15.2.1 Abstract

The Schindler case addresses the complex issue of crisis management for Western multinationals operating in Asian settings. In June 2006 a deadly accident killed a high school student in Minato Ward, Japan. As a result of a software flaw, the boy was slammed between the doors of a Schindler elevator. Besides the technical

S. Rothlin, D. McCann, *International Business Ethics*,
DOI 10.1007/978-3-662-47434-1_15

failure, the Japanese public opinion condemned the company's reaction because it showed insensitivity toward the victim's family. Schindler was blamed for focusing on its potential legal liability, rather than the moral issues. The late apology and the poor communication between the local branch and Schindler headquarters resulted in a PR disaster, which had serious repercussions for its business in Japan. Indeed, the ensuing sales drop and erosion of the firm's reputation significantly halted its progress in developing Japan as a strategic market in the elevator industry.

15.2.2 Keywords

Schindler, Minato Ward, Takeshiba building, Elevator accident, PR crisis

> "When you climb a new mountain, you are responsible for knowing the way; the mountain is not responsible for you," Schindler said. "And in this case, of course, the mountain is Japan and it has ears and eyes, and in a globalized environment one could expect that it would be slightly less . . . demanding, or maybe a little bit more tolerant, as people from far away…who do not necessarily have the same knowhow as they should have." (Otake 2009)

15.2.3 One Tragic Summer Evening

Hirosuke Ichikawa was 16 the day he became the innocent victim of an unforgiving equipment failure. It was June 3, 2006, and Hirosuke would never have imagined it would be his last day. The high school boy, perched on his bicycle, had just begun to back out of the lift at his family's condominium in "City Heights Takeshiba," Minato Ward. He did not even have time to realize what was going on. In a matter of nanoseconds, the elevator suddenly closed up, and a young life was lost. Because of a software glitch, the iron cage operated by Schindler Elevator K. K., the Japanese branch of the Swiss elevator manufacturer, unexpectedly crushed him to death (*Japan Times Online* 2006).

15.2.4 Fast Excuses, Late Apologies

In the days immediately following the accident, the only response from Schindler K. K. was a press release tersely stating that the company "would like to stress that we are convinced there is no reason to attribute the accident to either the design or the installation of the elevator" (*Japan Times Online* 2006). All Japanese TV channels broadcast footage showing Ken Smith, the president of Schindler Elevator K. K., repeatedly evading the questions of journalists (Fukushige 2006). He would later offer the excuse that answering directly seemed "not appropriate" in that situation (Kobayashi 2006). Smith's behavior, however, reinforced the widespread belief among Japanese people that multinational companies are more concerned about legal issues, rather than their moral responsibilities (Fukushige 2006).

Strongly criticized for the delay in acknowledging what had happened, the Swiss parent company directly intervened in the local crisis. Nine days after the failure of the Minato Ward elevator, Roland W. Hess, at that time president of the Management Committee for Elevators and Escalators of Schindler Holding, Ltd., apologized both to Ichikawa's family and to the residents of the condominium (*Japan Times Online* 2006). "Our thoughts are with the victim and his family. We pray for him and extend our condolences to the family involved in this tragic accident," declared Hess (Negishi 2006). Nevertheless he also echoed an earlier press release defending Schindler's product quality, with the observation that "we have never had a serious accident or fatality due to product design error" (Negishi 2006).

Schindler's local management team did not react favorably to the intervention from company headquarters. Since no investigation had been carried out yet, Schindler's Japanese employees tried to show their loyalty by opening their own inquiry into what went wrong (Kalbermatten and Haghirian 2011). Tomoyuki Nishimura, head of the New Installation Division, publicly acknowledged the recent retrieval of a defective control panel installed in a lift in Tokyo. "We cannot deny at this point the possibility that there may have been a problem with the control circuit," according to Nishimura (Negishi 2006). When Schindler's top management in Switzerland did not support their efforts, many employees quietly withdrew from the company, and some eventually attempted suicide (Kalbermatten and Haghirian 2011). A few months later, Ken Smith resigned his post because he felt that it would be impossible for him to continue managing the firm, inasmuch as he had lost everyone's confidence in his leadership. In December, Hess announced the appointment of the former president of Henkel Japan, Gerhard Schlosser, in place of Smith (*Kyodo News* 2006a). Given Schlosser's long-standing expertise in doing business in Japan, many could not understand why he accepted the position (Harris 2008).

15.2.5 Countering the Panic, Investigating the Causes

In the days following the Minato Ward accident as the news reached the public, there was a panic about elevators and their safety. Major lift makers and real estate groups were confronted with the pressing need to restore confidence in the safety of their equipment and buildings. In order to respond to the numerous inquiries, Toshiba Elevator provided its customers with free facilities checks on request. Other firms involved in the industry, such as Mitsubishi and Hitachi, did the same (*Asia Times* 2006). Meanwhile, as instructed by Japan's Ministry of Land, Infrastructure, Transportation, and Tourism (MLIT), local governments engaged in massive reinspections of Schindler equipment (*Japan Times Online* 2006). In response, Hess conceded that Schindler elevators have been involved in a number of fatalities. However, he pointed out that accidental deaths caused by stalled passengers trying to get out of elevators occurred at a comparatively higher rate than deaths directly attributable to maintenance problems (Negishi 2006). Nevertheless, the management of the Takeshiba building resolved to replace the three Schindler elevators with Mitsubishi equipment. Two of them had already been removed by the end of November 2006. The Mayor of Minato Ward, Masaaki Takei, attended the installation ceremony and took a symbolic ride to reassure the public about the safety of Mitsubishi's lifts (*Kyodo News* 2006b).

Meanwhile, MLIT set up a task force to determine the causes of the Minato Ward accident (Nakamura 2006). The bulk of discussion revolved around the handling of the elevator's maintenance, which came to be regarded as the critical factor. Although Schindler was initially in charge of maintenance, in 2005 that contract was awarded to another firm, SEC Elevator, as a result of the competitive bidding process mandated by Minato Ward (Nakamura 2006). Although the Fair Trade Commission had required elevator manufacturers to disclose the outsourcing of maintenance services and to convey all relevant information to the firms in charge of maintenance, the industry's compliance with the new provision was spotty at best (Nakamura 2006). Therefore while Schindler pointed to the maintenance provider's culpability, the provider alleged that Schindler had withheld the necessary information for the effective maintenance of its products (Nakamura 2006). Neither firm was willing to accept responsibility for the accident.

15.2.6 Mapping a New Way Forward

Notwithstanding the enormity of its public relations disaster, Schindler did not consider the option of winding down its Japanese operations (*Asia Times* 2006). Although the company accounted for a mere 1% share of Japan's market for elevators and escalators when the accident occurred (Fukushige 2006), it was responsible for maintaining 18,000 units and had no intention of abandoning them. Since Japan's potential market for their products and services remained huge, shutting the door on further business in the country would have had a significantly negative impact on Schindler's global competitiveness. Hess made this clear even at the peak of the scandal: "Regarding Schindler Japan, of course, we want to grow in this country. This is an extremely important country in the elevator industry. We would like to play an important role in this country" (*AFX News* 2006). However, the crisis did not come without a cost. Schindler's sales immediately dropped, and people start referring to its products as "murdering elevators" (Otake 2009). Moreover, the increasingly negative perception of the Schindler brand in Japan spilled over in its deteriorating reputation as an employer, making it difficult for the company to recruit and retain skilled Japanese workers (Kalbermatten and Haghirian 2011). Alfred Schindler, the chairman of the parent company, Schindler Holdings, tried to blame the firm's troubles on the fact that it had been "'bashed' in the Japanese media": "After the accident there was some kind of witch hunt" (Tucker and Soble 2009). Nevertheless, a few months later—in May of 2009—Schindler personally made his condolences to Ichikawa's relatives during a trip to

Japan while still insisting on the firm's innocence in the Minato Ward accident (Kyodo News 2009).

There's no doubt that the Minato Ward accident precipitated a heavy round of "Schindler bashing" in Japan. Impassioned outbursts of nationalist reactions against foreign manufacturers swamped various attempts to achieve an unbiased reading of the case (Otake 2009). Few were willing to acknowledge the strained relationship between Schindler and the Japanese firm, SEC Elevator, which had taken over responsibility for maintenance services at the Takeshiba housing complex. In the same way, few took into account the fact that at the time the accident occurred, the headquarters of Schindler Holding, Ltd. in Switzerland was on public holiday (Otake 2009). Besides, Hess did not dismiss the concerns of the Japanese people and himself pressed for clarifications: "They are entitled to feel unhappy when an accident like this happens, and entitled to answers" (Negishi 2006). He also attributed the public's strong reaction to the high safety standards to which Japan is accustomed, compared with other countries in the region (Negishi 2006). Chairman Alfred Schindler went further in recognizing the cultural dimension of his mistakes, "When you are educated in, let's say, a multicultural environment as I was, and mainly in the United States, apologizing is always the admission of guilt. So not only by training as a lawyer, but genetically we are preprogrammed never to apologize until it is clear you are guilty" (Otake 2009). Noburo Gohara, law professor at Toin University and former practitioner, tried to interpret Hess's and Schindler's statements in a conciliatory mood. Without entering into further details, he pointed out the biases in typical Japanese reactions to the disaster. According to Gohara, "a number of factors became intertwined with each other and led to the calamity. But because Japanese society has no system of objectifying the accident, all the blame fell on Schindler's shoulders" (Otake 2009).

Nevertheless, Tatsumi Tanaka from the Japanese PR firm, Recruit Co., broadened the criticism of Schindler's response. "Japan is a country in which you are forgiven if you apologize quickly," Tanaka explained (Kobayashi 2006). He added that worrying about legal aspects at the expense of a sincere expression of sympathy might worsen the outcome of crisis management. According to Tanaka, "companies should remember that any trial would be held in Japan," meaning not only that public opinion would play a major role in shaping final judgment but also that the legal assumptions held at headquarters in Switzerland might not offer the best way forward in Japan (Kobayashi 2006). Tanaka's argument appears to amplify the opinion of one of the residents at the Takeshiba complex: "Instead of accusing Schindler, I have watched how the company dealt with the accident and what kind of measures it took.... I am not satisfied yet" (Kobayashi 2006). Whatever else it would take to satisfy Japanese public opinion, the way forward would clearly involve a sincere apology.

15.2.7 Conclusion: Unanswered Questions

The Schindler case gives us reasons to reflect upon crisis management in Asian markets. The disastrous consequences for the company's reputation suggest that its response to the deadly accident at Minato Ward was especially misguided.

Japanese people felt outraged by the fact that it took Schindler's management over a week after the accident to offer an apology to the victim's family, thus creating the impression that the company's top priority was to minimize the risk of a lawsuit. What do you think about the timing of Schindler's responses? In your opinion, what role did cultural values play in the Japanese public's negative reaction to Schindler's response? Just how significant are such cross-cultural misunderstandings? Do you think that Schindler's response raises any issues for business ethics? What is the role of economic nationalism or the informal protectionism by which foreign multinational corporations are hobbled in their attempts to compete fairly in Japan and other Asian nations? Schindler may be faulted for making serious mistakes, but what about the Japanese news media's eagerness to pounce on them?

In hindsight, the intervention from on high by top management from Schindler Holding, Ltd. worsened the firm's position in Japan. The manufacturer's reputation suffered serious damage both with its direct and indirect customers, as well as with its employees and local managers. What is your view of the declarations of Roland W. Hess, in contrast with the various reactions of Schindler's Japanese staff? Should the local staff have spoken up, as they tried to do, when Japanese public opinion was demanding immediate answers? What do you think of Ken Smith's reactions to the accident? What do you think about his reason for resigning his position at Schindler K. K.? Was that the appropriate thing to do, or was it a lame attempt to avoid accepting his responsibility?

If you had been advising Hess, what would you recommend that he do to retake control of the events that were threatening Schindler's future in Japan? Is there anything more he could have done to balance the legal and financial risks while also taking responsibility? The accident at Minato Ward proved to be a serious setback to Schindler's growth in the Japanese market. Notwithstanding the need to rebuild trust and credibility with Japanese people, Hess did not choose to appoint a Japanese national as the company's new president. Instead, the choice went to former Henkel Japan director, Gerard Schlosser. Do you think this was an appropriate choice and why do you believe Hess made it? If you were Schlosser, what immediate measures would you take in order to set a positive tone for your presidency? Do you think that a review of Schindler's commitment to good business ethics might help it to regain competitiveness and trust in the Japanese market? What specific changes would you recommend?

15.2.8 Update

Today Schlosser is no longer president of Schindler K. K. He left in 2010 to become a consultant. Former Schindler Asia Pacific CFO Philippe Boué took his place. While the company's business in Japan, however, has shown modest growth since the 2006 scandal, Schindler K. K. has been involved in only a few public projects since then, among them, in 2008, an exclusive contract to build the 13 stations of the Nippori-Toneri transport line (Harris 2008). Getting rid of past ghosts is not easy in Japan. Every time Schindler's equipment is involved in minor accidents, criticisms run rampant (Harris 2008). The manufacturer's position was also worsened by the outbreak of a scandal in 2007. Although the international media coverage of the issue was relatively unsubstantial, the Japanese press used it to amplify lingering suspicions about Schindler K. K. (Kalbermatten and Haghirian 2011). In order to obtain proper licenses to operate, 53 Schindler inspectors lied about their number of years in the field. While the company tried to minimize the damage from negative press coverage, it could not totally offset voices claiming that the inspectors' lies were the result of an internal order by Schindler executives (Kalbermatten and Haghirian 2011).

On October 31, 2012, a new fatal accident occurred in Japan. A 63-year-old cleaning lady, Toshiko Maeda, fell out of a moving Schindler elevator at a hotel in Kanazawa, Ishikawa Prefecture. The elevator had been installed in 1998 (*Japan Today* 2012a, b). A Japanese official who witnessed the accident described how "the doors opened and she went to get in, but the cage was still moving up," causing her entrapment between the ceiling and the lift floor (*Japan Today* 2012a, b). Past experience at Minato prompted fast reaction from the company. Schindler K. K. immediately apologized to the relatives of the victim and issued a press release on its website a few hours after the accident. A comparison of the press releases issued by Schindler in the two instances shows the effects of the lesson learned from the 2006 accident.[1] However, the Japanese authorities were also quick to intervene. While the

[1] Here are the two press releases, each one issued after the accident, first, in 2006, and second, in 2012. Note that the first press release came 3 days after the event in Minato Ward, while the second was issued immediately on the same day as the accident in Kanazawa. Note also the differences in tone and the focus of Schindler's concerns.

1. "08.06.2006: Schindler Press Release: Fatal Accident in Tokyo, Japan:

   On Saturday night, June 3, 2006, a 16 year old boy died in a tragic accident involving an elevator manufactured by Schindler and maintained by a third party maintenance company in Tokyo, Japan. The boy was deadly injured when the elevator abruptly moved upwards with open doors while he was leaving the elevator. The Schindler Group deeply regrets this accident and offers its condolences to the family of the boy. Schindler fully supports the local Authorities and welcomes the investigation to establish the root-cause of the accident.

   The tragic accident happened in a Tokyo government housing development equipped with six Schindler elevators installed in 1998. For more than a year the elevators are no longer serviced by Schindler, but by two different local third party maintenance companies.

   Schindler has no design related user fatalities on record. Fatal accidents in the elevator industry are mainly due to inappropriate maintenance or dangerous user behavior in the context of entrapment. The elevator involved in the accident is a state-of-art product fully certified by various international Authorities and in use in many markets around the world.

   Schindler is moving safely over 700 million people per day or the equivalent of the Japanese population every 4 h. The risk of having a fatal accident with an elevator is lower than with any other means of transportation. Safety is Schindler's most important value" (Schindler 2006).

police raided the company's office at Nagoya, Minister of Transport, Yuichiro Hata, announced that 5,500 Schindler elevators would be checked. "We will make emergency checks of all the Schindler elevators on the basis of investigations into the cause of the accident," he declared (AAP 2012). One of the comments posted after an online version of the news reads, "I think Schindler can close their Japanese Branch after this" (*Japan Today* 2012a, b).

Nevertheless, Schindler K. K. has not been closed. Even so, there is no mention, let alone any positive news from it, in the Schindler Group's most recent documents, a fact sheet (Schindler 2014) summarizing its financial performance and the annual Group Review 2013. Apparently, since the 2012 accident, there has not been a single new order placed with Schindler K. K., despite the overall pattern of significant sales growth in the Asia Pacific region and India (Schindler 2013). It's still to be seen whether Schindler K. K. is sustainable, given the skepticism of the Japanese people. With a new CEO, Philippe Boué, at the helm, Schindler K. K. has yet another opportunity to show how well it responds to the cultural challenges of operating in the Japanese social environment.

15.3 Case Study Discussion

When Alfred Schindler visited Hong Kong in February 2009 in order to celebrate the opening of the new 118-storey International Commerce Centre, he wasn't just touring the elevators that Schindler had installed in that building. He also scheduled an extended meeting with Asian journalists—as part of a "charm offensive," if you will—at which he was asked to comment on the Minato Ward accident of 2006, at that time still under investigation. Schindler apparently got "off message" and complained that his company had been the victim of a "witch hunt" in the Japanese media, which was his explanation for its sharp drop in sales there (Tucker and Soble 2009). This was, perhaps, not the most appropriate time and place to give vent to his frustrations, for he also said that the purpose of the meeting was to "to provide the Japanese media with an opportunity to develop a [better] informed opinion of our company, that we are not bad guys" while also indicating that their one-sided

2. "31.10.2012: Schindler Press Release: Fatal accident in Japan:

Today, shortly after midnight (local time), a fatal accident occurred in Kanazawa, Japan, involving a Schindler elevator. A 60-year-old woman, who was employed at the hotel where the accident occurred, died as a result. Schindler very much regrets this accident.

At the present time, the cause of the accident is not known and, therefore, we cannot provide further information concerning the course of events. Schindler is fully supporting the authorities in trying to establish the cause of the accident. The elevator in question was installed in 1998.

In Japan, the media have already reported on this tragic incident. In addition, Schindler has held a press conference to apologize to the family and to offer our sincere condolences" (Schindler 2012).

coverage of foreign businesses made it very difficult for Schindler K. K. to compete in Japan. The Minato Ward case, in his view, ought to be about economic protectionism and the way Japanese public opinion is manipulated to exclude foreign competition where regulatory measures prove ineffective. "We are fighting for equal access, a level playing field," he said.

As we have seen, Japanese public opinion was focused on Schindler's failure to deliver a prompt and formal apology to the family of Hirosuke Ichikawa. Both Japanese journalists and their readers regarded the attitudes and behaviors exhibited by Schindler's representatives as proof that the firm was more interested in minimizing its exposure to potential lawsuits than in expressing any sincere concern for the victim's grieving family. When Schindler's representatives finally realized their mistake and tried to make an apology to the family as well as the people of Japan, it was commonly regarded there as too little and too late. What, then, can we learn from these conflicting interpretations of the aftermath of the accident at Minato Ward? Was Schindler the victim of a "witch hunt" designed to drive them out of business in Japan? Or was Schindler the victim of its own cultural insensitivity and therefore deserved the "bashing" that its reputation suffered in Japan? Or is there merit in both interpretations? Do both challenge us to dig deeper into the subtleties of becoming top-notch players in international business?

In trying to reconcile the two perspectives, one point should be obvious. Accidents involving elevators almost inevitably will attract an inordinate amount of media attention. The fear of elevators is listed as one of a large number of phobias that have been analyzed by clinical psychologists for diagnosis and treatment. It is a specific fear related to "claustrophobia" ("fear of enclosed spaces") and "agoraphobia" ("fear of being trapped in a situation in which escape would be difficult or impossible should a panic attack occur") (Fritscher 2014). While the fear of elevators is by no means unique to Japanese culture, it may be compounded there by an East Asian "tetraphobia"—based on the fact that the number four (*shi*) sounds identical to the word for death (*shi*), in both Japanese and Chinese languages. In order to minimize the risk of tetraphobia, most elevators in these countries do not list floor numbers four (4), thirteen (13), fourteen (14), or higher numbers with four in them. In spite of these cultural differences, certain patterns of anxiety, including symptoms of panic in extreme cases, are common in all cultures where people have been forced to rely on elevators.

These psychological perspectives are hardly unknown to companies that market, manufacture, install, and maintain elevators. An article in *The New Yorker* magazine (April 21, 2008), "Up and then down: The lives of elevators," goes into great detail on the history of elevators, their mechanical principles, their generally outstanding safety record, and the extent to which manufacturers, like Otis (USA) and Schindler (Switzerland), study the range of human responses to the experience of riding an elevator (Paumgarten 2008). Since user interface—including considerations of psychological comfort and cultural differences—is clearly a major component in the design of elevator systems, it does seem strange that Schindler K. K. apparently was ill prepared to deal with the predictable consequences of the accident in Minato Ward. Hindsight, of course, is uncanny when investigating an accident that has already occurred; nevertheless, top management at Schindler appears to have been clueless about the potentially negative consequences of its rather flat-footed response to initial reports of the accident. Any story involving an elevator accident is likely to draw media attention, but when the story involves a multinational corporation whom the Japanese public has already learned to suspect as inferior—allegedly offering a product with lower standards at a lower price than its Japanese rivals—any mistakes made in managing the firm's response to the accident are likely to be magnified. In the mind of Japanese public opinion, Schindler became synonymous with "murdering elevators" (Harris 2009).

Schindler's defense, also predictably, was too complex and subtle to reverse Japanese public opinion, once it had turned against the firm. Commentators have also pointed out that while an apology may have been necessary, it likely would not have been sufficient to enable Schindler K. K. to move beyond the crisis. As we shall see in the following section, there are right ways and wrong ways of making an apology, if it is to be credible and effective. Many Japanese firms are reported to have made mistakes mishandling apologies (Tanaka, 2007). Given their failures in various crises over the years, it is not likely that Schindler's mistakes can truthfully be blamed on cultural biases, either those of its top management or those of the Japanese news media. Cultural insensitivity, to be sure, complicates the challenge faced by Schindler K. K.'s new leadership, but when the firm's response to the Minato Ward is uncannily similar to the mistakes made by Japanese firms in other crises, who suffer similar punishments at the hands of Japanese public opinion, the problem may have to be redefined, if a solution is to be found.

15.4 Ethical Reflection

In Chap. 3, we introduced some of the standard categories used to map the field of applied ethics. Ethics, you will recall, is itself a scientific field, broadly understood as the study—both descriptive and normative, as well as metaethical—of morality, which is what people actually think and do, as they express their moral concerns. Anyone's willingness to offer an apology, when appropriate, clearly falls under the category of morality. Like all such human interactions, apologies are culturally embedded, that is, they reflect and extend cultural values with their sometimes overlapping and sometimes diverging indications of what is the right thing to do. The three main types of theories developed in normative ethics are based on logical differences in what people intend to communicate when they make judgments about which attitudes and behaviors are good and bad ("teleological ethics"), right and wrong ("deontological ethics"), and appropriate and inappropriate ("hermeneutical ethics").

15.4.1 Apologies in Business Ethics: Western Perspectives

Given these categories, we may consider the ethics of making (as well as demanding and accepting) apologies. What, then, is an apology? The *Internet Encyclopedia of Philosophy* defines an apology as "the act of declaring one's regret, remorse, or sorrow for having insulted, failed, injured, harmed or wronged another" (Mihai 2013). There are four basic types of apologies, based on differences in the givers and receivers of such declarations: "one to one," "one to many," "many to one," or "many to many." With such differences, the philosophical question is whether the "validity conditions" for an "authentic apology" are the same in all four types. In "one to one" or interpersonal apologies, here are the normal expectations: they must contain "an acknowledgement that the incident in question did in fact occur and that it was inappropriate; a recognition of responsibility for the act; the expression of an attitude of regret and a feeling of remorse; and the declaration of an intention to refrain from similar acts in the future." The purpose of such declarations is "to recognize the equal moral worth of the victim. While the offence cannot be undone, the act of acknowledging it recognizes the offended as an equal moral agent." The recognition of "the equal moral worth of the victim," of course, is necessary to restore "her self-respect," without which trust, mutuality, and reciprocity become virtually impossible.

Corporate apologies, such as the one that Schindler mishandled in its response to the Minato Ward accident, fall within the "many to many" or "many to one" type, which also include other "collective agents such as churches, professions, or the state." Compared with interpersonal apologies, the challenge of determining the validity conditions for such "collective apologies" includes the question of representation, that is, who specifically should represent the institution that is giving the apology and the community who is receiving it. Furthermore, analysis of "collective apologies" indicates that they have "both a symbolic function (recognition of the offended group as worthy of respect) and a utility function (the apology might bring about reparations to the victims and might lead to better inter-group relations)." Given the convergence of these functions, it becomes clear that the role of emotional demonstrations of personal contrition is less important in "collective apologies" than "changes in the norms and practices of the collective reparations, compensation, or memorialization projects [that] give concreteness to the symbolic act of apologizing." Over and above the purposes specified for interpersonal apologies, "collective apologies" aim to reaffirm the institution's commitment to "the fundamental moral principles of the community" (Mihai 2013). On these assumptions, had Schindler properly apologized for the Minato Ward accident, it would have made a symbolic gesture demonstrating the firm's commitment to honor the expectations embedded in Japanese culture, backed up by a timely and appropriate offer of compensation to the victim's family.

Practical advice on how to apologize successfully is consistent with this philosophical analysis mapping the types and validity conditions for apologies. Daryl Koehn, a widely regarded American business ethicist, recommends that the CEO make a public apology as part of any realistic strategy for "bouncing back" from either a personal mistake or a corporate failure (Koehn 2013). As she observes, "a good apology aims at winning back stakeholder trust." How to make a successful corporate apology therefore depends on knowing who the firm's stakeholders actually are, as well as their expectations. What will it take to win back their trust? Emotional demonstrations of remorse are not essential, she believes, when the CEO is apologizing for a corporate failure for which he or she may bear no direct responsibility. Nevertheless, "stakeholder skepticism" needs to be addressed, if not with emotional appeals, certainly with "a prompt response," in spite of any perceived risks of "litigation." If the stakeholders have become cynical, in light of a firm's previous attempts "to lie its way out of trouble," then the successful apology must "show somehow that the firm has significantly changed how it does business."

Koehn also notes briefly the importance of acknowledging "cultural differences," for example, in dealing with "Japanese audiences," and rightly advises CEOs to take these into account in "drafting a persuasive apology." Her remarks are addressed to "resilient CEOs," that is, to CEOs who understand the importance of staying "focused on what they can change," without getting "distracted by external forces outside of their control." Had Koehn been advising Alfred Schindler on how to conduct his "charm offensive" in Hong Kong (Tucker and Soble 2009), no doubt she would have told him to set aside his personal frustration over the "witch hunt" that Japanese journalists allegedly waged against Schindler K. K. He may have been right about what he perceived to be the lack of "equal access" or "a level playing field" for foreign companies competing in Japan. But no attempt to educate the Japanese media "that we are not bad guys" was likely to change their bias against Schindler K. K. As Koehn points out, the CEO would have been better advised to make a forward-looking apology "with details concerning the measures they are taking to fix the problem." When yet another death occurred, in 2012, in an unrelated accident involving a Schindler elevator in Japan, the firm was faced with an "external factor" literally "beyond its control." Under such circumstances, as Koehn reminds us, "there can be no guarantee that a CEO apology will restore trust, however well-considered and well-drafted that statement is."

Bruce Weinstein is widely known in the USA as "The Ethics Guy." His columns appear regularly in *Bloomberg Businessweek* and the *Huffington Post*. The central notion that animates his various posts is the concept of "ethical intelligence." He believes that business people can learn to extend their "emotional intelligence" by following five basic principles: "(1) Do No Harm, (2) Make Things Better, (3) Respect Others, (4) Be Fair, (5) Be Loving." Weinstein observes—in what can be taken as a concise summary of the overall argument of this book—that "we know these principles already," that "they're the basis of both religious traditions and secular societies," and that "they're tremendously difficult to live by" (Weinstein 2011: 6). One of the blogs he has written to illustrate these principles is "The Right and Wrong Ways to Apologize" (Weinstein 2013).

Weinstein's essay has the merit of describing in detail "How NOT to Apologize." He identifies five types of "non-apology": (1) "Say that 'mistakes were made'"; (2) "Change the subject"; (3) "Drag your feet"; (4) "Deny there is a problem"; and (5)

"Blame someone else." The first, "mistakes were made," involves the use of the passive voice, which "absolves the speaker of any responsibility." While in some languages, for example, German, use of the passive voice is far more common than in English, Weinstein is correct in alerting us to its inappropriateness if we mean to communicate an ethically intelligent apology. The other non-apologies that he lists should be obvious enough and need no further comment. Weinstein proceeds then to offer advice on "How to Apologize with Ethical Intelligence": (1) "Admit your mistake quickly and take personal responsibility for it"; (2) "Apologize first to the person you have wronged"; (3) "Speak from the heart"; (4) "Avoid repeating the mistake"; (5) "Know that a meaningful apology is a sign of integrity, not weakness"; and (6) "Don't be afraid to ask for help" (Weinstein 2013).

The relationship between Weinstein's "ethical intelligence" and "emotional intelligence" should be apparent from the emphasis that he gives to sincerity, as in recommendations three and five. "Speaking from the heart" involves a concrete demonstration of sincerity. As Weinstein points out, "An insincere apology is as bad as no apology at all. People can tell when you really mean it, even if you think you're a good actor and can fool everyone. If you don't think you're wrong, don't apologize—but be prepared to defend your position." Schindler's eventual apology for the Minato Ward accident came across as "half-hearted," because the company wasn't prepared to admit its share of responsibility. If Weinstein is correct about the characteristics of an ethically intelligent apology, then Schindler's problem wasn't a lack of cultural sensitivity. The CEO need not have excused himself because of his allegedly American education. If Weinstein is correct, Schindler's apology would no more have been accepted at face value in the USA than it was in Japan.

15.4.2 Apologies in Business Ethics: Japanese Perspective

We have explored in detail these Western discussions of corporate apologies in order to set up a comparison with Japanese practices. Tatsumi Tanaka, who was quoted in the case study commenting on the Schindler apology, wrote a book advising Japanese companies on the art of making an apology, *Sonna shazai de wa kaisha ga abunai—Apologizing that way will endanger your company* (Jones 2007). He, too, lists both apologies that don't work and those that do, while analyzing them both with case studies involving Japanese businesses. Here is his list of "bad" or "ineffective apologies": (A) "Apologies that Include Rebuttals or Excuses," (B) "Apologies that Include Lies or Deceptions," (C) "Apologies that are Vague," (D) "Apologies by the Wrong People," (E) "Misdirected Apologies," (F) "Apologizing Too Late," (G) "Disorganized Apologies," (H) "Apologies Preceded by Offers of Compensation," (I) "Apologies Without Other Action," and (J) "Apologizing Too Soon." Noteworthy about this list is the fact that Tanaka criticizes each of these ineffective apologies for reasons that parallel those we've already seen in the three Western presentations on corporate apologies. This finding is significant in that all of Tanaka's examples, and the literature analyzing them, are taken from exclusively

Japanese sources. His book was not written for an international audience, but was intended as a practical guide to Japanese business executives.

If there are significant cultural differences in the right way to apologize in Japan and the West, we would expect them to surface in Tanaka's book. But what we find is that his practical advice to Japanese businesses is uncannily similar to what was given by our Western ethicists, Mihai, Koehn, and Weinstein. When Tanaka turns to the typical characteristics of "effective apologies," we may expect to see some differences emerge. After all, a successful apology, in his view, involves "the right combination of what [he] calls heart (*kokoro*), technique (*waza*), and organization (*karada*)" (Jones 2007). Anyone with even a passing familiarity with Japanese culture will recognize the importance of *kokoro,* whose kanji character (心) is identical to the mandarin (心) signifying the Chinese notion of *xīn*, similarly translated as "heart." While there are subtleties in *kokoro* that are specific to Japanese culture,[2] Tanaka emphasizes its role in "removing the natural fear of apologizing." *Kokoro*, then, alerts Japanese business executives to concerns similar to those expressed by our Western ethicists over "sincerity" and how to achieve an appropriate and credible expression of it. Tanaka's point is similar to Weinstein's who observed that "a meaningful apology is a sign of integrity, not weakness." American English has recently coined a telling new phrase to express a similar insight: "man up" (Zimmer 2010). It takes courage to admit one's mistakes and own up to them. When others urge us to "man up," they are challenging us to find within ourselves the "heart" or, if you will, the "intestinal fortitude," which enables us to do the right thing, in this case, offering a sincere apology. Here, too, apparent cultural differences on what is required to make "effective apologies" seem to converge toward a moral consensus.

Tanaka's advice regarding technique (*waza*) and organization (*karada*) is similarly convergent, even though it is expressed in idioms indicative of Japanese culture. His advice on technique (*waza*) consists in three points: (1) "First, know your sins"; (2) "Set goals and lay a course"; and (3) "Approach the apology after thinking about it analytically." His overall approach is that making an apology should be understood as a "risk management strategy." Tanaka's use of the word, "sin," should not be dismissed as a translator's concession to a Western audience. A successful apology cannot be conjured up as some sort of public relations trick. If the corporate culture is lacking in ethical intelligence, the CEO cannot simply fake it. "Soul-searching is at the core of apologizing properly—understanding and accepting what you and your company have done wrong… This type of moral introspection and recognition of fault may be hard to build into a company's system of controls and procedures, yet the step is crucial to apologizing effectively."

The corporate culture must be transformed, so that its underlying moral vision becomes visible and actionable throughout the firm's governance structure. If effective apologies depend on such a transformation, it must be institutionalized in advance

[2] Lafcadio Hearn attempted to convey these to the West in his pioneering work on Japanese culture, aptly titled *Kokoro: Hints and Echoes of Japanese Inner Life*, originally published in 1896 (New York: Cosimo Classics, 2005).

of any need to apologize for anything. This general advice on the urgency of developing a corporate conscience is reinforced with specific advice on what to do when the need for an apology arises. "Setting goals and laying a course" means making adequate preparation for the press conference at which the apology will be offered. The ritual of apologizing should not be performed "until a management decision has been made as to where the company wishes to end up."

Analysis, according to Tanaka, indicates there are four phases to an apology: First is the comfort (*iyasu*) phase, in which you must subject "yourself to the emotions of angry and resentful victims (or their surviving family members)." Next is "the comprehension (*fu ni ochiru*) phase," in which disclosure of information is crucial, "since victims want to know what happened and why." The third phase is contingent on the successful completion of the previous two, since it consists in "forgiveness (*yurusareru*) and closure." The victims cannot reach this phase if they have serious misgivings about either the first or the second or both. The final phase is "the incident being forgotten (*wasureru*)." It is clear that Schindler's apology in 2006 had not enabled the Minato Ward victims to forget the accident, for when another unrelated accident occurred 6 years later, all the lingering negative emotions from the earlier one resurfaced, much to the detriment of Schindler's business in Japan.

Tanaka's third point on organization (*karada*) elaborates further on the development of a capacity for effective apology as part of the firm's risk management strategy. His advice concerns the kind of advisors the firm—and specifically its CEO—should turn to when managing the kind of crisis that may require an apology. "Have wise men from other fields." Since the prospect of making an apology is likely to provoke defensive reactions on the part of the firm's senior staff, it is "crucial" to turn to those "who can view the problem from broader perspective." Such broader perspectives, he insists, will not be found within the firm. Tanaka therefore advises CEOs to cultivate friendships with experienced persons from a variety of fields, who may contribute fresh thinking precisely because they have not been involved in the firm's routine operations. Similarly, "Choose outside experts based on their expertise." Expertise rather than reputation should be the deciding factor on who should be consulted. Lawyers in particular are to be kept at arm's length as the CEO deliberates on how to manage the crisis: "Lawyers should never be allowed to make the decision about whether to apologize. Not apologizing for legal reasons can lead to a roasting by the media with possibly disastrous results." So Tanaka urges CEOs "Don't let your experts get too close." He is wary of all "outsiders" since it is difficult for them "to remain objective, particularly in the context of a long-standing relationship that may have come to include personal friendship." Tanaka's remarks suggest that trusted friends or "wise men" are not in the same category as "experts," whose expertise may be counterproductive. Finally, as to the firm's own employees, he recommends, "Get rid of the sychophants.... These are the people who will tell you what you want to hear, even though their advice may conflict with the company's or even your own best interests." While there may be universal appeal in Tanaka's advice on how to organize the firm for more effective risk management, it is clear that in this area his thinking also reflects commonly perceived problems in Japanese styles of management. The further up one goes in the corporate hierarchy, the lonelier it gets, and the more indispensable becomes the question of who do you trust.

15.4.3 Converging Perspectives Pinpoint the Challenge for Schindler in Japan

Our point in comparing Tanaka's advice with that given by Western academics and pundits like Mihai, Koehn, and Weinstein is to suggest that Schindler's apology didn't fail primarily because of cultural insensitivity. If cultural insensitivity were the problem, then it would be safe to assume that had the elevator accident occurred in Germany or anywhere else in the EU or the USA, Schindler's reaction would have been accepted as appropriate, without further damage to the firm's reputation or prospects for doing business. Our alternative hypothesis—based on the convergence in approaches offered by a Japanese expert as well as Western ethicists—is that Schindler was unprepared to make an apology in any venue, because of an unaccountable weakness in its corporate culture or management style. Schindler may have been so focused on the financial health of the company, as well as the need for continuous innovation in the technological design of its products, that it was curiously out of touch with their symbolic resonance—the anxieties of the millions of people who must use their elevators and escalators—that so easily may create a public relations disaster for them whenever an accident like the one at Minato Ward occurs. Simply put, had they approached the risks they faced with a higher degree of ethical intelligence, they would have known that (a) accidents do happen, even or especially in the use of technologically advanced products and services and (b) that the firm should already have in place some kind of strategy for making effective apologies, ready for implementation when managing the fallout from such accidents. Instead, Schindler was caught flat-footed, as if it simply could not believe that any of its products might be involved in a serious accident.

Lacking an appropriate risk management strategy, informed by the kind of ethical intelligence advocated by both the Western ethicists and the Japanese expert, Schindler was unable to offer an effective apology in a timely manner. That failure, to be sure, became glaringly evident when it was played out in the context of the firm's Japanese operations and their dealings with the Japanese news media and Japanese public opinion. Cultural insensitivity may have compounded Schindler's problem in Japan, but the root of the problem was a failure of ethical intelligence.

If Schindler's management is to learn from this disaster, we would advise them to focus first on instilling a greater degree of ethical intelligence throughout their business, from its headquarters in Switzerland, through all its branches worldwide. Since the problem with Schindler's apology is not local—or exclusive to Schindler K. K.'s operations in Japan—the solution needs to be global rather than local. To be sure, throughout all its operations worldwide, Schindler must become aware of the problem of cultural insensitivity and must seek to address it by consulting more effectively with its local managers—especially those who themselves have been formed by the local cultures—and revising its policies so that cultural diversity is embraced as part of the solution rather than part of the problem of doing business globally. But working to eliminate cultural insensitivity is not likely to be effective unless it is founded upon a heightened sense of ethical intelligence.

15.5 Conclusion

Cross-cultural communication is an open-ended challenge. Despite all the discussions on how to overcome culture shock (Shelley and Makiuchi 1992), the fact remains that it can be a painful and protracted process. Many will be tempted simply to give up and go home (Williams 2014). It is especially galling for seasoned veterans to be told that they are culturally insensitive and in need of some serious rethinking of their attitudes and behaviors. If an appropriate response to cultural differences is to be achieved, it must be based on truthfulness and intellectual honesty. Pundits suggesting that all cultures are equally valid make as much sense as marketers who insist that the customer is always right. At best, these are but half-truths, and we cannot allow them to lull us into thinking that we have achieved any great insight by embracing them.

One of the most impressive aspects of this era of globalization is how it has enabled so many businesses to become working laboratories in the development of cross-cultural understanding. Managers in multinational corporations have plunged into the challenge of cross-cultural communication and, without much advice or encouragement from academics, have been able to find ways to do business while overcoming, or at least muddling through the anxieties and misunderstandings that may discourage others from trying. Inevitably, there will be mistakes made, and not just by Europeans attempting to do business in Japan and other East Asian venues. Much to its chagrin, Toyota discovered just how costly such mistakes can be, when it ignored a sexual harassment problem that had occurred in one of its plants in California, USA (Orey 2006). Though the case involved a Japanese manager who allegedly assaulted one of his Japanese subordinates there, her lawsuit in an American court resulted in Toyota paying her a rumored US$190 million to settle all claims in the matter (Maynard 2006). Toyota's management apparently was insufficiently aware of the seriousness with which sexual harassment charges are viewed in the USA, specifically in the cultural setting of California. The challenge of cross-cultural understanding is a two-way street. Both Schindler and Toyota paid a heavy price that year for their cultural insensitivity.

Nevertheless, our discussion in this chapter should give people involved in international business reasons for hope. After examining the details of Schindler's failed apology, we tried to determine whether there is any common ground in practicing the art of offering and accepting genuine apologies. By comparing the practical advice given by both Western ethicists and a Japanese expert, we came to realize that cultural insensitivity was more a symptom than the root cause of the problem.

The underlying problem was a failure of ethical intelligence that can be corrected by recovering a deeper understanding of the ethical rules that top-notch players should follow, regardless of their cultural differences. Schindler needs to dig more deeply into its own cultural values, those of its founders as well as their successors. But when it does, we believe that they will discover quite a bit of overlap with the values cherished by their Japanese customers and other stakeholders. Once again, we see the wisdom of Stephan Rothlin's formulation of one of his original rules for top-notch players: "If you strive to understand the value of different cultures, you will find common points." It may not require a PhD to discover that common ground but perhaps more "heart" than we previously realized.

References

AAP. (2012, November 2). Japan death prompts elevator checks. *Couriermail.com.* Retrieved November 3, 2012, from http://www.couriermail.com.au/news/breaking-news/japan-death-prompts-elevator-checks/story-e6freoo6-1226509519384?from=public_rss

AFX News. (2006, June 12). Schindler defends record after deadly elevator accident in Japan. Retrieved October 29, 2012, from http://www.finanznachrichten.de/nachrichten-2006-06/6554579-schindler-defends-record-after-deadly-elevator-accident-in-japan-020.htm

Agence France-Press. (2006, June 13). Schindler sorry for lift death. *The Standard.* Retrieved October 30, 2012, from http://www.thestandard.com.hk/news_detail.asp?we_cat=6&art_id=20655&sid=8377296&con_type=1&d_str=20060613&fc=2

Asia Times Online. (2006, June 13). Elevator firms in Japan cope with fatal accident. Retrieved October 29, 2012 from http://www.atimes.com/atimes/Japan/HF13Dh01.html

Fritscher, L. (2014, June 4). Health Phobias: What is the Fear of Elevators? *About.com.* Retrieved July 8, 2014, from http://phobias.about.com/od/phobiasatoh/f/What-Is-The-Fear-Of-Elevators.htm

Fukushige, S. (2006, June 8). How not to manage a PR crisis situation in Japan. *Fukumimi Blog.* Retrieved October 29, 2012, from http://fukumimi.wordpress.com/2006/06/08/how-not-to-manage-a-pr-crisis-situation-in-japan/

Harris, P. (2008, July 3). Going up? *Japan Inc.* Retrieved October 29, 2012, from http://www.japaninc.com/mgz_july_2008_schindler_japan

Hearn, L. (1896). *Kokoro: Hints and echoes of Japanese inner life* New York: Cosimo Classics (2005).

Japan Today. (2012a, November 1). Woman killed in elevator accident in Kanazawa; police raid Schindler office. Retrieved November 4, 2012, from http://www.japantoday.com/category/national/view/woman-killed-in-schindler-elevator-accident-in-kanazawa/comments/popular/id/2745662

Japan Today. (2012b, November 3). Govt to inspect 5,500 Schindler elevators after fatal accident. Retrieved November 5, 2012, from http://www.japantoday.com/category/national/view/govt-to-inspect-5500-schindler-lifts-after-fatal-accident

Jones, C. (2007, Spring). Book Review: Apologies and Corporate Governance in the Japanese Context—Tatsumi Tanaka's Sonna shazai de wa kaisha ga abunai [Apologizing that way will endanger your company]. *Brigham Young University International Law and Management Review.* Retrieved on July 10, 2014 from http://www.law2.byu.edu/ilmr/articles/spring_2007/BYU_ILMR_spring_2007_5_Jones.pdf

Kalbermatten, P., & Haghirian, P. (2011). Schindler elevators and the challenges of the Japanese market. In *Case Studies in Japanese Management*. World Scientific Press http://www.world-scientific.com/worldscibooks/10.1142/8097#t=aboutBook

Kobayashi, K. (2006, June 17). Schindler's tardy apology offers cautionary tale. *The Japan Times Online*. Retrieved on October 28, 2012 from http://www.japantimes.co.jp/text/nn20060617b6.html

Koehn, D. (2013). Why saying "I'm sorry" Isn't good enough: The ethics of corporate apologies. *Business Ethics Quarterly, 23*, 239–268. doi:10.5840/beq201323216.

Kyodo News. (2006a, December 15). Schindler elevator chief of Japan army exits over fatality. *The Japan Times Online*. Retrieved October 29, 2012, from http://www.japantimes.co.jp/text/nn20061215a9.html

Kyodo News. (2006b, November 21). Deadly Schindler elevator replaced. *The Japan Times Online*. Retrieved October 26, 2012 from http://www.japantimes.co.jp/text/nn20061121a8.html

Kyodo News. (2009, May 9). Schindler chief denies guilt in elevator death. *The Japan Times Online*. Retrieved November 3, 2012, from http://www.japantimes.co.jp/text/nn20090509a6.html

Maynard, M. (August 5, 2006). Automaker reaches settlement in sexual harassment suit. *The New York Times*. Retrieved July 15, 2014, from http://www.nytimes.com/2006/08/05/business/worldbusiness/05harass.html

Mihai, M. (2013). Apology. In *Internet encyclopedia of philosophy*. Retrieved July 11, 2014 from http://www.iep.utm.edu/apology

Nakamura, T. (2006). *Schindler elevator accident*. Failure Almanac 2006. Retrieved October 29, 2012 from http://www.shippai.org/eshippai/html/index.php?name=nenkan2006_04_SchindlerE

Negishi, M. (2006, June 13). Schindler executive apologizes after fatal accident. *The Japan Times Online*. Retrieved October 28, 2012, from http://www.japantimes.co.jp/text/nn20060613a2.html

Orey, M. (May 21, 2006). Trouble at Toyota. *Bloomberg Businessweek Magazine*. Retrieved July 15, 2014 from http://www.businessweek.com/stories/2006-05-21/trouble-at-toyota

Otake, T. (2009, March 8). When scandal strikes a firm. *The Japan Times Online*. Retrieved October 30, 2012 from http://www.japantimes.co.jp/text/fl20090308x1.html

Paumgarten, N. (2008, April 21). Up and then down—The lives of elevators. *The New Yorker*. Retrieved July 9, 2014 from http://www.newyorker.com/reporting/2008/04/21/080421fa_fact_paumgarten?currentPage=all

Schindler. (2006, June 8). Fatal accident in Tokyo, Japan. Retrieved on November 1, 2012 from http://www.schindler.com/com/internet/en/media/press-releases-english/press-releases-2006-2000/fatal-accident-in-tokyo-japan.html

Schindler. (2012, October 31). Fatal accident in Japan. Retrieved on November 4, 2012 from http://www.schindler.com/com/internet/en/media/press-releases-english/2012/fatal-accident-in-japan.html

Schindler. (2013). Group Review 2013. Retrieved July 7, 2014 from http://www.schindler.com/content/dam/web/com/pdfs/reports-factsheets/2013/Schindler2013AR_Group_Review_EN.pdf

Schindler. (2014). Fact sheet: Schindler Group in Brief. Retrieved on July 7, 2014 from http://www.schindler.com/content/com/internet/en/investor-relations/reports/_jcr_content/rightPar/downloadlist_9f3b/downloadList/59_1345709659270.download.asset.59_1345709659270/Schindler_IR_factsheet2014.pdf

Schindler. Our history. Retrieved October 31, 2012, from http://www.schindler.jp/jpn_en/jpn-index/jpn-kg-entry/jpn-kg-his.htm

Shelley, R., & Makiuchi, R. (1992). *Culture shock! Japan (Culture shock! A survival guide to customs and etiquette)*. Portland: Graphic Arts Center Publishing Company.

Shimizu, K. (2006, June 15). Schindler lists six other elevator malfunctions. *The Japan Times Online*. Retrieved October 22, 2012 from http://www.japantimes.co.jp/text/nn20061215a9.html

Suzuki, H. (2006, June 7). Japan orders nationwide inspection of Schindler-made elevators. *Bloomberg*. Retrieved October 27, 2012 from http://www.bloomberg.com/apps/news?pid=newsarchive&sid=aUqWlBoNlFu4&refer=japan

The Japan Times Online. (2006, June 14). Schindler apologizes to Minato Ward. Retrieved on October 28, 2012 from http://www.japantimes.co.jp/text/nn20060614b3.html

Tucker, S., & Soble, J. (2009, February 2). Schindler says sales hurt by 'witch hunt'. *The Financial Times*. Retrieved October 30, 2012 from http://www.ft.com/cms/s/0/1c487604-f150-11dd-8790-0000779fd2ac.html#axzz2Al8U3Ylb

Weinstein, B. (2011). *Ethical intelligence*. Novato: New World Library.

Weinstein, B. (2013, January 29). The right and wrong ways to apologize. Retrieved July 10, 2014, from http://theethicsguy.com/2013/01/29/the-right-and-wrong-ways-to-apologize/

Williams, Y. (2014). Culture shock: Definition, stages & examples. Retrieved July 12, 2014 from, http://education-portal.com/academy/lesson/culture-shock-definition-stages-examples.html

Zimmer, B. (2010, September 3). The meaning of 'Man Up'. *The New York Times*. Retrieved July 11, 2014, from http://www.nytimes.com/2010/09/05/magazine/05FOB-onlanguage-t.html

Chapter 16
The Social Environment: Ethics and Information Technology

> *"Ongoing changes in information technology require new forms of loyalty."* (Stephan Rothlin, *Eighteen Rules for Becoming a Top Notch Player*, 2004)

16.1 Prelude

Clearly, the social environment is rapidly changing, not only in Asia but also throughout the world. The digital revolution in technology has raised new questions about the moral limits to information gathering, specifically, whether human dignity entails a right to privacy that businesses, no less than governments and other international organizations, must respect. The case study that opens our discussion of these questions concerns the allegations of phone hacking routinely practiced by the Murdoch media group in order to obtain news stories in the UK. The technology is currently available to go well beyond what the Murdoch group allegedly did, but the story does dramatize the question of the moral limits to the use of information technology, including social media, in a digital age. In considering this question, the chapter will seek to clarify the purpose(s) for which information is gathered and whether any alleged right to privacy establishes or ought to establish credible limits to such practices. If a firm—or an agency, governmental or NGO—is accused of violating personal privacy, what should be done about it? Should such companies be subject to criminal prosecution? Should the management of information technology firms or departments within firms develop policy guidelines for such activities? If so, how can the firms conduct their legitimate information gathering activities while also respecting the privacy of the persons who are the focus of their investigations?

S. Rothlin, D. McCann, *International Business Ethics*,
DOI 10.1007/978-3-662-47434-1_16

16.2 Case Study: End of the World—Phone-Hacking Scandal Shuts Down Murdoch's *News of the World* After 168 Years

16.2.1 Abstract

Prince "William pulled a tendon in his knee after last week's kids' kickabout," read a small 2005 article in the British tabloid *News of the World* (Friedman 2011). This relatively mundane report landed its author and others in jail; led to the editor's resignation and a shake-up of senior management; caused the shutdown of the top selling 168-year-old paper; subjected its parent company to a litany of lawsuits, parliamentary probing, and significant expenses associated with internal investigations; and tarnished the reputations of a media mogul, a British Prime Minister, and arguably the entire newspaper industry (Owles et al. 2011).

Why did such a simple story wreak so much havoc? Once investigations were launched, they revealed that the intrusions into the Royal Family's privacy were trivial in comparison with the way tabloids like *News of the World* were hacking the telephones of ordinary people—and not just celebrities—who had been the victims of crimes and other personal catastrophes. The most egregious of these cases involved Milly Dowler, a murdered teenager who went missing in 2002 (Davies and Hill 2011). Once the hacking of her personal voice mail by an investigator hired by *News of the World* was discovered—confirming how widespread the practice actually was and dramatizing the serious harm done to the Dowler family as they struggled with the loss of their daughter—the scandal became synonymous with some of the UK's most pressing ethical concerns, namely, invasion of privacy, the misuse of technology, the corruption of big business, the manipulation of social media, and the problems of poor leadership in both business and government. The *News of the World* scandal affords readers a chance to explore how international business ethics approaches such issues and the prospects for creating company policies consistent with high standards of ethical responsibility, especially in the use of technology, treatment of privacy interests, oversight and whistle-blowing, leadership development, and decision-making.

16.2.2 Keywords

Phone hacking, Workplace surveillance, Right of privacy, Tabloid journalism, Corporate espionage, Political influence, Cover-up

16.2.3 A Good Story Goes Bad and a Bad Story Gets Worse

In 2005, Clive Goodman reported regularly on the Royal Family for the UK tabloid *News of the World*, one of numerous newspapers owned by News Corp, a mass-media multinational consistently ranked among Fortune 500's largest US companies (Fortune 2012). By 2011, the phone hacking behind some of Goodman's stories resulted in his incarceration, the closing of *News of the World*, and triggering significant scrutiny of News Corp and some of its executives by different governmental bodies (the US Congress and the British Parliament) and regulatory agencies (the FBI, Australian Federal Police, and UK Police) (Owles et al. 2011).

A single incident of phone hacking by one overzealous reporter trying to make a professional splash with a big story on the Royals,[1] as wrong and illegal as it is, would probably result in the quiet dismissal of the employee and some form of company communication reminding people about acceptable and unacceptable methods of investigative reporting. It was, however, much more than a single incident since as many as 4,000 different people had their phones hacked at one time or another (Bergstrom n.d.). When the Leveson Report, "An Inquiry into the Culture, Practices and Ethics of the Press" (2012), was finished, it highlighted the distress and genuine suffering inflicted on the families of crime victims like the Dowlers, who—over and above the false hope that their daughter might still be alive,[2] based on some unexplained changes in her voice mail recordings after she had gone missing—were hounded by photographers and reporters seeking to sensationalize and profit from their tragedy. The British press, for the most part, was indifferent to the harms done by such practices. According to Justice Leveson, "the family came to be treated as little more than a commodity in which the press had an unrestricted interest" (Leveson 2012, Vol 2: 540).

While the culprit who hacked into Milly Dowler's voice mail was identified as Glenn Mulcaire, a private investigator employed full time by *News of the World*, it is clear that he was but one player on a team that used phone hacking and other

[1] Ironically, the stories that led to Goodman's demise—one about Prince William tweaking his knee playing soccer followed soon after by another about him borrowing some "broadcasting equipment from journalist friend Tom Bradby" (Newsmax 2011)—were anything but splashy, until Goodman himself became the story and made quite a splash indeed.

[2] The original story that reported the allegation that News Corps' private investigator had deliberately erased voice mail messages in Milly Dowler's telephone account, thus creating the "false hope" that she was still alive, in order to maintain reader interest, was later proved to be wrong, and a retraction was published by *The Guardian* (The Guardian 2011). In the case study on Milly Dowler's disappearance, featured in the Leveson Report, the allegation was not only refuted, but a meticulous and convincing explanation of what actually happened to Dowler's voice mail account was offered. Justice Leveson, however, wisely observed that, in spite of the *News of the World*'s exoneration on this one point, it did not absolve them for their "egregious" pattern of "unethical journalistic conduct" (Leveson 2012, Vol. 2: 539).

covert surveillance techniques on a routine basis to develop their sensational stories. Clive Goodman, once convicted for his role in violating Prince William's privacy later admitted "that all of the stories he wrote over his final two years at *News of the World* were based on phone hacking" (Rayner and Hughes 2012). Subsequent inquiry identified other phone-hacking journalists, who bribed police officers and paid private investigators assisting their efforts, along with company managers (even senior executives) who did nothing despite their awareness of the practice (Owles et al. 2011).

The phone hacking was also used to get much more than little tidbits about the Prince's less noteworthy endeavors like a doctor's appointment to check on his sore knee or some inane celebrity gossip. In fact, it apparently involved a coordinated effort to uncover sensitive information about various public figures, politicians, and police in order to influence the political and social landscape (Owles et al. 2011). Such objectives might sound a bit ambitious for a Sunday-only tabloid, but this tabloid was *News of the World,* which at one time was the "best selling English language newspaper in the world with circulation still close to 3,000,000 per week in 2010" (Robinson 2011).

And finally, it was not just the tabloid *News of the World*, but its parent News International and their holding company, News Corp, the world's largest mass-media conglomerate with over 300 assets spread across the English-speaking world, consisting in televisions stations, broadcasting companies, satellite and cable channels, magazine and book publishers, movie studios, radio stations, sports teams, and, of course, telephone and newspaper operations with an estimated value of US$62 billion (Fortune 2012). The breadth, diversity, positioning, and prestige of News Corp's media holdings and the strong political ties and great wealth of its chairperson, Rupert Murdoch, endowed it with a level of power and persuasion over political preferences and public opinion that left many uncomfortable even before the phone-hacking scandal surfaced. The subsequent exposure of the extent and purpose of the practice, perpetrated at a time when society was especially suspicious of bad and collusive behavior by big business—as in, for example, controversies over the bank bailouts and economic crises in the USA and Europe—and of various excesses alleged against the much-maligned mass media, combined to create a perfect storm of moral outrage that continues to suck public figures and politicians into its vortex.

So the question is not so much did Clive Goodman and other reporters do something wrong or unethical by hacking certain phones to get newspaper scoops, but rather who else is responsible and to what degree? Who are the policy makers and other moral agents within *News of the World* and News Corp? What should they have done or should learn to do in the future? What about the other reporters who never confronted their peers or blew the whistle? Or does the fact that "everyone does it" provide a valid excuse since the practice was rampant at many papers in the industry (Chandrasekhar et al. 2012)? What is one to make of various editors who kept their heads in the sand, ignored the whispers, or even encouraged the practice by providing money to pay investigators and pay off police (Bergstrom n.d.)? What about the managers who had no policy in place, or did not enforce it, or even facilitated its violation? Or the executives who failed to intervene, then allegedly lied about their awareness, or even tried to cover up its occurrence?[3] Do you agree with Rupert Murdoch, the CEO of News Corp, that it was not his responsibility to prevent such practices, but that of the staff at *News of the World*? What about crisis management? How would you have advised Rebekah Brooks, Rupert Murdoch, and business leaders in general to deal with serious problems when they go public? And more importantly, what policies or practices would you implement in any business to avoid such a misuse of technology from ever happening again?

16.2.4 "Dark Arts" or "Good Magic"? Business Uses of Technology

The magical potential of technology often gives way to the "dark arts," a euphemism—derived from the Harry Potter novels—for the nefarious ways that private investigators work with media companies to access confidential information for stories (Stauffer 2012). Yet, many businesses do in fact authorize supervisors to listen to employee's phone calls and voice mail, to read their email and text messages, to monitor their activity on various social networks, to keep track of their key strokes and Internet usage, to videotape various parts of an office, and even to pinpoint their whereabouts via GPS (Rosenblat et al. 2014). The use of technology in this fashion, employers explain, promotes efficiency, improves safety, discourages improper behavior, and serves as an assessment or teaching tool. For example, employees will be less likely to steal from the office—whether tangible supplies or intangible files—if they realize that it can be traced back to them so easily. Employee monitoring arguably increases production and performance by inhibiting people from wasting time playing video games, surfing the Internet, or attending to social networks. Businesses similarly utilize technology in their dealings with customers and suppliers under the auspices of improving consumer service, market awareness, and dispute resolution. Background checks also investigate everything from credit reports, medical records, social activities to *Facebook* pages, drug tests, and resume review. In fact, Patricia Dunn, the Chairperson of Hewlett Packard, deployed some of these methods upon her own Board of Directors in order to determine who was revealing confidential information (Kaplan 2006).

[3] Here is a short list of people who declared ignorance or that it was only one "rogue" reporter only to have those statements refuted: (1) *News of the World* editor Andy Coulson who resigns; (2) Rebekah Brooks, former editor of *News of the World* and its sister paper *The Sun*, later named chief executive of News International, News Corp's British arm, and then arrested with her husband for conspiracy; (3) the *News of the World* itself; (4) Les Hinton, chief executive of Dow Jones and former executive chairman of Murdoch's newspaper arm in Britain, tells a committee of legislators any problem with phone hacking was limited to the one, already well-publicized, case. He says they carried out a wide review and found no new evidence (Chandrasekhar et al. 2012); (5) James Murdoch (who later admits to paying hush money to Gordon Taylor, one of the victims of the hacks) (Chandrasekhar et al. 2012); and (6) even Piers Morgan (Owles et al. 2011).

Employees and customers counter that it is an invasion of privacy and thus inappropriate, unethical, and even illegal. This violation of one's presumptive right to privacy may also impair the relationship businesses have or hope to have with their stakeholders and the corresponding loyalty, which may in turn lead to the exact behaviors the company was hoping to prevent (theft, minimum production, and inefficiency) because of the adversarial culture it creates (Spitzmüller and Stanton 2006). Business is the driving force behind the creation and use of technology, so it must also work to be the guiding influence on its proper use and deterrent to its improper uses.

The phone-hacking scandal provides a great paradigm for many moral dilemmas in that a questionable choice often offers an immediate payoff (made even quicker with technology), while often carrying serious risks long term. Delayed gratification is considered a sign of moral maturity, while lack of impulse control signals the opposite. *News of the World* employed technology in a manner that helped to make it a very successful journalistic enterprise for many years, financially, politically, and in overall reputation. But they may have miscalculated the severe consequences their actions would entail. Financially, *News of the World* and/or News International has paid out millions to settle cases (even to the perpetrators Goodman and Mulcaire) with still more to come. Murdoch himself admits that "the corporate cleanup of the scandal had cost News Corp hundreds of millions of dollars" (*The Associated Press* 2012), not including the time and energy devoted to public hearings and the like that have nothing to do with running a newspaper. The scandal essentially sabotaged News Corp's previously approved bid to gain control over the UK's Sky Broadcasting (poetic justice, since Brooks was heavily involved in lobbying the government in order to get it approved in the first place). When *News of the World* was shut down on July 19, 2011, after 168 years, and News Corp replaced it with a new Sunday version of *The Sun* (one of its many other papers that was previously offered only five days a week), its sales did not match *News of the World* (Greene and Rivers 2012).[4] Even though the *Sun on Sunday* may recoup some of the lost revenue over time, the damage to News Corp's reputation will take even longer to rebuild.

"Should our company use this technology?" is a question confronting companies every day and will continue to do so for as long as technological advances continue to be made. Instead of asking "whether," the more important question might be "how" to use it, since most companies already do use technology for various forms of monitoring and the trend is likely to increase (Rosenblat et al. 2014). How does monitoring employees differ from the phone hacking? Are there differences between the two that would legitimize the one, while drawing the line against the other? What exactly is the right to privacy and how extensive is it? When does it apply and when is it legitimately restricted? Do privacy expectations and levels of protection vary for different people, under different circumstances, in different countries?

---

[4] In another display of his defiant bravado, Rupert Murdoch tweets that the edition sold 3.26 million copies (*The Associated Press* 2012).

16.2.5 Murdoch's Mass-Media Monster

As a business behemoth, ranked 91st on the *Fortune 500* list of largest US companies for 2012 (and 98th in 2005), with 2012 revenues of US$33 billion from operations in many countries (Fortune 2012), News Corp naturally exercises global economic and societal influence. Soon after gaining control of some media companies in the early 1970s, Rupert Murdoch, the CEO of News Corp, "unabashedly" used "his London Papers... to advance a generally conservative, pro-business line" and those political figures who would promote them, such as Margaret Thatcher and Tony Blair (Owles et al. 2011). Former British Prime Minister John Major later testified that "Murdoch tried to influence his government's dealings with the European Union, even hinting that Major could lose the support of Murdoch's newspapers if he didn't change direction" (*The Associated Press* 2012). Rebekah Brooks of News International "acknowledged that she used her access...to the country's most powerful political leaders...to lobby the British government over the BSkyB takeover deal" (*The Associated Press* 2012).

This power, potential or realized, is one reason the FBI, UK Police, the US Congress, and British Parliament all investigated the phone-hacking scandal. Even Scotland Yard fell under suspicion as it was found to have mishandled, delayed, and limited the investigation because it was compromised by their relationship with News Corp (and discovered that their own phones had been hacked by *News of the World* reporters) (Owles et al. 2011). The list of casualties from the inquiry provides further evidence of the extent of News Corp's influence in UK politics:

- Sir Paul Stephenson (Commissioner of Scotland Yard) and John Yates (Commissioner of London's Metropolitan Police) resigned amid allegations of mishandling the investigation, although both were cleared of any wrongdoing (Owles et al. 2011).
- David Cameron (Britain's Prime Minister supported by News Corp's various papers) was called to resign for his poor handling of the investigation and for appointing Mr. Andy Coulson as Director of Communications in his administration, since he was the editor of *News of the World* during the scandal (Owles et al. 2011).
- Culture Secretary Jeremy Hunt withstood calls for his resignation for how he handled News Corp's bid for BSkyB (Chandrasekhar et al. 2012).

News Corp's size and success may be enviable from a business perspective. But can a business be too big and too powerful? Many nations have laws against monopolies, but most excuse companies that achieve market dominance—like Microsoft with its Windows operating system and Apple with their iPad tablets—as long as they do not abuse their position to take undue advantage of competitors and customers, and undermine the market itself. What is your perspective on big business and big media? Compare and contrast how the phone-hacking scandal might be addressed under different systems, say the free-market system of Britain and the controlled capitalism of China?

What is your perspective on tabloid journalism? Does it qualify as a product offering anything of value; does it measure up to society's expectations of ethical responsibility? Or does it raise questions similar to some forms of advertising about the actual value it delivers? Or to stretch the analogy, are tabloids selling us something like cigarettes, alcohol, or junk food—potentially harmful products whose redeeming qualities beyond profit and jobs are questioned by many? To be sure, even if the tabloids are no different than companies providing these other questionable products, should they be prevented from doing so, especially when there is clearly a demand for what they have to offer?

16.2.6 Summary

Over and above the short-term losses incurred by the individuals and institutions caught up in the UK's phone-hacking scandal, we must consider carefully the strong public reaction against the reckless and illegal invasions of privacy suffered by citizens from all walks of life, but especially the victims of crimes and catastrophe, like Milly Dowler's family. As the Leveson Report mordantly observed, "the family came to be treated as little more than a commodity in which the press had an unrestricted interest." The violation of another's human dignity is always a cause for concern, but when all-powerful media empires willfully exploit the anguish and grief of ordinary people in their most vulnerable moments, the offense seems particularly heinous. Compared to the violation endured by the Dowlers and other victims,[5] the enormity of the corporate losses that piled up as the scandal wore on may seem rather small and their calculation small minded. Nevertheless, if the prospect of such losses can actually succeed in awakening the consciences of newspaper editors as well as the leadership and management of news organizations big and small, to their ethical responsibilities, then a full reckoning may yet serve a useful purpose.

This misuse of technology provides a backdrop for exploring the various ways technology circumvents personal privacy in commercial settings—the monitoring of employees and consumers being but one example. Thus, the *News of the World's* demise provides managers, lawmakers, ethicists, and students an opportunity to

[5] The Leveson Report provides an illuminating analysis of three "case studies" in which ordinary citizens were victimized by the tabloids, their investigators, and reporters. In addition to the Milly Dowler case, which we have mentioned here, there is also the case of the press' treatment of the McCann family subsequent to the apparent kidnapping of their daughter, Madeline, during the family's vacation in Portugal and other incidents. Here is Justice Leveson's comment: "In this Chapter, before proceeding to examine the evidence as a whole, I examine in detail a number of individual examples of press reporting in recent years. Some of those examples will be well known to many reading this report and include the reporting of the disappearance of Amanda (Milly) Dowler, the disappearance of Madeleine McCann, the arrest of Christopher Jefferies on suspicion of murder and the publication of details of the medical condition of the former Prime Minister, the Rt Hon Gordon Brown's son. The first three of those, at least, were chosen because they exemplified what might be described as the most egregious cases of unethical journalistic conduct" (Leveson 2012, Vol. 2: 539).

weigh proposed business policies that address the use of technology, the treatment of privacy concerns, and the related questions of government oversight. What are some long-term policies and procedures that you might propose in order to address such challenges in the future? As you imagine yourself in the shoes of managers confronted with the ethical issues involved in various surveillance technologies, consider your available resources and eliminate any questionable or sleazy strategies for evading the reckoning that must be made. Once you've thought through your own ideas on the responsible use of surveillance technology in business, you may want to develop a strategic plan delineating stages of implementation. Once you've done that, you can always apply for a job at News Corp. No doubt you will do a better job than your predecessors.

16.3 Case Study Discussion

The News Corp phone-hacking scandal exposed the predatory side of the business of mass communications. It is hard to imagine how anyone could morally justify invading people's lives simply in order to create newspaper stories that would promote increases in sales and profits. This case study raises issues in the world of digital technology that are parallel to those we discussed in the "Sanlu: Tainted Infant Formula Case" presented in Chapter Three. In both cases, the harm was deliberate, even if not directly intended. Sanlu's subcontractors who mixed melamine into their dairy production were only trying to maximize profits by adding an ingredient that would increase the milk's protein content and thus its market value. They probably did not directly intend to harm the babies who consumed the melamine-laced infant formula.

Similarly, the investigative reporters at News Corp who caused the phone hacking were only trying to maintain the competitiveness of their tabloid, *News of the World*. Their advancement depended on getting scoops, that is, stories that people would enjoy reading, stories that would sell newspapers, particularly on street corners. The best scoops were juicy bits of scandal involving the rich and famous—like members of the Royal Family—or inside details on various calamities that are the stuff that urban legends are made of. But getting such scoops had become increasingly difficult, especially when targeting the rich and famous, who were spending considerable sums trying to maintain their privacy. Phone hacking was a way of breaching their defenses and getting the stories they wanted, apparently without all the risks involved in conventional methods of spying. So what if their subjects' privacy was violated? If you are a public figure, your private life is fair game, or so they thought.

Those engaged in phone hacking, however, failed to consider society's predictable reaction when confronted with evidence that the basic human dignity of individuals—especially vulnerable and defenseless ordinary people like themselves—had been violated. The public's strong reaction may be an attempt to heal the wounds inflicted, since without some such reckoning a morally obtuse culture of disrespect may remain unchallenged. The moral outrage triggered by the phone-hacking scandal largely depended on who was doing it to whom and why. The *News of the World* was seen as crossing the line between spreading the embarrassments and peccadilloes of the Royal Family and other celebrities and preying upon innocent victims who needed their privacy respected especially in moments of grief and anguish. A private business, in other words, had gone rogue in an area where even legitimate acts of covert surveillance on the part of the government are heavily regulated. In the UK, for example, there is the Regulation of Investigatory Powers Act 2000 that, in theory, permitted government surveillance as "lawful interception" undertaken by duly authorized public bodies typically "on the grounds of national security, for the purpose of preventing or detecting serious crime and for the purpose of safeguarding the economic well-being of the United Kingdom" (*The Guardian* 2009). Since "lawful interception" is exceptional, it requires specific warrant from the relevant authorities charged with enforcing the Act.[6] Judged in light of this standard, it is clear that the use of similar methods, like phone hacking, by a private organization for purposes of fulfilling its profit-making business plan is clearly illegal.

But is it immoral? Why should a news organization, like News Corp, be prevented from doing what various UK government agencies are permitted to do in carrying out their responsibilities? The most fundamental objection concerns society's pledge to respect the human dignity of each and every human being. No matter who is involved, if the breach of privacy violates the rights and dignity of an individual, a group, a family, or an institution, it is immoral. The social contract implied in the government's legitimate authority ordinarily demands that any apparent suspension of human rights be warranted and carefully regulated. Despite News Corp's enormous political power, it cannot be regarded as a government agency. Different rules apply to governments and businesses, at least in the area of covert surveillance.

Either there is a valid distinction between private and public institutions, and their activities, or there is not. While both private and public institutions have a history of violating the rules that ought to govern their activities, the government's failure to achieve strict compliance with the Regulation of Investigatory Powers Act 2000 in no way justifies the actions of private organizations like the News Corp that simply ignore the law in order to maximize profits. It is a matter of common sense—or at least ought to be—that "two wrongs don't make a right." Even if News Corp were a government agency, it could not justify its malfeasance by pointing out that other agencies—for example, the Metropolitan Police Service or New Scotland Yard—had been accused of similar violations.

The fact is that News Corp is a private business and thus cannot—or at least, should not—get any sympathy because of the alleged failures of government agencies. To argue that public figures are fair game makes sense only if the game is fair. Trying to scoop competing newspapers and tabloids by exposing the scandalous

[6] Note the controversy over the relatively lax oversight of legal interception in the UK and the effort to require a formal court order to warrant any such activities (http://en.wikipedia.org/wiki/Regulation_of_Investigatory_Powers_Act_2000).

behavior of the rich and famous may be a game worth playing, but it becomes unfair if the methods used to get the scoop violate society's legitimate expectations regarding privacy, human dignity, and our right to their preservation.

Still other questions may come to the fore, when considering who is fair game for investigative reporters. If public figures are assumed to be fair game, is there any limit to who is or is not a public figure? Should anyone whose name appears in a news story be considered a public figure? People may be mildly amused or disturbed by, if not indifferent to, the tabloids' revelations concerning members of the Royal Family or even the size of a former Prime Minister's bank account. But what about that same Prime Minister's infant son and his struggle for life or the whereabouts of a kidnap victim like Milly Dowler? The public at large doesn't consider everyone a public figure, and judging by the outrage provoked by the News Corp's shabby treatment of the Dowler child and her family, they do believe that a moral boundary was violated, one that was meant to safeguard respect for personal privacy.

That the News Corp's editors and managers not only didn't restrain their investigative reporters but actively encouraged them to use any means necessary to get a story that would sell newspapers suggests a failure of basic business ethics, the kind of irresponsible behavior that invites increased government regulation. There are just two different ways of looking at News Corp's failure to enforce adequate standards of media ethics. Either they didn't know what was going on or they didn't care. At trial it became clear that the *News of the World*'s editors, Andy Coulson and later Rebekah Brooks, did know what was going on and, when the facts began to emerge, actively participated in the corporate conspiracy to cover it all up. If they cared about anything, their care extended no further than their own careers and personal reputations. In the face of such corporate malpractice, even the British government, with its all-too-cozy relationship to News Corp's top management, was forced to prosecute some of those responsible and to distance itself from Rupert Murdoch's pending business deals.

Our case study, however, does not focus exclusively on the phone-hacking scandal, but places it in the context of concern over expanded capacities for all forms of corporate surveillance. The issues raised appear not only in tabloid journalism and other forms of mass communications but also in the ways that businesses monitor the activities of their employees and other stakeholders. Why move the discussion onto these broader questions? At stake in all of them is a general concern over the right to privacy and the various ways in which advances in digital technology may undermine, if not actually abolish, that right. There are important differences, however, between journalists abusing phone-hacking technologies and businesses using similar technologies to monitor employee performance. The most important of these is that employee surveillance is commonly regarded as voluntary, while various forms of wiretapping, including phone hacking, are involuntary. Employees generally are informed of their employers' use of surveillance technologies and are required to consent to them as part of their employment contract. The victims of the *News of the World*'s phone-hacking scheme neither knew about nor were they given an opportunity to consent to the surveillance. The principle of informed consent, in short, makes for a crucial moral difference between all forms of phone hacking and some forms of employee monitoring.

Even so, one may also question just how genuine is an employee's consent to the monitoring of his or her online activities. If employment is conditional, pending an agreement to such methods of surveillance, employees may feel that they have been forced to give consent, along with a series of other invasions of their personal privacy, such as submitting to urinalysis as part of the employer's random drug testing policy, or recording the websites they visit while working online, or reviewing their *Facebook* posts for any evidence of disloyalty to the firm, indulgence in irresponsible behavior, or harboring opinions that may be deemed contrary to the firm's interests. When addressing the ethical issues raised by various employee surveillance strategies, the question is rarely whether such strategies are illegal or immoral in principle, but how invasive can they be without seeming to violate the current consensus on employee privacy rights. For example, while monitoring what websites employees are visiting at work may be regarded as reasonable and appropriate, installing surveillance cameras in their locker rooms in order to deter theft of one sort or another may create more problems than it solves. In the era before high-tech surveillance equipment was generally available, similar problems were raised about how far one could go in questioning a prospective employee about her marital status or her sexual preferences. The challenge was—and is, especially in an era in which high-tech surveillance is commonplace—just how far an employer can go in monitoring the performance of his or her employees without violating their presumed right to privacy?

As we can see from the case study, such discussions tend to focus primarily on a calculation of consequences. The advent of digital technologies has lowered the cost of monitoring employees and enabled employers to become less intrusive in their monitoring activities. Nevertheless, if certain forms of surveillance turn out to be counterproductive, that is, inadvertently provoking behaviors the company was hoping to prevent (e.g., as we saw in the case study, "theft, minimum production, and inefficiency"), they are not likely to be retained, especially if there is active resistance against them. What goes on at work, then, is based less on "mutual consent amongst all parties involved" than on "a mutual understanding or complicity in acknowledging what is happening as the boundaries of what is possible stretch uncomfortably into the blurry terrain of what is permissible and what is considered a violation…. There is an unchallenged assumption that employers monitor their employees simply because they can, and that they do so more intrusively for the same reason—especially as technologies evolve to enable more and more methods of surveillance" (Rosenblat et al. 2014). Thus, if studies can show that less invasive performance monitoring systems tend to make employees more productive, more loyal, and less dissatisfied with working conditions, then by all means opt for the less invasive. It is clearly more cost-effective. Rarely, however, is the question raised whether the employees' rights and dignity should serve to define the limits on how far one can go.

The recent deployment of high-tech methods for monitoring employee performance, and our pervasive complicity in accepting them as both inevitable and necessay, may help us understand how phone hacking—at the *News of the World*, at least—became an effective tool for enhancing investigative journalism. If workers are routinely monitored by private businesses in order to enhance their performance, what's to prevent a competitive news organization from using similar technologies in the course of their routine business activities? *News of the World* might protest in its defense: "We have a newspaper to get out. In our business everything depends on timing. We have to find the stories for our readers before anyone else does. If a new technology comes along that will help us get the stories we need, we'll use it, at least until we meet significant resistance from either the government or the public at large." They might have added, "Even if people have a right to privacy, they also have a right to know what's going on in our world. It's our job to provide them with a convenient and entertaining way of doing that." We need to go deeper, then, into the right to privacy and what ethical limits, if any, it imposes on the use of surveillance technologies.

16.4 Ethical Reflection

What is privacy and what does it mean to claim a universal right to it? This is a difficult question, not only because so many different definitions have been offered but also because expectations vary greatly from one culture to another. Such questions all too often are answered with a shrug, meaning, "I'll know it when I see it." But rather than stop there, we ought to consider the link between privacy and human dignity, since the outrage provoked by the phone-hacking scandal was primarily about the violation of human dignity.

16.4.1 Privacy: A Human Right Inherent in Human Dignity

As we have seen in previous chapters, the United Nations' *Universal Declaration of Human Rights* (UDHR) is based on a profound commitment to human dignity and rights guaranteeing its equal protection for all. The Declaration's "Preamble" asserts that the "recognition of the inherent dignity and of the equal and inalienable rights of all members of the human family is the foundation of freedom, justice and peace in the world." Article 1 asserts "All human beings are born free and equal in dignity and rights. They are endowed with reason and conscience and should act towards one another in a spirit of brotherhood." Human dignity, then, is inherent in being human; it is no less real in ordinary people than in the members of political, economic, and social elites who command the resources to protect themselves. Article 22 declares that "everyone, as a member of society, has the right to social security and is entitled to realization, through national effort and international co-operation and in accordance with the organization and resources of each State, of the economic, social and cultural rights indispensable for his dignity and the free development of his personality." Governments exist, in other words, in order to assure that everyone's dignity is respected through the legal protection of "economic, social, and cultural rights." Article 23 explicitly links human dignity to the government's role in managing the economy so that everyone not only has a right to work but also that anyone "who works has the right to just and favorable remuneration ensuring for himself and his family an existence worthy of human dignity, and supplemented, if necessary, by other means of social protection."

Article 12 of the *Universal Declaration* (UDHR) recognizes privacy in a series of rights—usually considered civil or political rights—that governments must respect, if they are fulfilling their purpose of protecting human dignity: "No one shall be subjected to arbitrary interference with his privacy, family, home or correspondence, nor to attacks upon his honor and reputation. Everyone has the right to the protection of the law against such interference or attacks." At the same time, the *Universal Declaration* (UDHR) asserts that for every right, there is a corresponding duty that establishes the limits involved in the exercise of these rights. Article 29 declares that since "everyone has duties to the community in which alone the free and full development of his personality is possible… everyone shall be subject only to such limitations as are determined by law solely for the purpose of securing due recognition and respect for the rights and freedoms of others and of meeting the just requirements of morality, public order and the general welfare in a democratic society." The right to privacy, then, is real, but it is hardly absolute. There are situations in which the right to privacy may be qualified, suspended, or otherwise restricted, but there will never be a situation that justifies the violation of human dignity as such. At least, there will never be, so long as the UDHR remains a credible statement of humanity's moral aspirations.

16.4.2 Legal Protection for the Right to Privacy

While human dignity itself may not easily be reduced to a single concept, universally recognized by all moral and spiritual traditions, it remains the only adequate foundation for understanding the right to privacy and its legitimate restrictions. Even in the USA, specific reference to a right to privacy in legal discourse goes back no further than the groundbreaking *Harvard Law Review* article by Louis Brandeis—who later served as an Associate Justice of the US Supreme Court (1916–1939)—and Samuel Warren, "The Right to Privacy" (Brandeis and Warren 1890). Brandeis and Warren argued that the right to privacy was implicit in various aspects of the common law tradition and well described as a "right to be left alone." What apparently prompted their reflections was the proliferation of cases in which an unregulated newspaper industry, and other technological advances such as the invention of photography, had done egregious harm to various individuals, whose remedies were unclear from existing tort laws safeguarding property rights. Brandeis and Warren argued that the right to privacy—which they regarded as but a logical extension of the maxim enshrined in the common law "An Englishman's home is his castle"—was "a part of the more general right to the immunity of the person, the right to one's personality." Transcending the narrow scope of property rights, it expresses a concern to honor each individual's "right to an inviolate personality," which alone can afford a suitably broad basis for certain legal protections against unwarranted personal interference, harassment, invasion, or surveillance.

More than a century after Brandeis and Warren's groundbreaking article, despite nearly universal recognition of the value of privacy, it remains a topic for philosophical and legal debate. In 2013, Judith DeCew summarized the results of these discussions, particularly reflecting concerns emergent in the USA, in the *Stanford Encyclopedia of Philosophy*'s article on "Privacy" (DeCew 2013). In her summary, she cites William Prosser's attempt to define "four different interests in privacy" evident in legal cases up until 1960. Each of these had claimed specific concern as a violation of the right to privacy:

- Intrusion upon a person's seclusion or solitude or into his private affairs
- Public disclosure of embarrassing private facts about an individual
- Publicity placing one in a false light in the public eye
- Appropriation of one's likeness for the advantage of another (Prosser 1960, 389)

According to DeCew, the philosophical debates concerned whether these four areas validate a single, distinctive claim to a right to privacy—as Brandeis and Warren had argued—or were better understood under a variety of other categories, for example, the violation of property rights or other torts. The lingering controversy over the nature of privacy rights, however, apparently also has practical consequences. DeCew argues that typically the USA and various Asian nations have "developed a limited system of privacy protection that focuses on self-regulation within industry and government so that personal information is often readily available," whereas by contrast, "the European Union (EU) and others have adopted an alternative vision highlighting consumer protection and individual privacy against the economic interests of firms and public officials," as is evident from the EU's development of its "comprehensive rules about data privacy enacted in the EU's Data Protection Directive in 1995":

> The US has generally stood behind efficiency arguments that business and government need unfettered access to personal data to guarantee economic growth and national security, whereas the EU has sent a coherent signal that privacy has critical value in a robust information society because citizens will only participate in an online environment if they feel their privacy is guaranteed against ubiquitous business and government surveillance. (DeCew 2013)

The lack of consensus in the USA regarding a single definition of the right to privacy, in short, seems to have reinforced a *laissez-faire* attitude that is reluctant to intervene particularly against businesses using surveillance technologies to advance their commercial interests.

Nevertheless, Brandeis and Warren's original formulation of a right to privacy based on "inviolate personality" is defended by philosophers—like ourselves—who appeal to a substantive notion of human dignity. As DeCew points out, "it is possible to give a general theory of individual privacy" understood as an expression of "one's essence as a human being and it includes individual dignity and integrity, personal autonomy and independence. Respect for these values is what grounds and unifies the concept of privacy." Indeed, we would argue that these values taken together are synonymous with human dignity, without which the right to privacy may remain vague and easily ignored. As Edward J. Bloustein contends, the "common conceptual thread linking diverse privacy cases prohibiting dissemination of confidential information, eavesdropping, surveillance, and wiretapping, to name a few, is the value of protection against injury to individual freedom and human dignity. Invasion of privacy is best understood, in sum, as affront to human dignity" (Bloustein 1964).

Given the fact that the "one's essence as a human being" is social as well as personal, it is no surprise that privacy is valued for its role in helping to "regulate social relationships such as intimate relations, family relationships, professional relationships including those between a physician and a patient, a lawyer or accountant and a client, a teacher and a student, and so on." Priscilla Regan, for example, emphasizes the social character of privacy and its indispensable role in helping to create and sustain a democracy:

> Privacy is a *common value* in that all individuals value some degree of privacy and have some common perceptions about privacy. Privacy is also a *public value* in that it has value not just to the individual as an individual or to all individuals in common but also to the democratic political system. Privacy is rapidly becoming a *collective value* in that technology and market forces are making it hard for any one person to have privacy without all persons having a similar minimum level of privacy. (Regan 1995, 213)

Privacy, then, in DeCew's words, has both "intrinsic and extrinsic value to individuals but also has instrumental value to society," insofar as "it heightens respect for individual autonomy in decision-making for self-development and individual integrity and human dignity, but also enhances the value of privacy in various social roles and relationships that contribute to a functioning society" (DeCew 2013).

Though privacy is highly valued, it is neither absolute nor fundamental, in the same way that respect for human dignity is and ought to be respected. If there is a right to privacy, it must be balanced by a concern to honor all other valid rights claims. Brandeis and Warren concluded their discussion of the right to privacy by citing four situations that must limit its enforcement, consisting chiefly in cases where the matter is genuinely "of public or general interest," such as testimony given in a court of law or other public assemblies. Furthermore, the law may ignore claims that one's privacy has been violated, when the matter involves "oral publication in the absence of special damage." There is a difference between gossip repeated by neighbors conversing over the back fence and gossip published in a mass circulation tabloid like *News of the World*. Finally, the right to privacy cannot be invoked after an individual has already consented to publication, as in the case when someone sells his or her story to the news media or agrees to tell it all before a television audience. In addition, Brandeis and Warren rule out two considerations often used to excuse or justify violations of the right to privacy: the truth of the matter disclosed is irrelevant, as is the absence of "malice" or "personal ill-will" on the part of the one who violated the privacy of another:

> The invasion of the privacy that is to be protected is equally complete and equally injurious, whether the motives by which the speaker or writer was actuated are taken by themselves, culpable or not; just as the damage to character, and to some extent the tendency to provoke a breach of the peace, is equally the result of defamation without regard to motives leading to its publication. (Brandeis and Warren 1890)

Since Brandeis and Warren focused on the "the invasion of privacy brought about by public dissemination of details relating to a person's private life," they are rightly regarded as laying "the foundation for a concept of privacy that has come to be known as control over information about oneself" (DeCew 2013). While the concept proposed by Brandeis and Warren is central to the moral argument and legal case against the phone-hacking scheme organized by News Corp, the other issues identified by Prosser are clearly related to their seminal insight, but take us beyond the scope of our case study and its discussion.[7]

16.4.3 Privacy in Hong Kong and the People's Republic of China

This review of the ethical presuppositions operative in asserting a right to privacy in law and morality should alert us to a broader question regarding its cultural relativity. Even in the USA, the right to privacy is not specifically mentioned in the Bill of Rights to the Constitution, but emerges in the words of Justice William O. Douglas in the Griswold v. Connecticut case, as a "'penumbral' right 'emanating' from the Constitution" (DeCew 2013). As we have seen, the right to privacy in the USA has evolved and continues to be controversial. But what of other venues? DeCew pointed out that the right is more protected in the EU than in either the USA or

---

[7] The role of the right to privacy in the decisions of the US Supreme Court regarding the legality of abortion, as in Roe v. Wade (1973), very much concerns the social dimension of the right to privacy identified by Priscilla Regan and others. The legality, under certain circumstances, of abortion in the USA depends on whether and at what point in a pregnancy the State has a right and duty to breach the presumed privacy that protects the interactions between a pregnant woman and her physician. Since the State, according to Roe v. Wade, has no compelling interest in breaching their privacy during the first trimester, abortion along with any other therapeutic interventions is legal during that time. But as the pregnancy develops, as the fetus becomes viable, the State not only has an interest but an affirmative duty to protect the life of the unborn child, a duty to intervene that, because it is in the public interest, overrides any concern for the privacy of the doctor-patient relationship. Whatever the strengths and weaknesses of the Roe v. Wade decision, it clearly illustrates the fact that a right to privacy is not and cannot be regarded as absolute either legally or morally.

various Asian venues. What, then, is the status of the right to privacy in China and the societies in which Chinese civilization has had a major formative influence? Let us begin with Hong Kong. How is the right to privacy regarded in Hong Kong, particularly after the territory's reintegration into the People's Republic of China, under the administration of the Basic Law of the HKSAR?

People who assume that there is no basis for valuing privacy in Chinese culture generally appeal to its etymology. "Privacy" in Chinese is *yǐn sī* (隐私), which sounds like an older word designating a "shameful secret." *Yǐn sī*, then, signifies privacy in the sense of an unwillingness to disclose matters preferably kept from public view. At the same time, however, it casts a suspicion on such a desire, as if shame were the only reason for keeping some things a secret. The word apparently also carries the suspicion that shameful doings involve illicit sex, of one form or another. This cluster of assumptions is nicely explored in Peter Wang's film, "A Great Wall" (1986), depicting a Chinese family reunion, in which the brother who had immigrated to the USA returns with his family to his sister's home in Beijing, where they all must contend with the mutual affection but also with the alienation and cultural misunderstandings that long absences may bring. In one scene, the wives are discussing their teenage children and how to bring them up properly when Mrs. Chao, the sister who has never left Beijing, indicates that she routinely opens her daughter's mail in order to make sure she is not involved in anything shameful. Mrs. Fang, a Chinese-American who is thoroughly comfortable with her life in San Francisco, asks, "But what about her privacy?" The conversation that follows suggests that Mrs. Chao has no clue about it, especially when it concerns her daughter's activities. Since the film is a comedy, with a charmingly light touch, learning the ins and outs of privacy is but one of a number of areas in which members of both families come to experiment with new and different ways of being themselves.

"A Great Wall," then, provides a symbol of what has actually been happening in Chinese societies. The evolution of the right to privacy in Hong Kong tends to mirror the script provided by the Fangs and the Chaos. However sacred may have been the traditional ideal of an Englishman's home being his castle, the administration of the Crown Colony of Hong Kong was remarkably obscure about any right to privacy, especially as it might relate to the activities of its Chinese subjects. Only toward the end of its tenure did the right to privacy surface in the Bill of Rights promulgated in 1991 for the citizens of Hong Kong. Article 14 asserts:

> Protection of privacy, family, home, correspondence, honour and reputation: (1) No one shall be subjected to arbitrary or unlawful interference with his privacy, family, home or correspondence, nor to unlawful attacks on his honour and reputation. (2) Everyone has the right to the protection of the law against such interference or attacks.

This Bill of Rights, of course, is meant to incorporate into Hong Kong law the *International Covenant on Civil and Political Rights,* adopted by the UN General Assembly on December 19, 1966.

While the wording of Hong Kong's right to privacy is taken directly from the International Covenant, its enactment in Hong Kong has been a matter of controversy, both before and after the colony's return to China. While the Basic Law now governing the HKSAR, in its "Chapter III: Fundamental Rights and Duties of the

Residents," contains both an acknowledgement of the right to privacy[8] and a commitment to the continued enforcement of the UN's International Covenant on Civil and Political Rights, it remains unclear how such a right is to be protected, in cases where government agencies are alleged to have breached "the freedom and privacy of communications of Hong Kong residents" in the course of their investigations. One major focus of concern has been certain alleged violations of privacy routinely committed by Hong Kong's Independent Commission Against Corruption (ICAC), which have been contested in court because of unresolved issues over procedures to be followed in cases involving evidence obtained through covert surveillance.[9]

The guarantees stipulated in the Basic Law, needless to say, are subject to judicial interpretation, consistent with the decisions of the Standing Committee of the National People's Congress (NPCSC), whose authority rests upon the Constitution of the People's Republic of China (PRC). What, then, is the status of privacy and its protection in the PRC? According to Cao Jingchun, "Chinese people, like others, need privacy. It is a concept that, though less developed, is not alien to Chinese society and culture. From shameful secrets to personal information, from arbitrary invasion of privacy to legal protection of privacy, the Chinese people and government have already done a lot in this area" (Cao 2005). Chinese law in various ways confirms the validity of Cao's observations. The Constitution of the PRC in Article 38, for example, affirms: "The personal dignity of citizens of the People's Republic of China is inviolable. Insult, libel, false charge or frame-up directed against citizens by any means is prohibited." Article 40 provides Constitutional protection for "the freedom and privacy of correspondence of citizens of the People's Republic of China":

> No organization or individual may, on any ground, infringe upon the freedom and privacy of citizens' correspondence except in cases where, to meet the needs of state security or of investigation into criminal offences, public security or procuratorial organs are permitted to censor correspondence in accordance with procedures prescribed by law. (People's Daily Online 2004)

While China's "General Principles of the Civil Law" (National People's Congress 1986) make no mention of either human dignity or privacy, they do list both a "right of portrait" (Article 100) and "right to reputation" (Article 101) that provide, in the

---

[8]Article 30 of the Basic Law guarantees the right to privacy: "The freedom and privacy of communication of Hong Kong residents shall be protected by law. No department or individual may, on any grounds, infringe upon the freedom and privacy of communication of residents except that the relevant authorities may inspect communication in accordance with legal procedures to meet the needs of public security or of investigation into criminal offences" (Basic Law, 2012). Note that Article 30 covers the activities of both governmental agencies and private organizations and individuals, and thus would be relevant, had the phone-hacking scandal erupted in Hong Kong rather than London.

[9]While the trend internationally has been toward obtaining specific warrants from the relevant court of law to authorize such activities, the HKSAR government as yet has been unable to resolve the issue, despite launching a significant public consultation on it, the results of which are ably summarized in a briefing paper, "Surveillance, Basic Law Article 30, and the Right to Privacy in Hong Kong," issued by the Hong Kong Human Rights Monitor in October 2005 (Kellogg 2005).

opinion of some observers (Ishimaru & Associates 2012), a basis for protections equivalent to the right to privacy in other countries.

Cao, for example, offers a well-informed comparison of Chinese and Western legal theories on the right to privacy, pointing out the importance of respect for human dignity in Chinese law and morality as establishing a promising common ground for further reforms. Specifically, he analyzes specific legal cases in China, as well as local legislation, which suggest the realism of developing a right to privacy in the Chinese Civil Code. There is already a basis, then, not only for guaranteeing general protection for personal privacy but also for remedies against the misuse of personal data by private companies, including their involvement in practices of covert surveillance. While the evolution of Chinese law is likely to favor broad exemptions for the government, based on its Constitutional responsibility for "national security" and related exigencies, private businesses that would engage in similar activities in order to maximize their profits may risk rigorous prosecution, under tort law, both criminal and civil. As we have seen in other areas of concern for international business ethics, despite the obvious differences between the moral and spiritual traditions of China and the West, the evolution of Chinese law continues to trend toward the recognition of universal standards regarding the value of privacy and the protections to be afforded it. The developmental challenge in this area, as well as the others we have reviewed, is primarily in the area of law enforcement (Cao 2005).

16.5 Conclusion

The value of privacy has increased, almost to the point of becoming a moral absolute, as the processes of modernization were unleashed, first in Europe and North America and later throughout the world. While the protection of privacy in China and other Asian venues may be, as Cao remarked, "at least 10 years behind that of Western countries," it is clear that China—in this area, as in so many others—is catching up fast. At a time when the advance of digital technologies in some Western countries may be rendering modern assumptions about a universal right to privacy obsolete and perhaps unworkable, responsible business leaders everywhere must learn, first of all, to respect human dignity and never underestimate its importance to the various stakeholders whose interests and rights they must balance, as they try to fulfill their own legitimate business goals. Second, they must realize that, if there is a right to privacy, it must be honored along with a host of other rights that may not always be smoothly integrated with each other. Protecting privacy is terribly important, but it is not ultimately important or absolute. Knowing how to act responsibly in this area will depend on a wise assessment of the uses and potential abuses of digital technologies, which provide business organizations with powers that only recently seemed well beyond anyone's reach.

Business leaders, no matter how powerful they become, must also learn to face the limits of that power and how easily it can collapse in the wake of major scandals and other transgressions. Business, however masterful it may become in adopting digital innovations, is still not government. Different rules apply; different excuses may be given, based on different expectations. No business, for example, is likely to get away with defending its covert surveillance tactics on the basis of "national security." It is hard to say what went wrong at News Corp, when top management turned a blind eye to phone hacking and other forms of covert surveillance targeting innocent and vulnerable people, like the Dowler family. The Leveson Report, as we have seen, offers convincing evidence that, at bottom, there is a problem with the news media's corporate culture that cries out for a serious reexamination of media ethics. Going forward, what we can learn from News Corps' failure and subsequent losses is the cost of failing to respect the limits of corporate power, even in—or especially in—a world where the ongoing revolution in digital technology may inadvertently promote the illusion of omnipotence.

References

Bergstrom, G. (n.d.). Case study: Hacking and bribery scandal destroys news of the world. *About. com.* Retrieved June 21, 2012, from http://marketing.about.com/od/case_studies_and_tips/a/Case-Study-Hacking-and-Bribery-Scandal-Destroys-The-News-of-the-World.htm

Bloustein, E. (1964). Privacy as an aspect of human dignity: An answer to Dean Prosser. *New York University Law Review, 39*, 962–1007; as cited in DeCew, J. (2013). Privacy. *The Stanford encyclopedia of philosophy*. Retrieved November 3, 2014 from http://plato.stanford.edu/entries/privacy/

Brandeis, L., & Warren, S. (1890, December 15). The right to privacy. *Harvard Law Review, 4*(5). Retrieved November 3, 2014, from http://faculty.uml.edu/sgallagher/Brandeisprivacy.htm

Cao, J. (2005). Protecting the right to privacy in China. *Victoria University of Wellington Law Review, 36*(3). Retrieved November 3, 2014, from http://www.victoria.ac.nz/law/research/publications/vuwlr/prev-issues/pdf/vol-36-2005/issue-3/jingchun.pdf

Chandrasekhar, I., Wardrop, M., & Trotman, A. (2012, July 23). Phone hacking: Timeline of the scandal. *The Telegraph*. Retrieved October 21, 2014, from http://www.telegraph.co.uk/news/uknews/phone-hacking/8634176/Phone-hacking-timeline-of-a-scandal.html

Davies, N., & Hill, A. (2011, July 5). Missing Milly Dowler's voicemail was hacked by News of the World. *The Guardian*. Retrieved November 12, 2014, from http://www.theguardian.com/uk/2011/jul/04/milly-dowler-voicemail-hacked-news-of-world

DeCew, J. (2013). Privacy. *The Stanford encyclopedia of philosophy*. Retrieved November 3, 2014, from http://plato.stanford.edu/entries/privacy/

DeGeorge, R. (2002). *Ethics of information technology and business* (1st ed.). Hoboken: Wiley-Blackwell.

Fortune Magazine. (2012, May 21). Annual ranking of America's Largest Corporations. *Fortune Magazine*. Retrieved June 22, 2012, from http://money.cnn.com/magazines/fortune/fortune500/2012/full_list/

Friedman, U. (2011, July 7). Some phone hacking scoops that doomed news of the world. *The Atlantic Wire*. Retrieved June 22, 2012, from http://www.theatlanticwire.com/global/2011/07/some-phone-hacking-scoops-doomed-news-world/3968

Greene, R., & Rivers, D. (2012, February 26). Murdoch launches paper to replace disgraced tabloid. *CNN World*. Retrieved October 22, 2014 from http://www.cnn.com/2012/02/26/world/europe/uk-murdoch-sun/

Hong Kong Human Rights Monitor. (1991). Hong Kong Bill of Rights Ordinance. Retrieved November 3, 2014, from http://www.hkhrm.org.hk/english/law/eng_boro2.html

Hong Kong Special Administrative Region (HKSAR). (1997). The basic law full text: Chapter III: Rights and duties of the residents. Retrieved on November 18, 2014 from http://www.basiclaw.gov.hk/en/basiclawtext/chapter_3.html

Ishimaru & Associates. (2012, July). Overview of China privacy rules. *July China Bulletin*. Retrieved November 20, 2014, from http://ishimarulaw.com/overview-of-china-privacy-rulesjuly-china-bulletin/

Kaplan, D. A. (2006, September 17). Suspicions and spies in Silicon Valley. *Newsweek Magazine*. Retrieved June 24, 2012, from http://www.thedailybeast.com/newsweek/2006/09/17/suspicions-and-spies-in-silicon-valley.html

Kellogg, T. (2005, October). Surveillance, Basic Law Article 30, and the Right to Privacy in Hong Kong. Hong Kong Human Rights Monitor. LC Paper No. CB(2)259/05-06(01). Retrieved November 19, 2014, from http://www.legco.gov.hk/yr05-06/english/panels/se/papers/secb2-259-1e.pdf

Koffman, J., & Smith, C. (2011, July 9). News of the World is no more. *ABC News.Com*. Retrieved June 21, 2012, from http://abcnews.go.com/International/news-world-closed-telephone-hacking-scandal/story?id=14037284

Lawrence, A. T., & Weber, J. (2010). *Business and society: Stakeholders, ethics, public policy* (13th ed.). New York: McGraw-Hill/Irwin.

Leveson, B. (2012, November). *Leveson Inquiry: Report into the culture, practices and ethics of the press. Vols. I–IV*. London: The Stationery Office. Retrieved November 3, 2014, from https://www.gov.uk/government/publications/leveson-inquiry-report-into-the-culture-practices-and-ethics-of-the-press

National People's Congress. (1986, April 12). General principles of the civil law of the People's Republic of China. Retrieved November 20, 2014 from http://www.china.org.cn/china/LegislationsForm2001-2010/2011-02/11/content_21898337.htm

Newsmax. (2011, July 8). Prince William's voice mails led to hacking scandal. *Newsmax*. Retrieved November 21, 2014 from http://www.Newsmax.com/InsideCover/Prince-William-knee-injury/2011/07/08/id/402894/#ixzz3JGoGbcNL

Owles, E., Delviscio, J., Jacquette, R. F., & Donaldson, N. (2011, November 29). Anatomy of the News International Scandal. *The New York Times*. Retrieved June 22, from http://topics.nytimes.com/top/reference/timestopics/organizations/n/news_of_the_world/index.html

People's Daily Online. (2004). The Constitution of the People's Republic of China (Updated March 22, 2004; Adopted December 2, 1982). Retrieved November 20, 2014 from http://english.people.com.cn/constitution/constitution.html

Prosser, W. (1960). Privacy. *California Law Review, 48*, 383–423; as cited in DeCew, J. (2013). Privacy. *The Stanford encyclopedia of philosophy*. Retrieved November 3, 2014 from http://plato.stanford.edu/entries/privacy/

Rayner, G., & Hughes, M. (2012, February 23). Phone hacking: News of the world bosses ordered emails to be deleted. *The Telegraph*. Retrieved on June 21, 2015 from http://www.telegraph.co.uk/news/uknews/phone-hacking/9102231/Phone-hacking-News-of-the-World-bosses-ordered-emails-to-be-deleted.html

Regan, P. (1995). *Legislating privacy*. Chapel Hill: University of North Carolina Press, p. 213; as cited in DeCew, J. (2013). Privacy. *The Stanford encyclopedia of philosophy*. Retrieved on November 3, 2014 from http://plato.stanford.edu/entries/privacy/

Robinson, J. (2011, July 11). News of the World to close as Rupert Murdoch acts to limit fallout. *The Guardian*. Retrieved June 23, 2012 from http://www.guardian.co.uk/media/2011/jul/07/news-of-the-world-rupert-murdoch

Rosenblat, A., Kneese, T., & Boyd, D. (2014, October 8). *Workplace surveillance*. Data & Society working paper prepared for: Future of Work Project supported by Open Society Foundations. Data and Society Research Institute. Retrieved `October 22, 2014 from http://www.datasociety.net/pubs/fow/WorkplaceSurveillance.pdf

Spitzmüller, C., & Stanton, J. M. (2006). Examining employee compliance with organizational surveillance and monitoring. *Journal of Occupational and Organizational Psychology, 79*(2), 245–272. Retrieved June 22, 2012 from http://onlinelibrary.wiley.com/doi/10.1348/096317905X52607/abstract.

Stauffer, Z. (2012, March 27). A private investigator explains the "Dark Arts" of Tabloid News. *Frontline.* Retrieved October 21, 2014 from http://www.pbs.org/wgbh/pages/frontline/media/murdochs-scandal/a-tabloid-pi-explains-the-dark-arts/

The Associated Press. (2012, June 28). Developments in the British Phone Hacking Scandal. *Fox News*. Retrieved October 22, 2014, from http://www.foxnews.com/us/2012/06/28/developments-in-british-phone-hacking-scandal/

The Guardian. (2009, January 19). "Regulation of Investigatory Powers Act 2000." *The Guardian*. Retrieved November 19, 2014 from http://www.theguardian.com/commentisfree/libertycentral/2009/jan/14/regulation-investigatory-powers-act

The Guardian. (2011, December 20). *Corrections and clarifications*. Retrieved on June 21, 2015 from http://www.theguardian.com/theguardian/2011/dec/20/corrections-and-clarifications

UN General Assembly. (1966, December 19). International Covenant on Civil and Political Rights. Retrieved November 19, 2014, from https://treaties.un.org/doc/Publication/UNTS/Volume%20999/volume-999-I-14668-English.pdf

Zhu, G. (1997). The right to privacy: An emerging right in Chinese law. *Statute Law Review, 18*(3), 208–214. Retrieved November 3, 2014 from http://papers.ssrn.com/sol3/papers.cfm?abstract_id=1664935

Chapter 17
The Social Environment: Philanthropy

"Care for your Business by Caring for Society"
(Stephan Rothlin, *Eighteen Rules for Becoming a Top Notch Player*, 2004)

17.1 Prelude

Should private firms be expected to engage in philanthropic activities as a normal part of their business activities? Was Milton Friedman right to recommend that philanthropy ought to be a private activity, one that is best left up to the firm's individual investors and beneficiaries? Or should philanthropy be regarded as a moral obligation incumbent upon businesses, an activity that deserves serious consideration in international business ethics? If it is a normal part of business, how should it be related to the firm's other activities? Is it just a marketing strategy that may or may not be useful in creating good will in various business environments? Is it something more—a hallmark of a good company, an indication of the firm's intention to honor high standards for corporate citizenship? How, then, does philanthropy differ from corporate social responsibility? In order to focus attention on such questions in Asian business settings, we have selected a case study devoted to the Tata Trusts, their history, underlying rationale, and purposes in relationship to the Tata family businesses that support them. Now that the Tata Group is poised to become a major player in the global marketplace, should it rethink its traditional commitment to philanthropy, or should it extend such efforts to all the venues in which one or more of its members are active? Our purpose in devoting a full chapter to philanthropy is to suggest, not only that philanthropy is different from CSR, but also that philanthropic activities can and ought to be integrated into the strategic plans of all businesses competing in the global marketplace.

S. Rothlin, D. McCann, *International Business Ethics*,
DOI 10.1007/978-3-662-47434-1_17

17.2 Case Study: Tata Group: Philanthropy with Purpose

17.2.1 Abstract

Tata Group is an Indian conglomerate that throughout its history has combined business success with a positive model of "philanthropy with a purpose." That purpose has evolved from seeking to assist India's masses in overcoming centuries of foreign domination and colonialism, to supporting various efforts in social uplift during the contemporary period of rapid economic and social development. Under the leadership of Ratan Tata, the Group has attempted to remain faithful to its legacy of familial and cultural values, while also globalizing the scope of its business activities. Crucial to that attempt are the JN Tata Endowment and related Trusts, which control 66 % of the shares in the Tata Sons holding company. These institutions embody the Tata Group's continuing commitment to philanthropy. With the appointment of Cyrus Mistry to succeed Ratan Tata upon his retirement, the Tata Group is now faced with the challenging prospect of a change in leadership. As the Group charts a new course for the future, the question is whether the Tata family's reputation for doing well while doing good, including its strong commitment to philanthropy, can be maintained in the years ahead. Is "philanthropy with a purpose" still possible, when the Group is no longer to be managed by a member of the founders' family, when its businesses are rapidly evolving to seize the opportunities afforded by globalization?

17.2.2 Keywords

Tata Group, Ratan Tata, Philanthropy, Corporate Social Responsibility (CSR), Social Investment, Communal Development.

17.2.3 The Tata Group

Tata Group is an India based multinational conglomerate made up of "over 100 operating companies in seven business sectors: communications and information technology, engineering, materials, services, energy, consumer products and chemicals." For 2013–2014, Tata companies reported total revenues of over US$103 billion, while employing over 581,000 workers on six continents (Tata Group 2014a).

In the late 1860s, founder Jamsetji Tata (1839–1904), a native of Gujarat, abandoned the family tradition of Parsee priesthood to try his hand at business. Tata wrote that he began his business career at a time in India when "passive despair engendered by colonial rule was at its peak" (Tata Group 2014b). Ultimately, this historical context would provoke his drive to found enterprises that developed

India's industrial skills. Since the most effective long-term strategy for liberating India involved creating a workforce that eventually might help manage an independent nation's affairs, Jamsetji would establish the Tata companies as a framework for tutoring Indians in three major areas: steel production, electric power generation, and scientific research.

In 1892, the JN Tata Endowment was created in order to support higher education for young Indians and with it began the Tata Group's first philanthropic initiative. Jamsetji Tata explained his vision of philanthropy: "There is one kind of charity common enough among us… It is that patchwork philanthropy which clothes the ragged, feeds the poor, and heals the sick. I am far from decrying the noble spirit, which seeks to help a poor or suffering fellow being… [However] what advances a nation or a community is not so much to prop up its weakest and most helpless members, but to lift up the best and the most gifted, so as to make them of the greatest service to the country" (Tata Group 2014c). Later on, JRD Tata (1904–1993), who served as Chairman of Tata Sons (1938–1991), adopted and adapted Mahatma Gandhi's idea of "trusteeship" in order to institutionalize the relationship between the Tata philanthropies and the Tata Group of businesses (Sarukkai 2012). For the past century, Tata Sons has adhered to this philanthropic model with the aim of enabling people to succeed in their own fields, while supporting not only the growth of the Group but also the common good of India as a whole.

17.2.4 Modern Day Advancements

India's economic reforms in the 1990s introduced by the then Finance Minister Manmoham Singh and the then Prime Minister Narasima Rao coincided with the ascension in 1991 of a new chairman, Ratan Tata. On the eve of globalization, the Tata Group was viewed as being trustworthy, but not agile enough to globalize. Encroaching foreign competition in India's domestic markets led many to question the viability of the Tata model (Engardio 2007). However, the Group responded by diligently cultivating a pool of competent staff, managers, and engineers, in addition to developing innovative technologies.

Ratan Tata's appointment provoked substantial controversy. Many criticized his lack of experience. Russi Mody, chairman of Tata Steel and a good friend of Jamsetji, likened Ratan to a clown in a circus (Chandok 2013). Contrary to the skeptics' expectations, under Ratan's leadership the Group became renowned for its global acquisitions such as Jaguar, Land Rover, and Corus Steel. In justifying the Group's globalization strategy, Ratan pledged "to preserve and build upon our heritage and competitiveness" while "keeping the [acquisitions'] identities intact" (Timmons 2008a). Though some observers (Bajaj 2012) have praised Tata's global strategy on pragmatic grounds—it has been remarkably successful in the turnaround executed by Jaguar Land Rover—others have emphasized how seeking to build "Unity in Diversity," reflects cultural values deeply rooted in India's history (Suman Kumar 1992). For millennia, various civilizations, religions, and regimes have held sway in India, but the core culture remains intact. The Tata Group, apparently, seeks to encourage as much local autonomy as possible in the management of its overseas acquisitions.

Diversification has enabled the Tata Group to become one of the largest players in the tea and steel industries, while also developing a leadership position in the field of software engineering. Even as the Group's revenues have increased from US$5.8 billion to US$103.27 billion (Tata Group 2014g), it has also maintained a strong commitment to addressing societal needs alongside its business objectives. In 2010, for example, Tata Group donated US$50 million to the Harvard Business School (HBS), the largest donation ever received from an overseas organization (Kumar and Yu 2010). Many Indian and American scholars recognize that Ratan Tata's personal interest in such projects is long-standing. But making a gift to HBS is a new departure consistent with the Tata Group's strategy of globalization. In the words of Fareed Zakaria, an editor-at-large of TIME magazine, "the $50 million donation to the Business School is part of Tata's general efforts at expanding the international scope of his conglomerate. Tata is ultimately a worldwide company, so the Harvard Business School is a natural place to make an impact."

17.2.5 The Tata Philosophy in Action

The Tata Group's good intentions, as well as the unexpected challenges involved in fulfilling them, can be seen in its attempt to manufacture and market the world's cheapest car, the Tata Nano (BBC 2011a). Launched in 2009 with remarkable fanfare, the Nano represents the Group's hope of serving the real needs of society, not only in India but also throughout the developing world. A compact family car, initially priced at one lakh (100,000 rupees, or approximately US$2500), the Tata Nano was meant to provide Indian families a safe alternative to motorcycles, which are as pervasive as they are dangerous, given the state of India's roads. Such good intentions, however, are never easy to fulfill. Some critics have disparaged the vehicle as a "poor man's car" (*The Times of India* 2013), while others have criticized its safety record, in light of a recent failure in an internationally recognized crash test conducted in Germany (Oltermann and McClanahan 2014). Still others question the environmental impact of the Nano, were Tata Motors to succeed in achieving its sales goals (Kamenetz 2009). Clearly, the Nano will generate more air pollution than the motorcycles it is expected to replace; but can that trade-off be accepted when the car has serious safety issues of its own?

Then there's the controversy over Tata Motors' initial decision to build the Nano in West Bengal. Production had to be moved to Gujarat because local farmers and their political allies regarded the factory as detrimental to West Bengal's overall development (Bhaumik 2009). When Ratan Tata made the decision to relocate to Gujarat, he did so ostensibly "because of the risks to employees from the protests" (Chandran and Dahr 2008). Locals had complained about building an industrial center in an area devoted primarily to farming, but the protests soon were politicized and became violent. The relationship between the agricultural and industrial sectors is a major point of friction in the country, as two-third of Indians still rely on farming for their livelihood (Chandran and Dahr 2008). West Bengal's government had seized 400 ha of farmland for the factory site, while promising compensation to its previous owners. The flashpoint sparking the protests was a dispute over 160 ha, owned by farmers who refused to give up their lands. When they threatened violence against workers preparing the factory site, Tata decided to relocate the factory to Gujarat. While the relocation caused a delay in Nano's launch, some observers praised Tata's decision as yet another indication of the Group's concern for its stakeholders at every point in the supply chain. To be sure, the farmers' victory also meant the loss of industrial jobs desperately needed to rejuvenate the West Bengal economy. In that light, while the local government blamed the opposition party for irresponsibly "spearheading the protests," the politicians supporting the protests wondered why Ratan Tata had pulled the rug out from under the project so abruptly. Despite disappointing sales and other setbacks,[1] Tata Motors has reaffirmed its commitment to the Nano as an innovative attempt to provide basic transportation to people newly emerging from poverty.

Tata is busy addressing other social problems as well. The Group has sought to improve the living standards of those most in need, for example, through initiatives aimed at improving access to the very source of life: water. Tata spent over a decade developing the "Swach" water filtration system (BBC 2009). The company hopes to impact the lives of the almost one billion people worldwide who lack clean water by decreasing the economic and social costs of eliminating water contamination. Swach was first introduced in India where deaths due to unsafe drinking water are higher than those due to AIDS (Tata Chemicals 2009). In fact, Swach won a gold medal at the Asian Innovation Awards in 2010, because of its low cost and positive societal impact. Tata Swach enables the purification of one liter of water for one tenth of a rupee and does not require electricity. Furthermore, the addition of a lock system prevents its usage with counterfeit modules that could jeopardize the efficacy of the process.

A telling aspect of the Tata philosophy emerges from the idea that greater education is the key to sustainable development. The Educational Quality Improvement Project (EQUIP), organized by Tata Steel, educates students in three realms: improvement through problem solving, executing tasks, and innovation (Wadia 2011). Tata also sponsors an annual convention of Indian Schools, where students can display best practices in sustainable development and learn from each other. Deepali Misra, a consultant to Tata Quality Management Services (TQMS) which

[1] At this time (2014), it is clear that Ratan Tata himself blames Mamata Banerjee, the opposition leader in West Bengal, for the failure of the Nano. The farmers' agitation aided and abetted by Banerjee and other politicians forced the shift to a site at Sanand in Gujarat. The subsequent delay, in Tata's opinion, meant that all the hopes generated by the Nano's launch have evaporated. His anger over the declining fortunes of the Nano is one thing that apparently has not evaporated in the years since then (Moitra 2014).

hosts the event, explained, "The best part is that schools will learn from each other and share positive things. Our main motive is to implement and promote the concept of quality and performance in all their activities" (*The Telegraph* 2012). At the 2012 convention, 21 schools participated, showcasing a total of 73 best practices. Tata asserts that the end goal of such projects is to help people help themselves.

The Group's work in education, water technology, and in the development of an affordable car demonstrates the company's awareness of what is important not only to its customers, but also to society as a whole. Tata operates under the belief that innovation provides for an improved standard of living for all, culminating in continuous development.

17.2.6 The Organization of Corporate Philanthropy

Tata's mission statement asserts "At the Tata Group we are committed to improving the quality of life of the communities we serve. We do this by striving for leadership and global competitiveness in the business sectors in which we operate. Our practice of returning to society what we earn evokes trust among consumers, employees, shareholders and the community. We are committed to protecting this heritage of leadership with trust through the manner in which we conduct our business" (Tata Group 2012).

The guiding principles instilled by Ratan Tata's predecessors have not changed while the Group has grown under his direction. What has changed is the way they are implemented. Striving to impose organizational rigor, Ratan Tata has given the Trusts a cohesive governance structure, which focuses on integrating philanthropy with modern ideas of corporate accountability. The Trusts—beginning with the JN Tata Endowment (1892) that continues to fulfill its original mission in higher education by providing annually some 120 scholarships to Indian students for post-graduate study abroad—are today organized in two main clusters. The first consists in the Sir Dorabji Tata Trust (1932) and Allied Trusts (SDTT) that make substantial philanthropic grants to various agencies and individuals, supporting non-profit organizations focused on the following areas: "natural resource management and rural livelihoods, urban poverty and livelihoods, education, health, civil society, governance and human rights, media, art, and culture" (Tata Group 2014f). The other cluster consists in the Sir Ratan Tata Trust (SRTT, founded in 1919) and the Navajbai Ratan Tata Trust (NRTT, founded in 1974). The SRTT and the NRTT "seek to be a catalyst in development through giving grants to institutions" in various areas and for programs focused on improving "rural livelihoods and communities, education, health, enhancing civil society and governance, arts and culture, and sports" (Tata Group 2014f).

Given the overlapping leadership of the Trusts and the Tata Sons holding company, a question immediately arises regarding the relationship between the businesses and the philanthropies they support. How is that relationship managed? Tata spokespersons indicate that 75 % of the Trusts' funds come from dividends from their shares in Tata Sons, with the rest representing the yield on the Trusts' own investments. The Trusts, then, operate independently of the businesses upon which they depend for the bulk of their income. "Our trusts don't handle corporate social responsibility; they are more of a funding agency, like the Ford Foundation." The SDTT, for example, "supports different kinds of NGOs—some do social work, some research, while others are community based—usually for a period of three to five years." The Tata Group reports that both clusters "have stringent appraisal, assessment, accounting and auditing requirements for the NGOs they fund. Projects must be aimed towards sustainability for the community, and money is always released in a phased manner that meets the requirements of recipients" (Tata Group 2014f).

The head of the SDTT, Sarosh N. Batliwala, indicates that the Trusts and the holding company are kept at arms length, with the Trusts not usually encouraging or supporting projects run by Tata companies. Nevertheless, in special cases they may collaborate, and—in the words of the SDTT Programmes manager, Arun Pandhi—"there is a sharing of knowledge." The conflicts of interest, that could occur were this relationship to be mismanaged, are minimized by their common commitment to Tata's "Core Values"—"Integrity," "Understanding," "Excellence," "Unity," and "Responsibility"—which are animated by Jamsetji Tata's original pledge to "return to society what we earn." In support of the Core Values, both the Trusts and the businesses since 1998 have adhered to the Tata Code of Conduct (Tata Group 2014e), a lengthy document consisting in some 25 clauses, covering virtually all aspects of management and corporate governance. In addition, they both participate in the Tata Council for Community Initiatives which was founded in 1996 in order to create "structured approaches and specific processes… embracing a range of sustainable development initiatives such as community outreach, environmental management, biodiversity restoration, climate change initiatives and employee volunteering" (Tata Group 2014d). Among their most promising achievements is the establishment, in collaboration with the UN Global Compact in India, and the UN Development Program (India), of auditing and assessment procedures—the Tata Index for Sustainable Human Development Taxonomy, and the Tata Index for Sustainability—that significantly improve the performance of both the Trusts and the businesses in meeting their goals for both CSR and philanthropic activities.

The force behind these initiatives meant to achieve consistency among the diverse businesses and philanthropic activities is, of course, Ratan Tata himself. More than 20 years ago, when he crafted the Group's globalization strategy, he well understood (Kripalani 2004) that it would require an unprecedented level of coordination to ensure that the Tata trademark would remain "a uniform symbol of excellence across a group of diverse and independently run companies" (Kamath 2014). He therefore established Tata Quality Management Services (TQMS) as the leverage point for institutionalizing "the Tata Way" throughout the organization (Pednekar 2005). Through this unit, the ideals historically pursued by the company have been promoted systematically using the Tata Business Excellence Model (TBEM)—a program inspired by the USA's Malcolm Baldridge National Quality

Award—to provide "a group-wide platform that would encourage, support and recognise companies working to embed the tenets of business excellence in their operations" (Kamath 2014). The greatest single achievement of Ratan Tata's career, then, may be his success in developing TBEM as a model of accountability that goes beyond a narrow focus on compliance issues by enabling the Group to maintain its distinctive corporate culture while deepening its commitment to excellence in all aspects of its operations, social as well as financial.

17.2.7 Light and Shadows

Ratan Tata has gained respect all over the world thanks to his success in extending the Group's commitment to the good of Indian society. He has never been perceived as a public figure, but rather as a conscientious businessman and benefactor. Prior to 2010, there had been no hint of scandal related to Ratan Tata's personal conduct or his management of the Tata Group as a whole. However, in that year, Rajeev Chandrasekhar, a member of India's Parliament, who had been Tata's competitor in the past, filed an accusation against Ratan Tata for his alleged involvement in the Indian telecom scandal that had been festering since 2008 (India Knowledge at Wharton 2010). A report from India's top auditor—the Comptroller and Auditor General of India—claimed that there had been substantial irregularities in the allocation of the 2G mobile-phone spectrum, which cost the government an estimated US$40 billion in lost revenues.

Chandrasekhar alleged that Tata purchased underpriced licenses in order to increase the value of shares in Tata Teleservices, then in the process of being sold to the Japanese NTT Docomo. Although there was no proof that Ratan Tata did anything immoral or illegal in acquiring the licenses, the Tata Group profited substantially when Docomo bought shares in Tata Teleservices. A taped conversation between Ratan Tata and the Group's PR representative and lobbyist, Niira Radia, seemed to indicate that the firm had a stake in the election of the Telecom Minister, Andimuthu Raja (Thottam 2010). It was on Raja's watch that the 2G licenses were sold to numerous private Indian companies, while not following the Prime Minister's guidelines on an acceptable price range. Raja resigned as a consequence of the harsh criticisms that followed. In response to Chandrasekhar's sworn testimony, Ratan Tata wrote an open letter denouncing the allegations as "based on untruths and distortion of facts." He concluded, "I can hold my head high and say that neither the Tata Group nor I have at any time been involved in any of these misdeeds" (Thottam 2010). Despite Ratan Tata's denials, and the finding in the auditor's report confirming that Raja had not given Tata any special treatment, the investigation remains ongoing.

Possible discrepancies between the Group's professed commitment to the Tata Business Excellence Model and the complexities of managing large-scale industrialization projects are evident in the controversies surrounding the Tata Mundra

Ultra Mega Power Project in Gujarat. Tata Power is the largest electric power producer in India. When fully operational, the project will have added 4000 MW for a total of nearly 7000 MW generating capacity in Tata Power, of which 852 MW or roughly 12 % come from "clean sources such as hydro, wind and solar" (Moneycontrol 2012). Tata Power claims that the project actually will reduce the carbon emissions caused by thermal power generation, since Mundra will use 1.7 million tons of coal less in generating the same amount of power as conventional coal plants. Advanced technologies as well as the importation of higher-grade coals from Indonesia will enable the reduction in emissions.

The anticipated gains in environmental quality, however, are accompanied by fresh allegations at Mundra, concerning a disruption of the environment for dairy farming, on the one hand, and coastal fisheries, on the other. Tata Power, apparently, has been able to address the concerns of dairy farmers who had lost half of their grazing lands in the area as a result of constructing the power plant. After consulting with the villagers who had been affected by the disruption, Tata created another charitable trust. This trust enabled the affected dairy farmers to purchase fodder supplies for their cattle, instead of continuing their struggle to produce fodder on the marginal lands earmarked for the plant. Tata's response to the dairy farmers has been analyzed by scholars at the Indian Institute of Management Bangalore, who praise the firm for its effectiveness in coordinating its business operations with its philanthropic trusts in order create a model of best practice for "companies to engage responsibly with communities in particular when infrastructure requires acquisition of large land holdings" (Gupta and Srinivasan 2011). Tata's problems with the fisherfolk, however, have not yet yielded such a happy outcome.

The Mundra site is located on the Gulf of Kutch in Gujarat. Proximity to the Gulf allows Tata Power to accept deliveries of Indonesian coal by ship. The seawater of the Gulf also provides water for the plant, which generates power using steam-driven turbines, based on super-critical boiler technology. The fishing villages adjacent to the power plant will bear the brunt of a series of "environmental and social [impacts], including deterioration of water quality and fish populations, displacement of fishermen, community health impacts due to air emissions, and destruction of natural habitats" (Bank Information Center 2013). A report by an independent fact-finding team on the Tata Mundra project, "The Real Cost of Power" (Dutta 2012), documents the allegations made by MASS—the *Machimar Adhikar Sangharsh Sangathan* ("Association for the Struggle for Fishworkers' Rights") who have protested the projects' disruption of their traditional way of life, as well as the general deterioration in environmental quality. Their allegations are significant insofar as they claim that the Tata Group and its partner, the International Finance Corporation of the World Bank, used their influence to subvert the environmental impact assessment processes that would have indicated the problems inherent in the site chosen for the project. The World Bank's own Compliance Advisor Ombudsman (CAO) has since corroborated MASS's findings, though the IFC's response is not yet clear. Since the CAO's findings also concern the due diligence of the IFC's "client," namely Coastal Gujarat Power Limited (CGPL), a wholly owned subsidiary of Tata Power, they raise unavoidable questions about the effectiveness and sincerity of the Tata Group's various commitments to sustainability and respect for local rural communities in India. Was "the Tata Way"—epitomized in the Tata Business Excellence Model (TBEM)—somehow lost in the decision to go forward with Tata Mundra? Is Tata Mundra, as its critics allege, "making a mockery of accountability"? (Patel and Damle 2014)

17.2.8 A Promising Future?

Inevitably, the Tata Group will face even greater challenges in the future. For all the strides made by Ratan Tata, the task of becoming a company with a truly international outlook will still confront his successor, Cyrus Mistry (Kannan 2011). The son of an Indian billionaire—who is the single largest individual shareholder in Tata Sons—Cyrus Mistry has strong ties to the Tata Group since his sister is married to a member of the Tata family (Hill 2011). Additionally, Mistry belongs to the same Parsee community as the Tatas, and their families share a common commitment to the Zoroastrian religion. When Mistry's appointment was announced in an article, "Mystery Ends, Mistry Begins" (*The Economic Times of India* 2011a), it noted how Tata chose continuity in leadership, by refusing to abandon the familial and cultural legacies that have animated the Group from its founding. The play on "Mystery" and "Mistry" prompted one observer to comment: "The superiority of Tata's Indian model and the reluctance of Western businesses to learn from Tata was indicated as the true 'Mystery', especially in light of the ways in which it has helped sustain Tata's success throughout its long history" (Hill 2011).

When Mistry took the helm, however, it was estimated that in the aggregate Tata's capital over the past few years has been underperforming, and that, like a spreading banyan tree, this vast enterprise with its 182 subsidiaries needs to be pruned—an operation more in the tradition of GE's former chairman Jack Welch's ruthless philosophy of "kill, cure or sell" (*The Economist* 2012b). At the same time, the Tata Group contains some outstanding performers, such as Tata Consultancy Services (TCS) whose shareholder return of 150 % in 2010, prompted its recognition as one of the world's best performing technology companies (*The Economic Times of India* 2010b). Tata subsidiary companies have won numerous awards, both for philanthropic business, corporate governance, and for innovative ideas. But the "Triple Bottom Line" that has been institutionalized in the Tata Business Excellence Model requires that the Group's performance be measured not just in terms of return on investments. Over the long haul, the challenge for Cyrus Mistry, once he's out from under the giant shadow cast by Ratan Tata, is whether Tata's financial performance can keep pace with the growing needs of the Tata Trusts, and their own efforts to live up to the standards indicated in the Tata Business Excellence Model (TBEM).

17.2.9 Summary

The Tata Group's history indicates that it is possible to combine business success with a robust commitment to corporate philanthropy. The reports examined in this case study show how addressing needs at the bottom of the economic pyramid and contributing to national development can be translated into competitive advantages in international business. Personal leadership, however, appears to be an important component of the formula for success. Given Chairman Ratan Tata's retirement, it is uncertain whether Tata's new leadership can continue to build on the same values while also achieving global competitiveness. As the Tata Group continues to grow, and with it the revenues of the Tata Trusts, both will be challenged to continue upholding the Tata's legacy of commitment to India's economic, social, and cultural development, while also embracing the expectations for transparency and accountability in all aspects of their corporate governance and management. Despite occasional lapses—as indicated, for example, in the controversies involving Tata Mundra—there is reason to hope that Cyrus Mistry's commitment to the Tata Business Excellence Model (TBEM) will enable to Group as well as the Trusts to make continuous improvements in meeting these goals. As Mistry recently declared, "TBEM has been the glue in binding the group together and enhancing the Tata brand" (*Tata Group* 2014h).

17.3 Case Study Discussion

The Tata Group's saga challenges us to reexamine moral arguments for and against corporate philanthropy because the Tata Trusts, which control nearly two-thirds of the Group's shares, are the single largest cluster of philanthropic institutions in India, if not also throughout southern and eastern Asia. Since the Trusts in one form or another have a history going back nearly 125 years, they also allow us the opportunity to understand how corporate philanthropy has evolved, especially in response to new social challenges. Now that he is retired from chairing the Tata Group, Ratan Tata devotes himself exclusively to managing the Tata Trusts. His chief objective is to improve the effectiveness of the Trusts by introducing management methods similar to those promoted in the Tata Business Excellence Model (TBEM): "One hopes that one can treat the philanthropic activities of the trusts as a corporate entity: setting goals, looking at efficiencies, monitoring the outcome and benefits of what we're doing… Operating traditionally is perhaps the greatest weakness of the trusts; there's a tremendous resistance to change, and I have not shaken that attitude just yet," he admits. "A priority is to go out and look at what other foundations are doing, broaden our thinking and benchmark ourselves against others" (*Philanthropy Age* 2014).

As Ratan Tata surely knows, managing the Trusts involves some challenges different from coordinating the diverse industries that constitute the Tata Group. One of these, as we have seen, is the need to distinguish while also relating the

Group's corporate social responsibility (CSR) and the Trusts' philanthropic activities. The failure to distinguish these creates unnecessary confusion, since in practice they can and ought to be related in various situations. The problems that Tata Motors encountered in West Bengal over the location of the plant manufacturing the Nano, and similarly Tata Power's problems with local communities of dairy farmers and fisherfolk at the Tata Mundra site in Gujarat, should be approached as CSR problems. The Tata Trusts may provide some resources for solving these problems, but philanthropy alone will hardly resolve these issues.

Within the Tata Way, the distinction comes down to this: "Philanthropy is about contributing the best way you can to improve the well-being of the people who have been placed in your path," says Kishor Chaukar, managing director of Tata Industries and the chairman of the Tata Council for Community Initiatives (TCCI). "Corporate social responsibility, by contrast, is about linking a business or a company's activities to the well-being of the communities it operates within" (Chacko 2011). The contrast consists in observing the "thick line separating the world of corporate Tata from the work that the Tata trusts support." Such metaphors may not yet communicate much to those unfamiliar with "the Tata Way." But our case study indicates that Tata's philanthropic commitment to "improving the well-being of the people who have been placed in your path" means that the Trusts will seek to respond to social and cultural needs in any venue where the Tata Group is active. The philanthropy is no longer exclusively focused on the people of India. On the other hand, the "linking [of] a business or a company's activities to the well-being of the communities it operates within" means that the Tata Group will acknowledge its CSR obligations to all its stakeholders, whenever and however they may be impacted by the firms' business activities.

One indication of what the distinction means in practice is that a strict separation is maintained between the finances of the two, as well as their management structures. Officers in the Trusts are not to work directly with the Tata companies on their CSR programs. A.N. Singh—managing trustee of the Sir Dorabji Tata and the Allied Trusts—explains, "We maintain an arm's-length distance from corporate Tata because it would amount to a curious sort of situation if we were to fund some of these companies and their programmes…Their money comes to us in the form of dividends. We cannot route it back to them; that would be unethical" (Chacko 2011). On the other hand, as we have also learned, there is a sharing of knowledge and information, especially about local needs and how best to address them. While Ratan Tata clearly is committed to the firm's separation of CSR and philanthropy, his attempt to modernize the Trusts, by introducing the TBEM's methods for benchmarking their performance, will inevitably tend to reduce the differences. Tata himself seems eager to do more. He admits that while 4 % of the total annual budget of the Tata Group is earmarked for CSR activities, the Tata Trusts have averaged only US$92 million a year in their disbursements, albeit the largest single contribution among Indian philanthropies.

The Tata Trusts also stand out because of their relationship to Mahatma Gandhi's idea of trusteeship, as the most practical way of dealing with the problem that great wealth creates for those who possess it, while also addressing the needs of the masses of people, first in India, but also throughout the world, who for one reason or another lack access to it. We will examine Gandhi's actual proposal further on in this chapter, but for now it is important to recognize some of the issues that arise from the Tata family's attempt to put it into practice. As we've noted in a few places, the Trusts hold nearly two-thirds of the shares in the Tata Sons holding company, a proportion that dwarfs the ownership stake retained by various individual shareholders, including members of the Tata family. The Trusts' ownership stake is now reflected in the Articles of Association that give them a majority on the selection committee charged with appointing the Tata Group's Chairman (Chatterjee 2013). Since Ratan Tata currently holds the Chairmanship of the Tata Trusts, it would appear that even in retirement he retains the deciding vote over the Group's executive leadership. The bottom line is that, in seeking to maximize its return to shareholders, the Tata Group is working for the Trusts, and not the other way around. The Tatas' commitment to maintaining a "thick line" of separation between the Tata Group and the Trusts, in the end, then, rests upon the personal integrity of the executive leadership in both entities. Apparently, we will have to take Ratan Tata at his word on whether this line is thick enough to minimize, if not eliminate, all possible conflicts of interest.

Undeniably, the Tata Trusts are the single largest philanthropic group operating in India. In 2009–2010, for example, their grants and contributions amounted to roughly US$105 million (Chacko 2011). But given the fact that the trusts control nearly two-thirds of the shares in a business empire that generated US$67.4 billion in revenues that year, and a net profit of roughly US$2.3 billion (*The Economic Times of India* 2010a), one question is whether the Trusts could be doing more? A review of the Trusts' Annual Reports for 2010–2011 provides credible evidence, not only of the levels of transparency and accountability already achieved, but also of the relatively low costs of administering them. Out of the US$30.6 million in income received by the Sir Dorabji Tata Trust, only US$1.1 million (or 3.63 %) went for administrative expenses. Similarly in the Allied Trusts (SDTT), of US$61.8 million in income received, only US$1.3 million (or 2.1 %) went for administrative expenses (SDTT Annual Report 2011). When we turn to the other Tata Trusts, the same picture emerges. Over the same period, the Sir Ratan Tata Trust (SRTT) reports administrative expenses of US$510 thousand (or 2.68 %), while the Navajbai Ratan Tata Trust reports administrative expenses of US$190 thousand, or less than 1 % (SRTT Annual Report 2011). By contrast, in the USA it is estimated that "charities actually spend 36.9 cents on the dollar" for administrative expenses including fundraising. Of course, the Tata Trusts do not incur fundraising expenses, given their relationship to the Tata Sons holding company, but even so, their effectiveness in allocating grants and other benefits to the philanthropic objects for which they were intended is impressive.[2]

[2] The Annual Reports of the Tata Trusts are well worth further study, since they are publicly available for a number of years starting in 2006–2007 for the SDTT reports (SDTT 2013) and 1999–2000 for the SRTT and NRTT reports (SRTT 2014), and quite detailed in their assessments of all aspects of their operations. The annual reports allow observers to study how the Trusts have developed, particularly during the chairmanship of Ratan Tata, under whose leadership these annual reports were developed (SRTT 2014).

Despite their impressive success—or perhaps, precisely because of it—the story of the Tata Trusts raise questions regarding whether they should be regarded as a model for other philanthropists, particularly in southern and eastern Asia. Even if Milton Friedman's philosophic objections against corporate philanthropy can be set aside—as we hope to do in the next section—there are questions that emerge from Tata's role in India's struggle against colonialism and neocolonialism. Would their founders have established the Trusts, had India not found itself occupied and dominated by a foreign colonial power? In today's India, now struggling to assert itself in an era of globalization, can the same vision that animated the Tata Trusts still inspire similar efforts with similar results? Another way of asking the same question may emerge from a consideration of the Tatas' Zoroastrian faith and practice. The Parsi communities in India[3] are known for their business acumen, their sense of social responsibility, and their philanthropic activities. The Tata family's commitment to philanthropy—among Parsis at least—though exceptional is hardly unique. But is such a commitment likely to find imitators among the vast majority of Indians who are not Parsis? If the Tata Trusts are to be a philanthropic model for others to copy, how is the case to be made for it?

A crucial claim made by the Tata brand overall is that the Trusts' extraordinary commitment to philanthropy is completely consistent with the Tata Group's exemplary business practices. The Tata Business Excellence Model (TBEM) and other programs testify to the Group's efforts to make good on that claim. The Tatas mean to set a high moral standard in business ethics as well as in philanthropy. Such claims to moral leadership, of course, also provoke increased scrutiny. The recent difficulties that the Tata Group has encountered, for example, in the launch of the Tata Nano and the development of the Tata Mundra Power Plant, among other things, suggest that there's a price to be paid for raising the public's expectations. Firms that would consider developing their own philanthropies should also recognize that achieving an impressive reputation for philanthropic leadership will not suffice to cover up any shortcomings in their business ethics. On the contrary, building a good reputation for philanthropy is likely to raise expectations concerning the ethical standards operative throughout the firm's business practices. The lesson to be learned is not therefore to avoid involvement in philanthropic activities, but to be prepared to fulfill the high expectations that such activities generate in all aspects of one's business. Once we recognize the heightened level of scrutiny that philanthropic leadership will provoke, we can give credit to the Tata Group for how remarkably free of scandal and ethical controversy their operations have been. Mistakes have been made, but given the scale and scope of the Group's operations, they are relatively few and far between.

[3]For useful background study of the Parsis and the cultural assumptions governing the Tata family's business philosophy, see *The Good Parsi: The Fate of a Colonial Elite in a Postcolonial Society* (Luhrmann 1996).

17.4 Ethical Reflection

One lingering question can now be answered, in light of the relationship between the Tata Group and the Tata Trusts. What is the difference between philanthropy and corporate social responsibility (CSR)? Following "the Tata Way" we've seen an answer that is more practical than theoretical: the programs funded by the Trusts are kept strictly separate from the operations of the Tata Sons holding company. While the total budget for CSR activities within the Tata Group is reported to be approximately 4 % of net profits, these activities are understood and managed by the member firms as "social development programs" that are part of their ordinary and ongoing business strategy (Chacko 2011). The Trusts, on the other hand, as we have seen, are focused on addressing the needs of various groups and individuals in society as a whole, and not directly related to the businesses of the Tata Group. Though there may be significant overlap in the beneficiaries served by these two different strategies, as well as significant "sharing of knowledge" through joint participation in the Tata Council for Community Initiatives (TCCI), their financial structures and management are rigorously differentiated.

The policies developed by the Tata Group and the Trusts are consistent with various attempts internationally to make a theoretical distinction between philanthropy and CSR. The first major distinction is between "charity" and "philanthropy," in which "charity" refers to personal acts of loving response to the needs of others. Charity usually involves an immediacy of unconditional giving that is concerned to relieve symptoms, whereas philanthropy involves some kind of organized effort to determine the causes of the distress and address these as well. As the Confucian proverb has suggested, charity is giving a man a fish when he is hungry, whereas philanthropy is teaching a man to fish so that he need not be hungry again.

The second major distinction concerns the nature of corporate—as opposed to individual—philanthropy. "Corporate philanthropy" of the sort represented by the Tata Trusts embodies the original altruistic meaning of philanthropy (literally, "love of humanity"), and it is regarded as "'purely ethical' because it is not based on economic, legal or political considerations." Nevertheless, since it involves the use of corporate funds, such donations are made with the expectation minimally of "good governance by the beneficiaries" (Leisinger and Schmitt 2011). In contrast to CSR activities, corporate philanthropy "goes far beyond what bottom line duties require" in order to demonstrate "the management's value framework, company culture and core values." Nevertheless, since corporate philanthropy can and does "generate positive 'moral capital' among communities and stakeholders beyond the company's direct business relationships," these desirable side-effects can be managed to achieve consistency with the firm's business objectives. The more the management of corporate philanthropy is strategically aligned with the firm's objectives, the closer it gets to CSR. Substantial overlap between the two seems virtually inevitable.

When a scholar from the prestigious Chicago school of economics, Milton Friedman (1912–2006) rejected the very idea of CSR, his target was not primarily

CSR, but corporate philanthropy. He argued that "there is one and only one social responsibility of business--to use its resources and engage in activities designed to increase its profits so long as it stays within the rules of the game, which is to say, engages in open and free competition without deception or fraud" (Friedman 1970). As a defender of individual freedom, Friedman did not reject in principle the idea of charity or philanthropy—as if such activities were immoral or irresponsible—but in his view these were only legitimate as a personal choice of individuals. For a business or its executive leadership to allocate the firm's resources for CSR, in his view, is to impose a tax upon the owners or investors, depriving them of their fair share of its profits. For this reason, he described CSR as pursuing "collectivist ends… without collectivist means." What Friedman might have said about the Tata family's decision to found the various Tata Trusts is anyone's guess, since these were the result of personal decisions by each successive Chairman of the Tata Group, designed to make good on the family's commitment to their longstanding Parsi religious and cultural values. Conceivably, Friedman might have approved of the Tata Trusts, since the decisions that supported them did not necessarily preempt the rights of the other shareholders—like Cyrus Mistry's father, with an 18 % ownership stake in Tata Sons—to make other decisions about what to do with shares. On the other hand, as we have seen in Chap. 12, Friedman no doubt would object to the Tata Group's aggregate annual budget for CSR activities, prior to any dividends paid to any of the shareholders, including the Tata Trusts.

17.4.1 Corporate Philanthropy: Andrew Carnegie's Gospel of Wealth

When we attempt to locate the rationale for the Tata family's commitment to corporate philanthropy in the spectrum of arguments that have circulated globally, it may be useful to begin with the example of Andrew Carnegie (1835–1919). Carnegie's famous pamphlet, "The Gospel of Wealth" (Carnegie 1889), provides a modern, pragmatic rationale for philanthropy, and the philanthropist's role in managing their activities. A Scotsman who immigrated to the USA in 1848, Carnegie laid the foundation for one of the USA's first great industrial corporations, which later became U.S. Steel. With the proceeds of the sale of his company to J. P. Morgan in 1901, Carnegie turned to philanthropy, establishing a prodigious number of libraries, museums, universities, and foundations. Where Carnegie's "Gospel of Wealth" differs from Friedman's view is not in thinking differently about the nature of business corporations or the markets in which they operate, but in showing why and how the wealthy should exercise their moral responsibilities. He felt strongly that, at an opportune moment, the wealthy should retire from active management of their businesses in order to distribute the wealth they had amassed, through projects or foundations of their own choice, intended to advance the social progress of humanity as a whole.[4] Their personal involvement Carnegie regarded as essential, since their success had likely taught them the managerial skills needed to ensure that the wealth would be allocated wisely.

Carnegie's "Gospel" was meant to address the social conditions symbolized in the widening gap between the rich and the poor, resulting from the nineteenth century's unprecedented increase in productivity achieved, in his view, through the advent of modern industrial capitalism. Influenced by Herbert Spencer's philosophy of Social Darwinism, he believed that both the dramatic increase in wealth and its destructive impact on the traditional bonds of social solidarity were not only inevitable historically but also beneficial as society continued to evolve. Modern industrial capitalism, therefore, should not be overthrown by a revolution that willfully ignores the facts of human nature. Instead, each individual—particularly successful individuals—were to use the resources at their disposal to overcome its destructive consequences by distributing their wealth in ways that would be of genuine benefit to others.

Carnegie believed that wealth represented a moral hazard for the individuals and their families who succeeded in accumulating it. Social Darwinism, in his view, suggested that conspicuous consumption on the part of the wealthy was ultimately self-destructive, since its enervating effects could not be reconciled with the rigorous discipline required for the "survival of the fittest." Since wealth had to be redistributed, in order to avoid its toxic effect upon those who possessed it, the real question, then, was to determine how to avoid its negative consequences even in the act of sharing it.

Though Carnegie is remembered as a great philanthropist, he was clearly unsentimental—if not cynical—in his view of charity, as well as bequests, and their impact on both donors and recipients. He contended, "One of the serious obstacles to the improvement of our race is indiscriminate charity." By that he meant random "almsgiving" that can only "encourage the slothful, the drunken, the unworthy." Into this category, he also placed those who stood to inherit their fortunes, on the basis of nothing more than familial relationships. "Why should men leave great fortunes to their children? If this is done from affection, is it not misguided affection? Observation teaches that…great sums bequeathed oftener work more for the injury than for the good of the recipients." Thus a "thoughtful man must shortly say, 'I would as soon leave to my son a curse as the almighty dollar,' and admit to himself that it is not the welfare of the children, but family pride, which inspires these enormous legacies." For this reason, he proposed raising "death-duties" or inheritance taxes on a graduated basis with a top rate of at least 50 %. His point was that if moral arguments cannot persuade the wealthy to distribute their wealth wisely

---

[4] One telling example of what he had in mind was his offer to donate US$20 million to the Philippines in order to prevent its annexation by the USA as a result of the treaty ending the Spanish-American War of 1898. The USA had agreed to pay Spain the US$20 million to compensate for its loss of the Philippines, and to vindicate its own occupation of the islands. Carnegie was a strong supporter of the American Anti-Imperialist League that lobbied Congress against the annexation (Carnegie 1920).

during their lifetimes, then the threat of confiscatory tax policies upon their death may move them to do so.

The challenge, then, was one Carnegie personally had to face upon the sale of his Carnegie Steel Company, at that time the single largest commercial transaction ever recorded. What was one to do with all that money? Carnegie outlined his options as follows: "There are but three modes in which surplus wealth can be disposed of. It can be left to the families of the decedents; or it can be bequeathed for public purposes; or, finally, it can be administered during their lives by its possessors." He reasoned that, given the downside risks involved in the first two options, the only sensible choice was the third, that is, to manage the distribution of one's wealth through foundations that promised to make a difference in addressing the social problems exacerbated by the triumph of modern industrial capitalism:

> This, then, is held to be the duty of the man of Wealth: First, to set an example of modest, unostentatious living, shunning display or extravagance; to provide moderately for the legitimate wants of those dependent upon him; and after doing so to consider all surplus revenues which come to him simply as trust funds, which he is called upon to administer, and strictly bound as a matter of duty to administer in the manner which, in his judgment, is best calculated to produce the most beneficial results for the community—the man of wealth thus becoming the mere agent and trustee for his poorer brethren, bringing to their service his superior wisdom, experience and ability to administer, doing for them better than they would or could do for themselves (Carnegie 1889).

Carnegie's personal experience had taught him that humanity's spiritual hunger was far more compelling than any other needs and desires. Since only universal access to education, to literature and art, and philosophic enlightenment could satisfy that hunger, it is not surprising that his philanthropy tended to focus on the establishment of public libraries, museums, and educational institutions.

17.4.2 Corporate Philanthropy: Mahatma Gandhi's Concept of Trusteeship

Whether the Tata founders were familiar with Carnegie's "Gospel of Wealth" is not known, but there is clear evidence that J.R.D. Tata knew and was inspired by the remarkably similar thinking of Mahatma Gandhi (Sarukkai 2012). One point of convergence linking Carnegie and Gandhi is the notion of trusteeship. As Carnegie had said, "Individualism will continue, but the millionaire will be but a trustee for the poor; entrusted for a season with a great part of the increased wealth of the community, but administering it for the community far better than it could or would have done for itself." Gandhi had taught a similar notion of trusteeship:

> As for the present owners of wealth, they would have to make their choice between class war and voluntarily converting themselves into trustees of their wealth. They would be allowed to retain the stewardship of their possessions and to use their talent to increase the wealth, not for their own sakes, but for the sake of the nation and, therefore, without exploitation. The State would regulate the rate of commission which they would get commensurate

> with the service rendered and its value to society. Their children would inherit the stewardship only if they proved their fitness for it.... Supposing India becomes a free country tomorrow, all the capitalists will have an opportunity of becoming statutory trustees. But such a statute will not be imposed from above. It will have to come from below (Kelkar 1960).

This was Gandhi's statement, made in his weekly publication, *Harijan*, in 1946 on the eve of India's final struggle for independence from the British Empire.

The path that led Gandhi to espouse trusteeship was partly similar and partly different from Carnegie's. Both men had personal experience of divesting their personal fortunes, and hoped to get others to do the same. Both were very concerned about the destructive social consequences of the widening gap between rich and poor. Both believed that possessing wealth beyond anything reasonably necessary for fulfilling one's own needs was corrupting, spiritually as well as morally. Both, furthermore, respected the abilities of those capable of amassing great wealth and recognized that their talents would be focused better on stewardship for the sake of society as a whole. But there were also differences, based primarily on their diverging cultural backgrounds and philosophical interests. Gandhi's appeal to India's wealthy families was meant to provide them with an alternative consistent with the philosophy of non-violence (*Ahimsa*), his lifelong work dedicated to the liberation of India. The opportunity for a genuinely peaceful revolution would simply be lost, if India went the way of Russia in forcibly suppressing the wealthy:

> Society will be the poorer, for it will lose the gifts of a man who knows how to accumulate wealth. Therefore the non-violent way is evidently superior. The rich man will be left in possession of his wealth, of which he will use what he reasonably requires for his personal needs and will act as a trustee for the remainder to be used for society. In this argument honesty on the part of the trustee is assumed.
>
> As soon as a man looks upon himself as a servant of society, earns for its sake, spends for its benefit, then purity enters into his earnings and there is *Ahimsa* in his venture. Moreover, if men's minds turn towards this way of life, there will come about a peaceful revolution in society, and that without any bitterness (Kelkar 1960).

The purification that Gandhi promised those who embrace their stewardship responsibilities emerged from his extended meditations on the Hindu classic, the *Bhagavad Gita*. He believed that the *Gita*'s message to the wealthy was a simple invitation: "Enjoy Thy Wealth by Renouncing It." He explained: "Earn your crores by all means. But understand that your wealth is not yours; it belongs to the people. Take what you require for your legitimate needs, and use the remainder for society." Clearly, this is an insight that Carnegie might have endorsed, had it been presented to him, but it would have been rejected outright by Friedman, given his absolutist notion of private property rights. As an economist, however, Friedman would not, and did not, condemn personal acts of charity, or anything else on which the wealthy might spend their money, however silly or serious. Theirs was a free choice, and nobody else had the right to challenge them on it. Both Gandhi and Carnegie, by contrast, did make it their business to challenge them. They agree that the wealthy can achieve meaningful and fulfilling lives if, during their lifetimes, they put their money to work in the service of humanity as a whole.

The Tata family had already created the first of the Trusts when they encountered Gandhi and his philosophy of trusteeship. In 1909, when Gandhi was active in the anti-apartheid movement in South Africa, Sir Ratan Tata had sent him a donation of 25,000 rupees to support his work. Later, after Gandhi's return to India, in 1925 he visited Jamshedpur, the Tatas' model industrial city. Despite their religious differences and cultural differences, the Tatas and Gandhi were in profound agreement not only about India's national liberation, but also on various issues related to economic development, including the welfare of laborers and the high moral responsibilities of those who employ them. Though there were tensions between the two regarding just how reasonable it was to hope that capitalists could achieve high standards of business ethics in the absence of government regulation, Gandhi apparently appreciated the need for productivity and economic incentives, if sufficient wealth were to be created so that trusteeship could make a difference (Sarukkai 2012). Trusteeship, then, was meant to be universal in its applicability. Ordinary workers were trustees over their own labors, just as owners and managers were trustees over the capital and other resources that they contributed.

Years later, reflecting back on his career, J.R.D. Tata reaffirmed the family's commitment to trusteeship:

> I must say that I have always been basically in agreement with Gandhi's concept of trusteeship and have throughout my career tried to live up to it. In fact, our group of companies have, to the extent possible, officially adopted it as part of their credo. As I told you when we met, my only doubts have been in regard to the practical effect that can be given to such a concept, particularly considering, on the one hand, the ethical standards, or lack of them, that seem to prevail today amongst large sections of the business community of our country, and on the other hand, the dogmatic view of socialism and the resultant hostility toward private enterprise adopted by our government (Sarukkai 2012).

The Tatas and Gandhi agreed that, for trusteeship to be effective and play its intended role in India's development, it would have to be done voluntarily in the spirit of *Ahimsa* or nonviolence. J.R.D. Tata's contribution to this effort was to create a credible model for institutionalizing trusteeship. His practical approach involved adopting policies, particularly in the Tata Iron and Steel Company (TISCO), which were consistent with the egalitarian aspirations of trusteeship. It would take approximately 30 years on average for TISCO's policies, which were pioneering, voluntary experiments, to be adopted generally into India's labor law.

17.5 Conclusion

Unlike corporate social responsibility (CSR), which ought to be required of every business, philanthropy may not be for everyone. It requires moral leadership that is not content merely to meet the legal and customary obligations of businesses to their various stakeholders. Those obligations are properly acknowledged and fulfilled under the heading of CSR, for they are meant to make good on any legitimate business' claim to do no harm, or conversely, to do good while doing well.

Philanthropy, of course, is both personal and corporate. While personal philanthropy is the act of an individual seeking to share his or her personal wealth with others; corporate philanthropy acts on that same desire on behalf of a business organization, usually through a trust or a foundation established to improve conditions for society as a whole. Our focus in this chapter has been on corporate philanthropy, what motivates it, and how it fits into the overall picture of a business' relationships with the society in which it operates.

Corporate philanthropy attempts to go beyond what businesses are obliged to do with and for their various stakeholders. It is not an attempt to compensate those who have been adversely impacted by a business' routine operations. Nor is it an attempt to obtain the goodwill of the communities in which it operates, through gifts or grants designed, at least in part, to enhance the firm's business prospects. The impulse to engage in corporate philanthropy stems from a proper understanding of civic virtue, namely, that good citizenship—or, if you will, patriotism—calls us to do what we can to build up the community that all may flourish in it. In both its personal and corporate forms, philanthropy concerns the appropriate use of accumulated wealth, since the wealthy are both saddled with the burden and blessed with the opportunity to do this service. In both forms, it expresses a recognition of social solidarity, that is, the awareness that everyone's fate—the rich, the poor, and everyone in between—is interdependent. If we can make a difference in the quality of life for others, we ought to do so.

Whatever the specific religious, cultural, and philosophical assumptions animating philanthropic activities our study of them suggests that a global consensus is emerging not only as to the purpose of corporate philanthropy, but also the appropriate means for fulfilling this purpose. Though they come from different worlds, the Carnegies and the Tatas agree in principle about what to do and how to do it. Such philanthropists seek to make the ideal of trusteeship—or stewardship in the management of their contributions—practical and concrete. That their example, and that of many unnamed others, continues to attract wealthy individuals is evident from the growing interest globally, for example, in "The Giving Pledge" that Bill Gates and Warren Buffet have developed, inviting billionaires to commit at least half their wealth to philanthropy (Lane 2013). While the Pledge does not require the wealthy to become directly involved in managing these activities, it does reflect the values promoted by the Tata family. We hope that a careful consideration of the legacy of the Tata Trusts will inspire others throughout Asia to join in the effort to ensure that their growing wealth actually serves the common good.

References

Bajaj, V. (2012, August 30). Tata Motors finds Success in Jaguar Land Rover. *The New York Times*. Retrieved on August 13, 2014, from http://www.nytimes.com/2012/08/31/business/global/tata-motors-finds-success-in-jaguar-land-rover.html

Bank Information Center. (2013). *Tata Mundra Power Plant*. Retrieved on August 15, 2014, from http://www.bicusa.org/feature/tata-mundra-power-plant/

BBC News. (2009, December 7). India's Tata launches water filter for rural poor. Retrieved on May 8, 2012, from http://news.bbc.co.uk/2/hi/business/8399692.stm
BBC News. (2011a, November 21). Revamp for India's Tata Nano—The World's cheapest car. Retrieved on May 8, 2012, from http://www.bbc.co.uk/news/world-asia-15815850
BBC News. (2011b, June 20). India: Tata becomes India's wealthiest Group. Retrieved on May 7, 2012, from http://www.bbc.co.uk/news/world-south-asia-13838362
BBC News. (2012, January 5). India car boss Ratan Tata admits Tata Nano 'mistakes'. Retrieved on May 8, 2012, from http://www.bbc.co.uk/news/world-asia-india-16427707
Bhaumik, S. (2009, September 1). Tata seeks compensation over Nano. *BBC News*. Retrieved on May 8, 2012, from http://news.bbc.co.uk/2/hi/south_asia/8231972.stm
Carnegie, A. (1889). *The Gospel of Wealth*. Retrieved on June 16, 2014, from http://carnegie.org/fileadmin/Media/Publications/PDF/
Carnegie, A. (1920). *The autobiography of Andrew Carnegie*. London: Consn & Co., Ltd.
Chacko, P. (2011, May). Trust quotient. *Tata Group*. Tata Trusts/Feature Stories. Retrieved on August 17, 2014, from http://www.tata.com/ourcommitment/articlesinside/v3fvyGw4b5Q=/TLYVr3YPkMU=
Chandok, Ish. (2013, September 9). Ratan Tata—The profile of a Leader. *India Opines*. Retrieved on August 13, 2014, from http://indiaopines.com/ratan-tata-profile-leader/
Chandran, R., & Dhar, S. (2008, September 2). West Bengal protests lead Tata to halt all work on Nano car factory. *The New York Times*. Retrieved on June 3, 2012, from http://www.nytimes.com/2008/09/02/business/worldbusiness/02iht-tata.4.15840470.html
Chatterjee, D. (2013, April 11). Trusts to have sweeping powers to select, remove Tata Sons chairmen. *The Business Standard*. Retrieved on August 4, 2014, from http://www.business-standard.com/article/companies/trusts-to-have…g-powers-to-select-remove-tata-sons-chairmen-113041100023_1.html
Corporate Eye. (2008, May 20). Tata Group—A company that lives integrity. Retrieved on June 20, 2012, from http://www.corporate-eye.com/blog/2008/05/tata-group-a-company-that-lives-integrity/
Dutta, S. (2012). *The real cost of power*. The Bank Information Center. Retrieved on August 15, from http://www.bicusa.org/wp-content/uploads/2012/07/Real+Cost+of+Power.pdf
Engardio, P. (2007, August 2). The last Rajah. *Bloomberg Businessweek*. Retrieved on June 21, 2015, from http://www.bloomberg.com/bw/stories/2007-08-02/the-last-rajahbusinessweek-business-news-stock-market-and-financial-advice
Friedman, M. (1970, September 13). The social responsibility of business is to increase its profits. *The New York Times Magazine*. Retrieved on June 16, 2014, from http://www.umich.edu/~thecore/doc/Friedman.pdf
Gopalakrishnan, R. (2004, March). The challenge of growing. *Tata Group*. Retrieved on May 6, 2012, from http://www.tata.com/article.aspx?artid=RZMDxjGlK9Y=
Gupta, A., & Srinivasan, V. (2011). *When principles pay: Tata Power Plant Mundra* (Working Paper: 346). Indian Institute of Management Bangalore. Retrieved on August 7, 2014, from http://www.iimb.ernet.in/research/sites/default/files/WP%20No.%20346.pdf
Hill, A. (2011, November 28). Tata can take a long view on succession. *The Financial Times*. Retrieved on June 21, 2012, from http://www.ft.com/cms/s/0/a04030ce-1762-11e1-b00e-00144feabdc0.html#axzz1yiVws36Y
Hindustan Times. (2012, April 27). Tatas to raise R&D spending, cut costs. Retrieved on May 10, 2012, from http://www.hindustantimes.com/business-news/CorporateNews/Tatas-to-raise-R-amp-D--spending-cut-costs/Article1-847308.aspx
India Knowledge@Wharton. (2010, December 2). India's 2G telecom scandal spans the spectrum of abuse. Retrieved on July 15, 2012, from http://knowledge.wharton.upenn.edu/india/article.cfm?articleid=4549
Kamath, G. (2014, July). The excellence journey. *Tata Group*. Feature stories. Retrieved on August 15, 2014, from http://www.tata.com/company/articlesinside/The-excellence-journey

Kamenetz, A. (2009, March 23). Tata Nano: What's the environmental impact of 14 million more cars in India? *Fast Company*. Retrieved on August 5, 2014, from http://www.fastcompany.com/1229612/tata-nano-whats-environmental-impact-14-million-more-cars-india

Kannan, S. (2011, November 30). Can Mistry transform TATA's global brand? *BBC*. Retrieved on July 13, 2012, from http://www.bbc.co.uk/news/business-15959912

Kelkar, R. (Ed.). (1960, April). *M. K. Gandhi on Trusteeship*. Published by Jitendra T. Desai Navajivan Mudranalaya, Ahemadabad-380014 India. Retrieved on June 14, 1914, from http://www.mkgandhi.org/ebks/trusteeship.pdf

Kripalani, M. (2004, July 25). Ratan Tata: No one's doubting now. *Bloomberg Businessweek Magazine*. Retrieved on August 15, 2014, from http://www.businessweek.com/stories/2004-07-25/ratan-tata-no-ones-doubting-now

Kumar, G. S., & Yu, X. (2010, October 28). Tata's top executive embraces philanthropy. *The Harvard Crimson*. Retrieved on June 23, 2012, from http://www.thecrimson.com/article/2010/10/28/tata-business-school-group/

Lane, R. (2013, February 19). The Giving Pledge goes global—Warren Buffet details America's latest 'export'. *Forbes*. Retrieved on June 19, 2014, from http://www.forbes.com/sites/randalllane/2013/02/19/the-giving-pledge-goes-global-warren-buffett-details-americas-latest-export/

Leisinger, K. M., & Schmitt, K. (2011, April 17). Corporate responsibility and corporate philanthropy. *United Nations Organization*. Retrieved on July 25, 2014, from http://www.un.org/en/ecosoc/newfunct/pdf/leisinger-schmitt_corporate_responsibility_and_corporate_philanthropy.pdf

Luhrmann, T. M. (1996). *The good Parsi: The fate of a colonial elite in a postcolonial society*. Cambridge, MA: Harvard University Press.

Marlow, I. (2011, August 24). Telecom scandal shakes India's most beloved industry. *The Globe and Mail*. Retrieved on August 15, 2014, from http://www.theglobeandmail.com/report-on-business/telecom-scandal-shakes-indias-most-beloved-industry/article591884/?page=all

Mazumdar, R. (2011, November 24). Cyrus Mistry is mature enough to handle responsibility: KC Mehra, resident director Shapoorji Pallonji Group. *The Economic Times*. Retrieved on July 13, 2012, from http://articles.economictimes.indiatimes.com/2011-11-24/news/30437735_1_cyrus-mistry-ratan-tata-sir-nowroji-saklatvala

Moitra, S. (2014, August 7). Ratan Tata blames Mamata Banerjee for failure of Nano; TMC reacts by calling him 'delusional'. *DNA India*. Retrieved on August 13, 2014, from http://www.dnaindia.com/money/report-ratan-tata-blames-mamata-banerjee-for-failure-of-nano-tmc-reacts-by-calling-him-delusional-2008685

Moneycontrol.com. (2012, October 8). Tata Power synchronises third 800 MW unit at Mundra UMPP. Retrieved on August 8, 2014, from http://www.moneycontrol.com/news/business/tata-power-synchronises-third-800-mw-unit-at-mundra-umpp_766254.html

Nadkarni, A. G., & Branzel, O. (2008, March). The TATA way: Evolving and executing sustainable business strategies. *Ivey Business Journal*. Retrieved on June 18, 2012, from http://www.iveybusinessjournal.com/topics/strategy/the-tata-way-evolving-and-executing-sustainable-business-strategies

Oltermann, P., & McClanahan, P. (2014, January 31). Tata Nano safety under scrutiny after dire crash test results. *The Guardian*. Retrieved on August 8, 2014, from http://www.theguardian.com/global-development/2014/jan/31/tata-nano-safety-crash-test-results

Parsi Khabar. (2011, August 15). The story of India through powerful leaders: Ratan Tata. Retrieved on July 13, 2012, from http://parsikhabar.net/individuals/the-story-of-india-through-powerful-leaders-ratan-tata/3279/

Patel, B., & Damle, H. (2014, June 20). Tata Mundra: Making mockery of accountability. *Bretton Woods Project*. Retrieved on August 15, 2014, from http://www.brettonwoodsproject.org/2014/06/tata-mundra-making-mockery-accountability/

Pearson, N. (2012, March 8). Tata prefers clean-energy projects over coal in chase for growth. *Bloomberg*. Retrieved on May 10, 2012, from http://www.bloomberg.com/news/2012-03-08/tata-prefers-clean-energy-projects-over-coal-in-chase-for-growth.html

Pednekar, M. C. (2005). *Corporate social responsibility & business strategy—A case study on the Tata Group under Mr Ratan Tata*. Babasaheb Gawde Institute of Management Studies. Retrieved on June 22, 2012, from http://www.mmbgims.com/docs/full_paper/5_Mahesh_pp.pdf

Philanthropy Age. (2014, February 6). Ratan Tata: India's icon. Retrieved on July 25, 2014, from http://www.philanthropyage.org/2014/02/06/indias-icon/

Sarukkai, S. (2012). JRD Tata and the Idea of Trusteeship. In: Murzban Jal (Ed.), *Zoroastrianism: From antiquity to the modern period, PHISPC (Project of History of Indian Science, Philosophy, and Culture)* 2012. Retrieved on August 11, 2014, from http://eprints.manipal.edu/78163/1/Zoroastrianism_-_JRD_Tata_%26_the_idea_of_trusteeship-_SS-textbook.pdf

SDTT. (2013). Annual Reports. *Sir Dorabji Tata Trust and the Allied Trusts*. Retrieved on August 20, 2014, from http://www.dorabjitatatrust.org/id/85/Annual%20Report/

SDTT Annual Report. (2011). *Sir Dorabji Tata Trust and the Allied Trusts—Caring for what matters—Annual report for 2010–2011*. Retrieved on August 20, 2014, from http://www.dorabjitatatrust.org/pdf/SDTTAnnualReport2010-11.pdf

Shaaw, R. K., & Philip, S. (2011, November 24). Tata names Mistry to succeed Ratan as chairman, ending yearlong search. *Bloomberg*. Retrieved on June 20, 2012, from http://www.bloomberg.com/news/2011-11-23/mistry-will-replace-ratan-tata-as-head-of-india-s-biggest-business-group.html

SRTT. (2014). Downloads. *Sir Ratan Tata Trust & Navajbai Ratan Tata Trust*. Retrieved on August 20, 2014, from http://www.srtt.org/downloads/download.htm

SRTT Annual Report. (2011). *Annual report 2010–2011—Sir Ratan Tata Trust & Navajbai Ratan Tata Trust*. Retrieved on August 20, 2014, from http://www.srtt.org/downloads/annual/srttannualreport2010-11.pdf

Sullivan, P. (2012, August 15). Survey: Charities should spend 23 % on overhead. *The NonProfitTimes—The Leading Business Publication for Nonprofit Management*. Retrieved on August 20, 2014, from http://www.thenonprofittimes.com/news-articles/survey-charities-should-spend-23-on-overhead/

Suman Kumar, T. K. (1992). *India: Unity in diversity*. New Delhi: Anmol Publications, Publishers & Distributors.

Tata Chemicals. (2009). Tata Swach. Retrieved on June 18, 2012, from http://www.tatachemicals.com/products/tata_swach.htm

Tata Group. (2012). Tata code of conduct. Retrieved on August 11, 2014, from http://www.tata.com/aboutus/articlesinside/Tata-Code-of-Conduct

Tata Group. (2014a). Leadership with trust. Retrieved on August 11, 2014, from http://www.tata.com/aboutus/sub_index/Leadership-with-trust

Tata Group. (2014b). The giant who touched tomorrow. Retrieved on August 11, 2014, from http://www.tata.com/aboutus/articlesinside/AapOEYsYNwI=/TLYVr3YPkMU=

Tata Group. (2014c). The quotable Jamsetji Tata. Retrieved on August 11, 2014, from http://www.tata.com/article/inside/The-quotable-Jamsetji-Tata

Tata Group. (2014d). Values and purpose. Retrieved on August 15, 2014, from http://www.tata.com/aboutus/articlesinside/Values-and-purpose

Tata Group. (2014e). A tradition of trust. Retrieved on August 14, 2014, from http://www.tata.com/aboutus/articlesinside/A-tradition-of-trust

Tata Group. (2014f). The Tata Council for Community Initiatives. Retrieved on August 11, 2014, from http://www.tata.com/ourcommitment/articlesinside/Tata-Council-for-Community-Initiatives

Tata Group. (2014g). Tata Group Financials. Retrieved on August 13, 2014, from http://www.tata.com/htm/Group_Investor_GroupFinancials.htm

Tata Group. (2014h, July). TBEM has been the glue binding the group together. Retrieved on August 17, 2014, from http://www.tata.com/article/inside/TBEM-has-been-the-glue-in-binding-the-group-together

The Economic Times of India. (2010a, August 6). Tata Group: The numbers. Retrieved on August 20, 2014, from http://economictimes.indiatimes.com/top-10-tata-group-companies-by-revenues/tata-group-the-numbers/slideshow/6264312.cms

The Economic Times of India. (2010b, June 13). TCS ranked fifth in Bloomberg Businessweek's Tech 100. Retrieved on July 16, 2012, from http://articles.economictimes.indiatimes.com/2010-06-13/news/27632754_1_tech-100-shareholder-return-tcs

The Economic Times of India. (2011a, November 24). Mystery ends, Mistry begins. Retrieved on July 17, 2012, from http://epaper.timesofindia.com/Repository/getFiles.asp?Style=OliveXLib:LowLevelEntityToPrint_ETNEW&Type=text/html&Locale=english-skin-custom&Path=ETM/2011/11/24&ID=Ar00100

The Economic Times of India. (2011b, June 23). Tata group leaders praise Ratan Tata's leadership. Retrieved on May 10, 2012, from http://articles.economictimes.indiatimes.com/2011-06-23/news/29694693_1_ratan-tata-salt-to-software-managing-director-kishor-chaukar

The Economic Times of India. (2012, March 6). Tata Steel India's most admired company: Fortune. Retrieved on May 7, 2012, from http://articles.economictimes.indiatimes.com/2012-03-07/news/31127909_1_tata-steel-india-tata-tech-hay-group

The Economist. (2012a, February 11). Megahurts. Retrieved on July 15, 2012, from http://www.economist.com/node/21547280

The Economist. (2012b, December 1). From pupil to master: Ratan Tata's successor, Cyrus Mistry, has some dirty work to do. Retrieved on August 16, 2014, from http://www.economist.com/news/21567390-ratan-tatas-successor-cyrus-mistry-has-some-dirty-work-do-pupil-master

The Telegraph. (2012, February 15). Lessons in good practices on display. Retrieved on June 22, 2012, from http://www.telegraphindia.com/1120215/jsp/jharkhand/story_15134578.jsp

The Times of India. (2013, November 29). Ratan Tata: Marketing Nano as 'cheapest car' was a mistake. Retrieved on August 15, 2014, from http://timesofindia.indiatimes.com/business/india-business/Ratan-Tata-Marketing-Nano-as-cheapest-car-was-a-mistake/articleshow/26588240.cms

Thottam, J. (2009, April 13). The world's cheapest car debuts in India. *TIME*. Retrieved on May 13, 2012, from http://www.time.com/time/magazine/article/0,9171,1889168,00.html

Thottam, J. (2010, December 14). War of words escalates in India's telecom scandal. *TIME*. Retrieved on June 2, 2012, from http://www.time.com/time/world/article/0,8599,2036867,00.html

Timmons, H. (2008a, March 26). Ford sells Land Rover and Jaguar to Tata. *New York Times*. Retrieved on May 10, 2012, from http://www.nytimes.com/2008/03/26/business/worldbusiness/26cnd-auto.html

Timmons, H. (2008b, January 4). Tata pulls Ford units into its orbit. *New York Times*. Retrieved on May 10, 2012, from http://www.nytimes.com/2008/01/04/business/worldbusiness/04tata.html?_r=1

Wadia, J. (2011, October). Excellence in education—A unique initiative launched by Tata Steel aims at promoting excellence in education. *Tata Group/Sustainability/Feature Stories*. Retrieved on August 13, 2014, from http://www.tata.com/article/inside/jB!$$$$!S!$$$!Ra8Bxs=/TLYVr3YPkM=

Chapter 18
The Social Environment: Welfare and Corporate Social Responsibility

"Reduce the gap between rich and poor by developing a new social security system." (Stephan Rothlin, *Eighteen Rules for Becoming a Top Notch Player*, 2004)

18.1 Prelude

Pronto moda is a controversial new style among garments marketed under the "Made in Italy" label. The style is controversial not just because the garments are cheap and ephemeral; the controversy also focuses on the way they are manufactured, that is, by Chinese migrant and immigrant workers who have flocked to the old industrial city of Prato. Should cheap garments manufactured by Chinese migrants, in factories that some have accused of being sweatshops, be permitted to use the "Made in Italy" label? How should the city of Prato cope with the large influx of migrants, whose labors are certainly revitalizing some industries while also transforming the city's social environment? Our case study on Prato seeks to document not only the situation in Prato but also the responses of various groups to the challenges represented by the sudden appearance of an Asian immigrant community in their city. There are tensions to be explored, of course, but there are also stories of cooperation and mutual support involving the churches, businesses, and government agencies seeking to realize the common good in and for Prato.

This chapter takes its cues from this case study because the Prato story helps define the kind of considerations that must be addressed, if the common good is to be pursued in a global marketplace where the labor itself is now capable of migrating across national boundaries in search of new opportunities. Can universal moral standards seeking to protect the rights and human dignity of workers still be adhered to, when local traditions and institutions are overwhelmed by a massive influx of migrant workers coming from other countries with markedly different histories and cultures? What standard of care does any community owe the new arrivals whom they now must host? What do the migrants and their community leaders owe to the communities where they intend to create a new home for themselves? How do their responsibilities converge in a new search for the common good in a globalizing society?

S. Rothlin, D. McCann, *International Business Ethics*,
DOI 10.1007/978-3-662-47434-1_18

18.2 Case Study: Prato Meets China, in Search of the Common Good

18.2.1 Abstract

Chinese immigrants in the traditional textile district of Prato, Italy, form one of the largest Chinese communities in Europe today. Their arrival has fostered a wave of innovative entrepreneurship in the "Made in Italy" apparel industry. Chinese entrepreneurs have introduced a model of "fast fashion" production, which departs from the Italians' traditional standards of quality. Opinions regarding the phenomenon go in two directions. On the one hand, Chinese are perceived as a systemic threat; on the other hand, they are considered a resource for the survival of an industry now confronted with the challenges of globalization. The case addresses several critical issues when dealing with foreign investment and migrant workers: immigrant attitudes toward local laws, new jobs and wealth that do not contribute to those living in the area, preservation of traditional crafts, difficult communication between host and immigrant communities, and ways to build an effective cross-cultural dialogue.

18.2.2 Keywords

Made in Italy, Prato, Textile, Chinese immigrants, Workers' safety, Foreign investment, Intercultural dialogue, Rule of law

18.2.3 Prato

As the second largest city in Tuscany, Prato has the third highest population density in central Italy, surpassed only by Rome and Florence (*Unione Industriale Pratese* 2012a). Long ago, the area earned a reputation for its vibrant textile industry. For centuries, countless waves of immigrants have flooded to Prato seeking jobs. Prato's specialization in textiles began in the twelfth century, with the development of a local trade organization known as the Wool Guild of Merchants. In the nineteenth century, following a 200-year period of political instability, the industry was transformed from craftsmanship to mechanized production, which resulted not only in an increase in output but also in a rising demand for nonspecialized industrial labor. In the 1960s and 1970s, members of neighboring towns began to merge with Prato. The demographic boom was augmented by the arrival of southern Italians in 1981. During this transition, the distinctive nature of the area's competitive advantage changed, which till then had consisted of textile processing and production.

The markets Prato served, however, were also evolving, and consequently, the city needed to diversify its investments beyond its traditional focus on carded wool. This move provoked a crisis that persisted until the 1990s. However, the modest economic recovery did not last; Prato entered the new millennium in the midst of a deep depression with decreases in demand that are usually attributed to competition from developing economies (Dei Ottati 2009). In spite of Prato's vulnerability to ever-changing market conditions, various adjustments and technological innovations sustain its status as a global leader in fashion and textiles. However controversial, even the development of a Chinese district specializing in mass-market items alongside local high-end retailers provides solid evidence of Prato's ability to reinvent itself. The textile sector's current value is estimated to be a total of 4,352 million euros, enabling the participation of approximately 50,000 workers (*Unione Industriale Pratese* 2012b).

18.2.4 The Arrival of the Chinese

In recent years Prato has become the setting for unprecedented change in the composition of its workforce. Though the city accommodates large numbers of Albanians, Romanians, and Pakistanis, the population of Chinese nationals now surpasses any other foreign group, as their number increased from only 38 in 1989 to over 10,000 a decade later. Out of a total population of 187,000, there are approximately 11,500 legal Chinese residents. However, the local Bureau of Statistics estimates that there are 25,000 more illegal immigrants, the vast majority of whom are indeed coming from China (*Comune di Prato* 2012). Prato is the most successful Chinese community in Europe in terms of per capita income.

The entrepreneurial drive of the Chinese immigrant community has not gone unnoticed by Prato's Italian residents. At first the locals observed the newly established "Chinatown" with curiosity and quiet suspicion. In time, however, expressions of discontent have become more explicit, and the newcomers have started to be perceived as an economic threat as well as a social emergency (Dei Ottati 2009). Emergency or not, the Chinese impact on Prato is decidedly different in comparison with other immigrant groups, who have focused mainly on accepting whatever low-skill, low-paid jobs were available.

18.2.5 Takeover or Revitalization?

Chinese migrants, primarily from the Zhejiang region, identified Prato as an ideal base from which to set up an extensive network for garment distribution across Europe (Dei Ottati 2009). Heavy downsizing and the search for innovation to renew Prato's competitiveness laid the ground for the introduction of a new concept: *Pronto moda* or "fast fashion" (Donadio 2010).

Pronto moda follows a simple logic: exploit cheap inputs and sell products at low prices in order to earn on volume rather than margin. However, the traditional Italian interpretation of the fashion business prizes quality and uniqueness over mass merchandising. This is the reason why, for once, innovation came from outsiders rather than from home businesses that were unwilling to compromise their identity.

Chinese manufacturers, importing cheap raw materials from their home country, are producing fashion items sold worldwide under the reputable "Made in Italy" label. The meaning of "Made in Italy" goes far beyond geographic origin; in the fashion world, it is synonymous with uncompromising quality and unique couture—which are not the drivers of *Pronto moda*'s success. Those committed to traditional Italian ways of marketing and manufacturing fear that *Pronto moda* may gradually undermine the "Made in Italy" image in their customers' minds and thus put further pressure on domestic companies to adapt by imitating the success of their "foreign" competitors.

No doubt, the success of *Pronto moda* has enabled a dramatic increase in the number of Chinese manufacturers; over the past two decades, Chinese-owned factories grew to 3,200, while Italian owned have dwindled to 3,000. Between 2000 and 2010, Prato's *Confindustria*—the local industrial association—reported that the number of Italian textile factories was halved. If on the one hand the Chinese business model showed a path to restore local industry's competitiveness, on the other it is regarded as a threat to Italy's distinctive position in the global marketplace for fashion (Dei Ottati 2009).

Motivated by worries over the sustainability of their business in the face of "unfair competition" and prompted by allegations of workforce abuses and illegalities among the newcomers, Pratese entrepreneurs asserted that Chinese enterprises were in breach of Italian labor laws (Poggioli 2011). The National Council of Economy and Labor confirmed the widespread exploitation of labor in sweatshops and exposed these in a series of unannounced blitzes in the factories. The report contended that in order to sustain their advantageous pricing policies, numerous businesses neglected working hour limits and paid monthly salaries scarcely reaching 500 euros per month (Mottola 2011).

In addition, suspicions of rampant tax evasion provoked calls for greater governmental oversight. Riccardo Marini, leader of Prato's *Confindustria*, laments the competition coming from a "China without borders," at the same time adding, "the Chinese are very clever. They're not like other immigrants, who can be pretty thick" (Donadio 2010). He conceded that Italy's relatively underdeveloped institutional framework—which, in his opinion, is not the case in other European countries such as the UK and France (Dinmore 2010a)—may be to blame for the apparent disrespect of Italian labor laws by Chinese businesses.

Prompted by the controversies generated by the loud protests of local inhabitants and the defensive reactions of the accused, Prato's municipal government has increased the number of controls and inspections year by year in an attempt to reduce illegal violations (158 in 2008, 233 in 2009, and 400 in 2010). The biggest police operation, known as "Money to Money," uncovered a system of tax fraud and embezzlement culminating in unauthorized money transfers that channeled 238 million euros from Italy to China within a span of 2 years (2007–2009) (*China Daily* 2010). However, Mayor Roberto Cenni, an apparel company owner himself, pointed out how the complexity of evasions put in place by Chinese criminal organizations often running the factories renders countermeasures ineffective. For example, he cited the Chinese practice of registering new businesses when inspected ones are denied a license to operate. Furthermore, the compatibility of the organizational, family-based structure of the Chinese mafia and the Italian mafia has resulted in a collaboration based on the mutual sharing of networks, resources, and human capital.

Nevertheless, numerous Chinese business owners have refused to engage in black or gray market activities and instead work within the established regulatory system. Chinese textile manufacturer Xu Qiu Lin is one of them. Known in the city by the Italian name "Giulini," he was the first to become a member of *Confindustria*, and his business model encourages the hiring of both Chinese and Italian workers. He is keen to emphasize quality over quantity in order to avoid the diminishing returns associated with the production of cheap textiles. "My company is Italian," argued Giulini when interviewed, "because 'Made in Italy' is the style, fashion. And I need Italian taste, I need an Italian designer who could draw and create a model. Production no, that's outsourced" (*Italoblog* 2009). By integrating entrepreneurship Wenzhou style with the "Made in Italy" label, businessmen such as Xu may come to be regarded as renovators as opposed to systemic threats. "If the Chinese hadn't gone to Prato, would there be *Pronto moda*?" asks Matteo Wong, an Italian-born Chinese running a consulting firm for Chinese companies in Prato (Donadio 2010). The question implied in that statement is whether the district would have survived without *Pronto moda*.

Vinicio Bacio, the coordinator of special projects for the Italian investment agency, *Invitalia*, is the main promoter of a constructive atmosphere between Italian and Chinese businesses in Prato. He sees great potential in their collaboration, which, however hesitatingly, has already begun. Chinese and Italian businesses, in his view, are active at different stages of the supply chain and can maximize overall efficiency and profitability by leveraging technology transfers, sharing resources, and improving social solidarity. In Bacio's own words "the presence of the Wenzhounese community can be a great opportunity, if [the communities] develop rules and mechanisms for developing the economy and improving social cohesion, then closeness to China may be the key towards an innovative textile economy" (Gardner 2010).

In order to prompt integration and a shared sense of legality, the project IES (Immigration and Sustainable Economy) was introduced to address the state of Chinese entrepreneurs. IES is run by Prato's municipal government and financed by the Ministry of Internal Affairs (*Toscana TV* 2012a). The response by Chinese business owners has been greater than expected. The initial estimate determined 30 people would participate in the program. Real attendance was double that. Mayor Cenni saw this as an encouraging sign. Chinese business owners understood the need for a "zero tolerance" toward criminal activity paired with a proactive "information and formation" campaign, in order to achieve legitimacy in the eyes of their Italian neighbors.

18.2.6 Social Transformation

The Chinese wave in Prato goes well beyond narrowly defined economic consequences. Macroeconomic changes are self-evident and give ground to both rising fears and future hopes concerning the destiny of the Prato area. The number of Chinese-owned shops has soared with repercussions for the city's future development. Chinese hairdressers, restaurants, retailers, and food stores have become a noticeable part of the town.

Not surprisingly, remittances from such enterprises constitute a major friction point between the Pratese and Chinese inhabitants. An examination of data from the Bank of Italy and ISTAT (National Institute of Statistics) revealed 250 million euros have been remitted to China in 2011; by contrast, before the global financial crisis took full effect, the figure for 2009 was 500 million (*Chamber of Commerce of Prato* 2012). The income generated by the Chinese is used to support families in their home country, instead of being spent and reinvested locally. Some observers thus contend that the expanded economic activity is not mirrored by correspondingly dramatic increases in social capital at the community level.

Employment and security seem to be at the crux of the grievances heard within the Pratese communities. Chinese workers are often accused of stealing Italian jobs and isolating themselves so that even the market created by so many new consumers is primarily an advantage to fellow Chinese. Locals point to the fact that jobs at Chinese factories are primarily absorbed by new arrivals and do nothing to curb Prato's rising unemployment due to the closure of Italian factories. Currently, the Chamber of Commerce registry of foreign enterprises in the area has shown a 180 % increase in the ten years prior to 2012 (*Unione Industriale Pratese* n.d). Services covering real estate, insurance and credit, communications, business solutions, and travel are significantly expanding, though along the nationality divide. On the other hand, Prato is ranked among the biggest offenders in terms of increased abuses and illegalities, which—in the National Report on Criminality—are attributed to the presence of Chinese immigrants (*Notizie di Prato* 2011).

Though often overlooked in the attempt to legitimize or delegitimize the Chinese immigrants in public opinion, there is a growing convergence between the two communities. Thirty-two percent of newborns in Prato's hospitals have at least one Chinese parent. The percentage of foreign students in local schools surpass the Italian national average by far, reaching up to 70 % in primary schools within the city's historic center (Hooper 2010). This suggests the willingness of families to raise their children as Italians and Chinese at the same time, in the hope that the children will be able to bridge the cultural gap. Furthermore, the University of Wenzhou has opened a branch at the University of Florence Prato, with the intent of promoting dialogue and student exchanges between the two countries.

Nevertheless, in the opinion of some observers, Chinese society remains quite closed. Language is a major barrier, followed by differences in lifestyle and Italy's lax regulatory system. The Chinese live apart in the *Macrolotto zero* area of Prato and rarely respond to the suspicions nurtured by their Italian neighbors. Xu Qiu Lin sees this as a setback for both parties. He understands that enhancing communication might dramatically increase the potential for cross border collaboration. Chinese who settle down in Prato can learn from Italy's industries and social resources and can share what they learn in China through their network of relationships. At the same time, Italian entrepreneurs may come to understand Chinese culture and experiment by working together on a small scale. This was the idea that moved Xu Qiu Lin to set up the Centre for Made in Italy in Nanjing not far from his hometown, Hangzhou, which would ideally serve the needs of Italian companies pursuing business operations in China (*Italoblog* 2009). Marini praises Xu's initiatives that give him reasons to hope for the future, although he remains skeptical about the incentives enabling dishonest people to participate in such efforts (*Unione Industriale Pratese* 2009). Xu, however, embraces the zero-tolerance policy indicated by Mayor Cenni. He well understands the delicate situation in which he is a player. In fact, Xu was victim of two violent episodes, one in 2009 against his warehouse and the other in 2011 against his family (*La Nazione* 2011). "The Union of Industrialists," said Marini at the second National Conference on Immigration in 2009, "welcomes whoever wants to operate in the respect of legality to the enhancement of the industry, without nationality based distinctions" (*Unione Industriale Pratese* 2009), and he concluded with the wish there would be others like Xu, ready to raise their voices in the Chinese community while demonstrating their loyalty to shared values and beliefs.

As a pivotal institution linking Chinese and Italian cultures, the Chinese Catholic community also promotes integration. Prato's Chinese Church led by Fr. Francesco Wang, himself a native of Jilin, China, has worked hard to accommodate factory-working parishioners by setting up late masses for those who come off of the night shift, providing translation services, offering Italian lessons, and even connecting illegal aliens with Italian lawyers (Brunetti 2009). The Italian Episcopal Conference and the local *Caritas* office of the Pratese Diocese have supported the Chinese Church's development since its inception, enabling the creation of an independent pastoral presence. As the Chinese Catholic Church in Prato grows, so do levels of trust and channels of communication. The formation of laymen plays an important role as they become vehicles to spread a message of solidarity and as they develop into active members of the community (Brunetti 2009).

18.2.7 Summary

The Prato story illustrates the difficulties that emerge when diverse cultures collide in a single location and industry. The increasing tension between the Chinese and local Italian communities is motivated by both economic and cultural concerns. The pressures of competition in a globalizing economy, in particular, expose the perennial need to devise institutional measures that would address the many issues that impede the successful integration of the communities of Prato. Nevertheless, few people seem capable of extricating themselves from the polarized status quo and directly engaging in a dialogue to breach the wall of intolerance. Xu Qiu Lin is among them. How do you think entrepreneurs like Xu, who have decided to "play the game by the rules," can exert a positive role in the Chinese community? By the same token, how can Italian institutions like Vinicio Bacio's project at *Invitalia* engage in a fruitful collaboration with immigrants? Do you consider a "zero-tolerance policy" that may discourage Chinese immigration a sufficient response to the challenges and opportunities at Prato, or would you recommend alternative solutions? How would you seek to locate the common good in Prato's changing economy and society?

18.3 Case Study Discussion

The development of *Pronto moda* presents us with a classic story raising moral issues usually associated with globalization: An organized group of immigrants arrives on foreign shores in order to take advantage of new economic opportunities. Their activities provoke a range of responses from the locals, mostly wary and suspicious. Are the newcomers stealing jobs from the locals? Is their competition unfair? Will hard-won victories in defending workers' rights and basic human dignity be eroded by an influx of migrants for whom such standards may seem like a cruel joke, mocking their very real struggle just to survive? Were the migrants to be deported or forcibly excluded from employment opportunities in the countries where they have landed—one interpretation of a "zero-tolerance" policy—would that be fairer or more just than the present situation, with all its moral ambiguity, hypocrisy, and corruption?

Should the situation in Prato be regarded as a justification for resisting globalization by any means necessary? Would the highly regarded "Made in Italy" label be more effectively preserved, if globalization could be suppressed? Whether we are for or against globalization as such, the moral issues raised by Prato's transformation are not dissimilar from those found in other places where significant changes in local populations have occurred as a result of this process. We could focus, for example, on the controversies over Turkish *Gastarbeitern* in Germany, or Mexican farm laborers in the USA, or Filipina and Indonesian domestic helpers working in Hong Kong. Macro-level concerns regarding social justice and the common good—particularly with reference to workers' rights and basic respect for human dignity—inevitably have surfaced in these cases, just as they do in Prato's struggle over the impact of Chinese immigrants on its textile and apparel industries.

The problem with shifting from the specific challenges to be faced in Prato to a general discussion of the ethics of globalization is that such discussions are likely to become as borderless as the concerns giving rise to them. If our discussion is to contribute to the development of international business ethics, we may have to examine the details of the case, in order to determine whether the businesses operating in Prato, and their managers, are acting responsibly to create a win-win situation for everyone involved. Of course, creating a win-win situation, or trying to balance the legitimate concerns of all stakeholders, is but another name for pursuing the common good.

Rather than speculate about globalization in general, we should focus our inquiry on specific questions of moral agency. Who is responsible, for what are they responsible, and how can their exercise of responsibility enable the communities of Prato to make progress toward achieving the common good? Who, then, specifically is identified as a moral agent in our Prato case study, and what do we think of their activities? We have been introduced to at least three individuals representing different stakeholders, whose actions qualify them for consideration as moral agents: Mayor Roberto Cenni, who is also the owner of an apparel company, was observed expressing the concerns of the host community, the locals in Prato, who see themselves threatened by the influx of Chinese immigrants. Xu Qiu Lin, a Chinese entrepreneur originally from Hangzhou, known by his Italian name "Giulini," appeared to have done more than any other member of the immigrant community to reach out to the local communities in Prato. Finally, we also observed Fr. Francesco Wang, pastor of the Chinese Catholic parish, whose work is supported by the Italian Episcopal Conference as well as the Diocese of Prato. Fr. Wang's activities are significant because he represents a faith community rooted in Italy for nearly two millennia that has also been a significant part of Chinese history for close to 500 years. Each of these three community leaders is converging toward a constructive response to the challenges raised by Prato's changing demographics.

As we have seen, the challenges they face are multiple and complex. They involve ongoing controversies over the rights of immigrants, the desires of both individuals and groups for economic advancement, the rights and obligations of the communities that are forced to accommodate the new arrivals, and the possible irrelevance of ethical and legal standards historically identified with the Universal Declaration of Human Rights (UDHR). Beyond these, there is a basic philosophical question about human freedom and its limits. Should everyone be free to choose whatever will advance their immediate personal interests, so long as they are willing to live with the consequences? If an immigrant's desire to earn a living for his or her family conflicts with the desires of locals who want to do the same for their families, whose desire should be honored? If an immigrant is willing to accept lower wages or forego previously mandated social benefits, why should an employer be prevented from profiting from his or her choices? If I am willing to compete for a job by offering my services more cheaply than others, why shouldn't I be free to choose what I think is best for me and my family? Perennial questions regarding the freedom of labor contracts inevitably arise when the whole point of immigration is to improve one's position economically. This, of course, is the concrete reality of competition in a global labor market, and beyond the question of freedom, inevitably, it raises the question of fairness.

The moral agents featured in our story—Cenni, Xu, and Fr. Wang—are significant from the point of view of international business ethics because not only do they know the reality of competition on a day-to-day basis but they are also trying to respond to that reality while preserving and enhancing basic moral values. If you were in Cenni's shoes—or Xu's—what would you do? What would you say to your colleagues and coworkers who are looking to you for moral leadership? Since you are expected to represent one or the other community's business interests, just how moral can your leadership be? Can you rise above a one-sided defense of the hopes and fears of those whom you represent? Should you even attempt it, especially if criminal syndicates are making threats against you and your family? If you agree that everyone should orient their activities toward the common good, which policies would you support as promising and which would you criticize as counterproductive? Where, if at all, do you think the leaders need to do more? If so, what precisely? Among the three, Fr. Wang's leadership may be crucial, for he is a Catholic priest and therefore a community leader with ties to both the local and immigrant communities. Though he is not directly responsible for a business, he may be able to help the other two achieve their legitimate business goals while also working toward the common good.

Previously, in Chap. 4 on "Moral Decision-Making in Business," we proposed a six-step model for integrating ethical analysis into sound business decision-making. Adapted from Peter Drucker's classic, first published in 1954, *The Practice of Management*, the model may help us understand specifically the challenge faced by a particular moral agent. Let us use this model to learn from the experience of Prato's "Giulini," the Chinese entrepreneur, Xu Qiu Lin. We organize our comments on his actions under each of the six steps:

1. What is the problem? Xu has already demonstrated leadership by becoming the first of the immigrant Chinese businessmen to join *Confindustria*. His intention seems clear: he expects to settle his family permanently in Prato and support them by developing a business that combines Chinese manufacturing techniques with Italian designs in order to reinvigorate the "Made in Italy" fashion brand. Because he is committed to making Prato a success, he has attempted to diversify his workforce, employing both local Italians and Chinese immigrants, thus making his firm a social experiment for discovering how to integrate these groups successfully into a single workforce. Because his efforts are producing some success—for example, his collaboration with local authorities seeking to enforce Italian labor laws and other regulations—Xu has been the victim of violence directed against not only his warehouse but also his own family. This is the problem: faced with threats to his family's safety, should Xu continue his effort to improve working conditions and community relations in Prato, or should he quietly withdraw and, as they say, mind his own business? Obviously, Xu's efforts have provoked resistance, but from whom? He needs to know precisely who is behind the violence: resentful elements in either the Pratese or the Chinese groups or in both. Both would have a stake in seeking to discourage Xu's support for fair and even-handed law enforcement. Since both the Italian mafia and the Chinese triads are known to have a stake in preserving a status quo that treats workers as little more than slaves, Xu may need to find ways to preserve

his business, while working to improve the social environment by confronting the power of organized crime.

2. What are the resources for a solution? Xu is fortunate that his activities have already earned him quite a bit of favorable publicity, for his local prominence may be the best protection against the threats he is facing. Xu is known personally by leaders in the local Pratese business community, who refer to him as "Giulini" and who acknowledge his efforts to meet local law enforcement agencies halfway. These efforts create resources that he will need in achieving his ultimate goal of integrating the Chinese into the Pratese community. The organization that he has started in Nanjing, the "Centre for Made in Italy," appears to be a promising vehicle for educating Chinese seeking to do business in Italy and Italians seeking to do business in China. By using his unique position to facilitate the interactions of other entrepreneurs in both groups, Xu can create the kind of supportive environment in which he may become increasingly less vulnerable to personal attack. His most important resource, however, is the firm he has already established in Prato. The more successful he is in showing his Chinese colleagues that playing by the rules, and establishing positive relationships in the local community, can lead to long-term prosperity for all concerned, the more convincing he will be in representing their interests in his interactions with the Pratese community. He must strive therefore to become the change that he wants to see, by making his business a model of excellence in every possible way, including but hardly restricted to moral leadership.
3. Range of possible solutions: Here, we brainstorm anything that might address Xu's problem, moral or immoral, legal or illegal. Here are some options; they are for purposes of illustration. If Xu is worried about his family's safety, perhaps he should send them back to China. Or if security at the warehouse is a problem, perhaps he should negotiate a secret alliance with the Chinese triads. They will leave him alone, if he agrees to pay a hefty "tax" for their protection. Perhaps, there are other groups unhappy with Xu. Bribery is as old a tradition in Italy as it is in China. Why not just pay off whoever can provide whatever protection he needs to stay in business? Of course, there may also be positive solutions to explore, options more consistent with Xu's apparent philosophy and his stated goals. A major concern is convincing members of the Chinese business community to follow his leadership in developing cooperative relationships with local businesses, the press, various government agencies, etc. Transparency is very important here, in order to build trust. But making the first step toward transparency is very difficult, especially for people whose cultures have learned—for very good reasons—to be suspicious of it. Yet unless Xu can show others how to stand up to the threats posed by criminal elements in Prato, they will only be able to make as much progress as the triads and the mafia will allow. Unless Xu's own good example can inspire similar efforts within the Chinese business community in Prato, there seems little hope that integration can be achieved there. In this step, we want to explore as many solutions as anyone can imagine. What concretely might advance the cause of integration in Prato, without rendering Xu even more vulnerable to violent reprisals?

4. Eliminate the "sleaze," that is, eliminate any solutions that fall below the standards implicit in the resources identified in Step 2. Bribing the Chinese triads or setting up some kind of protection racket with them seems contrary to everything that Xu is attempting to achieve. It would certainly discredit any claim to moral leadership. Similarly, since Xu is committed to modeling moral leadership, he must consistently reject any solution that would compromise his basic moral principles or his sense of social responsibility.
5. From the remaining options, choose the one solution that makes the most business sense: Xu's first option, namely, sending his family back to China, may be understandable, but it is so narrowly focused on personal security that it does nothing specific to solve the problem facing his business. Arguably, Xu cannot achieve his business goals without creating or maintaining a social network among both Chinese and Pratese business people that is supportive of his community integration strategy. His own way of doing business, in short, will inevitably be undermined, if he withdraws from efforts to form a supportive social network. Conversely, the effort to go forward with creating a supportive social environment may be the key to securing a future for his business.
6. Implementation: While Xu's initial efforts at community integration and development show genuine moral leadership, the challenge is how to consolidate the gains that have already been made and use them as a platform for further progress. Moving on to the next step is never easy. Xu cannot do it alone. At this point he needs to step up his collaboration with the other leaders that we have identified as moral agents, namely, Mayor Cenni and Fr. Wang. The resistance that they have met from organized criminal gangs can only be overcome by creating new forms of solidarity, personally, as well as within and among the communities who look to them for leadership.

The Prato case study's focus on moral agency—highlighting, that is, the willingness of individual persons to act together for the common good—confirms our general thesis regarding the natural priority of moral virtue in human affairs, particularly in international business ethics. As we proceed further into the details of any situation or case study, we often find that the challenge actually does involve the perennial struggle of good versus evil. People have been enslaved and exploited for as long as human civilization has existed. While the evils apparent in some forms of globalization are nothing new, their scale and scope are greatly expanded—as is, of course, the scale and scope of opportunities for doing good. That a Chinese immigrant community has an opportunity to restore the apparel industry in a key area for manufacturing in central Italy could only have occurred as a result of globalization. But by the same token, the challenges to be faced in seizing this opportunity are themselves symptomatic of globalization. A focus on moral agency will determine whether and how the leaders in Prato will respond to these challenges.

The main point in case studies like this in international business ethics is to convince future business managers that they can do well while doing good. Not every challenge in business requires them to abandon their sense of personal integrity in order to achieve their business goals. Becoming a top-notch player, we believe, means acquiring the habit of examining any challenging situation for ways to harmonize both moral excellence and business success. Xu Qiu Lin seems to have understood this point and may serve as a role model for others in both the Chinese and the Pratese business communities. To be sure, we may be skeptical of role models in business, but it would be shortsighted and meanspirited to simply dismiss any reports of doing well while doing good, as if such an outcome by definition were impossible in a globalizing economy. We all have a stake in the virtuous circle that seems to be forming in Prato.

18.4 Ethical Reflection

Prato's effort to pursue a common good in which the legitimate interests of all the communities, both indigenous and immigrant, can be identified and secured probably could not have come even this far without the active participation of the Catholic Church. As its local representative in the Chinese immigrant community, Fr. Francesco Wang in 2009 was appointed associate pastor to the parish of the Ascension (*Parocchia Dell'Ascensione*) in Prato. His ministry clearly has expanded beyond meeting the immediate spiritual needs of Catholics in the Chinese community, to addressing problems in the social environment, both inside and outside the church, that have impeded the full integration of Prato's Chinese. Fr. Wang appears to have been particularly effective in alerting Catholic communities throughout the world to the importance of the struggle ongoing in Prato.

18.4.1 Modeling Catholic Social Teaching in Prato

Fr. Wang's report on "Chinese Migrants in Prato" was included in an issue of *Tripod*—a publication of the Catholic Diocese of Hong Kong—commemorating the 120th anniversary of the Vatican's publication of Pope Leo XIII's *Rerum novarum* (1891), commonly regarded as the point of departure for the development of Catholic social teaching. His brief sketch of the situation in Prato expresses the hope that the church's involvement, especially through the establishment of a "Chinese pastoral center," will enable various groups, including the vast majority of non-Catholic immigrants, to work together for "a bright future." Fr. Wang is very frank about the difficult situation of the Chinese workers in Prato:

> Due to the language barrier, most of the Chinese laborers choose to work in Chinese factories. The working environment is very bad, and is even worse for the illegal workers, who do not have the right of abode. They are not entitled to public holidays; they have no medical insurance; they receive low wages; they are exposed to textile fiber, heat, cold, noise and to a 15 to 16 hour work day. The only motivation that drives them to work so hard is the salary that is more than ten times higher than what they could earn in China. (Wang 2011)

He is similarly frank about the fears and resentments of the Italian communities in Prato and their potential for provoking further violent reactions:

> From 2009 onwards, tension between the town of Prato and the Chinese migrants has escalated. Many of the Chinese factories were closed down or are being investigated. The Italians have a bad impression of the Chinese. Many look upon the Chinese as tax evaders, those who snatch away their job opportunities, or who cheapen Italian brands. Moreover, criminal activities where the Chinese team up with Italian organized crime groups, have also mounted. These include not only the illegal import of textile products, but also people smuggling, prostitution, gambling, and money laundering. Other places in Italy also keep an eye on the situation in Prato, and the things mentioned above increase the hostility of the local people towards the Chinese. (Wang 2011)

Rather than attempt to hide the problems of the Chinese immigrants and their vulnerability to exploitation by criminal elements in both communities, Fr. Wang apparently believes that transparency and accountability are necessary first steps toward building collaborative relationships that may converge toward a harmonious society.

Fr. Wang's personal efforts, since his appointment as associate pastor at the *Parocchia dell'Ascensione*, have yielded mixed results. While some of his requests to the Diocese of Prato and other Catholic institutions have not been granted, for example, his appeal for financial support to allow five immigrants to participate in the Church's World Youth Day (August 2011) in Madrid or his petition to shorten the length of time for converts taking instructions in the Catholic faith and practice before accepting them into the church through the sacrament of baptism, others have been successful, such as the opening of a community center for the Chinese immigrants at the parish. Mindful of the national minorities in China and the diversity among their spoken languages, Fr. Wang has insisted that all Chinese religious services be held in Putonghua or Mandarin, the sole official language of the PRC. For his efforts, Fr. Wang has received increasingly favorable treatment by the news media in Prato.[1] As heartening as his increasing recognition may be, his experience gives us an opportunity to examine the Catholic social teaching that so clearly animates his service in Prato.

[1] One telling example is the story of Xie Guofa, characterized in the press as "the other Godenzio" in order to distinguish him from Hu Li Xia, whose homeless existence has made him an urban legend and the butt of too many cruel jokes throughout central Italy, including Rome (Cochi 2014a). By contrast, Fr. Wang discovered Xie Guofa on the steps of the parish hall and eventually persuaded him to take some food and shelter there. Meanwhile, Fr. Wang made inquiries in the Prato Chinese community and, using his connections in China, was able to reunite Xie with his family who were able to take him home. Xie apparently had suffered from an industrial accident in Prato that had left him unable to care properly for himself (Cochi 2014b). Rather than turn his back on Xie as not worth his time and effort, Fr. Wang apparently saw in him the suffering Christ to whom Christians must respond, "Whatsoever you do to the least of my brothers, that you do unto me" (Matthew 25: 31–46). Fr. Wang seems to be a true example of Christian virtue, flourishing in the midst of Prato's Chinatown.

18.4.2 *The Enduring Relevance of Pope Leo XIII's* Rerum novarum

It is not a coincidence that Fr. Wang's report should appear in an edition of *Tripod* celebrating the 120th anniversary of *Rerum novarum*,[2] for *Rerum novarum* (1891) was the first papal social encyclical to address the problems of workers in the capitalistic industrial economy that had developed so dramatically in Europe during the second half of the nineteenth century. One of the *Tripod* articles, "Pope Leo XIII's Encyclical *Rerum novarum* and the Challenges for China" (Ticozzi 2011), explores the relevance of the encyclical to the dramatic changes that have occurred in China during this era of economic and social reform. Since these changes, as China moves away from a "socialist economy" through reforms bent on "liberalization," the "serious negative side effects" are uncannily similar to the evils addressed by Leo XIII. *Rerum novarum*, in Ticozzi's view, provides a sound advice on five "main challenges" that China is facing today:

1. "Agreements between employers and employees on a 'Just Salary'"—*Rerum novarum*'s answer to the problem of "exploitation of the workers" consists not only in an explanation of what justice demands for wages—ultimately that they be sufficient to support "a frugal and well-behaved wage-earner" and his family—but also that they be subject to negotiation through collective bargaining, in which "workers associations" genuinely function to preserve the workers' rights (*Rerum novarum*, paragraph 57). In this context, Ticozzi specifically mentions the plight of "Chinese migrants being forced to work long hours in Chinese-owned factories in several countries, without proper remuneration and good living conditions." He also notes the progress that has been made recently in China, specifically, "the 12th Five-Year Program," adopted by the Communist Party of China's Central Committee, in October 2010, which assured the protection of workers' rights.
2. "Cooperation between employers and employees, instead of social conflict or 'class struggle'"—Under the leadership of Hu Jintao, China's 11th Five-Year Plan (2006–2010) endorsed the concept of a "harmonious society" committed to "peaceful development" instead of Chairman Mao's advocacy of perpetual "class struggle." In so doing, the Communist Party's ideology is now consistent with *Rerum novarum* (no. 19). But as Ticozzi points out, they differ still on the role of religion in cultivating a harmonious society:

[2] *Rerum novarum*, usually mistranslated as "of new things," refers to the revolutionary changes then occurring in Europe, impacting especially the conditions of the working class. The focus of the encyclical is not on revolution, but on how society should think about and respond to these changes, in the hope of creating greater justice and peace and easing the miseries of workers and their families. The general introduction to *Tripod*'s articles, "Revisiting Rerum novarum in its 120th Year," by Joseph Cardinal Zen Ze-Kuin, former Bishop of the Catholic Diocese of Hong Kong, is an excellent guide to the basic message of the encyclical and its relevance today (Zen 2011).

> The role of the State is to promote social justice and order through protection of the rights of citizens, while religion, and the churches, must provide the correct social principles for ensuring the just solution of conflicts, moral guidance to temper the free operations of market forces and to prevent abuses, as well as providing charitable services to ensure a harmonious cooperation among the people. (Ticozzi 2011)

As Ticozzi points out, while "the role of religion and churches in building up a harmonious society has been officially recognized by the Chinese authorities on several occasions," the churches have yet to be allowed "the range of autonomy and free initiative" necessary to ensure their effectiveness in carrying out their mission.

3. "Obligations to justice by both employers and employees: Professional Ethics"—Unlike other Western philosophies that tend to regard rights as entitlements pure and simple, *Rerum novarum* and the subsequent tradition of Catholic social teaching insist that for every right, there is a corresponding duty or responsibility. Thus, in addition to defending workers' rights, Leo XIII outlined the duties specific to both workers and their employers:

> Of these duties, the following bind the proletarian and the worker: fully and faithfully to perform the work which has been freely and equitably agreed upon; never to injure the property, nor to outrage the person, of an employer; never to resort to violence in defending their own cause, nor to engage in riot or disorder; and to have nothing to do with men of evil principles, who work upon the people with artful promises of great results, and excite foolish hopes which usually end in useless regrets and grievous loss.
>
> The following duties bind the wealthy owner and the employer: not to look upon their work people as their bondsmen, but to respect in every man his dignity as a person ennobled by Christian character. They are reminded that, according to natural reason and Christian philosophy, working for gain is creditable, not shameful, to a man, since it enables him to earn an honorable livelihood; but to misuse men as though they were things in the pursuit of gain, or to value them solely for their physical powers—that is truly shameful and inhuman. Again justice demands that, in dealing with the working man, religion and the good of his soul must be kept in mind. Hence, the employer is bound to see that the worker has time for his religious duties; that he be not exposed to corrupting influences and dangerous occasions; and that he be not led away to neglect his home and family, or to squander his earnings. Furthermore, the employer must never tax his work people beyond their strength, or employ them in work unsuited to their sex and age.
>
> His great and principal duty is to give every one what is just. Doubtless, before deciding whether wages are fair, many things have to be considered; but wealthy owners and all masters of labor should be mindful of this—that to exercise pressure upon the indigent and the destitute for the sake of gain, and to gather one's profit out of the need of another, is condemned by all laws, human and divine. To defraud any one of wages that are his due is a great crime which cries to the avenging anger of Heaven. "Behold, the hire of the laborers… which by fraud has been kept back by you, crieth; and the cry of them hath entered into the ears of the Lord of Sabaoth." Lastly, the rich must religiously refrain from cutting down the workmen's earnings, whether by force, by fraud, or by usurious dealing; and with all the greater reason because the laboring man is, as a rule, weak and unprotected, and because his slender means should in proportion to their scantiness be accounted sacred. (*Rerum novarum*, no. 20)

Leo XIII firmly believed, and Catholic social teaching unwaveringly teaches, that a harmonious society is possible, if only employers as well as workers were to abide by their basic moral obligations to one another. It is useful to note that in addition to wage justice and the elimination of all forms of cheating or fraud perpetrated by members of either group, *Rerum novarum* insists that workers be given sufficient time to perform their religious duties—which, as we have seen, has been one of Fr. Wang's major concerns in his negotiations with the Chinese employers of Prato. Such concerns are not trivial or merely "spiritual," if we agree that the kind of genuinely ethical reciprocity, cultivated in the churches and other religious institutions, is the ultimate key to achieving a harmonious society.

4. "Human rights and private property"—Ticozzi lists the various "socioeconomic rights" of all workers, outlined in *Rerum novarum*, "namely, the right to human dignity (nos. 16, 40), the right to justice (nos. 33, 36), the right to welfare (no. 34), the right to enjoy freedom (no. 40), the right to work (no. 44), the right to good and safe working conditions (nos. 33, 36), the right to a living wage and a just salary (nos. 43, 45), the right to private property (nos. 10, 11, 38, 47), the right to proper rest (no. 41, 42), the right to savings (no. 38, 46), the right to protest (no. 39), the right to equal taxation (no. 39, 47), the right to social security (nos. 36, 40, 47), the right to association (no. 47), the right to equality and to be protected by public authorities (nos. 33, 37, 40), and the right of children to a true education (no. 42, against child labor), etc." (Ticozzi 2011). Private property, we must note, is not an obstacle to fulfilling these rights, as if their realization could only be achieved through the abolition of private property. On the contrary, "the principle of private ownership must be held sacred and inviolable" (no. 46), for without it, the other rights are vulnerable to the vagaries of the state policy. This lesson has also been learned in China, through bitter experience, and "after years of controversy, in 2007, the National People's Congress adopted the Property Law," protecting "ownership rights, use rights, and security rights" in the various forms of "state, collective, and private" property. Where Catholic social teaching differs from China's current policies on private property is in recognizing that it "is not simply a right given to people by the State, but it is a right of all human beings because of their human nature. It is a right which the State must respect, guarantee, and favour. This shift of attitude and mentality is a critical challenge for the Chinese authorities" (Ticozzi 2011). Once again, there is genuine progress toward consensus, but major philosophical differences remain unresolved.
5. "The gap between the rich and the poor"—*Rerum novarum* recognized that the concentration of wealth as a result of the Industrial Revolution in Europe had the effect of laying "upon the teeming masses of the labouring poor a yoke little better than that of slavery itself" (no. 3). The encyclical regarded this as a revolutionary change that needed to be overcome, but not by adopting the revolutionary alternative represented by socialism. Instead, the only way forward was to restore society's commitment to the common good, which would entail taking specific measures to preserve human dignity and enhance human solidarity: "If working people can be encouraged to look forward to obtaining a share in the land and property, the consequence will be that the gulf between vast wealth and sheer poverty will be bridged over, and the respective classes will be brought nearer to one another… (no. 47)."

In Ticozzi's view, struggling to overcome the desperate poverty of China's masses, Chairman Mao and his associates attempted to establish a revolutionary regime that not only demoralized the Chinese people but ultimately widened "the wealth gap between rich and poor," once the era of economic reform was underway. If China is to overcome not only the wealth gap but also "the increasing social inequality between urban and rural areas, as well as the income gap among workers in various industries," it must attempt a genuine renewal of moral education, with the support of many institutions, including the churches. China's Catholic community has "the Church's best kept secret"—Catholic social teaching—to contribute.[3] China's rulers should not be paralyzed by fear of what they regard as the subversive potential of this foreign ideology. As we have seen, there are remarkable convergences between Catholic social teaching and the laudable aspirations of many in China's current government for economic and social reform. The struggle to achieve a harmonious society inevitably requires us to overcome past fears and suspicions in order to see the common good that is increasingly evident in the work of the Chinese Catholic Church and its affiliated churches overseas.

18.4.3 Catholic Social Teaching on Immigration and Globalization

No less impressive is Catholic social teaching's concern to address the problems of migrant workers, who must bear a disproportionate share of the burdens imposed by globalization. The *Compendium of the Social Doctrine of the Church* (Pontifical Council for Justice and Peace 2004), for example, reaffirms Catholicism's perennially positive attitude toward immigration, including "the immigration of people looking for a better life," that is, migrant workers: "In most cases, however, immigrants fill a labour need which would otherwise remain unfilled in sectors and territories where the local workforce is insufficient or unwilling to engage in the work in question" (*Compendium*, no. 297). Without attempting to resolve all the thorny political issues involved in the rights and responsibilities of governments to regulate migrations within and through their jurisdictions, Catholic social teaching urges "institutions in host countries" to resist "the temptation to exploit foreign labourers, denying them the same rights enjoyed by nationals, rights that are to be guaranteed to all without discrimination":

> Regulating immigration according to criteria of equity and balance is one of the indispensable conditions for ensuring that immigrants are integrated into society with the guarantees required by recognition of their human dignity. Immigrants are to be received as persons and helped, together with their families, to become a part of societal life. (*Compendium*, no. 298)

[3] The Vatican's Justice and Peace Commission has recently published a Chinese translation of the *Compendium of the Social Doctrine of the Church* (Wong 2011). The Chinese translation is now available online (Catholic Truth Society–Hong Kong 2011).

Consistent with its commitment to respecting human dignity and solidarity, as well as implementing the principle of subsidiarity, the *Compendium* emphasizes the need to preserve and enhance family life. Thus, it specifically urges that "the right of reuniting families should be respected and promoted," while also advising governments and other agencies to collaborate in fostering "increased work opportunities in people's place of origin," so that people would have less incentive to take up the often difficult and dangerous path of immigration (*Compendium*, no. 298).

Catholic social teaching's current perspective on the rights and responsibilities of workers and the challenges of immigration converges through the prism afforded by a positive understanding of globalization. As the *Compendium* observes, "if it is true that Globalization is neither good nor bad in itself, but depends on how it is used, it must be affirmed that a globalization of safeguards, minimum essential rights and equity is necessary" (*Compendium*, no. 310). Since globalization is "one of the most important causes of change in the organization of work," its impact must be understood, if these "safeguards, minimum essential rights, and equity" are to remain viable and relevant. Globalization is "an unprecedented transformation that determines a change in the structure of work itself":

> The reorganization of time, its standardization and the changes currently underway in the use of space—comparable in extent to the first Industrial Revolution insofar as they involve every sector of production, on every continent, independent of their level of development—are therefore to be considered a crucial challenge, also at the level of ethics and culture, in the area of defining a renewed system for the defence of work. (*Compendium*, no. 311)

Defining the elements or social institutions indispensable for "the defense of work" is especially difficult, given that globalization "requires greater flexibility in the labour market and in organizing and managing production processes" (*Compendium*, no. 312). Further complicating the task is the fact that the changes are asymmetrical with various impacts "in developing countries and countries with economies in transition" and yet entirely other trends in "the economic systems of the more developed countries, [that are] going through a phase that marks the passage from an industrial-type economy to an economy essentially built on services and technological innovations" (*Compendium*, no. 313).

Under such circumstances, neither the wholesale condemnation of globalization nor its uncritical embrace—as if market forces alone were enough to produce fair and efficient outcomes—is appropriate. Globalization and the challenges it poses should not be approached in a fatalistic or "deterministic manner." By contrast, Catholic social teaching rightly emphasizes "the subjective dimension of work," that is, the fact that ultimately "the decisive factor and 'referee' of this complex phase of change is once more the human person, who must remain the true protagonist of his work" (*Compendium*, no. 317). Moral agency, as we have insisted throughout this book, by no means has been rendered obsolete:

> The historical forms in which human work is expressed change, but not its permanent requirements, which are summed up in the respect of the inalienable human rights of workers. Faced with the risk of denying these rights, new forms of solidarity must be envisioned and brought about, taking into account the interdependence that unites workers among themselves. (Compendium, no. 319)

Catholic social teaching's view of where the new forms of solidarity can emerge may be surprising to some, for the *Compendium* closes its reflections on globalization by noting that "people's natural tendency to establish relationships" may actually be enhanced through the revolution in digital communications technology that "has allowed the relational aspect of work to spread throughout the world, giving to Globalization a particularly rapid rhythm":

> The ultimate foundation of this dynamism is the working person, who is always the subjective—and never the objective—element… the anthropological foundation of the inherent relational dimension of work. The negative aspects of the Globalization of work must not damage the possibility opening up for all people: that of giving expression to a humanism of work on a planetary scale, to solidarity in the world of work on this same level, so that working in similar contexts, spread throughout the world and interconnected, people will understand ever better their one, shared vocation. (*Compendium*, no. 322)

18.5 Conclusion

In our discussion of the Chinese immigrants in Prato, we have found no easy recipe for producing a harmonious society or pursuing the common good. Instead, we have focused on the personal decisions and activities of people whom we have identified as key moral agents in the situation, that is, people whose leadership may determine whether or not the communities in Prato resolve the challenges that globalization has tossed in their direction. Mayor Cenni has to decide whether he will stoke the fears of the Italian communities in order to achieve short-term political goals—winning elections and consolidating the kind of power that will make it easier for his businesses to prosper—or whether he will defy local prejudices and enter into a genuinely constructive dialogue with leaders in the Chinese immigrant community. The entrepreneur, Xu Qiu Lin, known generally as "Giulini," has to decide whether he can continue his efforts to demonstrate good business ethics and a sense of social responsibility within the immigrant Chinese community and how to stay the course while facing up to the very real threats made against him and his family by the organized crime elements who stand to lose if he succeeds in these efforts. Fr. Francesco Wang, now 5 years into his pastoral assignment at the *Parocchia Dell' Ascensione* in Prato, has to figure out how to translate his initial success in creating a community center for all the Chinese immigrants into a full experiment in implementing Catholic social teaching's vision of a harmonious society, an experiment in uniting all the workers of Prato, locals and immigrants alike, in a shared commitment to their common good. We wish each of them well and have high hopes for the emerging Chinese leadership in Prato. But we also realize that for each one of them, in different ways, their virtue will surely be tested with each new challenge they face. But this is what it means to accept the challenge of moral leadership in business and government and in the religious institutions that genuinely seek the good of all the people. We expect to learn more from their ongoing efforts.

References

Abbate, C. (2011, March 17). L'offshore cinese di Prato. *Panorama: Settimanale d'Opinione: Milano*. Accessed online on January 17, 2015 at http://www.fiscooggi.it/files/u27/rassegna-stampa/07.03.2011_10_3.pdf

Battista, A. (2011, September 2). *Prada or Prato? The blurred divide between "Made in Italy" and "Made in China"* [Personal Blog]. Retrieved on May 27, 2012, from http://irenebrination.typepad.com/irenebrination_notes_on_a/2011/09/prada-or-prato-bath-lecture.html

Bilsky, P. (2011, April 4). *Investigation of Chinese sweatshops in Italy* [Video file]. Retrieved on May 30, 2012, from http://www.youtube.com/watch?v=PGMXBnlukHY&feature=related

Brunetti, S. (2009, February). La comunita' cinese a Prato. *Fondazione Migrantes*. Retrieved on June 1, 2012, from http://www.chiesacattolica.it/documenti/2009/06/00014666_la_comunita_cinese_a_prato_s_brunetti.html

Camera di Commercio di Prato. (2012, January). *L'Imprenditoria Straniera in Provincia di Prato*. Retrieved on May 20, from http://www.po.camcom.it/doc/public/2012/stranieri_11.pdf

Catholic Truth Society—Hong Kong. (2011). *The compendium of the social doctrine of the church, Chinese Translation*. Accessed online on February 17, 2015 at http://www.vatican.va/roman_curia/pontifical_councils/justpeace/documents/rc_pc_justpeace_doc_20060526_compendio-dott-soc_zh.pdf

Chen, C. (2011). Made in Italy (by the Chinese): Economic restructuring and the politics of migration. *Inter Asia Papers, 20*, 1–34. Retrieved from http://ddd.uab.cat/pub/intasipap/20131747n20/20131747n20p1.pdf

China Daily. (2010, July 5). Italian financial police launch investigation over Chinese the money-laundering. Retrieved on May 27, 2012, from http://www.china-daily.org/International-News/Italian-financial-police-launched-operations-against-the-Chinese-money-laundering/

Cochi, G. (2014a, May 21). *La vera storia di Godenzio raccontata dai frati di Chinatown: "Non deridetelo su Facebook, dategli piuttosto un paio di pantaloni"*. Prato: TV Prato. Accessed on December 9, 2014 at http://www.tvprato.it/2014/05/la-vera-storia-di-godenzio-raccontata-dai-frati-di-chinatown-non-deridetelo-su-facebook-dategli-piuttosto-un-paio-di-pantaloni/

Cochi, G. (2014b, June 8). *L'altro Godenzio, la storia di Xie il senzatetto cinese che ha ritrovato la strada di casa*. Prato: TV Prato. Accessed online at http://www.tvprato.it/2014/06/laltro-godenzio-storia-di-xie-il-senzatetto-cinese-che-ha-ritrovato-la-strada-di-casa/

Comune di Prato. (2012). Guida alla consultazione dei dati sull'immigrazione cinese a Prato. Retrieved on May 30, 2012, from http://www.comune.prato.it/immigra/guide/htm/cinesi.htm

Dei Ottati, G. (2009, December). An industrial district facing the challenge of globalization: Prato today. *European Planning Studies, 17*(12), 1817–1835.

Dinmore, G. (2010a, February 9). *Tuscan town turns against Chinese immigrants* [Personal blog]. Retrieved on May 27, 2012, from http://guydinmore.wordpress.com/2010/02/09/tuscan-town-turns-against-chinese-immigrants/

Dinmore, G. (2010b, June 28). Chinese Gangs exploit niche left by Mafia. *Financial Times*. Retrieved on May 27, 2012, from http://www.ft.com/intl/cms/s/0/a8cb4784-82de-11df-b7ad-00144feabdc0.html#axzz1n0Aust8h

Donadio, R. (2010, September 10). Chinese remake the 'Made in Italy' fashion label. *The New York Times*. Retrieved on May 27, 2012, from http://www.nytimes.com/2010/09/13/world/europe/13prato.html?pagewanted=all

Drucker, P. (1986). Making decisions. In *The practice of management*. New York: HarperCollins/Perennial Library.

Gardner, B. (2010). How Chinese companies in Prato, Italy are revitalizing the textile economy. *Invest In*. Retrieved on May 27, 2012, from http://www.investin.com.cn/invest-in-how-chinese-companies-in-prato-italy-are-revitalizing-the-textile-economy.html

Giannoni, F. (2009, May 7). Toscani D'Adozione: Xu Qiu Lin. *Toscana OGGI*. Retrieved on May 30, 2012, from http://www.toscanaoggi.it/notizia_3.php?IDNotizia=11245&IDCategoria=326

Gold Sea. (2010). Italy's Chinese enclave suffers from debt crisis. Retrieved on May 27, 2012, from http://goldsea.com/Text/index.php?id=12124

Hooper, J. (2010, November 17). Made in little Wenzhou, Italy: The latest label from Tuscany. *The Guardian*. Retrieved on May 27, 2012, from http://www.guardian.co.uk/world/2010/nov/17/made-in-little-wenzhou-italy

Italoblog. (2009, March). Il made in Italy di Xu Qiu Lin. Retrieved on June 6, 2012, from http://www.italoblog.it/2009/03/il-made-in-italy-di-xu-qiu-lin/

La Nazione. (2011, January 21). Primo imprenditore cinese iscritto a Confindustria. Retrieved on June 11, 2012, from http://www.lanazione.it/prato/cronaca/2011/01/21/446654-primo_imprenditore_cinese_iscritto.shtml

La Nazione. (2012, January 1). Centro storico: Al via la riqualifica dei suoi vicoli. Retrieved on July 22, 2012, from http://www.lanazione.it/prato/cronaca/2012/01/11/651019-centro_storico.shtml

Leo XIII. (1891, May 15). *Rerum novarum*. Libreria Editrice Vaticana. Retrieved on December 9, 2014, from http://w2.vatican.va/content/leo-xiii/en/encyclicals/documents/hf_l-xiii_enc_15051891_rerum-novarum.html

Mallet, V., & Dinmore, G. (2011, June 8). Europe: Hidden economy. *Financial Times*. Retrieved on May 27, 2012, from http://www.ft.com/intl/cms/s/0/efc3510e-9214-11e0-9e00-00144feab49a.html#axzz1n0Aust8h

Meichtry, S. (2011, June 22). Italian police raid Chinese businesses. The *Wall Street Journal*. Retrieved on May 27, 2012, from http://online.wsj.com/article/SB10001424052702304887904576399900158034890.html

Mottola, G. (2011, May 19). La mafia cinese è come la 'ndrangheta. *Liberainformazione*. Retrieved on May 30, 2012, from http://www.liberainformazione.org/news.php?newsid=14808

Notizie di Prato. (2011, November 1). Prato maglia nera per l'incremento di reati. Petrella (IdV): "Bisogna cambiare la strategia d'approccio in tema di sicurezza". Retrieved on May 30, 2012, fromhttp://www.notiziediprato.it/2011/11/prato-maglia-nera-per-lincremento-di-reati-petrella-idv-bisogna-cambiare-la-strategia-dapproccio-in-tema-di-sicurezza

People's Daily. (2010, December 22). Crackdown in Italy's 'Little China'. Retrieved on May 27, 2012, from http://english.peopledaily.com.cn/90001/90778/90861/7238789.html

Poggioli, S. (2011, June 15). 'Fast Fashion': Italians wary of Chinese on their turf. *National Public Radio*. Retrieved on May 27, 2012, from http://www.npr.org/2011/06/15/137107361/fast-fashion-italians-wary-of-chinese-on-their-turf

Polchi, V. (2011, November 28). Se gli immigrati "fanno impresa" e assumono lavoratori italiani. *La Repubblica*. Retrieved on May 30, 2012, from http://www.repubblica.it/cronaca/2011/11/28/news/cnel_immigrati-25708639/

Pontifical Council for Justice and Peace. (2004). *Compendium of the social doctrine of the church* (English translation). Retrieved on June 23, 2015 from http://www.vatican.va/roman_curia/pontifical_councils/justpeace/documents/rc_pc_justpeace_doc_20060526_compendio-dott-soc_en.html

Potter, A. (2007, December 12). Designer labels' sweatshop scandal. *Sunday Mirror-UK*. Retrieved from http://www.sweatfree.org/news_SM-12-2-07

Principi d'Italia (n.d.). Xu Qiu Lin. Retrieved on June 11, 2012, from http://www.iprincipiditalia.com/xu-qui-lin.html

Sacchetti, S., & Tomlinson, P. R. (2009, December). Economic governance and the evolution of industrial districts under globalization: The case of two mature European industrial districts. *European Planning Studies, 17*(12), 1837–1859.

Santini, C., Rabino, S., & Zanni, L. (2011). Chinese immigrants socio-economic enclave in an Italian industrial district: The case of Prato. *World Review of Entrepreneurship, Management and Sustainable Development, 7*(1), 30–51.

Smith, T. (2004, February 19). Crisis in Tuscany's China town. *BBC*. Retrieved on July, 2012, from http://news.bbc.co.uk/2/hi/europe/3500285.stm

The Independent. (2010, September 25). Welcome to China, Italy: Photographer Gerd Ludwig tours a very industrious community. Retrieved on May 27, 2012, from http://www.independent.co.uk/life-style/fashion/features/welcome-to-china-italy-photographer-gerd-ludwig-tours-a-very-industrious-community-2086594.html?action=Gallery

The Telegraph. (2010, June 29). Chinese gangs step into gap left by Mafia. Retrieved on May 30, 2012, from http://www.telegraph.co.uk/news/worldnews/europe/italy/7859991/Chinese-gangs-step-into-gap-left-by-mafia.html

Ticozzi, S. (2011). Pope Leo XIII's Encyclical Rerum Novarum and the Challenges for China. *Tripod: Spring 2011 Vol. 31—No. 160 Rerum Novarum 120th Anniversary*. Accessed on December 9, 2014 at http://www.hsstudyc.org.hk/en/tripod_en/en_tripod_160_05.html

Tilikka, J. (2010, December 9). Inward outsourcing/case: Prato. *Hanna Saren*. Retrieved on May 27, 2012, from http://hannasaren.net/thestudio/inward-outsourcing-case-prato/

Toscana TV. (2012a, February 7). Legalita' per le imprese straniere, iscrizioni sopra le aspettative. Retrieved on May 30, 2012, from http://www.toscanatv.com/leggi_news?idnews=NL134279

Toscana TV. (2012b, March 8). Il ministro Riccardi ai cinesi di Prato: 'Rispetto delle regole e lingua italiana'. Retrieved on May 30, 2012, from http://www.toscanatv.com/leggi_news?idnews=NL135504

Unione Industriale Pratese. (2009, September 25). Comunicato Stampa sulla 2a conferenza italiana sull'immigrazione. Retrieved on June 11, 2012, from http://www.ui.prato.it/unionedigitale/v2/areastampa/areastampa-dett.asp?doc=UIP035521.doc

Unione Industriale Pratese. (2012a). Evolution of the Prato textile district. Retrieved on May 17, 2012, from http://www.ui.prato.it/unionedigitale/v2/english/presentazionedistrettoinglese.pdf

Unione Industriale Pratese. (2012b). Prato industry in numbers. Retrieved on May 27, 2012, from http://www.ui.prato.it/unionedigitale/v2/english/numbers.asp

Wang, F. S. (2011). Chinese migrants in Prato. *Tripod: Spring 2011 Vol. 31—No. 160 Rerum Novarum 120th Anniversary*. Accessed on December 9, 2014 at http://www.hsstudyc.org.hk/en/tripod_en/en_tripod_160_07.html

Wong, F. (2011, March 22). *Hong Kong issues Chinese social doctrine compendium.* Zenit: The World Seen from Rome. Accessed online on February 17, 2015 at http://www.zenit.org/en/articles/hong-kong-issues-chinese-social-doctrine-compendium

Zen, J. (2011). Revisiting Rerum Novarum in its 120th Year. *Tripod: Spring 2011 Vol. 31—No. 160 Rerum Novarum 120th Anniversary*. Accessed on December 9, 2014 at http://www.hsstudyc.org.hk/en/tripod_en/en_tripod_160_04.html

Chapter 19
The Natural Environment: Ethics and the Environment

"Long-term success urgently calls you to constantly care for the environment." (Stephan Rothlin, *Eighteen Rules for Becoming a Top Notch Player*, 2004)

19.1 Prelude

Once regarded as "the silent stakeholder," with each passing day the natural environment grows more strident in the warnings that emanate from it regarding the destructive consequences of unsustainable and irresponsible economic development. A concern for the environment was once dismissed in Asian business circles as a luxury that only prosperous or economically developed nations can afford. The case study introducing this chapter examines the story of the great spill in 2005 of hazardous chemicals into China's Songhua River and the immediate responses to the spill on the part of government agencies, businesses, and residents along the river. While the severity of the spill and its toxic consequences for residents was minimized at first, the effort to deal with it increased dramatically as the pollution reached the border with Russia and threatened to become an international incident. One important issue raised by this case is the need for long-term efforts to clean up the riverbed after the polluted water has already flowed away. Besides caring for "the silent stakeholder"—in this case, the ecological sustainability of the river itself—the case study shows the harmful consequences of seeking to cover up the disaster, thus making it difficult for businesses and the communities along the way to protect themselves and their water supplies. The chapter will then proceed to argue the merits of a robust concept of environmental responsibility that is incumbent upon all stakeholders, and will point out examples of how businesses in particular can exercise their stewardship responsibilities for the natural environment.

S. Rothlin, D. McCann, *International Business Ethics*,
DOI 10.1007/978-3-662-47434-1_19

19.2 Case Study: Pollution, Politics, and Prevention—Lessons from the Songhua River Catastrophe

19.2.1 Abstract

On November 13, 2005, an explosion at the China National Petroleum Corporation (CNPC)'s Jilin branch contaminated the water of the Songhua River. The large-scale pollution affected millions of Chinese and Russians living along the river-banks and cost local economies millions of *yuan*. In the aftermath of the explosion, local Chinese authorities initially denied that dangerous pollutants had been released. However, the carcinogenic nature of the spill became known and led to increased public anxiety and distrust of the local government. It was not until several weeks after the incident that the central government finally intervened in cleanup efforts, however, not without increased public criticism. The Songhua case highlights the issue of environmental responsibility in China. The toxic contamination of the Songhua River not only created health problems but also spread social panic and provoked an international crisis. Our particular concern is with the responses of businesses affected by environmental catastrophes and the emergence in China of a civil society capable of playing a role in promoting environmental responsibility on the part of both government and business. For a number of reasons, as we shall see, the Songhua River catastrophe may mark the tipping point in China's efforts to enforce environmental legislation and promote environmental awareness in society as a whole.

19.2.2 Keywords

Songhua River, Amur River, CNPC, SEPA, MEP, Corporate responsibility, Environmental responsibility, Emergency relief, Cleanup

19.2.3 Water of Life

The Songhua River basin is located in northeast China. It has a drainage area of 556,800 km^2 and is essential for the irrigation and transport of agricultural products. The Songhua River flows through Heilongjiang Province, Inner Mongolia, and three regions of Jilin Province, supplying drinking water to several million people between Jilin and Harbin (Heilongjiang People's Government 2007). The Songhua River merges with the Heilong River, which flows into Russia. Once in Russia, it is known as the Amur River marking the border between the two countries. As a strategic shipping and transportation route, the Songhua's banks are home to many factories. CNPC was just one of the firms stationed close to the Songhua River.

19.2.4 Explosion and Contamination

China National Petroleum Corporation is China's largest oil and gas producer and supplier. It is a state-owned enterprise and parent company of PetroChina, its publicly traded subsidiary. The Chinese government is CNPC's most important stakeholder, and as such they work very closely together. The CNPC's commitment to environmental responsibility is prominently displayed on its website, where its mission is described: "While providing energy products and services, we strive for harmonious relationships between operation and safety, energy and the environment, and corporate and community interests" (CNPC 2014a). Conscious of the dangers involved in the petroleum industry, CNPC claims that employee safety "has become the core of our corporate culture"[1] (CNPC 2014b). This commitment is situated within a comprehensive set of coordinated policies on "health, safety, and the environment," which begins with the reassurance that "CNPC has always believed that people and the environment are our two most important resources" (CNPC 2014c).

Despite these good intentions—or, perhaps, before they had assumed great urgency in CNPC's strategic plans for the future—a violent explosion occurred on November 13, 2005, at the aniline unit of the double benzene plant at the firm's Jilin location. The explosion was due to a fire in the P-102 tower that had resulted from improper handling of hazardous materials. Zhao Haifeng, vice general manager of the Jilin branch, attributed the explosion to "a blockage in the chemical plant's processing tower and a worker's botched attempt to clear it" (Yong and Na 2005). The blasts led to the release of 100 tons of carcinogenic chemicals into the Songhua River as a toxic cloud hovered over Jilin City (Chen 2009). The incident resulted in five deaths, 30 injuries, and the evacuation of over 10,000 residents from the surrounding area (China Daily 2005a).

Of immediate concern following the explosion were the potentially harmful pollutants released into the atmosphere and river water. Addressing these concerns fell to Wang Wei, deputy mayor of Jilin City. Under his direct control were the Municipal Economic Council, the City Labor and Social Security Bureau, and the Municipal Supervisory Bureau for Work Safety (*The Epoch Times* 2005). To dampen the frenzy set off by the blast, Wang organized the evacuation of nearby residents. The next morning, however, Wang told the media that the explosion "did not produce large-scale pollution... Water [quality] has not changed" (Ansfield 2005).

---

[1] The CNPC website appears to have been revised, beginning in 2009, in light of the painful lessons learned from the Songhua River disaster. As evidence of its commitment to safety, the firm claims that in 2014, "for four consecutive years, CNPC has launched 'Safety and Environmental Protection Year' campaign, focusing on human-centered safety principles." These include an impressive list of risk assessment and training initiatives designed to prevent accidents before they occur and to support "emergency response" capabilities, when there are accidents or other catastrophic events. "Safety" for CNPC includes not only environmental responsibility but also providing reasonable levels of security for employees working abroad who are vulnerable to terrorist attacks and other hostilities (CNPC 2014b).

The following day, November 14, CNPC released a statement consistent with that of Wang's: "The accident did not affect the main business of the CNPC Jilin Branch and according to environmental monitors, the air quality surrounding the accident site meets standards" (*CNPC* 2005).[2]

Despite assurances that there were no harmful pollutants released from the explosion, widespread panic ensued. Harbin residents downstream rushed to buy emergency supplies. Water and bread went out of stock in large supermarkets. Even beer was quickly sold out. Zhang Ping, an employee at Century Mart, described the situation to *China Daily*: "People started to pour in [at] 1 pm. By 3 or 4 pm, all the drinks sold out" (Li 2005). Craig Hutchinson, a foreign teacher resident in Harbin, confirmed that "the city was full of ridiculously large queues. People were buying water in massive quantities" (*BBC* 2005a). As a consequence of the rapidly diminishing supply, bottled water prices skyrocketed. A local brand, *Chunzhongchun*, for example, previously available for half a *yuan*, was sold for at least double the original price (Li 2005).

19.2.5 Flowing Across Borders

In the immediate aftermath of the explosion, factory managers and local government representatives repeatedly denied that toxins had been released into the Songhua River. Instead, CNPC managers and local officials, including Wang, tried to manage the pollution on their own. Without notifying officials in Beijing, they

[2] Months later, PetroChina's *Annual Report for 2005*, issued in March 2006, described the Songhua River explosion, and the actions taken to cope with it, in its list of "Major Events" for the year: "On November 13, an explosion broke out in Jilin Petrochina Benzene Production Plant. The incident caused serious personal injuries and deaths, loss of property and water pollution of the Song Huajiang. The Company dispatched an operation team and a specialist team to the site immediately after the incident. The Company also activated the contingency plan to minimize the loss and the number of injuries and deaths. At the same time with the handling of the incident, the Company quickly organized a large-scale inspection of safety standards in production, focusing on "anti-breach of rules, inspection of hidden risks and procurement of rectification", and put into effect various measures for safety in production in winter. The Company has learned a lesson from the incident and has strengthened its efforts at ensuring safety in production and environmental protection" (PetroChina 2006). The only other mention of the Jilin accident in the Annual Report is a statement acknowledging the company's potential liabilities arising from it: "The impact of the accident is undergoing government investigation. The incident shows that the Company needs further strengthening of its operational safety and environmental protection. The Company has realized the seriousness of the issue and has stepped up its efforts in securing operational safety and environmental protection. The Company will bear resultant liabilities caused by the explosions based on the results of the investigation" (PetroChina 2006). After a very rocky start, the firm's response to the crisis suggests a dramatic change in its perception of the role of environmental responsibility in creating and maintaining an image favorable to international expansion and foreign investment.

"drain[ed] reservoir water into the Songhua in an attempt to dilute the contaminants" (Green 2009).

On November 18, 5 days after the explosion, the central government sent environmental experts to report on the state of the spill. However, the public was not notified until the pollution reached Harbin on November 21 (Green 2009). On that day, the Harbin Municipal Government informed residents that tap water would not be available for 4 days, on account of routine maintenance on the city's water supply facility (*Harbin People's Government* 2005). By this time, residents had become skeptical about water safety because of the media reports challenging the Harbin government's assurances (Green 2009). Later that same day, the local government reversed itself and issued an emergency statement declaring that the explosion at CNPC had indeed resulted in toxic water pollution (Chen 2009).

The Songhua's contamination put at risk the nearly four million residents of Harbin, who rely on the river for drinking water (Ansfield 2005). Anticipating the crisis that would occur when the pollution reached the city, the Harbin city government in the previous 12 h had created a reserve water supply to meet the needs of local residents, who also were urged to evacuate on a voluntary basis (Jiang 2005). As the toxic chemicals made their way downstream toward Harbin, it was clear that the river pollution posed a much greater health threat than the regional government had suggested. There is, of course, a fine line between curbing social panic and sharing timely information. How well did the managers at CNPC and local government leaders walk that line? Had you been in their shoes, how far would you have gone in an effort to inform the public?

No matter what action might have been taken at Harbin, there was no stopping the flow of the Songhua as it carried the pollution further along. On November 24, 9 days after the accident, Xie Zhenhua, the director of the State Environmental Protection Agency (SEPA), officially informed the Russian ambassador that the benzene contamination had reached across the border between China and Russia. Russia's Emergency Situations Ministry immediately responded to the potential public health crisis. The Russian Ministry of Natural Resources set up a task force to address the approaching pollution (*Asia Times* 2005). An estimated 70 Russian cities were put at risk by the spill. Cities along the border, like Kazakevitch, built dikes to prevent contaminated water from mingling with the city's supply of drinking water (Kirschner and Grandy 2006). At Khabarovsk, a city of 600,000 residents now besieged by the benzene slick making its way down the Amur River, a spokesman for the regional government commented that this was not the first time Chinese chemicals had polluted the waters of Russia (*Asia Times* 2005).

In a move that contrasted with the local government's initial response to the crisis in Jilin City, then Chinese Foreign Minister Li Zhaoxing gave a "rare and well-publicized apology" to the Russian ambassador and offered assistance in preventing the further spread of the pollutants (Jie 2006). The Russian government provided China a list of chemicals to be monitored. Chinese President Hu Jintao was determined to maintain peaceful Sino-Russian relations. "We will take all necessary and effective measures and do our utmost to minimize the pollution and reduce the damage to the Russian side," he declared in his address to Russian officials (UNEP 2005). President Hu also provided Russia water testing and purifying equipment (Chen 2009), and 3,000 Chinese nationals were enlisted to build a dam along the Fuyuan waterway linking the Heilong and the Ussuri Rivers, in order to protect the water supply of Khabarovsk (Kirschner and Grandy 2006).

19.2.6 No More Cover-Ups

On November 26, SEPA representatives attended the United Nations Environmental Programme (UNEP) meeting in Nairobi. Under the direction of Xie, the Chinese delegation provided the UN with information on the extent of the pollution and measures underway to contain and clean up the spill (Green 2009). Meanwhile, back home, the public's anger over the government's apparent mishandling of the crisis was growing. Much confusion was evident over who's to blame for the disaster, as if assigning blame would undo the damage caused by water pollution. Even Premier Wen Jiabao, when he visited Harbin, became the object of some bloggers' scorn (Jie 2006), and unfairly so, since it was his personal intervention that persuaded the local officials to inform the public fully about the extent of the threat to their city's water supply (Jiang 2005). Some news media criticized officials who initially lied about the extent of the pollution. Beijing's *Zhongguo Jingji Shibao* (*China Economic Times*), for example, editorialized, "If individual leaders tell irresponsible lies, [it] is an extremely terrible crime against society, because any rumor could trigger a social disaster! [The pollution cover up] is about to come out into the open, and by then, those who have lied will certainly be punished severely" (*BBC* 2005b).

The Chinese government's move to punish those responsible for the Songhua River crisis, however, resulted in administrative changes, but no criminal proceedings. Local officials as well as CPNC managers involved in the plot to conceal the dangerous pollutants were dishonorably removed from their posts. The sanctions they faced were meant to limit their prospects for career advancement in both the corporate world and the Party cadres (*BBC* 2006). Among those dismissed was Wang Wei, the deputy mayor of Jilin, who had declared that no harmful pollution occurred as a result of the CNPC explosion (Pan 2005). Just before the arrival in Jilin of the central government's investigators, Wang was found dead in his home. However obscure the circumstances, what is known is that when the police went to his home to question him, Wang's body was found hanging (*The Epoch Times* 2005). Two anonymous Chinese sources stated that Wang had been set up to take the fall for others who led local efforts to "gloss over the crisis." "The Jilin provincial government came to the conclusion that Wang Wei should be held entirely responsible," said one of the informants. "He decided to commit suicide to prove he was innocent" (Ansfield 2005).

Newsweek reported that Wang's death was conspicuously missing from the headlines in China because of its political sensitivity (Ansfield 2005). According to P. C. Lo, the director of the Centre for Applied Ethics at Hong Kong Baptist University, traditional Confucian philosophy accepts "self-regarding suicide, namely, dying to avoid humiliation and disgrace" as a praiseworthy act of countercultural protest (Lo 1999). Even the traditional celebration of the Dragon Boat Festival commemorates the life of Qu Yuan, a poet and statesman said to have drowned himself to defend his good name. The story of Wang taking his own life to prove his innocence may be consistent with this ancient tradition.

However that may be, the fact is China's central government had just announced an uncompromising stance toward those who tried to hide relevant information concerning the pollution (Pan 2005). "Any cover-up of the accident, and any negative attitude toward the probe, will be considered cheating the public and ignoring the authority of the government," announced Li Yizhong, secretary general of the State Production Safety Supervision Agency and head of the Songhua investigative team (Pan 2005). Wang's death did not occur until after Li stated the government's intention to track down and punish those responsible—which is enough for some to believe he committed suicide merely to avoid retribution. What do you think of Wang's suicide? Was his an ethical protest, or was he merely trying to escape the consequences of his actions?

19.2.7 Cleaning Up the Songhua River Basin

Once the immediate problem of minimizing the damage caused by the spill had passed, China's Ministry of Environmental Protection (MEP) initiated a series of measures to clean up the Songhua River, committing a total of CNY7.84 billion yuan to it. However, the government's efforts still met with a degree of skepticism from environmental experts (*Global Times* 2011). For example, Gu Jidong, an environmental toxicology expert based in Hong Kong as well as a Harbin native, explained that the effects of the pollution would occur in two phases. The first phase is watercourse pollution, the second, riverbed pollution. "It is not as simple as saying that the chemicals have now passed the city and the water is now safe," said Gu. "The local government is talking about the first stage, but not about the second stage." Removing toxins gradually released by the riverbed would require a long-term commitment to cleanup operations (*Asia Times* 2005). There is ample evidence since then, however, suggesting that the MEP has begun to address both stages in the pollution cleanup effort and in so doing is creating a model for managing environmental protection efforts that can be used to address similar problems in other parts of China.[3]

Back in December 2005, such a response was still in its formative stage. The change in policy required a comprehensive reassessment of China's previous development model and the lack of incentives for local government officials to focus on any other goal besides annual growth in GDP (Zhou 2011). That reassessment began with statements released by the Party and the State Council admitting that SEPA "did not attach enough importance to the [Songhua] accident and did not adequately anticipate the possible severe consequences of the accident, and therefore should be held responsible for the losses" (Jie 2006). In response to these negative statements, Xie Zhenhua resigned from his position as director of SEPA. Following Xie's resignation, the State Council released "The Decision on Implementing the Scientific Concept of Development and Stepping Up Environmental Protection," which may mark the tipping point in China's struggle to demonstrate a serious commitment to environmental protection. The "Decision" document highlighted environmental issues needing immediate attention, including drinking water safety, river basin contamination control, and water pollution prevention and response (*World Bank* 2007).

In January 2006, the Songhua basin officially was registered on the priorities listing for programs in the Five-Year Plan supporting Chinese water pollution control and prevention, and a new approach to pollution prevention plan was drafted. Zhou Shengxian, newly appointed director of SEPA, asserted that the plan's main aim was, "to let all people drink clean water" (Li 2006). As part of this initiative, 11 enterprises were publicly reprimanded by SEPA for creating environmental hazards, and an additional 127 chemical plants were subjected to environmental risk examination (*World Bank* 2007). Since 2007, SEPA has closed down an additional 316 plants and suspended 513 plants involved in pollution-related challenges (*Xinhua* 2009b).

[3] A 2011 report from Zhou Shengxian, the minister of Environmental Protection, "Investigations on the Progress in Rehabilitation of Songhua River," demonstrates the ways in which the MEP, following up on the instructions of the State Council, has intensified its efforts to coordinate policies and priorities among the provinces most directly impacted by the Songhua disaster. The statistics on measured reductions in the discharge of pollutants, plus the implementation of a new concept for rehabilitating the river, as specifically demanded by China's 11th Five-Year Plan (2006-2011), are very impressive, as is the MEP's pledge to honor certain "basic principles" in the rehabilitation project, including "giving priority to people, improving people's life, obeying the rule of nature, revitalizing the river, adopting systematic management and integrated treatment approaches, and controlling the pollution sources and intercepting the wastewater, and optimizing the industrial mix" (Zhou 2011). The progress reported by Zhou is confirmed by outside monitoring agencies, for example, the World Bank's 2007 Report on "Water Pollution Emergencies in China: Prevention and Response," which made ten specific recommendations for improving coordinated responses to emergency situations, particularly in the areas of (1) overall institutional reform, (2) risk management and prevention, and (3) response and mitigation, which have helped to guide the implementation of the MEP's efforts (World Bank 2007). Similarly, the Asian Development Bank's 2012 Monitoring Report on the "Songhua River Basin Water Pollution Control and Management Project, Jilin Component" gives a detailed account of how the ADB's loan was used to develop infrastructure to assist in the long-term rehabilitation of the river (ADB 2013).

Besides demanding changes in the way industrial plants managed the pollutants they were generating, *China Daily* indicated the need for increased coordination among local departments and regulatory bodies and suggested that the companies should be sanctioned more heavily for failing to live up to their individual responsibilities (Jiang 2006). When China's State Environmental Protection Agency issued its year-end report in 2006, the results were still not satisfactory, for even a full year after the Songhua disaster, it admitted that similar incidents, although of much smaller scope, occur every 2–3 days throughout China (*Xinhua* 2006a). The intractability of China's pollution problem, according to Guo Huaicheng from Peking University, can only be overcome by seeking to balance economic growth with greater environmental sensitivity. Guo believes that Chinese grassroots initiatives may help restore the proper balance: "The Chinese people, or at least the Chinese media, are becoming more and more alert to environmental problems and are now a strong force in China's environmental protection campaign" (*Xinhua* 2006a). SEPA's newly appointed director, Zhou Shengxian, apparently agrees that businesses should become part of the solution to China's environmental problems. During an onsite visit to Jiamusi City in Heilongjiang Province, Zhou said, "The pollution of the Songhua River water is a pain like cutting flesh.... Businesses shouldn't pose development against environmental protection" (Jing 2005b).

19.2.8 Short-Term Punishments, Long-Term Consequences

In the immediate aftermath of the Songhua disaster, the State Council and the Jilin provincial government formed a joint investigation team to interrogate Yu Li, general manager of CNPC's Jilin branch (Jing 2005a). The investigation sought to determine who was responsible for the "improper handling" that led to the explosion, deaths, pollution, and cover-up. A report released by CNPC found Yu liable for the accident and he was removed from his post as general manager. Shen Dongming and Wang Fang, responsible for the benzene facility and a safety workshop at the Jilin plant, were also removed from their positions (*The New York Times* 2005). The comment from Jiang Jiemin, CNPC chairman, declared that those terminated from the CNPC "aroused huge attention from the international community and tarnished the overall image of CNPC" (*China Daily* 2005d), suggesting that his concern was primarily with managing the public relations fallout from the disaster. Jiang, however, was not held responsible for the explosion in any capacity.

The CNPC paid the highest fine at that time under Chinese environmental law for polluting the Songhua River basin—a mere CNY one million *yuan*. However, none of the penalty fine went toward cleanup operations. As a result, a debate ensued regarding who should bear the costs for cleaning up the pollution. Provincial enforcement was criticized as too outdated to meet present needs. Among the critics was Wang Jin, who sued the CNPC for an additional payment of CNY10 billion *yuan*. In theory the sum would be used to discharge the company's responsibilities toward the environment; however, Wang's case was rejected in court (*Asia News* 2007).

The total costs of the Songhua River disaster are still being calculated. Pollutants embedded in the riverbank may slowly be released from the soil for years to come, causing further damage to human health and local agriculture. In Harbin during its 4 days without running water, 29 companies completely stopped production, while 23 others slowed production. The average loss during the period was almost CNY100 million *yuan* a day (Chen 2009). According to the *China Economic Times*, the direct costs related to the river pollution totaled CNY1.5 billion *yuan*, although indirect costs remain too difficult and long term to calculate (Chen 2009).

Ding Ning, a Harbin citizen, filed a civil suit against the CNPC. He asked for a compensation of CNY15 *yuan* and a public apology from the company. "A formal apology would be valued by me and my fellow residents," Ding said, "while the monetary compensation is only symbolic." Following Ding's call for an apology, Zeng Yukang, deputy general manager of the CNPC's Daqing Petroleum Administration Bureau, went to Harbin, where he met with Heilongjiang provincial officials to express regret for the company's mishandling of the Songhua accident (*Xinhua* 2005b). Do you think a sincere apology is enough to offset the environmental damage caused by the CNPC? Do you think Ding Ning was right to demand such an apology? What more should the company do to carry out its responsibilities toward the environment?

Environmental activists like Wen Bo from Pacific Environment—an environmental organization based in San Francisco, California—declared, "many local people actually think this pollution accident was a blessing in disguise" (Worldwatch Institute 2013). The Songhua crisis increased awareness of the risks of water pollution and the urgency of measures designed to reduce these risks. Nevertheless, Wen believes people like Xie Zhenhua and Wang Wei became "scapegoats" sacrificed to protect a flawed system (Worldwatch Institute 2013). Hu Kanping, a journalist from *China Green*, gave a similar opinion when talking about Xie's resignation from SEPA: "Though he is not at primary fault for what happened, it shows an improving situation for government accountability in China. This resignation will likely be followed by more resignations and increasing accountability in corporate environmental responsibility. This means better industry performance and safer production and will likely expedite the government's resolution of environmental conflicts." Hu further expressed his approval regarding the choice of Zhou Shengxian to lead reform efforts at SEPA. According to Hu, Zhou is first and foremost "a very honest worker" (Worldwatch Institute 2013). From your understanding of the case, do you agree with Wen that Xie and Wang were made "scapegoats"? While the Songhua disaster did happen on their watch, as they say, did they deserve to be fired for their role in it? Would it have been better to have them stay at their posts and use their experience to manage the cleanup? What would you have recommended to their superiors?

19.2.9 Conclusion

As a result of the Songhua River disaster, certain changes occurred in China's environmental policies that, however subtle, may actually yield long-term improvement. First of all, in 2008, SEPA became a cabinet level Ministry of Environmental Protection (MEP). The new agency reports directly to the State Council, China's chief administrative authority, and is responsible for implementing the nation's environmental policies and enforcing all relevant laws and regulations. The change in status for this department is more than a mere name change. The five regional environmental inspection and enforcement centers now must report directly to the MEP and not to the provincial governments. The MEP, apparently, will now be able to demand compliance at the provincial and regional levels, in ways that seemed impossible in the previous administrative structure.

The MEP has also been active internationally, having secured funds for a joint pollution prevention program from the Asian Development Bank (ADB), whose 2011 Report confirms substantial progress in developing effective water pollution control infrastructure for Jilin and the surrounding area. The ADB had approved loans of up to US$146.6 million to Tongfang Water Engineering (TWE), which was charged with the task of restoring the water supply and water treatment in the Songhua basin. The ADB's investment was used to construct an additional 70 urban sewage treatment plants with an impressive daily capacity of processing 295 million tons of water. The treatment plants span all 36 counties along the Songhua River basin (*Xinhua* 2009b). Philip Erquiaga of the ADB believes this project would change the lives of people living around the Songhua River: "Treating more waste water and improving the supply of potable water will reduce pollution in the urban environment around the Songhua River Basin, and improve the health and quality of life for millions of residents" (*WASH News* 2010).

Like many other environmental disasters, the Songhua River incident was a result of human error. However, the resulting social panic, widespread pollution, and ineffective cover-up brought international attention to China's environmental protection policies. Instead of communicating the dangers of the toxic spill in a timely manner, the central and local governments' attempt to minimize the scale of the problem met with scorn in the court of public opinion. After the Songhua spill, Wang Wei was discovered dead, Xie Zhenhua resigned as SEPA director, and several CNPC managers were fired. These events, on the one hand, illustrate the extensive consequences one company's negligence can have, while on the other hand, they also demonstrate how genuine change for the better can result, once both business and government recognize the true costs of paying only lip service to environmental responsibility. The change underway in China, as a result of the actions taken in response to the Songhua River disaster, may yet turn out to be a "blessing in disguise," not only for alerting everyone to the need to concern ourselves with preserving the natural environment but also for improving the health of Chinese and foreign citizens, as well as national and international political and social relations.

19.3 Case Study Discussion

The Songhua River disaster, to be sure, is not the greatest environmental disaster ever endured by China, and it certainly is not the greatest ever in the world. For sheer loss of life and horrible long-term consequences, the explosion at the Union Carbide plant in Bhopal, India, in 1984 remains the worst ever, with basic questions of moral and legal responsibility—not to mention the completion of an effective cleanup effort—still not fully resolved (*The Hindu* 2014).

Nor are such disasters still only occurring in developing countries like China and India. The Upper Big Branch Mine disaster that happened in West Virginia in 2010 involved the death of 29 of the 31 miners at the site (*Charleston Gazette* 2014), the worst coal mine disaster in the USA since 1970. In both the Bhopal and Upper Big Branch explosions, the firms involved—Union Carbide and Massey Energy—have had to answer charges of criminal liability for their negligence. Compared to the ways these businesses have responded to the disasters resulting from their operations, after a shaky start, both the CNPC and the MEP seem to have turned over a new leaf, when it comes to facing up to the need for effective environmental protection.

Of course, the outrageous failures of other businesses and regulatory agencies cannot absolve either the CNPC or the MEP—as well as local and provincial leaders—of their mistakes, of their responsibility for what they could have done to prevent the Songhua River disaster, and of how they responded once the explosion occurred. As the old saying goes, two wrongs don't make a right. What, then, are the lessons that apparently have been learned in China, and how can everyone learn from the experience of the CNPC and the MEP?

The first great lesson is the importance of information, its timely release and its credibility. Those who believed that a cover-up could work were proven wrong. The basic geography of the Songhua River made it impossible to contain either the spill or the need for accurate information about it securely within China's borders. Once the benzene slick threatened cities downstream in Russia, the disaster inevitably became international and threatened China's reputation and aspirations as an emerging superpower. But if the Russian authorities were owed the truth about the disaster coming their way, what about the Chinese people, the citizens of Jilin, Harbin, and other cities, towns, and villages that depend upon the river for their water? Had Premier Wen Jiabao not intervened to end the failed attempts at a cover-up, the legitimacy of China's central government might have faced new and even greater challenges. It was good that China's leadership ended the cover-up; it would have been better had they done it even sooner in the initial phase of the disaster.

A second important lesson is to face up to the fact that the PetroChina Benzene Production Plant in Jilin was an accident waiting to happen. The explosion wasn't simply the result of one worker's "bungled attempt" to unblock a channel in the nitration tower (Yong and Na 2005). As various investigations moved forward, it became obvious that years of negligence, born of complacency, corruption, and a subordination of all other concerns to meeting production quotas, had created circumstances in which a demonstration of "Murphy's law"—"If something can go wrong, it will"—was sure to happen. While there is probably no way absolutely to guarantee that something will never go wrong, there are many ways to minimize the risks of an accident, through prudent planning and training in risk assessment and management. Clearly these concerns are now prominently displayed in the CNPC's approach to "HSE" concerns. That is good. Lessons have been learned and mistakes have been corrected. But never again should anyone be lulled into complacency. If something can go wrong, it will.

A third lesson is for businesses, like the CNPC, to accept the principle that the "polluter pays." When and if an industrial accident occurs causing pollution or other forms of environmental damage, the firm ought to pay the full cost of the cleanup. If firms, however large or small, cannot pay, then they should not have engaged in such risky ventures in the first place. If this principle is adopted, then at the very least, businesses must either buy insurance to cover the known risks of doing business or otherwise indemnify themselves against potential liabilities. Among the more ethically suspect of the strategies for maximizing profits is trying to shift the costs—and risks—involved in doing business upon others, such as the public at large or the taxpayers, who have little or no way of defending themselves against predatory business practices.

A fourth lesson concerns the ethical significance of the "polluter pays" principle. A firm's commitment to protect the environment should not be praised as an example of corporate social responsibility. The "polluter pays" principle places environmental responsibility right at the core of sound business ethics, whose first principle is "Do No Harm." If harm is done in the course of your business activities, if you injure someone or damage some good, public or private, you ought not only to pay fair compensation to those you've injured, but also to do everything in your power to prevent such accidents from happening again. As children, we may have learned, "If you make a mess, you've got to clean it up." It's the only fair thing to do. Businesses that try to hide the messes they've made, or otherwise deny that they caused them, are acting like spoiled children in need of some serious punishment.[4]

[4] CNPC's apparent change of heart, embracing transparency and accountability, however hesitant at first, may be contrasted with British Petroleum (BP)'s attempt to evade responsibility for the Deepwater Horizon disaster, in which one of their oil rigs exploded, resulting in an estimated 4.9 million barrels of oil spilling into the Gulf of Mexico during the 87 days it took to reseal the oil well (April 20–July 15, 2010). BP's attempt to minimize its liability for the spill is ongoing and involves using every conceivable legal maneuver to shift the costs of the spill upon others, including its business partners in constructing the Deepwater Horizon rig. It is estimated that, if BP's legal maneuvers continue to fail, as seems likely, the firm's eventual costs for cleanup and compensation will exceed US $43 billion. A complete archive of stories reporting the events of the BP oil disaster is available at *The Guardian*'s website (*The Guardian* 2014). BP's response to the Deepwater Horizon disaster, through all its vicissitudes, deserves condemnation on moral grounds and the punishment that it is currently receiving in the US courts of law. Had BP recognized the principle of "polluter pays" and institutionalized it within the firm's corporate culture and risk management policies, they might have saved their investors billions in cleanup costs and penalties that one way or another eventually will be extracted from them, if they hope to continue operating in the USA.

Those that step forward and acknowledge their mistakes in good faith should be praised not for exemplary moral leadership, but simply for doing what every business is required to do, consistent with sound business ethics.

A fifth lesson concerns the intrinsic connection between environmental responsibility and the struggle against corruption. The attempted cover-up of the Songhua River spill might have been dismissed out of hand had it not been for the all-too-cozy relationship between local and regional officials, charged with enforcing China's environmental protection laws and the businesses they were supposed to regulate. Negligence in the form of inspections only superficially undertaken, whose results were falsified or simply ignored, could only encourage a false sense of security among plant managers, who wrongly assumed that their friendly ties with the regulators would protect them in the event of an accident. Corruption is not simply an act of bribery, it is a form of spiritual pollution that lulls everyone involved into a false sense of security. Corruption will never prevent bad things from happening. On the contrary, corruption increases the likelihood that disasters will occur, for it fosters complacency and a cynicism about the need to be diligent in carrying out one's responsibilities. If the inspectors can be bought off—so the cynic mistakenly assumes—there's no need to worry about what might happen to the environment or whether one's own career might be at risk if anything bad happens. In China, as elsewhere around the world, the struggle against corruption and the struggle for environmental protection are two sides of the same coin.

A final lesson to be drawn from the Songhua River disaster and its aftermath is that, as hard as they are to achieve, good intentions are never enough. Even if all the parties involved had been virtuous—that is, sincere in their desire to the serve the people in and through their various responsibilities, honest in their dealings with one another, and genuinely committed to transparency and accountability—there is no guarantee that the explosion at the PetroChina Benzene Production Plant in Jilin would not have happened, and no guarantee that the resulting spill could have been quickly and efficiently overcome. All the good intentions in the world are not likely to guarantee a positive outcome, if the accountability structures—the ways in which the various agencies of business and government interact and on how the flow of information among them is managed—are outmoded or seriously deficient. Real change began to appear in the long-term rehabilitation of the Songhua River basin only after the accountability structures were updated and reformed, primarily with the administrative reorganization that transformed SEPA into an MEP exercising credible authority. A change of heart is always a necessary first step, but the second step must involve a reexamination of organizational structures to remove whatever obstacles—so-called bottlenecks—preventing the agencies from fulfilling their legitimate purposes.

What had begun as a public relations disaster for China, yet one more shameful incident highlighting the nation's corruption and incompetence, was turned around, so that today an honest appraisal of the Songhua River disaster must acknowledge the progress that has been made in rehabilitating the river, and how that progress has been achieved, starting with the moral leadership shown by Premier Wen Jiabao and President Hu Jintao and following through with the determined efforts of Zhou

Shengxian at the MEP, as well as the rethinking of the CNPC's commitments to "HSE"—health, safety, and environmental—programming. It would be nice to think that the lessons learned in the Songhua River disaster have carried over into the way PetroChina dealt with subsequent accidents involving significant levels of water pollution. But such reassurance is not yet possible, given the company's less than straightforward responses to the pipeline break that polluted the Chishui River in 2009 (Chao and Zhu 2010) and the pipeline explosions in 2010 at the port of Dalian at Xingang Harbor (Wong 2010). In both cases, alas, there were delays in making adequate information available to the public and charges of attempted cover-up. As the CNPC's statement on "safety" insists, "high risks in oil industry mean that hard work has to be done to ensure safety," and all surely would agree with that. What remains to be seen is whether PetroChina can truthfully claim, as it does in the sentence that follows, "Safety has become the core of our corporate culture." Would that it were true.

19.4 Ethical Reflection

Let us begin our reflections with the notion of a "silent stakeholder." The term originated in the USA, partially in response to Rachel Carson's groundbreaking effort to create an environmental movement, *Silent Spring* (Carson 1962). Springtime in the USA, like the months immediately following Chinese New Year, witnesses the reawakening of nature in all its blooming, buzzing confusion, when the earth is alive with the noisy exaltation of new birth. The prospect of a "silent" Spring is Carson's image of an environment that is dying, from the self-inflicted wounds of a humanity that has grown heedless of its existential dependence upon nature. As the environment slowly dies from DDT and the other chemical pesticides and fertilizers that Carson lobbied so strenuously against, eventually springtime itself falls into silence. Once it was recognized—thanks to Carson and other environmental activists—that everyone, and not just governments, shared a serious obligation to preserve the life that sustains us all on this planet, the environment came to be regarded as "the silent stakeholder" as part of the ethical redescription of business' managerial responsibilities understood within the stakeholder theory.

19.4.1 The Silent Stakeholder

The distinguished American philosopher, Robert C. Solomon, clarified the significance of the "silent stakeholder" for business ethics:

> Concern for the environment has become an inescapable concern for the free-enterprise system. Thirty years ago, it was at most a marginal aesthetic issue for most industries. Today it is or it should be part of every corporate mission. In current business ethics terms,

> the environment has become a "stakeholder" in the corporation, one of the sources of obligation and responsibility.
>
> The environment does not have a voice or a vote in running our society. It is not a stockholder and has no say in the running of our corporations. Nevertheless it provides the atmosphere, many of the resources, the very ground and climate within which all business and all human activity takes place. It is, therefore, the silent stakeholder of every corporation, or rather, the precondition for every corporation's very existence. (Solomon 1997: 264)

If Solomon is correct in regarding our natural environment as "the silent stakeholder in every corporation," then the challenge for international business ethics is to determine how our responsibilities to this stakeholder are to be reconciled with all the other stakeholders who make legitimate claims—as we have seen in previous chapters—upon the exercise of moral responsibility in business.

What once may have been regarded as the silence of this "silent stakeholder" appears to have been broken. The measurable collective impact of various forms of water and air pollution has been linked directly with the prospect for catastrophic climate change. Each new disturbance in "normal" weather patterns, each new disruption in the ecosystems supporting the plant and animal life upon which our own existence depends, must be regarded as significant communication demanding a rethinking of our relationship to this most indispensable of all stakeholders. Business corporations, as well as governments, and all of us ignore nature's distress signals at our own peril. The silence has been broken; the ultimate stakeholder has raised her voice in protest; now what must we do, in order to acknowledge our environmental responsibilities and balance them with the concerns of our other stakeholders?

The Songhua River disaster, like the Bhopal explosion, and BP's catastrophic oil spill in the Gulf of Mexico should teach all business managers that the silent stakeholder cannot be ravaged without creating serious problems with all other stakeholders. Toxic chemicals released into rivers, lakes, and the oceans negatively impact other industries, as well as farmers, fisherfolk, and others whose livelihood depends upon the health and integrity of those waterways and their ecosystems. When the drinking water supply for major cities in the Songhua-Amur river basin was endangered by the CNPC explosion, China was faced with an international crisis, as dangerous as it was embarrassing. When the poor of Bhopal suffered loss of life and livelihood because of the Union Carbide disaster, the resulting legal struggle over liabilities has continued to dog the firm's activities in India and that of its successor, Dow Chemical. When the Deepwater Horizon oil rig blew up in the Gulf of Mexico, BP was forced to pay unprecedented amounts in compensation to the businesses—tourism and fishing, mostly—that were seriously damaged as the oil made its way to the shores of the Gulf states, Louisiana, Alabama, and Florida. Even if the ecosystems themselves stood by silently suffering these atrocities, there were other stakeholders determined to make the polluters pay, who had damaged them and the environments they depend on.

19.4.2 *Management, Stewardship, and Sustainability*

Situating management's concern for the environment within the range of its responsibilities for all other stakeholders, of course, implies that sound business ethics—here as elsewhere—must steer a course between moral absolutism and ethical relativism. The claims of the "silent stakeholder" may be existential and ultimate, but they are not absolute. While some philosophers may object to the alleged "anthropocentrism" or "speciesism" suggested by that relatively modest claim (Stanford Encyclopedia)—as if nature as such had greater "intrinsic value" than any concern for humanity and its flourishing—we believe that an ethic of responsibility provides a far more realistic and effective approach, one that places the idea of environmental "stewardship" or "sustainability" at the core of sound business practice. As every farmer knows, there is a significant difference between cultivation and exploitation. Cultivation is a form of stewardship in which we seek to meet our own basic human needs while also taking care to preserve and enhance the environment which supports them. Cultivation seeks to be sustainable. Exploitation, by contrast, seeks an immediate payoff, heedless of the costs to others or to the degradation inflicted on the environment. Taken literally, as we have seen in previous chapters, profit maximization is an unsustainable form of exploitation. While it offers no false guarantee regarding increased profits, cultivation gives us a reasonable chance to do well, while not destroying the very basis of our future prosperity.

Stewardship, then, consists in a moral vision, a general commitment to use the things of this earth—including our own intelligence and virtually limitless capacity for good work—in ways that enable all of us to flourish together. Stewardship embraces an attitude of cultivation[5] that progressively distances itself from exploitation. Stewardship, unlike the utopian visions animating some environmentalists, carries no preference for preserving a pristine state of nature, as if the earth would be more perfect were humanity simply to disappear. Stewardship makes no romantic distinction between nature and our actual environment, the result of millennia of human interactions, good and bad. It simply directs us to do the best we can with what we have been given acknowledging that whatever may have gone on before, ours is the task of managing wisely, preserving and enhancing the environment wherever and whenever possible, by seeking to achieve a harmony between human

[5] The prophets and sages of all the great religious and spiritual traditions have recognized that embracing an ethic of stewardship is impossible apart from the pursuit of wisdom. One such sage is Peter Maurin, who along with Dorothy Day founded the Catholic Worker Movement. Maurin's *Easy Essays* (Maurin 2010) and other writings often note the proper relationship of "cultivation" with "cult" and "culture"—meaning the relationship of stewardship particularly in the form of agriculture, with religion and education (Zwick L. & M. 1996). The virtues necessary for sustaining an ethic of stewardship, or the proper spirit of cultivation, must be grounded in the successful performance of the duties prescribed by cult and culture. Though Maurin was an Orthodox Catholic, his thoughts on cultivation, cult, and culture reflect values enshrined in Confucian tradition as in, for example, Book IX on "The Conveyance of Rites" (*Li Yun*: 禮運), containing a description of the ideal commonwealth state (*dàtóng*: 大同): "When the perfect order prevails, the world is like a home shared by all."

flourishing and nature's own continued good health. Stewardship presupposes that proper management is essential to achieving the good life as well as fulfilling nature's own destiny, insofar as that can be determined.

Wise management consists not in the relentless pursuit of short-term goals like profit maximization, at the expense of all other values. As we have seen time and again in previous chapters, there's nothing intrinsically wrong with trying to make a profit. It all depends—to paraphrase Confucius (Analects 4: 5)—on the doing it in the right way, that is, in a way that is consistent with one's ethical responsibilities. Identifying the environment as the "silent stakeholder," therefore, does not cancel the rights and legitimate concerns of all other stakeholders. Management must still satisfy the legitimate expectations of the firm's owners or investors, its employees, its suppliers, its customers, as well as the communities in which it operates and the government agencies that monitor its compliance with the law. But each of these now must be squared with another stakeholder's concern, namely, our common existential need to sustain the natural environment without which no stakeholder's interest is sustainable.

Inevitably, there will be trade-offs, as each stakeholder group must be persuaded by management to accommodate its expectations to the legitimate concerns of all other stakeholders, including especially the interests of the "silent stakeholder." Scientifically based risk management practices, for example, impose additional costs, at least initially. Pollution control devices that monitor a plant's discharge of waste water, or the effectiveness of its water treatment facilities, will cost money and may force investors to recalculate their anticipated returns. But recognizing these trade-offs and adjusting the firm's forecasts are nothing new. If commodity prices change and key raw materials cost more or less than what had been assumed, adjustments will be made. If the results of collective bargaining with the employees require that wages be increased, adjustments will be made. Factoring in the costs of environmentally friendly policies and procedures may challenge management's ingenuity, but the challenge is not essentially different from responding credibly to the concerns of all other stakeholders. Besides, reports on the adoption of environmentally friendly or "green" technologies show that they yield many unexpected benefits and may end up paying for themselves. The case for embracing an ethic of stewardship is simply another chapter in the ongoing struggle to do well while doing good.

19.4.3 Stewardship as Corporate Social Responsibility

Exercising moral leadership in business can be divided roughly into two great areas of responsibility, namely, those that are internal and external to a business' ordinary and routine operations. This division may be regarded as the distinction between business ethics as such and corporate social responsibility (CSR). Basic business ethics follows directly from the first principle governing the morality of all human activities: "Do No Harm (primum non nocere)." Corporate social responsibility

(CSR) refers to a business' citizenship responsibilities, its share in our collective pursuit of the common good. Both areas must be honored in an ethic of stewardship or environmental responsibility. Because of the nature of the Songhua River catastrophe, our discussion emphasized the internal dimension, namely, a business'—in this case, CNPC's—responsibility not only for cleaning up after any accidents caused by its routine operations but also for seeking ways to prevent or at least minimize the risk of repeat occurrences in the future. If the principle of "Do No Harm" is fully embraced, a business' strategic planning must address both of these concerns, as part of the cost of staying in business. What, then, of the other dimension, the CSR dimension of an ethic of environmental responsibility?

CSR policies are meant to demonstrate the firm's commitment to good citizenship. It is committed to the common good, by contributing its fair share in taxes to support the operations of the government; by collaborating with government agencies, civic groups, and nongovernmental organizations (NGOs) to formulate and implement policies that support a sustainable environment; and by offering its expertise and other resources to civic groups to help them define and address local environmental problems more effectively. Such positive contributions qualify as examples of effective CSR programming when and if they are not directly related to the firm's basic and routine business operations and when and if they are undertaken primarily as a demonstration of the firm's concern to secure the good will of the local community.[6] One promising example is the leadership many businesses and institutions have shown in trying to understand their "carbon footprint," that is, the ways in which their diverse activities may contribute positively or negatively to the sustainability of the environment.

Nothing is too trivial to be measured as part of the firm's "carbon footprint," including the management of food services and cafeterias for employees, whether composting solid wastes is part of their garbage disposal procedures, or, to cite another example, the use of renewable energy technologies—solar panels and wind turbines come to mind—to reduce the firm's dependence on the region's conventional power grid whose consumption of fossil fuels, coal and oil, contributes significantly to air and water pollution. Such activities may include an assessment of the transportation needs of employees and whether the firm can reduce its "carbon footprint" by encouraging employees to carpool and use public transportation or even bicycles, rather than assume that owning and using their own private automobile is the only way to get to and from work each day. By the same token, a firm that is committed to environmental responsibility will likely assign staff to conduct

[6]The webpages of most corporations aspiring to global leadership in their industries, as CNPC clearly is in the energy industry, are filled with testimony to their CSR activities. As we have seen in Chap. 12, it is surely legitimate for a business to demand an effective and efficient use of the resources that it allocates for such activities; it is also understandable that they will weigh the strategic advantages of various programs in light of the firm's core competencies and long-term business plan. Nevertheless, the desire to be of service to the community by contributing to the common good of all must be credible, transparent, and accountable to all stakeholders. CSR programming should not be used to cover up the mistakes and other forms of wrongdoing for which the firm has been responsible.

ongoing research on new, energy-saving technologies or the programs promoting their use by government agencies and private foundations supporting the switch toward a sustainable environment. Participation in such programs may yield competitive advantages, particularly to firms that are early adopters of the energy-saving innovations.

19.4.4 Exercising the Principle of Subsidiarity in and for the Environment

For a firm to find its own way of contributing to the common good, developing its own effective strategies for exercising environmental responsibility—from the perspective of international business ethics—conforms to the principle of subsidiarity that should govern all social interactions. First emergent in the tradition of Catholic social teaching, the principle of subsidiarity ostensibly sets a limit to the role of governments in achieving the common good. But there's far more to it than that. Appeals to the principle of subsidiarity make it clear that individuals and groups at the local level bear their own responsibilities for the common good and should not wait passively for the government to intervene before playing their own part in achieving it. But if, as the principle suggests, everyone is generally responsible for the common good, how then are each of us to understand our specific responsibilities for it? The danger is that if everyone is responsible for the common good in principle, no one in particular is likely to step forward first.

The principle of subsidiarity does not offer a detailed blueprint for overcoming this problem. Instead, it encourages coordination and communication among individuals and groups. It invites us to create new and more effective levels of transparency and accountability in our mutual interactions. Governments will not necessarily retreat from the scene, as if their interventions were neither necessary nor welcome. On the contrary, governments will continue to intervene, but only in ways that enhance—rather than usurp or preempt—the participation of the individuals and local groups involved and in ways that provide genuine support and assistance, as the Latin root of "subsidiarity" implies.

The principle of subsidiarity affords us a way of analyzing what went wrong and—just as significantly—what went right, for example, in China's response to the Songhua River disaster. Businesses can learn to implement this principle, so that similar mistakes may be avoided and similar progress achieved. The chief lesson is the priority of local response to a disaster in the making. CNPC and local officials in Jilin were right to respond, without waiting for the central government to intervene. They were wrong to try covering up the extent of the catastrophe. They needed the central government's help, and the sooner, the better. Had they been able to coordinate and communicate more effectively, the disaster might have been mitigated in its initial stages. Once the central government got involved, things began to get better. A major international crisis with Russia was averted; the threat to water supplies downstream was mitigated, hesitantly, in the case of Harbin, but with increasing effectiveness at Khabarovsk and other points north; and international agencies were allowed to participate in the long-term rehabilitation effort, involving the construction of new waste management facilities and other infrastructure improvements along the Songhua.

None of the successful efforts would have been possible without the intervention of China's central government and top political leadership. What the principle of subsidiarity requires is that all such interventions be conceived and executed with the intent of empowering local communities to act more effectively in pursuit of the common good. The principle of subsidiarity, in principle, seeks to define the politics of environmental responsibility beyond the sterile contrast between totalitarianism and laissez-faire liberalism. There is a role for strong government leadership, of course, but, it, too, must be understood as a form of stewardship. Stewardship, in the political arena, means empowering all other groups and individuals to exercise their own distinctive responsibilities for the common good.

19.5 Conclusion

We have seen at least one observer characterize the Songhua River disaster as a "blessing in disguise." In retrospect, this seems to be a fair and accurate verdict on it, since the responses of the various agents involved, after some initial hesitation, seem to represent a turning point in China's determination to address its environmental problems responsibly. Exercising environmental responsibility, as we have seen, is everyone's business, but making progress in it may require all concerned to move beyond "business as usual" attitudes and practices. Undeniably, there has been a change at the CNPC and not just in its embrace of the rhetoric of CSR. There has also been a change in the central government's approach, as indicated by the new mandate granted to the MEP recognizing the need for coordination among agencies, local, provincial, regional, national, and international, both public and private. Effective coordination, of course, cannot be achieved without real gains in transparency and accountability at all levels. The transformation apparently underway, we hope, is a sign that an ethic of stewardship with Chinese characteristics may emerge among China's leaders in business, government, and its civic institutions.

References

ADB. (2013). Songhua river basin water pollution control and management project: Jilin component: Environmental Monitoring Report (2012). Retrieved on June 23, 2015 from http://www.adb.org/projects/documents/songhua-river-basin-water-pollution-control-and-management-project-jilin-component-emr-2012

Ansfield, J. (2005, December 18). Who's to blame? *Newsweek*. Retrieved on June 23, 2015 from http://www.newsweek.com/whos-blame-113957

Ansfield, J. (2007, January 11). Xie Zhenhua's unsystematic return and other curious moves. *China Digital Times*. Retrieved on July 24, 2012, from http://chinadigitaltimes.net/2007/01/xie-zhenhuas-unsystematic-return-and-other-curious-moves/

Asia News. (2007, January 26). Company only fined for benzene slick in Songhua River. Retrieved on July 23, 2012, from http://www.asianews.it/news-en/Company-only-fined-for-benzene-slick-in-Songhua-River-8333.html

Asia Times. (2005, November 30). Northeast cleans up after chemical blast. Retrieved on July 12, 2012, from http://www.atimes.com/atimes/China_Business/GK30Cb06.html

Batson, A. (2006, March 29). China considers tradable pollution-rights permits. *The Wall Street Journal*. Retrieved on July 13, 2012, from http://www.washingtonpost.com/wp-dyn/content/article/2006/03/28/AR2006032801565_pf.html

BBC. (2005a, November 23). Toxic leak threat to Chinese city. Retrieved on July 15, 2012, from http://news.bbc.co.uk/2/hi/asia-pacific/4462760.stm

BBC. (2005b, November 24). Chinese papers condemn Harbin 'lies'. Retrieved on July 23, 2012, from http://news.bbc.co.uk/2/hi/asia-pacific/4465712.stm

BBC. (2006, November 24). China punishes river's polluters. Retrieved on July 14, 2012, from http://news.bbc.co.uk/2/hi/asia-pacific/6179980.stm

Bezlova, A. (2005, November 30). Pollution grows along with China's economy. *China Environmental Digest*. Retrieved on July 13, 2012, from http://china-environmental-news.blogspot.it/2005_11_01_archive.html

Caijing.com. (2005, March). Reform pollution law and let the rivers roll. Retrieved on July 12, 2012, from http://english.caijing.com.cn/2007-03-05/100043227.html

Carson, R. (1962). *Silent spring*. Boston: Houghton Mifflin Harcourt.

CBS News. (2009, February 11). China: Punishment for pollution. Retrieved on July 12, 2012, from http://www.cbsnews.com/2100-202_162-1075739.html?tag=contentMain;contentBody

Chao, X., & Zhu, C. (2010, January 14). Defending the Yellow River. *Caixin Online*. Accessed on February 17, 2015, at http://english.caixin.com/2010-01-14/100108202.html

Charleston Gazette. (2014, November 13). Timeline of Upper Big Branch mine disaster events. Retrieved on December 24, 2014, from http://www.wvgazette.com/article/20141113/GZ01/141119618

Chen, G. (2009). *Politics of China's environmental protection: Problems and progress*. Singapore: World Scientific Publishers.

China Daily. (2005a, November 14). One dead, 5 missing in chemical plant blasts. Retrieved on December 11, 2014, from http://www.chinadaily.com.cn/english/doc/2005-11/14/content_494329.htm

China Daily. (2005b, November 25). Citizen sues China petroleum for polluting river. Retrieved on July 22, 2012, from http://www.chinadaily.com.cn/english/doc/2005-11/25/content_498057.htm

China Daily. (2005c, November 25). Commentary: Cover-up can't hide murky water truth. Retrieved on December 11, 2014, from http://www.chinadaily.com.cn/english/doc/2005-11/25/content_498002.htm

China Daily. (2005d, December 6). CNPC sacks three responsible for blast. Retrieved on December 18, 2014, from http://www.chinadaily.com.cn/english/home/2005-12/06/content_500802.htm

CNPC. (2005, November 15). CNPC announcement. Retrieved on July 23, 2012, from http://www.petrochina.com.cn/resource/EngPdf/BulletinBoard/gg051116e.pdf

CNPC. (2014a). CNPC>Environment & Society. Retrieved on December 18, 2014, from http://www.cnpc.com.cn/en/environmentsociety/society_index.shtml

CNPC. (2014b). CNPC>Environment & Society>Safety. Retrieved on December 18, 2014, from http://www.cnpc.com.cn/en/safety/common_index.shtml

CNPC. (2014c). CNPC>Environment & Society>Our Commitment to HSE. Retrieved on December 18, 2014, from http://www.cnpc.com.cn/en/ourhse/OurCommitmenttoHSE_index.shtml

Da, S. (2005, December 14). Songhua pollution sparks rethink of industrial distribution. *China.org.cn*. Retrieved on July 15, 2012, from http://www.china.org.cn/english/2005/Dec/151978.htm

Dan, L. (2005, November 26). China's cover up of accident unveiled. *The Epoch Times*. Retrieved on August 16, 2012, from http://www.theepochtimes.com/news/5-11-26/35021.html

Gleick, P. H. (2009). China and water. In *The world's water 2008-2009* (chap. 5). Chicago: Island Press.
Global Times. (2011, June 2). China invests 7.84 bln yuan to treat Songhua River pollution. Retrieved on July 15, 2012, from http://business.globaltimes.cn/industries/2011-06/661460.html. Retrieved on December 20, 2014, from http://wikileaks.org/gifiles/docs/33/3349155_-os-china-econ-gv-china-invests-7-84-bln-yuan-to-treat.html
Green, N. (2009, March). A China environmental health project brief. Positive spillover? Impact of the Songhua River Benzene incident on China' s environmental policy. *China Environmental Forum*. Retrieved on August 8, 2012, from http://www.circleofblue.org/waternews/wp-content/uploads/2011/03/songhua_march09.pdf
Griswold, E. (2012, September 21). How 'Silent Spring' ignited the environmental movement. *The New York Times*. Retrieved on December 24, 2014, from http://www.nytimes.com/2012/09/23/magazine/how-silent-spring-ignited-the-environmental-movement.html
Harbin People's Government. (2005, November 22). Harbin People's government notice to stop water supply. Retrieved on July 22, 2012, from http://www.harbin.gov.cn/info/news/index/detail/234194.htm
Heilongjiang People's Government. (2007, July 5). The mountains range river of Heilongjiang province. Retrieved on July 23, 2012, from http://www.hlj.gov.cn/cylj/system/2007/07/05/000043392.shtml
Jakes, S. (2006, October 24). When the Yellow River runs red. *TIME World*. Retrieved on July 14, 2012, from http://www.time.com/time/world/article/0,8599,1550046,00.html
Jiang, W. (2005). The cost of China's modernization. *China Brief, 5*(25). Retrieved on August 8, 2012, from http://www.jamestown.org/programs/chinabrief/single/?tx_ttnews%5Btt_news%5D=3915&tx_ttnews%5BbackPid%5D=195&no_cache=1
Jiang, P. (2006, July 31). Give law greater clout in battle against pollution. *China Daily*. Retrieved on July 13, 2012, from http://www.chinadaily.com.cn/opinion/2006-07/31/content_653096.htm
Jie, Y. (2006). The environmental yellow peril. *China Rights Forum 2006, No.1 - China's Environmental Challenge*. Retrieved on December 12, 2014, from http://23.253.170.136:11781/sites/default/files/PDFs/CRF.1.2006/CRF-2006-1_Yellow.pdf
Jing, D. (2005a, December 6). Head of CNPC's Jilin branch dismissed. *Gov.cn*. Retrieved on August 10, 2012, from http://english.gov.cn/2005-12/06/content_118698.htm
Jing, D. (2005b, December 13). Songhua River pollution "painful": Official. *Gov.cn*. Retrieved on August 10, 2012, from http://english.gov.cn/2005-12/13/content_125121.htm
Kirschner, L. A., & Grandy, E. B. (2006). The Songhua River Spill: China's pollution crisis. *Parsons Behle & Latimer Law Firm*. Retrieved on July 14, 2012, from http://www.parsonsbehlelaw.com/CM/Articles/The-Shonghua-River-Spill.asp
Li, F. (2005, November 22). Water stoppage in Harbin sparks panic buying. *China Daily*. Retrieved on July 23, 2012, from http://www.chinadaily.com.cn/english/doc/2005-11/22/content_496761.htm
Li, F. (2006, January 10). Cleaning up Songhua River is a priority. *China Daily*. Retrieved on July 15, 2012, from http://www.chinadaily.com.cn/english/doc/2006-01/10/content_510877.htm
Liu, J. R., et al. (2009). Organic pollution from the Songhua River induces NIH 3T3 cell transformation: Potential risks for human health. *Journal of Toxicology and Environmental Health Sciences, 1*(4), 060–067.
Lo, P. C. (1999). Confucian ethic of death with dignity and its contemporary relevance. *The Annual of the Society of Christian Ethics, 19*(Nov. 1999), 313-333. Retrieved on August 20, 2012, from http://arts.hkbu.edu.hk/~pclo/article/a1999_ceodw.pdf
Matisoff, A. (2012, February). *Crude beginnings: An assessment of China National Petroleum Corporation's environmental and social performance abroad*. Retrieved on August 17, 2012, from http://www.scribd.com/doc/102327304/Crude-Beginnings
Maurin, P. (2010). *Easy Essays* (Catholic Work Reprint). Eugene: Wipf and Stock.
McCann, D. (2014). Who is responsible for the common good? Catholic social teaching and the praxis of subsidiarity. In D. Solomon & P. C. Lo (Eds.), *The common good: Chinese and American perspectives* (pp. 261–289). Dordrecht: Springer.

Pan, P. (2005, December 7). Official in China spill case is dead. *The Washington Post*. Retrieved on July 23, 2012, from http://www.washingtonpost.com/wp-dyn/content/article/2005/12/07/AR2005120702356.html

PetroChina. (2006, March 20). 2005 annual report. Retrieved on December 17, 2014, from http://www.petrochina.com.cn/enpetrochina/ndbg/201404/8de0a9c658f84d698db0ee671c00fbc8.shtml

Solomon, R. C. (1997). *It's good business: Ethics and free enterprise for the new millennium*. Lanham: Rowman and Littlefield.

Taipei Times. (2005, December 8). CCP warns against cover-ups. Retrieved on July 24, 2012, from http://www.taipeitimes.com/News/world/archives/2005/12/08/2003283496/2

Tang, H. (2005, August 25). Why Chinese firms don't apologize. *Chinadialogue*. Retrieved on July 14, 2012, from http://www.chinadialogue.net/article/show/single/en/3787-Why-Chinese-firms-don-t-apologise

The Epoch Times. (2005, December 10). Jilin PetroChina explosion under investigation, vice-mayor of Jilin City reported dead. Retrieved on July 22, 2012, from http://www.theepochtimes.com/news/5-12-10/35620.html

The Guardian. (2014). BP oil spill. Retrieved on December 23, 2014, from http://www.theguardian.com/environment/bp-oil-spill

The Hindu. (2014, December 2). Editorial: No closure for Bhopal. Retrieved on December 18, 2014, from http://www.thehindu.com/opinion/editorial/no-closure-for-bhopal/article6652304.ece

The New York Times. (2005, December 5). Chinese chemical company boss fired over toxic spill. Retrieved on July 23, 2012, from http://www.nytimes.com/2005/12/05/world/asia/05iht-web.1205china.html

UNEP. (2005, December). *The Songhua River spill. Field mission report*. Nairobi: UNEP. Retrieved on July 14, 2012, from http://www.unep.org/PDF/China_Songhua_River_Spill_draft_7_301205.pdf

WASH News. (2010, June 15). China, Songhua river basin: ADB providing $146.6 million loan to privatise and improve water supply and wastewater treatment. Retrieved on July 15, 2012, from http://washasia.wordpress.com/2010/06/15/china-songhua-river-basin-adb-providing-146-6-million-loan-to-privatise-and-improve-water-supply-and-wastewater-treatment/

Watts, J. (2005, November 26). Officials say sorry to Harbin for toxic spill in face of media fury. *The Guardian*. Retrieved on July 23, 2012, from http://www.guardian.co.uk/world/2005/nov/26/china.jonathanwatts

Wong, E. (2010, July 23). China acts to reduce oil spill threat. *The New York Times*. Accessed on February 17, 2015, from http://www.nytimes.com/2010/07/24/world/asia/24china.html?_r=0

World Bank. (2007, June). *Water pollution emergencies in China*. Retrieved on August 6, 2012, from http://siteresources.worldbank.org/INTEAPREGTOPENVIRONMENT/Resources/Water_Pollution_Emergency_Final_EN.pdf

Worldwatch Institute. (2013). *In wake of Songhua disaster, environmentalists divided over future of environmental protection in China*. Retrieved on December 17, 2014, from http://www.worldwatch.org/node/1089

Wu, J. (2007, January 10). Recycling officials: Is it right? *China Daily*. Retrieved on July 24, 2012, from http://www.chinadaily.com.cn/china/2007-01/10/content_779115.htm

Xinhua. (2005a, November 24). CNPC, Jilin apologize for river pollution. Retrieved on July 23, 2012, from http://news.xinhuanet.com/english/2005-11/24/content_3831294.htm

Xinhua. (2005b, November 24). CNPC official apologizes for river pollution. Retrieved on July 15, 2012, from http://china-environmental-news.blogspot.it/2005/11/cnpc-official-apologizes-for-river.html

Xinhua. (2006a, December 11). Yearender: Environmental protection in China: A Spate of catastrophes and a glimmer of hope. Retrieved on July 13, 2012, from http://news.xinhuanet.com/english/2006-12/11/content_5469285.htm

Xinhua. (2006b, February 2). Songhua pollution goes on to be tackled. Retrieved on July 15, 2012, from http://www.chinadaily.com.cn/english/doc/2006-02/02/content_516794.htm

Xinhua. (2009a, March 25). More investment to control pollution in Songhua River Basin. Retrieved on July 15, 2012, from http://www.china.org.cn/environment/news/2009-03/25/content_17501089.htm

Xinhua. (2009b, August 26). Sewage treatment plants built along Songhua River. Retrieved on August 17, 2012, from http://www.china.org.cn/environment/news/2009-08/26/content_18408080.htm

Yong, W., & Na, H. (2005, November 15). Cause of Jilin chemical blasts found. *China Daily.* Retrieved on August 15, 2012, from http://www.chinadaily.com.cn/english/doc/2005-11/15/content_494601.htm

Zhou, S. (2011, August 2). Investigations on the progress in rehabilitation of Songhua river. *Ministry of Environmental Protection*. Retrieved on July 12, 2012, from http://english.mep.gov.cn/Ministers/Speeches/201108/t20110815_216048.htm

Zwick, L. & M. (1996, August 1). Peter Maurin, Saint and Scholar of the Catholic worker. *Casa Juan Diego: Houston Catholic Worker, XVI*(4), July-August 1996. Accessed on December 27, 2014 from http://cjd.org/1996/08/01/peter-maurin-saint-and-scholar-of-the-catholic-worker/

Chapter 20
Toward a New Paradigm of Business Economics

"If you want to become a top notch player, learn from the success of social businesses." (Stephan Rothlin)

20.1 Prelude

Our concluding chapter focuses on the possibility of a new paradigm of economics, based on the systematic integration of the basic moral concerns identified in the spiritual traditions of Asia adapted to the challenges of international business ethics. We believe that a convergence of insights from the traditions of virtue ethics, to which we have appealed in various ways throughout the chapters of this book, provide the best chance of securing the ethical foundations for this new paradigm. What makes the paradigm new is that it seeks to overcome the sterile dichotomy that sees business exclusively in terms of profit maximization and ethics exclusively in terms of punitive legal sanctions against irresponsible practices. The new paradigm, in short, rejects the idea that business is simply war by other means. By contrast, the new paradigm seeks to enlist the efforts of all stakeholders in the search for innovative ways to achieve our economic goals while enhancing the moral development of society as a whole. Our case study on the ACCU's success in establishing credit unions in the Philippines gives us reasons to be cautiously optimistic about the actual effectiveness of businesses founded upon the premises of the new paradigm. The credit unions have demonstrated the practicality of microfinance as offering a way out of grinding poverty and destitution. With every success, of course, comes new challenges, especially the need for ever-greater attention to business ethics and managerial responsibility, as the credit unions have grown in the scope and scale of their activities. We believe that the business model developed by the ACCU credit unions is sustainable economically as well as ethically. They offer not just the Philippines but all of Asia a way forward toward successful business that is sustainable precisely because it strives to compete with integrity. They illuminate one important dimension of the new paradigm of business economics.

S. Rothlin, D. McCann, *International Business Ethics*,
DOI 10.1007/978-3-662-47434-1_20

20.2 Case Study: Credit Unions and Credit Cooperatives in the Philippines

20.2.1 Abstract

Credit unions are microfinance institutions aimed at "helping people to help themselves." Their small scale and their altruistic motivation make them a perfect tool for community development. After a general introduction to the cooperative model for financing, the case study focuses on the Filipino experience. The reader is challenged to understand the dynamics of social networking underpinning successful credit unions and to make suggestions to overcome the limits of inherited governance structures.

20.2.2 Keywords

Credit unions, Credit cooperatives, Microfinance, ACCU, NATCCO, PFCCO

20.2.3 A Success Story in Plaridel

Nita Morequio is the chapter leader in Plaridel, Misamis Occidental Province, of the Paglaum Multi-Purpose Cooperative (PMPC). She's been a member of PMPC for 10 years, during which her life has taken an entirely new course. Nita remembers when she used to make 50 pesos a day by selling fish caught by her husband. "Then I got a loan for a pump-boat," she recalls, "and now I have three pump-boats. I got a motorbike for my husband and have paid off the loan. Now I make enough money every day that I can afford to make my payments on the 100,000 pesos loan I got to build my new house. And now I have two kids and I can send them both to college" (Evie 2009). The websites of most Filipino cooperatives and credit unions feature success stories like that of Ms. Morequio. They have helped many people in various ways. The question, however, is whether and how the cooperatives and credit unions can play a role in Asian economic and social development. What is happening in the Philippines is a good example of both the promise and the pitfalls of such grassroots organizations.

Paglaum Multi-Purpose Cooperative (PMPC), to which Ms. Morequio belongs, is affiliated with the Association of Asian Cooperatives and Credit Unions (ACCU), the organization, you may recall from Chapter Two, that Andrew So helped establish more than 40 years ago. Mr. Gadwin E. Handumon founded PMPC in 1992 with the mission of "giving hope to the seemingly hopeless." In its 20 years of operation, it has seen its membership grow from 35 to 30,000 and its P2,000 initial capital increase to P100M (PMPC 2014). PMPC is active in multiple areas. It offers, among other services, microfinance tools to its members, training to indigenous farmers, and programs for the disabled. It also provides training and financial education to the villagers it serves. The coop has several chapters across Zamboanga del Norte and Misamis Occidental provinces, typically organized within the local "barangay"—a Filipino term for "village" that describes the basic unit of civic administration. Working within the barangays, PMPC has reached many Filipinos who otherwise might remain invisible to the prevailing system of commercial banking.

20.2.4 *Credit Unions and Cooperatives: An Innovation in Microfinance?*

The PMPC's success is part of a much larger story that has been unfolding in many places for more than a century. Such credit unions and cooperatives are part of the development of a strategy for transforming social capital into the financial resources needed to lift enterprising people out of poverty. "Microcredit, or microfinance, is banking the unbankables, bringing credit, savings and other essential financial services within the reach of millions of people who are too poor to be served by regular banks, in most cases because they are unable to offer sufficient collateral" (Van Maanen 2004). A professor at Chittagong University, Bangladesh, Mohammed Yunus proved to the world that even poor people are "bankable." According to Yunus and the Grameen Bank that he founded to demonstrate this idea, the risk involved in making loans to the poor is no greater than making loans to the rich. The bank's motto succinctly captures Yunus' vision: "Empowering people. Changing lives. Innovating for the world's poor." Since its establishment in 1983, the Grameen story has raised interest in microfinance on the global scene, thus meriting Yunus the Nobel Peace Prize for 2006 (Perkins 2008).

The basic principles animating microfinance, however, are not especially new. Savings and credit groups based on mutualist ideas have existed for centuries all over the world. The Grameen Bank may have improved on these ideas, specifically by showing how loans can be managed by using the borrowers' social networks as accountability structures. When these networks are managed properly, the risks involved in lending to the poor are significantly reduced. Banks routinely face high agency costs in assessing the credit worthiness of individuals, verifying the success of their business plans, and collecting repayments. While these are compounded when the borrowers are poor, Grameen's development of a joint liability strategy tends to minimize these costs not only for banks but also for borrowers (Sengupta and Aubuchon 2008).

Credit unions and cooperatives are different from banks insofar as their clients—savers as well as borrowers—are members of the organization and must contribute to its success. Their origin dates back to the 1800s in Europe. Hermann Schulze-Delitzsch and Friedrich Wilhelm Raiffeisen set up the first genuine credit unions in order to support people affected by the famine of 1846–1847 (WOCCU 2012).

At that time, Raiffeisen was the mayor of a small town in Germany. Having experienced poverty himself, he was determined to help citizens find a way out of it. Raiffeisen turned first to wealthy individuals, but he soon realized their philanthropy would provide only temporary relief. A sustainable solution, he believed, would only emerge from an act of social solidarity. Entrepreneurs had to join forces against the common crisis by working together to negotiate better prices and maintain competitiveness. Raiffeisen described the peculiar nature of the unions saying: "Credit Unions must not confine themselves to granting loans. Their main objectives should be to control the use of money, and to improve the moral and physical values of people, and also, their will to act by themselves" (Mizis 2001).

The strength of his argument rested on the concept of "social capital," in contrast to "finance capital." Raiffeisen understood that, for those included in the circle of mutuality and trust, "social capital" is the key to acquiring access to finance capital. Those with the right "social capital" could get loans to finance their projects, because they were known to be credit worthy. Overcoming poverty meant expanding the circle known to possess "social capital," so that it could facilitate the financing necessary to sustain enterprise development. Raiffeisen's idea spread rapidly throughout Europe, where it was adapted to the needs of each country. At the dawn of the twentieth century, the cooperative phenomenon reached Canada and shortly after the USA. A Canadian citizen, Alphonse Desjardins, organized the first credit union (*caisse populaire*) in Levis, Quebec, in response to social conditions similar to those that confronted Raiffeisen. Quebec's economy was floundering, and people could not afford to borrow at the interest rates then on offer by commercial banks.

Reinforced by his initial success at Levis, Desjardins founded many other cooperatives throughout North America. His ideas influenced Edward E. Filene, a Boston Merchant, and Pierre Jay, the Massachusetts banking commissioner. Desjardins helped them to import the credit union model into Massachusetts (CNCUL 2015). Their efforts quickly attracted national attention. Soon after President Franklin D. Roosevelt approved the Federal Credit Union Act in 1934, the US Credit Union National Association (CUNA) was organized (DESCO 2012). CUNA helped promote the model in developing countries through its World Extension Department. By the 1950s, credit unions had become accepted worldwide as a viable tool for community development (WOCCU 2012).

20.2.5 How Credit Unions and Cooperatives Work

How the credit unions' cooperative approach works is evident in the local success stories celebrated in the Philippines, such as that of the Tubao Credit Cooperative (TCC). In 1966, a missionary priest, Father Jaime Quatannens, founded this organization in La Union Province, Philippines (DeLeon and Bitonio 2012). He had studied cooperativism in Europe and saw its potential for raising ordinary people from poverty. While the Tubao economy relied heavily on agriculture, the farmers were kept poor because of loan sharking and usury. Father Jaime formed a group of

39 people, who established the TCC with an initial capital of 314,000 pesos. At first, membership was restricted to the inhabitants of Tubao. Subsequently, the TCC opened several branches in nearby villages and membership was extended to outsiders. As of December 2011, the registered members were 25,392. The governance system evolved as the cooperative organized additional services to the community beyond financial ones. Membership on the TCC's board of directors expanded from 5 to 11 in order to meet the needs arising from greater complexity. The board supervises the activity of the cooperative and works through committees structured to handle specific matters, such as credit evaluation.

Father Jaime instilled in the cooperative a strong sense of fraternity, based on shared religious convictions. Indeed, the TCC lists "Divine Guidance" as the first factor explaining its success, understood as a concrete demonstration of the principles of "self-reliance," true "Christian spirit," and "apostolic sacrifice," embraced by its members (DeLeon and Bitonio 2012). A deep sense of gratitude is evident from the testimonials of TCC clients like Florante Abad: "Words cannot express how grateful we are to the Tubao Credit Cooperative. The cooperative enabled us to fulfill our dreams in life of having a passenger jeep and a house, which we can call our own. From the amount of 125,000P as our initial loan, we bought a jeep, which is now earning more or less 1,000P a day. The following years, due to our prompt repayment, we were allowed to renew yearly so we had a total loan of 665,000P. Out of these loans we were able to construct a beautiful house and feel proud that out of the earnings of the jeep, we are able to send our children to private schools. We are able to pay monthly our loans because we don't have any loans from other lending organizations, be it government or non-government, except the Tubao Credit Cooperative" (TCC 2009). Like the Morequio family in Plaridel, the Abads used loans from the TCC to begin or expand a local business, whose success eventually provided the resources for fulfilling the family's other aspirations.

Credit union supporters have identified four determinants for their success: services for lifetime asset growth, mixed outreach, savings mobilization, and a full service array of loan products (Branch and Evans 1999). Each of these relates to the fact that credit unions operate in local communities for the betterment of the community's inhabitants. Every credit union is organized at the local level as a network of chapters or branches, each of which may be further subdivided into clusters. Chapter leaders and bookkeepers are elected democratically and report to higher levels in the cooperative (Diaz et al. 2011). Members must commit themselves to full repayment of the loans and will make themselves accountable to their peers in their cluster group. In case a group member fails in repaying the loan, the whole group will absorb the loss. While most loans are for relatively small amounts, some unions expand the capital needed to increase their membership by opening a line of credit at a commercial bank (Balkenhol 1999). Usually, credit unions require their members to be either employed or engaged in some economic activity. This reduces the risk of default. Diversity of membership also helps to spread the additional risks associated with calamities or cyclical downturns in local industries and the national economy (Branch and Evans 1999).

Since its founding in 1971, the Association of Asian Confederation of Credit Unions (ACCU) has worked "in partnership with its members to strengthen and promote credit unions as effective instruments of socio-economic development of the people" (ACCU 2015). Such support includes the development of management tools that enable local credit unions to improve their social and economic performance. Once such innovation is the ACCU's certification program qualifying the best cooperatives as "ACCESS Brand," an acronym signifying "A-1 Competitive Choice for Excellence in Service and Soundness according to Global Standards." Only cooperatives that demonstrate sustainable business practices along with a clear commitment to the solidarity principle are awarded this recognition (NATCCO 2015b).

In order to promote ACCESS Brand certification, ACCU provides its members with an assessment tool comprising 86 performance indicators in four areas: Finance, Learning & Growth, Customer-Member Processes, and Internal Business Processes. This measurement tool is known to standard businesses as the "Balance Scorecard." The Balance Scorecard identifies the links between financial sustainability and managerial practices, using both quantitative and qualitative measures. ACCU intends to raise the bar for the cooperatives' operations by means of their professionalization, particularly in order to achieve financial sustainability. Members can use the ACCESS Balance Scorecard to evaluate their performance, track improvements, and strive to achieve positive outcomes in all four areas. Once those are achieved, they will get their certification (NATCCO 2015b).

20.2.6 Credit Unions in the Philippines

In spite of its early start, the history of the Filipino cooperative sector was not to be easy (SOEMCO 2012). The Philippine Credit Union League (PHILCUL), formed by merely 44 credit unions in 1960, had grown dramatically by 1965 to represent 1/3 of all Filipino cooperatives when it became affiliated with CUNA (USAID). In 1969, it also became a founding member of the World Council of Credit Unions (WOCCU) and joined ACCU 2 years later. When the Marcos regime issued its "Magna Carta of Social Justice and Economic Freedom," Filipino cooperatives were officially recognized as a central element in the national development strategy. Nevertheless, when Martial Law was declared in 1972, the Filipino cooperative sector came under government control. Following the Presidential Decree, "Strengthening the Cooperative Movement" (P.D.175), PHILCUL was shut down, and both the ACCU and WOCCU suspended their activities in the Philippines. With the end of the Martial Law period in 1982, PHILCUL, now reincorporated as PFCCO (Philippine Federation of Credit Cooperatives), once again took up its mission to "intensify and promote credit unions as helpful vehicles for community and economic development of people." (PFCCO 2010).

Once the credit unions' autonomy was restored, the need for tighter supervision became glaringly obvious. Many credit unions and cooperatives displayed poor governance practices and had become overly reliant on governmental financial stimuli for poverty reduction (Morales 2004). In order to address these problems, the Philippine government's Cooperative Development Authority (CDA) established the Philippine Cooperative Center (PCC) to regulate all Filipino cooperatives (Teodosio 2009). ACCU's performance benchmarks for external and internal governance provided the CDA a basis for new regulations (Salvosa 2007). The introduction of compulsory licensing by the CDA also decreased the number of cooperatives in many areas. In Bukidnon, for example, the number was cut down to 700 in 1997, after it had expanded to 1,000 in 1995 thanks to incentives from the Land Bank, a government-owned bank that serves principally fishermen and farmers (Morales 2004). The CDA also introduced compulsory training programs designed to reduce mismanagement and criminal fraud.

The Tagum Cooperative provides a model of financial management that has worked well. According to the Cooperative's annual report, the total assets increased by P310 million in one short year, from 2010 to 2011. Further, it registered a 9.3 % rise in net surplus in a year and a half timespan, reaching P102.18 million in May 2012. The surplus is used to fund the development of the cooperative and extension of its services. Newly elected cooperative chair Norma Pereyras attributes Tagum's success to a substantial improvement in governance (Colina IV 2012). The cooperative has also applied for ACCU's ACCESS Brand certification. Its multilayered auditing system is designed to elicit maximum trust and respect among the cooperative's members. Tagum avails of both an internal and an external auditing body. The double check is meant to guarantee the absence of any conflict of interest. Pereyras has no doubt "that [financial documents] should pass through stringent scrutiny" and sees achieving ISO standards like ACCESS Brand as a possible next step to reinforcing the strength of their commitment to full transparency and competitive management. ACCESS Brand is not just a certification program but also a management tool based on stakeholder theory. Fulfilling each of the ACCESS Brand expectations requires the cooperative to focus in specific ways on its responsibilities to each of its stakeholder groups.

20.2.7 Obstacles to Credit Union Development

In spite of its great promise, the credit cooperative model remains challenging to implement. Tagum and Paglaum should be regarded as bright lights contrasting with the shadows that linger elsewhere. Notwithstanding the increased oversight by CDA, problems of governance still hinder the development of credit unions. The ACCU estimates that the delinquency rate among Filipino cooperatives is the highest in Asia. Half of the 300 cooperatives operating in the Cebu area, for example, are underperforming (Borromeo 2008). CDA Central Visayas Regional Director Marlene Estrella points to mismanagement as the main cause of their failure. Arsenio Pacana, former chairman of the City Council Committee on Cooperatives, agrees there is a link between loan defaults and budget problems. Managers in the cooperatives do not receive adequate training that will make them more effective in collecting repayments in full from their members (Borromeo 2008).

In a brainstorming session with NATCCO representatives, Tita Viesca from the Novaliches Development Cooperative ("NOVADECI") tried to show how she tackles this vexing problem. Viesca insists on the business nature of the cooperatives, saying: "Friendship ends where business begins!" (NATCCO 2012). She stressed the need to be clear about the true meaning of "solidarity." Making one's payments in a timely manner, for example, is part of the rights and duties arising from the social contract underlying the cooperative model. A general manager remarked: "Old officials of the cooperative are high-risk, especially Directors and founders." This is attributed to the fact that cooperatives cannot charge a fee for the defaults committed by their own employees. Indeed, Filipino law restricts government agencies from deducting for private organizations (NATCCO 2012), thus leaving the credit unions with few options for collecting payments owed on loans made to their own officers and employees. This loophole leaves ample space for corruption, which can only be overcome with a strong commitment to the social contract implicit in a proper understanding of "solidarity."

Nevertheless, the story of the Cordova Multipurpose Cooperative, also based in Cebu City, contains lessons on how to overcome such problems, despite the loopholes in the law and the underlying cultural obstacles. When Aurea de Ramayo became general manager in 1987, the Cordova coop was on the edge of failure. "I've seen a dying co-op," explains Aurea, "the co-op would have been closed because of net loss and mismanagement." Then, "they asked me to take over as a volunteer manager. I said yes" (International Dispatch 2011). De Ramayo first assembled a team committed to saving the cooperative. Then she persuaded them to pay back all the coop's debts to outside financial institutions—debts that had masked the coop's problems by creating the illusion of liquidity. At that point, Cordova was left with a mere P300 operating capital and no physical assets to dispose of. So Aurea appealed to the community's sense of solidarity: "We began caroling door-to-door to our members, asking for deposits, for loan repayments and for support." The rescue team collected 3,000 pesos in 7 days. Members agreed to pay back one peso on each old loan every day, two for a new loan. As the delinquency rate was reduced from a catastrophic 95 % to a worrisome but manageable 40 %, the capital available for new loans and other activities gradually increased. The Cordova coop was saved. Today, it has over 900 members and is considered a model in the Cebu area. However, de Ramayo believes there is room for improvement. Her current priority is to reduce further the delinquency rate to 10 % (International Dispatch 2011). What do you think of her response to the crisis that faced the cooperative? Do you think her success in saving it can be replicated elsewhere?

The Cordova case suggests how mutual help and solidarity can enhance the power of standard turnaround measures. Aurea started by reducing the coop's debts, an essential move to get back full control and independence. She first assessed the situation and put together a task force to deal with the problem. She created a sense of urgency and hope at the same time. The door-to-door collection week served as a memorable episode in the cooperative's history and laid the groundwork for a new culture of accountability. This made possible an organizational change that was accepted as necessary by all members of the cooperative. The members' trust and mutual support enabled the effective definition and implementation of a strategy to regain competitiveness. As she had in reducing the delinquency rate on loans, Aurea set out concrete and measurable targets for achieving other goals. All of these correspond to the steps indicated by leading consultants for successful business turnarounds (Treace 2012).

In light of what we've seen in these stories from the Philippines, formal education and managerial training for cooperative members and employees are urgently needed. Nevertheless, their extent has to be complemented by the strong commitment of the cooperatives' member to work together and stay loyal to each other. As Michael Rama, Mayor of Cebu, urged all officials celebrating "Cooperative Month" in October 2008, "United we stand, divided we fall" (Borromeo 2008). There's no better formula for a successful cooperative, so long as it is understood that such unity inevitably entails a commitment to mutual accountability.

20.2.8 Summary

Credit unions and credit cooperatives are microfinance institutions aiming at community development. Although of European origin, they've enjoyed substantial popularity all over the world thanks to their adaptability to local systems and folkways. What, in your opinion, are the main professional and ethical challenges involved in managing a cooperative? How do you think they vary from one culture to another?

The early adoption of the credit union model in the Philippines, for example, has delivered mixed results. On the one hand, successful cooperatives provide us with stories of hope and change. The principle of empowerment has worked well, for example, in the cases of Nita Morequio and Florante Abad. They can now send their children to college, which would have been unthinkable until they joined their cooperatives. Do you believe empowerment can expand people's life horizons, besides enhancing their economic stability? What incentives do people have to pay back their loans? How far should credit unions rely on gratitude as an incentive? What else, if anything, may be needed?

On the other hand, many attempts at implementing the credit union model have failed because of financial mismanagement. In order to address the issue of poor governance, the Cooperative Development Authority (CDA) in the Philippines, since the 1990s, has tried to foster the professionalization of cooperatives through regulatory reform and compulsory training. Do you think these will be sufficient to improve the overall performance of this sector? How would you interpret the economic significance of Mayor Rama's call for solidarity? What concrete steps can be taken to help the credit unions and cooperatives implement standard practices of good business management? Are there useful lessons to be learned from the Cordova cooperative turnaround?

20.3 Case Study Discussion

What kind of a business is a credit cooperative or union? What are its goals and how does it work to achieve them? Does it intend to make a profit? If so, how does it differ from other profit-making enterprises? If not, what are appropriate benchmarks for measuring its success or failure? Remember Peter Drucker on the role of profit in business: while it is not the purpose of a business, it is an important measure of business success or failure. Profit is simply a way of keeping score. Owners and investors pay close attention to a business' quarterly reports, because they must know the score if they are to make prudent investment decisions. What about not-for-profit organizations? They, too, must keep score. Their performance must also be measured so that their investors—call them "donors"—can make prudent decisions about which organizations to support, with what purposes in mind.

If we ask whether credit cooperatives and unions are for-profit or not-for-profit, the answer may not be so obvious once we get into the details, and in any case—if Drucker's understanding of profit is correct—it may not be particularly significant. Yunus, for example, insisted that social businesses should be not-for-profit. But many microfinance institutions, like credit cooperatives and unions, often pay dividends to their members, in proportion to the savings or other funds they have contributed to the coop. The coop's ability to pay dividends, of course, depends on how well it has managed the loans and other financial services that it provides to its members. Were no dividends to be paid out, it might indicate that the organization was failing. On the other hand, it might mean that the surplus revenues earned in the last reporting period have been reinvested in the coop in order to expand its activities and thus fulfill its mission more effectively, that is, by lessening the need to borrow funds (and pay interest on loans) from banks or other outside institutions.

The purpose of the credit cooperative or union is to serve its members, as Raiffeisen declared, by controlling "the use of money, and [improving] the moral and physical values of people, and also, their will to act by themselves." Such a purpose is broader than that of banks that expect to make money by providing financial services to customers willing and able to pay for them. Controlling the credit cooperative members' "use of money" involves not simply making loans to people who have sufficient "social capital" to demonstrate their credit worthiness. It also entails educating people to the importance of savings and helping them to achieve the level of self-discipline required to pay back their loans according to a schedule mutually agreed upon. It requires cultivating relationships among members, who must hold each other mutually accountable through social networks related to the coop and its activities. Only then will the credit cooperative have assisted its members by "[improving their] moral and physical values, and also, their will to act by themselves." Access to finance capital, and a growing capacity to manage it well, is indispensable for achieving the freedom or autonomy "to act by themselves," no longer at the mercy of their impoverished circumstances and their unsatisfied desires.

The credit cooperative or union, then, must measure its successes comprehensively in terms of the actual empowerment that its members experience in using money wisely to take control of their own lives. Of course, once the members of a coop grasp the possibility of genuine freedom, they must also learn to exercise it responsibly. The moral challenges involved in managing a credit cooperative or union are not simply focused on ensuring that its members will repay their loans in a timely manner, they also demand that the coop enhance and preserve the integrity of its own internal accountability procedures and structures. With the possibility of freedom comes the likelihood not just of success but also of moral failure, one form or another of a betrayal of the trust inherent in the acceptance of managerial responsibility. Such betrayals, as we have learned from our case study, are just as likely to occur in not-for-profit organizations as they are in other businesses. They may actually be more likely to occur in these, since a business' owners and investors may be more alert to the possibilities for fraud, theft, embezzlement, and other financial crimes than are a coop's donors and members.

The struggle against corruption is not a peripheral issue in credit cooperatives and unions. Even coops praised for their sound management practices may find themselves victimized by a murky combination of poor record keeping, reluctance to investigate irregularities, and misplaced trust in its officers and managers. In June 2012, for example, ANTRECCO—the Agusan del Norte Teachers, Retirees, Employees and Community Cooperative, in Butuan City—became embroiled in a dispute with its former cashier, after an audit revealed that P2.6 million pesos was missing and apparently stolen by him (Samonte 2012a). Though the funds had been missing since September 2011, formal action against the cashier was only taken 9 months later, culminating in his dismissal for "breach of trust" after a formal investigation authorized by ANTRECCO's board of directors (Samonte 2012b). Though the cashier refused to file a report accounting for the missing funds, his termination of employment appears to have been the end of the incident, which, of course, was highly embarrassing since the coop previously had applied for the ACCU's ACCESS Brand certification and had been regarded as exceptionally well managed. As we learned from other reports alleging delinquencies in loan repayments and management irregularities among Philippine credit cooperatives, creating the kind of accountability structures that will enable a coop to fulfill its mission may require a long-term process of cultural transformation that will go well beyond implementing the theories and models that have been successful elsewhere. If the credit union movement is to fulfill its promise in the Philippines, those involved as either members or managers will have to acknowledge the moral significance of "solidarity."

Those who have struggled with the challenges of economic and social development will be the first to admit that there's no magic formula for guaranteeing "solidarity," particularly its active contribution to the common good. The word itself suggests a "union or fellowship arising from common responsibilities and interests, as between members of a group or between classes or peoples" (*Dictionary.com* 2014). Fellowship, like friendship and other social bonds developed outside one's immediate family, is inherently good, but it can also become morally ambivalent when the "common responsibilities and interests" are too narrowly conceived. The proverbial "honor among thieves" acknowledges that solidarity exists among predators, who may protect each other's interests, while scheming to victimize others. Such antisocial solidarity, when it achieves sufficient strength, is capable of corrupting all other groups, by undermining the rule of law and other instruments of public morality. Genuine solidarity—that is, a form of solidarity that actually promotes participation in the common good—must be based on more than a common interest in protecting members of the group from outsiders. Genuine solidarity seeks to achieve a higher goal transcending personal loyalties. It is incompatible with any "Code of Silence" that would shield group members from the consequences of their actions, ranging from sheer incompetence and the commission of honest but costly mistakes to crimes deliberately meant to breach the trust that has been invested in them. Transparency and accountability must be achieved at all levels of the organization, with the activities of no individual or group exempt from proper review and public scrutiny.

For credit cooperatives and unions to succeed in their noble purpose, their members must learn to distinguish between morbid and healthy forms of solidarity, between corruption and integrity in the management of their business affairs, and between fake and genuine expressions of moral leadership. The challenges described in our case study tend to focus attention on a serious problem: With the many advantages marking the birth of the movement of the coop in the Philippines, why have so many of these institutions failed? Why has there been so much delinquency at all levels of accountability? Why have too many borrowers felt no moral obligation to pay back their loans, in full, in a timely manner? Why have too many coop managers succumbed to the temptation to steal—or otherwise misallocate funds—from the organizations entrusted to them? No doubt, there are complex cultural analyses that might help explain away these failures—the lingering but no less lethal effects of colonialism and neocolonialism, the mutually reinforcing tendencies of idealism and cynicism, and the sheer inertia of traditional cultures whose persistent influence has slowed the development not only of Philippine national identity but also of any loyalty higher than nationalism. But the bottom line is that, however illuminating such theories may be, the challenge remains one of basic moral education, particularly in shaping the professionalization of cooperative management.

The lessons to be drawn from our case study, then, should highlight the efforts of those within the credit union movement who continue to struggle to define and implement appropriate standards of mutual accountability, among members and managers alike. The unflagging efforts of the ACCU, working closely with the Philippine government's Cooperative Development Authority (CDA), are designed to improve the coop's internal governance procedures. They provide especially welcome support and accountability through licensing, certification, and training programs. The CDA's statement of the "Core Values" (CDA 2014b) that ought to animate the Philippine cooperative movement—*Excellence* ("Giving one's best performance and achieving the desired outcome through effective and efficient management of resources"), *Commitment* ("High dedication and proactive involvement in the realization of the Agency's mandate"), *Integrity* ("Maintain personal conduct, beyond reproach"), and *Teamwork* ("Working collectively and harmoniously to achieve synergy in an environment conducive to the achievement of organizational goals")—is certainly commendable. As is the CDA's "Performance Pledge" (CDA 2014c), establishing specific expectations for evaluating its own operations also provides a model of transparency and accountability for its member coops.

Finally, the CDA provides a useful analysis of the causes for failure among Philippine coops,[1] supporting the conclusion that "the fundamental cause of failure in a cooperative enterprise is the lack of proper understanding of the principles and true aims of cooperative associations, and the non-adherence to them in the actual operation of cooperative enterprises" (CDA 2014a). Our case study suggests that the CDA's list of specific problems in "the early cooperatives" is not merely of historical interest. They identify chronic challenges that even today stand in the way toward the full realization of the Philippine coop movement's admirable goals. These challenges suggest that the training programs and other services offered by the CDA must include innovative efforts in basic moral education that would address the movement's desire to empower people for personal and social responsibility.

20.4 Ethical Reflection

Our case study often suggested the influence of Roman Catholicism on the development of credit cooperatives and unions in the Philippines. The Tubao Credit Union (TCC), as we learned, for example, was founded by Father Jaime Quatannens, a missionary priest who instilled in the cooperative a strong sense of fraternity, based on shared religious convictions. The specific inspiration animating the TCC was evident in its testimony acknowledging "Divine Guidance" as the primary explanation for its success—expressed in the coop's commitment to the principles of "self-reliance," true "Christian spirit," and "apostolic sacrifice." Such appeals to Catholic faith and practice are not at all unusual in the Philippines, which is far and away the most Catholic country in Asia, measured in terms of religious affiliation (Religion Facts 2014). Since the ACCU—which helped develop the credit union movement in the Philippines—was itself established by lay Catholic leaders in

[1] The CDA's historical overview lists thirteen different reasons for the failures of "early cooperatives in the Philippines": "Incompetent management; Lack of proper understanding of the principles, practices true aims, and purposes of cooperative associations; Improper use of credits by the borrowers who, instead of using money borrowed for production, spent it for fiestas or luxuries; Defective securities; Political interference particularly in the collection of overdue accounts; Lack of compensation of officers; Inadequate character and moral responsibility in handling the other fellow's money; Lack of adequate safeguard against unscrupulous officers who took advantage of their position to grant loans to themselves and their compadres which later proved disastrous to the system; The dominance of the individualistic attitude instead of the spirit of cooperation among the people; Inability of cooperatives to secure adequate capital; Their dependence on alien suppliers and distributors; Ineffectiveness of the government and promotion of cooperative organizations; Inadequate marketing facilities" (CDA 2014a).

Asia, understanding how and why Catholicism became so closely identified with co-ops may provide additional resources for improving their performance. What is the significance, then, of credit cooperatives and unions in Catholic social teaching (CST)?

At other points in this book, we have mentioned CST in passing, usually in order to establish convergences between European ethical traditions and Chinese moral philosophy. We have seen that through Aristotle and Confucius, they share many insights into the nature of virtue ethics, as well as a social vision that honors the pursuit of the common good. We have seen that CST supports a robust understanding of universal human rights while also resisting any temptation to consider these in the abstract as absolute entitlements. Like Confucian and other forms of Asian moral wisdom, CST emphasizes a strict correlation of rights and duties or responsibilities that reflect a broader vision of the meaning of human life and happiness. Like these other Asian traditions, CST claims that its vision is grounded objectively and normatively in human nature; unlike them, it understands human nature as "made to the image and likeness of God" (Genesis 1:26). Despite differences in metaphysics concerning the reality of God, or the Great Ultimate, Catholic social teaching demonstrates close convergences with the ethical practices that constitute the proper way (*Dào*: 道) for human beings to achieve their purpose in life.

20.4.1 Human Dignity and Solidarity: Core Concepts in Catholic Social Teaching

There are two key themes in CST that reflect the practical implications of its moral vision of humanity created as "the image of God," namely, human dignity and solidarity. Human dignity is inherent in human nature, understood as our natural or God-given capacity to act rationally, or with purpose, consistent with the conscience or "heart" instilled in us by the Creator. Though the capacity for moral agency or responsibility symbolized as "the image of God" can be corrupted and distorted through evil acts—which are usually self-destructive as well as harmful to others—it can never be destroyed. Human dignity must be respected by all, including any governments that people choose to form, as an expression of their solidarity—and thus mutual accountability—to one another. Human dignity thus may be developed and perfected through collective action, but it is not bestowed or established through the decrees or policies of any state. All legitimate governments rest upon the consent of the governed.

Given these assumptions, the state may assist the development and perfection of individuals and groups while respecting the limits of its own role in their activities. While natural associations, starting with the family, are the primary expressions of human dignity and solidarity—and thus a direct manifestation of "the image of God" in humanity—they are not established by the decrees of the state. The state's role is to assist the development of these natural associations through appropriate regulation, and not to usurp or suppress their proper activity. This is the meaning of CST's "principle of subsidiarity" which seeks to promote the common good pursued in regimes of ordered liberty, which stand equally opposed to both totalitarianism and libertarianism. The fault in these failed ideologies, according to CST, is both theoretical and practical: theoretical, insofar as both presuppose an atheistic view of humanity that is incompatible with a proper understanding of human dignity, and practical, insofar as neither understands or respects the natural bonds of solidarity that people exercise through the establishment of free and responsible institutions.

The common good, like the related terms "justice" and "social harmony," is vulnerable to misunderstanding, if not deliberate co-optation, when it is detached from a proper anchoring in human dignity, solidarity, and subsidiarity. CST describes the common good as "the sum of those conditions of social life which allow social groups and their individual members relatively thorough and ready access to their own fulfillment" (Vatican II 1965. Par. 26). The practical import of this abstract formulation immediately follows: "Every social group must take account of the needs and legitimate aspirations of other groups, and even of the general welfare of the entire human family." The common good cannot be truly common, if my pursuit of it prevents others also from pursuing it. In other words, the common good is incompatible with all forms of zero-sum thinking and acting. Governing society in accordance with the principle of subsidiarity means using the power of the state to empower social participation by creating "win-win" situations enabling all groups to flourish. While "social justice"—a commitment long honored by CST—may "demand from each individual all that is necessary for the common good" (Pius XI 1937: Par. 51), a proper understanding of human dignity and solidarity also demands that appeals to the common good not be used to justify suppressing any legitimate human rights or usurping any legitimate individual responsibilities.[2]

[2] CST's understanding of the common good thus must be distinguished from the moral visions proposed by either utilitarianism or Kantianism. As is often pointed out in philosophical discussions of the basic utilitarian principle, "The greatest good for the greatest number," there is no limit to the sacrifices that the state may impose on individuals provided that the benefit to society as a whole is maximized. Similarly, Kantianism's categorical imperative, "Treat persons as ends and never as means only," tends to absolutize human rights insofar as it lacks a systematic answer to the problem that inevitably occurs when one right conflicts with another, within either an individual person's conscience or society as a whole. Both utilitarianism and Kantianism, standing alone, therefore tend to exacerbate zero-sum thinking in ethics, that is, by emphasizing moral dilemmas and quandaries. Such might be approached more effectively by focusing on the common good and practicing the principle of subsidiarity. Throughout this book, whenever conventional appeals to utilitarian and Kantian ethical principles have been discussed, we have noted how and why an exclusive appeal to one or the other system yields less than satisfactory results and have favored the so-called "mixed" deontological approach identified with "justice" in applied moral philosophy. This approach is adequate for responding to the kinds of challenges described in our case studies, provided that it is animated by a robust commitment to the common good. Best practice, however, requires that the pursuit of the common good be informed by a serious commitment to the cultivation of the moral virtues shared by CST along with Confucian moral philosophy and most other traditions of moral wisdom grounded in spirituality.

20.4.2 The Common Good and the Cultivation of Moral Virtue

In order for individuals to contribute to the common good, their exercise of moral responsibility must be informed by an ongoing effort to cultivate the moral virtues. CST presupposes the morality enshrined in the "perennial philosophy" emerging from Hellenistic Antiquity in the schools of Plato, Aristotle, and the Stoics that focused on the importance of the so-called cardinal virtues of "prudence," "justice," "fortitude," and "temperance." The exposition of these virtues in Chapter Two presupposes the understanding of them outlined in *The Catechism of the Catholic Church*,[3] where they serve as the moral basis for envisioning the common good and seeking to organize society consistent with it. Above all, the pursuit of the common good requires the virtue of "prudence," since moral discernment is indispensable for identifying and enhancing those social conditions that are genuinely "win-win," thus enabling human beings to fulfill their purpose, individually and collectively. The catechism identifies the common good's "three essential elements": first, "respect for the person as such," which means "respect for fundamental and inalienable rights…[especially] the right to act according to a sound norm of conscience and to safeguard…privacy, and rightful freedom also in matters of religion"; second, "the social well-being and development of the group itself" in which the governing "authority… should make accessible to each what is needed to lead a truly human life: food, clothing, health, work, education and culture, suitable information, the right to establish a family, and so on"; and third, "peace, that is, the stability and security of a just order" whose "complete realization" occurs in the establishment of "political community"—"It is the role of the state to defend and promote the common good of civil society, its citizens, and intermediate bodies." The order envisioned as the common good, finally, "must be subordinate to the order of persons, and not the other way around. This order is founded on truth, built up in justice, and animated by love" (Libreria Editrice Vaticana 2003: Par. 1905–1912).

The interrelated concepts of human dignity, solidarity, the common good, and the principle of subsidiarity thus may be understood as presenting CST's version of the ideal commonwealth or Grand Union (*dàtóng*: 大同) presented, as we saw in Chapter Two, in the *Lǐ Yun* (禮運) section of *The Record of Rites* (*Lǐjì*: 禮記). While CST's vision of the common good is convergent with the Confucian ideal

[3]The cardinal virtues are introduced in "Part Three: Life in Christ" in "Section One: Man's Vocation Life in the Spirit." Article Seven in Chapter One on "The Dignity of the Human Person" identifies them as "The Human Virtues" to distinguish them from "The Theological Virtues"—"Faith," "Hope," and "Charity"—which the Catholic Church regards as having God "for their origin, motive, and object" (Libreria Editrice Vaticana 2003: Par. 1812). The human virtues, by contrast, "are acquired by human effort." They are described as "firm attitudes, stable dispositions, habitual perfections of intellect and will that govern our actions, order our passions, and guide our conduct according to reason and faith. They make possible ease, self-mastery, and joy in leading a morally good life. the virtuous man is he who freely practices the good" (Libreria Editrice Vaticana 2003: Par. 1804). The cardinal virtues are those around which all other virtues are grouped. Similar to the virtues characteristic of a Confucian jūnzǐ (君子), they play a "pivotal role" in becoming an "exemplary person" capable of moral leadership.

commonwealth, CST tends to emphasize the moral principles involved, while the Confucian *dàtóng* (大同) vividly describes the social consequences of living virtuously. We believe that Andrew So has been right to sense the convergences between the two perspectives and to seek to harmonize them in his own career of public service in Hong Kong. His commitment to the ACCU's pioneering work in promoting cooperatives and credit unions throughout East Asia witnesses to the ongoing power of this vision, at once truly Chinese and authentically Catholic.

Organizing credit unions is an important, if not indispensable, element in realizing the common good in today's world. The common good can no longer be understood as exclusively the responsibility of the state. Even if the state had the power to do so, it cannot unilaterally impose its own version of the common good without violating the principle of subsidiarity. If the common good is the goal of political community, broadly understood, the principle of subsidiarity indicates the appropriate means for pursuing it. Cooperatives and credit unions are a very useful example of the principle of subsidiarity in action, since they are voluntary associations, usually NGOs, that attempt to capitalize local resources necessary for real improvements in the lives of their members. In order to fulfill their mission, such co-ops must do things differently from the conventional practices of either businesses or governments. While they may require economic support in the form of loans from commercial banks or political support in the form of government regulation, the effectiveness of the co-ops depends on their capacity for identifying and developing "social capital" in the communities they serve. Their mission reflects the principle of subsidiarity, insofar as they are both rooted in natural associations at the local level and yet assisted through the proper mediation of larger economic and political institutions.

20.4.3 Credit Unions and the Creation of "Social Capital"

CST has long understood the importance of such voluntary associations and their crucial role in the formation of the "social capital" indispensable for economic and social development. The practical proposals advanced by CST begin with *Rerum novarum*'s advocacy of "workingmen's unions" (Leo XIII 1891: Par. 48–51). As CST developed, *Quadragesimo anno* appealed to Pope Leo's perspective in order to offer constructive criticism[4] of Italy's experiment in a state-sponsored "system of syndicates and corporations" (Pius XI 1931: 91–97). Later on, *Mater et magistra* endorsed the establishment of "cooperative associations" (John XXIII 1961: Par. 84), urging their development specifically among "farm workers [in order] to benefit from scientific and technical methods of production and protect the prices of their products" (Par. 146). In his encyclical letter *Centesimus annus* commemorating the 100th anniversary of *Rerum novarum*, Pope John Paul II reiterated CST's

[4] Note that this criticism exemplifies the principle of subsidiarity just enunciated (Par. 79–80). Explain the context in Pius XI's growing awareness of the serious defects in the ideology and practice of Italian Fascism.

understanding of the "natural human right to form private associations." Those who participate in such efforts "represent *a great movement for the defence of the human person* and the safeguarding of human dignity" (John Paul II 1991: Par. 3). They have "made a notable contribution in establishing producers', consumers' and credit cooperatives, in promoting general education and professional training, in experimenting with various forms of participation in the life of the work-place and in the life of society in general" (John Paul II 1991: Par. 16).

Not until Pope Benedict XVI issued *Caritas in veritate* (Benedict XVI 2009) do we find the exercise of the right to form private associations like co-ops described in terms of social capital and its development. At first, Benedict mentions the loss of social capital that was exacerbated, though hardly initiated, by the financial collapse of 2007–2008. He observes that "the systemic increase of social inequality" undermines "social cohesion," thus "placing democracy at risk" while also undermining the economy "through the progressive erosion of 'social capital': the network of relationships of trust, dependability, and respect for rules, all of which are indispensable for any form of civil coexistence" (Benedict XVI 2009: 32). The breach of trust involved in the collective default of public morality marked by the financial collapse demonstrated that "if the market is governed solely by the principle of the equivalence in value of exchanged goods, it cannot produce the social cohesion that it requires in order to function well. *Without internal forms of solidarity and mutual trust, the market cannot completely fulfil its proper economic function.* And today it is this trust which has ceased to exist, and the loss of trust is a grave loss" (Benedict XVI 2009: Par. 35). Since social capital has been squandered—in addition to the widely acknowledged losses of finance capital—how can it be restored or renewed?

20.4.4 Toward a Business Economy Based on "Mutualist Principles"

Pope Benedict's answer was built upon the work of his predecessors who advanced proposals for promoting "private associations." Pope John Paul II, in particular, urged an understanding of social reality as "a system with three subjects: the market, the State, and civil society" in which civil society is "the most natural setting for an *economy of gratuitousness* and fraternity"—in other words, the most natural setting for the development of social capital:

> Today we can say that economic life must be understood as a multi-layered phenomenon: in every one of these layers, to varying degrees and in ways specifically suited to each, the aspect of fraternal reciprocity must be present. In the global era, economic activity cannot prescind from gratuitousness, which fosters and disseminates solidarity and responsibility for justice and the common good among the different economic players. It is clearly a specific and profound form of economic democracy. Solidarity is first and foremost a sense of responsibility on the part of everyone with regard to everyone, and it cannot therefore be merely delegated to the State. (Benedict XVI 2009: Par. 38)

From this perspective, Pope Benedict argued the case for "social businesses"—or, in his terms, "commercial entities based on mutualist principles"—in which the intent is to increase the social capital necessary for both the markets and the state to function effectively:

> What is needed, therefore, is a market that permits the free operation, in conditions of equal opportunity, of enterprises in pursuit of different institutional ends. Alongside profit-oriented private enterprise and the various types of public enterprise, there must be room for commercial entities based on mutualist principles and pursuing social ends to take root and express themselves. It is from their reciprocal encounter in the marketplace that one may expect hybrid forms of commercial behaviour to emerge, and hence an attentiveness to ways of *civilizing the economy*. Charity in truth, in this case, requires that shape and structure be given to those types of economic initiative which, without rejecting profit, aim at a higher goal than the mere logic of the exchange of equivalents, of profit as an end in itself. (Benedict XVI 2009: Par. 38)

CST's social vision, thus, presupposes that the systemic differences among markets, the state, and civil society reflect divergent "logics" from whose interplay a new paradigm of business economics may emerge. Realizing the benefits of "gratuitousness"—or the logic of cooperative interaction—is the key "to defeat underdevelopment":

> Action is required not only on improving exchange-based transactions and implanting public welfare structures, but above all on gradually *increasing openness, in a world context, to forms of economic activity marked by quotas of gratuitousness and communion*. The exclusively binary model of market-plus-State is corrosive of society, while economic forms based on solidarity, which find their natural home in civil society without being restricted to it, build up society. The market of gratuitousness does not exist, and attitudes of gratuitousness cannot be established by law. Yet both the market and politics need individuals who are open to reciprocal gift. (Benedict XVI 2009: Par. 39)

"Individuals who are open to reciprocal gift" is an unmistakable appeal for moral leadership. The common good cannot be achieved without individuals and groups willing and able to act upon the principle of gratuitousness—or, if you will, the spirit of cooperation that flows naturally from the cultivation of true virtues. What better description is there of what motivates those who in good faith try establishing and managing cooperatives and credit unions?

If such "enterprises based on mutualist principles" can emerge from a healthy civil society, the result will be a new paradigm of business economics grounded in good business ethics. Benedict calls for "an ethics which is people-centered" and sees hopeful signs that it is emerging in the wake of the financial crisis:

> Today we hear much talk of ethics in the world of economy, finance and business. Research centres and seminars in business ethics are on the rise; the system of ethical certification is spreading throughout the developed world as part of the movement of ideas associated with the responsibilities of business towards society. Banks are proposing 'ethical' accounts and investment funds. 'Ethical financing' is being developed, especially through micro-credit and, more generally, micro-finance. These processes are praiseworthy and deserve much support. Their positive effects are also being felt in the less developed areas of the world. (Benedict XVI 2009: Par. 45)

The new paradigm, however, is not yet mature. In his view, there is great need of "discernment," since the word "ethics…can lend itself to any number of interpretations, even to the point where it includes decisions and choices contrary to justice and authentic human welfare." CST "can make a specific contribution, based as it is on an affirmation of man's creation 'in the image of God' (Gen 1:27), a datum which gives rise to the inviolable dignity of the human person and the transcendent value of natural moral norms." Lacking proper orientation to these assumptions, business ethics "risks becoming subservient to existing economic and financial systems rather than correcting their dysfunctional aspects" (Benedict XVI 2009: Par. 45).

Rather than dwell on the ambiguities of today's renewal of concern for business ethics, Pope Benedict focused on the promise of "enterprises based on mutualist principles":

> In recent decades a broad intermediate area has emerged between the two types of enterprise. It is made up of traditional companies which nonetheless subscribe to social aid agreements in support of underdeveloped countries, charitable foundations associated with individual companies, groups of companies oriented towards social welfare, and the diversified world of the so-called "civil economy" and the "economy of communion". This is not merely a matter of a "third sector", but of a broad new composite reality embracing the private and public spheres, one which does not exclude profit, but instead considers it a means for achieving human and social ends. Whether such companies distribute dividends or not, whether their juridical structure corresponds to one or other of the established forms, becomes secondary in relation to their willingness to view profit as a means of achieving the goal of a more humane market and society (Benedict XVI 2009: Par. 46)

The resulting *plurality of institutional forms of business*, Pope Benedict hopes, will give *rise to a market which is not only more civilized but also more competitive*.

20.5 Conclusion

The new paradigm of business economics is new, only in the sense that it departs from the assumptions governing conventional thinking about business and government, namely, profit maximization and an ever-increasing reliance on the rule of law to compensate for businesses' worst excesses. The new paradigm is actually quite old, harkening back to a vision of society based on cooperative assumptions, the memory of which CST has been cultivated as a possible contribution to international business ethics. From the Medieval guilds and other associations to the cooperatives and credit unions that have emerged in response to the challenges of modern economic and social development, CST consistently has pointed out that there are specific solutions—institutional as well as personal—to the problems that confront us. We have argued throughout this book of case studies in Asian business ethics that the key to grasping these solutions and assuming the risks involved in implementing them requires a change in attitude, a return to our traditions of spiritual and moral wisdom, and a recovery of virtues that remain the key to personal integrity and moral leadership. That change in attitude, as we argued from the beginning, may depend upon which metaphor we accept for illuminating the proper way (*Dào*: 道) to conduct business. Is business really more like a war or more like a game properly understood? We reject the idea that business is warfare. It has a different end in view and employs different means. Above all, it is not well understood by those who cannot advance beyond zero-sum thinking. In the 20 case studies we have considered in this book, we hope to have shown you where a change in attitudc might lcad. It is up to you to find your own way (*Dào*: 道) to makc a success of it.

References

ACCU. (2015). *Introduction*. Retrieved on January 3, 2015, from http://www.aaccu.coop/introduction.php

Balkenhol, B. (1999). *Credit unions and the poverty challenge: Extending outreach, enhancing sustainability*. Geneva: ILO.

Benedict XVI. (2009). *Caritas in veritate* (On Integral Human Development in Charity and Truth). Libreria Editrice Vaticana. Retrieved on January 15, 2015, from http://www.vatican.va/holy_father/benedict_xvi/encyclicals/documents/hf_ben-xvi_enc_20090629_caritas-in-veritate_en.html

Borromeo, R. U. (2008, October 4). About 150 coops in Cebu City are 'mismanaged'. *The Freeman*. Retrieved on January 5, 2015, from http://www.philstar.com/cebu-news/404730/about-150-coops-cebu-city-are-mismanaged

Branch, A., & Evans, A. C. (1999, August 13). *Credit unions: Effective vehicles for microfinance delivery*. Madison: World Council of Credit Unions.

CDA. (2014a). *History*. Republic of the Philippines Cooperative Development Authority. Retrieved on January 8, 2015, from http://www.cda.gov.ph/index.php/transparency/overview/historical-background

CDA. (2014b). *Core values*. Republic of the Philippines Cooperative Development Authority. Retrieved on January 8, 2015, from http://www.cda.gov.ph/index.php/transparency/overview/core-values

CDA. (2014c). *Performance pledge*. Republic of the Philippines Cooperative Development Authority. Retrieved on January 8, 2015, from http://www.cda.gov.ph/index.php/transparency/transparency-seal/120-transparency/transparency-seal/i-cda-mandate-powers-and-functions-citizen-s-charter-and-contact-information/c-citizen-s-charter

CNCUL. (2015). *Credit unions: For people, not profit: History of the credit union movement*. California and Nevada Credit Union Leagues. Retrieved on January 5, 2015, from http://www.ccul.org/consumers/cuhistory.cfm

Colina IV, A. L. (2012, April 30). Tagum coop posts 9 percent growth in net surplus. *Sun.Star Davao*. Retrieved on August 8, 2012, from http://www.sunstar.com.ph/davao/business/2012/04/30/tagum-coop-posts-9-percent-growth-net-surplus-219042

DeLeon, J., & Bitonio, J. (2012, January). *Success story of Tubao Credit Cooperative*. Cooperative Development Authority, Dagupan Extension Office. Retrieved on August 15, 2012, from http://www.slideshare.net/jobitonio/success-story-of-tubao-credit-cooperative

DESCO. (2012). *History of credit unions*. DESCO Federal Credit Union. Retrieved on August 16, 2012, from http://www.descofcu.org/s01p010.php

Diaz, J. N., Ledesma, J. M., Ravi, A., Singh, J., & Tyler, E. (2011, September). *Saving for the poor in the Philippines*. New American Foundation. Retrieved on January 5, 2015, from http://www.microsave.net/files/pdf/Savings_for_the_Poor_in_the_Philippines.pdf

Dictionary.com. (2014). Solidarity. *Dictionary.com Unabridged*. Retrieved on January 07, 2015, from website: http://dictionary.reference.com/browse/solidarity

Duron-Abangan, J. (2012, March 30). *Tagum Cooperative eyes ISO certification*. Ugnayan. Philippine Information Agency. Retrieved on January 3, 2015, from http://www.ugnayan.com/ph/DavaodelNorte/Tagum/article/1J9C

Evie. (2009, February 11). *The hundred thousand peso house*. Kiva Fellows Blog. Retrieved on January 5, 2015, from http://pages.kiva.org/fellowsblog/2009/02/11/the-hundred-thousand-peso-house-0

Grameen Foundation. (2015). *About Grameen Foundation*. Retrieved on January 5, 2015, from http://www.grameenfoundation.org/about

International Dispatch. (2011, June 30). *On a quest for excellence*. Retrieved on August 9, 2012, from http://archive.constantcontact.com/fs036/1102316589700/archive/1106288753042.html

ISO. (2015). *About ISO*. Retrieved on January 5, 2015, from http://www.iso.org/iso/home/about.htm

John XXIII. (1961). *Mater et magistra* (On Christianity and Social Progress). Libreria Editrice Vaticana. Retrieved on January 15, 2015, from http://w2.vatican.va/content/john-xxiii/en/encyclicals/documents/hf_j-xxiii_enc_15051961_mater.html

John Paul II. (1991). *Centesimus annus*. (On the Hundredth Anniversary of *Rerum novarum*). Retrieved on January 14, 2015, from http://www.vatican.va/holy_father/john_paul_ii/encyclicals/documents/hf_jp-ii_enc_01051991_centesimus-annus_en.html

Labie, M., & Perillleux, A. (2008). Corporate governance in microfinance: Credit unions. In *Solvay Business School* (CEB Working Paper No. 08/003). Retrieved on June 23, 2015 from https://ideas.repec.org/p/sol/wpaper/08-003.html

Leo XIII. (1891). *Rerum novarum* (On Capital and Labor). Libreria Editrice Vaticana. Retrieved on January 13, 2015, from http://w2.vatican.va/content/leo-xiii/en/encyclicals/documents/hf_l-xiii_enc_15051891_rerum-novarum.html

Libreria Editrice Vaticana. (2003, November 4). *Catechism of the Catholic Church*. Retrieved on January 14, 2015, from http://www.vatican.va/archive/ENG0015/_INDEX.HTM

Libreria Editrice Vaticana. (2004). *Compendium of the social doctrine of the Church*. Pontifical Council for Justice and Peace. Retrieved on January 13, 2015, from http://www.vatican.va/roman_curia/pontifical_councils/justpeace/documents/rc_pc_justpeace_doc_20060526_compendio-dott-soc_en.html

Llanto, G. M. (1994, July). *The financial structure and performance of Philippine Credit Cooperatives* (Discussion Paper Series No. 94-04). Philippine Institute for Development Studies. Retrieved on August 16, 2012, from http://dirp4.pids.gov.ph/ris/dps/pidsdps9404.pdf

Mizis, N. (2001, June 21). *Credit unions—Philosophy, policy and regulation*. NIS Policy Forum on Microfinance, Law and Regulation, Krakow, Poland. Retrieved on January 3, 2015, from http://www.microfinancegateway.org/sites/default/files/mfg-en-paper-credit-unions-philosophy-policy-and-regulation-jun-2001_0.pdf

Morales, B. (2004). *Microfinance and Financial Institution in Bukidnon*. Department of Agricultural and Applied Economics. University of Wisconsin-Madison. Retrieved on January 5, 2015, from http://pdf.usaid.gov/pdf_docs/PNADE771.pdf

NATCCO. (2012). *Credit management seminar shows how to defeat delinquency*. Retrieved on August 17, 2012, from http://www.natcco.coop/index.php?option=com_content&view=article&id=128:credit-mgmt-seminar-shows-how-to-defeat-delinquency&catid=1:latest-news&Itemid=80

NATCCO. (2015a). *Profile*. Retrieved on January 5, 2015, from http://www.natcco.coop/index.php/about-us/history-2

NATCCO. (2015b). *Access branding*. Retrieved on January 5, 2015, from http://www.natcco.coop/index.php/product-services/allied-services/training-supervision/access-branding

Perkins, A. (2008, June 3). Katine it starts with a village: A short history of microfinance. *The Guardian*. Retrieved on August 8, 2012, from http://www.guardian.co.uk/katine/2008/jun/03/livelihoods.projectgoals1

PFCCO. (2010). *Vision and mission*. Retrieved on January 5, 2015, from http://overridehost.com/portfolio/pfcco/

Pius XI. (1931). *Quadragesimo anno* (On reconstruction of the social order). Libreria Editrice Vaticana. Retrieved on January 15, 2015, from http://w2.vatican.va/content/pius-xi/en/encyclicals/documents/hf_p-xi_enc_19310515_quadragesimo-anno.html

Pius XI. (1937). *Divine redemptoris* (On atheistic communism). Libreria Editrice Vaticana. Retrieved on June 23, 2015 from, http://w2.vatican.va/content/pius-xi/en/encyclicals/documents/hf_p-xi_enc_19031937_divini-redemptoris.html
PMPC. (2014). *History of Paglaum multi-purpose cooperative*. Retrieved on January 5, 2015, from http://www.paglaumcoop.org.ph/aboutus.html
Religion Facts. (2014). *Religion statistics by country*. http://www.religionfacts.com/religion_statistics/religion_statistics_by_country.htm
Salvosa, C. R. (2007). *Bridging the governance divide in the Philippines: Perspectives from the cooperative sector*. Centre for Cooperative Study at University of Saskatchewan. Retrieved on August 15, 2012, from http://usaskstudies.coop/socialeconomy/files/congress07/salvosa.pdf
Samonte, P. (2012a, June 20). Cashier in trouble for failure to account P2.6m. *Mindanao Daily News*. Retrieved on January 7, 2015, from http://issuu.com/mindanaodaily/docs/june_20
Samonte, P. (2012b, July 23). Coop fires cashier. *Mindanao Daily News*. Retrieved on January 7, 2015, from http://issuu.com/mindanaodaily/docs/july_23/3
Sengupta, R., & Aubuchon, C. (2008, January/February). The microfinance revolution: An overview. *Federal Reserve Bank of St. Louis Review, 90*(1), 9–30. Retrieved on August 15, 2012, from http://research.stlouisfed.org/publications/review/08/01/Sengupta.pdf
SOEMCO. (2012). *History of Philippine Cooperatives*. Socorro Empowered Peoples Cooperative. Retrieved on January 5, 2015, from http://www.soemco.coop/history-of-philippine-cooperatives
TCC. (2009). *Testimonials > Jeepney*. Retrieved on August 15, 2012, from http://www.tubaocreditcooperative.com/content.php?content_id=18
Teodosio, V. A. (2009). *Community participation through cooperatives in addressing basic services: The Philippine experience*. United Nations. Retrieved on August 16, 2012, from http://www.un.org/esa/socdev/egms/docs/2009/cooperatives/Teodosio.pdf
Treace, J. R. (2012, January 9). Five steps for successful business turnaround. *The Recruiter*. Retrieved on August 16, 2012, from http://www.recruiter.co.uk/expert-advice/2012/01/five-steps-for-successful-business-turnaround/
Van Maanen, G. (2004). *Microcredit, sound business or development instrument?* Oikocredit. Retrieved on January 3, 2015, from http://www.microfinancegateway.org/sites/default/files/mfg-en-paper-microcredit-sound-business-or-development-instrument-sep-2004.pdf
Van Steenwyk, M. (1987, May 1). Cooperatives in the Philippines: A study of past performance, current status and future trends. *USAID/Philippines*. Retrieved on August 16, 2012, from http://pdf.usaid.gov/pdf_docs/PNAAY599.pdf
Vatican Council II. (1965, December 7). *Gaudium et spes: Pastoral constitution on the church in the modern world*. Retrieved on January 14, 2015, from http://www.vatican.va/archive/hist_councils/ii_vatican_council/documents/vat-ii_cons_19651207_gaudium-et-spes_en.html
WOCCU. (2011, May 3). *Asian CU Confederation turns 40*. WOCCU. Retrieved on August 15, 2012, from http://www.woccu.org/newsroom/releases/Asian_CU_Confederation_Turns_40
WOCCU. (2012). *International credit union day: A brief history*. Retrieved on August 8, 2012, from http://www.woccu.org/events/icuday/history

Glossary of Terms for International Business Ethics: Focus on China

"ACCESS Brand" is the name of the certification program that the Association of Asian Confederation of Credit Unions (ACCU) offers to its members in order to demonstrate their implementation of sustainable business practices, consistent with the mission of credit unions (see Chap. 20).

Accountability is the kind of moral obligation that people owe to each other for their actions. An individual or organization should be prepared to provide an explanation for its activities to whomever is owed such an explanation. Normally, accountability means accepting responsibility by disclosing one's actions in a transparent manner to whatever stakeholders are owed an explanation. In standard business practice, accountability typically includes responsibility for money or other entrusted property.

Allocative efficiency is a benefit that results from properly functioning markets whose operations provide an optimal distribution of goods and services, responding to consumer preferences. It means that the market allocates scarce resources in a way that responds to the needs and desires of the buyers and sellers who participate in it. Market failure occurs when the allocation of goods and services is inefficient for various reasons, including the impact of various corrupt practices that block the development of free and fair competition (see Chap. 14).

Amakudari is a Japanese term that literally means "descent from heaven." It refers to the practice of businesses hiring bureaucrats recently retired from the government agencies that regulate them. Such a practice establishes a revolving door between businesses and government that some critics believe undermines the integrity of Japanese regulatory agencies (see Chap. 10).

Apologies in business settings are expected and offered when a firm must take responsibility for some accident or other negative impact of its operations. Since apologies involve social rituals that are embedded in diverse cultures, they can easily be mishandled, thus creating additional problems for the firm, especially in its foreign operations. Such problems may be avoided by adopting various

S. Rothlin, D. McCann, *International Business Ethics*,
DOI 10.1007/978-3-662-47434-1

policies that cultivate a genuine respect for cultural diversity, especially in its local management teams (see Chap. 15).

Art of self-cultivation refers to East Asian, primarily Confucian, strategies of moral education. Self-cultivation assumes that progress in moral development is not primarily about learning the rules and how to apply them, but about nurturing "the sprouts" from which the moral virtues sanctioned as the way (*Dao*) can be acquired and refined. Confucian teaching on the art of self-cultivation especially in the tradition of Mencius assumes that all people are naturally good, but in need of improvement based on genuine insight into human nature and its possibilities (see Chap. 2).

Association of Asian Confederation of Credit Unions (ACCU) was founded in 1971 in order to coordinate the development and continuous improvement of credit unions in Asia. By 2012, there were over 20,000 affiliated organizations serving the needs of over 37 million members. The ACCU is highly valued for its role in helping millions of Asian families to lift themselves out of poverty by helping them develop their own social capital, thus providing access to the financial capital they need to take control of their own lives (see Chap. 20).

Asymmetrical reciprocity describes the condition typically experienced in human relationships. Reciprocity is meant to be mutual in the relationship, but the assistance actually given and expected is rarely symmetrical. The primary relationships in which Confucian morality traditionally unfolds are usually asymmetrical, for example, parent-child, older sibling-younger sibling, husband-wife, older friend-younger friend, and ruler-subject. Rituals establish the recognition of asymmetrical responsibilities as, for example, a child starts out in life totally dependent upon its parents, who eventually may become totally dependent on him. The reciprocity is genuine, but its unfolding is asymmetrical over time (see Chap. 2).

Bankruptcy laws vary from one legal jurisdiction to another. They are designed to provide legal protection for individuals and businesses that must reorganized their finances because of their inability to pay their debts. There are various efforts underway to harmonize bankruptcy laws internationally, since globalization makes it possible for businesses to operate simultaneously in different nations. While bankruptcy laws provide a degree of legal protection, they generally do not completely absolve any individual or institution from the obligation to pay its debts. Rather, the laws generally establish a priority list among the creditors, thus determining who will be paid first and to what extent when it becomes impossible to pay all debts in full (see Chap. 7).

Bretton Woods system, toward the end of World War II, was established in order to regulate commercial and financial relations among the nations involved in international trade. The regulatory system focused on the coordination of monetary policy, including the management of exchange rates among various currencies and the balance of payments, in order to stabilize the development of international trade. The International Monetary Fund (IMF) and the World Bank are the two institutions created to administer the Bretton Woods system (see Chap. 9).

Bribery: Originally, bribery was defined as the act of promising, giving, receiving, or agreeing to receive money or some other item of value, in order to influence a public official in the conduct of his or her official duties. Bribery is usually distinguished from extortion: If a public official demands money and threatens to withhold his or her service until he gets it, the act is one of extortion since it is assumed to be involuntary on the part of the one who must pay. For example, it is extortion when a corrupt customs official refuses to allow your goods to cross the border unless he or she receives a "gratuity" of some sort. On the other hand, when someone initiates the offer of a "gratuity" in exchange for the benefit he or she expects to receive, that is bribery. If I offer a "gratuity" to a customs official in order to get his or her cooperation allowing me to smuggle goods across the border, I am guilty of bribery.

Business-as-usual attitude: the phrase, "business is business," generally suggests the erroneous assumption that the conduct of business as such is amoral, operating in a sphere of interactions—the marketplace—that is exempt from normal ethical considerations. The chief mistake is to assume that there are any areas of human interaction that are exempt from ethical expressions of approval or disapproval. Business is never just business, but always already involves moral matters of conscience, however well or poorly formed, among those who engage in it.

Business bluffing: Albert Z. Carr's article on business bluffing argued that business is like a game of poker, in which bluffing is an acceptable and expected part of the game. Carr may be right in thinking that business, like games, follows rules that may be different, in some cases, from other forms of rule governed behavior, like marriage and family. But he is wrong in thinking that the game of poker should determine the basic rules of business ethics. Cheating, for example, occurs in all games, but the actions that are regarded as cheating in business may not be justified simply by equating them with bluffing in a game of chance. See Chap. 7.

Carbon footprint is a measurement of the total sets of greenhouse gas emissions caused by an organization, event, product, or person. While controversy continues to rage over whether such measurements can ever be done accurately, attempts to establish policies designed to reduce one's carbon footprint are generally regarded as a positive sign that an organization is trying to bear its share of society's environmental responsibility. See Chap. 19

Carrot and stick approach: This metaphor describes the process of achieving compliance with any set of rules and regulations that rely on both positive ("carrots") and negative ("sticks") incentives. Just as a stick alone is not likely to persuade a stubborn mule to comply with its master's orders, so the threat of punishments or legal sanctions are not likely to guarantee compliance. People must be persuaded to comply with rules and regulations, primarily by showing them that they have an ownership stake in the desired outcomes. Enlightened self-interest, in which people identify with the rules and regulations, may be the best way to achieve compliance with them (see Chap. 11).

Category mistake is a philosophical term indicating a type of informal fallacy in which things belonging to one category are mistakenly interpreted as belonging to another. Describing business as if it were a form of warfare—as some observers have attempted to do in applying Sunzi's *Art of Warfare* to strategic management—is overly simplistic and a category mistake leading to systematic misunderstandings of what does and does not happen in the routine conduct of business. If the nature of business is categorically misunderstood, any lessons regarding business ethics based on such a mistake will be both misleading and counterproductive (see Chap. 1).

Catholic Social Teaching (CST) is a body of Roman Catholic statements focused on questions of economic and social development that have been issued primarily in the form of encyclical letters, beginning with Pope Leo XIII's *Rerum Novarum* (1891) and Pius XI's anniversary commemorative, *Quadragesimo Anno* (1931). In more recent times, CST has responded to the challenges of globalization, as these are addressed in Paul VI's *Populorum Progessio* (1967), as well as in John Paul II's *Solicitudo Rei Socialis* (1987) and Benedict XVI's *Caritas in Veritate* (2009). Throughout its development, CST highlights the moral dimensions of the social question, by urging everyone to consider the importance of human dignity and solidarity, and related core values and principles designed to safeguard personal integrity while also advancing the common good of society as a whole (see Chaps. 8, 18, 19 and 20).

Caveat emptor is the original formulation in Latin of the idea "Let the Buyer Beware." It is usually paired with *Caveat venditor,* which means "Let the Seller Beware." The twin principles suggest that business ethics includes moral obligations that are the responsibility of both buyers and sellers. Both buyers and sellers must interact in ways that benefit all concerned, while also preserving the integrity of the markets in which they interact.

Charity and philanthropy should be distinguished, roughly on the basis of the ways in which each is organized. Charity tends to be personal, that is, an individual's attempt to help other individuals through gifts or personal donations. Philanthropy, on the other hand, tends to be corporate, that is, the activity of an organization—a business or private foundation—seeking to assist other institutions directly involved in providing resources to improve the lives of others, particularly the poor and the marginalized (see Chaps. 12 and 17).

Cheating typically occurs in games and other forms of rule-governed behavior. It refers to acts deliberately intended to break the rules in order to secure benefits not obtainable by following the rules. Cheating is a form of theft, usually involving some form of deception, apart from which the cheating would readily be detected and penalized. Cheating imposes losses upon anyone trying to play by the rules of the game and is usually subject to sanctions. Cheating occurs in market exchanges whenever buyers or sellers attempt to gain an advantage through one form or another of fraudulent activity (see Chap. 5).

Civil society refers to the social sphere that may be distinguished from the institutions of both the state and the market. Within that sphere are the aggregate of nongovernmental organizations (NGOs) that manifest the diverse interests of a nation's citizens. Civil society begins with the natural association of the family and includes other associations organized for the pursuit of various private and public interests outside and beyond the family. Churches and other religious institutions, as well as private foundations, and other organizations whose membership is voluntary, form elements of civil society (see Chaps. 16, 18, and 20).

Class struggle: Marxist social analysis assumes that changes in history can be explained as resulting from class struggle, that is, the often violent conflict in material interests identified with one social class or another resulting from the fact that some social classes are subdued as slaves for the rest of the society. The class struggles that Marxism analyzed were primarily a conflict between workers and the owners of industry, or labor and capital. Marxist theory assumed that class struggle was not only inevitable but that changes in the development of industry—relations of production and means of production—would precipitate a social revolution in which labor would triumph over capital, in which private ownership of the means of production would be abolished (see Chap. 18).

Codes of ethics are a major part of the effort to improve international business ethics, especially for firms operating in a globalizing economy and in political and social contexts where the rule of law is either weak or inexistent. Codes of ethics seek to establish ethical norms that are valid cross-culturally, that is, principles that are readily recognized and embraced in a variety of cultural settings. The attempt to formulate codes of ethics for businesses and industries is best understood as part of the ongoing effort to professionalize management. Codes of ethics can be very effective in managing a corporate culture, so long as they respect the diversity of cultures represented among those who must comply with them.

Collateralized debt obligations (CDOs) are a type of structured asset-backed security in which various forms of debt—bonds, mortgages, car loans, etc.—are repackaged so that they can be sold to investors. The market for these securities was made up of investors seeking higher returns than what could be obtained by holding the original fixed income assets upon which the CDOs were based. Many blamed the recent global financial crisis on the proliferation of these securities, whose risks were either not fully understood or seriously misstated by those promoting them (see Chap. 7).

Commercial bribery refers to business transactions, in which contracts or agreements have been concluded on other than economically rational considerations, for the sake of personal benefits of one form or another. A purchasing agent, for example, who signs a contract with one firm because of the money offered as a personal inducement, rather than the economic benefits to the firm he or she represents, may be regarded as having corrupted the transaction by accepting a bribe. Commercial bribery is condemned in international business ethics as both illegal and immoral because it creates obstacles to both economic development and international trade conducted on a free and fair basis. In actual practice, it is often difficult to distinguish bribes from gifts and other gratuities; there may be differing standards from one culture to another, which must be taken into account, in determining the extent of corrupt practices in one setting or another (see Chap. 14).

Common sense may be defined as the ability to think and behave in a reasonable way to make good decisions. It may be identified with the virtue of prudence or practical wisdom. Common sense is essential in an ethic of responsibility, in which moral agents must make decisions that are often unscripted, that is, decisions that require us to think beyond the mere application of rules. Common sense is closely related to the idea of conscience, that is, the assumption that a reasonably intelligent person is capable of thinking and acting on the basis of moral norms in the absence of detailed instructions from some set of rules (see Chap. 3).

Community development is the ultimate goal of the movement to institute credit unions and credit cooperatives, especially in service to the poor whose need for financial services is either ignored by commercial banks or exploited by predatory usurers or "loan sharks" (see Chap. 20).

Commutative justice is the justice that is expected in exchange relationships conducted in a marketplace. As theorized by Aristotle and Aquinas, and more recently, by F. A. von Hayek, the expectation is that equality is achieved when both parties to the exchange receive equal satisfaction of their needs or desires—thus creating, as it were, a "win-win" situation. For such to be realized, the transaction must be free and fair, that is, based on a mutual agreement as to the worth of the goods or services to be exchanged. Though, like gifts, the exchange is voluntary, unlike gifts market transactions involve the creation of debts or mutual obligations on both sides to render full value, as specified in the agreement (see Chap. 5).

Compensatory damages is a legal concept specifying the expectation that when someone is injured by another, he or she is owed compensation for the harm suffered. The point of compensatory damages is to render the injured party whole and may be contrasted with punitive damages that are meant to punish the party inflicting an injury upon another. Usually awards in civil court cases for punitive damages are much higher than simply for compensatory damages (see Chap. 9).

Compliance rules are designed to insure that policies are enforced on all parties subject to them. Establishing reasonable and effective compliance rules, including penalties against any incidents of noncompliance, is an essential task of corporate governance. Compliance rules are meant to insure that no one will profit from ignoring policies, or breaking them, in order to gain some personal advantage contrary to the policies in question (see Chap. 13).

Compromise is an indispensable feature of moral maturity or ethical responsibility both on an individual and on a social level. Knowing when and how to compromise, without sacrificing one's personal integrity or organizational mission, is the result of cultivating the virtue of prudence. One may make compromises for the sake of preserving social harmony or because one realizes that insisting on one's rights may cause more problems than it solves. Compromises may be temporary—for example, postponing the fulfillment of some goal—or permanent, which may result from reexamining one's goals and revising them on the basis of further insight. The greater a person's moral wisdom, the higher a person's skill in exercising the virtue of prudence, the more likely that his or her compromises will increase rather than undermine personal integrity and the common good (see Chap. 4).

Compulsory licensing is one set of strategies for achieving compliance with certain organizational policies. There are two chief examples of compulsory licensing in our case studies. One is the Doha Declaration, explored in Chap. 13, which permits states to break patents in public health emergencies, by requiring drug manufacturers to make available the drugs specifically needed to address the emergency. The other is the policy of the Cooperative Development Authority (CDA) of the Philippines, which requires the licensing of credit unions, in order to achieve compliance with regulations designed to minimize the risks of fraud and mismanagement (see Chap. 20).

Conflict of interest is a term that generally refers to a situation in which a person or an organization has multiple responsibilities that may diverge from one another, making it difficult or impossible to satisfy all of them in an equal and impartial manner. As a legal term, conflict of interest occurs when a public official or a person with fiduciary responsibilities acts contrary to his or her obligations, thus exploiting the relationship for personal benefit, financial, or otherwise. Failure to acknowledge or resolve conflicts of interest is generally regarded as a sign of corruption or malfeasance in office (see Chaps. 7 and 17).

Confucian ethics is the primary tradition in Chinese moral philosophy inspired by the study of the writings of Confucius (551–479 BCE) and his major disciples especially Mencius and Xunzi. The *Analects* (*Lun Yu*), a collection of aphorisms and observations based upon conversations with his first disciples, is attributed to Confucius. It is the most authoritative text for the study of Confucian ethics. Confucius is a major figure in the history of virtue ethics and is celebrated for his original formulation of the so-called Golden Rule, "What you do not wish for yourself, do not do unto others." His understanding of human nature, the unity of the virtues that develop from it, and his insights into the challenges involved in following the Way (*Dao*), practicing the art of self-cultivation, are a permanent and indispensable contribution to the teaching of ethics and convergent with the ethical traditions of the various forms of Christian humanism that emerged in the West (see Chap. 2).

Conscience may be defined as the virtually universal experience of an inner sense of what is right and wrong in one's conduct or motives, impelling a person toward right action. While debates over the origin of conscience may seem interminable—does it stem from "nature" or "nurture"? from God or from social convention—conscience seems to be coextensive with the human mind or "heart" (Chinese: *Xin*; Japanese: *Kokoro*). The universality of conscience does not necessarily entail uniformity in the moral sentiments that it promotes. Although a spark of humanity or conscience may be latent in all human persons, that spark can be snuffed out or smothered or distorted in various ways. Corruption is also a process of spiritual deterioration, in which conscience can be suppressed, if not entirely eliminated. By the same token, conscience can also be cultivated and refined, as we learn greater sensitivity to the purpose of life and the needs of humanity (see Chaps. 2 and 15).

Consumer rights and responsibilities: The moral exercise of rights and responsibilities tends to be differentiated according to the various roles a person assumes in life. The role of consumer—which defines one category of stakeholders that all businesses must acknowledge—carries its own set of rights and responsibilities that have been codified over the past fifty years. The point of such codes is to make everyone involved aware of the basic morality underlying the relationship between consumers and producers or customers and the firms that seek to do business with them (see Chap. 6).

Copyright is one type of intellectual property rights intended to protect the written expression of ideas. A writer may register his copyright covering his writings, establishing his claim to any royalties or other proceeds that may be earned by the publication of his works, over a set period of time. In principle a copyrighted work may not be published legally without the permission of its author. Because the means of expressing ideas and publishing them have expanded dramatically over the past several decades, copyright laws now extend to a variety of creative products, including tape recordings, films, videotapes, video compact discs, computer programs, and virtually all forms of digitalized information, as well as works of art (see Chap. 13).

Core competencies refer to the basic skills assembled and coordinated in any firm in order to achieve its business objectives. An inventory of a firm's core competencies may be useful in developing an effective strategy for exercising one's corporate social responsibilities (CSRs). A firm whose core competencies are in the area of computer software development, for example, may be wise to focus its CSR programming on providing resources that may help create synergies between the business and the communities in which it operates. Infosys' initiation of a "Computers@Classrooms" program is not only an important contribution to the schools in its area but also an indirect way of enhancing its own core competencies in the long term, by enabling students to make a pathway toward careers in software development (see Chap. 12).

Corporate espionage: This term refers to unauthorized or illegal surveillance activities—typically involving the use of advanced digital technologies—conducted by a business in order to learn the trade secrets and other proprietary information of its competitors, for commercial purposes. It should be distinguished from the forms of espionage conducted by national governments in the alleged interest of national security, as well as from the kinds of workplace surveillance of employees using similar technologies, which may or may not be illegal or unethical (see Chap. 16).

Corporate malpractice is any form of corporate wrongdoing—violation of compliance rules, mandated codes of ethics and corporate policy, etc.—that violates legal standards or ethical expectations enshrined in the implied social contract between a business and its stakeholders. The term, corporate malpractice, typically implies that the wrongdoing is authorized by corporate management in an attempt to fulfill its business goals, such as profit maximization. Absent any effective structures for sharing information between management and a firm's workers, corporate malpractice often gives rise to incidents of whistle-blowing, which can be risky for all concerned (see Chaps. 10 and 16).

Corporate social responsibility (CSR) is the term referring to business' interaction with the social environment in which it operates. The policies and programs identified as examples of CSR typically are closely related to the firm's business plan and its need to manage well its relationships with all its external stakeholders. From a business' point of view, CSR programs are designed to demonstrate that the firm takes its citizenship responsibilities seriously and thereby intends to earn and retain the goodwill of the communities in which it is active. CSR represents a multiplicity of responsibilities that may be understood as a "CSR Pyramid" ranging from compliance with basic moral and legal obligations to philanthropic social and environmental initiatives. Typically, CSR is a form of social development programming designed to further the firm's long-term business plan (see Chap. 12).

Corruption in general signifies a defect in something in itself considered good or useful. Political power, for example, is good because it enables society to make progress toward the common good, but abusing that power means prostituting one's public office for personal gain, which is bad. Corruption therefore can be compared to cancer. Just as the human body can be corrupted by cancer, so can the State or any organization be more and more deeply debilitated by the cancer of corruption. Ultimately, corruption is a form of spiritual pollution, because it involves the decision to set aside one's responsibilities—for example, the impartial administration of justice or the rule of law—in exchange for illegitimate gifts, payments, or other benefits. Corruption can occur not only in the public sector but also in private sector business transactions, when the parties collude to subvert free and fair market competition, in exchange for bribes, kickbacks, etc. (see Chap. 14).

Cost-benefit analysis is a tool used in business decision-making based on the calculation of anticipated consequences, both positive and negative, as assessed from the perspective afforded by the firm's specific business plan. It is distinguished from utilitarianism, considered as a method of ethical analysis, which assesses anticipated consequences from the perspective of the common good or the interests of society as a whole. Cost-benefit analysis, therefore, has a limited scope that is not as broad as the utilitarian principle of the "the greatest good for the greatest number" (see Chap. 4).

Cover-up refers to the efforts of an organization to obscure its involvement in or responsibility for a negative result of its policies or business plan. Cover-ups usually seek to shift the blame for such results to others in the hope that the firm will be able to escape paying whatever compensation may be due its victims. As the demand for transparency in corporate governance grows, along with more effective policies supporting transparency, cover-ups become increasingly risky and counterproductive (see Chaps. 10 and 19).

Credit default swaps are the most common form of credit derivative developed in order to manage the risks involved in buying and selling fixed income financial instruments, based on debts, like mortgages, loans, and other credit transactions. Credit default swaps are like insurance policies underwritten by banks and purchased by investors, in order to hedge their exposure to the risks involved in holding such instruments (see Chap. 7).

Credit enhancement is the process designed to improve the credit profile of a structured financial transaction, by creating a bundle of debts with different ratings of credit worthiness. In theory, the bundle mixing less risky (higher credit rating) notes with more risky ones with lower credit ratings will enhance the overall credit worthiness and hence the value of the package as a whole. Credit enhancement was done on a large scale in creating the financial instruments whose value was severely challenged during the subprime mortgage crisis that precipitated the global financial crisis of 2007–2008 (see Chap. 7).

Credit unions and credit cooperatives are membership organizations, usually not-for-profit, that provide financial services, primarily savings accounts and loans, as well as basic education in financial management, in order to empower people who otherwise may have little or no access to the finance capital they need to meet major expenses or to start businesses of their own. The purpose of such organizations is to promote thrift and thereby increase access to the capital required to become financially independent or self-sustaining (see Chap. 20).

Culture of accountability describes a corporate culture that is structured in such a way that one's personal, institutional, and social responsibilities are not only clear, but also enhanced by the organization's governance structure in accordance with local laws. A culture of accountability, among other things, enables employees, both managers and workers, to succeed by providing timely feedback and adequate supervision, as well as open channels of communication to support everyone's participation in fulfilling the organization's specific mission.

Customers may be distinguished from consumers, insofar as a customer is invited to develop a relationship of trust with a business, thus motivating him or her to do more business transactions with it. According to Peter Drucker, the purpose of a business is to create a customer. A business can succeed in achieving its economic goals, only if it enables consumers to become customers (see Chap. 6).

Cynicism is an attitude in which distrust of others and a tendency to emphasize negative feelings toward virtually everything are predominant. In Chinese moral philosophy, the small-minded person (*Xiaoren*) exhibits cynicism in assuming that the only way to get ahead is by taking advantage of others before they take advantage of you. In Hellenistic moral philosophy, cynicism is a form of sophistry—literally, adopting a doglike attitude—whose distortions undermine respect for moral values, assuming that they are nothing more than social conventions, imposed by the rich and powerful upon the poor and powerless. Cynicism is a major obstacle to cultivating an ethic of virtue in business, since the cynic assumes that businesses inevitably must lie, cheat, and steal, in order to achieve their objectives.

Deontological method is used in applied ethics to determine the moral obligations or duties of a specific person or moral agent, including businesses and other organizations. It is especially useful for establishing priorities in cases where a moral agent is confronted with multiple and possibly conflicting moral obligations (see Chap. 4).

Deontological override is a rule for applying justice in situations where both moral obligations and good or desirable outcomes are evident, but not well sorted out as priorities. The deontological override stipulates that any valid claims regarding obligations should be addressed first, before moving on to a utilitarian analysis of desirable outcomes (see Chap. 4).

Distributive justice, in Hellenistic moral philosophy starting with Aristotle's *Nicomachean Ethics*, is the kind or species of justice that a public official or administrator seeks to achieve when distributing social benefits. While the general aim of justice is equality—that is, treat equals equally—in distributive justice, some may receive more benefits and others less, depending on their different needs, or merit, or contribution or other relevant factors. Aristotle theorizes that distributive justice is proportional, in contrast to commutative justice—which governs market exchanges—which is arithmetical. In allocating retirement benefits, for example, the government may calculate the amount an individual citizen receives based on his or her previous contributions to the system, resulting in the distribution of unequal payments (see Chap. 5).

Do no harm (*primum non nocere*) is often cited as the first principle of business ethics. The reason for this emphasis is that market transactions are typically private and voluntary. No one is compelled to enter into them, in the same way one is compelled to pay one's taxes. Since they are private, intending a mutual benefit to the parties involved, they are restricted only by the concern that neither party deliberately attempt to harm the other and that the mutual agreement of the transacting parties should not harm any third parties, including society as a whole. Following the economic logic of market exchanges, the assumption is that free and fair market transactions will generally benefit all concerned, with the contracting parties benefiting immediately and directly, and the rest of society benefiting long-term and indirectly. In theory that is expected outcome, so long as no one seeks to use the market deliberately to harm anyone else, for example, by profiting through exploitation or various forms of fraud (see Chap. 7).

Due diligence is the standard for achieving financial transparency that anyone entering into a business transaction is expected to exercise, in order to verify through investigation the claims made for the specific products or services to be bought or sold. If one party to an exchange is offering payment for a product or service, the other party should verify his or her credit worthiness or ability to pay as promised. On the other hand, if one party is offering a product or service in exchange for payment, the other party should verify that the product or service is what is claimed, without defects or other diminishment that would reduce the value of what is offered for sale. The twin principles of *caveat emptor* and *caveat venditor* implicitly reflect the expectation that buyers and sellers will act prudently in their mutual self-interest, thus performing due diligence to ensure that their transactions are successfully completed (see Chap. 6).

Duty to preserve a market's integrity is assumed, in theory, by all those participating in it, buyers and sellers alike. The development of markets is assumed to be part of the common good, when free and fair transactions collectively result in optimizing allocative efficiency. Anything that distorts or subverts the market's operations—for example, by deliberately seeking to create a monopoly or by erecting political barriers to international trade, as in various forms of "protectionism"—undercuts the market's integrity and, therefore, merits condemnation as a form of corruption (see Chap. 14).

Ecological sustainability is the goal of businesses and other organizations seeking to exercise their environmental responsibilities. Ecological sustainability refers to preserving or enhancing the capacity of an ecosystem—for example, a river estuary—to maintain its essential functions and processes, while retaining biodiversity for the foreseeable future (see Chap. 19).

Equal Employment Opportunities Commission (EEOC) and Title VII of the Civil Rights Act of 1964 refer to legislation in the USA prohibiting all forms of discrimination in employment and creating institutions to monitor compliance with it. Besides discrimination based on race or religion, Title VII and the EEOC are concerned with discrimination based on gender and/or sexual orientation, as well as all forms of sexual harassment in the workplace. This legislation and its enforcement are but one dimension of ongoing effort to acknowledge the human dignity and human rights of workers (see Chaps. 8 and 9).

Embezzlement is a form of theft done by one who has fiduciary responsibility for funds or property entrusted to him or her by another. The embezzler dishonestly converts the funds or property for his or her own use, without the knowledge or authorization of the person or agency that had entrusted them. Embezzlement differs from larceny—which is theft pure and simple—since it involves funds or property that were originally entrusted legally. The crime occurs when the funds or property are then converted to the embezzler's use or exclusive benefit.

Employee monitoring is a form of workplace surveillance greatly enhanced by the development of digital technologies that enable managers to keep an eye on the activities of employees by using programs designed to record the employees' use of computers, cell phones, and other digital technologies allocated to them for business purposes. Employees have been monitored since time immemorial, often in ways that violate their human dignity if not their human rights, but the development of digital technologies has greatly expanded the scale and scope of such surveillance. Such practices are at stake in contemporary debates over the right to privacy, its scale and scope, and how to balance employee rights with the rights of employers (see Chap. 16).

Entrepreneurship is the art of identifying and responding to market opportunities for starting up a business and making its sustainable. Entrepreneurship is commonly regarded as the key to economic development, to the extent that new businesses generate economic activity as well as increase profits and employment opportunities, which in turn stimulate more investment and further development. Successful entrepreneurs recognize the competitive nature of business and seek to optimize profits within the rules governing market competition, by creating innovative products and services that will attract paying customers.

Environmental responsibility, as one of the hallmarks of sustainable economic development, requires a business or other agency to organize its activities so that they are consistent with the goal of ecological sustainability. An environmentally responsible business or organization will seek to reduce its "carbon footprint" and otherwise reduce waste and emissions known to cause deterioration in the natural environment. Environmental responsibility means transforming a business or other agency's relationship with nature from exploitation to cultivation, that is, aiming toward a harmonious relationship that will preserve the environment for future generations (see Chap. 19).

ESG responsibilities are a set of environmental, social, and governance criteria used in capital markets and among investors to evaluate corporate performance. ESG responsibilities are nonfinancial indicators providing investors with access to information that will have a bearing on the firm's future financial performance. The European Federation of Financial Analysts Societies (EFFAS) has identified nine general areas of accountability indicative of ESG performance (see Chap. 11).

Ethical intelligence and emotional intelligence are distinct but related capacities whose convergence is closely realized in the traditions of virtue ethics of Confucianism and Hellenistic moral philosophy. High ethical intelligence coupled with low emotional intelligence can result in a morality that is excessively rigid and rule bound, whereas high emotional intelligence coupled with low ethical intelligence can result in a morality that is manipulative, opportunistic, and unscrupulous. Creating a harmonious relationship between the two may be a useful way to think about the goal of virtue ethics, in which the pursuit of wisdom becomes characteristic of a person capable of exercising moral leadership (see Chaps. 2 and 15).

Ethical relativism is a philosophical theory that denies the existence of moral absolutes and binding universal values, claiming instead that whether an action is right or wrong depends exclusively on the changing current moral norms of a given society. Social convention, in short, provides a complete explanation for moral judgment and ethical behavior. Such a theory is a mistake because it confuses cultural diversity, which clearly is a fact, with a conclusion that does not necessarily follow from it. Cultural practices may be diverse, but they may also reflect an underlying moral imperative that is common to all sustainable cultures. Bribery, for example, may be defined differently in different cultures, resulting in diverse judgments as to which transactions are bribes and which are gifts. But the underlying concern to restrict or place sanctions on the abuse of power by those who use public office for personal gain may be common to all of them. Among its other shortcomings, ethical relativism as a theory cannot account for how or why moral norms change or develop within a given society. If ethical relativism were true, it would be virtually impossible to account for how and why, for example, there is a growing moral consensus cross-culturally that sexism is wrong and that traditional forms of sexual abuse, such as harassment and human trafficking, can and ought to be punished (see Chaps. 9, 15 and 16).

Ethical theory is divided into three major areas, descriptive ethics, normative ethics, and metaethics. Descriptive ethics examines the actual moral beliefs and practices of various groups, much in the same way that anthropology and the social sciences study them, but with the intent of clarifying their moral logic. Normative ethics examines what ought to be, much in the same way that philosophy does, but with the intent of identifying moral principles and the logic of their application to specific situations. Metaethics analyzes the meaning of moral terms, the nature of ethical properties, statements, attitudes and judgments, in order to achieve clarity about what morality itself is and whether and how moral norms respond to specific social and political situations. Descriptive ethics thus focuses on understanding the practices that people regard as right and wrong; normative ethics, on making judgments whether something is right or wrong; and metaethics, on understanding the nature—the analytic presuppositions of such practices and judgments (see Chap. 3).

Fair and unfair competition within the marketplace may be distinguished on the basis of whether the competitors compete on a level playing field, that is, a market in which the competition is open to all, where the same rules apply to all, where competition cannot be restricted by some competitors seeking an unfair advantage over the others. The distinction between the two is another indication that business is more like a game, in which rules determine the nature of the competition and what it means to win or lose, than like warfare that typically unfolds in the absence of such rules (see Chap. 1 and 5).

Fair Labor Association (FLA) is a nonprofit collaborative project involving universities, civil society organizations (NGOs), and businesses, seeking to promote compliance with international and national labor laws. Member firms pledge to uphold the FLA Workplace Code of Conduct, based on the standards established by the International Labour Organization (ILO) designed to monitor workplace conditions in order to promote their improvement for the sake of the workers' health, safety, and well-being (see Chap. 8).

Fiduciary responsibility is a concept defining the obligations that an agent—usually a financial advisor or broker—undertakes when managing other people's money. At the core of this cluster of obligations is the idea of fiduciary duty, which is the obligation—legal as well as moral—of an agent to act in the best interests of his or her principal, that is, someone to whom an agent has promised this service. A fiduciary is a person who is entrusted with the care of another person's money or property (see Chap. 11).

Fixed income instruments are financial securities that provide a return in the form of fixed periodic payments and the eventual return of the principal at maturity. Bonds are an example of a fixed income security. Though the global financial collapse of 2007–2008 was a result of certain irregularities in the production and marketing of fixed income instruments, there is nothing inherently wrong with such securities, provided that the markets in which they are bought and sold are properly regulated and subject to the basic norms of international business ethics and international law (see Chap. 7).

Foreign Corrupt Practices Act (FCPA) is a legislation originally passed by the US Congress in 1977 in order to enforce the standards of accounting transparency previously established in the 1934 Securities Exchange Act and to criminalize the practice of bribing foreign officials by US businesses operating internationally. The FCPA was a milestone in efforts to minimize corruption in a globalizing economy still in the early stages of its development. Meanwhile most other countries have passed similar legislation (see Chap. 14).

Fraud is deliberate deception in order to secure unfair or unlawful gain. It is, in law, both a civil wrong and a criminal offense. Fraud consists in a false representation of a matter of fact, whether by words or conduct or false and misleading claims or by concealment of something that should have been disclosed. The result is deception of another intending to get the other to act against his or her best interest. Fraud is a basic offense against commutative justice, since it creates a deception as to a matter of fact without which the true value of the transaction cannot be determined. It is a form of theft or stealing that achieves its purpose through deliberate deception rather than coercion, as in an act of robbery (see Chaps. 5 and 7).

Freedom and fairness are the two basic conditions indicative that justice has been achieved in a market transaction. Both parties must be free in the sense of having the capacity to act on their own self-interest; the transaction must be fair insofar as neither party has attempted to deceive the other or coerce the other into a transaction that is contrary to their own self-interest. Freedom may be defective, for example, in sales contracts made with minors whom the law regards as incapable of acting in their own self-interest. Fairness may be lacking, for example, when a seller deliberately conceals the defects in the goods or services for sale, in order to charge a higher price for them (see Chap. 5).

Game theory is the study of strategic decision-making, modeled on the interactions that occur among participants in various games. Game theory research has mapped the various types of games, particularly cooperative and noncooperative games, as well as positive sum and zero-sum games. The interactions of buyers and sellers in the marketplace can usefully be understood as falling within the purview of game theory, since they are involved in a form of interactive decision-making that seeks to create a "win-win" situation or positive outcome for all those involved (see Chap. 1).

Gamesmanship is distinguished from sportsmanship, insofar as gamesmanship aims at winning at all costs, by fair means or foul, usually by doing things that seem unfair but that are not actually against the rules. This use of aggressive or dubious tactics differs from the ideal of sportsmanship that not only respects the letter and spirit of the rules of the game but also seeks to protect the integrity of the game. If winning at all costs is characteristic of gamesmanship, sportsmanship is best captured in the saying, "It doesn't matter whether you win or lose, but how you play the game" (see Chap. 1).

Gandhi's idea of trusteeship promoted the notion that the rich should regard their wealth as held in trust for the benefit of the people as a whole. Gandhi believed that the wealthy could be persuaded to become trustees, who dedicate their wealth to projects that would help the poor. Like Andrew Carnegie, Gandhi understood that great wealth created a moral hazard for those who possessed it, especially through inheritance. He proposed that wealthy families should establish trusts voluntarily and manage the funds allocated to them in support of projects that will actually make a difference in the lives of the poor and marginalized. The skills acquired by successful entrepreneurs who had become rich could then be focused on ensuring that the trusts were well managed and effective in meeting their social goals. Warren Buffett and Bill Gates are recognized as global drivers of such trusteeship (see Chap. 17).

Globalization is the worldwide process enabling the convergence or integration of economic activity, financial networks, international trade, and communications. Globalization involves a never-ending search for strategic advantage in marketing and other business functions, where competition results in the free—or at least relatively unrestricted—transfer of capital, goods, and services and most recently the unhindered movement of labor across national borders. Globalization remains controversial because the benefits it promises for global economic and social development come with certain costs that may or may not be acceptable. Not only are the benefits shared unevenly, but they also tend to disrupt local cultures and societies. Not yet resolved is the question whether globalization can be managed so that it enhances the common good of the entire human family (see Chap. 18).

Greenwashing is a term describing the pretense of environmental responsibility. Greenwashing occurs when a business or organization makes false or exaggerated claims about its "green" activities seeking to create a positive impact on its public relations, without actually allocating the resources needed to make a positive impact on the environment (see Chaps. 14 and 19).

Guanxi is a Chinese term indicating relationship. In business it means networking among people who have a connection, based on kinship, or other forms of association. The point of using *guanxi* networks in business is to capitalize on the presumed trustworthiness of associates within the network and thus minimize the risk of doing business with strangers. In the absence of the rule of law, where contracts are enforced by the threat of lawsuits or where one can routinely expect economic crimes to be punished—for example, a breach of fiduciary duties or various other forms of fraudulent activity—the reliance on *guanxi* networks may be the most effective way to minimize such risks (see Chaps. 4 and 5).

Harmonious society (*héxié shèhuì*) is based on the Confucian ideal represented, for example, in the description of the Grand Union (*Dàtóng*) found in the *LǐYun*—Book IX of *The Book of Rites* (*Lǐjì*). This ideal has been developed recently as a key feature of PRC government ideology, where it is meant to raise awareness of the problems of social injustice and inequality in China that, if unaddressed, carry the risk of social conflict. Highlighting the importance of establishing a harmonious society involves shifting development goals from economic growth at all costs to overall social balance, with the intent of facilitating moderate prosperity for all, rather than perpetuating extremes of wealth and poverty. The notion of creating a harmonious society is hardly unique to Chinese tradition, since the common good envisioned by Catholic Social Teaching (CST) intends a similar goal (see Chap. 18).

HSE concerns reflect the cluster of issues related to health, safety, and environmental challenges faced by workers throughout the world. A good business is one that seeks to address HSE concerns, so that working conditions will enable employees to perform their assigned tasks responsibly and without avoidable risk of harm to their health and personal safety, thus sustaining a good environment for all its workers (see Chap. 19).

Human dignity refers to the inherent worth of human persons that must be respected in any moral and social order. The Universal Declaration of Human Rights proclaimed by the United Nations in 1948 begins with this assertion: "Whereas recognition of the inherent dignity and the equal and inalienable rights of all members of the human family is the foundation of freedom, justice and peace in the world." While the importance of respecting human dignity may be universally recognized, its actual meaning and scope are variously understood in different cultures. Both the Roman Catholic Church and the government of China (PRC), for example, demand respect for human dignity, while Catholic Social Teaching (CST) understand it primarily in theological terms. The Biblical claim that human beings are made to "the image and likeness of God underscores the value of each human being and his or her inalienable human rights. Chinese philosophers as well as the Communist Party of China, on the other hand, regard it as inherent in a human nature capable of moral development. This capacity, well described in the Confucian classics, is the basis for humanity's inherent nobility and stateliness. It is manifest in the principles of Heaven inherent in basic goodness of human nature. Understanding the diversity of such affirmations of human dignity may help explain differences regarding human rights and how they are to be enforced around the world (see Chaps. 16 and 20).

Ideal Commonwealth State or Grand Union (*Dàtóng*) summarizing the Confucian social philosophy is found in the *LǐYun*, in Book IX of *The Book of Rites* (*Lǐjì*). It describes a harmonious society in which Confucian moral virtues are practiced by all, thus establishing a community consisting not only of exemplary moral persons but also one in which social problems can be managed without recourse to a legal system dispensing rewards and meting out punishments. As *The Book of Rites* observes, the Ideal Commonwealth State is utopian; nevertheless, it expresses a yearning for a world in which the triumph of good over evil is both spontaneous and complete. By contrast, the world as we know it—and as Confucius knew it—is poised precariously between becoming either a "small tranquility" (*xiǎokāng*) or an "infirm state" (*cīguó*). The "small tranquility" is a state in which there is sufficient order to insure that everyone is "well-off," while an "infirm state" is one characterized by massive corruption and disorder, neither of which is ideal by Confucian standards.

Improper advantage defines the goal of any attempt at bribery or extortion, either in public affairs involving government officials or in private business transactions. Advantage is the natural outcome of successful negotiations and competition in business; advantage becomes improper when it is achieved by deliberately corrupting the processes or institutions in which it is sought (see Chap. 14).

Independent Commission Against Corruption (ICAC) is an agency of the Hong Kong government, directly accountable to Hong Kong's Chief Executive, charged with cleaning up corruption through law enforcement, prevention, and community education. After it was established in 1974 in order to combat corruption in the police force, the ICAC expanded its mission so that it now enforces the Prevention of Bribery Ordinance not only in cases involving government officials but also in private business transactions. With its wide investigative powers, the ICAC has been effective in changing the public's perception that bribes and kickbacks are the normal way to get things done in dealings either with government agencies or private businesses (see Chaps. 14 and 16).

India's Companies Act of 2013 is a comprehensive legislation passed by the parliament regulating the incorporation of a business organization, its responsibilities and those of its directors, and the procedures for dissolution of a company. The Act is noteworthy for mandating that every company of a certain size must set aside at least 2% of its average net profit to fund corporate social responsibility (CSR) activities, which are defined in Schedule VII of the Act with its special focus on poverty alleviation (see Chaps. 12 and 17).

Informal protectionism is an accusation usually made by business firms to explain that the barriers they face operating in a foreign country are cultural rather than legal. Usually, in this view, they blame their inability to succeed in foreign markets on the skepticism and hostility of local news media whose reporting on their activities plays upon the fears of the local population, who for one reason or another may resist their goods and services. Even if informal protectionism could be proven—which is highly unlikely—protesting against it may be ineffective. Instead, any firm trying to establish itself in a foreign country and encountering such resistance would do well to reexamine its marketing strategy and the tacit cultural assumptions behind it (see Chap. 15).

Insider trading is a form of malpractice in the financial industry in which traders with access to nonpublic information about a public company buy or sell its stock or other securities in order to maximize gains or minimize losses prior to the public release of material information. Insider trading is illegal when an insider makes the trade, while the information is still nonpublic or under embargo. Insider trading is legal once the information has been released to the public, thus cancelling any unfair advantage that the insider may have had over other investors. Even when such trading is legal, insiders who engage in it are often required to report their transactions to the appropriate regulatory authority—as in the USA, the Securities Exchange Commission (SEC). The rules on insider trading differ from one financial center to another, often depending on previously established practices in various financial cultures (see Chap. 7).

Institutional investors are organizations whose activities in the financial markets move large blocks of shares and thus have significant influence on the markets' performance. Institutional investors pool large amounts of capital from their various clients—other organizations and wealthy individuals—and invest it on their behalf, in the expectation that the institutional investors are generally more knowledgeable about the markets and the various stocks, bonds, and other securities bought and sold on them than individual or noninstitutional investors who manage their investments either personally or through a broker or financial advisor (see Chap. 7).

Integrity is a characteristic ascribed to persons respected for their honesty and strong moral principles. A person valued for his or her integrity is someone who tries to do the right thing at all times and in all circumstances, whether or not anyone is watching. Integrity implies the capacity to act impartially or to achieve fairness in all one's dealings, in business or otherwise. While a person valued for his or her integrity is surely someone to be trusted, he or she is also likely to welcome whatever measures will ensure both transparency and accountability so that others can be assured that their trust is well placed. A sense of integrity, as recognized by others and discovered in oneself, is the natural outcome of the ongoing processes of self-cultivation recommended in the wisdom traditions that sustain virtue ethics (see Chap. 2).

Intellectual property rights (IPR) are the property rights enjoyed by persons who have produced intellectual creations that may be valued as property by themselves and others. The World Intellectual Property Organization (WIPO) defines intellectual property as "creations of the mind, such as inventions; literary and artistic works; designs; and symbols, names and images used in commerce." The property rights granted to those who create such works are codified in law and regulated by both national governments and international agencies. Like all other property rights, intellectual property rights are never absolute and must be balanced or adjusted in relationship to other valid rights claims (see Chap. 13).

Investment rating agencies, also known as credit rating agencies, were established to provide investors with reliable information on the degrees of risk associated with various debt securities. The agencies—for example, Standard and Poors (S&P), Moody's, and Fitch—were expected to investigate the securities, verify the claims, and provide an easily understood letter grade, ranging from AAA on down the alphabet, signifying their assessment of the risks involved. The failure of the investment rating agencies to perform as expected is regarded as a major contributing factor in the global financial crisis of 2007–2008.

Investor's Bill of Rights (IBOR) is a concept proposed to further the reform of financial markets by making them more transparent and accountable to investors. Analogous to the Bill of Rights attached to the Constitution of the USA, an IBOR is meant to define the rights and responsibilities both of those who provide financial services—for example, banks, brokerages, insurance companies, and others—and their clients. Though no IBOR has been enacted into law and incorporated into the system of government agencies regulating financial services, many such firms have developed their own IBOR statements in order to reassure their clients and demonstrate their commitment to best business practices (see Chap. 11.)

Initial public offering (IPO) refers to the first sale of stock by a private company to the public at large. An IPO typically involves an underwriting firm that assists the company trying to launch its stock by advising it on the type of security to issue, the best offering price, and the timing of its initial offering. IPOs are generally regarded as more risky than ordinary stock market transactions because there may be relatively less information available upon which to estimate the value of the stock being offered. IPOs can be mismanaged, resulting in significant losses, as was the case initially with the IPO done for *Facebook* in May 2012 (see Chap. 7).

Joint venture (JV) is a legal business organization in which the participating parties (individuals or firms) agree to share the costs as well as any profits from their new partnership. Normally both parties to a joint venture contribute assets and share the risks as well as rewards from the business. Joint ventures are widely used by firms seeking to do business in foreign markets. The foreign company will partner with a domestic company already doing business locally, with the foreign company contributing capital as well as new technologies and business practices, and the domestic company contributing its network of relationships with government agencies and other local businesses (see Chap. 4).

Jūnzǐ, often translated as "gentleman" or "morally refined person," refers to the Confucian ideal of a person whose exemplary moral character is second only to that of a sage or legendary wisdom figure. A *jūnzǐ* has mastered the moral virtues achieved by Confucius and thus may be relied upon to teach these by personal example. *Jūnzǐ* is contrasted with *xiǎorén*, that is, a small or petty person who cannot grasp the importance of cultivating the moral virtues and thus seeks only his own immediate gain. By not considering the consequences of his actions in the overall scheme of things, the *xiǎorén* usually ends up creating problems for himself, whereas the *jūnzǐ*'s wisdom and self-discipline allows him to exercise leadership over others (see Chap. 2).

Just Wage or Just Salary refers to a concept in Catholic Social Teaching (CST), defined in Pope Leo XIII's *Rerum Novarum* (1891) and elaborated in Pope John Paul II's *Laborem Exercens* (1981), according to which justice in wages, salaries, or other compensation is the amount needed to support a thrifty and upright worker plus his family. CST in general is well aware that wages generally reflect the laws of supply and demand as they operate in labor markets. The tradition also realized that labor market outcomes usually reflect asymmetries in bargaining power between individual workers and their employers. Workers had to take whatever they could get and were rarely if ever in a position to make demands upon their employers. The idea of a Just Wage or Just Salary—often expressed today in campaigns to achieve a "Living Wage"—was meant as a protest against the immorality of treating labor as just another commodity, to be bought and sold in the marketplace. CST advocates the formation of community organizations, like workingmen's associations, in which workers and their employers could learn to respect each other's human dignity and together discover ways to achieve greater justice in wages and salaries for all (see Chap. 18).

Just War is an ethical theory outlining the rules of combat governing the conduct of the armed forces of a given state. The theory was developed as part of Christian ethics in an attempt to regulate (and thus minimize) the use of the military in conflicts with other states. The tradition focuses on two major questions, the right to go to war (*jus ad bellum*) and right conduct in warfare (*jus in bello*). It generally regards the use of military force as a last resort when all other means to resolve such conflicts have failed and clearly places the moral burden of proof upon any state that would start a war for any reason. The theory seeks to promote respect for the rights of noncombatants, who are not to be deliberately targeted for attack in any act of war. It is also invoked in situations where using military force against terrorists and religious extremists may be justified only when the violence cannot be stopped by peaceful means. We argue that Just War theory is also relevant for understanding the morality of whistle-blowing, which is often regarded by business corporations as an act of warfare against them (see Chap. 10).

Lawful interception refers to legitimate acts of covert surveillance, usually those conducted by governments in the interests of national security. The existence of legislation regulating such acts presupposes the difference between state agencies and private businesses, making it clear that forms of covert surveillance that may be legitimate when done by governments may also be illegitimate when done by private individuals or corporations (see Chap. 16).

Level playing field is an expression that refers to the ethical expectation of fairness or impartiality in business competition. In sports, a level playing field is one in which the rules of the game are observed by all participants and interpreted as well as applied impartially by the referees or umpires, without favoring one side or another. In international business ethics, the expression refers to circumstances in which a firm in competition with others may complain that it is being restricted or penalized unfairly, particularly by the ways in which local markets function or are regulated. Such circumstances violate the expectation of a level playing field (see Chaps. 5, 14, and 15).

Loan sharking is a practice typical of predatory lenders who charge exorbitant rates of interest, either legally or in clear violation of laws that, in some jurisdictions, set a limit to such interest rates. Those engaged in loan sharking typically target the poor who are unable to establish sufficient creditworthiness or collateral to apply for needed loans from commercial banks. Credit cooperatives and credit unions were established in order to provide financial services to the poor, particularly opportunities for savings and loans, at reasonable interest rates usually well below those charged by loan sharks or predatory lenders (see Chaps. 2 and 20).

Loyalty to an employer is an ethical expectation implicit in the act of accepting employment in exchange for wages, salary, or other benefits. Such loyalty requires an employee to carry out whatever tasks or responsibilities may be assigned, with due care, reasonable effort, or wholeheartedness. A loyal employee will not try to minimize his or her compliance with assigned tasks or responsibilities, by sticking to the letter of his or her job description, but instead will seek to respond intelligently to whatever obstacles stand in the way of successful performance. The nature of one's loyalty to an employer is changing in some respects. Employers should not expect blind loyalty, and employees are not obligated to do things that a reasonable person would regard as immoral or illegal. Employers must do more today to earn the loyalty of their employees, by creating working conditions and supporting a management style that credibly demonstrate respect for workers' rights and their human dignity (see Chaps. 8, 9, 10, and 18).

Marketing vs. selling is a distinction memorably developed by Theodore Levitt in an essay originally published in the *Harvard Business Review* (1960) as "Marketing Myopia." Selling is oriented to the needs of the seller, primarily to close the sale in order to move the product from his inventory to the buyer so that he can maximize profits. Marketing, on the other hand, is oriented to the needs of customers, which the seller must understand in order to shape all phases of his relationship with them, starting with the very design of the product. The point of marketing is to achieve competitive advantage by creating a highly loyal set of customers. If marketing is done properly, profits will be maximized without reliance upon predatory or unethical sales practices (see Chaps. 6 and 7).

Match-fixing is one of a number of ways of cheating in organized sports competition, committed by either players or referees. It involves playing the game in order to achieve a completely or partially predetermined outcome, for example, hitting a desired points spread between the winner and loser of a particular match. **Match-fixing** usually is motivated by the interests of gamblers or organized crime syndicates who pay bribes to players or referees in order to guarantee the predetermined outcome, the assurance of which enables them to place their bets without fear of losses. Match-fixing not only harms those who lose their bets but it also deprives sports competition of any meaning as a game and symbol of fairness (see Chap. 1).

Mengzi (372–289 BCE) is the most famous Confucian scholar beyond Confucius himself. His contribution to the Confucian classics, *The Book of* Mencius, is crucial for the development of Chinese virtue ethics, inasmuch as it declares the innate goodness of human nature and demonstrates how the virtues, when cultivated properly, grew from "sprouts" universally present in all human beings. Since Mengzi's father died when he was very young, the formation of his exemplary moral character is attributed to the influence of his mother, Zhǎng, who is revered in stories recounting the lengths to which she would go in order to find a proper environment in which to educate her son (see Chap. 2).

Method of applying justice involves a synthesis of deontological and teleological theories in applied ethics. Doing justice is rarely simple and direct, since it usually involves seeking a harmonious compromise among competing moral claims, analyzed in either theory. The method of applying justice must enable moral agents to identify all the claims being made, in order to evaluate them and prioritize among them impartially. The theory of justice proposed by John Rawls proposes a method of applying justice basically as fairness, integrating both a principle of equality, maximizing a system of the most extensive basic liberty for each individual compatible with the same liberty for others, and a principle for allocating differences so that these be advantageous to all concerned and that competition for these be open to all (see Chap. 4).

Microfinance is a general term referring to financial services targeted to low-income individuals or those who do not have access to the services offered to customers by commercial banks. Microfinance projects are an important element in social and economic strategies intending to overcome poverty and marginalization, inasmuch as they not only provide the finance capital required by small entrepreneurs to start their own businesses but also strengthen the social networks that enable their beneficiaries to demonstrate accountability through the repayment of their loans and the accumulation of capital for others in similar circumstances (see Chap. 20).

Monopoly is an attempt to create conditions that undermine market competition in favor of a single supplier of valued goods or services. Monopoly, literally meaning "a single seller," occurs when one firm is able to eliminate all other competitors who provide or could provide the same or similar goods or services. Since the formation of monopolies tends to defeat the promised allocative efficiencies that allow markets to contribute to the common good, they are often restricted by law and subject to intensive regulation.

Moral agency reflects a person's capacity for making moral judgments based on commonly accepted notions of right and wrong and for becoming responsible for their actions. A moral agent is any person who is believed to be capable of acting morally, that is, acting responsibly in light of these commonly accepted notions. Individual human beings, having acquired the use of reasoning, are assumed to be moral agents unless proven otherwise; other entities, such as business corporations, may be regarded as moral agents insofar as their actions reflect the internalization of a similar capacity in their corporate cultures. Business ethics advances the idea of moral agency in business by assisting in the development of accountability structures that are responsive to moral considerations, over and above the fear of legal sanctions for noncompliance with government regulations.

Moral leadership is a capacity that persons of exemplary moral character may demonstrate, particularly in the responsibilities they exercise in various social and organizational settings. The primary quality exhibited in moral leadership is a commitment to service for the common good, that is, a focus on strengthening the capacities of others and removing obstacles to their successful performance, within the organization. This service takes shape in policies and actions designed to enhance transparency and accountability, as the moral leader demonstrates care for those to whom and for whom he or she is responsible (see Chaps. 2, 17, and 18).

Mortgage-backed securities (MBS) are a type of financial instrument, specifically debt obligations, that represent claims to the cash flows from pools of mortgage loans, most commonly on residential property. In creating an MBS, mortgages are purchased from banks, mortgage companies, and other originators, from which pools are assembled by various agencies, for example, the government's Federal Home Loan Mortgage Corporation (Freddie Mac), or investment banking firms like Bear Stearns. Once an MBS is created, the agency creating it transfers the claims on the principal and interest payments made by the borrowers to those purchasing the securities. This process is known as securitization (see Chap. 7).

Mortgages are loans granted to the buyers of real estate in order to obtain the funds required to complete the purchase of the property. The real estate serves as the collateral on the loan and is subject to foreclosure if the buyers default upon the mortgage loan. Mortgages enable buyers to purchase real estate, typically in order to become homeowners, while lacking the funds necessary to pay the full purchase price up front. In obtaining a mortgage from a bank or other financial institution, the homeowner usually makes a substantial down payment and borrows the remainder of the price from the lender. Subprime mortgages are a subset of mortgage loans made to individuals with poor credit histories, who otherwise would not qualify for a conventional mortgage. Since such borrowers with poor credit histories represent a higher risk for the lenders, the mortgages issued to them—known as subprime mortgages—charge interest rates above the prime lending rate (see Chap. 7).

Mozi (470–391 BCE) is a Chinese philosopher of the "Hundred Schools of Thought" period who argued that exemplary moral virtue consisted primarily in developing a capacity for impartial care or universal love (*jian'ai*) achieved through self-reflection, rather than the cultivation of filial piety (*xiào*) through Confucian ritual practices. Mozi apparently believed that Chinese people by nature were already too attached to their family and kin and thus thought that they should be challenged to lead a life of asceticism and self-restraint in which they would learn to care for all people equally. Since Mozi's philosophy shares many assumptions in common with Confucianism, their relationship should be understood as complementary rather than antagonistic. In appreciating Mozi's wisdom, one need not feel constrained to repudiate the wisdom of Confucius and his disciples (see Chap. 2).

Murphy's Law is a colloquial expression stating that if anything can go wrong, it will go wrong. The point of Murphy's Law is not so much to encourage passivity, but to warn against complacency. Human schemes will not achieve their goals, if they are left unattended, without adequate monitoring or supervision (see Chap. 19).

Organized crime refers to criminal organizations—be they transnational, national, or local—whose purpose is to engage in illegal activities, usually for profit. Some such organizations, like terrorist networks, are politically motivated, but most are strictly business, such as the Japanese Yakuza, the Russian mafia, the Italian Camorra, and Mexico's Sinaloa drug cartel (see Chap. 18).

Outsourcing production involves creating a supply chain in which goods to be marketed in one country are produced and assemble in other countries. The technological revolutions associated with globalization have made outsourcing production both cost-effective and manageable. Outsourcing production is challenging, but it offers no legitimate excuse for any deterioration in quality controls (see Chaps. 6 and 15).

Overtime regulations refer to the guidelines issued by various regulatory agencies concerning the number of hours an employee may work in any given week or month. While the specifics of such regulations may vary from one venue to another, collectively they are intended to enforce certain basic standards safeguarding the human dignity of workers and their human rights (see Chap. 8).

Patent is one form of coverage extended by intellectual property rights. Patents grant inventors exclusive rights over the use of their inventions—for example, whether and how they can be marketed—for a limited period of time in exchange for detailed disclosure of the invention, its formulas, designs, or other information needed to reproduce them. Once the limited time afforded by patent protection has expired, others may reproduce the invention legally for their own business purposes (see Chap. 13).

Patriarchal or sexist attitudes reflect long-standing but increasingly obsolete cultural assumptions enforcing gender discrimination and sexual harassment. Policies designed to overcome these forms of abuse generally include programs of consciousness raising meant to challenge these attitudes in favor of cultivating more egalitarian and professional relationships among men and women working together in a business or organization. Another example of such attitudes is the strong preference for male offspring which is still prevalent in Asian cultures. It may be challenged as a questionable hangover of obsolete cultural assumptions perpetuated in a distorted understanding of Confucian thinking (see Chap. 9).

Philanthropy, the practice of giving money and time to help make life better for other people, is an activity often supported by enlightened businesses desiring to share their success and wealth with the communities in which they operate. Philanthropy on the part of businesses may be understood as a form of civic virtue, an attempt to demonstrate the firm's commitment to the values of good citizenship and patriotism. Businesses supporting philanthropic activities usually attempt to distinguish these from activities demonstrating corporate social responsibility (CSR). Though these often overlap in specific cases, CSR is linked directly to a firm's business plan and is meant to maximize strategic advantages inherent in that plan; philanthropy, on the other hand, is usually oriented to unmet needs in the community and therefore tends to demonstrate altruistic rather than self-interested motives, from the perspective of the businesses engaged in them. Those businesses that seek to engage in both philanthropy and CSR usually strive to keep them separate in terms of their organization, accountability, and transparency (see Chap. 17).

Phone hacking is a surveillance technique that specifically involves the interception of telephone calls or unauthorized access to voicemail messages, usually without the knowledge or consent of the persons making the calls. Phone hacking by private organizations, such as the news media seeking stories to publish, is widely condemned as a violation of human dignity, especially the right to privacy that private persons are assumed to possess. Phone hacking of this sort should not be confused either with legitimate or regulated forms either of employee monitoring or government wiretapping in the interests of national security (see Chap. 16).

Polluter pays is the principle, supported by both law and morality, that seeks to promote environmental responsibility by making the party responsible for pollution pay the costs of its cleanup, including compensation to others who have been harmed by the damage done to the environment, whether or not that damage was deliberate or merely the result of an accident (see Chap. 19).

Predatory lending is the unfair, deceptive, or fraudulent practices of some lenders that sometimes occur when borrowers apply for a loan. Usually, such practices are association with the loan origination process for home mortgage loans. The predator seeks to convince the borrower to apply for a loan that the borrower is unable to repay consistent with the terms of the loan. While the borrower is often unaware of the situation because of the deception, the lender not only clearly understands it but also exploits it in order to reap greater profits, in the form of commissions, loan origination fees, and various incentives encouraging the resale of subprime mortgages for packaging in mortgage-backed securities (see Chap. 7).

Prima facie evidence is a legal term suggesting that you have enough evidence to support a presumption of fact unless other evidence emerges to refute it. The term is also used similarly in applied ethics where it is necessary to establish facts sufficient to warrant a particular moral judgment of right or wrong. Prima facie evidence is usually contrasted with all things considered evidence, which indicates that the process of weighing the evidence is complete and a moral judgment or legal verdict may now be rendered (see Chap. 8).

Principle of informed consent is a standard enshrined first in bioethics or medical ethics, in order to guarantee that the patient's basic human dignity is respected throughout any medical procedure performed by his or her doctor in the course of treatment. Informed consent means that after the procedure is explained and the patient's questions are answered, the patient is asked to approve the procedure recommended, prior to its performance. Consistent with the Hippocratic Oath, which forbids doing harm to anyone seeking help, the principle of informed consent is meant to protect both doctors and patients by confirming the patients' consent to the procedures to be performed. The principle of informed consent also has broad application in international business ethics, especially in the understanding of a firm's responsibilities toward its customers. All forms of deceptive advertising or otherwise fraudulent representations violate the principle of informed consent, since customers are prevented from making their choices on the basis of accurate information (see Chaps. 5, 6, 7 and 16).

Principle of subsidiarity was first formulated in Catholic Social Teaching (CST), in Pope Pius XI's encyclical letter *Quadragesimo anno* (1931). The principle was formulated in order to clarify both the necessity of government intervention in the affairs of other institutions, including families, and its limits. The help to be given (*subsidium*) must support the proper functioning of these institutions and not preempt them, usurping their autonomy in order to aggrandize the power of the state. As a contribution to political philosophy, the principle of subsidiarity positions CST in opposition to the theories of government identified with both totalitarianism (too much) and laissez-faire liberalism (too little). Government regulation of credit unions, as in the Philippines' Cooperative Development Authority (CDA), is an example of the principle of subsidiarity in action, because the CDA is meant to assist in the strengthening of such coops, so that they can achieve their own stated purposes more effectively (see Chaps. 18, 19 and 20).

Principles for Responsible Investment (PRI) is an initiative of the United Nations Environmental Program (UNEP) and the UN's Global Compact promoting the relevance of ESG (environmental, social, and governance) performance standards for evaluating the sustainability of proposed investments. The Principles are six in number, pledging the signatories to appropriate compliance with ESG concerns. While these principles are voluntary and aspirational, they have been acknowledged by over a thousand signatories—asset owners, investment managers, and service providers—who claim to manage over US$45 trillion in investments (see Chap. 11).

Private property is the legal ownership of property by nongovernmental entities ranging from individual citizens, families, to businesses and the institutions of civil society. The right to private property is regarded by Catholic Social Teaching (CST) as inherent in human dignity, along with all other human rights. While the origins of private property remain obscure, theoretical justification for this right usually emphasizes the role of human labor—individual or organized—in creating something of value from the goods of this earth. Empty and unoccupied wasteland, for example, may become private property if and when an individual or a group cultivates the land, sets its boundaries, and put it to productive use. Private property is regarded as an indispensable means for preserving and enhancing the autonomy of the nongovernmental entities that possess it. A legal claim to private property usually means that the legal owner has an exclusive right to determine its uses, including any decision to buy or sell it (see Chaps. 13 and 18).

Pro-cyclical and countercyclical economic policies are distinguished according to whether they are designed to be neutral—having no impact upon the cycle of market activity—or negative, countering or otherwise intervening to adjust this cycle. If the cycle of economic expansion and contraction is to be managed, countercyclical economic policies are required. The lack of such policies may be an indication of an economic philosophy that believes that markets achieve optimal results when left alone ("laissez-faire") by government intervention (see Chap. 9).

Product safety standards are enshrined in sets of regulations—usually enacted by government agencies—focused on the design and manufacture of consumer products in order to ensure the safety of those who purchase and use these products. The concern for consumer product safety is another expression of the ethical principle, do no harm, which the public expects all businesses to honor. When a defect or other violation of these standards is detected, firms usually will be required to announce—or will voluntarily cooperate in—a product recall in which the defects are either fixed or an upgraded product is offered as compensation (see Chap. 6).

Professionalism refers to the competence or skill expected of someone claiming to be a professional or member of a profession. In premodern times the professions were fewer in number, primarily in the fields of law, medicine, teaching, and religious ministry. More recently, the number has increased dramatically with the advent of professional education in other fields especially related to business. Given the assumptions regarding the skills required of a professional, modern societies have tended to regard the professions as self-regulating, that is, organized into associations capable of monitoring the performance of their members and imposing appropriate discipline or additional training requirements as needed. Since professionals are expected to maintain high ethical standards, as part of their basic skill set, professionalization in business has been among the most important factors increasing awareness of international business ethics, through the development of codes of conduct within the various business specializations seeking professional recognition, as well as in the development of corporate cultures (see Chap. 11 and 20).

Pronto moda, literally "fast fashion," is the name given in Italy to the production of cheap, ready-to-wear apparel goods, in which the time taken for the design, as well as manufacturing, of such goods has been shortened dramatically, through the use of digital technology and the importation of foreign labor, primarily Chinese immigrants. *Pronto moda* remains controversial, with some regarding it as a threat to Italy's traditional apparel industry with its reputation for high-quality goods and others regarding it as providing a pathway for the redevelopment of an older industry that otherwise cannot survive the competitive pressures of globalization (see Chap. 18).

Public morality refers to the moral and ethical standards enforced in a society, by law or social pressure, especially as these are applied to public life, that is, to the institutions of government and civil society that are expected to model socially responsible behavior for society as a whole. The standards of public morality are no different in principle than those expected in private relationships; nevertheless, the glare of publicity more readily exposes the hypocrisies usually involved in any breach of public morality.

Public relations is a strategic communications process that manages the spread of information between an individual or organization and their publics, in order to build mutually beneficial relationships among them. For such relationships to be successful, public relations firms must be committed to working truthfully, which means that they cannot tell lies or try to deceive the public, even as they attempt to interpret their clients' policies and actions in the best possible light. Those engaged in public relations work generally seek recognition as professionals, whose activities are regulated by various codes of ethics and professional associations (see Chap. 5).

Rectification of names is the basic strategy for ethical improvement advocated by Confucian moral philosophy. Since the ethical norms needed to guide any activity or relationship are implicit in the names given to them, rectification or reform occurs when people attempt to live up to the requirements embedded in the name. For example, the ethical norms for acting properly as a father or son are implicit in what it means to be a father or son. Understanding the name enables a person to become the reality (see Chap. 2).

Registered Investment Advisers (RIAs) are those investment advisers who are licensed or registered by the Securities Exchange Commission (SEC) or other government agencies. Such advisers by law must adhere to a fiduciary standard of care, that is, they must serve a client's best interest with the intent of eliminating all potential conflicts of interest that might prompt them to favor their own interests over a client's (see Chap. 7).

Respect people as ends and not as means only is one key formulation of the Kantian categorical imperative, which conveys the basic philosophical meaning of deontological obligations meant to ensure that the dignity of each human being is respected (see Chap. 4).

Reverse engineering is the process of extracting knowledge or design information from any product and then reproducing it or something similar based on that information. The legality of reverse engineering varies significantly from one jurisdiction to another, as well as from one product to another (see Chap. 13).

Right to privacy is explicitly stated in Article 12 of the Universal Declaration of Human Rights. The right has been described in various ways as a right to be left alone, a right to inviolate personality, and the right to control information about oneself. The right to privacy has generally been inferred from the moral obligation to respect human dignity and is generally intended to protect individuals from unwarranted and undesired surveillance and publicity. Like all other human rights, the right to privacy is not absolute, either in law or in morality, since it may conflict with the rights of other parties and may be suspended or forfeited under some circumstances (see Chap. 16).

Risk management is the systematic analysis and assessment of unacceptable risks, in order to minimize or eliminate these through the assertion and extension of managerial control. Risks are usually defined as the impact of uncertainties on an organization's ability to achieve its goals, for example, accidents, project failures, legal liabilities, credit risks, natural disasters, and acts of warfare or terrorism. Such risks may be managed, by putting into practice policies designed to reduce exposure to uncertainties or at least to meet them effectively, if and when they occur (see Chap. 15).

Rule of law is often contrasted with rule by law. When a government rules by law, its citizens are subject to administrative regulations that do not necessarily apply to the rulers or their agents as well. When a government observes the rule of law, it is committed to the principle that everyone is subject to the same administrative regulations, including the rulers and their agents. Rule of law is meant to protect citizens from the arbitrary decisions of government officials that are neither transparent nor accountable and are lacking in due process for adjudicating grievances or other alleged miscarriages of justice or malfeasance in office.

Saving face refers to the all-too-human desire to avoid humiliation or embarrassment, to maintain dignity or preserve reputation. The intensity of this desire and the lengths to which people will go to save face vary significantly from one culture to another. Face is often equated with respect, and it can be given to others, lost because of some misdeed, and regained by good deeds recognized by others (see Chap. 10).

Scapegoat is someone who is unfairly blamed for something others have done. While the practice of scapegoating is found in all cultures, the term's origins are Biblical (Leviticus 16:8) where it refers to a ritual involving a goat whose head is symbolically laden with the sins of the people before it is let loose in the wilderness. Creating a scapegoat is a way of relieving oneself of responsibility for correcting the wrongs one has done to others (see Chaps. 3 and 19).

Secrecy is the practice of concealing information from some individuals or groups. Such concealment may be done for various purposes, some of which are legitimate morally and legally while others are not. In business, the right to protect trade secrets is recognized as a part of intellectual property rights, while secrecy in order to avoid the detection of a fraud or other financial irregularity is both immoral and illegal. Transparency and accountability are generally encouraged as values contrasting with illegitimate forms of secrecy (see Chaps. 6, 7, and 19).

Securities and Exchange Commission (SEC) is an agency of the US government, holding primary responsibility for enforcing existing federal securities laws, proposing regulations for the securities industry, and monitoring its activities. The SEC was established through the Securities Exchange Act of 1934 in order to bring legal action against individuals and firms alleged to have committed accounting fraud, provided false information, and engaged in insider trading and other financial crimes occurring in the financial markets. Other countries, such as the Philippines, have established similar agencies with similar purposes (see Chap. 7).

Securities fraud refers to deceptive practices or frauds committed in the buying and selling of stocks, bonds, and other financial instruments. Like all forms of fraud, it seeks to achieve its criminal intent by conveying false information to investors, whose reliance on such information causes them to lose rather than gain from their investments (see Chap. 7).

Securitization is the process by which a financial instrument is created by combining other financial assets into a package that can be resold to investors. Mortgage-backed securities (MBS) are an example of securitization, in which mortgages with varying degrees of risk and reward are combined in a large pool of assets intended to minimize the risk and maximize the reward for investors (see Chap. 7).

Sexual discrimination is a comprehensive term inclusive of civil rights violations based on sexism or prejudice against a person's sex or gender. While it includes sexual harassment, sexual discrimination usually refers to the act or policy of rejecting a person's application for employment on the basis of sex or gender, when these characteristics are clearly irrelevant to the qualifications required of the applicants for a particular job (see Chap. 9).

Sexual harassment refers to forms of sexual abuse that occur within an organization, in relations between employers and employees, or teachers and students, or physicians and their patients, etc. Sexual harassment consists in unwelcome sexual advances, in the context of interactions usually involving a superior and a subordinate. For example, an employee is pressured into having sex with his or her boss as a condition of employment, with the implied threat that resistance will be met with retaliation. In this example, the form of sexual harassment is termed *quid pro quo*, because one thing is exchanged for another, sexual favors for job security or advancement. The other major form is the creation of a hostile work environment. In that case, the parties at work may have freely consented to their affair, but their activity creates a situation in which other employees are made uncomfortable or feel unfairly discriminated against because of the special relationship enjoyed by the employee and his or her boss. Sexual harassment is commonly regarded as a form of bullying, an effort to assert dominance over others, and not as the result of an excess of erotic desire. It is condemned both in law and in morality as a basic violation of human dignity (see Chap. 9).

Skepticism is a philosophical theory that doubts systematically conventional claims to the truth of facts and the validity of moral norms. While questioning facts and moral norms is an indispensable part of the development of critical thinking skills, skepticism often encourages attitudes that refuse to accept certain established facts and values, once all reasonable objections have been answered. For example, remaining skeptical of the heliocentric view of the solar system, once its truth was demonstrated, was a sign not of superior critical thinking skills but of willful irrationality. Currently, the lingering doubts about the reality of catastrophic climate change and the role of human activities in causing it is an example that most people would regard as unwarranted skepticism.

Social business is a term, popularized by the Nobel Peace Prize winning economist, Muhammad Yunus, to describe enterprises created and designed to address a social problem, usually on not-for-profit basis. Yunus' own work in the Grameen Bank demonstrates how such a business can be successful, that is, financially self-sustainable, with its profits reinvested in the business itself rather than distributed to its investors. Other, even older enterprises based on mutualist principles, such as credit unions and credit cooperatives, may be regarded as social businesses, whose relationships with their members who are depositors may or may not conform to Yunus' not-for-profit business plan (see Chap. 20).

Social capital is an important concept for understanding how credit unions and credit cooperatives actually succeed in meeting their goals. Social capital, primarily in the form of basic trust and mutual accountability, is believed to be common or at least accessible to all human persons. Under proper conditions, social capital can be transformed into finance capital, when the relationships of trust and accountability are used to demonstrate the credit worthiness of members of a network, organized through the credit union or cooperative. Social capital functions to guarantee that loans will be repaid, even in the absence of conventional forms of collateral (see Chap. 20).

Social contract theory began in early modern European history as an explanation of how individuals form governments and consent to be governed by them. The term, social contract, has been expanded to cover the relationship between a business and its stakeholders, particularly, the public at large, who consent to the activities of a business corporation, if and when they recognize that the business is making a contribution to the common good. The social contract between business and society begins with the firm's commitment to the basic principles of business ethics, that is, fair dealing in all its business operations, and ranges through its participation in various programs of corporate social responsibility (CSR) and philanthropy (see Chaps. 12 and 17).

Social Darwinism is a philosophy, popular in the late nineteenth century, which claimed to apply biological concepts of natural selection to the history of human societies. The ruling idea was that "survival of the fittest" was the imperative operative in both biological and social evolution. Andrew Carnegie, for example, believed that social Darwinism indicated the inevitability of modern industrial capitalism and the extraordinary accumulation of wealth it made possible. Carnegie, however, did not appeal to social Darwinism to justify such wealth, but recommended that those most successful in accumulating it—the fittest who had survived in the struggle to dominate competitive markets—should create foundations and other organizations to enable the rest of society to share in their success, through greater access to education and other social benefits (see Chap. 17).

Socrates, in the history of European philosophy, stands as the model of a wise and humble man, who in response to the Oracle at Delphi sought to discover anyone wiser than him by interrogating all others who claimed to dispense wisdom to their followers. His Socratic method of questioning and engaging people from different walks of life in philosophical dialogue was not only amusing to his youthful disciples but also profoundly irritating to those whose claims he questioned. Socrates' death, forced upon him in his refusal of any punishment for his alleged corruption of youth and other impieties, is celebrated as an example of the true philosopher's commitment to integrity in the pursuit of truth.

Solidarity is the feeling of unity between people who have the same interests, goals, standards, and sympathies. Solidarity is not based primarily on ties of kinship, as in families, but on communities of belief and shared practice. Solidarity in the late twentieth century was the name given to the Polish trade union movement that eventually precipitated the collapse of the Soviet hegemony in eastern Europe. As one of the core values of Catholic Social Teaching (CST), solidarity expresses the tradition's commitment to the importance of forming a civil society composed of voluntary associations that conform to the social logics of neither governments nor businesses. Such associations, according to CST, play an indispensable role in assisting families and individuals to participate in achieving the common good or natural institutions such as the family. Solidarity, however, can be antisocial as well as social, for example, when organized crime syndicates create conditions that prevent the common good (see Chaps. 18 and 20).

Sportsmanship is the ideal of fair play, respect for opponents, and a commitment to the integrity of a sport, by those competing within it. Sportsmanship means a commitment to abide by the rules of the game, whether one is winning or losing, at any given moment in any given match. Sportsmanship is moral leadership among participants in a sport who take responsibility for preserving the good reputation and goodwill engendered by free and fair competition (see Chap. 1).

Stakeholder is any person or group who has a legitimate interest or concern in how an organization conducts its activities. The term, "stakeholder," was adopted in management theory in contrast to "stockholders," that is, the owners or investors in a business, in order to understand the complex and multiple responsibilities that managers have in enabling the firm to meet its goals. Stakeholder theory concerns the ways in which stakeholder interests may conflict and how management must seek to deal with all of them in a responsible way (see Chaps. 4, 15, and 19).

Stewardship emphasizes the responsible planning and management of resources. The steward is a manager, that is, one who acts as a surrogate for the owner, especially by managing his or her property or financial affairs, etc. Just as stewardship may include a manager's responsibilities toward all stakeholder groups, so it may also comprehend a firm's environmental responsibilities, on the assumption that the environment is the "silent stakeholder" in all businesses that profit from the development of natural resources (see Chap. 19).

Supply chain management involves comprehensive supervision of the entire process of production, from supplier to manufacturer to wholesaler to retailer to consumer. Successful supply chain management coordinates and integrates the flow of interactions within this process, as it unfolds both within the firm and among the companies forming its supply chain. International business ethics is concerned about supply chain management because the firm must establish, monitor, and enforce its ethical standards throughout the process. Ethical lapses within the supply chain are the responsibility of the firm that has organized the process, as well as the companies participating in it (see Chap. 6).

Sustainability is the capacity of systems and processes to endure, meaning, to continue growing while maintaining their basic identity, in response to various challenges both external and internal by an organization seeking to sustain its activities. Sustainable development usually is the result of interactions in four interconnected domains: ecology, economics, politics, and culture (see Chaps. 11 and 12).

Sweatshop is a negative term used as an accusation against firms alleged to be operating a workplace with socially unacceptable working conditions. Sweatshops are characterized by a lack of respect for human dignity, evidenced by lack of concern about worker health and safety issues, including the amount of overtime work demanded, or the adequacy of housing and other amenities provided to the workers (see Chaps. 8 and 18).

Tabloid journalism is a type of journalism that appears in tabloids, that is, in newspapers with a compact page format. Tabloid journalism generally tends to emphasize topics such as sensational crime stories, astrology, and gossip columns about the personal lives of celebrities. The now defunct *News of the World* is but one example of the genre, which is often to be found for sale in supermarkets and news and magazine kiosks at various transportation hubs (see Chap. 16).

The blame game is not a game, but an attempt to avoid sole responsibility for some undesirable event by blaming everyone else involved in it. Given the generally complex accountability structures typical of business corporations, it is not surprising that managers and other employees often resort to the blame game in order to cover up their involvement when something goes wrong.

The right of abode is an individual's freedom from immigration control in a particular country. The right of abode in a certain country is generally restricted to those who are citizens and, within certain limits, those who have been granted the status of permanent residents (see Chap. 18).

The sanctity of contracts is a term recognized in the English common law tradition and its derivatives, meaning that once a contract has been entered into, the obligations stipulated in the contract must be honored. To default upon such obligations is to be in breach of contract, with penalties sanctioned by both law and morality (see Chap. 4).

Tip of the iceberg is a colloquial expression meaning that the problem one sees may be only a small part of a larger, hidden problem. Problems, like icebergs floating in the sea, may have only a small part—the tip—visible, even though the greater menace remains invisible (see Chap. 14).

Tobin tax, named after its original proponent, the Nobel Prize winning economist, James Tobin, was intended to discourage short-term currency speculation, by imposing a small charge on international currency transactions. More recently, proposals have extended it to all stock and bond transactions, and their derivatives, in order to fulfill the same intent, namely, to discourage speculative trading (see Chap. 11).

Top-notch player is the term developed by Stephan Rothlin to describe the ideal of a successful business practitioner, whose capacity for moral leadership matches his or her technical skills in doing business. Just as a top-notch player in any game is one who embodies the ideal of sportsmanship, so a manager or entrepreneur becomes a top-notch player in business by cultivating the virtues that enable him or her to do well while doing good (see Chaps. 1 and 2).

Tort law covers torts or wrongs that unfairly cause someone else to suffer loss. Tort law provides a remedy for such wrongs, by awarding damages to the injured party. Since torts may be committed against persons and property, the compensation for damages may impose significant costs on those found guilty of a tortious act (see Chap. 16).

Trade-offs occur in situations in which there are both gains and losses and where the one cannot be obtained without also acquiring the other. Facing trade-offs, understanding them, and compromising in order to achieve the best result are usually regarded as signs of moral maturity or an ethic of responsibility (see Chaps. 4 and 19).

Trafficking is a general term referring to trade in something illegal, such as drug trafficking. Human trafficking is trade in people, whose basic human rights are violated by the coercive nature of the trade—that is, people are forced into it against their wills—for purposes of commercial exploitation. Human trafficking is a modern-day form of slavery and stands condemned universally both in law and in morality.

Transparency International (TI) is an international nongovernmental organization (NGO) devoted to combating corruption by focusing on prevention and the reform of organizations through education. TI has pioneered the use of international rankings systems, or indices, in order to alert people to the level of corruption reported in the various nations participating in their surveys. TI annual publishes the Bribe Payers' Index and the Corruption Perception Index in order to spur further efforts at reform (see Chap. 14).

Transparency, a term used in the science, engineering, business, the humanities, and more generally in various social contexts, is a value highlighting the desire for organizations to operate in such a way that it become easy for others to see how they carry out their policies and actions. Transparency implies a commitment to openness, effective communication, and accountability.

Triple bottom line is an accounting framework involving three parts: social, environmental, and financial. By contrast, "the bottom line" in the past usually referred exclusively to financial accounting. Proposals to audit all three areas reflect a growing concern for sustainability in business, on the assumption that such depends on successful interactions in all three, sometimes referred to as "people, planet, and profits" (see Chap. 17).

Trusteeship is a legal term referring to any person who holds property, authority, or a position of trust or responsibility for the benefit of another person or third party. A trustee agrees to do certain tasks in order to protect the interests of the beneficiaries, while also agreeing not to use this office in order to pursue his or her own interests.

Type A and type B problems in business ethics ought to be distinguished, according to Laura Nash, so that they can be addressed more effectively. Type A problems are situations properly regarded as "moral dilemmas," whose resolution may require the use of managerial decision-making models and methods of analysis proposed in the discipline of applied ethics. Type B problems, however, are situations in which a person knows the right thing to do but fails to do it, because of lack of virtue, particularly courage, or other deficiencies in his or her personal development. Addressing type B problems may require active engagement in the forms of self-cultivation available in the wisdom traditions of various religions and philosophies (see Chaps. 2, 3, and 4).

Usury traditionally referred to lending money in exchange for repayment including interest. While Islamic banking practice continues to honor the Biblical prohibition against usury, modern commercial banks and their regulators regard it as lending at excessive or illegal rates of interest. Usurious loans are considered immoral because they unfairly enrich the lender. Those engaged in such predatory lending are commonly referred to as loan sharks (see Chap. 20).

Utilitarianism is an ethical theory that advocates seeking "the greatest amount of good for the greatest number of people." This principle of maximization is applied by measuring the consequences of various courses of action, calculating the amount of good and bad that is likely to occur, and choosing those courses that promise the greatest amount of good over bad. In the discipline of applied ethics, utilitarianism is fully developed through categories differentiating specific acts from policies or rules of practice. Utilitarianism is usually contrasted with Kantianism, highlighting the difference between good consequences and moral obligations. Kantian ethics insists that valid moral obligations must be fulfilled regardless of the consequences, resulting in an unresolved philosophical dispute over which of the two theories is more adequate and comprehensive. Applied ethics' approach to justice seeks to embrace both of these perspectives and to harmonize them in reference to specific problems and their solutions (see Chaps. 4 and 20).

Values education, according to UNESCO, is a pedagogy designed to achieve two basic outcomes: "Helping students to better understand the values that guide their own daily lives, and contributing to changes in values held collectively by communities and personally by individuals." Values education, therefore, plays an important role in the development of strategies supporting the renewal of moral education in various countries (see Chaps. 18 and 20).

Vested interest may be defined as an interest in influencing something so that you can continue to benefit from it. In legal usage, it means a right or a title to the present or future possession of an estate or some form of tangible or intangible property. Specifically, it also refers to the entitled benefit that employees may enjoy as a matter of right granted under their employer's provision of a pension plan for them.

Vicarious liability is a legal term referring to the doctrine in tort law that imposes responsibility upon one person for the failure of another, with whom the person has a special relationship. An agent, for example, who is acting on behalf of his or her principal or employer, may cause harms to another, who then may have a legal tort case against the employer. Legal jurisprudence in the USA has imposed the standard of vicarious liability on businesses that have been lax in enforcing laws against sexual discrimination and sexual harassment. In such cases, not only is the individual who is accused liable for damages but also the employer may be have vicarious liability, if the individual is found guilty (see Chap. 9).

Virtue ethics is one of three major approaches to normative ethics, the other two being deontological and utilitarian forms of moral reasoning. Virtue ethics emphasizes the primary importance of moral character formation, without which the acquisition of moral reasoning skills may not be sufficient to advance the cause of moral education and reform. Virtue ethics is common to culturally diverse traditions of moral wisdom and spirituality. It is the common ground where those influenced by Socrates, Plato, and Aristotle meet Confucius and his disciples (see Chap. 2).

Whistle-blowing is another significant term in business ethics derived from the world of sport. Whistle-blowing is the attempt, usually initiated by an employee, to correct some action or policy that isn't right—something illegal, in particular something that may be harmful to any of the firm's stakeholders. Once generally regarded as an act of disloyalty to one's employer, whistle-blowing—when it involves going outside the firm in order to make a disclosure in the public interest—is increasingly regarded as "civic minded" and thus worthy of praise. Nevertheless, given the risks involved and the potential harms that may be done by those engaged in it, it is important to develop an ethic of whistle-blowing that distinguishes when it is morally permissible and when it is morally obligatory, from situations when it may be unfair and irresponsible (see Chap. 10).

World Trade Organization (WTO) is an intergovernmental organization that regulates international trade. Its mission is to facilitate international trade by providing a framework for negotiating trade agreements and a dispute resolution process for achieving compliance with WTO agreements. Among these is the Trade-Related Aspects of IPR Agreement (TRIPS) that governs trademarks, copyrights, and patents and international disputes arising from conflicting claims about them (see Chap. 13).

Zero-tolerance policy is a term describing policies designed to achieve strict compliance with rules or laws. The range of situations in which such policies have been proposed or enacted range from enforcing rules of conduct in various educational institutions to combatting illegal drug sales and possession and to prosecuting undocumented aliens or illegal immigrants. Zero-tolerance policies remain controversial since they lack the flexibility that may be necessary for effective compliance and law enforcement. Their lack of flexibility, in short, may be counterproductive (see Chap. 18).

Printed by Printforce, the Netherlands